SOCIAL MEDIA

Sara Miller McCune founded SAGE Publishing in 1965 to support the dissemination of usable knowledge and educate a global community. SAGE publishes more than 1000 journals and over 800 new books each year, spanning a wide range of subject areas. Our growing selection of library products includes archives, data, case studies and video. SAGE remains majority owned by our founder and after her lifetime will become owned by a charitable trust that secures the company's continued independence.

Los Angeles | London | New Delhi | Singapore | Washington DC | Melbourne

SOCIAL MEDIA

a critical introduction

2nd edition

CHRISTIAN FUCHS

Los Angeles | London | New Delhi
Singapore | Washington DC | Melbourne

Los Angeles | London | New Delhi
Singapore | Washington DC | Melbourne

SAGE Publications Ltd
1 Oliver's Yard
55 City Road
London EC1Y 1SP

SAGE Publications Inc.
2455 Teller Road
Thousand Oaks, California 91320

SAGE Publications India Pvt Ltd
B 1/I 1 Mohan Cooperative Industrial Area
Mathura Road
New Delhi 110 044

SAGE Publications Asia-Pacific Pte Ltd
3 Church Street
#10-04 Samsung Hub
Singapore 049483

Editor: Michael Ainsley
Editorial assistant: John Nightingale
Production editor: Imogen Roome
Copyeditor: Neil Dowden
Proofreader: Leigh C. Timmins
Indexer: Silvia Benvenuto
Marketing manager: Lucia Sweet
Cover design: Jen Crisp
Typeset by: C&M Digitals (P) Ltd, Chennai, India
Printed by: CPI Group (UK) Ltd, Croydon, CR0 4YY

First edition published 2014

This second edition published 2017

Library of Congress Control Number: 2016949804

British Library Cataloguing in Publication data

A catalogue record for this book is available from
the British Library

ISBN 978-1-4739-6682-6
ISBN 978-1-4739-6683-3 (pbk)

At SAGE we take sustainability seriously. Most of our products are printed in the UK using FSC papers and boards.
When we print overseas we ensure sustainable papers are used as measured by the PREPS grading system.
We undertake an annual audit to monitor our sustainability.

CONTENTS

WHAT IS A CRITICAL INTRODUCTION TO SOCIAL MEDIA?

KEY QUESTIONS

- What is social about social media?
- What does it mean to think critically?
- What is critical theory and why is it relevant?
- How can we approach critical theory?

KEY CONCEPTS

Social media

Critical theory

Marxist theory

Critical political economy

OVERVIEW

What is social about social media? What are the implications of social media platforms such as Facebook, Google, YouTube, Wikipedia and Twitter for power, the economy and politics? This book gives a critical introduction to studying social media. It engages the reader with the concepts needed for critically understanding the world of social media with questions such as:

- Chapter 2: What is social about social media?
- Chapter 3: How meaningful is the notion of participatory culture for thinking about social media?
- Chapter 4: How useful are the concepts of communication power and mass self-communication in the network society for thinking about social media?
- Chapter 5: How does the business of social media work?
- Chapter 6: What is good and bad about Google, the world's leading Internet platform and search engine?

- Chapter 7: What is the role of privacy and surveillance on Facebook, the world's most successful social networking site?
- Chapter 8: What is the role of Twitter in respect to new forms of politics, democracy and potentials and limits to the revitalization of the political public sphere?
- Chapter 9: What are the features of the political economy of Chinese social media platforms such as Weibo in the context of the development of the Chinese economy and Chinese society?
- Chapter 10: What is the role of online sharing in contemporary capitalism, including the ideology of sharing, sharing platforms such as the commercial flat-sharing platform Airbnb and the taxi-location-sharing app Uber, and non-capitalist potentials of online sharing?
- Chapter 11: What forms and principles of collaborative knowledge production are characteristic for Wikipedia, the world's most widely accessed wiki-based online encyclopedia?
- Chapter 12: How can we achieve social media that serve the purposes of a just and fair world, in which we control society and communicate in common?

This book introduces a theoretical framework for critically understanding social media that are used for discussing social media platforms in the context of specific topics: being social (Chapter 2), participatory culture (Chapter 3), communication and media power (Chapter 4), political economy (Chapter 5), political ethics (Chapter 6), surveillance and privacy (Chapter 7), democracy and the public sphere (Chapter 8), global capitalism (Chapter 9), the gift- and sharing economy (Chapter 10), power and collaborative work (Chapter 11) and the commons (Chapter 12).

Let us consider three examples where social media play a role: *The Huffington Post*, Jeremy Corbyn's social media campaign and Internet/social media surveillance in the age of Edward Snowden.

UNPAID LABOUR FOR *THE HUFFINGTON POST*

The Huffington Post (HP) is the most popular news blog in the world. Arianna Huffington started it in 2005. It has been based on the contributions of many unpaid voluntary bloggers (Fuchs 2014a). In 2011, AOL bought HP for US$315 million and turned it into a profit-oriented business. The writer Jonathan Tasini, who had contributed to HP, filed a $105 million class action suit against HP, arguing that it unjustly enriched itself from its bloggers' unpaid contributions when it was turned into a business and acquired by AOL. Tasini stated: "In my view, the Huffington Post's bloggers have essentially been turned into modern-day slaves on Arianna Huffington's plantation. [. . .] She wants to pocket the tens of millions of dollars she reaped from the hard work of those bloggers."[1] Arianna Huffington, in contrast, argued that bloggers work without payment for fun and to get recognition: "People blog on HuffPost for free for the same reason they go on cable TV shows every night for free: either because they are passionate about their ideas or because they have something to promote and want exposure to large and multiple audiences. [. . .] Our bloggers are repeatedly invited on TV to discuss their posts

---

1 www.forbes.com/sites/jeffbercovici/2011/04/12/aol-huffpo-suit-seeks-105m-this-is-about-justice/ (accessed on 14 October 2015).

and have received everything from paid speech opportunities and book deals to a TV show."[2] The opinions on working for for-profit online sites without remuneration differ widely: Is it the exploitation of unpaid digital labour? Or is it a new form of participatory online journalism that pays writers by recognition rather than with money?

THE JEREMY CORBYN CAMPAIGN AND SOCIAL MEDIA

In September 2015, the socialist Member of the British Parliament Jeremy Corbyn became the Labour Party's first left-wing leader in a very long time. He has faced a very hostile mainstream media campaign that portrayed him unfairly as an old-fashioned socialist whose policies are outdated and do not work in the twenty-first century, who wants to create a centralized, state-bureaucratic economy, is a sympathizer of extremists, dictators, terrorists, racists, Islamists and anti-Semites, and is a vegetarian hippie, eco-zealot and clown, who dresses badly, has no style, hates cars, and celebrates immigration and multiculturalism.

The British press described Jeremy Corbyn, for example, as someone who "can hardly see a terrorist without wanting to kiss their butt" (*Sun*, 6/9/15), a "left-wing nutter" (*Sun*, 7/9/15), "a danger to national security" (*The Times*, 7/9/15), "a gormless Marxist who delights in describing as 'friends' every possible enemy of this country" (*Sun*, 9/9/15), "a vegetarian" who "looks halfdead" (*Sun*, 11/9/15), looking like "a grandfather popping down to the local garden centre for some extra compost" (*Daily Mail*, 11/9/15), "Jez What Do You Look Like Corbyn" (*Sun*, 12/9/15), "Jezbollah" (*Daily Mirror*, 12/9/15), "Jeremy Cor bin-Laden" (*The Times*, 13/9/15), "the left's Duracell Bunny" (*The Times*, 13/9/15), "several times winner of the Worst Dressed MP award" (*Independent*, 4/9/15) and a "malevolent clown" (*Daily Telegraph*, 1/9/15).

Corbyn's campaign has been a mass movement in which hundred of thousands became involved, especially young people and those who oppose right-wing austerity politics. Such neoliberal policies want to make everyday people pay for the capitalist crisis by cutting public support and expenditures, while at the same time reducing taxes for the rich and corporations. Activists describe Corbyn as honest, decent, advancing a new style of politics, socially just and an everyday person. The voices of these activists, who also call themselves Corbynites, have almost never been heard in the mainstream media. They therefore in the Corbyn campaign made heavy use of social media, especially Facebook and Twitter, for internal and public communication. On Twitter, the hashtag campaigns #Jeremy4Leader and #JezWeCan were created.

Jeremy Corbyn has been contested on social media. Whereas some use social media to support him, others spread anti-socialist ideology online regarding him (for a detailed analysis, see Fuchs 2016d). Some examples from Twitter are:

- "The radical extreme left wing lunacy of Jeremy left wing lunacy left wing loony lefty extreme radical Corbyn"
- "Bloody pinko"
- "Jeremy Corbyn ..... A communist fraud .... hope he goes the way of Trotsky #Mexico1941 #NeverForget"

---

2 http://latimesblogs.latimes.com/technology/2011/04/arianna-huffington-on-jonathan-tasini-writer-lawsuit-there-are-no-mertis-to-the-case.html (accessed on 14 October 2015).

- "When will everyone realise that #Corbyn is a communist bastard? He's gonna fuck this country up if he gets in power #Labour"
- "Corbyn is a left wing socialist scumbag."
- "Loony leftie, he should be arrested."
- "He is Stalin resurrected."
- "Fuck off Corbyn you terrorist loving twat!"
- "Corbyn this filthy Marxist enemy of Britain."
- "It is clear that commie Corbyn is a terrorist and should be locked up as soon as possible!"
- "BREAKING NEWS: THE UNITED KINGDOM LITERALLY JUST BECAME A PROLETARIAN DICTATORSHIP! JEREMY 'STALIN II' CORBYN HAS BEEN ELECTED LABOUR LEADER."
- "CORBYN. Communism is back baby! Prepare the Gulags."

Corbyn supporters challenge such emotional, irrational, anti-socialist attacks that are devoid of arguments and often link to biased tabloid articles with strategies such as humour, satire, pointing out the absurdity of the claims, associating Corbyn with positive values and reversing the claim that Corbyn is an extremist. Some examples from Twitter are:

- "In an era when Thatcher was calling Mandela a terrorist, Jeremy Corbyn was protesting against apartheid."
- "Corbyn suggests peaceful & non-violent solutions and he's a terrorist ally? Is war the only way we communicate?"
- "World according to UK right wing media fascists is black/white upside/down. War Criminal #Blair is moderate. #Corbyn is dangerous extremist."
- "Jeremy Corbyn's anti-austerity plans are sound & the austerity agenda is extremist."
- "Congratulations to Corbyn. Unity, equality, social justice."
- "Corbyn to consult women on train harassment => extremist loon. Workers may not even get 1% pay rise => not a problem."
- "SHOCK, HORROR! Corbyn would respect international human rights law."
- "Corbyn sure seems like a decent fella."
- "David Cameron is also a supporter of human rights abuses in Saudi Arabia."

Corbyn supporters do not agree what role social media should play in campaigns: the left-wing journalist Owen Jones argues that social media are not enough and that Corbyn needs a media strategy in order to be present in traditional media that reach out to the non-activist public. "But without engaging with the mainstream media it is almost impossible to get a message to the as-yet unpersuaded. [...] We can't just want retweets and packed halls, after all, but to change the world."[3] Ben Seller, who led Corbyn's social media campaign, objects to Jones:

> I think Owen is absolutely wrong in his assessment of social media as an
> "echo chamber" of the left. [...] Social media has been likened to a very large

---

3 Owen Jones: If Jeremy Corbyn's Labour is going to work, it has to communicate. *Guardian* online. 16 September 2015. www.theguardian.com/commentisfree/2015/sep/16/jeremy-corbyn-labour-twitter-media (accessed on 27 September 2016)

pub, with everyone talking at once – tens of thousands of conversations at once. That's not a bad analogy. The key to making sense of it, of how to create some movement out of all those disparate voices, is about how it's organised.[4]

EDWARD SNOWDEN AND THE SURVEILLANCE-INDUSTRIAL INTERNET COMPLEX

In June 2013, the computer expert Edward Snowden revealed with the help of *The Guardian* the existence of large-scale Internet and communications surveillance systems such as Prism, XKeyscore and Tempora. According to the documents he leaked, the National Security Agency (NSA), through the Prism programme, obtained direct access to user data from eight online/ information and communications technology (ICT) companies: AOL, Apple, Facebook, Google, Microsoft, Paltalk, Skype and Yahoo![5] The Powerpoint slides that Edward Snowden leaked refer to data collection "directly from the servers of these U.S. Service Providers".[6] Snowden also revealed the existence of a surveillance system called XKeyScore that the NSA can use for reading emails, tracking web browsing and users' browsing histories, monitoring social media activity, online searches, online chat, phone calls and online contact networks, and following the screens of individual computers. According to the leaked documents, XKeyScore can search both meta-data and content data.[7] Snowden worked for Booz Allen Hamilton, a profitable private security company entangled in the surveillance-industrial complex that is based on the co-operation of state institutions and corporations in the surveillance of citizens' communications.

The documents that Snowden leaked also showed that the Government Communications Headquarters (GCHQ), a British intelligence agency, monitored and collected communication phone and Internet data from fibre optic cables and shared such data with the NSA.[8] According to the leak, the GCHQ, for example, stores phone calls, emails, Facebook postings and the history of users' website access for up to 30 days and analyses these data.[9] Further documents indicated that in co-ordination with the GCHQ, intelligence services in Germany (Bundesnachrichtendienst (BND)), France (Direction Générale de la Sécurité Extérieure (DGSE)), Spain (Centro Nacional de Inteligencia (CNI)) and Sweden (Försvarets radioanstalt (FRA)) developed similar capacities.[10]

---

4 Ben Sellers: That's one hell of an "echo chamber": Why I disagree with Owen Jones on social media. https://theworldturnedupsidedownne.wordpress.com/2015/09/24/thats-one-hell-of-an-echo-chamber-why-i-disagree-with-owen-jones-on-social-media (accessed on 14 October 2015).

5 NSA Prism program taps in to user data of Apple, Google and others. *Guardian* online. 7 June 2013. www.theguardian.com/world/2013/jun/06/us-tech-giants-nsa-data. (accessed on 27 September 2016).

6 Ibid.

7 XKeyscore: NSA tool collects "nearly everything a user does on the internet". *Guardian* online. 31 July 2013. www.theguardian.com/world/2013/jul/31/nsa-top-secret-program-online-data (accessed on 27 September 2016).

8 GCHQ taps fibre-optic cables for secret access to world's communications. *Guardian* online. 21 June 2013. www.theguardian.com/uk/2013/jun/21/gchq-cables-secret-world-communications-nsa?-guni=Article:in%20body%20link (accessed on 27 September 2016).

9 Ibid.

10 GCHQ and European spy agencies worked together on mass surveillance. *Guardian* online. 1 November 2013. www.theguardian.com/uk-news/2013/nov/01/gchq-europe-spy-agencies-mass-surveillance-snowden (accessed on 27 September 2016).

1.1 WHAT IS SOCIAL ABOUT SOCIAL MEDIA?

Questions that many people immediately ask when one employs the term "social media" are: What is social about social media? Are not all media social? These questions have to do with another question: What does it mean to be social?

INFORMATION AND COGNITION

Are human beings always social, or only if they interact with others? In sociological theory, there are different concepts of the social (see Chapter 2). Some say that all media are social because they are part of society and aspects of society are present in the technological artefacts we use. This means that if you sit alone in front of your computer, type a document in your word processor and are not connected to the Internet, your activities are perfectly social: the ideas you think and write up refer to ideas of other people and what is happening in society; the word processor has certain features and functions that were all designed by humans for certain reasons and under specific working conditions. So cognition is a social activity. The computer you use may have been assembled in China and the raw materials out of which its components were made may come from mines in Africa. You cannot see all the labour that goes into the computer, but nonetheless it is a tool that was created in society by humans who experience certain working conditions. If we employ this broad understanding of sociality, then not just Facebook is social, but also television, the radio, the telegraph, posters, books, wall paintings and all other forms of information.

COMMUNICATION

Other people say that not all media are social, but only those that support communication between humans. Communication is a reciprocal process between at least two humans, in which symbols are exchanged and all interaction partners give meaning to these symbols. Computer-mediated communication did not start with Facebook and Twitter: Ray Tomlinson sent the first Internet email from one computer to another in 1971.[11] If we understand social activity to mean communication or symbolic interaction, then not all media use is social. Based on this understanding, it is not social if you write a document alone, but it is social to send an email or chat with a friend on Facebook. Communication is a basic feature of all societies and all human activity. We cannot live and survive without communication, just like we cannot survive without food and water. Communication takes place routinely in everyday life.

COMMUNITY

Some communications that take place repeatedly result in something more than just social relationships – they involve feelings of belonging together or friendship. Communication turns this form of the social into community. A certain share of the communications on Facebook is part of communities of personal friends, political activists, hobby or fan groups.

---

11   See http://openmap.bbn.com/~tomlinso/ray/firstemailframe.html and http://openmap.bbn.com/~tom-linso/ray/ka10.html (accessed on 14 October 2015).

But online communities are not new; they existed already in bulletin board systems such as the WELL (Whole Earth 'Lectronic Link) in the 1980s.

COLLABORATION AND CO-OPERATIVE WORK

A fourth form of sociality is collaboration, or co-operative work. The research area of computer-supported co-operative work (CSCW) was founded in the 1980s and deals with how computers enable human co-operation. Collaborative work, as for example the co-operative editing of articles performed on Wikipedia or the joint writing of a document on Google Docs, is not new in computing, although the popularity of Wikipedia and wiki platforms such as Mediawiki, PBWorks and Wikispaces is a more recent development. CSCW was already the subject of academic discussions in the 1980s when a conference series started with the first ACM (Association for Computing Machinery) Conference on Computer and Communications Security that took place in December 1986 in Austin, Texas. The concept of the wiki is also not new: the first wiki technology (the WikiWikiWeb) was introduced by Ward Cunningham in 1995.

INFORMATION, COMMUNICATION, COLLABORATION AND COMMUNITY ARE FORMS OF SOCIALITY, BUT WHAT IS NOW SOCIAL ABOUT FACEBOOK?

There are different forms of the social, such as information, communication, communities and collaboration. When we talk about "social media", we have to be careful to specify which meaning of the term "social" we are employing. Therefore, studying social media is in need of social theory and social philosophy. These tools of thought allow us to come to grips with the basic meaning of terms such as sociality, media, society, power, democracy, participation, culture, labour, communication, information, the public sphere and the private realm that are often employed when discussing social media, but often poorly understood.

All computing systems, and therefore all web applications, as well as all forms of media can be considered as social because they store and transmit human knowledge that originates in social relations in society. They are objectifications of society and human social relations. Whenever a human uses a computing system or a medium (also if s/he is alone in a room), s/he cognizes based on objectified knowledge that is the outcome of social relations. But not all computing systems and web applications support direct communication between humans, in which at least two humans mutually exchange symbols that are interpreted as being meaningful. Amazon mainly provides information about books and other goods one can buy; it is not primarily a tool of communication, but rather a tool of information, whereas Facebook has in-built communication features that are frequently used (mail system, walls for comments, forums, etc.).

Social media is a complex term with multi-layered meanings. Facebook contains a lot of content (information) and is a tool for communication and for the maintenance creation of communities. It is only to a minor degree a tool for collaborative work, but involves at least three types of sociality: cognition, communication and community. Chapter 2 focuses more in depth on the concept of social media.

Understanding social media critically means, among other things, to engage with the different forms of sociality on the Internet in the context of society. If one compares the most frequently accessed websites in 2013 to the ones that were popular in 2000, then one sees that the most accessed sites in 2000 were MSN, Yahoo!, Excite, AOL, Microsoft, Daum, eBay and

Altavista,[12] whereas in 2015 the most accessed websites in the world include Google, Facebook, YouTube, Baidu, Yahoo!, Amazon, Wikipedia, QQ, Amazon, Twitter, Taobao, Live.com, Sina, LinkedIn and Weibo.[13] The difference is that these platforms now include social networking sites (Facebook, LinkedIn), video-sharing sites (YouTube), wikis (Wikipedia) and microblogs (Twitter, Weibo). There are relatively new companies in the Internet business that did not exist in 2000. What makes platforms such as Facebook, Weibo, Twitter, Instagram, Pinterest, LinkedIn, Snapchat, Tumblr, Vine, Diaspora, Ello, Google+, VK, Academia, ResearchGate, Blogger, Wordpress and Foursquare distinct is that they are integrated platforms that combine many media and information and communication technologies, such as webpages, webmail, digital image, digital video, discussion group, guest book, connection list or search engine. Many of these technologies are social network tools themselves. Social networking sites, sharing sites for user-generated content, blogs, microblogs and wikis, just like all other media, are social in the broad understanding of the term as information. Some of them support communication, some collaborative work, content sharing or community building. These latter three forms of sociality have, due to the rise of platforms like Facebook, LinkedIn, Wikipedia or YouTube, become more important on the World Wide Web (WWW).

The discussion shows that understanding social media requires asking and engaging with a lot of theoretical questions. This book invites the reader to engage with theory and philosophy for understanding contemporary media. Social theory not only allows us to understand the meaning of concepts, it also allows us to ask important questions about the world, and it can be fun to theorize and to discuss theories with others. And the best questions we can ask are critical ones. But what does critical thinking mean? And why does it matter?

1.2 WHAT IS CRITICAL THINKING AND WHY DOES IT MATTER?

When discussing the question "What does it mean to be critical?" with academic colleagues, many have the immediate reaction: we are all critical because we ask critical questions and criticize the work of our academic colleagues. Scholars who characterize themselves as critical thinkers or critical theorists often question these claims. They emphasize the term "critical" and the need for being critical in order to stress that in their view not everyone is critical and that a lot of thought (academic or not) is uncritical. Their basic argument is that not all questions really matter to the same extent for society and that those whom they call uncritical or administrative researchers often focus on questions and research that is irrelevant, or even harmful, for improving society in such a way that all can benefit. They are concerned with questions of power.

POWER

Power is a complex concept, discussed in more detail in Chapter 4, which focuses on communication power. Power has to do with who controls society, who is taking important decisions,

---

12   According to alexa.com, version from 15 August 2000, archived on http://web.archive.org/web/20000 815052659/, www.alexaresearch.com/clientdir/web_reports/top_websites_nonclient.cfm (accessed on 2 July 2013).

13   According to alexa.com, version from 14 October 2015.

who owns basic resources, who is considered as being influential, who has the reputation to influence and change society, who is an opinion maker or who defines dominant norms, rules and values. The question "Who is in power?" immediately begets the question "And who lacks the capacity to influence and change things?". Power asymmetries mean that there are groups of people who benefit in society at the expense of others, by using them for their own ends and deriving advantages that do not benefit society as a whole or those who are being used.

It makes a difference whether one asks questions about society with a concern for power or not. Let's come back to the topic of social media. One can ask a lot of questions that ignore the topic of power. For example:

- Who uses social media?
- For what purposes are social media used?
- Why are they used?
- About what do people communicate on social media?
- What are the most popular social media?
- How can politicians and parties best use social media for obtaining more votes in the next elections?
- How can companies use social media for improving their advertisements and public relations so that they make more profits?
- How much average profit does one click on a targeted ad that is presented on Facebook or Google bring a company?
- How can a company make a profit by crowdsourcing work to users and employing free and open source software?

Such questions are not uncommon, but rather quite typical. Yet they include two problems. First, many of them ignore the topic of power. They do not ask the question who benefits and who has disadvantages from the use of social media, the Internet and ICTs and how the benefits of some are based on the disadvantages of others. Second, such questions are based on a particularistic logic: they are concerned with how certain groups, especially companies and politicians, can benefit from social media, and ignore the question of how this use benefits or harms others and society at large. So uncritical questions ask, for example, how *companies* can benefit from social media, but do not discuss the working conditions in these companies – the wealth gap between the well-off, managers and shareholders, on the one hand, and the large number of the unemployed, the homeless and precarious workers on the other hand, and the rising inequality in the world.

Let's go back to the three examples of social media in the Arab Spring, the Occupy movement and *The Huffington Post*. What does it mean to ask critical questions in the context of these examples?

ASKING CRITICAL QUESTIONS ABOUT UNPAID WORK FOR *THE HUFFINGTON POST*

- What is a commodity and what is the process by which something is turned into a commodity (= commodification)?
- How does commodification work on social media such as *The Huffington Post*?

- What is the role of advertising in these models? What is the role of users' activities in these models?
- Why is commodification in general, and on social media in particular, problematic?
- What are the negative implications of crowdsourcing and targeted advertising?
- What does exploitation of labour mean?
- In what way is the labour of users on social media exploited?
- How can the use of Facebook be exploited labour even though I am not paid for it, I do it in my free time and I find that it is a fun activity that is helpful in my everyday life?
- How can Facebook use be labour even though it is so different from working in a coal mine and feels more like singing a song with friends at a campfire?
- Can something be exploitation even though it does not feel like exploitation and is fun? Do users actually think about corporate social media use as labour?
- Do they see any problems? If so, what problems? If not, why not?
- How do trade unions, data protection agencies, privacy advocates, consumer protection groups and social movements react to the existence of this digital labour?
- Are there any alternatives to commercial social media? What are the opportunities and limitations of alternative social media?

ASKING CRITICAL QUESTIONS ABOUT THE JEREMY CORBYN CAMPAIGN AND SOCIAL MEDIA

- How is anti-socialist ideology expressed and challenged on social media in respect to Jeremy Corbyn?
- What is the role of articles published in right-wing versions of online newspapers and other right-wing news sources in social media postings about Jeremy Corbyn that express anti-socialist ideology?
- What power structures are underlying contemporary social movements such as the Corbynite movement?
- How do they influence the use of social media?
- What are the realities, opportunities and risks of social movements' social media use?
- Does the corporate character of platforms like Facebook, Twitter and YouTube negatively impact social movements' use of social media? What are the risks and opportunities of social movements' corporate social media use?
- If so, how?
- How should activists such as Jeremy Corbyn's supporters best deal with the contradiction that mainstream media misrepresent them, but that they reach a broad public and that not everyone actively uses social media?
- How do activists such as the Corbynites think about non-commercial social media platforms in contrast to for-profit platforms?
- Which problems and limits do such alternative platforms face in capitalist society, in which the control of resources (money, time, attention, influence, etc.) is asymmetrically distributed?
- How can the asymmetrical communication power that critical social movements such as the Corbynites face, be overcome?

ASKING CRITICAL QUESTIONS ABOUT EDWARD SNOWDEN AND THE SURVEILLANCE-INDUSTRIAL INTERNET COMPLEX

- What is the role of surveillance in modern societies? Why does it exist? What is the role of corporations and the state in surveillance?
- How do capitalist corporations and state institutions collaborate in the surveillance-industrial Internet complex whose existence Edward Snowden revealed?
- What are the problems of Internet surveillance?
- Why has surveillance been intensified and extended so much since 9/11? On what kind of ideological assumptions and myths about surveillance are these developments based?
- What are the causes of crime and terrorism? Are law-and-order politics and the increased control and monitoring of communications the solution? What are alternative approaches to the politics of surveillance, warfare and control as attempted solutions?
- What can be done against the surveillance-industrial complex? How can an alternative Internet that is not controlled by the state and corporations be created?

The list of questions is exemplary and far from complete. It shows that many critical questions can be asked about social media and need to be asked. Thinking critically about society and the media is concerned with creating structures of society and the media where everyone can benefit.

1.3 WHAT IS CRITICAL THEORY?

Critical theory is a specific form of critical thinking. Why is it relevant for understanding computer technologies?

The history of communication and transport technologies is not a progressive success story. Although many people today benefit in mutual ways from using books, telephones, trains, cars, television, radio, computers, the Internet or mobile phones, the history of these technologies is deeply embedded into the history of capitalism, colonialism, warfare, exploitation and inequality. Winseck and Pike (2007) show, with the example of the global expansion of cable and wireless companies (such as Western Union, Commercial Cable Company, Atlantic Telegraph Company or Marconi) in the years 1860–1930, that there was a distinct connection between communication, globalization and capitalism. Edwin Black (2001) has shown in his book *IBM and the Holocaust* that by selling punch-card systems to the Nazis, International Business Machines (IBM) assisted them in their attempt to extinguish the Jews, ethnic minorities, communists, socialists, gay people, the handicapped and others. The Nazis used these systems for numbering the victims, storing and processing where they should be brought, what should happen to them, and for organizing their transport to extermination camps such as Auschwitz, Bergen-Belsen, Buchenwald, Dachau, Majdanek, Mauthausen, Ravensbrück or Sachsenhausen. IBM made an international business out of mass murder (*I-B-M*) by accumulating profits from selling data storage and processing machines to the Nazis. The punch cards covered information on where a victim would be deported, the type of victim he/she was (Jew, homosexual, deserter, prisoner of war, etc.) and his/her status. Code status 6 was "*Sonderbehandlung*" (special treatment), which meant death in the gas chamber. Black has shown that the system was delivered and maintained by IBM and that IBM New York and the German Nazi state made rental contracts. Black (2001, 9) says that there was a "conscious involvement – directly and through its subsidiaries –" of IBM "in the Holocaust, as well as [. . .] in the Nazi war machine that murdered millions of others throughout Europe". The computer and the Internet have their origins in the military-industrial complex and were later commercialized. They both first served the interest of war before companies discovered the profitability of these technologies. The examples show that corporate, military or state interests often stand above the communicative interest of humans.

This book is based on a concern for human interests and for overcoming the global problems of society. We live in turbulent times that are shaped by worldwide inequality, global economic crisis, global ecological crisis, war and terrorism, high unemployment, precarious living and working conditions, rising poverty levels, etc. Can all benefit in this situation from social media? Or is it likely that only some benefit at the expense of others? In this book, I ask questions about power and (in)equality in contemporary society. I want to stress that it is important to be concerned about alleviating inequality and creating a society of equals, in which all benefit and lead a good life. The book is based on the normative assumption that we need a society and social media that benefit not just some of us, but all of us. This universal concern makes this book a critical book. Therefore it is called *Social Media: A Critical Introduction*.

Critical theory is especially connected to one name: Karl Marx.

YOU WANT ME TO READ KARL MARX? ARE YOU CRAZY? WHY SHOULD I DO THAT?

Karl Marx does not need much introduction. He was a thorough theorist and fierce critic of capitalism, a public intellectual, a critical journalist, a polemicist, a philosopher, an economist, a sociologist, a political scientist, a historian, a Hegelian, an author (with Friedrich Engels) of the *Communist Manifesto* (1848) and *Capital* (1867, 1885, 1894), a leader of the Communist League and the International Workingmen's Association, and one of the most influential political thinkers in the nineteenth, twentieth and twenty-first centuries.

But wasn't Marx responsible for the horrors of Stalin and the Soviet Union? Marx did not live in the 1930s, when Stalin organized show trials and killed his opponents. So he cannot really be blamed for what happened more than 50 years after his death. Furthermore, in many of his writings Marx was deeply concerned with humanism and a democratic form of socialism, whereas Stalin and his followers were arguably not (for a thorough discussion of why prejudices against Marx are incorrect, see Eagleton 2011).

The capitalist crisis that started in 2008 has made clear that there are huge gaps between the rich and the poor, owners and non-owners of capital, and that there are big problems of capitalism. The Occupy movement has made class an important topic. Occupy Wall Street argues that there is a "corrosive power of major banks and multinational corporations over the democratic process" and that "the role of Wall Street in creating an economic collapse [. . .] has caused the greatest recession in generations".[14] Occupy movements emerged in many parts of the world. Anti-austerity protests such as 15-M in Spain, the Indignant Citizens

---

14 www.occupywallst.org/about/ (accessed on 14 October 2015).

Movement in Greece that gave rise to the left-wing Syriza government in 2015, UK Uncut, the People's Assembly against Austerity, the movements supporting Bernie Sanders and Jeremy Corbyn, the 2015 anti-austerity student protests in Montreal, and contemporary labour protests in China and other countries that demand better working conditions have shown the limits of capitalism. Such developments have come along with an increased interest in Karl Marx's works that remain very topical in the twenty-first century because capitalism creates crises and inequalities. In media and communication studies, this interest in Marxist political economy has resulted in publications such as *Reading Marx in the Information Age: A Media and Communication Studies Perspective on Capital Volume 1* (Fuchs 2016b), *Reconsidering Value and Labour in the Digital Age* (Fisher and Fuchs 2015), *Digital Labour and Karl Marx* (Fuchs 2014a), *Marx is Back: The Importance of Marxist Theory and Research for Critical Communication Studies Today* (Fuchs and Mosco 2012), *Marx in the Age of Digital Capitalism* (Fuchs and Mosco 2016a), *Marx and the Political Economy of the Media* (Fuchs and Mosco 2016b), *Cyber-Proletariat: Global Labour in the Digital Vortex* (Dyer-Witheford 2015) and *Labor in the Global Digital Economy: The Cybertariat Comes of Age* (Huws 2014). Marx analysed how class, capitalism, crisis and power work and what the potentials of struggles for a better world are. Occupy and the reality of capitalism make Marx's themes very topical. The engagement with Marx can help us to better understand the situation we are in today, the problems society is facing and how struggles for a better future can be organized.

But wasn't Marx a nineteenth-century thinker? Why should I read him if I want to understand social media? Obviously, Marx did not use Facebook. So why should I care about his works today?

SO, YOU TELL ME THAT MARX INVENTED THE INTERNET?

Some scholars have said that Marx never commented on networked media (McLuhan 2001, 41). But Marx discussed the implications of the telegraph for the globalization of trade, production and society, was one of the first philosophers and sociologists of technology in modern society, anticipated the role of knowledge labour and the rise of an information society and was himself a critical journalist. This shows that somebody who cares about the analysis of media and communication has many reasons to engage with Marx. Marx stressed the importance of the concept of the social: he highlighted that phenomena in society (such as money or markets and, today, the Internet, Facebook, Twitter, etc.) do not simply exist, but are the outcome of social relations between human beings. They do not exist automatically and by necessity because humans can change society. Therefore, society and the media are open for change and contain the possibility of a better future. If we want to understand what is social about social media, then reading Marx can help us a lot.

In his work the *Grundrisse*, Marx described a global information network in which "everyone attempts to inform himself" about others and "connections are introduced" (Marx 1857/1858, 161). Such a description not only sounds like an anticipation of the concept of the Internet, it is also an indication that Marx's thought is relevant for Media/Communication Studies and the study of the Internet and social media. This passage in the *Grundrisse* is an indication that although the Internet as technology was a product of the Cold War and Californian counter-culture, Marx already anticipated its concept in the nineteenth century – *Karl Marx invented the Internet!*

SOCIAL MEDIA AND CAPITALISM

In 2014, the Internet researcher danah boyd (2014) published the book *It's Complicated: The Social Lives of Networked Teens* that analyses the implications of teenagers' uses of social media. The focus is on topics such as identity, privacy, crime, safety and security discourses, and bullying. For boyd, capitalism is an irrelevant topic for the study of social media:

> I also take for granted, and rarely seek to challenge, the capitalist logic that underpins American society and the development of social media. Although I believe that these assumptions should be critiqued, this is outside the scope of this project. By accepting the cultural context in which youth are living, I seek to explain their practices in light of the society in which they are situated. (boyd 2014, 27)

According to statistics, 28 per cent of those in the age group 65+ and 93 per cent of those aged 16–24 in Britain had at least one social media profile in autumn 2014 (Ofcom 2015a). In 2015, 90 per cent of young US adults used social media and 35 per cent of those aged 65 and older (PewResearchCenter 2015). Children and teenagers spend substantial amounts of their free time online, predominantly on commercial platforms. They are not just young people, but also young consumers growing up in consumer capitalism, in which they are almost constantly confronted by commodity consumption and advertising. Given the amount of time young people stay on social media, advertisers are particularly interested to present ads and sell commodities to them via such platforms. Young people who leave school or finish studying at university need to find paid labour in order to survive in a capitalist system. It is a tendency that they find work in the media, cultural and digital industries very attractive, but that such labour is, although often self-fulfilling, frequently so-called precarious labour: labour that is low paid, insecure, irregular, can involve working long hours, and is often freelance work.

One situation that young people particularly frequently report as feeling uncomfortable about is when employers or potential employers access employees' and applicants' social media profiles (Fuchs 2009b). A capitalist market for the online surveillance of job applicants has emerged (Allmer 2015, 91–92). In a survey of young Internet users, 53.1 per cent disagreed or strongly disagreed that it is okay that companies screen job applicants on the Internet and on social networking sites, whereas only 23.1 per cent agreed or totally agreed (Kreilinger 2014, 81). Labour and commodity culture are two fundamental aspects of capitalism and of the life of young people (and others) in contemporary society. Given the importance of labour and commodity culture in young people's lives, it is striking that boyd is not interested in their analysis. Young people do not just grow up and form identities; in doing so they are also confronted with consumer capitalism, the logic of competitive individualism, and the imperative to acquire skills to be employable for the capitalist labour market. Capitalist production, markets, and commodity culture in complex ways contextualize social media use. Under neoliberal conditions, these imperatives play a particularly important role. Karl Marx's works still today in the age of social media help us to understand the role the logics of capitalism, class and commodities play in everyday life.

HOW CAN ONE DEFINE CRITICAL THEORY?

Ben Agger (2006, 4–5) argues that critical social theory is based on seven foundations:

- It is a critique of positivism and of the assumption that theory is value free.
- It argues for the possibility of a better future without domination and exploitation.
- It sees domination as a structural phenomenon.
- It shows how humans, who live in structures of domination, tend to reproduce these structures in false consciousness.
- It is interested in everyday life such as the workplace and the family.
- It conceives structure and agency as dialectical.
- It sees liberation as a process that must be accomplished by the oppressed and exploited themselves.

Relating these aspects to Marx's works, we can identify six dimensions of a critical theory:

1   critical ethics;
2   critique of domination and exploitation;
3   dialectical reason;
4   struggles and political practice;
5   ideology critique;
6   critique of the political economy.

1 CRITICAL THEORY HAS A NORMATIVE DIMENSION

Criticism "measures individual existence against essence" (Marx 1997, 61–62). This means that critical theory is normative and realistic, it argues that it is possible to logically provide reasonably grounded arguments about what a good society is, that the good society relates to conditions that all humans require to survive (the essence of humans and society), and that we can judge existing societies according to the extent they provide or fail to provide humane conditions.

2 CRITICAL THEORY IS A CRITIQUE OF DOMINATION AND EXPLOITATION

Critical theory questions all thought and practices that justify or uphold domination and exploitation. Domination means that one group benefits at the expense of others and has the means of violence at hand that they can use for upholding the situation where the one benefits at the expense of others. Exploitation is a specific form of domination, in which one group controls property and has the means to force others to work so that they produce goods or property that they do not own themselves, but that the owning class controls.

An example is a slave-owner who owns a slave as property and owns all products that the slave creates; it even allows killing her/him if s/he refuses to work. A somewhat different example is Facebook Inc., a company controlled by private shareholders who own the Facebook platform. Facebook's users create data whenever they are online that refers to their profiles and online behaviour. This data is sold to Facebook's advertising clients who are enabled to present targeted advertisements on users' profiles. Without Facebook users, there would be no profit. So, one can say that users create the monetary value and profit of Facebook. But they do not own this profit, which is rather controlled by Facebook's shareholders. So, also, Facebook users are exploited.

Marx formulated the categoric imperative of critical theory "to overthrow all conditions in which man is a degraded, enslaved, neglected, contemptible being" (Marx 1997, 257–258). Critical theory wants to show that a good life for all is possible and that domination and exploitation alienate humans from achieving such a society. Marx therefore identifies the "task of philosophy [. . .] to unmask human self-alienation" (Marx 1997, 251). In deconstructing alienation, domination and exploitation, critical theory also makes demands for a self-determined, participatory and just democracy. Participatory democracy is a society in which all decisions are made by those who are concerned by them and all organizations (workplaces, schools, cities, politics, etc.) are controlled by those who are affected by them. Such a society is not only a grassroots political democracy, that is a society controlled by all people, but also an economic democracy in which producers control the production process and the means and outcomes of production. Critical theory wants to make the world conscious of its own possibilities. The "world has long dreamed of something of which it only has to become conscious in order to possess it in actuality" (Marx 1997, 214).

3 CRITICAL THEORY USES DIALECTICAL REASONING AS A METHOD OF ANALYSIS

Dialectical reasoning is a philosophical method for understanding the world. The dialectical method identifies contradictions. Contradictions are "the source of all dialectics" (Marx 1867, 744). Dialectics tries to show how contemporary society and its moments are shaped by contradictions. A contradiction is a tension between two poles that require each other to exist, but have opposing qualities. Basic contradictions are, for example, those between being and nothingness and life and death: all things have a beginning and an end. The end of one thing gives rise to a new thing. So, for example, the music industry's trial against the Napster file-sharing platform resulted in the end of Napster, but not in the end of the filesharing technology, as the rise of related technologies such as Kazaa, Napster, BitTorrent and the PirateBay platform has shown.

Contradictions result in the circumstance that society is dynamic and that capitalism assures the continuity of domination and exploitation by changing the way these phenomena are organized. Dialectics "regards every historically developed form as being in a fluid state, in motion, and therefore grasps its transient aspects as well" (Marx 1867, 103). The "movement of capitalist society is full of contradictions" (Marx 1867, 103). In a contradiction, one pole of the dialectic can only exist because the opposing pole exists: they require and exclude each other at the same time. In a dominative society (such as capitalism), contradictions cause problems and are to a certain extent also the seeds for overcoming these problems. They have positive potentials and negative realities at the same time.

Marx analysed capitalism's contradictions, including those between the following: non-owners/owners, the poor/the rich, misery/wealth, workers/capitalists, use value/exchange value, concrete labour/abstract labour, the simple form of value/the relative and expanded form of value, social relations of humans/relations of things, the fetish of commodities and money/fetishistic thinking, the circulation of commodities/the circulation of money, commodities/money, labour power/wages, subject/object, labour process/valoriza-tion process, subject of labour (labour power, worker)/the object of labour (the means of production), variable capital/constant capital, surplus labour/surplus product, necessary labour time/surplus labour time, single worker/co-operation, single company/industry sector, single capital/competing capitals, production/consumption and productive forces/relations of production.

The tension between opposing poles can be resolved in a process that Hegel and Marx called "sublation" and "negation of the negation". Sublation is a difficult concept that helps us to understand how change happens. For example, it can be used for explaining what is new and old about the contemporary form of social media. The German philoso-pher Georg Wilhelm Friedrich Hegel first introduced this concept. It is difficult because its meaning is not intuitively clear. This has to do with the fact that the term comes from the German word *Aufhebung*, which cannot be directly translated to English. It has three meanings: (a) to eliminate, (b) to preserve and (c) to lift up. Hegel used this notion as a language game in order to express that change of something means that (a) the current state is eliminated, (b) some aspects of the old state are preserved in the new state and (c) a new quality emerges in the new state. Marx applied the concept of sublation to soci-ety in order to explain how it changes.

Take the example of Facebook. It is a sublation of earlier Internet platforms: (a) It eliminated the dominance of other Internet technologies, such as guest books on websites. Nowadays it is much more common that users write on the walls of their Facebook friends. But (b) the guest book has also been preserved on Facebook: the wall is a kind of guest book. And (c) Facebook is more than just a guest book for commenting; it also includes features such as email, photo and video sharing, discussion forums, fan pages and the friends list.

Marx was concerned with dialectical relations in society. So, for example, there is a dia-lectical relation between labour power and wages: labour power is the capacity to work; work is the transformation of nature by human activity so that goods emerge. In capitalism, a lot of labour power is organized as wage labour. So wages exist only in relation to labour power (for paying labour power), and capitalism forces workers to earn wages in order to have money for buying goods. Labour and wages cannot exist without one another in capitalism. Workers, however, do not have the power to determine their wages. Marx (1867) argued that the power of the owners of firms that employ workers results in the circumstance that they only pay parts of the work the labourer performs, only a certain number of hours a day, whereas the other part is unpaid. The work that is performed unpaid is called surplus labour and the unpaid work time (measured in hours) surplus value. Surplus labour is a specific form of labour that emerges from the relation of labour power and wages in capitalism. The production of surplus value is the source of profit. For example, if workers in a company produce goods that are sold for €10,000, but their wages are only €5000, then there is an unpaid surplus labour that has produced a profit/surplus of €5000. Marx considers the unpaid production of surplus by workers and the appropriation of this value by capitalists to be the main scandal and injustice of capitalism. He therefore argues that there is a class relation (contradictory interests) between workers and capitalists.

Capitalism's class relation is another dialectical contradiction. Marx says that its subla-tion is not possible within capitalism, but requires to overcome this type of society and to build a new society. We will come back to the concept of surplus value in Chapter 5.

There are contradictions in capitalism that are persistent and not frequently sublated. They are at the heart of human misery in capitalism. Their sublation can only be achieved by political struggle and means the end of capitalism. These are especially the antagonisms between productive forces/relations of production, owners/non-owners, the poor/the rich, misery/wealth, workers/capitalists, dominated groups/oppressors. The contradiction between productive forces and relations of production is partly sublated in crisis situations, but reconstitutes itself right in the crisis. Its true sublation can only be achieved by the overthrow of capitalism. If, in capitalism, an important contradiction is the one between the owning class that exploits the non-owning class, then the goal of critical theory is the representation of the interest of oppressed and exploited groups and the overcoming of class society. "It can only represent a class whose historical task is the overthrow of the capitalist mode of production and the final abolition of all classes – the proletariat" (Marx 1867, 98).

In formulating a critique of exploitation and domination, critical theory develops "new principles for the world out of the principles of the world" (Marx 1997, 214). Dialectical thinking argues that the foundations of a classless society develop already within capitalism; that capitalism, on the one hand, produces new forms of co-operation that are, on the other hand, within class relations, forms of exploitation and domination. In capitalism, the forces of production are at the same time destructive forces.

4 CRITICAL THEORY IS CONNECTED TO STRUGGLES FOR A JUST AND FAIR SOCIETY: IT IS AN INTELLECTUAL DIMENSION OF STRUGGLE

Critical theory provides a "self-understanding [. . .] of the age concerning its struggle and wishes" (Marx 1997, 315), it can "show the world why it actually struggles" and is "taking sides [. . .] with actual struggles" (Marx 1997, 214). This means that critical theory can help to explain the causes, conditions, potentials and limits of struggles. Critical theory rejects the argument that academia and science should and can be value-free. It rather argues that political worldviews shape all thought and theories. There are deeply political reasons why a person is interested in a certain topic, aligns himself/herself with a certain school of thought, develops a particular theory and not another one, refers to certain authors and not others because modern society is shaped by conflicts of interests, and therefore, in surviving and asserting themselves, scholars have to make choices, enter strategic alliances and defend their positions against others. Critical theory holds not only that theory is always political, but also that critical theory should develop analyses of society that struggle against interests and ideas that justify domination and exploitation.

5 IDEOLOGY CRITIQUE: CRITICAL THEORY IS A CRITIQUE OF IDEOLOGY

Ideologies are practices and modes of thought that present aspects of human existence, especially those having to do with domination, that are historical and changeable as eternal and unchangeable. In *Capital*, Marx argued that capitalism is inherently ideological because in it, social relations tend to appear as things such as money and commodities sold on markets. This creates the impression that capitalism is a natural state of affairs, has always existed and cannot be changed. He termed this phenomenon the fetishism of commodities: the social relations between workers' labour appear not "as direct social relations between persons in their work, but rather as material relations between persons and social relations between things" (Marx 1867, 166). A commodity is a peculiar thing that is "strange" (Marx 1867, 163), "metaphysical" (163), "mystical" (164) and "mysterious" (164) because its value "transcends sensuousness" (163) so that the commodity "stands on its head" and "grotesque ideas" (163) about the nature of the commodity can emerge. Many ideologies are a form of fetishism: they make social relations appear as unchangeable, fixed and determined by static laws.

It is possible, for example, to claim that there is no alternative to Facebook and that the organizational model of Facebook, which uses targeted advertising, is the only possible form of a social networking site. Facebook is so dominant and has more than a billion users. Many of its users have several hundred contacts. It is difficult to imagine that there could be an alternative to Facebook because we are afraid to lose the possibility of communication with these contacts. But what if one could import all these contacts to another platform that does not have complex privacy policies, does not use targeted advertising and where all Facebook contacts are available? Ideologies claim that things cannot be changed, have always been or need to be the way they are now. Marx, in contrast, argued that everything in society is social, which also means that it can be changed by humans and that all things have a beginning and an end.

Ideology critique wants to remind us that everything that exists in society is created by humans in social relationships and that social relationships can be changed. It wants to bring "problems into the self-conscious human form" (Marx 1997, 214), which means that it wants to make humans conscious of the problems they are facing in society and the causes of these problems. Arguments like "there is no alternative to capitalism, neoliberalism, competition, egoism, racism, etc. because man is egoistic, competitive, etc." forget about the social character of society and create the impression that the results of social activity are unchangeable things. Critical theory provides an "analysis of the mystical consciousness that is unclear about itself" (Marx 1997, 214).

6 CRITICAL THEORY IS A CRITIQUE OF THE POLITICAL ECONOMY

Critical theory analyses how capital accumulation, surplus value exploitation and the transformation of aspects of society into commodities (commodification) work and what the contradictions of the capitalist mode of production are. A commodity is a good that is exchanged with other goods in a certain quantitative relationship: x amount of commodity A = y amount of commodity B. "In the critique of political economy, therefore, we shall examine the basic categories, uncover the contradiction introduced by the free-trade system, and bring out the consequences of both sides of the contradiction" (Engels 1843/1844, 175). Critical political economy is concerned with how resources are produced, distributed and consumed, and which power relations shape these resources. These resources can be physical productions, such as a car, but also non-physical goods, such as information. The information uploaded to Facebook is produced by users, but not owned and controlled by them: Facebook obtains the right to sell data about the uploaded information and your usage behaviour to other companies. It controls the profits derived from this process. Also, attention has its own political economy on the Internet: not everyone has the same power to be heard, seen and read on social media. Powerful actors such as CNN or *The New York Times* have much more visibility than a single political blogger. George Orwell was describing an animal kingdom, in which some animals are "more equal than others" (Orwell 1945, 85). On capitalist social media such as Google,

Facebook, Twitter and YouTube, some users are more equal than others – which means that there is inequality. Marx's political economy is not just a critique of the commodity form. It is also a critique of commodity fetishism, that is of ideologies associated with capitalist society, and an intellectual form of social struggle for a fair, just and participatory democracy.

1.4 CRITICAL THEORY APPROACHES

THE FRANKFURT SCHOOL: NOT A SAUSAGE, BUT A CRITICAL THEORY

The Frankfurt School is a tradition of critical thinking that has its origins in the works of scholars like Herbert Marcuse, Max Horkheimer and Theodor W. Adorno (for introductions see Fuchs 2016a, Held 1980, Wiggershaus 1995). All six dimensions of Marx's theory can be found in the Frankfurt School's understanding of critique and can be exemplified by studying Marcuse's (1988, 134–158) essay "Philosophy and Critical Theory", Horkheimer's (2002, 188–252) essay "Traditional and Critical Theory", Marcuse's (1988, 43–87) article "The Concept of Essence" and the section "The Foundations of the Dialectical Theory of Society" in Marcuse's book *Reason and Revolution* (1941, 258–322). These texts are apt because they describe the fundamentals of how the thinkers of the Frankfurt School thought one should study society.

Critical theory is *ethical*. It has a "concern with human happiness" (Marcuse 1988, 135). It is a *critique of domination and exploitation*. It holds that "man can be more than a manipulable subject in the production process of class society" (Marcuse 1988, 153). The goal of critical theory is the transformation of society as a whole (Horkheimer 2002, 219) so that a "society without injustice" (221) emerges. Like Marx, critical theory makes use of *dialectical reason*. It argues that concepts that describe the existence of capitalism (profit, surplus value, worker, capital, commodity, etc.) are dialectical because they "transcend the given social reality in the direction of another historical structure which is present as a tendency in the given reality" (Marcuse 1988, 86). Critical theory wants to advance *struggles and political practice*. "The materialist protest and materialist critique originated in the struggle of oppressed groups for better living conditions and remain permanently associated with the actual process of this struggle" (Marcuse 1988, 141). It advances a *critique of ideology* by trying to show that capitalism's central phenomena in many presentations of reality "do not immediately appear to men as what they are 'in reality', but in masked, 'perverted' form" (Marcuse 1988, 70). Critical theory bases its ideas on Marx's *critique of the political economy* (Horkheimer 2002, 244).

Jürgen Habermas built his approach on the classical Frankfurt School and at the same time worked out the concept of communicative rationality, by which he went beyond the classical tradition (Fuchs 2016a). Habermas (1984, 285–286) distinguishes between instrumental (non-social, success-oriented), strategic (social, success-oriented) and communicative action (social, oriented on understanding). Habermas (1971, 53) conceives instrumental action and communicative action as the two fundamental aspects of social praxis.

Communication is certainly an important aspect of a society free of domination. It is, however, in capitalism also a form of interaction, in which ideology is, with the help of the mass media, made available to dominated groups. Communication is not automatically progressive. Habermas differentiates instrumental/strategic reason and communicative reason, whereas Horkheimer draws a distinction between instrumental reason and critical reason (Horkheimer 1947) and, based on that, between traditional and critical theory (Horkheimer 2002). Habermas splits off communication from instrumentality and thereby neglects that, in capitalism, the dominant system uses communication just like technology, the media, ideology or labour as an instrument for defending its rule (for a critique of Habermas's critical theory of communication, see Fuchs 2016, chapters 1, 6 and 7). Communication is not pure and left untouched by structures of domination; it is antagonistically entangled into them. For Horkheimer (based on Marx), critical theory's goal is man's "emancipation from slavery" (Horkheimer 2002, 249) and "the happiness of all individuals" (248). Horkheimer has in mind the emancipation of communication just like the emancipation of work, decision-making and everyday life. His notion of critical rationality is larger than Habermas's notion of communicative rationality which risks becoming soaked up by non-critical approaches that use Habermas's stress on communication for instrumental purposes. The concept of communication can be critical, but is not necessarily critical, whereas the concept of a critique of exploitation and domination is necessarily critical.

CRITICAL POLITICAL ECONOMY OF MEDIA AND COMMUNICATION: STUDYING THE MEDIA AND COMMUNICATION CRITICALLY

Dwayne Winseck (2011) provides a map of the landscape of Political Economy research in Media and Communication Studies by identifying four approaches and speaking of Political Economies of Media:

* Neoclassical Political Economy of the Media;
* Radical/Marxist/Critical Political Economy of the Media;
* Schumpeterian Institutional Political Economy of the Media;
* The Cultural Industries School.

Speaking of Political Economies of Communication and the Media in the plural, as Winseck does, creates the impression that all these approaches are equally important and desirable. There is, however, a big political difference between, for example, neoclassical political economy that favours capitalist ownership of the media and Marxist political economy that opposes it. In media and communication research, radical/Marxist/critical political economy has historically and up until today been the most important approach. Winseck's pluralization of the political economy of the media and communication downplays the political and academic importance of Marx and Marxist theory.

In his seminal introduction to the field, Vincent Mosco defines the Political Economy of Communication as the "study of the social relations, particularly the power relations, that mutually constitute the production, distribution, and consumption of resources, including communication resources" (Mosco 2009, 2). Marxian Political Economy of Communication decentres the media by "placing in the foreground the analysis of capitalism, including the development of the forces and relations of production, commodification and the production of surplus value, social class divisions and struggles, contradictions and oppositional movements" (Mosco 2009, 94). Graham Murdock and Peter Golding (2005) argue that the Critical Political Economy of Communications analyses "the interplay between the symbolic and the economic dimensions of public communications" (60) and "how the making and taking of meaning is shaped at every level by the structured asymmetries in social relations" (62). For Jonathan Hardy (2014, 3–4), the Critical Political Economy of the Media is a

> tradition of analysis that is concerned with how communication arrangements relate to goals of social justice and emancipation. [...] I take the critical political economy approach to encompass studies that consider political and economic aspects of communications and which are critical in regard to their concerns with the manner in which power relations are sustained and challenged.

A critical political economy of social media is particularly interested in the power relations that govern the production, distribution and use of information of platforms such as Facebook, Google, YouTube, Weibo, QQ, LinkedIn, Pinterest, Tumblr, Blogger/Blogspot, Wordpress, Wikipedia, WikiLeaks, Snapchat, Instagram, Vine, Youku, RenRen, Douban, Tudou, WeChat, WhatsApp, Baidu, Vk, Reddit and Imgur.

The following terms have been used for naming this field: (Critical) Political Economy of Communication (Mosco 2009), (Critical) Political Economy of Communication(s) (Wasko 2004; Wasko et al. 2011), Political Economy of Culture (Calabrese and Sparks 2004), Political Economy of Information (Garnham 2011; Mosco and Wasko 1988), Political Economy of Mass Communication (Garnham 1990) and (Critical) Political Economy of the Media (Golding and Murdock 1997b; Hardy 2014; McChesney 2008). All of these approaches refer mainly to Winseck's second approach.

The Critical Political Economy of Communication studies media communication in the context of power relations and the totality of social relations and is committed to moral philosophy and social praxis (Mosco 2009, 2–5). It is holistic, historical, cares about the public good and engages with moral questions of justice and equity (Murdock and Golding 2005, 61). Golding and Murdock (1997a) mention five characteristics of the Critical Political Economy of the Media:

- holism;
- historicity;
- realist and materialist epistemology;
- moral and philosophical foundations;
- a focus of the analysis on cultural distribution and on the distribution between the private and public control of communications.

Important topics of the Critical Political Economy of Communication include: media activism; media and social movements; the commodification of media content, audiences and communication labour; capital accumulation models of the media; media and the public sphere; communication and space-time; the concentration of corporate power in the communication industry; the media and globalization; the media and imperialism; the media and capitalism; media policies and state regulation of the media; communication and social class, gender, race; hegemony; the history of communication industries; media commercialization; media homogenization/diversification/multiplication/integration; media and advertising; and media power (Garnham 1990, 1995/1998, 2000; Hardy 2010, 2014; Mosco 2009; Wasco 2004).

Dallas Smythe (1981, xvi–xviii) identified eight core aspects of a Marxist political economy of communications: materiality, monopoly capitalism, audience commodification and advertising, media communication as part of the base of capitalism, labour power, critique of technological determinism, consciousness, arts and learning.

CRITICAL POLITICAL ECONOMY AND THE FRANKFURT SCHOOL ARE TWO CRITICAL THEORIES, BUT DO WE REALLY NEED TWO OF THEM?

There are connections between Critical Political Economy and the Frankfurt School's stress on ideology. For Murdock and Golding (1974, 4), the media are organizations that "produce and distribute commodities", are the means for distributing advertisements, and they also have an "ideological dimension" by disseminating "ideas about economic and political structures". The approaches of the Frankfurt School and of the Critique of the Political Economy of Media and Communication should be understood as being complementary. There has been a stronger focus on ideology critique in the Frankfurt School approach for historical reasons. For Horkheimer and Adorno (2002), the rise of German fascism, the Stalinist praxis and American consumer capitalism showed the defeat of the revolutionary potentials of the working class (Habermas 1984, 366–367). They wanted to explain why the revolutionary German working class followed Hitler, which brought up their interest in the analysis of the authoritarian personality and media propaganda. The Anglo-American approach of the Political Economy of the Media and Communication was developed by people like Dallas Smythe and Herbert Schiller in countries that did not experience fascism, which might be one of the factors that explain the differences in emphasis on ideology and capital accumulation. Whereas North American capitalism was based on pure liberal ideology and a strong consumer culture, German capitalism after 1945 was built on the legacy of National Socialism and a strong persistence of authoritarian thinking.

Horkheimer's (1947) notion of instrumental reason and Marcuse's (1964) notion of technological rationality open up connections between the two approaches. Horkheimer and Marcuse stressed that in capitalism there is a tendency that freedom of action is replaced by instrumental decision-making on the part of capital and the state so that the individual is expected to only react and not to act. The two concepts are grounded in Georg Lukács's (1923/1972) notion of reification, which is a reformulation of Marx's (1867) concept of fetishism. Reification means "that a relation between people takes on the character of a thing and thus acquires 'phantom objectivity', an autonomy that seems so strictly rational and all-embracing as to conceal every trace of its fundamental nature: the relation between people" (Lukács 1923/1972, 83).

Capitalist media are modes of reification in a double sense. First, they reduce humans to the status of consumers of advertisements and commodities. Second, culture is, in capitalism, to a large degree connected to the commodity form: there are cultural commodities that are bought by consumers and audience commodities that the media consumers become themselves by being sold as an audience to the capitalist media's advertising clients (see the debate about audience commodification: Murdock 1978; Smythe 1977). Third, in order to reproduce its existence, capitalism has to present itself as the best possible (or only possible) system and makes use of the media in order to try to keep this message (in all its differentiated forms) hegemonic. The first and second dimensions constitute the economic dimension of instrumental reason, the third dimension the ideological form of instrumental reason. Capitalist media are a means of advertising and commodification and spaces of ideology. Advertisement and cultural commodification make humans an instrument for economic profit accumulation. Ideology aims at instilling the belief in the system of capital and commodities into humans' subjectivity. The goal is that human thoughts and actions do not go beyond capitalism, do not question and revolt against this system and thereby play the role of instruments for the perpetuation of capitalism. It is of course an important question to what extent ideology is always successful and to what degree it is questioned and resisted, but the crucial aspect about ideology is that it encompasses strategies and attempts to make human subjects instrumental in the reproduction of domination and exploitation.

A critical theory of media and technology analyses "society as a terrain of domination and resistance and engages in critique of domination and of the ways that media culture engages in reproducing relationships of domination and oppression" (Kellner 1995, 4). It is "informed by a critique of domination and a theory of liberation" (Kellner 1989, 1; see also Feenberg 2002; Kellner 2009).

CRITICAL THEORY AND CRITIQUE OF THE POLITICAL ECONOMY OF SOCIAL MEDIA

Frankfurt School Critical Theory and the Critical Political Economy of Media/Communication have both developed critiques of the role of media communication in exploitation, as means of ideology and potential means of liberation and struggle. Both traditions are valuable, important and complementary approaches for studying social media critically. The approach presented in this book is methodologically grounded in a combination of Frankfurt School Critical Theory and the Critique of the Political Economy of Media/Communication/Information/Culture (for this approach see also Fuchs 2009a, 2011b).

Marx developed a Critique of the Political Economy of Capitalism, which means that his approach is:

(a) an analysis and critique of capitalism;
(b) a critique of liberal ideology, thought and academia;
(c) transformative practice.

The globalization of capitalism, its new global crisis, the new imperialism and the role of knowledge and communication in capitalism (anticipated by Marx's notions of the means of communication and the General Intellect) have resulted in a renewed interest in Marx that should also be practised in Media and Communication Studies (Fuchs 2011b). To a certain extent, the German tradition of the Critique of the Political Economy of Communication has engaged with Marx and connected these works to the analysis of the role of communication in capitalism (see e.g. Holzer 1973, 1994; Knoche 2005). The problem is that these approaches, due to limited resources, have hardly been translated into English, which has left their impact limited to national levels and has resulted in a lack of international diffusion (for a recent English translation of one of Knoche's key works, see Knoche 2016). Horst Holzer (1994) spoke of Marxian analysis as the forgotten theory of communication in the German world (Holzer 1994).

Holzer (1973, 131, 1994, 202ff.) and Manfred Knoche (2005) distinguish four functions of the media in capitalism that are relevant for the Marxist Critique of the Political Economy of the Media and Communication:

1 capital accumulation in the media industry;
2 advertising, public relations and sales promotion for other industries;
3 legitimization of domination and ideological manipulation;
4 reproduction, regeneration, and qualification of labour power.

Holzer and Knoche have provided a good framework that could add the dimension of social struggles.

A more complete task for a Critical Theory and Critique of the Political Economy of Communication, Culture, Information and the Media is to focus on the critique and analysis of the role of communication, culture, information and the media in capitalism in the context of

● processes of capital accumulation (including the analysis of capital, markets, commodity logic, competition, exchange value, the antagonisms of the mode of production, productive forces, crises, advertising, etc.),
● class relations (with a focus on work, labour, the mode of the exploitation of surplus value, etc.),
● domination in general,
● ideology (both in academia and everyday life)

as well as the analysis of and engagement in

● struggles against the dominant order, which includes the analysis and advancement of
● social movement struggles and
● social movement media that
● aim at the establishment of a democratic socialist society that is based on communication commons as part of structures of commonly owned means of production. (Fuchs 2011b)

The approach thereby realizes that in capitalism all forms of domination are connected to forms of exploitation (Fuchs 2008a, 2011b).

Based on the methodological combination of Critical Theory and Critique of the Political Economy with a special interest in Karl Marx's works and dialectical philosophy, this book presents a critical theory of social media, which means that it outlines the predominant forms of capital accumulation of social media, the class relations and modes of surplus value exploitation underlying these capital accumulation models, and analyses the ideologies underlying capitalist social media and the potentials and limits for alternative social media and struggles for a just society that enables commons-based digital media.

"Philosophy is preserved in science as critique" (Habermas 1971, 63). If we want to conduct a critical analysis of social media, then we require a critical philosophy as a foundation. The tradition that goes back to Hegel and Marx is the most suitable critical philosophy tradition for such a project. Dialectical philosophy can provide a strong philosophical and theoretical grounding of Critical Media and Communication Studies (Fuchs 2011b,

Chapters 2 and 3). It is well suited for helping to bridge gaps in the field of Critical Media and Communication Studies (between the focus on structure and agency, subject and object, reason and experience, technology and society, economy and culture, pessimism and optimism, risks and opportunities, work and pleasure/joy, alienation and self-actualization, etc.) and for avoiding one-sided approaches.

Critical theory "never simply aims at an increase of knowledge as such" (Horkheimer 2002, 249). The task of this book is therefore not simply to produce new knowledge about social media, but to enable critical insights into the potentials and limits of social media that can enter into struggles for a just society. Critical theory wants to bring "to consciousness potentialities that have emerged within the maturing historical situation" (Marcuse 1988, 158). It analyses "the tension between potentiality and actuality, between what man and things could be and what they are in fact, [since this] is one of the dynamic focal points of this theory of society" (Marcuse 1988, 69). This book analyses the actuality of social media in contemporary capitalism and the potentials and limits for overcoming the corporate character of social media and for establishing a truly participatory Internet within the context of a participatory democracy.

Economic theory becomes critical theory by the insight that capitalism's "natural objectivity is mere semblance" and that it "is a specific historical form of existence that man has given himself" (Marcuse 1941, 281). This book wants to contribute to the insight that the capitalist character of social media, that is their grounding in profit logic, commodity logic, (targeted) advertising and exploited labour, is not a necessity, but a historical consequence of the commercial and capitalist organization of the Internet. Deconstructing the semblance of the necessity of corporate social media wants to contribute to the formation of consciousness about and struggles for a public, commons-based Internet.

RECOMMENDED READINGS AND EXERCISES

If you want to understand social media in a critical manner, it makes sense to start with foundational readings in critical theory. Therefore readings recommended in this section include works by Karl Marx, Herbert Marcuse, Max Horkheimer, Theodor W. Adorno and a debate between Adorno and Karl Popper on what the notion of the critical means in the social sciences.

Marx, Karl. 1843. Toward the critique of Hegel's philosophy of law: Introduction. In *Writings of the young Marx on philosophy and society*, 249–265. Indianapolis, IN: Hackett.

In this famous work Marx introduces his concept of ideology and argues that religion is the "opium of the people". Ask yourself:

- What does Marx mean by ideology? What are its characteristics?
- Give some examples of ideologies.
- What are important ideologies today?
- Where have social media merged with ideologies? Provide some examples. What exactly is the content of these ideologies? What claims are they making? What does reality look like and how can you determine what reality looks like in contrast to the claims made by social media ideologies? Search for examples and discuss them.

Marx, Karl. 1844. *Economic and philosophic manuscripts of 1844*. Mineola, NY: Dover.

This is one of Marx's earliest works on labour, capital, private property, estranged/alienated labour and communism. It is generally considered as his most important work for grounding a humanist critical theory that wants to create a society in which all humans live a good life. Questions for discussion and consideration:

- What is, for Marx, the most fundamental problem of capitalism?
- What does Marx mean by alienation (note: a synonymous term is estrangement)?
- How does Marx understand the term "communism"?
- How can Marx's concepts of capitalism, labour, alienation (and alternatives) be used for understanding social media critically?

Marcuse, Herbert. 1932. New sources on the foundation of historical materialism. In *Heideggerian Marxism*, 86–121. Lincoln, NE: University of Nebraska Press.

Although written in 1844, Marx's *Economic and philosophical manuscripts* were only published in 1932 (in German, later in English and other languages). Marcuse's text is one of the first reviews. It helps you to better understand Marx's philosophical text. Read first Marcuse and then Marx. Discuss in groups and compare the results:

- What do Marx and Marcuse (based on Hegel) mean by the essence of a thing? Try to give some examples of the essence of something.
- What is the difference between the essence and the existence of something in society? Try to give some examples.
- What is the essence of social media? What is the existence of social media? Is there a difference between the essence and the existence of social media?

Horkheimer, Max. 1937. Traditional and critical theory. In *Critical theory: Selected essays*, 188–243. New York: Continuum.

Marcuse, Herbert. 1937. Philosophy and critical theory. In *Negations: Essays in Critical Theory*, 134–158. Boston, MA: Beacon Press.

These two articles are two foundational texts of the Frankfurt School. They try to explain what critical theory is. Exercises:

- Every person in the classroom writes down how s/he defines "being critical". Compare the answers and make a list of which elements of criticism were identified.
- Discuss in groups and compare the results: How do Horkheimer and Marcuse define critical theory? What are the important elements of critical theory?
- Compare your own definitions of critique in the initial exercise to Horkheimer's and Marcuse's understandings. Argue what commonalities and differences there are.
- Discuss: What are purposes and tasks of a critical theory of the Internet and social media?

(Continued)

(Continued)

Marcuse, Herbert. 1941. The foundations of the dialectical theory of society. In *Reason and revolution: Hegel and the rise of social theory*, 258–322. Amherst, NY: Humanity Books.

In this chapter, Marcuse discusses how Marx used Hegel's dialectical philosophy for constructing a dialectical theory of society. Discuss in groups and compare the results:

- What is dialectical philosophy? Try to give some examples of how to apply dialectical philosophy to everyday phenomena.
- What is, for Marx, a dialectical theory of society? Try to find some examples of dialectical relationships and dialectical development in contemporary society.
- What are basic assumptions of a dialectical theory of the Internet and social media? Try to formulate a general concept and to give some examples.

Adorno, Theodor W., Hans Albert, Ralf Dahrendorf, Jürgen Habermas, Harald Pilot and Karl R. Popper. 1976. *The positivist dispute in German sociology*, 1–122, 288–296. London: Heinemann.

The positivist dispute was a debate in German sociology in the early 1960s about what it means to be critical. The main participants were Theodor W. Adorno and Karl Popper. Jürgen Habermas and others also contributed to the debate. Ask yourself:

- How does Popper define critique? What are basic elements of his understanding?
- How does Adorno define critique? What are basic elements of his understanding?
- On which aspects do Popper and Adorno agree and disagree?
- Which elements are needed for a critical theory of the Internet and social media? What are basic assumptions of such a theory if it is based on Adorno? What are its basic assumptions if it is based on Popper?

Read the first chapter in Karl Marx's most famous book, *Capital Volume 1*:

Marx, Karl. 1867. *Capital. Volume 1*. London: Penguin. Chapter 1: The Commodity (125–177).

It is not easy to understand Marx's writing style if it is the first time you have read him. It is even more difficult to think of how to relate his work to the realm of media and communications. The book *Reading Marx in the Information Age: A Media and Communication Studies Perspective on Capital Volume 1* is a chapter-by-chapter guide that makes reading and understanding Marx and relating his ideas to communications easier. Read, therefore, also as an accompanying guide to the first chapter in volume 1, the following chapter:

Fuchs, Christian. 2016. *Reading Marx in the Information Age: A Media and Communication Studies Perspective on Capital Volume 1*. New York: Routledge. Prefaces, Postfaces, and Chapter 1: The Commodity (pp. 15–51).

Marx introduces in Chapter 1 key categories for the critical theory and critique of the political economy of capitalism, such as the commodity, use-value, exchange-value, value, labour, abstract labour, concrete work, the forms of value, fetishism and ideology. Ask yourself and discuss:

- What is capitalism? What are particular features of contemporary capitalism?
- What roles do social media have in contemporary capitalism?
- What exactly is the commodity that social media corporations such as Google, Facebook, Twitter, Weibo or Baidu sell?
- What is social media's use-value, exchange-value and value?
- What is the (digital) labour that creates the social media commodity's value?
- What is the role of fetishism and ideology in the realm of social media?

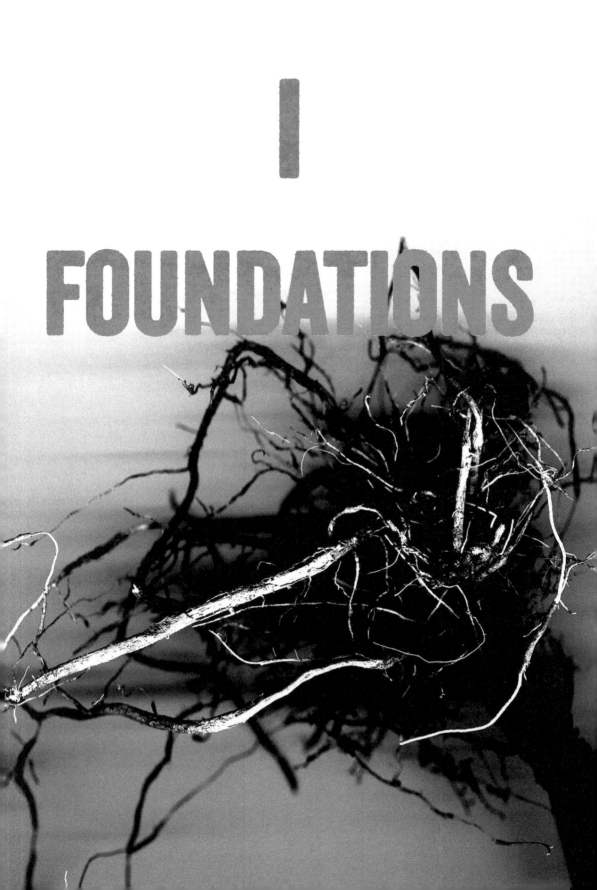

I

FOUNDATIONS

2 WHAT ARE SOCIAL MEDIA AND BIG DATA?

KEY QUESTIONS

- What does it mean to be social?
- What kinds of social theories exist?
- How can social theory help us to understand what is social about social media?
- How social is the web?
- What is big data? How is it related to social media? What are its implications for society and academia?

KEY CONCEPTS

Internet

Social media

Web 1.0

Web 2.0

Web 3.0

Émile Durkheim's notion of social facts

Max Weber's notions of social action and social relations

Ferdinand Tönnies's concept of community

Karl Marx's concept of co-operative work

Big data

OVERVIEW

This chapter introduces how one can think about social media. You will engage with the question: What is social about social media? One of the first reactions that many people have when hearing the term "social media" is to ask: "Aren't all media social?" This depends on how one conceives the social. In order to understand the meanings of this term, we need to go into sociological theory. This chapter presents some concepts of what it can mean to be social and discusses the implications of these concepts for understanding social media.

Mainly, sociological theory has asked the question of what it means to be social. Answering it therefore requires engagement with sociological theory. Specifically, I will introduce Durkheim's, Weber's, Marx's and Tönnies's concepts of sociality and apply them to providing an explanation of the social media concept.

Section 2.1 discusses the question of what new social media are and provides some basic features and criticisms of the terms "web 2.0" and "social media". In section 2.2, you can read different definitions of social media. I point out that we need social theory to understand what is social about social media. For this task, some sociological theory concepts are introduced that allow us to better understand the sociality of social media. I introduce four concepts developed by social theorists. Émile Durkheim (1858–1917) was a French sociologist who developed the concept of social facts. Max Weber (1864–1920) was a German sociologist who worked out a theory of social action and social relations. Karl Marx (1818–1883) was a social theorist who established a critical theory of capitalism. Collaborative work is one of this theory's concepts. Ferdinand Tönnies (1855–1936) was a German sociologist who is best known for his theory of community. Section 2.3 discusses how the concepts of these four thinkers can be used in constructing a model of social media. It also examines how one can empirically study the continuities and changes of the World Wide Web. Section 2.4 introduces a model of social media communication. Section 2.5 discusses the notion of big data and why it has become important.

2.1 WEB 2.0 AND SOCIAL MEDIA

WEB 2.0

The terms "social media" and "web 2.0" have in the past years become popular for describing types of World Wide Web (WWW) application, such as blogs, microblogs like Twitter, social networking sites, or video-/image-/file-sharing platforms or wikis. As the word "social" features prominently in the term "social media", the question arises: What is social about social media?

The term "web 2.0" was coined in 2005 by Tim O'Reilly (2005a, 2005b), the founder of the publishing house O'Reilly Media, which focuses on the area of computer technology. O'Reilly (2005a) lists the following as the main characteristics of web 2.0: radical decentralization, radical trust, participation instead of publishing, users as contributors, rich user experience, the long tail, the web as platform, control of one's own data, remixing data, collective intelligence, attitudes, better software by more users, play, undetermined user behaviour. He provides the following more formal definition:

> Web 2.0 is the network as platform, spanning all connected devices; Web 2.0 applications are those that make the most of the intrinsic advantages of that platform: delivering software as a continually-updated service that gets better the more people use it, consuming and remixing data from multiple sources, including individual users, while providing their own data and services in a form that allows remixing by others, creating network effects through an "architecture of participation", and going beyond the page metaphor of Web 1.0 to deliver rich user experiences. (O'Reilly 2005b)

O'Reilly creates the impression that the WWW, featuring BitTorrent, blogs, Flickr, Google, tagging, Wikipedia and so on, was in 2005 radically new and different from the earlier web (1.0). O'Reilly (2005a) consequently spoke of web 2.0 as a "new platform" that features "new applications".

In 2000, a crisis of the Internet economy emerged. The inflow of financial capital had driven up the market values of many Internet companies, but profits could not hold up with the promises of high market values. The result was a financial bubble (the so-called dot-com bubble) that burst in 2000, resulting in many start-up Internet companies going bankrupt. They were mainly based on venture capital financial investments and the hope of delivering profits in the future, and this resulted in a gap between share values and accumulated profits. The talk about the novelty of "web 2.0" and social media fits well into the post-crisis situation, in which investors had to be convinced to invest in new Internet start-up companies, which was difficult after the 2000 crisis. The ideology that web 2.0 is something new and different and that it has new economic and democratic potentials helped to convince investors. Web 2.0 and social media were therefore born in the situation of capitalist crisis as ideologies aimed at overcoming the crisis and establishing new spheres and models of capital accumulation for the corporate Internet economy. The talk about novelty was aimed at attracting novel capital investments.

Although Tim O'Reilly surely thinks that "web 2.0" denotes actual changes, he says that the crucial fact about it is that users, as a collective intelligence, co-create the value of platforms like Google, Amazon, Wikipedia or Craigslist in a "community of connected users" (O'Reilly and Battelle 2009, 1). He admits that the term was mainly created for identifying the need of new economic strategies for Internet companies after the "dot-com" crisis, in which the bursting of financial bubbles caused the collapse of many Internet companies. So he states in a paper published five years after the invention of the term "web 2.0" that this nomenclature was "a statement about the second coming of the Web after the dotcom bust". He was speaking at a conference that was "designed to restore confidence in an industry that had lost its way after the dotcom bust" (ibid.).

CRITIQUES OF WEB 2.0 AND SOCIAL MEDIA OPTIMISM

Critiques of web 2.0/social media optimism have, for example, stressed the following points:

- *Digital labour*: Online advertising is a mechanism by which corporations exploit Internet users' digital labour. Users form an Internet prosumer/produser commodity and are part of a surplus-value generating class that produces the commons of society that are exploited by capital (Fuchs 2008a, 2010c). Web 2.0 is based on the exploitation of free labour (Terranova 2004).
- *The branding of the self*: Most Internet users are part of a creative precarious underclass that needs economic models that assist them in making a living from their work (Lovink 2008). Blogging is mainly a self-centred, nihilistic, cynical activity (Lovink 2008). Alice Marwick (2013) argues that social media foster status-seeking behaviour and thereby "promote the infiltration of marketing and advertising techniques into relationships and social behavior" (93). Social media "is predicated on the cultural logic of celebrity, according to which the highest value is given to mediation, visibility, and

attention" (Marwick 2013, 14). The neoliberal logic of competition and individualism is expressed by the fact that on certain social media platforms one accumulates likes, followers, friends or check-ins, and the more of it one has, the higher one's cultural online capital and social online capital. Social capital is, according to Pierre Bourdieu (1986, 122), "a capital of social connections, honourability and respectability", whereas cultural capital has to do with reputation. Competitive social media foster the branding, quantification, marketization, commodification, capitalization of the self. Although we speak of "social" media, many contemporary "social" media platforms' logic is quite individualistic. They are called Facebook, YouTube or MySpace and not WeBook, OurTube or OurSpace because they are all about the self-presentation of the individual (networked) self. There is, however, also the potential to redesign social media away from the commodification of data and the self towards a collective "we"-logic, in which individuals encounter each other as partners, friends based on a logic of the commons, community and co-operation. So although dominant social media tend to foster the logic of individualization, as Marwick and Lovink stress, there are certainly alternative potentials.

- *Corporate imperialism*: Corporate media chains dominate the Internet economy (Stanyer 2009). Web 2.0 is contradictory and therefore also serves dominative interests (Cammaerts 2008). Web 2.0 optimism is uncritical and an ideology that serves corporate interests (Fuchs 2008a; van Dijck and Nieborg 2009). Corporations appropriate blogs and web 2.0 in the form of corporate blogs, advertising blogs, spam blogs and fake blogs (Deuze 2008).
- *Marketing and sharing ideology*: Web 2.0 and social media constitute a marketing ideology (Scholz 2008) that aims at attracting investors by trying to convince them that the Internet is constantly renewing itself and thereby bringing about new business opportunities. Both concepts have been arising in the aftermath of Internet economy's crisis in 2000 and have aimed to restore investors' confidence (Hinton and Hjorth 2013, Chapter 2). Facebook and other corporate social media use the notion of sharing for mystifying the logic of profit, advertising and commerce that is at the heart of their operation (John 2013).
- *The ideology of activity and creativity*: Web 2.0 users are more passive users than active creators (van Dijck 2009).
- *Simplistic notion of participation*: Web 2.0 discourse advances a minimalist notion of participation (Carpentier and De Cleen 2008).
- *Depoliticization*: Web 2.0 discourse is technological fetishism that advances post-politics and depoliticization in communicative capitalism (Dean 2005, 2010).
- *Techno-determinism*: Social media optimism is based on the techno-deterministic ideologies of cyber-utopianism and Internet-centrism (Morozov 2011) that only postulate advantages for businesses and society without taking into account the realities of exploitation and the contradictions of capitalism (Freedman 2012; Fuchs 2011b, Chapter 7).
- *Engineered, instrumental sociality*: José van Dijck (2013, 11) argues that social media automate the social by engineering and manipulating social connections. It would make "sociality technical" (van Dijck 2013, 12). Douglas Rushkoff (2010, 158) says that as a result "we are optimizing humans for machinery". "These days the social is a feature. It is no longer a problem (as in the nineteenth and twentieth centuries when the Social Problem predominated) or a sector in society provided for deviant, sick, and elderly people. Until recently, employing an amoral definition of the social was unthinkable" (Lovink 2011, 6).

HOW NEW ARE SOCIAL MEDIA?

Matthew Allen (2012) and Trebor Scholz (2008) argue that social media applications are not new and that their origins can be traced back to years earlier than 2005. Blogs were already around at the end of the 1990s, the wiki technology was suggested by Ward Cunningham in 1994 and first released in 1995, social networking sites already existed in 1995 (Classmates) and in 1997 (Sixdegrees), Google was founded in 1999. The discourse of ever newer versions would allow "products to claim to be new" (Allen 2012, 264), but at the same time also sustain "continuity and promise an easy transition from what came before" (ibid.). Versions would be ways of encouraging consumption. When talking about novelty, one has to be clear as to whether one talks about the novelty of technology, usage patterns or power relations.

Allen and Scholz argue that the technologies that constitute "social media"/"web 2.0" are not new. However, on the level of usage, these technologies were not popular in the 1990s and have become popular rather recently. On the level of the power relations of the Internet, it is just as unlikely that nothing changes at all as it is unlikely that there is radical change, because at a certain level of its organization capitalism requires change and novelty in order to stay the same (system of surplus value exploitation and capital accumulation) and continue to exist.

Tom Standage (2013), in his book *Writing on the Wall: Social Media – The First 2,000 Years*, takes a long-term perspective and argues that at the time of the Romans, social communication took on the form of "letters and other documents which were copied, commented on, and shared with others in the form of papyrus rolls" (1–2). Social media would therefore be at least 2,000 years old.

> The Romans did with with papyrus rolls and messengers; today hundreds of millions of people do the same things rather more quickly and easily using Facebook, Twitter, blogs, and other Internet tools. The technologies involved are very different, but these two forms of social media, separated by two millennia, share many of the same underlying structures and dynamics: they are two-way, conversational environments in which information passes horizontally from one person to another along social networks, rather than being delivered vertically from an impersonal central source. (3)

2.2 THE NEED OF SOCIAL THEORY FOR UNDERSTANDING SOCIAL MEDIA

DEFINITIONS OF WEB 2.0 AND SOCIAL MEDIA

Michael Mandiberg argues that the notion of "social media" has been associated with multiple concepts: "the corporate media favorite 'user-generated content', Henry Jenkins' media-industries-focused 'convergence culture', Jay Rosen's 'the people formerly known as the audience', the politically infused 'participatory media', Yochai Benkler's process-oriented 'peer-production', and Tim O'Reilly's computer-programming-oriented 'Web 2.0'" (Mandiberg 2012, 2).

Here are some example definitions of web 2.0 and social media that can be found in the research literature (in reverse chronological order, the list includes examples only and by no means claims to be complete):

- "I use the term social media to refer to the sites and services that emerged during the early 2000s, including social network sites, video-sharing sites, blogging and microblogging platforms, and related tools that allow participants to create and share their own content" (boyd 2014, 6).
- Social media means "networked information services designed to support in-depth social interaction, community formation, collaborative opportunities and collaborative work" (Hunsinger and Senft 2014, 1).
- Social media is an environment in which information is "passed from one person to another along social connections, to create a distributed discussion or community" (Standage 2013, 3). "Today, blogs are the new pamphlets. Microblogs and online social networks are the new coffee-houses. Media-sharing sites are the new commonplace books. They are all shared, social platforms that enable ideas to travel from one person to another, rippling through networks of people connected by social bonds, rather than having to squeeze through the privileged bottleneck of broadcast media" (Standage 2013, 250).
- "The very word 'social' associated with media implies that platforms are user centered and that they facilitate communal activities, just as the term 'participatory' emphasizes human collaboration. Indeed, social media can be seen as online facilitators or enhancers of human networks – webs of people that promote connectedness as a social value" (van Dijck 2013, 11). "As a result of the interconnection of platforms, a new infrastructure emerged: an ecosystem of connective media with a few large and many small players. The transformation from networked communication to 'platformed' sociality, and from a participatory culture to a culture of connectivity took place in a relatively short time span of ten years" (van Dijck 2013, 4).
- Social media represents "the technologies or applications that people use in developing and maintaining their social networking sites. This involves the posting of multimedia information (e.g., text, images, audio, video), location-based services (e.g., Foursquare), gaming (e.g. Farmville, Mafia Wars)" (Albarran 2013, 2).
- "Since at least 2004, the internet, and more specifically the web, has witnessed a notorious and controversial shift away from the model of the static web page towards a social web or Web 2.0 model where the possibilities of users to interact with the web have multiplied. It has become much easier for a layperson to publish and share texts, images and sounds. A new topology of distribution of information has emerged, based in 'real' social networks, but also enhanced by casual and algorithmic connections" (Terranova and Donovan 2013, 297).
- Social media "describes a specific set of internet-based, networked communication platforms. These use a business model of a database built by its own users. And they enable the convergence of public and personal communication. This definition includes Facebook and Twitter, Reddit and Tumblr, Pinteresta and Instagram, Blogger and YouTube, among others" (Meikle 2016, x). Social media tools feature "the elements of profile, contacts and interaction with those contacts", "blur the distinction between personal communication and the broadcast model of messages sent to nobody in

particular" (Meikle and Young 2012, 61). Social media "manifest a convergence between personal communication (to be shared one-to-one) and public media (to be shared with nobody in particular)" (Meikle and Young 2012, 68).

- "In the first decade or so of the Web's existence (from the 1990s to the early or mid-200s), websites tended to be like separate gardens. [. . .] Web 2.0 is like a collective allotment. Instead of in individuals tending their own gardens, they come together to work collaboratively in a shared space. [. . .] At the heart of Web 2.0 is the idea that online sites and services become more powerful the more they embrace this network of potential collaborators" (Gauntlett 2011, 4–5). It is characterized by the emergence of a "'making and doing' culture" (Gauntlett 2011, 11) and by "making and sharing our own media culture – I mean, via lo-fi YouTube videos, eccentric blogs, and homemade websites, rather than by having to take over the traditional media of television stations and printing presses" (Gauntlett 2011, 18). Making things online and offline would connect things together and involve "a social dimension and connect us with other people", the social and physical world (Gauntlett 2011, 3).
- "Social media indicate a shift from HTML-based linking practices of the open web to liking and recommendation, which happen inside closed systems. Web 2.0 has three distinguishing features: it is easy to use, it facilitates sociality, and it provides users with free publishing and production platforms that allow them to upload content in any form, be it pictures, videos, or text" (Lovink 2011, 5).
- "Social media is the latest buzzword in a long line of buzzwords. It is often used to describe the collection of software that enables individuals and communities to gather, communicate, share, and in some cases collaborate or play. In tech circles, social media has replaced the earlier fave 'social software'. Academics still tend to prefer terms like 'computer-mediated communication' or 'computer-supported co-operative work' to describe the practices that emerge from these tools and the old skool academics might even categorize these tools as 'groupwork' tools. Social media is driven by another buzzword: 'user-generated content' or content that is contributed by participants rather than editors" (boyd 2009).
- Social media and social software are tools that "increase our ability to share, to co-operate, with one another, and to take collective action, all outside the framework of traditional institutional institutions and organizations" (Shirky 2008, 20–21).

These approaches discussed above describe various forms of online sociality: collective action, communication, communities, connecting/networking, co-operation/collaboration, the creative making of user-generated content, playing, sharing. They show that defining social media requires an understanding of sociality: What does it mean to be and act in a social way? What is the social all about? There are different answers to these questions. The field concerned with these kinds of questions is called social theory. It is a subfield of sociology. To provide answers, we therefore have to enter the research field of social theory.

MEDIA AND SOCIAL THEORY

Media are not technologies, but techno-social systems. They have a technological level of artefacts that enable and constrain a social level of human activities that create knowledge that is produced, diffused and consumed with the help of the artefacts of the technological level. There is a recursive dynamic relation between the technological and the social level of the media. Media are based on what Anthony Giddens (1984) calls the duality of structure and agency (see Figure 2.1, Fuchs 2003b): "According to the notion of the duality of structure, the structural properties of social systems are both medium and outcome of the practices they recursively organise" (25) and they both enable and constrain actions (26). Media are techno-social systems, in which information and communication technologies enable and constrain human activities that create knowledge that is produced, distributed and consumed with the help of technologies in a dynamic and reflexive process that connects technological structures and human agency.

The Internet consists of both a technological infrastructure and (inter)acting humans. It is not a network of computer networks, but a network that interconnects social networks and

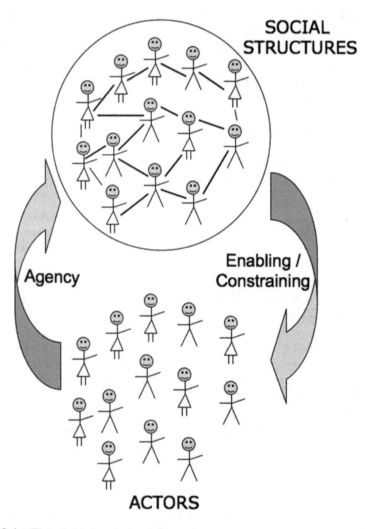

FIGURE 2.1　The dialectic of structure and agency

technological networks of computer networks (see Figure 2.2). The technical network structure (a global computer network of computer networks based on the TCP/IP (Transmission Control Protocol/Internet Protocol) protocol, a model that is used for defining how data is formatted, transmitted and received on the Internet) is the medium for and outcome of human agency. It enables and constrains human activity and thinking and is the result of productive social communication and co-operation processes. The technological structure/part of the Internet enables and constrains human behaviour and is itself produced and permanently reproduced by the human communicative part of the Internet. The Internet consists of a technological system and a social subsystem that both have a networked character. Together these two parts form a techno-social system. The technological structure is a network that produces and reproduces human actions and social networks and is itself produced and reproduced by such practices.

If we want to answer the question what is social about social media and the Internet, then we are dealing with the level of human agency. We can distinguish different forms of sociality at this level. They correspond to the three most important classical positions in social theory, the ones defined by Émile Durkheim, Max Weber and Karl Marx (Elliott 2009, 6–7).

ÉMILE DURKHEIM: THE SOCIAL AS SOCIAL FACTS

The first understanding of sociality is based on Émile Durkheim's notion of the *social* – social facts:

> A social fact is every way of acting, fixed or not, capable of exercising on the individual an external constraint; or again, every way of acting which is general throughout a given society, while at the same time existing in its own right independent of its individual manifestations. (Durkheim 1982, 59)

All media and all software are social in the sense that they are products of social processes. Humans in social relations produce them. They objectify knowledge that is produced in society, applied and used in social systems. Applying Durkheim's idea of social facts to computing means that all software applications and media are social because social structures are fixed and objectified in them. These structures are present even if a user sits in front

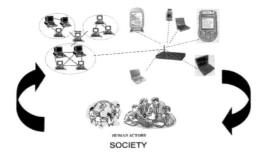

HUMAN ACTORS
SOCIETY

FIGURE 2.2 The Internet as duality of technological computer networks and social networks of humans

of a screen alone and browses information on the World Wide Web because, according to Durkheim, they have an existence of their own, independent of individual manifestations. Web technologies therefore are social facts.

MAX WEBER: THE SOCIAL AS SOCIAL RELATIONS

The second understanding of sociality is based on Max Weber. His central categories of sociology are *social action* and *social relations*: "Action is 'social' insofar as its subjective meaning takes account of the behavior of others and is thereby oriented in its course" (Weber 1978, 4). "The term 'social relationship' will be used to denote the behaviour of a plurality of actors insofar as, in its meaningful content, the action of each takes account of that of the others and is oriented in these terms" (Weber 1978, 26). These categories are relevant for the discussion because they allow a distinction between *individual* and *social activities*:

> Not every kind of action, even of overt action, is "social" in the sense of the present discussion. Overt action is not social if it is oriented solely to the behavior of inanimate objects. For example, religious behavior is not social if it is simply a matter of contemplation or of solitary prayer. [. . .] Not every type of contact of human beings has a social character; this is rather confined to cases where the actor's behavior is meaningfully oriented to that of others. (Weber 1978, 22–23)

Weber stresses that in order to constitute a social relation, behaviour needs to be a meaningful symbolic interaction between human actors.

FERDINAND TÖNNIES: THE SOCIAL AS COMMUNITY

The notions of community and co-operation, as elaborated by Tönnies and Marx, are the foundation for a third understanding of the social as collaboration. Ferdinand Tönnies conceives co-operation in the form of "sociality as community". He argues that "the very existence of *Gemeinschaft* [community] rests in the consciousness of belonging together and the affirmation of the condition of mutual dependence" (Tönnies 1988, 69), whereas *Gesellschaft* (society) for him is a concept in which "reference is only to the objective fact of a unity based on common traits and activities and other external phenomena" (Tönnies 1988, 67). Communities would have to work within a harmonious consensus of wills, folkways, belief, mores, the family, the village, kinship, inherited status, agriculture, morality, essential will and togetherness. Communities are about feelings of togetherness and values.

KARL MARX: THE SOCIAL AS CO-OPERATIVE WORK

Marx discusses community and collaborative aspects of society with the help of the notion of co-operative work. Marx and Engels argued that co-operation is the essence of society. In capitalism, it has become subsumed under capital so that it is alienated labour, and can only be fully developed in a free society. For Marx and Engels, co-operation is the essence of the social:

By social we understand the co-operation of several individuals, no matter under what conditions, in what manner and to what end. It follows from this that a certain mode of production, or industrial stage, is always combined with a certain mode of co-operation, or social stage, and this mode of co-operation is itself a "productive force". (Marx and Engels 1846, 50)

Co-operation is a foundation of human existence:

By the co-operation of hands, organs of speech, and brain, not only in each individual, but also in society, human beings became capable of executing more and more complicated operations, and of setting themselves, and achieving, higher and higher aims. (Engels 1886, 288)

But co-operation is also the foundation of capitalism: "A large number of workers working together, at the same time, in one place (or, if you like, in the same field of labour), in order to produce the same sort of commodity under the command of the same capitalist, constitutes the starting-point of capitalist production" (Marx 1867, 439).

Marx argues that capitalists exploit the collective labour of many workers by appropriating surplus value. Co-operation would therefore turn, under capitalist conditions, into alienated labour. This antagonism between the co-operative character of production and private appropriation that is advanced by the capitalist development of the productive forces is a factor that constitutes crises of capitalism and points towards and anticipates a co-operative society:

The contradiction between the general social power into which capital has developed and the private power of the individual capitalists over these social conditions of production develops ever more blatantly, while this development also contains the solution to this situation, in that it simultaneously raises the conditions of production into general, communal, social conditions. (Marx 1894, 373)

A fully developed and true humanity is, for Marx, only possible if man "really brings out all his *species*-powers – something which in turn is only possible through the co-operative action of all of mankind" (Marx 1844, 177). For Marx, a co-operative society is the realization of the co-operative essence of humans and society. Hence he speaks based on the Hegelian concept of truth (i.e. the correspondence of essence and existence, the way things should be and the way they are), of the "reintegration or return of man to himself, the transcendence of human self-estrangement", "the real *appropriation* of the *human* essence by and for man", "the complete return of man to himself as a *social* (i.e., human) being" (Marx 1844, 135). Marx (1875) speaks of such transformed conditions as the co-operative society.

The basic idea underlying Marx's notion of co-operation is that many human beings work together in order to produce goods that satisfy human needs and that, hence, also the ownership of the means of production should be co-operative. It is interesting that Marx already had a vision of a globally networked information system. Of course he did not speak of the Internet in the mid-nineteenth century, but he anticipated the underlying idea: Marx stresses that the globalization of production and circulation necessitates institutions that allow capitalists to inform themselves on the complex conditions of competition:

Since, "if you please," the autonomization of the world market (in which the activity of each individual is included), increases with the development of monetary relations (exchange value) and vice versa, since the general bond and all-round interdependence in production and consumption increase together with the independence and indifference of the consumers and producers to one another; since this contradiction leads to crises, etc., hence, together with the development of this alienation, and on the same basis, efforts are made to overcome it: institutions emerge whereby each individual can acquire information about the activity of all others and attempt to adjust his own accordingly, e.g. lists of current prices, rates of exchange, interconnections between those active in commerce through the mails, telegraphs etc. (the means of communication of course grow at the same time). (This means that, although the total supply and demand is independent of the actions of each individual, everyone attempts to inform himself about them, and this knowledge then reacts back in practice on the total supply and demand. Although on the given standpoint, alienation is not overcome by these means, nevertheless relations and connections are introduced thereby which include the possibility of suspending the old standpoint.) (The possibility of general statistics, etc.) (Marx 1857/1858, 160–161)

Although Marx here speaks of lists, letters and the telegraph, it is remarkable that he saw the possibility of a global information network in which "everyone attempts to inform himself" on others and "connections are introduced". Today the Internet is such a global system of information and communication, which represents a symbolic and communicative level of mechanisms of competition, but also poses new opportunities for "suspending the old standpoint".

Tönnies's and Marx's notions of the social have in common the idea that humans work together in order to produce new qualities of society (non-physical ones, i.e. shared feelings, in the case of Tönnies and material ones, economic goods, in the case of Marx).

2.3 EXPLAINING SOCIAL MEDIA WITH DURKHEIM, WEBER, MARX AND TÖNNIES

A MODEL OF HUMAN SOCIALITY

The three notions of sociality (Durkheim's social facts, Weber's social actions/relations, Marx's and Tönnies's co-operation) can be integrated into a model of human social activity. It is based on the assumption that knowledge is a threefold dynamic process of cognition, communication and co-operation (Hofkirchner 2013; see also Fuchs and Hofkirchner 2005; Hofkirchner 2002). Cognition is the necessary prerequisite for communication and the precondition for the emergence of co-operation. Or in other words: in order to co-operate you need to communicate and in order to communicate you need to cognize. Cognition involves the knowledge processes of a single individual. They are social in the Durkheimian sense because the existence of humans in society and therefore social relations shape human knowledge. Humans can only exist by entering into social relations with other humans. They exchange symbols in these relations – they communicate. This level corresponds to Weber's notion of social relations. A human being externalizes parts of its knowledge in every social relation.

As a result, this knowledge influences others, who change part of their knowledge structures and, as a response, externalize parts of their own knowledge, which results in the differentiation of the first individual's knowledge. A certain number of communications is not just sporadic, but continuous over time and space. In such cases there is the potential that communication results in co-operation, the shared production of new qualities, new social systems or new communities with feelings of belonging together. This is the level of co-operative labour and community. It is based on the theories of Marx and Tönnies.

Information (cognition), communication and co-operation are three nested and integrated modes of sociality (Hofkirchner 2013). Every medium can be social in one or more of these senses. All media are information technologies. They provide information to humans. This information enters into the human realm of knowledge as social facts that shape thinking. Information media are, for example, books, newspapers, journals, posters, leaflets, films, television, radio, CDs, DVDs. Some media are also media of communication – they enable the recursive exchange of information between humans in social relations. Examples are letters in love relations, the telegraph and the telephone. Brecht (1932/2000), Enzensberger (1970/1997) and Smythe (in his essay "After bicycles? What?"; Smythe 1994, 230–244) have discussed the possibility that broadcasting technologies are transformed from information into communication technologies.

Networked computer technologies are technologies that enable cognition, communication and co-operation. The classical notion of the medium was confined to the social activities of cognition and communication, whereas the classical notion of technology was confined to the area of labour and production with the help of machines (such as the conveyor belt). The rise of computer technology and computer networks (such as the Internet) has enabled the convergence of media and machines – the computer supports cognition, communication and co-operative labour (production); it is a classical medium and a classical machine at the same time. Furthermore, it has enabled the convergence of production, distribution (communication) and consumption of information – you use only one tool, the networked computer, for these three processes. In contrast to other media (like the press, broadcasting, the telegraph, the telephone), computer networks not only are media of information and communication, but also enable the co-operative production of information.

In discussions about the novelty, discontinuities and continuities of the contemporary WWW, one can find a lot of confusion about which notion of sociality one actually talks about. Furthermore, people often do not reflect on whether they talk about the technological level or the level of social relations when they speak of changes and continuities. The social level is also the level of power relations in society; that is, the level at which in heteronomous societies certain groups and individuals try to make use of resource advantages, violence and means of coercion (physical violence, psychological violence, ideology) in order to derive benefits at the expense of others. When talking about changes of media or the Internet, one should always specify which level of analysis (technology, power relations) and which dimension of sociality one is referring to. The question of whether the Internet and the WWW have changed in the past x number of years always depends on the level of analysis, the granularity of analysis and the employed understanding/dimension of sociality. Different assumptions about the novelty or oldness, the discontinuity and continuity of the media, the Internet and the WWW are based on different definitions of the social, different levels of analysis and different levels of granularity of the analysis. Most of these discussions are very superficial and lack an understanding of social theory and philosophy.

One hypothesis of this book is that in order to maintain the inequality of the power relations of capitalism and capital accumulation, capitalism needs to change its productive forces, which includes the change of its informational productive forces. Therefore the technological and informational structures of the Internet have to a certain degree changed in order to guarantee the continuity of commodity culture, exploitation, surplus value generation and capital accumulation. The changes of the media and the Internet are shaped by complex, dialectical and contradictory continuities and discontinuities.

WEB 1.0, WEB 2.0, WEB 3.0

If the web (WWW) is defined as a techno-social system that comprises the social processes of cognition, communication and co-operation, then the whole web is social in the Durkheimian sense because it is a social fact. Parts of it are communicative in the Weberian sense, while it is the community-building and collaborative part of the web that is social only in the most concrete sense of Tönnies and Marx. The part of the web that deals with cognition is exclusively Durkheimian without being Weberian, let alone Tönniesian–Marxian. The part that is about communication is Weberian and Durkheimian. And only the third, co-operative, part has all three meanings. Based on this distinction we can say that web 1.0 is a computer-based networked system of human cognition, web 2.0 a computer-based networked system of human communication, web 3.0 a computer-based networked system of human co-operation (Fuchs 2008a; Fuchs et al. 2010). Table 2.1 gives an overview of the application of the different concepts of sociality to the WWW. The distinction between the three dimensions of sociality is not an evolutionary or historical one, but rather a logical one. The use of the discourse of versions expresses the dialectical-logical connection of the three modes of sociality:

- Communication is based on and requires cognition, but is more than and different from cognition.
- Co-operation is based on and requires communication, but is more than and different from communication.
- Communication is a Hegelian dialectical *Aufhebung* (sublation) of cognition, co-operation is a dialectical *Aufhebung* of communication. *Aufhebung* means a relation between entities, in which one entity is preserved in the other and the other entity has an additional quality that is different from the first one (for a detailed discussion see Fuchs 2011b, Chapters 2.4 and 3.3). This difference also eliminates the first entity within the second, the preservation of qualities is at the same time an elimination – the two entities are different.

One, two or all three forms of sociality can (at a certain point of analysis) to a certain degree shape the WWW or any other medium. The task of empirical studies that are based on theoretical conceptions of the social is to analyse the presence or absence and the degree of presence of the three types of sociality in a certain medium.

The three forms of sociality (cognition, communication, co-operation) are encapsulated into each other. Each layer forms the foundation for the next one, which has new qualities. Figure 2.3 visualizes the encapsulation of the three dimensions of sociality on the WWW.

It is unlikely that the web (understood as a techo-social system that is based on the interaction of technological computer networks and social networks of power) has not changed in the years since 2000 because capital has reorganized itself as a result of the capitalist crisis

TABLE 2.1   Different understandings of sociality on the web

Approach	Sociological theory	Meaning of sociality on the WWW
1 Structural Theories	*Émile Durkheim:* Social facts as fixed and objectified social structures that constantly condition social behaviour.	All computers, the Internet and all WWW platforms are social because they are structures that objectify human interests, understandings, goals and intentions, have certain functions in society and effect social behaviour.
2 Social Action Theories	*Max Weber:* Social behaviour as reciprocal symbolic interaction.	Only WWW platforms that enable communication over spatio-temporal distances are social.
3 Theories of Social Co-operation	*Ferdinand Tönnies:* Community as social systems that are based on feelings of togetherness, mutual dependence, and values.	Web platforms that enable the social networking of people, bring people together and mediate feelings of virtual togetherness are social.
	Karl Marx: The social as the co-operation of many humans that results in collective goods that should be owned co-operatively.	Web platforms that enable the collaborative production of digital knowledge are social.
4 Dialectic of Structure and Agency *Émile Durkheim:* Cognition as social due to conditioning external social facts.	Web 1.0 as a system of human cognition.	The Web as a dynamic threefold system of human cognition, communication and co-operation.
Max Weber: communicative action.	Web 2.0 as a system of human communication.	
Ferdinand Tönnies, Karl Marx: Community-building and collaborative production as forms of co-operation.	Web 3.0 as a system of human co-operation.	

in 2000 so that it can survive and find new spheres of accumulation. It is also unlikely that the web is something completely new because, as we have seen, the Internet is a complex techno-social system with different levels of organization and sociality that have different speeds and depths of change within capitalism.

EMPIRICALLY STUDYING CHANGES OF THE WEB

If and how the web has changed needs to be studied empirically. Such empirical research should be based on theoretical models. I want to give an example for testing the continuity and discontinuity of the WWW. We want to find out to which degree cognition, communication and co-operation, the three modes of sociality, were featured in the dominant platforms that made up the technical structures of the WWW in the USA in 2002 and 2015. The statistics are based on the number of unique users in one month of analysis. According to the claims made by O'Reilly (2005a, 2005b), 2002 was a year in the era of 1998, and 2015 one in the era of web 2.0. By conducting a statistical analysis, we can analyse the continuities and discontinuities of the technical structures of the WWW. Table 2.2 shows the results.

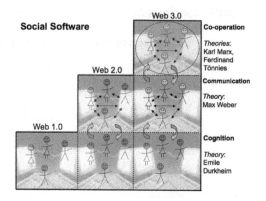

FIGURE 2.3   Three dimensions of the web's sociality

The analysis shows that there are continuities and discontinuities in the development of the dominant platforms of WWW in the USA in the years 2002 and 2015. In 2002, there were 20 information functions, 13 communication functions and one co-operation function available on the top 20 websites. In 2015, there were 20 information functions, 17 communication functions and six co-operation functions on the top 20 websites. The number of websites that were oriented towards pure cognitive tasks (like search engines) had decreased from seven in 2002 to three in 2015. In 2015, the number of websites that also had communicative or co-operative features (six) was larger than the one of the pure information sites (three). This shows that the technological foundations for communicative and co-operative sociality have increased quantitatively. The quantitative increase of collaborative features from one to six has to do with the rise of Facebook, Google+, Wikipedia and LinkedIn: collaborative information production with the help of wikis and collaborative software (Wikipedia, Google Docs) and social networking sites oriented towards community building (Facebook, Google+, LinkedIn). There are continuities and discontinuities in the development of the WWW in the period 2002–2015. The changes concern the rising importance of co-operative sociality. This change is significant, but not dramatic. One novelty is the rise of social networking sites (Facebook, LinkedIn, Google+, Douban, RenRen, VK, Ello, Diaspora, Vk, etc.). Another change is the emergence of blogs (Wordpress, Blogger/Blogpost, Tumblr, etc.), microblogs (Twitter, Weibo) and file-sharing websites (YouTube, Youku, Tudou), which have increased the possibilities of communication and information sharing in the top 20 US websites. Google has broadened its functions: it started as a pure search engine (in 1999), introduced communication features in 2007 (gMail) and its own social networking site platform (Google+) in June 2011.

The statistics indicate that the rise of co-operative sociality supported by social networking sites and wikis, and the differentiation of cognitive and communicative sociality (the emergence of file-sharing sites and blogs, including microblogs such as Twitter), have to a certain degree changed the technical structures of the WWW in order to enable new models of capital accumulation and the maintenance of the capitalist character of the WWW. Another significant change is the rise of the search engine Google, which has pioneered the web capital accumulation models by introducing targeted advertising that is personalized

TABLE 2.2   Information functions of the top 20 websites

9 December 2002 (three-month page ranking based on page views and page reach)			15 October 2015 (one-month page ranking based on average daily visitors and page views)		
Rank	Website	Primary information functions	Rank	Website	Primary information functions
1	yahoo.com	cogn, comm	1	google.com	cogn, comm, coop
2	msn.com	cogn, comm	2	facebook.com	cogn, comm, coop
3	daum.net	cogn, comm	3	youtube.com	cogn, comm
4	naver.com	cogn, comm	4	baidu.com	cogn, comm
5	google.com[1]	cogn	5	yahoo.com	cogn, comm
6	yahoo.co.jp	cogn, comm	6	amazon.com	cogn
7	passport.net	cogn	7	wikipedia.org	cogn, comm, coop
8	ebay.com	cogn	8	qq.com	cogn, comm
9	microsoft.com	cogn	9	twitter.com	cogn, comm
10	bugsmusic.co.kr	cogn	10	google.co.in	cogn, comm, coop
11	sayclub.com	cogn, comm	11	taobao.com	cogn
12	sina.com.cn	cogn, comm	12	live.com	cogn, comm
13	netmarble.net	cogn, comm, coop	13	sina.com.cn	cogn, comm
14	amazon.com	cogn	14	linkedin.com	cogn, comm, coop
15	nate.com	cogn, comm	15	yahoo.co.jp	cogn, comm
16	go.com	cogn	16	weibo.com	cogn, comm
17	sohu.com	cogn, comm	17	ebay.com	cogn
18	163.com	cogn, comm	18	google.co.jp	cogn, comm, coop
19	hotmail.com	cogn, comm	19	yandex.ru	cogn, comm
20	aol.com	cogn, comm	20	hao123.com	cogn, comm
		cogn: 20 comm: 13 coop: 1			cogn: 20 comm: 17 coop: 6

[1] Google's main communicative feature, the email service gMail, was launched in 2004. Its social networking site Google+ was launched in 2011.

to the interests of users and monitors their online behaviour and personal interests on the Internet. The change of the technical structures of the WWW has enabled the continuity of the logic of capital accumulation on the Internet after the dot-com bubble. Wikipedia, which is a non-profit and non-commercial platform funded by user donations, has entered the scene. It is the only successful WWW platform thus far that is not based on a capital accumulation model.

2.4 A MODEL OF SOCIAL MEDIA COMMUNICATION

The study of social media activity is due to the novelty of blogs and social networks like Facebook and Twitter, a relatively young endeavour (see Fuchs et al. 2012; Trottier 2012). Based on the theoretical assumptions about the information process (the model of information as cognition, communication and co-operation introduced in section 2.3) and society, we can describe social media communication based on social theory (see Fuchs 2015a, Chapter 8; Fuchs and Trottier 2015; Trottier and Fuchs 2015) based on social theory.

Some constitutive features of social media in modern society are the following.

INTEGRATED SOCIALITY

Social media enable the convergence of the three modes of sociality (cognition, communication, cooperation) in an integrated sociality. This means, for example, that on Facebook an individual creates a multimedia content like a video on the cognitive level, publishes it so that others can comment (the communicative level) and allows others to manipulate and remix the content, so that new content with multiple authorship can emerge. One step does not necessarily result in the next, but the technology has the potential to enable the combination of all three activities in one space. Facebook, by default, encourages the transition from one stage of sociality to the next, within the same social space.

INTEGRATED ROLES

Social media like Facebook are based on the creation of personal profiles that describe the various roles of a human being's life. In contemporary modern society, different social roles tend to converge in various social spaces. The boundaries between public life and private life as well as the workplace and the home have become porous. Habermas (1984, 1987) identified systems (the economy, the state) and the lifeworld as central realms of modern society. The lifeworld can be further divided into culture and civil society. We act in different social roles in these spheres: for example as employees and consumers in the economic systems, as clients and citizens in the state system, as activists in the socio-political sphere, and in the socio-economic sphere as lovers and consumers. We also act as family members in the private sphere, or as fan community members, parishioners, professional association members and so on in the socio-cultural sphere. A new form of liquid and porous sociality has emerged, in which we partly act in different social roles in the same social space. On social media such as Facebook we act in various roles, but all of these roles become mapped onto single profiles that are observed by different people who are associated with our different social roles. This means that social media are social spaces in which social roles tend to converge and become integrated in single profiles.

INTEGRATED AND CONVERGING COMMUNICATION ON SOCIAL MEDIA

On social media, various social activities (cognition, communication, co-operation) in different social roles that belong to our behaviour in systems (economy, state) and the lifeworld (the private sphere, the socio-economic sphere, the socio-political sphere, the socio-cultural sphere) are mapped to single profiles. In this mapping process, data about a) social activites within b) social roles are generated. This means that a Facebook profile holds a1) personal data, a2) communicative data, a3) social network data/community data in relation to b1) private roles (friend, lover, relative, father, mother, child, etc.), b2) civic

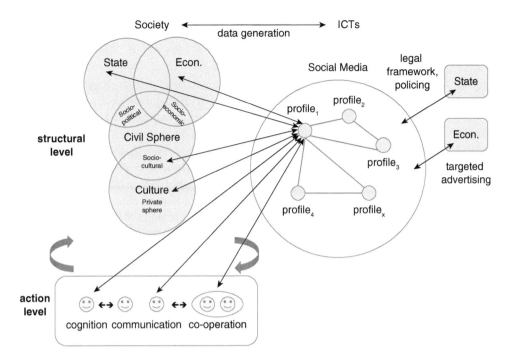

FIGURE 2.4 The process of social media communication in modern society

roles (socio-cultural roles as fans, community members, neighbourhood association members, etc.), b3) public roles (socio-economic and socio-political roles as activists and advocates) and b4) systemic roles (in politics: voter, citizen, client, politician, bureaucrat, etc.; in the economy: worker, manager, owner, purchaser/consumer, etc.). The different social roles and activities tend to converge, as for example in the situation where the workplace is also a playground, where friendships and intimate relations are formed and dissolved and where spare time activities are conducted. This means that social media surveillance is an integrated form of surveillance, in which one finds surveillance of different (partly converging) activities in different partly converging social roles with the help of profiles that hold a complex networked multitude of data about humans.

Figure 2.4 visualizes the communication process on one single social media system (such as Facebook) in modern society. The total social media communication process is a combination and network of a multitude of such processes. The integration of different forms of sociality and social roles on social media means that there are myriad possible social purposes that any single platform can serve. Individual citizens may use it to communicate with other citizens in the context of any number of social roles, as well as for purposes that may transcend roles. They may also communicate with organizations and institutions for the same purposes. They may also simply monitor the communication in which any of these social actors are engaged. Institutions, including branches of the state, may do all of the above as well.

2.5 BIG DATA

WHAT IS "BIG DATA"?

"Big data" is an even newer concept, trend, development, hype and ideology than "social media". According to Mayer-Schönberger and Cukier (2013), big data "refers to things one can do at a large scale that cannot be done at a smaller one, to extract new insights or create new forms of value" (6), "an important step in humankind's quest to quantify and understand the world", the "preponderance of things that could never be measured, stored, analyzed, and shared before is becoming datafied" (17–18). We would now be able to "manage far larger quantities of data than before, and the data [...] need not be placed in tidy rows or classic database tables" (6). For Manyika et al. (2011) big data "refers to datasets whose size is beyond the ability of typical database software tools to capture, store, manage, and analyze" (1). Big data refers to

> the major expansion in the contemporary era of the quantities of digital data that are generated as the products of users' transactions with and content generation via digital media technologies, as well as digital surveillance technologies such as CCTV cameras, RFID chips, traffic monitors and sensors monitoring the natural environment. (Lupton 2015, 94)

Big data "refers to the movement to analyze the increasingly vast amounts of information stored in multiple locations, but mainly online and primarily in the cloud" (Mosco 2014, 177). We can as a general definition say that big data are the vast amount of data generated by large-scale computing operations in order to analyse and predict the development of certain aspects of society or nature.

A related term is cloud computing. Whereas big data refers to large amounts of digital objects stored in computers, cloud computing refers to the way computing resources are used for storing big data. It is about devices for and the very processes of the storage, processing and distribution of data (Mosco 2014, 17), which often involves shared access to data among a certain group. It is also associated with the storage of vast amounts of data in data centres.

Uncritical accounts of big data explain its importance purely technologically as the effect of Moore's law that says computers' storage space and processing power doubles every 18 months. The rise of computing capacity would therefore result in an exponential growth of data storage. "Things really are speeding up. The amount of stored information grows four times faster than the world economy, while the processing power of computers grows nine times faster" (Mayer-Schönberger and Cukier 2013, 8)

NEOLIBERAL BIG DATA IDEOLOGY: NON-ECONOMIC ASPECTS SUCH AS PRIVACY, DEMOCRACY, WAR/PEACE, OR (IN)EQUALITY ARE MISSING

The big data ideology presents the massification of available, collected, stored and analysed data as a huge opportunity for the economy and society and tends to disregard negative aspects. One example is an economic reductionism that frames big data in terms of gross domestic product (GDP) and productivity growth:

Our research finds that data can create significant value for the world economy, enhancing the productivity and competitiveness of companies and the public sector and creating substantial economic surplus for consumers. [...] we are on the cusp of a tremendous wave of innovation, productivity, and growth, as well as new modes of competition and value capture – all driven by big data as consumers, companies, and economic sectors exploit its potential. (Manyika et al. 2011, 1–2)

An associated ideology is that big data is in a positivist manner first presented as a major change of society and as radically new and transformative, and second results in claims that big data only benefits society:

"Big data marks the beginning of a major transformation [...] Things really are speeding up. The amount of stored information grows four times faster than the world economy, while the processing power of computers grows nine times faster" (Mayer-Schönberger and Cukier 2013, 7–9). The "world of big data is poised to shake up everything from businesses and the sciences to healthcare, government, education, economics, the humanities, and every other aspect of society" (11). "The benefits to society will be myriad, as big data becomes part of the solution to pressing global problems like addressing climate change, eradicating disease, and fostering good governance and economic development" (17). Some non-economic issues are addressed here, but overall such approaches argue for a technological fix to economic, social, political and cultural problems. They are techno-deterministic.

BIG DATA'S POLITICAL ECONOMY

Critical political economy analyses the interconnection of economic and political dimensions of communications and digital media and discusses them in respect to history, society as totality, moral questions and ethical-political implications.

Big data stand in a broader societal – economic, political and ideological – context: 9/11 has advanced a culture of control, surveillance, fear-mongering, scapegoating and suspicion, competition and individualization, in which law-and-order politics and surveillance are seen as fixes to the complex societal problem of terrorism. This culture and ideology of surveillance and control has resulted in the emergence of a specific organizational form of the military-industrial-corporate complex, namely the surveillance-industrial Internet complex, in which secret services, communications corporations and private security companies collaborate in order to conduct large-scale surveillance of citizens' communications. Edward Snowden has revealed the existence of this complex that uses technologies and programmes such as Prism and XKeyScore.

Neoliberalism is on the one hand a market-fundamentalist ideology, but on the other hand also a form of governance that regulates the economy by strengthening the power of capital and weakening the power of labour. It advances the commodification and privatization of almost everything, the weakening of the idea of public services and the common good. The extension and intensification of advertising and consumer culture into the realm of online data is an expression of large-scale capitalist privatization and commodification under neoliberal condition. Facebook and Google collect and store vast amounts of data. They capture and hold all the information they can get about their users, because they are interested in commodifying it so that monetary profits can be derived. Facebook and Google are not communications companies. They do not sell access to communications, they sell big data for advertising purposes. They are the world's largest advertising agencies that operate as big data collection and commodification machines.

The collection, storage, control and analysis of "big data" stands in the context of the surveillance-industrial-complex and neoliberalism. Big data is a method for the economic and political control and targeting of individuals. They are targeted as consumers and as potential terrorists and criminals. Mark Andrejevic (2013) argues that big data stands in the context of big data surveillance of citizens, consumers and workers. Big data is the "paradox of 'total documentation'", in which the population as a whole is the target that is subjected to "population-level data capture" (35). Big data seen from a political-economic perspective of analysis means "data collection without limits" (36). For Vincent Mosco (2014, 10), big data and cloud computing are an expression of the combination of "surveillance capitalism" and the "surveillance state" in what he terms the military information complex (9).

BIG DATA'S DANGERS, PROBLEMS AND IMPLICATIONS IN A CAPITALIST WORLD

"While the technological sphere of social media is new, so is the global phenomenon of Big Data worship, the ethical question about 'accessing', privatizing, and commodifying the commons has been a time-honored concern that goes all the way back to the beginning of the capitalist world-system" (Qiu 2015, 1091). There are manifold dangers and implications that big data poses in a capitalist world.

CONSUMER CULTURE

The world is turned into a huge shopping mall. Humans are confronted with ads almost everywhere, capitalist logic colonizes the social, public and private world.

INSTRUMENTAL REASON

Algorithms' instrumental reason tries to calculate, plan and control human needs. David Chandler (2015) argues in this context that big data promises a posthuman world, in which not humans, but "'data' do the work" (848). The consequence would be an instrumental and administrative understanding of politics that "reduces governance to an ongoing and technical process of adaptation, accepting the world as it is" (835). It would advance a model of the governance of the self (838). We can add that individuals' and communities' self-help via big data suggests the neoliberal outsourcing of responsibility from the state to individuals and communities and is therefore a discourse that neoliberal governments, parties and politics uncritically embrace. Ideological parallels are the neoliberal philosophy that you should "do what you love" and the concept of a big society in which individuals form co-operatives, self-help groups, grassroots initiatives and other voluntary civil society projects that replace the welfare state. The problem is that such outsourcing of responsibility can create and enforce the attitude and impression that individuals and communities are responsible for social problems and their solutions, which distracts attention from actually existing power structures. There is no doubt that a state that enhances and supports participation and grassroots initiatives is a much-needed development. Under neoliberal governmentality, the tendency is, however, that such initiatives are seen not as complements to, but as substitutes for the welfare state.

In big data analytics, the "human comes into the picture relatively late in the process (if at all)" (Chandler 2015, 837). Algorithms play a central role. Big data analysis and research tends to be inductive, atheoretical, it works "'down' to the contextualisation of the individual case, thereby promising personalised or individualised health care, political campaigning or product purchasing information. Big Data 'drills' or 'mines' down from the mass of data to the individual case" (846).

In big data analytics, instrumental reason takes on such a form that algorithms become "actors" that make choices and define needs on behalf of humans and make assumptions about human thought and behaviour based on algorithmic logic. The problem is that algorithms and computers, unlike humans, do not have affects, ethics and morals and only act based on the purely instrumental linear logic "IF condition C THEN take action A". Given that humans are complex societal beings, such linear instrumental reasoning is error-prone and creates false positives. In economic and political life, algorithmic logic can have severe consequences such as humans being considered as criminals or terrorists although they are innocent, or being discriminated against by banks, corporations or public services. Algorithms tend to erect a new God's eye view that automates human decision-making and action and thereby creates totalitarian potentials. Given the impacts of big data, research urgently faces "the task of revitalising a critical approach" (Chandler 2015, 851).

INEQUALITY

The increased commodification coming along with big data means social inequality. There are new forms of discrimination that involve rational discrimination and cumulative disadvantage resulting from data recorded in databases that algorithms infer from predictions and that are error-prone (Gandy 2009). The Internet becomes a class-realm of exploitation. There is a "big data divide" (Andrejevic 2014) that concerns the ownership and control of data and poses advantages for the powerful and disadvantages for the less powerful.

SURVEILLANCE SOCIETY'S FASCIST POTENTIALS

Categorical suspicion turns the presumption of innocence into a fascist presumption of guilt so that one is "innocent until proven guilty" and a "terrorist until proven innocent". Terrorists are not so silly as to communicate their plans online, so the whole logic of big data surveillance is mistaken because there is no technological fix to political and socio-economic problems. Law and order politics fosters fascist potentials in society. Big data surveillance has intensified in times of capitalist crisis. Times of crisis are times of ideological scapegoating in order to distract attention from causes of social problems. Contemporary scapegoats include Romanian and Bulgarian workers, the European Union, benefits recipients, the unemployed, the poor, black youth, international students, immigrants, Muslims and Jews. Such ideologies deflect attention from social problems, inequality, precarious labour, unemployment, that is from the problems of capitalism. Crises are "ideologically constructed by the dominant ideologies to win consent" (Hall et al. 1978, 220–221). Surveillance society is associated with moral panics that are "the key ideological forms in which a historical crisis is 'experienced and fought out'" (221).

ENVIRONMENTAL PROBLEMS

Big data results in an exacerbation of environmental problems (Mosco 2014, 127–137, 2016, 520) because of the consumption of the large amounts of energy needed for keeping data centres and cloud storage going and the increase of digital media technology use with short life-time that is as e-waste dumped into developing countries. In 2012, data centres used electricity that equals the output of 30 nuclear power plants.[1] Data centres tend to use diesel generators as back-up power supply systems (Mosco 2014, 133, 2016, 520). They produce pollutants that are released into the air and the soil.

INCREASE OF UNEMPLOYMENT AND PRECARIOUS LABOUR

Big data and cloud computing can threaten jobs by outsourcing data storage and software provision and maintenance from companies' in-house IT departments to IT services (Mosco 2014, 155–174, 2016, 522–524). It can also result in the dismissal of knowledge workers if companies assume that big data analytics can provide better knowledge than these employees' expertise and skills. When corporations trust algorithms more than humans, this can have major consequences for employees. Because big data's digital positivism is prone to producing "big errors" (Mosco 2014, 199), substituting knowledge workers by algorithms also increases the risk of increasing economic vulnerability. Given the predominantly unregulated nature of digital labour, crowdsourcing labour to the cloud via platforms such as Amazon Mechanical Turk tends to create precarious, insecure labour that puts pressure on other jobs.

BIG DATA AND ACADEMIA: SOCIAL MEDIA RESEARCH AS BIG DATA ANALYTICS AND COMPUTATIONAL SOCIAL SCIENCE

The rise of big data and social media has also transformed academia. In the social sciences, it has resulted in what Deborah Lupton (2015) terms digital sociology. Digital sociology involves: a) professional digital practice, in which social scientists use "digital tools as part of sociological practice – to build networks, construct an online profile, publicise and share research and instruct students" (15); b) analyses of digital technology uses; c) digital data analysis. In the context of the latter it has also become fashionable to speak of digital methods (Rogers 2013). The fourth aspect of digital sociology is d) critical digital sociology, by which Lupton (2015, 16) understands the "reflexive analysis of digital technologies informed by social and cultural theory".

There are many forms of social and cultural theory and in a way all forms of social analysis are a reflexion on and of society. For me, critical digital sociology is a particular reflexion of and on digital technologies' role in society, namely one that is informed by critical and Marxist theory that tries to understand capitalism and domination as well as their possible alternatives. There is indeed a contradiction between critical sociology as digital sociology's fourth realm and big data analytics that is part of Lupton's third realm of digital sociology.

An important trend in Internet research is big data analytics that has a focus on collecting large amounts of data from social media platforms and analysing it in a predominantly quantitative manner. The new media research guru Lev Manovich has argued that Internet Studies should therefore be turned into the large-scale computational analysis of online data, an

---

1 www.nytimes.com/2012/09/23/technology/data-centers-waste-vast-amounts-of-energy-belying-industry-image.html (accessed on 27 September 2016).

approach that he terms Cultural Analytics (Manovich 2009) and Software Studies.[2] The obsession with quantification, computationalism and big data has also manifested itself as a preoccupation with attempts to develop new digital methods both in the humanities and social sciences: "Digital Humanities" often understands itself as humanities computing (Terras et al. 2013). The Collaborative Online Social Media Observatory (COSMOS) understands "social media research" explicitly as big data analytics, namely the analysis of "aggregate information in 'big social data' repositories, such as collective sentiment scores for sub-groups of twitter users".[3]

BIG DATA ANALYTICS' PROBLEMS

The trouble with many of these approaches is that they often do not connect statistical and computational research results to a broader analysis of human meanings, interpretations, experiences, attitudes, moral values, ethical dilemmas, uses, contradictions and macro-sociological implications of social media. There is a danger that a de-emphasis of philosophy, theory, critique and qualitative analysis advances administrative research (Lazarsfeld 1941/2004) that is predominantly concerned with how to make technologies and administration more efficient and effective. Paraphrasing Jürgen Habermas (1971), we can say that there is a danger that digital positivism advances an "absolutism of pure [digital, quantitative] methodology" (5), forgets about academia's educational role, falls short of fully understanding "the meaning of knowledge" (69) in the information society at large and is an "immunization of the [Internet] sciences against philosophy" (67). A further danger is that computational social science acts as an imperialism of computer science that aims to transform the social sciences into computer science. Once social science students spend time learning programming, there will not be enough time left for engaging thoroughly with critical social theory, philosophy, and qualitative methods.

Vincent Mosco (2014, 2016) describes the belief in big data analytics' radically transformative power as digital positivism and cloud sublime. Big data is "a myth, a sublime story about conjuring wisdom not from the flawed intelligence of humans, with all of our well-known limitations, but from the pure data stored in the cloud" (Mosco 2014, 193). The "hot new profession of data scientist knows only quantitative approaches" (Mosco 2014, 197).

> This is inherently flawed because subjective states such as happiness, depression, or satisfaction mean different things to different people […] It is uncertain which is worse: that big data treats problems through oversimplification or that it ignores those that require a careful treatment of subjectivity, including lengthy observation, depth interviews, and an appreciation for the social production of meaning. (Mosco 2014, 198)

"It also devalues research grounded in historical, theoretical and disciplinary understandings of a field" (Mosco 2016, 524) and "tends to neglect context and history" (Mosco 2014, 201). Digital positivism can have serious negative impacts on humans and society because big data "can contain and mask big errors with big consequences" (Mosco 2014, 205).

Pure quantitative analyses of big data collected from social media are often relatively meaningless. They show what dominant topics and actors there are and often draw nice and

---

2 http://lab.softwarestudies.com.

3 www.cs.cf.ac.uk/cosmos/ethics-resource-guide/.

colourful pictures such as network graphs, but lack an understanding of why users act in specific way, how ideologies are expressed and challenged, what meanings they give to data, what ethical implications developments in the world of data have for society and humans, what alternatives to associated problems exist and so on. I am not arguing against social media and online-data based research methods, but only caution that social media and big data do not outdate established social research methods such as interviews, surveys, focus groups, content analysis and critical discourse analysis. All of these methods are needed for understanding the role of digital media in the information society. However, it also makes sense to combine these methods with the collection of online data and critical, interpretative, creative, artistic, and theory-led online research methods and approaches. As well as conducting qualitative social research with social media users in order to learn about their experiences, interpretations and perspectives, it makes sense to also engage in collecting and analysing samples of data from social media platforms with the help of tools and services such as DiscoverText, HootSuite, DiscoverText, NodeXl, Gephi, NCapture/NVivo and Twitter Archiving Google Spreadsheet (TAGS). Instead of large-scale quantitative analysis of these data, critical digital sociology is well advised to utilize smaller samples and to analyse them with the help of qualitative analysis methods (critical visual analysis, ideology critique, critical discourse analysis, qualitative text/content analysis, etc.) and to critically interpret them with the help of social philosophy. We need a paradigm shift from big data analytics to critical social media research methods. Social media can also be used for engaging users in creating texts, images and videos as part of the research process. Thereby new potentials for creative, engaging and participatory research have emerged.

Social media content is a form of text that can be analysed in various ways. The usual way is to analyse big data corpuses in a predominantly quantitative way. At the same time, critical discourse analysis and ideology critique as research method has only been applied in a limited manner to social media data. Majid KhosraviNik (2013, 292) argues that "critical discourse analysis appears to have shied away from new media research in the bulk of its research". Critical discourse analysis has not just been weak on studying social media data, but is also a rather dogmatic and orthodox approach dominated by certain key figures not allowing much methodological flexibility in what is considered as being discourse analysis and what is excluded from it. Discourse is in general a rather strange, postmodern concept distant from the Marxist category of ideology that is much better suited for a critical theory of society. It is therefore better to speak of ideology critique instead of critical discourse analysis. Social media such as Twitter are still relatively new, which is one of the reasons why research about ideologies on social media has remained thus far limited. The mainstream in social media research is quantitative big data analysis, an approach that is very different from ideology critique that wants to understand the structure, context and implications of ideologies. The dominant paradigm of social media positivism has also posed limits for critical research. Developing critical social media research methods is an interesting aspect of critical digital and social media theory.

CRITICAL SOCIAL MEDIA RESEARCH AND RESEARCH ETHICS

Some scholars studying Internet ethics have argued that a lot of users do not read the terms of service. Some of them may therefore not be aware of the potential data use and may assume that their postings disappear in the mass of social media data, or find it offensive if their public social media content is quoted in an academic work without informed consent. The removal that the removal of identifiers is no guarantee of anonymity because of the possibility to search in repositories and meta-data and that large data archives can contain postings of private messages (Zimmer 2010a, 2010b; Zimmer and Proferes 2014). Differences between platform contexts have to be taken into account. Much of what happens on Facebook has for example a much more private feel than communication on Twitter.

SOCIAL MEDIA RESEARCH ETHICS: THE DILEMMA OF PRIVACY PROTECTION VS. CENSORSHIP OF CRITICAL RESEARCH

This debate shows that Internet research faces the problem that from an ethical perspective it should not harm users by its analyses, but Internet research ethics taken to an extreme can make the development of new research methods impossible and harm academic knowledge production, and in the case of critical studies also the possibilities for the critique of society. One should probably draw a distinction between the privacy implications of companies, the police and secret services conducting social media data analysis for commercial or national security interests and non-profit, non-commercial academic research. Commercial data analysis instrumentalizes and commodifies data. The police and secret services' analyses are often based on the problematic assumption that crime and terrorism can be predicted from online data, which can easily result in false positives. Privacy's context matters in social media analysis (Nissenbaum 2010). For social media research, we can, as the discussion shows, not assume that Twitter data analysis can never cause harm and that therefore anything goes. At the same time, privacy fundamentalism risks discarding social media analysis. A realistic approach is needed.

When large data archives with tens or hundreds of thousands of items are published as open data, then the problem arises that sensitive data may be included and linked to personal identifiers. A good practice is to read the data in these archives item by item and to anonymize the IDs and content of those that contain sensitive data. In citing social media data in publications, some scholars and institutions, such as the Collaborative Online Social Media Observatory,[4] have taken the approach to only quote data from public institutions and to not quote individual users, except if they provide informed consent. Often such approaches mean that content data is displayed in the form of word clouds or only based on aggregate statistical information, which poses problems for critical analyses that analyse language use online in the context of society. The Centre for the Analysis of Social Media at Demos regularly conducts studies of online politics and takes a somewhat different approach. It argues that it is good to present data in aggregated form and that it needs to be carefully considered if Twitter quotations can cause "harm or distress to the originator" (Bartlett et al. 2014, 37). If "invasive personal information" (ibid.) is revealed in tweets, then it does not use these postings. In some cases, it also "cloaks" the text so that originators cannot be identified (ibid.). In general, it argues that Twitter data "is in the public domain and can therefore be treated as carrying implicit informed consent" (Bartlett and Miller 2013, 60).

It is not an option for an ideology critique of Twitter data to only present results in aggregated form or as word clouds because this does not allow for understanding in detail how ideology works and is challenged. To obtain informed consent, for example,

---

4 www.cs.cf.ac.uk/cosmos/cosmos-ethics-statement/ (accessed on 2 June 2015).

for quoting racist, nationalist, fascist, fundamentalist, Nazist or right-wing extremist content may often result in rejection of informed consent and can endanger researchers. It is therefore easier for ideology critique to argue that Twitter data is public data. The danger of overdoing Internet research ethics is that it results in a de facto censorship and ethical prohibition of the critical investigation of ideologies. One can argue that Twitter's privacy policy already is a form of informed consent. Privacy scholars do, however, tend to see such policies as insufficient because it is not self-evident that everyone reads them in detail. The point of ideology critique is to study ideologies not in a personalized manner, but as structures in society. The actual user names of those expressing or challenging an ideology are therefore not relevant, except if these are people working for public institutions, such as politicians.

In the case of everyday users, Internet researchers should not mention user names, but rather employ pseudonyms so that they make no direct identification. Even if data is anonymized, user profiles can often be identified via searches (Zimmer 2010). It is infeasible to conduct no critical analyses at all of online data. Any such considerations have the problematic potential to forestall critique. To reformulate the content of postings results in inauthenticity and can be interpreted as fabricating data. Absolute privacy would either require not doing online critical research or fabricating data. The most feasible solution for this dilemma is in my view that everyday users' profile names are not mentioned, which means that one does not personally identify them in the paper or report one writes.

CRITICAL INTERNET RESEARCH ETHICS: REALISM

The British Psychological Society argues that online observation should only take place when and where users "reasonably expect to be observed by strangers" (BPS 2009, 13). It is often feasible to think about whether users in particular social media contexts expect to be observed by strangers or not. It is, for example, reasonable to assume that users who use specific hashtags (e.g. political hashtags) and direct their messages at the public for discussion therefore also reasonably expect to be observed by strangers such as journalists and researchers. Not revealing the profile names of everyday users, but instead using pseudonyms, seems in this context to therefore be a sufficient measure. The British Sociological Association argues in its ethical guidelines that informed consent and the blurring boundaries between the private and the public pose challenges in Internet research, and that researchers should inform themselves about "ongoing debates on the ethics of Internet research" (BSA 2002, §41). Reflecting on Internet research ethics highly matters whenever we analyse online data.

Internet research ethics should not be taken to an extreme on social media in general and Twitter in particular. It must see that there is a big interest among academics to conduct qualitative analyses of social media data; that simply ascertaining privacy violations does not help, is not a way forward and unnecessarily pits Internet researchers against Internet ethicists. The point is that a constructive and realist dialogue is needed about such questions. It is feasible to assume that most political online communication on Twitter has the attention to attract a large public because politics is a social, collective and public phenomenon. Just like the private is political, most politics is public and intended for public debate, commenting and analysis.

2.6 CONCLUSION

Analysing continuities and discontinuities of the web requires social theory foundations. The WWW is not social in a simple sense, but to certain degrees on certain levels of analysis that are grounded in sociological conceptions of sociality. If one compares WWW use in the late 1990s to the end of the first decade of the second millennium, one finds that the use patterns of the WWW are shaped by continuities and discontinuities. Information is continuously present, communication has been transformed, web technologies of co-operation have become more frequently used and important, but are certainly not dominant. The web is neither purely old nor purely new; it is a complex techno-social system embedded into power structures of capitalism that has to change to a certain extent at certain levels in order to enable the continuity of Internet-based capital accumulation.

This chapter dealt with the question: What is social media? Its main results are as follows:

- Dealing with the question "What is social media?" requires an understanding of what the social is all about. It is, in this respect, helpful to look at social theory for engaging with concepts of sociality in society. Relevant concepts of sociality include social facts (Émile Durkheim), social relations/social action (Max Weber), co-operative labour (Karl Marx) and community (Ferdinand Tönnies).
- Claims about the novelty and opportunities of "web 2.0" and "social media" like blogs, social networking sites, wikis, microblogs or content-sharing sites originated in the context of the dot-com crisis of the Internet economy and the resulting search for new business models and narratives that convince investors and users to support new platforms. The ideology of novelty intends to attract investors and users.
- Most social media technologies originated before 2005, when Tim O'Reilly established the concept of web 2.0. Wikis, blogs, social networking sites, microblogs and content-sharing sites have, however, become really popular since the middle of the first decade of the second millennium. It is both unlikely that in the years 2000–2010 the WWW has not changed at all and unlikely that it has radically changed. The capitalist Internet economy needs to change and innovate in order to guarantee the continuity of capital accumulation.
- The two concepts of participation and power have been used for characterizing social media (participatory culture, power and counter-power of mass self-communication). Class is another concept that is particularly suited. Great care should be taken to avoid techno-deterministic thinking, techno-centrism, techno-optimism, techno-pessimism and naturalization of domination in conceptualizing qualities of social media. Engaging with social theory, the history of concepts and the philosophical groundings of the Internet can provide help for developing concepts that describe structure, agency and dynamics of social media.
- Media are techno-social systems in which technological structures interact with social relations and human activities in complex ways. Power structures shape the media and the social relations of the media. When analysing social media, one should be clear about and should explicate the level of analysis.

RECOMMENDED READINGS AND EXERCISES

Making sense of social media requires a theoretical understanding of what it means to be social. Sociological theory offers different concepts of the social. The following suggested readings introduce you to various concepts of the social by thinkers such as Émile Durkheim, Max Weber, Ferdinand Tönnies and Karl Marx. Other readings focus on digital sociology and big data/cloud computing.

Durkheim, Émile. 1895. The rules of sociological method. In *Classical sociological theory*, ed. Craig Calhoun, Joseph Gerteis, James Moody, Steven Pfaff and Indermohan Virk, 139–157. Malden, MA: Blackwell.

In "The rules of sociological method", Émile Durkheim introduces some basic foundations of a functionalist social theory, such as the notion of social facts. Discuss in groups and compare your results:

- What is a social fact?
- Make a list of economic, political and cultural examples of social facts that can be found in contemporary society.
- Each group can choose one web platform (such as Google, Yahoo, Facebook, Twitter, Weibo, Wikipedia, etc.). Think in your group about how this platform works and what kind of activities it supports. Make a list of social facts that can be found on the platform.

Weber, Max. 1914. Basic sociological terms. In *Classical sociological theory*, ed. Craig Calhoun, Joseph Gerteis, James Moody, Steven Pfaff and Indermohan Virk, 139–157. Malden, MA: Blackwell.

In "Basic sociological terms", Max Weber introduces foundational categories of a sociological action theory, such as action, social action and social relations. Discuss in groups and compare your results:

- How does Max Weber define social action?
- Make a list of examples of online activities that correspond to Weber's theory of the social and non-social. Compare how Durkheim would characterize the sociality of these platforms.
- Try to find examples of the four types of social action that Weber identifies.
- Try to find examples of four types of online social action according to Weber.

Tönnies, Ferdinand. 2001. *Community and civil society*, 17–51. Cambridge: Cambridge University Press.

Rheingold, Howard. 2000. *The virtual community: Homesteading on the electronic frontier*. Cambridge, MA: MIT Press. Chapter 11: Rethinking virtual communities.

Ferdinand Tönnies first published *Community and Civil Society* in 1887. In this work, he draws a distinction between *Gemeinschaft* (community) and *Gesellschaft* (society). It is interesting to read this text in combination with Howard Rheingold's *The Virtual Community*, where he discusses the logic of community in the age of the Internet and how it is limited by the logic of commodities that Tönnies considered specific for what he termed society. Discuss in groups and compare your results:

- Identify basic characteristics of a community according to Ferdinand Tönnies. Construct a list of features of a community.
- Try to identify different groups that you are in contact with on Facebook or another social networking site. Which of these groups are communities according to Tönnies, which are not, and why? Try to test the applicability of all community features that you have identified.
- What are, according to Howard Rheingold, the basic features of a virtual community? In which respects is Facebook a virtual community, and in which respects not? What does Howard Rheingold mean by "commodification of community"? Having read his chapter, how do you think he assesses Facebook?
- Additional exercise: Organize a conversation with Howard Rheingold or another well-known Internet scholar about what s/he sees as the positive and negative features of social media.

Marx, Karl. 1867. *Capital. Volume I*. London: Penguin. Chapter 13: Co-operation.

Capital. Volume I is one of the most influential books in economic thought. It contains a chapter that discusses the phenomenon of collaborative work and its role in the modern economy. Discuss in groups and compare your results:

- Try to give a definition of what co-operation and collaborative work are (this requires that you also define the concept of "work").
- How does Marx see the role of co-operation in capitalism?
- How does co-operation work on Wikipedia? Try to identify commonalities and differences between the co-operation brought about by capitalism that Marx describes and co-operation on Wikipedia. What are the differences and commonalities?

Lupton, Deborah. 2015. Introducing digital sociology. In *Public sociology: An introduction to Australian society*, ed. John Germov and Marilyn Poole. Crows Nest: Allen & Unwin. Chapter 22.

Read this text and then ask yourself and discuss in groups:

- What kind of digital practices do academics such as students, teachers and senior researchers engage in? How do digital media shape your academic lives?
- How do you analyse digital technology use in society? What kind of approaches, models, theories and methods do you use?
- What role does digital data analysis and analytics play in your research? What potentials does it have? What are its problems?
- What is critical digital sociology? What should the role of critical theory be in it? How does critical digital sociology relate to digital sociology's other three dimensions (digital practices, the analysis of digital technology use in society, digital data analysis)? Why is the relationship between critical digital sociology and big data analytics problematic? What is the role of digital data analysis for critical theory and the role of critical theory for digital data analysis?

Mosco, Vincent. 2016. Marx in the cloud. In *Marx in the age of digital capitalism*, ed. Christian Fuchs and Vincent Mosco, 516–535. Leiden: Brill.

(Continued)

(Continued)

First, read Vincent Mosco's text. Second, work in groups: each group chooses one cloud storage service such as Amazon Web Services, Google Cloud, Apple iCloud, Microsoft Azure, Dropbox, IBM Cloud or VMware's vCloud. Inform yourselves what big data and cloud services these companies offer. Read also the services' terms of use and privacy policies. Ask yourself which of the dangers that Vincent Mosco identifies apply to these big data/cloud computing services. In which respect? What would alternatives look like and how could they be organized?

Chandler, David. 2015. A world without causation: Big data and the coming age of posthumanism. *Millennium: Journal of International Studies* 43 (3): 833–851.

Qiu, Jack L. 2015. Reflections on big data: "Just because it is accessible does not make it ethical". *Media, Culture & Society* 37 (7): 1089–1094.

These two texts by David Chandler and Jack L. Qiu discuss potential problems of big data analytics. First, read the two texts. Second, work in groups: Make a list of big data analytics' potential dangers. Each group searches for one case of how big data analytics is used in politics, the economy or culture. Discuss the following based on the list of potential dangers: How could such dangers affect the case of big data you are studying? What could be potential negative effects on human beings and society? What needs to be done politically in order to avoid such negative effects?

3 SOCIAL MEDIA AS PARTICIPATORY CULTURE

KEY QUESTIONS

* What is participatory culture? How have different scholars attempted to define it?
* How have scholars understood participatory culture within the realm of social media?
* What do scholars mean by "participatory democracy"?
* Are contemporary social media truly participatory?

KEY CONCEPTS

Henry Jenkins's notions of participatory culture and spreadable media
Participatory culture as ideology

Participatory democracy
Digital labour

OVERVIEW

Participatory culture is a term that is often used for designating the involvement of users, audiences, consumers and fans in the creation of culture and content. Examples are the joint editing of an article on Wikipedia, the uploading of images to Flickr or Facebook, the uploading of videos to YouTube and the creation of short messages on Twitter or Weibo.

The participatory culture model is often opposed to the mass media and broadcasting model typical of newspapers, radio and television, where there is one sender and many recipients. Some scholars argue that in the online world, culture and society are becoming more democratic because users and audiences are enabled to produce culture themselves and to not just listen or watch without actively making and creating culture:

* The Internet analyst Clay Shirky (2011a, 27) has argued that social media result in "the wiring of humanity", allow us to "treat free time as a shared global resource, and [let] us design new kinds of participation and sharing that take advantage of that resource".

- The Australian scholar Axel Bruns says that produsage, the combination of production and use, is characteristic of social media. As the result of social media he envisions a "produsage-based, participatory culture" (Bruns 2008, 256) and "a produsage-based democratic model" (372).
- Similarly, the business consultants Don Tapscott and Anthony Williams (2007, 15) argue that social media result in the emergence of "a new economic democracy [...] in which we all have a lead role".

All three statements have in common that they highlight positive aspects of social media and point out that these media are possible to make culture and society more democratic. This chapter critically questions these claims. Section 3.1 discusses the notion of participatory culture, section 3.2 deals with Henry Jenkins's focus on fan culture, section 3.3 addresses his discussion of social media and section 3.4 looks at how he sees the so-called digital labour debate, that is the role of unpaid user activities in value-generation.

3.1 THE NOTIONS OF PARTICIPATION AND PARTICIPATORY CULTURE

SOCIAL MEDIA AS SPREADABLE MEDIA

For Henry Jenkins, the main characteristic of "social media"/"web 2.0" is that they are spreadable media (Jenkins et al. 2009): "Consumers play an active role in 'spreading' content [...] Consumers in this model are [...] grassroots advocates for materials which are personally and socially meaningful to them" (Jenkins et al. 2009, part 2). Spreadable media are based on the logic "if it doesn't spread, it's dead" (Jenkins et al. 2013, 1) and involve audiences that "actively" shape "media flows" (2) so that culture becomes "far more participatory" (1). Sharing, co-creation, remixing, reuse and adaption of content on Facebook, YouTube and other online platforms are, for Jenkins, a manifestation of a gift economy.

He argues that spreadable media "empower" consumers and "make them an integral part" of a commodity's success (Jenkins et al. 2009, part 8). The "longer term" benefits would include the expansion of "the range of potential markets for a brand" and the intensification of "consumer loyalty by increasing emotional attachment to the brand or media franchise" (Jenkins et al. 2009, part 8).

Jenkins et al. (2013, xii) argue that they "accept as a starting point that the constructs of capitalism will greatly shape the creation and circulation of most media texts for the foreseeable future" and that those companies that "listen to [...] their audiences" will strive. They accept the logic of capitalism in a time of crisis, where trust in corporations is low and capitalism has shown that it organizes society necessarily in such a way that exploitation, misery and precariousness are a necessary reality for a significant share of people.

When Pepsi launched a marketing campaign in 2007, which allowed consumers to design the look of a Pepsi can that was featured on 500 million Pepsi cans around the United States, the task was not, as frequently claimed by management gurus, to create "a new economic democracy [...] in which we all have a lead role" (Tapscott and Williams 2007, 15; for a critique of this approach, see Fuchs 2008b), but to outsource design work and thereby surplus value-generation cheaply to consumers and to ideologically bind the emotions of the consumers to the brand so that more Pepsi could be sold and more profit be made. The Convergence Culture Consortium that includes GSD&M Advertising, MTV Networking and Turner Broadcasting funded Jenkins's study of spreadable media.

PARTICIPATORY CULTURE

For Jenkins, social media are also an expression of participatory culture. He defines participatory culture as culture "in which fans and other consumers are invited to actively participate in the creation and circulation of new content" (Jenkins 2008, 331). It also involves "participants who interact with each other" (Jenkins 2008, 3). Participation involves, for Jenkins, "new forms of participation and collaboration" (Jenkins 2008, 256). Jenkins points out, based on Pierre Lévy (1997), that those who engage in "participatory culture" pool resources and combine skills so that collective intelligence emerges as "an alternative source of media power" (Jenkins 2008, 4).

Jenkins defines participatory as a culture with:

1   relatively low barriers to artistic expression and civic engagement;
2   strong support for creating and sharing creations with others;
3   some type of informal mentorship whereby what is known by the most experienced is passed along to novices;
4   members who believe that their contributions matter; and
5   members who feel some degree of social connection with one another (at the least, they care what other people think about what they have created). (Jenkins et al. 2009, 5–6)

PARTICIPATORY DEMOCRACY

Jenkins has argued that increasingly "the Web has become a site of consumer participation" (Jenkins 2008, 137). A problem of the "participatory culture" concept is that participation is a political science term that is strongly connected to participatory democracy theory and authors such as Crawford Macpherson (1973) and Carole Pateman (1970). An article by Staughton Lynd (1965) that describes the grassroots organization model of the Students for a Democratic Society (SDS) made the earliest use of the term "participatory democracy" that I could trace in the literature. One should avoid a vulgar use of the term "participation". Internet Studies should relate the usage of the term to participatory democracy theory, in which it has the following dimensions (Fuchs 2011b, Chapter 7):

1   The intensification and extension of democracy as grassroots democracy to all realms of society.
2   The maximization of human capacities (Macpherson (1973) speaks of human developmental powers) so that humans become well-rounded individuals.
3   Extractive power as impediment for participatory democracy.
4   Macpherson (1973) argues that capitalism is based on an exploitation of human powers that limits the development of human capacities. The modern economy "by

its very nature compels a continual net transfer of part of the power of some men to others [for the benefit and the enjoyment of the others], thus diminishing rather than maximizing the equal individual freedom to use and develop one's natural capacities" (Macpherson 1973, 10–11).

5   Participatory decision-making: in a participatory organization, those who are affected by decisions take them together. An alternative, when there is a lack of time, resources or interest in all deciding on everything together, is that those affected choose or elect delegates, who are responsible for certain aspects of the organization and accountable to their base.

6   Participatory economy: a participatory economy requires a "change in the terms of access to capital in the direction of more nearly equal access" (Macpherson 1973, 71) and "a change to more nearly equal access to the means of labour" (73). In a participatory society, extractive power is reduced to zero (74). A democratic economy involves "the democratising of industrial authority structures, abolishing the permanent distinction between 'managers' and 'men'" (Pateman 1970, 43).

7   Technological productivity as material foundation of participatory democracy.

8   Participation as education in participation.

9   Pseudo-participation as ideology.

IGNORING OWNERSHIP, CAPITALISM AND CLASS: CULTURAL AND POLITICAL REDUCTIONISM

For Jenkins, participation means that humans meet on the net, form collectives, create and share content. He has a culturalistic understanding of participation and ignores the notion of participatory democracy, a term which has political, political economic and cultural dimensions. Jenkins's definition and use of the term "participatory culture" neglects aspects of participatory democracy; it disregards questions about the ownership of platforms/companies, collective decision-making, profit, class and the distribution of benefits. Jenkins et al. (2009, 9) mention community membership, production, collaboration and sharing as activities in participatory cultures, whereas ownership is not mentioned. The 11 skills listed as characteristics for literacy in participatory culture do not include critical thinking, but rather activities that can all work well in a company context (collective intelligence, networking, multitasking, play, performance, simulation, appropriation, distributed cognition, judgement, transmedia navigation, negotiation; Jenkins et al. 2009, xiv). Corporate platforms owned by Facebook, Google and other large companies strongly mediate the cultural expressions of Internet users. Neither the users nor the waged employees of Facebook, Google and others determine the business decisions of these companies. They do not "participate" in economic decision-making, but are excluded from it.

Jenkins's concept of participation is not theoretically grounded. Also, Nico Carpentier (2011), who advances a more nuanced approach that is grounded in political theory, disregards ownership aspects of the participation concept. He conceives participation as "equal power relations in decision-making processes" (Carpentier 2011, 69) and media participation as co-decision-making in the contexts of media technology, content, people and organizations (130). This notion of media participation is explicitly a political concept (354), focusing on involvement in media decision-making (355) and avoiding a broad definition of participation (69). Carpentier does not include aspects of media ownership, neither does he consider ownership questions as questions relating to participation. In contrast to Crawford MacPherson, Carpentier reduces participation to the political level. The problem of a purely political concept of (media) participation is that it implies that full "participation" can be achieved without letting people participate in the ownership of the organizations in which they work, as long as they are involved in decision-making. The topic of inequality of ownership and wealth is ignored and declared to be secondary or unimportant. A truly participatory media democracy must also be an ownership democracy (Fuchs 2011b, 2014a). Carpentier, although being theoretically versed and well read, just like Jenkins, ends up with a reductionist concept of media participation. Reductionism means that a certain aspect of the world is explained based on one specific dimension, although other dimensions also matter. In the social sciences, liberal and conservative scholars have often claimed that Marxism reduces explanations of society to the economy. At the same time, the same scholars often ignore aspects of class and capitalism and thereby reduce explanations of society either to politics (politicism, political reductionism) or culture (culturalism). Raymond Williams's approach of cultural materialism allows us to think about the relationship of the economy, politics and culture in a non-reductionist, truly dialectical and materialist way (see Fuchs 2015, 2016a for a detailed discussion and for how Williams's cultural materialism matters for the study of social media): the economy is a necessary foundation of politics and culture because all social systems, including political and cultural ones, are based on production processes. Politics and culture do, however, also go beyond the economy; they have emergent qualities and feed back on the economy. Williams (1977, 93) therefore speaks of the "material character of the production of a social and political order": all social systems are material because they are based on production processes.

Jenkins et al. (2013, 193) argue that participatory culture is relative and that we "do not and may never live in a society where every member is able to fully participate". This passage essentializes exclusion, as if it were a natural feature of every type of society. Essentialism is a form of argumentation that does not see phenomena as historical, which means that they have a beginning and an end and can be changed by human action. These phenomena (such as money, capital, domination, violence, egoism, competition, etc.) are declared to exist necessarily and forever. Karl Marx (1867) has termed this form of argumentation "fetish thinking": certain phenomena are treated like being things and the fact that they are social circumstances that can be changed by humans is ignored.

Participation means that humans have the right to be part of decisions and to govern and control the structures that affect them, and that such participation is not just a desire or goal, but a reality. Rights are always universal and not particularistic. For example, if human rights are only valid for some people but not others, then they are not rights at all. Similarly, participation is a universal political demand, not a relative category. Otherwise one could say that a dictatorship is a participatory democracy because a ruling elite is "participating", which is, however, only an extremely small part of the population.

When Jenkins writes about political goals, he remains rather vague with formulations such as the demand for "corporate responsibility" (Jenkins 2008, 259) or "a much greater diversity of opinion" (250; see also 268). He says it is important for "pressuring companies to change the products they are creating and the ways they relate to their consumers" (261), that there is an "alarming concentration of the ownership of mainstream commercial media" (18) and that "concentration is bad" (259).

The basic question is whether capitalist organizations can ever be responsible, given that they must necessarily be interested in reducing wages and investment costs in order to increase profits if they want to survive in the competition process. Marisol Sandoval's empirical study of corporate social responsibility in eight media corporations (Apple, AT&T, Google, HP, Microsoft, News Corporation, Vivendi, Walt Disney) concludes that the

> actual business practices of the media and communication companies revealed that while the companies were successful in reaching their profit goals, at the same time they failed to act socially responsible. The analysis [...] shows that, despite CSR, the business practices of media and commu- nication companies often conflict with the common good. [...] CSR serves as an ideology that diverts attention away from actual existing corporate social irresponsibilities and thereby strengthens the legitimacy of capitalism. Despite its reference to universal social values, current theories and prac- tices of CSR as such do not promote a socially responsible media system. (Sandoval 2014, 251, 252)

The notion of diverse opinion remains empty if one does not consider the question of whether a fascist opinion is equally desirable and valuable as a democratic socialist opinion. Capitalism is based on the need to increase productivity for increasing profits. But produc- tivity and competitive advantages tend to be asymmetrically distributed. As a result, compe- tition tends to turn into monopolies and capital concentration. Media and other concentration is not just something that is bad, but rather a structural feature of capitalism.

WHITE BOYS WITH "PARTICIPATORY" TOYS

Internet culture is not separate from political economy, but is to a large extent organized, controlled and owned by companies (platforms like Wikipedia are non-corporate models that are different from the dominant corporate social media model). Social media culture is a culture industry. Jenkins's notion of "participatory culture" is mainly about expressions, engagement, creation, sharing, experience, contributions and feelings, and not so much about how these practices are enabled by and antagonistically entangled into capital accumulation. Jenkins tends to advance a reductionist understanding of culture that ignores contemporary culture's political economy. Furthermore, he reduces the notion of participation to a cultural dimension, ignoring the broad notion of participatory democracy and its implications for the Internet. An Internet that corporations dominate by exploiting users and commodifying data can in the theory of participatory democracy never be participatory. The cultural expressions on it cannot be an expression of participation.

An argument that scholars frequently employ in this context is that despite social media's capitalist character, it can have positive political and cultural effects. Whereas Jenkins makes this argument in respect to culture, Jin and Feenberg apply it to politics:

> [D]espite the dispiriting commercialism of SNSs on the Internet, and the role of corporate and government surveillance in stripping us of the last vestiges of privacy, there is another encouraging side to the story. […] it is clear that social networking creates a new kind of democratic public sphere with considerable oppositional potential. (Jin and Feenberg 2015, 58–59)

Capitalism is not independent from cultural and political uses of social media, but constrains and limits them. Activists cannot trust capitalist platforms because they may not be their friends and are likely to co-operate with the police and secret services in monitoring activists (Fuchs 2014c). The logic of capitalism shapes the very cultural uses of social media in the form of a neoliberal culture of individualist and self-centred competition, in which users aim to accumulate reputation, likes, followers and so on. Capitalism does not determine political and cultural uses of the Internet, but it poses disadvantages for everyday users and progressive activists. Jin and Feenberg's argument is based on the mistaken techno-deterministic assumption that contemporary protests are Twitter and Facebook rebellions. Such authors argue that Facebook is both a realm of commodification on the one side and political activism and cultural expression on the other side. They say that the political and cultural phenomena are more important than the economic ones. They do not relate the two phenomena to each other and end up with a one-sided techno-optimism that sees struggles and resistance everywhere technology is and ignores that society faces contradictions.

Important goals for Jenkins seem to be that companies establish "stronger connections with their constituencies and consumers" (Jenkins 2008, 22), a "collective bargaining structure" (Jenkins 2008, 63) between fans and companies, brand communities that "empower" consumers to "assert their own demand on the company" (Jenkins 2008, 80), "experiments in consumer-generated content" that "have an influence on the mass media companies" (Jenkins 2008, 172), and that cultural entrepreneurs give "their consumers greater opportunities to shape the content and participate in its distribution" (Jenkins 2008, 268). Jenkins is deeply concerned with the question of whether consumers will be able to shape the content of cultural commodities according to their desires by engaging as active and creative prosumers in "participatory culture".

Jenkins's writings read much like a celebration of participatory culture as a structure that allows consumers "to participate in the production and distribution of cultural goods" (Jenkins 2008, 137). They do not much engage with or analyse the downsides of the Internet, such as the economic crisis; the exploitation of users; the exploitation of precarious freelancers conducting low-paid work via crowdsourcing platforms such as Amazon Mechanical Turk, Upwork, Freelancer, TaskRabbit, or PeoplePerHour (Fuchs 2014a, 2015a; Scholz 2017); concerns about privacy violations and surveillance; e-waste (Maxwell and Miller 2014); the exploitation of miners who often extract the minerals needed for the production of laptops, computers and other hardware under slave-like working conditions (this topic is also called "conflict minerals" because of the wars and interest conflicts that often underlie these working conditions); and the exploitation of hardware manufacturers who often are overworked, underpaid and conduct their jobs in toxic workplaces (Fuchs 2014a, Qiu 2016). Participatory democracy is a demand that speaks against such problems, whereas participatory culture is a rather harmless concept mainly created by and for white boys who love their toys.

3.2 ONLINE FAN CULTURE AND POLITICS

FAN CULTURE AS POLITICS?

Henry Jenkins sees fan communities in general, and online fan communities in particular, as "preparing the way for a more meaningful public culture" (Jenkins 2008, 239). He tends to idealize fan communities' political potentials and cannot explain why these communities should make fans more interested and active in politics. From the circumstances that "fans are viewers who speak back to the networks and the producers" and that they "know how to organize to lobby on behalf of endangered series" (Jenkins 1992, 284), it does not follow that fans have an interest in protesting against racism, neoliberalism, wage cuts, the privatization of education or welfare, lay-offs in the companies and so on. Toby Miller asks in this context, can "fans be said to engage with labour exploitation, patriarchy, racism, and neo-imperialism, or in some specifiable way make a difference to politics beyond their own selves, when they interpret texts unusually or chat about romantic frustrations?" (Miller 2008, 220).

Henry Jenkins mistakenly assumes an automatic connection of fandom in popular culture and political protest. He also mistakes politics with popular culture and sees politics taking place largely as micro politics within popular culture (such as the struggle of fans to make the culture industry respect their ideas in the design of plots). The protestors who brought about a revolution in Egypt in 2011 to a certain extent also made use of media (like Facebook, Twitter and mobile phones) for forming communities – not fan communities, but rather a political community engaging in street protests, strikes, blockades and the struggle against a regime. Their political practices have shown how a revolution works and that revolution is possible today. Not social media causes revolutions and protests. Such mediated communication is rather in complex ways related to offline interaction (see my study of the Occupy movement's use of social media; Fuchs 2014b). Fan communities played no significant role in the Egyptian revolution. Many passages in Jenkins's books (e.g. Jenkins 2006, 10–11) convey the impression that he wants to get rid of the heritage of Critical Studies having to be political in an analysis and that he feels the desire to engage purely with the fun of popular culture. But if academics do not engage with popular culture for political reasons (to establish a just society), what is really the goal and justification for it? This is why Stuart Hall wrote that popular culture matters in respect to socialism. "Otherwise, to tell you the truth, I don't give a damn about it" (Hall 1981/1988, 453).

Henry Jenkins (2008, 12) says that he is "not simply a consumer of many of these media products; I am also an active fan". He says that his living room is full of various media players and recorders, "a huge mound of videotapes, DVDs and CDs, game cartridges and controllers" (Jenkins 2008, 15). Fandom as such is not a problem, if the researcher, who is also a fan of his object of study, manages to maintain critical reflexivity. I am a fan of *The Simpsons*, Monty Python, 3WK Underground Radio or bands such as Mogwai, Radiohead and The Fall, but I do not think that it is political to watch these programmes or listen to these bands. In a lot of contemporary works on popular culture, one gets the impression that scholars want to rationalize their own fandom and their love for commodity culture by trying to identify progressive political aspects of the consumption and logic of cultural commodities. Because they like spending their work time and free time consuming popular culture, they tend to justify this behaviour as a form of political resistance. There is then no need to engage in, or support, the more risky activities of political movements because popular culture is declared to be a political movement itself. Most intellectuals are probably fond of some type of popular culture, but it makes a difference whether one sees and celebrates this fondness as an act of political resistance or not.

IS ONLINE FASCISM PARTICIPATORY CULTURE?

Cultural communities are not automatically politically progressive. An example is that document.no and an accompanying Facebook group are gathering places for Norwegian right-wing extremists, who oppose immigration to Norway and argue for advancing Islamophobia and the idea of cultural purity. The fascist terrorist Anders Behring Breivik, who killed 77 people in the Norwegian terror attacks on 22 July 2011, was one of the active members of this community. Jenkins does not much discuss the negative potentials and realities of online communities and cultural communities.

The Ultras soccer fan movement's discussion forum is www.ultras.ws. One can find anti-Semitic and racist jokes in the forum, and in a survey conducted in the forum 56 per cent said that it is no problem if fans shout "Jews" for characterizing opposing teams.[1] The following joke is typical and no exception, but rather the rule, in this forum:[2] "How do you get 30 Jews into a Trabi [= a small car common in East Germany under Soviet times]? Two in the front, three in the back and the rest in the ashtray." The concept of participatory culture has a focus on "community involvement" (Jenkins et al. 2009, 6). However, it idealizes community and fan culture as progressive and ignores the fact that the collective intelligence and activity of cultural communities and fandom can easily turn into a fascist mob, especially in situations of capitalist crisis that are prone to advance the growth and radicalization of right-wing extremism.

Jenkins has, thus far, mostly analysed the fan communities he likes and rather neglected those that have fascist potentials. Fascist communities do not seem to fit his concept of fandom and communities. Jenkins (1992, 290) says that fans are not necessarily progressive, but that they have the potential to be active (293) and that they "find the ability to question and rework the ideologies that dominate the mass culture" (290). There is no doubt that hooligan soccer fan groups are active (they actively inflict violence against other fans and immigrants, make active plans to harass, threaten or kill them, etc.), but activity and creativity of fans is not necessarily, as assumed by Jenkins in his deterministic and reductionist logic of argumentation, a questioning of ideologies; it can just as likely be a reproduction of dominant ideologies (like racism). The competitive character of organised sports, reality TV and entertainment, where teams or individuals fiercely contest each other, is not just a reflection of the logic of war, patriarchy and the soldier, but is also a breeding ground for fascism. The only progressive way forward is to overcome the culture of competition. Although Jenkins assures his readers in single sentences that fans are not always progressive, the structure of his examples and other formulations advance exactly the conclusion that they are progressive.

---

1 www.ultras.ws/umfrage-juden-jena-rufe-und-die-strafe-t4414.html (accessed on 1 August 2011).
2 www.ultras.ws/viewtopic.php?p=483232 (accessed on 29 July 2013).

3.3 SOCIAL MEDIA AND PARTICIPATORY CULTURE

SOCIAL MEDIA CAPITALISM

Although Henry Jenkins is to a certain extent aware that corporations exert greater power than consumers (Jenkins 2008, 3, 175), he focuses the reader's attention in most of his books on the presentation of hundreds of examples that want to assert to the reader that contemporary media empower consumers because they enable production processes, and that consumers successfully resist corporatism. He conceives media prosumption (productive consumption) as inherently participatory. Jenkins argues that increasingly "the Web has become a site of consumer participation" (Jenkins 2008, 137) and hardly gives any examples of corporate domination in culture or on the Internet. Therefore, the notion of participatory culture takes on a reified character in his works.

Jenkins argues that participatory culture advances cultural diversity (Jenkins 2008, 268), but overlooks that not all voices have the same power and that produced content and voices are frequently marginalized because visibility is a central resource in contemporary culture that powerful actors, such as media corporations, can buy. Jenkins assumes that diversity is the linear result of prosumption.

Jenkins simply constructs a dualistic "both . . . and" argument based on the logic that "Web 2.0 is both . . . and . . .": both pleasure and exploitation, both a space of participation and a space of commodification. Convergence is "both a top-down corporate-driven process and a bottom-up consumer-driven process. Corporate convergence coexists with grassroots convergence" (Jenkins 2008, 18). He wants to focus on the aspects of pleasure and creativity and to leave the topic of exploitation to others and does not, thereby, grasp the dialectics at work and the relations of dominance we find on web 2.0. The question is not only what phenomena we find on social media, but how they are related and to what extent and degree they are present. There is no doubt that web 2.0 users are creative when they generate and diffuse user-generated content. But the question is also how many web 2.0 users are active and what degree of activity and creativity their practices have. Ofcom (2015a, 91) found that in 2015 22 per cent of the Internet users in its survey uploaded or shared videos or photos at least once a week. In addition, 8 per cent of the users indicated that at least once a week they updated their own website or blog (38). Ten years earlier, in 2005, the level was 7 per cent (38). Such data shows that user-generated content creation is conducted by some users sometimes, but certainly not by all users all the time. During vast amounts of time users tend to use social media in a more consumptive manner. Consumption is also production of interpretations of contents, but not the production of content itself. That the potential for prosumption exists does not imply that users are prosumers all of the time. Social media have new potentials, but are often used as traditional media because new media do not eliminate old media, but sublate them so that old qualities persist in new media that also have emergent potentials and qualities.

Scholars like Jenkins tend to overstate the creativity and activity of users on the web. Creativity is a force that enables Internet prosumer commodification, the commodification and exploitation of the users' attentions, activities and the data they generate. Creativity is not outside or alongside exploitation on web 2.0. It is its very foundation.

YOUTUBE

Jenkins (2008, 274) argues that YouTube is a site "for the production and distribution of grassroots media" and that on YouTube "participation occurs at three distinct levels [. . .] – those of production, selection, and distribution" (275), without considering the fact that YouTube is owned by Google and that the revenues that are accumulated with online advertising on YouTube do not belong to the immediate content producers, but to the shareholders of Google. Jenkins here neglects ownership as a central aspect of participation. The most popular YouTube videos stem from global multimedia corporations like Universal, Sony and Walt Disney (see Table 5.1 in Chapter 5). Google and Facebook are based on targeted advertising models and a commercial culture, which results in huge profits for these companies. Politics on YouTube, Twitter and Facebook are possible, but are minority issues. The predominant focus of users is on non-political entertainment. Web 2.0 corporations and the usage they enable are not an expression of participatory democracy. As long as corporations dominate the Internet, it will not be participatory. The participatory Internet can only be found in those areas that resist corporate domination and where activists and users engage in building and reproducing non-commercial, non-profit Internet projects such as Wikipedia or Diaspora. Jenkins continuously ignores questions of who owns, controls and materially benefits from corporate social media.

Jenkins is aware of the topic of the exploitation of digital labour on the Internet (Green and Jenkins 2009; Jenkins 2009). He concludes, however, that the problem is that "YouTube pushes up content which receives support from other users" (Jenkins 2009, 124), which is only part of the truth, and ignores the fact that large corporate media companies' content is so popular because they have resource advantages in attaining recognition and attention over everyday users. Jenkins concludes that "a more collaborative approach" is needed that is based on a "negotiation of the implicit social contract between media producers and consumers, balancing the commodity and cultural status of creative goods" (Green and Jenkins 2009, 222). This view ignores the contradictory and crisis character of capitalism. The history of capitalism is a history of the colonization of societies and human spaces in order to create new spaces of commodification and capital accumulation and is a history of the crisis of capitalism. There can be no long-term peace between capital and consumers/workers/prosumers because the first has an inherent interest in exploiting the latter and accumulation leads to crisis, which is the ultimate disruption of temporary class compromises. Also, the world economic crisis in the 1970s brought an end to the welfare-oriented model of Fordist capitalism. Capitalism is inherently crisis-ridden.

BLOGS

In the corporate social media sphere, attention is unequally distributed: big companies, celebrities and well-known political actors enjoy attention advantages and the most active prosumers come from the young, educated middle class. Jenkins (2008, 227) celebrates blogs as a "means for their participants to express their distrust of the news media and their discontent with politics as usual", "potentially increasing cultural diversity and lowering barriers in cultural participation", "expanding the range of perspectives", as "grassroots intermediaries" that ensure "that everyone has a chance to be heard" (Jenkins 2006, 180–181). He forgets most political blogs' lack of visibility in the public sphere. Political blogs have hardly been able to reach the large numbers of readers of the websites of big corporate newsmakers like CNN and *The New York Times*. Statistics of the most frequently accessed web platforms (alexa.com, measured by a combined index of average daily visitors and page views over the past month, accessed on 24 October 2015) show that popular political blogs tend to get much less visibility and attention than mainstream news websites. Political blogs do not rank in the top 1000. Examples are: Daily Kos (#1,175), Raw Story (#2,251), ThinkProgress (#3,303), Mediaite (#4,602), Talking Points Memo (#3,899), Hot Air (#6,657), NewsBusters (#13,251), Crooks and Liars (#14,198), Power Line (#16,843), Wonkette (#17,428), Redstate (#18,975), LewRockwell (#22,078), Common Dreams (#25,440), Guido Fawkes (#31,861), AmericaBlog (#82,703), Little Green Footballs (#89,118), Eschaton (#119,829), Labourlist (#142,420), Left Food Forward (#216,176), Andrew Sullivan's Daily Dish (#265,989), Liberal Conspiracy (#1,409,173). In contrast, popular mainstream news sites achieve top rankings: CNN (#75), BBC Online (#85), *The New York Times* (#98), *Daily Mail* (#103), *Indiatimes* (#107), *Guardian* (#137), *Der Spiegel* (#300). This inequality shows that visibility and popularity on the web are stratified.

The political economy of online attention tends to privilege large media companies that have established brands and control a lot of resources. *The Huffington Post* (#11) started in 2005 as a blog project, acquired venture capital investment and so became a relatively popular site. It was purchased by AOL in February 2011 and thereby became part of the mainstream media market. Its business model is targeted advertising. The example shows that alternative online media can easily become commodified and transformed into capitalist businesses.

One can now argue that political blogs still gather a lot of attention and as a total phenomenon have a lot of readers. The advantage of a site like *The New York Times* is that it attracts the attention of a high number of people who all have the same information as a basis for discussion and opinion-formation. This does not mean that the information published in the mainstream media is superior and unproblematic. To the contrary, it is often more one-dimensional and distorted than the information on political blogs. But gathering a large number of people on one site is a power in itself, whereas gathering some people on many dispersed sites fragments the public, results in "a huge number of isolated issue publics" (Habermas 2006, 423) and risks "cultural relativism" that neglects that democracy is in need of "some common normative dimensions" and "more generalized media" (Garnham 1992, 369).

3.4 HENRY JENKINS AND DIGITAL LABOUR

The digital labour debate is a discourse that has emerged in Critical Media and Communication Studies with the rise of social media (see Arvidsson and Colleoni 2012; Fuchs 2010c, 2012c, 2014a, 2015, Scholz 2017; as well as the contributions in Burston et al. 2010; Fisher and Fuchs 2015; Scholz 2013). It focuses on the analysis of unpaid user labour and other forms of labour (such as slave labour in Africa, highly-exploited ICT manufacturing work) that are necessary for capital accumulation in the ICT industries. In this debate, the works of Dallas Smythe (1977, 1981/2006) have gained new significance (for a detailed discussion, see Fuchs 2012a). Smythe argued that audiences of advertising-financed newspapers, TV and radio stations work when giving attention to these media (audience labour) and produce themselves as a commodity (the audience commodity) that is sold to advertisers. In the book *Spreadable Media: Creating Value and Meaning in a Networked Culture* (Jenkins et al. 2013), Henry Jenkins and his colleagues engage with some of the arguments in the digital labour debate.

DALLAS SMYTHE, DIGITAL LABOUR AND HENRY JENKINS

Jenkins et al. (2013, 127) discuss Smythe's approach and comment that "companies are often profiting from this audience labor, but it's crucial not to paint this wholly as exploitation, denying the many ways audience members benefit from willing participation in such arrangements". They argue against representatives of the digital labour discourse that "free labour may be meaningful and rewarding" (57). The authors make the argument that users are not purely motivated by financial returns (58–59), but by the desire to "share with a larger audience", the "pride in their accomplishments" and the "desire for dialogue" (59).

Jenkins et al. insinuate that representatives of digital labour theory assume that the money logic drives users, which they definitely do not. The three authors miss the point that the profit orientation is inherent in capitalism, not in users or audiences, who are confronted with the commodity form in their everyday lives. Audience labour would be engaged, not exploited (60), and would be "labor[s] of love" (61). It would have much to do with worth, that is "sentimental investment" (71).

There is no doubt that users are motivated by social and communicative needs and desires to use social media. But the fact that they love these activities does not make them less exploited. Jenkins's argument follows the logic "if users like it, then it is no problem". That work is and feels like play does not mean that it is more or less exploited, but rather that the structures of work are changing. Exploitation is measured as the degree of unpaid labour from which companies benefit at the expense of labour. If exploitation does not feel like exploitation, then this does not mean that it does not exist. It is exploitation even if users like it. User labour is objectively exploited and, to a certain degree, at the same time enjoyed by the users. This does not diminish the degree of exploitation, but rather shows the contradictions of culture in capitalism. In Jenkins's terminology one can say that social media corporations capitalize on users' desire for social, intellectual and cultural worth in order to exploit their labour and make them create monetary value. In Jenkins's account, cultural worth is seen as legitimatization of exploitation: it is perfectly fine for him that users are exploited if they feel they are appreciated by other users and companies.

Jenkins and his colleagues argue that Smythe and the digital labour approach overlook that audience members benefit from the corporate web 2.0. But they disregard in this critique that money has a central importance in capitalism because it is a general equivalent of exchange: it is the only commodity that can be exchanged against all other commodities. It is the universal commodity and is therefore of specific relevance. One can directly buy food, games, computers, phones and so on with money. One can, at most, gain such goods indirectly by making use of reputation and social connections. Money is a privileged medium for achieving objectives in capitalism, which is why capitalism is an economy that is based on instrumental reason.

SOCIAL MEDIA AND FANS, FANS, FANS: DID OCCUPY, THE ARAB SPRING AND WIKILEAKS NEVER HAPPEN?

Jenkins et al.'s (2013) book *Spreadable Media* mainly uses examples from fan culture because "fan groups have often been innovators in using participatory platforms" (29). Reading this book, one gets the impression that the world is only inhabited by fans, as if the Arab Spring, WikiLeaks, Anonymous, the Occupy movement and the widespread protests and revolutions in the world during 2011 never happened. One wonders why Henry Jenkins advances a new form of elitism that privileges fans and disregards activists and citizens. The book, for example, discusses the online platform 4chan, but ignores the political hacking of Anonymous that was born on 4chan (Colemean 2015).

Jenkins (2014, 276) argues that Spreadable Media "cannot fully engage with the Arab Spring (which unfolded as the manuscript was nearing completion)". The Tunisian Revolution took place in December 2010 and January 2011, the Egyptian Revolution in January and February 2011. Spreadable Media's bibliography contains 21 references to works from 2011 and 2012, which shows that the actual writing must have extended until 2012. This would have allowed the possibility that Jenkins and his colleagues would engage with the Arab Spring, which they however did not do.

3.5 JENKINS'S RESPONSE TO CRITICISMS

JENKINS'S RESPONSE

Jenkins has responded to criticism of his works, especially *Convergence Culture*, arguing that today he has become more critical:

> Today, I am much more likely to speak about a push towards a more participatory culture, acknowledging how many people are still excluded from even the most minimal opportunities for participation within networked culture, and recognizing that new grassroots tactics are confronting a range of corporate strategies which seek to contain and commodify the popular desire for participation. As a consequence, elites still exert a more powerful influence on political decision-making than grassroots networks, even if we are seeing new ways to assert alternative perspectives into the decision-making process. (Jenkins 2014, 272)

He admits that he and others "underestimated the barriers to achieving what we see as the potential for transformative change emerging as the public has gained greater control over the means of cultural production and circulation" (Jenkins 2014, 273). "Today, I am far more focused on these mechanism of control, after five years' worth of debates over Web 2.0 platforms, than I was when I wrote Convergence Culture" (Jenkins 2014, 278).

Jenkins also writes that he has been doing more work focusing on political activism, including the Occupy Wall Street movement (Jenkins 2014, 286). It remains to be seen, however, whether Jenkins frames such movements merely as a positive development mediated by the Internet or if he also sees their failures (that have to do with the power of the state, corporations and ideologues that have, since the new world economic crisis started in 2008, intensified) and the limits put on social movement activities by state surveillance and corporate control of the Internet (see Fuchs 2014b for a detailed discussion).

JENKINS AND THE ENGAGEMENT WITH CORPORATIONS

Jenkins (2014b, 287) argues that critique should include "to engage directly with corporations" and to "intervene in corporate policies". Critical and cultural studies would too often remain theoretical and fail to "protect its independence from commercial interests at the cost of making meaningful interventions in public debates" (289). This would involve "working within rather than outside capitalist institutions" (290). Speaking critically with corporations is certainly not in itself wrong. That is also what trade unions do. They, however, have certain means of pressuring corporations, for example via the strike and the refusal of work, which they bring to the conversation. In intellectual debates, the problem is that corporations often are willing to speak with supporters and very modest critics, from whom they do not have to fear more fundamental criticisms. They will be willing to listen as long as their profit imperatives are not questioned and especially to those about whom they know that no fundamental questions and issues will be brought up. So if one has the opportunity to talk to corporations, then the question is what one says and suggests they should do.

Jenkins seems to approach corporations with a certain naivety that they surely welcome. When writing about corporations, his criticism tends to be very mild, arguing that corporations should listen more to their customers and employees.

> In management studies, the focus has been on creating stronger horizontal networks within companies that might allows employees to feel a greater stake in the firm's success and to be capable of contributing new insights that might inform strategic and tactical decision-making. (Jenkins 2014b, 271)

Writing in *GfK Marketing Review*, "an outstanding Marketing magazine directed at managers and market research professionals who are interested in new insight and methods of Marketing Research",[3] Jenkins (2014a) gives recommendations to brand managers of how to "prevent brand-damage" (38).

> To avoid becoming the target of grassroots resistance, brands should very carefully confirm that all their touchpoints are truly in line with the values they promote. [...] The best way to respond is not to shut them down, not to ignore them, but to get into the game. Keep in mind that in this age of networked communication, if it doesn't spread, it's dead. (Jenkins 2014a, 39)

---

3 www.gfk-verein.org/en/publications/gfk-marketing-intelligence-review (accessed on 26 October 2015).

Jenkins does not give tips that relate to equality issues such as paying fair wages, fostering tax justice (which under neoliberal conditions has to include increasing corporate taxation and making global Internet companies such as Facebook and Google, that are experts in tax avoidance, accountable to tax authorities in various parts of the world so that they pay their taxes), reducing the negative effects corporations have on the environment, fostering co-operative ownership as a form of economic democracy and so on. He rather focuses on telling companies how to communicate in order to prevent or contain criticisms that could harm profitability. He talks about strategic corporate communication and not strategic political change that brings about a fairer and more just world.

Jenkins acknowledges that right-wing movements (he mentions the Tea Party) also use networked technologies. "Granted, the practices of participatory culture can produce complicated and contradictory results when read according to traditional ideological categories" (Jenkins 2014b, 285). There "is nothing about participatory culture that would inevitably lead to progressive outcomes" (285). Jenkins here reduces participation to a neutral cultural category that is only focused on "insuring as many people as possible have access to the platforms" (285), which disregards that it matters what exactly platforms are used for and if these usages aim at fostering equality, justice and democracy or inequality, repression and fascism. A neutral concept of participation that does not relate it to the political notion of participatory democracy is disinterested in ethics and politically uncritical. Nico Carpentier distinguishes between participation and participatory democracy. He argues that Nazis using the Internet show that "participation can be outside a democratic culture" (Jenkins and Carpentier 2013, 19) and that the notion of participation should therefore be related to substantive democracy.

HENRY JENKINS AND NICO CARPENTIER: CULTURAL AND POLITICAL PARTICIPATION

In a conversation between Henry Jenkins and Nico Carpentier (2013), Carpentier points out that in discussions of participatory culture, participation, access and interaction are often mixed up. The "more radical (maximalist) meanings of participation were being annihilated when a simple museum visit (and gazing at a painting) was labeled participation" (271). Carpentier argues that "the political is always a dimension of all social processes" and that therefore "both institutionalized politics and cultural participation is always political" (271). Jenkins argues he is interested in such discussions because sites such as YouTube "fall far short of both my original sense of a participatory culture and your [Carpentier's] notion of participation as depending on equality between participants" (273). Carpentier responds to Jenkins that in this context the distinction between participation in and through the media is important. Participation "in YouTube is minimalist", but there may be certain potentials for participation through YouTube (10). Jenkins agrees with this distinction, arguing that it allows distinguishing between YouTube's organization and the "participatory communities" (275) that use it.

I want to go one step further and argue that not just are social systems political, but they all have an economic, a political and a cultural dimension because they are based on resources, decision-making structures and reputation-generating structures (Fuchs 2008a).

These economic, political and cultural structures enable and constrain practices that produce and reproduce social structures (Fuchs 2008a). Social systems are certainly political because they are about the distribution of economic political and cultural power. They are, however, even more political-economic in the sense that the economic is about humans' production and reproduction of structures in social systems and is always political because questions about how power (the power of ownership, the power of decision-making, the power of reputation) is distributed arise.

YouTube, like all social systems, has economic aspects of ownership and labour, decision-making and reputation-generation. It is in itself a complex social system in which managers, financial investors, employees, viewers and prosumers are involved. At the level of consumption and prosumption, a multitude of other social systems created by the audiences is structurally coupled to YouTube. Also these systems have their own distributions of power in economic, political and cultural respects. To talk about participation means for me to always ask questions about democracy; that is, how economic, political and cultural power in social systems is distributed. When we discuss YouTube, we should therefore analyse and consider both how power is distributed in YouTube as an organization and in the social systems coupled to it as well as how these two realms interact, enable and constrain each other to particular degrees. Both Jenkins and Carpentier tend to argue for a rather neutral concept of participation that is contextualized and over-determined by the political (in the case of Carpentier) and culture (in the case of Jenkins). My argument is that participation itself has to do with the question of how power is distributed in society and social systems and should therefore best be seen as a political-economic concept.

3.6 CONCLUSION

Jenkins's work stands in the celebratory Cultural Studies tradition that focuses on worshipping TV audiences (and other audiences) as "rebelling" and constantly "resisting" in order to consume ever more. Jenkins (2008, 259) opposes the approaches of political economists such as Noam Chomsky and Robert McChesney because their "politics of critical pessimism is found on a politics of victimization", whereas his own "politics of critical utopianism is founded on a notion of empowerment". It is incorrect to characterize the Critical Political Economy approach as disempowering because it frequently stresses the potential of political movements and their media use for bringing about transformation. Jenkins is a utopian thinker in respect of the circumstance that he sees resistance of consumers necessarily and almost always at work in popular culture and ignores aspects of exploitation and ideology. But he is certainly not a critical utopian, only a utopian. Critical Theory and Critical Political Economy do not, as claimed by Jenkins (1992, 291), read "the audiences from the structures of the text or in terms of the forms of consumption generated by the institutions of production and marketing"; they are, rather, in contrast to Jenkins, concerned about the phenomena of exploitation (of workers and audiences) and class inequality that are implicated by the commodity form of culture. They see deep inequalities at the heart of the commodity form and therefore question the logic of commodification and capital accumulation.

Media and Communication Studies should forget about the vulgar and reductionist notion of participation (simply meaning that users create, curate, circulate or critique content) and focus on rediscovering the political-economic notion of participation by engaging with participatory democracy theory. There was a time when Cultural Studies scholars were claiming about others that they are economic reductionists. Today, it has become overtly clear – and Jenkins's work is the best expression of this circumstance – that cultural reductionism has gone too far, that the cultural turn away from Critical Political Economy was an error and that Media and Communication Studies needs to rediscover concepts like class and participatory democracy. Stuart Hall, who died in 2014, in one of his last interviews argued in this context for the re-introduction of Marx in cultural studies:

> In its attempt to move away from economic reductionism, it [Cultural Studies] forgot that there was an economy at all. It is not in a wonderful position [. . .] They [Cultural Studies scholars] would have to go back and ask themselves: [. . .] What is the role of the economic in the reproduction of material and symbolic life? They'd have to ask themselves economic questions. [. . .] It's more like a return to what Cultural Studies should have been about and was in the early stages. It sort of lost its way very much. [. . .] I'm sounding like the headmaster I never wanted to be.[4]

We can summarize the main results of this chapter as follows:

- Henry Jenkins reduces the notion of participation to a cultural dimension, ignoring the broad notion of participatory democracy and its implications for the Internet. An Internet that is dominated by corporations that accumulate capital by exploiting and commodifying users can never, in the theory of participatory democracy, be participatory and the cultural expressions of it cannot be expressions of participation. Jenkins especially neglects ownership as an aspect of participation and does not give attention to aspects of class and capitalism.
- Jenkins mistakenly assumes an automatic connection of fandom in popular culture and political protest. He also mistakes politics with popular culture and sees politics taking place largely as micro politics within popular culture (as the struggle of fans for making the culture industry respect their ideas in the design of plots).
- Jenkins's account of participatory culture and social media as producers of participatory culture is a form of cultural reductionism and determinism that neglects structural constraints of human behaviour and the dialectic of structure and agency.
- In his arguments, Jenkins misses the central economic relevance of money in the economy and argues that the exploitation of users' digital labour is not really a problem if they have social benefits from platform usage.

---

4 Stuart Hall interviewed by Sut Jhally, London, 30 August 2012. http://vimeo.com/53879491 (accessed on 24 October 2015).

RECOMMENDED READINGS AND EXERCISES

Engaging with different texts is a good approach for understanding the topic of participatory culture. The suggested readings include works on participatory culture by Henry Jenkins and political theorists such as Carole Pateman and Crawford Macpherson, who engage with the notion of participatory democracy. Contrasting these texts allows us to work out different understandings of participation.

Jenkins, Henry. 2008. *Convergence culture.* New York: New York University Press. Introduction: Workshop at the altar of convergence: A new paradigm for understanding media change. Chapter 4: Quentin Tarantino's Star Wars? Grassroots creativity meets the media industry. Chapter 5: Why Heather can write: Media literacy and the Harry Potter wars. Conclusion: Democratizing television? The politics of participation.

Green, Joshua and Henry Jenkins. 2009. The moral economy of web 2.0: Audience research and convergence culture. In *Media industries: History, theory, and method,* ed. Jennifer Holt and Alisa Perren, 213–225. Malden, MA: Wiley-Blackwell.

Jenkins, Henry. 2009. What happened before YouTube. In *YouTube,* ed. Jean Burgess and Joshua Green, 109–125. Cambridge: Polity Press.

These readings give an introduction to Henry Jenkins's notion of participatory culture. Discuss in groups:

* First, make a list of the characteristics of Henry Jenkins's concept of participatory culture. Make the list systematic by introducing dimensions of participatory culture.
* Think about how to define the concept of culture and which aspects and dimensions it has. Go back to your list of characteristics of participatory culture and try to make it theoretically systematic by mapping the dimensions of culture you identified and the characteristics of participatory culture. Try to avoid overlapping categories/dimensions.
* Together, look at those passages and articles/chapters that mention social media/web 2.0 platforms. Use your typology/list of characteristics of participatory culture to identify what Jenkins sees as characteristics of participatory web culture.

Pateman, Carole. 1970. *Participation and democratic theory.* Cambridge: Cambridge University Press. Chapter IV: "Participation" and "democracy" in industry. Chapter VI: Conclusion.

Macpherson, Crawford Brough. 1973. *Democratic theory.* Oxford: Oxford University Press. Chapter I: The maximization of democracy. Chapter II: Democratic theory: Ontology and technology. Chapter III: Problems of a non-market theory of democracy.

Held, David. 2006. *Models of democracy* (3rd edition), 209–216. Cambridge: Polity Press.

Pateman, Carole. 2012. Participatory democracy revisited. *Perspectives on Politics* 10 (1): 7–19.

Crawford Brough Macpherson and Carole Pateman are two of the most important political thinkers who have written on the concept of participatory democracy. Their books *Democratic Theory* and *Participation and Democratic Theory* are classical works in political theory. David Held's reading is a supplementary text for better understanding the term "participatory democracy".

(Continued)

(Continued)

- Make a list of characteristics of the concept of participatory democracy, as introduced by Pateman and Macpherson. Try to make the list systematic by identifying dimensions of democracy, and avoid overlapping dimensions.
- Discuss where examples of participatory democracy can be found and in which respect these examples have the characteristics of participatory democracy that you identified. Are there examples for participatory democracy on the Internet?
- Try to think about what the Internet and social media would look like in a participatory democracy. What changes to society, the current Internet and current social media are needed in order to establish a participatory democracy and a participatory Internet/web? Compare such a concept of a participatory Internet to Henry Jenkins's concept of participatory culture.
- Conduct a search for reviews of Henry Jenkins's books in databases such as Social Sciences Citation Index, Communication and Mass Media Complete, Scopus, Sociological Abstracts, Google Scholar, etc. Distribute all the reviews you found among those participating in the exercise. After reading the reviews, construct a systematic and ordered list of points of criticism of Jenkins's works. Discuss these points in class.
- Search in Jenkins's books and articles to see if he refers to the authors who criticized him and, if so, how he responds to their criticism. If you find such responses, discuss them in class.

4 SOCIAL MEDIA AND COMMUNICATION POWER

KEY QUESTIONS

- What is power? What is counter-power?
- How does power relate to communication?
- How has social media influenced our conception of communication power?
- What has been the role of social media-communication power in the Arab spring and the Occupy movement?

KEY CONCEPTS

Power
Counter-power

Manuel Castells's concept of mass self-communication
Communication power

OVERVIEW

Power is a key concept in political theory, but it has been defined in different ways. Max Weber says that it is the "chance of a man or a number of men to realize their own will in a social action even against the resistance of others who are participating in the action" (Weber 1978, 926). For Jürgen Habermas, power has to do with the realization of collective goals, means of coercion, symbols of power and status, decision-making authorities, disadvantages, power of definition, counter-power, organization and legitimation (Habermas 1984, 1987). Niklas Luhmann (2000, 39) sees power as the achievement of inducing someone to act in a certain way when s/he wouldn't act that way normally and only does so due to the threat of possible sanctions. For these authors, power has to do with the capacity of one group to use means of coercion against others so that it asserts its will and interests.

Michel Foucault argued that such a definition of power ignores the fact that power is not only located in powerful bodies such as the state or companies:

> We must cease once and for all to describe the effects of power in negative terms: it "excludes," it "represses," it "censors," it "abstracts," it "masks," it "conceals." In fact, power produces, it produces reality, it produces domains of objects and rituals of truth. The individual and the knowledge that may be gained of him belong to this production. (Foucault 1977, 250)

He said that "there are no relations of power without resistance" (Foucault 1980, 142).

Anthony Giddens defines power as "'transformative capacity', the capability to intervene in a given set of events so as in some way to alter them" (Giddens 1985, 7), as the "capability to effectively decide about courses of events, even where others might contest such decisions" (ibid.: 9). So, for Giddens, as opposed to Weber, Habermas and Luhmann, power is a general concept – the capacity of humans to act and to thereby transform society.

No matter which of these definitions one follows, it is clear that power has to do with the question of who can influence what society looks like and who controls the means that allow such influence. In the information society, communication and communication technologies have become ubiquitous in everyday life and society. The question is therefore how power has been transformed in the information society and what communication power is.

Manuel Castells is one of the most cited authors in the social sciences and media/communication studies. This chapter focuses on Castells's approach and his concept of communication power in the context of social media. Manuel Castells worked for a long time in urban sociology and with the rise of the World Wide Web became a leading Internet researcher. He is Professor of Sociology at the Open University of Catalonia in Barcelona. He is also Professor of Communication Technology and Society at the University of Southern California's Annenberg School of Communication.

In his approach, Manuel Castells stresses the role of the Internet and social media in what he terms the network society. He has in this context worked out the concepts of communication power and mass self-communication. For him, social media communication is mass self-communication. He argues that the emergence of this type of communication has resulted in profound shifts in the power structures of society. In this chapter, I present, discuss and critically analyse the theoretical foundations of Castells's approach.

We will discuss the role of social theory in Castells's approach (in section 4.1), the concept of communication power (4.2), communication power on social media (4.3) and communication power in the Arab Spring and the Occupy movement (4.4).

4.1 SOCIAL THEORY IN THE INFORMATION AGE

WHAT IS SOCIAL THEORY?

My experience is that if one asks Internet and social media researchers what social theories they use, some of them will answer: Manuel Castells's theory. But what is social theory? Social theory is the systematic development and connection of "concepts with which to grasp social life, with identifying patterns in social relations and social action, with producing explanations for both specific features of life in society and changes in overall forms of society" (Calhoun et al. 2007, 3). It is an endeavour to understand events, institutions and trends in society, the connections between events, institutions and trends and the connection of personal life to society (Calhoun et al. 2007, 4). It is also concerned with "the nature of human action", interaction and institutions (Giddens 1984, xvii), the human being, human doing and the reproduction and transformation of society (xx). Philosophical debates and philosophical reasoning are important tools for social theory (Giddens 1984, xvii).

Sociology and social theory have their roots in philosophy (Adorno 2000, 176, 2002, 8, 54). Tasks of (critical) social theory include to point out and make people aware of society's unrealized potentials, to point out possibilities of action in contemporary society, to ask new and different questions about the present order of society (Calhoun 1995, 7–8), to strengthen the imagination of people about what a better society could look like, to point out and make people aware of contemporary problems of society that limit the realization of society's possibilities, to provide narratives about which society we live in and the main characteristics of this society so that discussions about the character and problems of contemporary society are enabled, and to analyse the relation between appearance (that which is/exists) and essence (that which should be) (Adorno 2002, 25).

Given the role of social philosophy in social theory and its role of providing guidance about questions that focus on which society we live in, it is important that each theory justifies why a certain concept is employed in a certain way and not in another way. This requires engagement with other theories and arguments relating to these theories. Castells only provides his own definitions without providing reasons why these definitions are superior to others.

CASTELLS: SOCIAL THEORIST OF THE INTERNET IN THE INFORMATION SOCIETY?

Castells's approach deals with life and communication in what he calls the "network society". He is author of the trilogy *The Information Age* (Castells 2000, 2004, 2010), which was followed up by *Communication Power* (Castells 2009). Castells says that *The Information Age* "does not present a formal, systematic theory of society, it proposes new concepts and a new theoretical perspective to understand the trends that characterize the structure and dynamics of our societies in the world of the twenty-first century" (Castells 2010, xix). So Castells does see his approach as a social theory. A social theory of the Internet in society needs to start by providing an understanding of questions like: What is society? How is a society made up? How does social transformation work in society? What are the roles of structures and agency in society? What is the relationship of the human individual and society? It can then move on to applying these questions first to modern society and then to contemporary society in order to have theoretical knowledge at hand that allows understanding, conceptualizing and criticizing the role of the Internet in contemporary society (see Fuchs 2008a). Castells mainly presents a history of the Internet and its context, whereas his work lacks a theory of society and a theory of modern society. He provides a brief, 13-page conceptual framework in the prologue of *The Information Age* (Castells 2010, 5–18) that describes the relationship of technology and society as consisting of structures of production (modes of production, modes of development), experience and power. It is, however, unclear whether Castells here talks about society in general or specific societies, because he talks about class relationships as part of production (15–16). Class is certainly an aspect of modern society, but, as Marx knew when talking about classless societies, is not necessarily present in all societies.

The task of *Communication Power* is to "advance the construction of a grounded theory of power in the network society" (Castells 2009, 5). Castells does not want to place himself in theoretical debates (he bases his approach on "a selective reading of power theories" (6)), does not want to write books about books (Castells 2009, 6; 2010, 25), and thinks that social theory books are contributing to the deforestation of the planet (Castells 2009, 6), which is just another way of saying that they are unimportant and not worth the paper they are printed on.

Lacking grounding in social theory, Castells cannot explain why he uses a certain definition of power, globalization, social movements and so on, and why he thinks we live in a network society rather than a post-industrial society, capitalist society, new capitalist empire/imperialism, finance capitalism, knowledge society and so on. It is simplistic to give single definitions and not to engage with the history of concepts. An approach is only adequately grounded if it can logically justify why it uses concepts in a certain way and not in another. Understanding contemporary society in meaningful ways requires engaging with social philosophy and the history of conceptualizing society. Castells's aversion to social theory discourses makes him fall short of providing a grounded and justified approach. His approach is neither a social theory nor adequately theoretically grounded, but rather an arbitrary and unsystematic form of conceptualizing and a collection of observations.

4.2 COMMUNICATION POWER IN THE NETWORK SOCIETY

CASTELLS ON POWER: AN ESSENTIAL FEATURE OF ALL SOCIETIES?

Castells (2009, 43–47, 418–420) introduces four kinds of power in the network society: networking power, network power, networked power, network-making power. Inspired by Max Weber, he defines power as "the relational capacity that enables a social actor to influence asymmetrically the decisions of other social actor(s) in ways that favor the empowered actor's will, interests, and values" (Castells 2009, 10). Power is for Castells associated with coercion, domination, violence or potential violence, and asymmetry. He refers to the power concepts of Foucault, Weber and Habermas, and argues that he builds on Giddens's structuration theory. However, Giddens conceives power in a completely different way, a way that Castells neither mentions nor discusses. For Giddens, power is "'transformative capacity', the capability to intervene in a given set of events so as in some way to alter them" (Giddens 1985, 7), the "capability to effectively decide about courses of events, even where others might contest such decisions" (9). Power is, for Giddens, characteristic of all social relationships; it "is routinely involved in the instantiation of social practices" and is "operating in and through human action" (Giddens 1981, 49–50).

In Giddens's structuration theory, power is not necessarily coercive, violent and asymmetrically distributed. Therefore, it becomes possible to conceive and analyse situations and social systems in which power is more symmetrically distributed, for example situations and systems of participatory democracy. Power understood as transformative capacity seems indeed to be a fundamental aspect of all societies. This also means that there is a huge difference between Castells's approach and Giddens's structuration theory, which is not problematic as such, but should also be explicated, especially because Castells (2009, 14) says that he builds on Giddens's structuration theory, which, in my opinion, he does not. The problem with

Castells's notion of power is that he sees coercive, violent, dominative power relationships as "the foundational relations of society throughout history, geography, and cultures" (Castells 2009, 9). Such power is for him "the most fundamental process in society" (10). Furthermore, Castells (13) dismisses the "naïve image of a reconciled human community, a normative utopia that is belied by historical observation".

Is it really likely that all history of humankind and all social situations and systems in which we live are always and necessarily shaped by power struggles, coercion, violence and domination? Relationships of love, intimacy and affection are in modern society unfortunately often characterized by violence and coercion, and are therefore frequently (in Castells's terms) power relationships. But isn't love a prototypical phenomenon, where many people experience feelings and actions that negate violence, domination and coercion? Isn't the phenomenon of altruism in love and civil society the practical falsification of the claim that coercive power is society's most fundamental process? My claim is that not coercive power, but co-operation is the most fundamental process in society (Fuchs 2008a, 31–34, 40–58), and that it is indeed possible to create social systems without coercive power (in Castells's terms) and with a symmetric distribution of power (in Giddens's terminology). If one is conceiving of power as violent coercion, then one naturalizes and fetishizes coercion and violent struggles as necessary and therefore not historical qualities of society. The problematic ideological-theoretical implication is that in the final instance war must exist in all societies and a state of peace is dismissed and considered as being categorically impossible. Castells surely does not share this implication, as his analysis of communication power in the Iraq war shows (Castells 2009).

POWER AND TECHNOCRATIC LANGUAGE

One problem regarding Manuel Castells's (2009) book *Communication Power* is that he tends to use rather technocratic language for describing networks and communication power – social networks, technological networks and techno-social networks are all described with the same categories and metaphors that originate in computer science and computer technology: program, meta-programmers, switches, switchers, configuration, inter-operability, protocols, network standards, network components, kernel, program code and so on. I have no doubt that Castells does not intend to conflate the difference between social and technological networks. He has argued in the past, for example, that social networks are a "networking form of social organization" and that information technology is the "material basis" for the "pervasive expansion" of social networks (Castells 2010, 500).

But even if the terminology that Manuel Castells now tends to employ is only understood in a metaphorical sense, it is a problem that he describes society and social systems in technological and computational terms so that the *differentia specifica* of society in comparison to computers and computer networks – that society is based on humans, reflexive and self-conscious beings that have cultural norms, anticipative thinking, and a certain freedom of action that computers do not have – gets lost. It is no surprise that, based on the frequent employment of such metaphors, Castells (2009, 45) considers Bruno Latour's actor network theory as brilliant. It is important that one distinguishes the qualities of social networks from the qualities of technological networks and identifies the emergent qualities of techno-social networks such as the Internet (Fuchs 2008a, 121–147).

Castells acknowledges that there is a "parallel with software language" (Castells 2009, 48), in his terminology, but he does not give reasons why he uses these parallels or why he thinks such parallels are useful. Obviously society is shaped by computers, but it is not a computer itself, so there is, in my opinion, simply no need for such a terminological conflationism. Computer metaphors of society can, just like biological metaphors of society, become dangerous under certain circumstances so, in my opinion, it is best not to start to categorically conflate the qualitative difference between society and technology. Technology is part of society and society creates, produces and reproduces technology. Society is more than just technology and has emergent qualities that stem from the synergetical interactions of human beings. Technology is one of many results of the productive societal interactions of human beings. It therefore has qualities that are, on the one hand, specifically societal but, on the other hand, different from the qualities of other products of society. It is a common aspect of social and technological networks that there are nodes and interactions in all networks. One should not forget the important task of differentiating between the various emergent qualities that technological networks and social networks have – emergent qualities that interact when these two kinds of networks are combined in the form of techno-social networks such as the Internet so that meta-emergent techno-social qualities appear.

The contradictions and fetishisms that one can partly find in Castells's work stem from a lack of engagement with social theory and show the importance of social theory as a theory of the Internet in contemporary society.

4.3 COMMUNICATION POWER, SOCIAL MEDIA AND MASS SELF-COMMUNICATION

MASS SELF-COMMUNICATION

Castells argues that mass self-communication is a novel quality of communication in contemporary society:

> It is mass communication because it can potentially reach a global audience, as in the posting of a video on YouTube, a blog with RSS links to a number of web sources, or a message to a massive email list. At the same time, it is self-communication because the production of the message is self-generated, the definition of the potential receiver(s) is self-directed, and the retrieval of specific messages or content from the World Wide Web and electronic networks is self-selected. The three forms of communication (interpersonal, mass communication, and mass self-communication) coexist, interact, and complement each other rather than substituting for one another. What is historically novel, with considerable consequences for social organization and cultural change, is the articulation of all forms of communication into a composite, interactive, digital hypertext that includes, mixes, and recombines in their diversity the whole range of cultural expressions conveyed by human interaction. (Castells 2009, 55; see also 70)

Castells theorizes that mass self-communication is based on Umberto Eco's semiotic model of communication as the emergence of "the creative audience" (Castells 2009, 127–135) that engages in the "interactive production of meaning" (132) and is based on the emergence of the figure of the "sender/addressee" (130).

AUTONOMY

Castells argues that the contemporary Internet is shaped by a conflict between the global multimedia business networks that try to commodify the Internet and the "creative audience" that tries to establish a degree of citizen control of the Internet and to assert the right of communicative freedom without corporate control (Castells 2009, 80, 97, 136). Castells (2009) first introduces the notion of autonomy in mass self-communication on page 129 of *Communication Power*, but does not define it, which leaves the reader wondering what Castells wants to tell her/him by using this normatively and politically connoted term (see also Castells 2009, 302). The meaning of the concept of autonomy is not self-explanatory. Is it autonomy in the sense of Kant, understood as the autonomy of the will as the supreme principle of morality (Kant 2002, 58), the "quality of the will of being a law to itself" (Kant 2002, 63)? Or does autonomy mean the "true individualism" that Hayek (1948) had in mind, in which capitalism is conceived as spontaneous order that should be left to itself and should not be shaped by political rules (Hayek 1988)? Does it refer to freedom of speech, taste and assembly – "the liberty of thought and discussion" – in line with the harm principle, as postulated by John Stuart Mill (2002)? Or is autonomy the existence of functionally differentiated self-referential subsystems of society (Luhmann 1998)? Or does it, in a less individualistic sense, refer to the combination of individual autonomy, understood as subjectivity – that is "reflective and deliberative" and "frees the radical imagination" from "the enslavement of repetition" (Castoriadis 1991, 164) – and social autonomy, "the equal participation of all in power" (Castoriadis 1991, 136; see also Castoriadis 1998)? Does Castells's notion of autonomy confirm one of the two poles of the theoretically unreconciled relationship of private autonomy and public autonomy that Habermas (1996, 84) has critically examined, or does it refer to the dialectic of autonomy that Habermas has in mind when he speaks of a "cooriginality of private and public autonomy" (Habermas 1996, 104) achieved in a "system of rights in which private and public autonomy are internally related" (Habermas 1996, 280) and "reciprocally presuppose each other" (Habermas 1996, 417)? Or does autonomy mean the "status of an organized people in an enclosed territorial unit" (Schmitt 1996, 19; for a critique of this approach see Habermas 1989a)? Or is autonomy a postmodern project of plural democracy with a multiplicity of subject positions (Laclau and Mouffe 1985)?

In short, there are all kinds of meanings of concepts such as autonomy, power, information and networks. It is one of the tasks of social theory to clarify which meanings of concepts are feasible and suitable for understanding and analysing contemporary society's situation. The problems of Castells's lack of engagement with social theory become apparent in his unreflected use of terms.

POWER AND COUNTER-POWER ON THE INTERNET AND SOCIAL MEDIA

Castells says that mass self-communication (2009, 413) allows subjects to "watch the powerful", but those in power "have made it their priority to harness the potential of mass self-communication in the service of their specific interests" (414). Therefore, they engage in enclosing the communication commons (414). Castells speaks of a dialectical process in relation to mass self-communication. On the one hand, "web 2.0" business strategies result in "the commodification of freedom", the "enclosing of the commons of free communication and selling people access to global communication networks in exchange for surrendering their privacy and becoming advertising targets" (421). On the other hand, "once in cyberspace, people may have all kinds of ideas, including challenging corporate power, dismantling government authority, and changing the cultural foundations of our aging/aching civilization" (420). The typical web 2.0 business strategy is not, however, "selling people access", but that providers give users free access and sell the data users generate as commodity to third parties in order to generate profit. This relationship is highly unequal. The actual power of corporations in web 2.0 "is much larger than the actual political counter-power that is exercised by the produsers. Castells acknowledges this in some instances, for example when he speaks of "unequal competition" (2009, 422), but he also contradicts this realism in some instances by a certain web 2.0 optimism, for example when he says that "the more corporations invest in expanding communication networks (benefiting from a hefty return), the more people build their own networks of mass self-communication, thus empowering themselves" (421).

There is an asymmetry between the power of corporations and other powerful groups and citizens' actual counter-power. The dialectic of power is only a potential, but not an automatic actual or necessary dialectic. Political counter-power on the Internet faces a massive asymmetry that is due to the fact that the ruling powers control more resources, such as money, decision-making power, capacities for attention generation and so on. Power struggles are struggles of the less powerful against the powerful. There is no guarantee that they can emerge, that they can mobilize significant resources so that they do not remain precarious, or that they will be successful. Power asymmetries are dialectical in the sense that they constitute social contradictions that are a necessary foundation of social struggles, but do not determine their emergence and outcome. There are examples of relatively successful counter-power struggles that have made use of the Internet, as Castells (2009) shows, but it is only a potential, not an automatism that citizens "overcome the powerlessness of their solitary despair by networking their desire. They fight the powers that be by identifying the networks that are" (431). The problem is that there are also forces of power in contemporary society, such as ideology and coercion, that might forestall such fights, that keep people occupied with struggling for survival so that they have no time, energy or thoughts for counter-power struggles. Communication counter-power should not be overestimated, but only assessed as potential.

MEDIA POWER AS CULTURAL POWER: JOHN B. THOMPSON

John B. Thompson (1995) distinguishes four forms of power (see Table 4.1). The problem of Thompson's approach is that the media's power is reduced to the symbolic dimension and that the relationship of violence and power is unclear. Symbolic power is an important dimension of the media: the media not only have form, but also communicate content to the public, which allows attempts to influence the minds of the members of the public. But ideology is not the only aspect of the media. Rather, the media are a terrain where different forms of power and power struggles manifest themselves: the media have specific structures of private or public ownership that tend to be concentrated. There are attempts

TABLE 4.1   John B. Thompson's four forms of power

Type of power	Definition	Resources	Institutions
Economic power	"Economic power stems from human productive activity, that is, activity concerned with the provision of the means of subsistence through the extraction of raw materials and their transformation into goods which can be consumed or exchanged in a market." (14)	Material and financial resources	Economic institutions
Political power	Political power "stems from the activity of coordinating individuals and regulating the patterns of their interaction". (14)	Authority	Political institutions (e.g. states)
Coercive power	"Coercive power involves the use, or threatened use, of physical force to subdue or conquer an opponent." (15)	Physical and armed force	Coercive institutions (military, police, carceral institutions, etc.)
Symbolic power	Symbolic power is the "capacity to intervene in the course of events, to influence the actions of others and indeed to create events, by means of the production and transmission of symbolic forms". (17)	Means of information and communication	Cultural institutions (church, schools, universities, media, etc.)

Source: Based on Thompson 1995, 12–18.

to politically control and influence the media and the media often have political roles in elections, social movement struggles and so on. Violence is a frequent topic in media content. The media are not just a realm of symbolic power, but socio-material spaces where structures and contradictions of economic, political, coercive and symbolic power manifest themselves. Nick Couldry (2002, 4) defines media power as "the concentration in media institutions of the symbolic power of 'constructing reality'". Like Thompson's definition of power, the one given by Couldry also focuses on the symbolic and cultural dimensions of the media.

MEDIA POWER AS MULTIDIMENSIONAL FORM OF ECONOMIC, POLITICAL AND CULTURAL POWER

It is unclear why Thompson defines violence as a separate form of power. He reduces violence to direct physical violence, exerted, for example, if one kills or beats somebody. Johan Galtung (1990, 292) defines violence, in contrast, as "avoidable insults to basic human needs, and, more generally to life, lowering the real level of needs satisfaction below what is potentially possible". According to Galtung (1990), violence can be divided into three principal forms: direct violence (through physical intervention; an event), structural violence (through state or organizational mandate; a process) and cultural violence (dehumanizing or otherwise exclusionary representations; an invariance). This means that in exerting violence one can physically coerce somebody (physical violence), exclude him/her from access to vital resources (structural violence) or manipulate his/her mind or ruin his/her reputation (ideological violence). Violence exists not only if it is actually exerted, but also if it is only a threat: "Threats of violence are also violence" (Galtung 1990, 292). The three forms of violence are forms of how people or groups try to accumulate different forms of power.

Different forms of violence can be exerted in order to accumulate different forms of power. In modern society, economic, political and cultural power can be accumulated and tend to be asymmetrically distributed. Table 4.2 gives an overview of these three forms of power. Karl Marx (1867) stresses that the logic of accumulation (getting more and more of something) is vital for modern society. It has its origins in the capitalist economy. But it also shapes the logic of modern politics and culture that are focused on the accumulation of political and cultural power. Capitalism is therefore not just an economic system, but also a form of society.

Pierre Bourdieu argues that modern society is based on the accumulation of economic, political and cultural capital:

> Depending on the field in which it functions, and at the cost of the more or less expensive transformations which are the preconditions for its efficacy in the field in question, capital can present itself in three fundamental guises: as *economic capital*, which is immediately and directly convertible into money and may be institutionalized in the form of property rights; as *cultural capital*, which is convertible, on certain conditions, into economic capital and may be institutionalized in the form of educational qualifications; and as *social capital*, made up of social obligations ("connections"), which is convertible, in certain conditions, into economic capital and may be institutionalized in the form of a title of nobility. (Bourdieu 1986/1997, 47)

Bourdieu bases his theory of society on the distinction between economy, politics and culture. One can argue that he generalized Marx's approach by pointing out that all of society's subsystems have (at least) in modern society their own economies because they are focused on the accumulation of certain forms of capital, which results in inequalities and a multidimensional class structure (see Fuchs 2003a, 2008a, Chapter 3). Structures of acculation are modern society's basic power structures.

Physical, structural and ideological violence can be used in any of the three dimensions/fields of modern society for trying to accumulate power at the expense of others. Many structures of modern society are based on specific forms of violence that help in accumulating power. For example, a corporation makes use of the structural violence of the market and private property in order to accumulate capital. Or the state uses the monopoly of physical violence and the institutional power of government institutions in order to make collective decisions.

The media and social media in contemporary society are shaped by structures of economic, political and cultural power:

- Social media have specific ownership structures. If social media's economic power is asymmetrically distributed, then a private class owns social media. If it is more symmetrically distributed, then a collective of users or all people own social media.
- Social media have specific decision-making structures. If social media's political power is asymmetrically distributed, then a specific group controls decision-making. If it is more symmetrically distributed, then all users or all people in society can influence decision-making.

- Social media have specific mechanisms for the generation of reputation and popularity. If social media's cultural power is asymmetrically distributed, then the reputation and visibility of certain actors are in contrast to the attention and visibility given to others. Social media can also act as conveyors of ideologies that misrepresent reality. If highly visible actors communicate such ideologies, then it is likely that they will have some effect. If cultural power is more symmetrically distributed, then all users have a significant degree of visibility and attention.

James Curran (2002, Chapter 5) has identified 11 dimensions of media power and seven dimensions of media counter-power. I have classified these dimensions according to the three dimensions of media power (see Table 4.3): economic media power, political media power and cultural media power. Curran stresses that media power is not just symbolic, but multidimensional. The distinction of three realms of society (economy, politics, culture) allows us to classify forms of media power (Table 4.3). Curran emphasizes the contradictory character of contemporary media: there are "eleven main factors that encourage the media to support dominant power interests" (Curran 2002, 148), but "the media are also subject to countervailing pressures which can pull potentially in the other direction" (Curran 2002, 151).

THE ASYMMETRIC DIALECTIC OF MEDIA POWER

The systematic typology of media power that is based on Curran's approach shows that modern media can best be viewed dialectically: they are subject to elite control, but have potentials for acting as, and being influenced by, counter-powers that question elite control. This form of struggle is a potential, which means that it does not automatically arise. The power of dominant and alternative media tends to be distributed unequally (see Fuchs 2010a; Sandoval and Fuchs 2010): alternative media are often facing resource inequalities and have to exist based on precarious labour and resource precariousness.

Social media are spaces where media power and counter-power are played out. Dominant platforms, such as Facebook, Google/YouTube and Twitter, are privately owned and there are economic, political and ideological forms of media power at play; private ownership, concentration, advertising, the logic of consumption and entertainment, the

TABLE 4.2 Three forms of power

Dimension of society	Definition of power	Structures of power in modern society
Economy	Control of use-values and resources that are produced, distributed and consumed.	Control of money and capital.
Politics	Influence on collective decisions that determine aspects of the lives of humans in certain communities and social systems.	Control of governments, bureaucratic state institutions, parliament, military, police, parties, lobby groups, civil society groups, etc.
Culture	Definition of moral values and meaning that shape what is considered as important, reputable and worthy in society.	Control of structures that define meaning and moral values in society (e.g. universities, religious groups, intellectual circles, opinion-making groups).

Source: Based on Curran 2002, Chapter 5.

TABLE 4.3   Power and counter-power in the media

Dimension of media power	Forms of media power	Forms of media counter-power
Economic media power	High entry and operation costs; media concentration; private media ownership; influence of companies on the media via advertising	Public media; alternative grassroots media; public funding for alternative media
	Market pressure to produce homogeneous (often uncritical) content with wide appeal; content that appeals to wealthy consumers	Staff power (e.g. critical journalism, investigative reporting)
	The unequal distribution of economic resources (money) allows economic elites more influence on and control of the media	Consumer power (e.g. by support of alternative media in the form of donations)
Political media power	State censorship of the media	Media regulation that secures quality, fair reporting, diversity, freedom of expression, assembly and opinion
	Public relations of large (political and economic) organizations results in bureaucratic lobbying apparatus that aims to influence the media	Alternative news sources
	The unequal distribution of political resources (influence, decision power, political relations) allows economic elites more influence on and control of the media	State redistribution of resources from the more powerful to the less powerful
Cultural media power	Focus on content covering prestige institutions, celebrities and others who have high reputation; dominant ideologies influence dominant media to a certain degree; the unequal distribution of cultural resources (reputation, prestige) allows economic elites more influence on and control of the media	Creation of counter-organizations that develop counter-discourses and operate their own media

high visibility of and attention given to elites and celebrities shape and filter communication on dominant social media platforms. At the same time, dominant structures are questioned by phenomena such as file-sharing, commons-based social media that are non-profit and non-commercial (e.g. Wikipedia, Diaspora*), social movements' use of social media for political purposes, the development of alternative social media, protests against the dominance of platforms like Google, protests and legal disputes over privacy violations, and so on. Contemporary social media is a field of power struggles in which dominant actors command a large share of economic, political and ideological media power that can be challenged by alternative actors that have less resources, visibility and attention, but try to make best use of the unequal share of media power they are confronted with in order to fight against the dominant powers.

MEDIA POWER AS CONTRADICTORY

Des Freedman (2014) argues for studying media power in capitalism as contradictory. There are "multiple contradictions within the commercial media" (28). Such an approach to media power emphasizes structures *and* agency, contradiction *and* action, consensus *and* conflict; an analytical framework that recognizes the existence of unequal power frameworks but acknowledges that they are not forever frozen; and a perspective that takes seriously the activities of producers and audiences while recognizing the existence of uneven consciousness. In short, the contradiction paradigm is needed to compensate for the misplaced optimism of pluralism, the occasional functionalism of the control paradigm and the unwarranted celebrations of the chaos scenario. (Freedman 2014, 29)

THE STRATIFIED ONLINE SPHERE

Castells (2009, 204) argues that in mass self-communication "traditional forms of access control are not applicable. Anyone can upload a video to the Internet, write a blog, start a chat forum, or create a gigantic email list. Access in this case is the rule; blocking Internet access is the exception". Visibility and the attention economy form a central filter of the Internet that benefits powerful actors. Although everyone can produce and diffuse information easily in principle with the help of the Internet because it is a global, decentralized, many-to-many and one-to-many communication system, not all information is visible to the same degree or gets the same attention. The problem in the cyberspace flood of information is how users are drawn to specific information that flows in the huge informational online ocean.

Alternet and Democracy Now!, two of the most popular alternative online news platforms, are ranked numbers 4,133 and 20,461 in the list of the most accessed websites, whereas CNN Online is ranked number 81, BBC #87, *The New York Times* # 99, the *Daily Mail* #106, *India Times* #114, *China Daily* #142, Fox News #195, *The Washington Post* #196, *Daily Telegraph* #231, *Bildzeitung Online* #293, Bloomberg News #301, *Spiegel Online* #319 (data source: alexa.com, top 1,000,000,000 sites, accessed on 26 October 2015). This shows that there is a stratified online attention economy in which the trademarks of powerful media actors work as powerful symbols that help the online portals of these organizations to accumulate attention. This is not to deny the heavy use of "mass self-communication" platforms such as Facebook, YouTube, LinkedIn, Vk, Twitter, Weibo, Blogspot/Blogger, Pinterest, Wordpress, Reddit, Tumblr, imgur and so on, but political information generation and communication on such sites is much more fragmented, which is the reason why Jürgen Habermas speaks in relation to the Internet of a danger of the "fragmentation of large but politically focused mass audience into a huge number of isolated issue publics" (Habermas 2006, 423). Social media are in a capitalist society, as will be discussed in Chapter 5, confronted by an asymmetric attention economy, in which large corporations, celebrities, politicians, governments and parties tend to receive much more attention and many more followers, likes, re-tweets and so on than everyday users.

WEB 2.0 AND 3.0

Castells employs the terms "web 2.0 and 3.0" (see e.g. Castells 2009, 34, 56, 65, 97, 107, 113, 421, 429), which he defines as "the cluster of technologies, devices, and applications that support the proliferation of social spaces on the Internet" (Castells 2009, 65). We should also ask critical questions about "web 2.0":

- To what extent are the claims about the "new web" ideological and to what extent do they serve marketing purposes?
- What is novel about "web 2.0" and how can this novelty be empirically validated?
- What does it mean exactly to say that the web has become more social?
- Which notions of the social are employed when people speak of "web 2.0"?
- Which notion of sociality underlies "web 1.0" and how does this idea differ from the idea of sociality that underlies the concepts of web 2.0 and 3.0?
- What are the differences between web 1.0, 2.0 and 3.0?

In short, the talk about "web 2.0", "social media" and "social software" compels us to answer some basic questions: What is social about the Internet? What are the different forms of sociality that we find on the Internet? To answer these questions, we need to enter conceptual sociological discussions, and therefore social theory is important for understanding the contemporary Internet. Users do have the counter-power capacities to use web 2.0 against the intentions of the corporate operators in progressive ways and political struggles, but the corporate platform owners possess the power to switch users off the networks or to switch off entire networks. Furthermore, they also have an interest in and power to permanently control the online behaviour and personal data of users in order to accumulate capital with the help of targeted advertising. Economic surveillance is at the heart of capital accumulation in web 2.0. The power relationship between the corporate media and the creative users that Castells describes is an asymmetrical one that privileges the former. There are different media that can be used for trying to mobilize others to attend demonstrations, visit Occupy camps, etc.: face-to-face communication, phone communication (voice, SMS) and various commercial and non-commercial forms of online communication. There are positive correlations between the frequency of usage of many of these types of mobilization communication, which shows that activists tend to not limit their mobilization communication to one medium, but use multiple media.

4.4 COMMUNICATION POWER IN THE ARAB SPRING AND THE OCCUPY MOVEMENT

2011: THE YEAR OF THE REBIRTH OF HISTORY AND DANGEROUS DREAMING

The year 2011 will be remembered in history. It was a year of persistent global crisis and, in this respect, was not different from the preceding years 2008, 2009 and 2010. What made 2011 stand out is that it was a year of revolutions, major protests, riots and the emergence of various social movements. Alain Badiou (2012) argues, in this context, that 2011 was the year of the rebirth of history, a year in which people tried to change history by their protests. Slavoj Žižek (2012) adds to Badiou's analysis that 2011 was the year of dreaming dangerously – the year in which people dared to try to make dreams of a different world a reality. History proved liberalism wrong. The new rebellious and revolutionary movements showed that "the world has long since dreamed of something of which it needs only to become conscious for it to possess it in reality" (Marx 1843b). The year 2011 was when dreams of a different world were put into political practice. Naturally, such developments are reflected in the intellectual realm by the publication of books that reflect on the causes, implications and consequences of the emergence of social movements. Manuel Castells's *Networks of Outrage and Hope: Social Movements in the Internet Age* (2012) is one of these books.

The Egyptian revolution resulted in the replacement of Hosni Mubarak's authoritarian government. The first free democratic presidential elections in June 2012 brought the candidate of the Muslim Brotherhood, Mohamed Morsi, to power. At the end of June 2013, a mass movement against Morsi emerged, which protested against his rule that members of the movement perceived to be yet another authoritarian regime. On 3 July, the Egyptian armed forces staged a brutal coup d'état and killed thousands. The chief of the Egyptian armed forces, Abdel el-Sisi, became the new president in 2014. Mubarak was released from prison, while Morsi and a significant number of his leading followers were sentenced to death. The 2011 Syrian protests against President Bashar al-Assad resulted in a long-lasting civil war on multiple fronts that gave rise to the Islamic State (ISIS, ISIL, Daesh) and has involved Iranian and Russian forces supporting al-Assad, Syrian oppositional forces, Sunni Islamist forces organized in the Army of Conquest (including the Al-Nusra Front, an Al-Qaeda branch operating in Syria), various Kurdish forces, a US-led Western coalition and so on. The complexity of this war did not just result in further destabilization of the constantly destabilized political situation in the Middle East, but also in large global tensions. The two examples of Egypt and Syria show that revolutions and rebellions are political, economic, ideological and societal ruptures in society with largely unpredictable outcomes. In such a situation, the future is relatively open, new struggles can unfold and unexpected events can take place. There is no automatism or guarantee that the overthrow of an authoritarian society results in a progressive economic and political system. Situations of fundamental change of society are real opportunities for establishing a fair society, but such opportunities can also be missed.

THE ARAB SPRING AND OCCUPY

Castells's (2012) *Networks of Outrage and Hope* analyses the role of social media and communication power in the Tunisian and Egyptian revolutions as well as in protests in Iceland, the Spanish 15-M movement and the Occupy Wall Street movement (for a detailed discussion and criticism, see Fuchs 2012b). To the second edition published in 2015, Castells (2015) added analyses of the Gezi Park movement in Turkey, the Brazilian anti-corruption movement, the Chilean student movement, the Mexican #YoSoy132 movement and Beppe Grillo's Five Star Movement in Italy. He argues that "the Arab uprisings were spontaneous processes of mobilization that emerged from calls from the Internet and wireless communication networks" (Castells 2012, 106). The Occupy movement "was born on the Internet, diffused by the Internet, and maintained its presence on the Internet" (168).

Castells puts a very strong emphasis on the mobilization capacities of the Internet. His argument implies that in the studied cases Internet communication created street protests, which means that without the Internet there would have been no street protests. In the concluding chapter, Castells generalizes for all analysed movements:

> The networked social movements of our time are largely based on the Internet, a necessary though not sufficient component of their collective action. The digital social networks based on the Internet and on wireless platforms are decisive tools for mobilizing, for organizing, for deliberating, for coordinating and for deciding. (Castells 2012, 229)

TWITTER AND FACEBOOK REVOLUTIONS?

Formulations, such as the ones that the Internet resulted in the emergence of movements, that movements were born on the Internet, that the Internet conveyed protests or that movements are based on the Internet, are based on the logic of technological determinism: technology is conceived as an actor that results in certain phenomena that have societal characteristics. Castells fails to see that it is not the Internet that creates sociality, but human actors who are embedded in antagonistic economic, political and ideological structures of society. The Internet is a techno-social system consisting of social networks that make use of a global network of computer networks. It is embedded in the antagonisms of contemporary society and therefore has no in-built effects or determinations. Collective social action that makes use of the Internet can have relatively few effects or dampen or intensify existing trends. The actual implications depend on contexts, power relations, resources, mobilization capacities, strategies and tactics as well as the complex and undetermined outcomes of struggles. Castells's model is simplistic: social media results in revolutions and rebellions. He shares the widespread ideological talk about "Twitter revolutions" and "Facebook rebellions" that, as already discussed, first became popular when the conservative blogger Andrew Sullivan (2009) claimed that the "revolution will be twittered" in the context of the 2009 Iran protests.

Society's reality is more complex than Castells's behaviouristic model of protest (Internet as the stimulus, critical consciousness and political action as the response) suggests. The media – social media, the Internet and all other media – are contradictory because we live in a contradictory society. As a consequence, their effects are actually contradictory. They can dampen/forestall or amplify/advance protest or have not much effect at all. Also, different media (e.g. alternative media and commercial media) stand in a contradictory relation and power struggle with each other. The media are not the only factors that influence the conditions of protest – they stand in contradictory relations with politics and ideology/culture that also influence the conditions of protest.

CASTELLS FALSIFIED: EMPIRICAL RESEARCH ON THE ROLE OF THE MEDIA IN SOCIAL MOVEMENTS

The Tahrir Data Project (http://tahrirdata.info) conducted a survey with Tahrir Square activists (N = 1056). Wilson and Dunn (2011) present data from the Tahrir Data Project, in which a survey (N = 1056) was conducted among Egyptian activists. The survey shows that face-to-face interaction (93 per cent) was the most important form of activists' protest communication, followed by television (92 per cent), phones (82 per cent), print media (57 per cent), SMS (46 per cent), Facebook (42 per cent), email (27 per cent), radio (22 per cent), Twitter (13 per cent) and blogs (12 per cent). Interpersonal communication, traditional media and telecommunications were more important information sources and communication tools in the revolution than social media and the Internet. Another part of the survey showed that Egyptian revolutionaries perceived phone communication, followed by face-to-face talk, as most important for their own protest, most informative and most motivating for participating in the protests. Facebook, email and Twitter were considered to be less important, less informative, less used and less motivating.

The Occupy General Survey that was conducted among Occupy Wall Street activists (see www.occupyresearch.net/2012/10/18/orgs-data-facet-browser/, accessed on 2 July 2013) showed that face-to-face communication and the Internet were activists' most important means of obtaining information about the Occupy movement. Facebook, word of mouth, websites and email played an especially important role. Both direct face-to-face interaction and mediated interaction have been crucial news sources for Occupy activists. This result was confirmed by the OccupyMedia! Survey (Fuchs 2014b). Broadcasting and newspapers had a much less important role than the Internet. Facebook was a very popular source of information; however, older online media (email, websites) played a much more important role than YouTube, blogs, Twitter and Tumblr, which shows that one should not overestimate the role of what some have called "web 2.0" in protests. These empirical results falsify Castells's speculative argument that contemporary social movements emerged from and are largely based on the Internet, and live and act through digital media.

Sara Salem (2015) conducted 20 semi-structured interviews with activists who participated in the Egyptian revolution. Online and offline media would both have been important and would have been used together for spreading protest information:

> The initial call for protests on January 25 was spread through social media. [...] Posters, banners and videos were shared widely through e-mail, blogs and Facebook. On Twitter, the hashtag #Jan25 was publicised. The 'We Are all Khaled Said' [Facebook] page created an event for the January 25 protest, to which more than fifty thousand confirmed their attendance. Most of the respondents had heard about the protests through online media, predominantly the Facebook event. [...] The links between online and offline communication should not be under-emphasised. Efforts towards mobilisation were also being made offline, through the spread of pamphlets, text messages and – most importantly – word of mouth. [...] The spread of information through word of mouth is a crucial aspect of the revolution that is often ignored. Its importance became especially clear when the government cut off the Internet during the uprising. (Salem 2015, 178–179)

The Egyptian state tried to monitor activists on social media, used it itself as a propaganda tool, sent out mass text messages, and shut down the Internet and mobile phone networks. Salem argues that activists used proxies and landline connections to try to circumvent control. "Blogs gave advice about how to use dial-up on mobile phones and laptops, and suggested connecting to the Internet service provider Noor, which was left operational as it was used by the Egyptian stock exchange and Western companies. To facilitate communication by protesters some of its subscribers even removed their password for Wi-Fi access" (della Porta and Mattoni 2015, 57). State control of the Internet would have had effects on online mobilization and would have extended the protests because many people were infuriated by the government's control tactics. This backfired, however, and led to many people taking to the streets to find out what was happening because they could no longer rely on social media to stay informed. "Blocking the Internet infuriated me, and showed me and other people how much the regime could suppress and oppress people. This was a major driving force for people to go to the protests" (Salem 2015, 183).

THE OCCUPYMEDIA! SURVEY

The OccupyMedia! Survey studied the role of social media in Occupy movements. I published its results in the book *OccupyMedia! The Occupy Movement and Social Media in Crisis Capitalism* (Fuchs 2014b). A total of 429 respondents, who participated in the Occupy movement, took part in the survey. One task was to find out what the actual role of social media is in social movements such as Occupy. There has been too much talk and not enough profound empirical research on this question. It can also not be answered by studying the amount, content and structure of communication networks of tweets, Facebook and other social media postings because such analyses cannot tell us anything about the role of offline communication.

One of the questions asked to the survey participants was the following one: If you think back to a month in which you were involved in Occupy protests, then how often did you engage in certain media activities for trying to mobilize people for a protest event, discussion, demonstration or the occupation of a square, building, house or other space? The results are shown in Table 4.4.

The data indicates that face-to-face communication, Facebook, email, phone, SMS and Twitter are the most important media that Occupy activists employ for trying to mobilize others for protests. Activists use multiple media for mobilization-oriented communication. These include classical interpersonal communication via phones, email, face-to-face and private social media profiles as well as more public forms of communication such as Facebook groups, Twitter and email lists. Posting announcements on alternative social media is much more uncommon than doing the same on Twitter and Facebook: whereas 42 per cent of the respondents posted protest announcements frequently on their Facebook profiles, only small numbers of respondents used non-commercial alternative platforms; only 4.4 per cent did so on Occupii, 3.1 per cent on N-1 and 1.1 per cent on Diaspora*; 25.8 per cent frequently posted protest announcements on their friends' Facebook profiles, whereas only 1.3 per cent did so on Occupii, 2.2 per cent on N-1 and 0.8 per cent on Diaspora*; 35.6 per cent frequently posted protest announcements on Occupy pages/groups on Facebook, 3.7 per cent on Occupii, 2.5 per cent on N-1, 1.1 per cent on Diaspora*. The data indicate that the big corporate social media are more attractive to activists in mobilization communication. The reason could be that these platforms have a large number of users and that the activists have a relatively large contact network there, whereas alternative social media are not used that much and as a consequence tend to feature smaller contact networks. Although there are various forms of protest mobilization communication, one should not overestimate this form of communication. There is a significant proportion of respondents who did not engage in mobilization communication: 29.8 per cent of the respondents never sent mobilization messages via email, 36.9 per cent never did the same via the phone, 49.7 per cent never via SMS, 46.2 per cent never via email lists, 44.0 per cent never posted announcements on Facebook groups, 53.1 per cent never wrote such messages on Facebook profiles of their friends, 52.0 per cent never used Twitter for this purpose. There is a significantly large share of activists who engage in protest mobilization communication, but this type of communication, although fairly common, is not common to all activists.

I also conducted a correlation analysis of the variables that cover protest mobilization communication. Some of the correlation results are presented in Table 4.5.

Correlation analysis shows that a higher level of protest activity tends to result in a higher level of media use for protest mobilization. Political positioning does not have a lot of

TABLE 4.4 Frequency of usage per month of specific forms of communication in the mobilization of protest

	Infrequently (0)	Medium (1–6)	Frequently (>6)
I had a personal face-to-face conversation in order to mobilize others	15.0%	37.60%	47.40%
I sent an email to personal contacts	29.8%	40.40%	29.80%
I phoned people	36.9%	39.50%	23.60%
I sent an SMS to my contacts	49.7%	27.00%	23.30%
I posted an announcement on an email list	46.2%	29.90%	23.90%
I posted an announcement on my Facebook profile	25.2%	32.40%	42.00%
I posted an announcement on Facebook friends' profiles	53.1%	21.10%	25.80%
I posted an announcement in an Occupy group on Facebook	44.0%	20.50%	35.60%
I posted an announcement on Twitter	52.0%	15.90%	32.10%
I created an announcement video on YouTube	85.9%	11.10%	3.00%
I posted an announcement on my own profile on the social networking site Occupii	86.1%	9.40%	4.40%
I posted an announcement on friends' profiles on the social networking site Occupii	91.3%	7.40%	1.30%
I posted an announcement in an Occupy group on the social networking site Occupii	85.3%	11.00%	3.70%
I posted an announcement on my own profile on the social networking site N-1	90.9%	5.90%	3.10%
I posted an announcement on friends' profiles on the social networking site N-1	93.3%	4.60%	2.20%
I posted an announcement in an Occupy group on the social networking site N-1	93.9%	3.60%	2.50%
I posted an announcement on my own profile on the social networking site Diaspora*	94.3%	4.70%	1.10%
I posted an announcement on friends' profiles on the social networking site Diaspora*	95.7%	3.50%	0.80%
I posted an announcement in an Occupy group on the social networking site Diaspora*	95.7%	3.20%	1.10%
I wrote an announcement on a blog	69.0%	22.20%	8.80%
I informed people on meetup.com	87.5%	10.70%	1.80%
I informed others by using one of the movement's chats	73.8%	17.40%	8.90%
I posted an announcement on one of the movement's discussion forums	67.6%	22.00%	10.30%
I made an announcement with the help of a Riseup tool (chat, email lists)	84.7%	11.00%	4.30%
I made an announcement on an InterOccupy teleconference	86.1%	11.00%	2.80%
I made an announcement with the help of the OccupyTalk voice chat	95.3%	2.90%	1.80%

Source: Data from OccupyMediaSurvey!, Fuchs 2014b.

influence on the media use in protest mobilization, with the exception of announcements on N-1. Mobilization in face-to-face communication tends to positively influence other forms of mobilization communication, with the exception of non-commercial social media platforms such as Occupii, N-1 and Diaspora*. Posting announcements on Facebook in order to mobilize

TABLE 4.5 Correlations between the frequency of specific forms of protest mobilization communication, activism intensity as well as political positioning (Spearman's rho)

	Intensity of activism, significance	Political positioning	Face-to-face conversations with friends	Announcement on my Facebook profile	Announcement video on YouTube	Announcement on my Occupii profile
OccupyTalk	0.072, 0.232	0.72, 0.233	−0.084, 0.161	0.098, 0.106	0.154*, 0.010	0.320**, 0.000
InterOccupy teleconference	0.283**, 0.000	0.100, 0.093	0.111, 0.062	0.172**, 0.004	0.210**, 0.000	0.236**, 0.000
Riseup tool	0.290**, 0.000	0.013, 0.832	0.189**, 0.002	0.104, 0.086	0.233**, 0.000	0.030, 0.625
Movement discussion forum	0.335**, 0.000	0.096, 0.108	0.206**, 0.001	0.319**, 0.000	0.293**, 0.000	0.191**, 0.000
Movement online chat	0.313**, 0.000	0.029, 0.632	0.182**, 0.002	0.306**, 0.000	0.318**, 0.000	0.273**, 0.000
Meetup.com	0.066, 0.274	0.151*, 0.01	0.009, 0.876	0.193**, 0.001	0.130*, 0.031	0.065, 0.287
Blog post	0.225**, 0.000	−0.078, 0.190	0.177**, 0.003	0.231**, 0.000	0.257**, 0.000	0.179**, 0.000
Occupy group on Diaspora*	0.059, 0.329	0.035, 0.561	0.067, 0.265	0.093, 0.124	0.226**, 0.000	0.184**, 0.000
Friends' profiles on Diaspora*	−0.004, 0.941	0.054, 0.369	0.015, 0.798	0.060, 0.322	0.263**, 0.000	0.250**, 0.000
Own profile on Diaspora*	0.020, 0.734	0.086, 0.153	0.052, 0.387	0.072, 0.235	0.228**, 0.000	0.220**, 0.000
Occupy group on N-1	0.101, 0.092	0.184**, 0.002	0.033, 0.584	0.140*, 0.021	0.242**, 0.000	0.361**, 0.000
Friends' profiles on N-1	0.019, 0.748	0.160**, 0.007	0.029, 0.629	0.082, 0.175	0.240**, 0.000	0.400**, 0.000
Own profile on N-1	0.006, 0.926	0.123*, 0.038	0.051, 0.395	0.116, 0.052	0.204**, 0.000	0.339**, 0.000
Occupy group on Occupii	0.159*, 0.006	0.106, 0.067	0.047, 0.424	0.231**, 0.000	0.325**, 0.000	0.697**, 0.000
Friends' profiles on Occupii	0.085, 0.143	0.115*, 0.047	0.020, 0.733	0.223**, 0.000	0.310**, 0.000	0.653**, 0.000
Own profile on Occupii	0.128*, 0.028	0.027, 0.644	0.048, 0.410	0.278**, 0.000	0.346**, 0.000	—
Video on YouTube	0.294**, 0.000	0.026, 0.660	0.167**, 0.004	0.305**, 0.000	—	0.201**, 0.000
Twitter	0.340**, 0.000	0.030, 0.605	0.243**, 0.000	0.440**, 0.000	0.339**, 0.000	0.293**, 0.000
Occupy group on FB	0.481**, 0.000	0.125*, 0.031	0.304**, 0.000	0.697**, 0.000	0.349**, 0.000	0.293**, 0.000
Friends' FB profiles	0.307**, 0.000	0.080, 0.171	0.371**, 0.000	0.708**, 0.000	0.354**, 0.000	0.255**, 0.000
My Facebook profile	0.337**, 0.000	0.061, 0.288	0.318**, 0.000	—	0.305**, 0.000	0.278**, 0.000
Email mailing lists	0.431**, 0.000	0.043, 0.460	0.415**, 0.000	0.374**, 0.000	0.240**, 0.000	0.149*, 0.011
SMS	0.389**, 0.000	0.074, 0.206	0.420**, 0.000	0.419**, 0.000	0.260**, 0.000	0.087, 0.140
Phone calls	0.428**, 0.000	−0.011, 0.856	0.554**, 0.000	0.342**, 0.000	0.191**, 0.001	0.082, 0.161
Personal email	0.443**, 0.000	−0.103, 0.075	0.570**, 0.000	0.385**, 0.000	0.182**, 0.002	0.136*, 0.020
Personal conversation	0.497**, 0.000	−0.092, 0.109	—	0.318**, 0.000	0.167**, 0.004	0.048, 0.410

Source: Fuchs (2014b).

others tends to positively impact other forms of mobilization communication, with the exception of some of the non-commercial platforms. Posting videos on YouTube for mobilization tends to have positive effects on the frequency of all other analysed forms of mobilization communication. Usage of the non-commercial platform Occupii for mobilization communication tends to positively influences usage of most other forms of online communication on commercial and non-commercial platforms. It does not have a positive impact on the usage of face-to-face and phone communication for mobilization.

The frequency of activism tends to positively influence the frequency of media use for informing oneself about the movement, sharing user-generated content online, communication between activists using various media and using media for protest mobilization communication. The use of face-to-face communication and online communication tend to mutually reinforce each other. The use of various online media for information, the sharing of user-generated content and protest mobilization also tend to mutually reinforce each other. We can therefore not say that online communication either determines protest or is unimportant. There is a *dialectic of online and offline protest communication*: activists use multiple online and offline channels for obtaining information, discussing protests and trying to mobilize others. Online communication and face-to-face communication for these purposes tend to mutually reinforce each other.

JEFFREY JURIS, PAOLO GERBAUDO AND MIRIYAM AOURAGH: FOR OR AGAINST CASTELLS?

Jeffrey Juris (2012), a former PhD student of Castells, conducted participant observation at Occupy Boston. He says that whereas the global justice movement primarily used mailing lists and was based on a logic of networking, the Occupy movement is based on a logic of aggregation, based on which social media result in "the viral flow of information and subsequent aggregations of large numbers of individuals in concrete physical spaces" (Juris 2012, 266). Individuals would "blast out vast amounts of information", make use of "ego-centered networks" so that "the use of Twitter and Facebook [. . .] tends to generate 'crowds of individuals'" (Juris 2012, 267). Like Castells, Juris assumes that social media "generate" protests. He claims that "social media such as Facebook, YouTube, and Twitter became the primary means of communication within #Occupy" (266), without empirically validating this claim.

In his book *Tweets and the Streets: Social Media and Contemporary Activism*, Paolo Gerbaudo (2012) challenges, on theoretical and empirical grounds, the assumption of Castells and others that the Internet brings about leaderless movements. He interviewed 80 activists in the USA, Egypt, Spain, the United Kingdom, Tunisia and Greece about their use of social media in protests and found that although contemporary social movements claim that they are leaderless networks, there are soft leaders who make use of social media for choreographing protests and "constructing a *choreography of assembly*" (Gerbaudo 2012, 139): "a handful of people control most of the communication flow" (135). The choreography of assembly means "the use of social media in directing people towards specific protest events, in providing participants with suggestions and instructions about how to act, and in the construction of an emotional narration to sustain their coming together in public space" (12). The movements' spontaneity would be organized "precisely because it is a highly mediated one" (164). The ethical problem would not be this movement choreography, but the denial that there are leaders, because this would result in unaccountability.

W. Lance Bennett and Alexandra Segerberg (2012, 2013) argue that Occupy and many other contemporary protest movements are based on the logic of connective action, in which there is no or little hierarchy and organization coordination, social media take "the role of established political organizations" (Bennett and Segerberg 2012, 742) and are realms through which "easily personalized ideas" (e.g. "We are the 99%"), which the authors term personal action frames, are shared and spread. Bennett and Segerberg oppose the logic of connective action to the logic of collective action and thereby over-stress individualization and separation. But do protest movements not necessarily have specific collective features? This thought becomes evident if one thinks about Occupy Wall Street's occupation of a common space and its collective demands for "direct and transparent participatory democracy", "personal and collective responsibility", empowerment, education as human right, open technology, culture and knowledge.[1] Collective goals, values and identities are the outcome of discussion and communication processes in social movements. Bennett and Segerberg's approach creates the impression that Occupy has no collective identities, goals or values at all and is a pure combination of individualized politics. They also neglect how contemporary social movements are facing the collective power of institutions such as the state, the police, corporations, banks, tabloid media and so on. Mimicking Margaret Thatcher's slogan "there is no such thing as society",[2] they are convinced that in Occupy and comparable movements there is no such things as collectivity. Occupy is a movement that aims at reclaiming the commons of society. It is therefore a movement for making privatized and privately controlled resources collectively available to all. Occupy's networked action has a collective dimension – the common coming-together in public space through which collective values, demands and goals are formed in order to reclaim and strengthen the commons. It is in this sense that Jodi Dean (2012), in contrast to individualistic interpretations, argues that Occupy is a movement oriented on the commons.

Miriyam Aouragh (2012, 529) argues that the

> overt fascination with social media gave the impression that the revolutions were mainly middle class and secular. Western experiences were taken as the model for Arab revolutions evaluated through the lens of modernity going hand in hand with the idea that social media plays an important role in developing a sense of modernity or, as this fascinating analysis claims.

Overcoming short-circuited analyses of the role of social media in revolutions would require a dialectical and historical Marxist analysis:

> A widespread and deep anger over the regional politics overlapped with domestic issues and grew deeper as the economic impact of the neoliberal (IMF/WB) privatisation combined with the price increases caused by the global financial crisis. (Aouragh 2012, 529)

Miriyam Aouragh shares Paolo Gerbaudo's analysis, but connects it, in contrast to him, to a Marxist theory framework:

---

1 Occupy Wall Street Principles of Solidarity, http://www.nycga.net/resources/documents/principles-of-solidarity/ (accessed on 26 September 2016).
2 Margaret Thatcher, Interview for *Woman's Own*, September 23, 1987. http://www.margaretthatcher.org/document/106689 (accessed on 26 September 2016).

I argued, echoing Rosa Luxemburg, that revolutionary change does not rely on spontaneous unorganized acts: it needs organizers, leaders, determination, and accountability. Discipline and structured organizing enables activists to generalize from complex and uneven realities and they are imperative for the survival of political movements. The activist networks do not confirm the view of leaderless swarms as often remarked when "new" Internet structures for political activism are concerned. It is mostly because it looked like it was a new, youth, non-ideological, online, horizontal movement that it gained attention and perhaps for many disillusioned with mainstream politics to give it the benefit of the doubt. (Aouragh 2012, 534)

SOCIAL MOVEMENTS IN TURKEY, BRAZIL, CHILE, MEXICO AND ITALY

Castells (2015) added two new chapters to *Networks of Outrage and Hope*'s second edition. He focuses on the analysis of the Turkish Gezi Park movement in 2013, the Brazilian anti-corruption movement in 2013/2014, the Chilean student movement in 2011–2013, the Mexican #YoSoy132 movement and the Italian Five Star Movement. He stresses the role of the Internet and social media as tools of political communication and networking in these movements.

He argues that a common characteristic of such movements is that

the diffusion of Internet-based social networks is a necessary condition for the existence of these new social movements in our time. But it is not a sufficient condition. […] Presence on social networks is simply a way of life for the majority of the young population of the planet for all kinds of purposes in the diverse range of human activity. And so, when they protest, they also do it on the social networks that they inhabit. But they do not necessarily protest. […] So, I believe it can be safely said that given enough social unrest and rebellious potential in a given society, the widespread use of social media allows individual rebellions to become social protests and ultimately social movements. (Castells 2015, 226)

In the book's second edition Castells also overestimates the importance and role of social media in social movements. If Internet-based social networks are, as Castells says, a necessary but not sufficient condition for new social movements of our time, then this implies that in cases where governments or Internet corporations block, censor or strictly monitor social media so that movements can no longer use them, social movements have to necessarily break down. The example of the Egyptian 2011 revolution shows that such assumptions are not true. When the Mubarak regime shut down the Egyptian Internet on 27 January, which was the first shutdown of the Internet across an entire country in the history of the network, the protests grew in size (Salem 2015): many people were angry about the blockage of online communication, others wanted to find out what had happened by taking to the streets.

Castells argues that far-right movements such as the Front National in France, the Finns Party in Finland, the Tea Party in the USA, the Five Star Movement in Italy, the UK Independence Party or Golden Dawn in Greece (226–227, 272–284) that also use the Internet as organization, communication and mobilization tools are not real social movements because they would not be autonomous social revolts, but political groupings having strong centralized leadership structures. They would not be "networked social movements", but rather "reactionary populist movements" (277). Their emergence would have to do with the lack of existence of strong autonomous social movements. This assumption cannot be sustained: Greece's Nazi-movement Golden Dawn emerged at the time of large anti-austerity protests. In the United Kingdom, the People's Assembly Against Austerity organized a movement that helped the socialist Jeremy Corbyn to become the Labour Party's leader, while at the same time the anti-European and xenophobic UK Independence Party led by Nigel Farage was very popular.

I certainly agree with Castells that right-wing movements are politically reactionary. Castells, however, tries to interpret the networked character of movements as inherently democratic. But a network can have hubs and even leadership structures that are more influential than other parts. Paulo Gerbaudo's (2012) analysis of social movements and social media has shown that leadership structures emerge in many progressive social movements. Todd Wolfson (2014) in his book *Digital Rebellion: The Birth of the Cyber Left* adds to this analysis that grassroots democratic structures are not just often a myth in left-wing movements, but tend to take away energy, time and resources from mobilization and organization so that accountable and elected leaders would be a preferential option for social movements (see Fuchs 2015b for a review of Wolfson's book). Democratic leadership structures can benefit social movements and do not automatically result in right-wing movements.

Wolfson (2014) questions the tendency of contemporary social movements to "uncritically celebrate" the "logic of horizontality as a deeply democratic form of movement building" (20). Social movement fetishism not just focuses on the organizational dynamic of movements, but also sees the Internet as an appropriate means supporting grassroots democracy. The blind spot of the optimism that Wolfson's book questions is that social movements exist within a global capitalist world, in which access to space, resources, attention, money and power are asymmetrically distributed, which creates a political economy of asymmetrical resource distribution, by which all social movements are confronted. Social movements, unlike companies, do not sell anything and so cannot count on monetary resource inputs. They also do not have the privileged access to law-making and public resources that political parties have. They cannot count on sympathetic media coverage and often only become subjects of the media as part of scandalizing tabloid coverage that wants to discredit them and portrays them as chaotic and violent with the help of one-dimensional and distorted reports. Most activists or sympathizers have to earn a wage in order to survive, which limits their possibilities of and time for doing politics, a phenomenon that under conditions of neoliberalism and precarity becomes even more problematic. Occupations are, for example, time- and energy-consuming, which is further reinforced by the fact that the wage form is the main means of survival in a capitalist world. Activist and citizen media tend to have fewer resources and receive less attention than mainstream media. They are harder to maintain and often struggle with the difficulty of how to survive. The history of media activism and alternative journalism is also a story of voluntary, self-exploited and precarious knowledge labour (Sandoval and Fuchs 2010).

If activists rely on established mainstream media, then they are confronted with the fact that capitalist media's managers are part of the 1 per cent and may not favourably view movements critical of capitalism. Such conditions do not mean that all capitalist media always censor, exclude or distort information about social movements, but that there is a significant risk and a power asymmetry. Left-wing activists are, of course, smart in seeking ways of how to try to overcome such structural restrictions, but it is clear that capitalism's political economy poses problems and limits for activism. The lack of resources and time can easily result in unacknowledged power structures, under which those who control the scarce resources or have more time or speaking skills than others develop into de facto leaders, whereas the official ideology is that there are no leaders because one is a grassroots movement.

It is more honest to acknowledge that some form of hierarchy, democratic representation and political organization is inevitable and beneficial given the resource precarity that social movements face in capitalism. If these problems are not acknowledged, then a gap between on the one hand a strange ideology of horizontality that remains a mere discourse and on the other hand unacknowledged centralization and hierarchy that form the actual practices can easily develop. The real issues of external power and political economy are then not adequately addressed, which can result in a fundamentalism of horizontalism and radicalism that accuses specific individuals or factions of hierarchism or reformism. Such misrecognition of how structural conditions impede social movement agency can weaken or cause the end of movements. Grassroots democracy is a nice idea, but within capitalism often does not work as an organizational principle because there is a lack of time, resources and money. Being preoccupied with themselves, horizontalist movements often turn into political sects whose immanent struggles weaken their transformative capacities within society. Todd Wolfson (2014) argues in this context that most "Cyber Left institutions have weak organizational structures with little collective decision-making power because they have dismissed, a priori, centralized power and structures of accountability and leadership of any kind" (24). One of the effects of the ideology of practising decentralization and participatory democracy within a world whose macro-societal structures are centralized and undemocratic is an "isolated localism that is in tension with democratic decision making" (155).

Castells wants to reserve the terms "social movements" and "networked movements" to the social movements he sympathizes with. But the far-right movements that have become so strong in many parts of the world also use network logic and are social in many respects: they are social groups reaching out to various social groups in society, they use networking as social systems online and offline, they often more than some other parties argue for social welfare policies for national citizens (and an exclusion of immigrants and refugees from the welfare state), and so on. Neither the term social nor the term network is automatically politically progressive. What distinguishes movements such as the anti-austerity protests in Greece, Spain, the UK and other countries and parties such as Syriza, Podemos and the Labour Party under Corbyn, from Donald Trump's white supremacist supporters, Golden Dawn, UKIP, the Freedom Party of Austria, the Danish People's Party, Jobbik in Hungary, the Sweden Democrats, the Finns Party, the Tea Party and so on is that they struggle with various means for an inclusive, democratic form of socialism, whereas the right-wing parties aim at a discriminatory, xenophobic, nationalist, closed society. In the end, the difference boils down to that between democratic socialism and fascism. The important category is then not the one of the social movement, but the one of socialism. We need a democratic socialism for the twenty-first century in order to shape power in such a way that a fair, just and participatory society can be established. We may today very well again have come to a crossroads comparable to the one that Rosa Luxemburg, citing Friedrich Engels, identified 100 years ago: "Bourgeois society stands at the crossroads, either transition to socialism or regression into barbarism" (Luxemburg 1916, 388).

4.5 CONCLUSION

Manuel Castells conceives of "social media" as a form of mass self-communication and as a social realm where communication power and counter-power are exerted. There are doubts about Castells's use of social theory, his notion of power, the use of computer science terms for analysing society, the assessment and categorical description of the power distribution between global multimedia corporations and the creative audience, the feasibility of the notion of web 2.0, and the centrality of informationalism and communication power.

The global economic crisis resulted in a return of the importance of economic questions, which are also questions about class, in social theory, and has shown the huge power that the global financial and economic networks wield over our lives. The central political task might now be to develop counter-power against the commodification of everything and the step-by-step fascistization of the world. The task for social theory in the contemporary situation is to develop analyses of power and potential counter-power. Manuel Castells reminds us that the role of communication certainly should not be neglected in such endeavours. However, I have serious doubts that Castells's approach can advance the critical analysis of contemporary society or provide help for creating a better society.

We can summarize this chapter's main conclusions:

- Castells mainly presents a history of the Internet and its context, and his work lacks a theory of society and a theory of modern society. His approach is neither a social theory, nor adequately theoretically grounded, but rather an arbitrary and unsystematic form of conceptualizing and collection of observations. Castells's concept of social media lacks an engagement with social theories that conceptualize power, autonomy, society, sociality and capitalism.
- Castells conceives of power and communication power as coercive, asymmetric and violent features of all societies. He thereby naturalizes domination and overlooks the possibility of dominationless communication and a dominationless society.
- Manuel Castells uses computing language (terms like program, switches, protocols, kernel) for describing society. He conflates the logic of society with the logic of computing and cannot account for the special role of humans in society.
- In his discussion of social media in the Arab Spring, the Occupy movement and other 2011 uprisings, Castells shares the techno-euphoria and techno-determinism of thinkers like Clay Shirky (2008, 2011a, 2011b) and Andrew Sullivan (2009) by advancing the assumption that contemporary social movements emerged from and are largely based on the Internet and live and act through digital media.

A critical theory of social media and society is needed. Neither Jenkins nor Castells have provided such an approach. This book tries to contribute to the creation of some foundations of a critical theory of social media.

RECOMMENDED READINGS AND EXERCISES

Gaining an understanding of the concept of communication power can be achieved by engaging with the works of various thinkers, such as Manuel Castells, those who offer criticisms of Castells and the idea of the network society, thinkers who have theorized power and violence (e.g. Max Weber, Anthony Giddens, John P. Thompson, Johan Galtung, James Curran) and those who have studied social media in revolutions.

Castells, Manuel. 2010. *The rise of the network society. The information age: economy, society and culture*, Volume I (2nd edition with a new preface). Malden, MA: Wiley-Blackwell. Preface to the 2010 edition. Prologue: The Net and the self. Conclusion: The network society.

Jessop, Bob. 2003/2004. Informational capitalism and empire: The postMarxist celebration of US hegemony in a new world order. *Studies in Political Economy* 71/72: 39–58.

Webster, Frank. 2002. The information society revisited. In *Handbook of new media*, ed. Sonia Livingstone and Leah Lievrouw, 22–33. London: SAGE.

Fisher, Eran. 2010. Contemporary technology discourse and the legitimation of capitalism. *European Journal of Social Theory* 13 (2): 229–252.

Fuchs, Christian. 2013. Capitalism or information society? The fundamental question of the present structure of society. *European Journal of Social Theory* 16 (4): 413–434.

Fuchs, Christian. 2009. Some reflections on Manuel Castells' book "Communication power". *tripleC: Open Access Journal for a Global Sustainable Information Society* 7 (1): 94–108.

Golding, Peter. 2000. Forthcoming features: Information and communications technologies and the sociology of the future. *Sociology* 34 (1): 165–184.

Garnham, Nicholas. 2000. "Information society" as theory or ideology. *Information, Communication & Society* 3 (2): 139–152.

Castells's *The Network Society* is the book that made his work appealing to a wide audience. It introduces the idea that we live in a network society. Critical theorists are often critical of this notion, which is expressed in reviews of Castells's book. Eran Fisher contextualizes the network discourse and argues that it is a new ideology. Christian Fuchs stresses that it is important to talk about capitalism when discussing information technologies and that one needs a dialectical analysis for understanding their impact on society. He questions Castells's notion that the network society is a new society. Read the texts and discuss the following questions in groups:

- What is an ideology? Try to give a definition. You can search for and consult literature for this task.
- In what respects are the information society and the network society ideologies? Which ideologies do the authors identify in the work of Castells? Construct an ordered and systematic typology of ideologies of the information and network society.
- Find examples of how the ideologies identified in the previous task can be found in public discourses about social media. Find examples by consulting media, debates, press releases, news clips, websites, etc.
- Do we live in an information society or not? Give reasons for your answer.

(Continued)

(Continued)

- How should contemporary society be characterized? What is your individual opinion and what is your group's opinion? What prefix should be used for characterizing contemporary society and why? Note: A prefixing term (as in "information society", "knowledge society", "modern society", "industrial society", "agricultural society", "reflexive society", "postmodern society", "digital society", "global society", "postindustrial society", "capitalist society", "labour society", "fascist society", "authoritarian society", "hyperreal society", "education society", "dynamic society", "functionally differentiated society", "flexible society", "adventure society", "divided society", "polycentric society", "risk society", "transcultural society", "multicultural society", "surveillance society", "transparent society", "responsible society", "virtual society", "ICT society", "Internet society", "cyber society", "world society", etc.) of society indicates that the prefix is the main characteristic of the society that is being described.

Castells, Manuel. 2009. *Communication power*. Oxford: Oxford University Press. Chapter 1: Power in the network society. Conclusion: Toward a communication theory of power.

In *Communication Power*, Castells provides an analysis of power in the context of social media.

- Search for reviews and criticisms of Castells's book with the help of Social Sciences Citation Index, Communication and Mass Media Complete, Scopus, Sociological Abstracts, Google Scholar, etc. Work in groups and construct a systematic and ordered list of points of criticism. Discuss these criticisms first in groups and then compare the results with the class.

Weber, Max. 1981. Selections from *Economy and Society*, volumes 1 and 2; and General economic history. In *Classes, power, and conflict: Classical and contemporary debates*, ed. Anthony Giddens and David Held, 60–86. Basingstoke: Macmillan.

Giddens, Anthony. 1984. *The constitution of society: Outline of the theory of structuration*. Cambridge: Polity Press. Chapter 1: Elements of the theory of structuration. Chapter 5: Change, evolution and power.

Giddens, Anthony. 1990. *The consequences of modernity*. Cambridge: Polity Press. Chapter II.

Max Weber and Anthony Giddens are two of the twentieth century's most important social theorists. They have both provided theories of society that include important concepts of power.

- Compare Weber's and Giddens's concepts of power. What are commonalities and differences?
- Compare both Weber's and Giddens's concepts of power to Castells's concept of communication power.
- Find examples of communication power on social media based on a Weberian understanding of power.
- Find examples of communication power on social media based on a Giddensian understanding of power.

Movie: Manuel Castells: Lecture about "Communication power in the network society", https://www.youtube.com/watch?v=xoMam-oFOzY

Watch the video lecture. Ask yourself if there are aspects you agree with and why and what points of criticism you have. Discuss the lecture in groups. Present the discussion results.

Work in groups: Try to find an example of communication power and counter-power on social media and look for a short video about this example that can be presented in the classroom. Prepare a presentation that focuses on the following:

- What is communication power? What is communication counter-power? How can the two terms be defined? Which definition should be employed – the one by Castells or another one, and why?
- Prepare an example of communication power and communication counter-power on social media. Use a short YouTube video that can be presented to your colleagues that is connected to the topic of communication power.
- Discuss aspects of communication power and communication counter-power in relation to your example video.
- Each group presents its example video and explains what aspects of communication power and communication counter-power can be found in the example and how these terms can best be understood.

Castells, Manuel. 2012. *Networks of outrage and hope: Social movements in the Internet age*. Cambridge: Polity Press. Chapters: Opening: Networking minds, creating meaning, contesting power; The Egyptian revolution; Occupy Wall Street: Harvesting the salt of the earth; Changing the world in the network society.

Fuchs, Christian. 2012. Some reflections on Manuel Castells's book "Networks of outrage and hope: Social movements in the Internet age". *tripleC: Communication, Capitalism & Critique: Open Access Journal for a Global Sustainable Information Society* 10 (2): 775–797.

Networks of Outrage and Hope is Castells's analysis of social media's role in the 2011 revolutions and uprisings. I have published the first English review of this book.

- Read the chapters listed above in Castells's book. Note especially how he uses the terms "power" and "communication power". Work in groups and compare these passages to the definitions of communication power in his previous book, *Communication Power* (2009). How exactly does Castells apply this concept? What kind of definition of power does he advance in the books? Are the definitions the same or do they vary?
- Read my criticism of Castells. Search for additional reviews and criticisms with the help of Social Sciences Citation Index, Communication and Mass Media Complete, Scopus, Sociological Abstracts, Google Scholar, etc. Work in groups and construct a systematic and ordered list of points of criticism. Discuss these criticisms first in groups and then compare the results.

Thompson, John B. 1995. *The media and modernity: A social theory of the media*. Cambridge: Polity Press. Chapter 1: Communication and social context.

(Continued)

(Continued)

Galtung, Johan. 1990. Cultural violence. *Journal of Peace Research* 27 (3): 291–305.

John B. Thompson's *The Media and Modernity* is an influential book in media sociology. Chapter 1 includes a discussion of power. Johan Galtung is the founder of Peace and Conflict Studies and has written extensively on questions of violence. The works of these two thinkers are a helpful starting point for discussing the role of power and violence in the media. Read these two texts and discuss the following:

• How should the terms power and violence best be defined (try to give your own views and definitions)?
• Which forms of power are there (try to give your own views and definitions)?
• Which forms of violence exist (try to give your own views and definitions)?
• How can the relationship of power and violence best be conceptualized (try to give your own views and definitions)?
• Discuss how different forms of power and violence play a role in social media. Try to find examples and explain which forms of power and violence play a role and what role they have.

Curran, James. 2002. *Media and power.* London: Routledge. Chapter 5: Renewing the radical tradition.

Freedman, Des. 2014. *The contradictions of media power.* London: Bloomsbury Academic. Chapter 1: Approaches to media power.

James Curran's book *Media and Power* discusses the multidimensional character of power in capitalism and how its economic, political and ideological dimensions relate to the media. Des Freedman's book discusses media power as contradictory.

• Discuss James Curran's dimensions of media power and media counter-power and compare them to Table 4.3 in this chapter. Try to find examples for all forms of media power and media counter-power in the context of social media.
• Discuss: Which approaches to media power does Des Freedman identify? What are their commonalities and differences? How can the approach of media power as contradictory force be applied for understanding social media in a critical manner?

Fuchs, Christian. 2014b. *OccupyMedia! The Occupy movement and social media in crisis capitalism.* Winchester: Zero Books.

• Read the *OccupyMedia!* study. Ask yourself: What are important protest movements at the moment? Are there questions asked by the *OccupyMedia!* study about the Internet and social media that are also relevant in the context of these movements. If so, which are these? If only partly or not, then which other questions need to be asked?
• How can these questions best be empirically studied in the context of one specific movement that is relevant at the moment?

OCCUPYMEDIA! SURVEY'S DATASET

SPSS format: http://fuchs.uti.at/wp-content/Occupy Media!_Dataset.sav

CSV format: http://fuchs.uti.at/wp-content/Occupy Media!_Dataset.csv

Open Database License (ODbL) v1.0 http://opendatacommons.org/licenses/odbl/1.0/

The OccupyMedia! Survey's full questionnaire can be found at:

http://fuchs.uti.at/wp-content/questionnaire.pdf

Rules and guidelines for the usage of the dataset:

http://fuchs.uti.at/wp-content/DataUsageGuide.pdf

Description of the dataset:

http://fuchs.uti.at/wp-content/mapping_questions_variables.pdf

- Acquaint yourself with the OccupyMedia! Survey's questionnaire and dataset. I have published the dataset using an Open Database License, which allows others to analyse it. Also have a look at the data usage guide.
- There are lots of qualitative answers to questions in the dataset. Work in groups: each group asks one particular qualitative question about the dataset. For example: How do the activists in the survey argue about police surveillance of the Internet and social media? Identify keywords that you can use for finding relevant results in the dataset. Identify all corresponding relevant entries. Conduct a qualitative analysis. Present the results.

Aouragh, Miriyam. 2012. Social media, mediation and the Arab revolutions. *tripleC: Communication, Capitalism & Critique: Journal for a Global Sustainable Information Society* 10 (2): 518–536.

Gerbaudo, Paolo. 2012. *Tweets and the streets: Social media and contemporary activism.* London: Pluto Press. Introduction, Chapters 1 and 2.

Juris, Jeffrey S. 2012. Reflections on #occupy everywhere: Social media, public space, and emerging logics of aggregation. *American Ethnologist* 39 (2): 259–279.

Murthy, Dhiraj. 2013. *Twitter: Social communication in the Twitter age.* Cambridge: Polity Press. Chapter 6: Twitter and activism.

The four texts by Miriyam Aouragh, Paolo Gerbaudo, Jeffrey Juris and Dhiraj Murthy provide analyses of the role of social media in the 2011 revolutions and protests.

- Read the four texts. Compare all four positions to Castells's conceptualization of the role of social media in the Arab Spring and the 2011 protests.
- Compare the four authors' analyses to each other. What commonalities and differences are there? What role does critical thinking and theorizing play?

(Continued)

(Continued)

Trottier, Daniel and Christian Fuchs, eds. 2015. *Social media, politics and the state: Protests, revolutions, riots, crime and politics in the age of Facebook, Twitter and YouTube.* New York: Routledge.

The collected volume *Social media, politics and the state: Protests, revolutions, riots, crime and politics in the age of Facebook, Twitter and YouTube* documents case studies of social media's contradictory power structures. Read first Trottier and Fuchs's introduction and and choose one specific case study. Discuss after you have read the case study:

- What aspects of power can be identified in this specific case? In which respect is this power contradictory?
- How do different forms of power and power structures and their contradictions relate to social media in the example case?

II

APPLICATIONS

5 THE POWER AND POLITICAL ECONOMY OF SOCIAL MEDIA

KEY QUESTIONS

- What are the ideologies and common myths that surround social media?
- What is meant by the political economy of social media and how does this work?
- What is digital labour and what role does it play within the political economy of social media?

KEY CONCEPTS

Political economy of social media
Digital labour
Social media ideologies
Corporate colonization of social media
Prosumption
Audience commodity

Internet prosumer commodity
Targeted advertising
Prosumer surveillance
Panoptic sorting
International division of digital labour

OVERVIEW

Political economy analyses the structural features of capitalism, such as the causes of crises. Ideology critique analyses the claims that are made about reality and how true they are. If one wants to understand power, then one needs to analyse both ideology and political economy. For a critical analysis of social media, this means that we have to take a look at both ideological aspects and political economy.

In strict terms, critical political economy and ideology are not two separate realms of analysis, but are interconnected. Karl Marx in his opus magnum *Capital, Volume 1* starts the analysis with the commodity. He argues that the commodity is capitalism's cell form: "The wealth of societies in which the capitalist mode of production prevails appears as an 'immense collection of commodities'; the individual commodity appears as its elementary form" (Marx 1867, 125). In the same chapter, he argues that commodity structures tend to be naturalized so that they appear as natural parts of society and not as constructs that serve to legitimate power structures. Ideologies that are disseminated by the media are a specific form of fetishism. Analysing the commodity form of the media and ideologies in the media belongs together in an analysis that uses critical political economy (Fuchs 2015a, Chapter 3).

This chapter's task is to provide an introduction to the critical power structure analysis of social media. For this purpose, it will explain how surplus value production and exploitation work on corporate social media platforms; that is, aspects of labour and capital accumulation are analysed. I point out the limits of the participatory social media hypothesis (in section 5.1) and introduce Marx's cycle of capital accumulation (5.2), which I apply to social media (5.3). I discuss the connection of unpaid user labour to other forms of labour (5.4) and finally, draw some conclusions (5.5).

5.1 SOCIAL MEDIA AS IDEOLOGY: THE LIMITS OF THE PARTICIPATORY SOCIAL MEDIA HYPOTHESIS

SOCIAL MEDIA: PARTICIPATION AS IDEOLOGY

Techno-deterministic approaches that assume that the rise of these technologies results in a more democratic society dominate studies of "web 2.0" and "social media". This becomes especially clear when representatives of this approach speak of "participatory social media". For example, Jenkins argues that increasingly "the Web has become a site of consumer participation" (Jenkins 2008, 137), Shirky (2008, 107) says that on web 2.0 there is a "linking of symmetrical participation and amateur production", Tapscott and Williams (2007, 15) argue that "the new web" has resulted in "a new economic democracy", Howe (2008, 14) speaks of social media crowdsourcing as a "manifestation of a larger trend toward greater democratization of commerce", Benkler (2006, 15) states that due to commons-based peer production "culture is becoming more democratic: self-reflective and participatory", Bruns (2008, 17) says that Internet produsage allows "participation in networked culture", Deuze (2007, 95) concludes that "new media technologies like the Internet have made visible [. . .] the participatory engagement of people with their media". To be fair, one has to say that Deuze (2008) has also written contributions in which he stresses the "corporate appropriation of participatory culture" (contribution title).

Approaches such as the ones just mentioned miss a theoretically grounded understanding of participation. They use claims about implications for democracy, but miss that in political theory mainly the approach of participatory democracy theory (Held 2006) uses the term "participation". The earliest use of the term "participatory democracy" that I could trace in the literature is an article by Staughton Lynd (1965) that describes the grassroots organization of the student movement. Participatory democracy theory (for a more detailed discussion and its implications for the analysis of social media, see Fuchs 2011b, Chapter 7) has two central features:

- the broad understanding of democracy as encompassing areas beyond voting, such as the economy, culture, and the household; and
- the questioning of the compatibility of participatory democracy and capitalism.

THE LIMITS OF YOUTUBE

One should analyse the political economy of social media platforms when making judgements about their participatory character. If there are, for example, asymmetries in terms of visibility and attention, then it is questionable that corporate social media are truly participatory. It is therefore not enough to stress enabling and limiting potentials of the Internet, but one rather needs to analyse the actual distribution of advantages and disadvantages. It is also important to analyse the negative aspects of social media in order to temper the uncritical social media optimism that is an ideological manifestation of the search for new capital accumulation models that wants to exploit user labour in order to raise the profit rate in the digital media industry. Critics have stressed in this context that web 2.0 optimism is uncritical and an ideology that serves corporate interests (Fuchs 2011b; van Dijck and Nieborg 2009) or that web 2.0 users are more passive users than active creators (van Dijck 2009).

Analysis of the ten most viewed videos on YouTube (see Table 5.1) shows that transnational media corporations, the organized exploiters of artists and consumers' surplus value-generating labour, control YouTube's political attention economy. The first edition of this book contained the same table with the most viewed YouTube videos based on a search conducted on 1 March 2013. The music video "Gangnam Style" was already the most viewed video back then, two years and eight months earlier. The number of views almost doubled during this time period from 1.37 billion to 2.44 billion. In 2013, there was also one private user-generated video among the top 10, "Charlie bit my finger – again!". In 2015, the top 10 were exclusively music videos whose copyright is owned by four large transnational multimedia companies (Universal, Sony, YG, Warner). We can say that YouTube is the new MTV, as music is the most popular YouTube content. Entertainment and music are very popular on YouTube and Facebook (see also Table 5.2), whereas politics is a minority interest.

TABLE 5.1 The most viewed YouTube videos of all time

Rank	Title	Type	Owner	Views
1	Psy – Gangnam Style	Music	YG Entertainment (distributed by Universal)	2,440,465,911
2	Taylor Swift – Blank Space	Music	Universal	1,240,590,445
3	Justin Bieber – Baby	Music	Universal	1,229,111,754
4	Katy Perry – Dark Horse	Music	Universal	1,149,792,020
5	Taylor Swift – Shake It Off	Music	Universal	1,119,564,553
6	Katy Perry – Roar	Music	Universal	1,115,067,711
7	Enrique Iglesias – Bailando	Music	Universal	1,113,157,219
8	Mark Ronson – Uptown Funk	Music	Sony	1,106,637,888
9	Wiz Khalifa – See You Again	Music	Warner Music	1,089,576,146
10	Meghan Trainor – All about that Bass	Music	Sony	1,084,945,283

Source: youtube.com (accessed on 29 October 2015).

TABLE 5.2   The most popular fan groups on Facebook

Rank	Facebook fan group	Type	Number of fans
1	Facebook for every phone	IT	513.2 million
2	Facebook	Internet	165.7 million
3	Cristiano Ronaldo	Sports	107.4 million
4	Shakira	Music	103.1 million
5	Vin Diesel	Entertainment	95.8 million
6	Coca-Cola	Brand	93.5 million
7	Eminem	Music	92.4 million
8	FC Barcelona	Sports	87.4 million
9	Real Madrid C.F.	Sports	84.9 million
10	Rihanna	Music	81.5 million
	Michael Moore	Alternative media producer	1,256,469
	Karl Marx	Political philosopher, communist	1,231,823
	Noam Chomsky	Political intellectual	1,051,453
	Jeremy Corbyn	Socialist politician	298,887

Source: Data from http://socialbakers.com (accessed on 29 October 2015).

THE LIMITS OF FACEBOOK

Technology, sports, music, entertainment and brands are very popular on Facebook (see Table 5.2). Powerful politicians, such as President Obama, dominate the attention given to the political Facebook groups, whereas alternative political figures, such as Michael Moore, Karl Marx, Noam Chomsky and Jeremy Corbyn, have a much lower numbers of fans (Table 5.2).

THE LIMITS OF GOOGLE

The top search keywords used on Google in 2010 show that the 12 most used keywords did not contain political topics. Instead, there was more interest in Whitney Houston, Gangnam Style, Hurricane Sandy, iPad 3, Diablo 3, Kate Middleton, Olympics 2012, Amanda Todd, Michael Clarke Duncan, Big Brother Brazil 12.[1] The most searched Google keywords in 2014 were Robin Williams, World Cup, Ebola, Malaysia Airlines, ALS Ice Bucket Challenge, Flappy Bird, Conchita Wurst, ISIS, Frozen, Sochi Olympics. Seven of the ten most searched keywords have to do with entertainment, two with catastrophes (Ebola virus epidemic, crash of Malaysia Airlines flights 370 and 17) and just one with politics (ISIS).

THE LIMITS OF TWITTER

Twitter is one of the most popular social media platforms. Blogger Andrew Sullivan wrote after the Iranian protests of 2009 that "the revolution will be twittered", which contributed to

---

1 www.google.com/zeitgeist/ (accessed on 2 July 2013).

TABLE 5.3   Twitter user profiles with the highest number of followers

Rank	Twitter user profile	Followers
1	Katy Perry @katyperry	77.0 million
2	Justin Bieber @justinbieber	68.9 million
3	Taylor Swift @taylorswift13	65.3 million
4	Barack Obama @barackobama	65.3 million
5	YouTube @youtube	56.1 million
6	Rihanna @rihanna	52.2 million
7	Lady Gaga @ladygaga	51.9 million
8	Justin Timberlake @jtimberlake	49.5 million
9	Ellen DeGeneres @theellenshow	49.0 million
10	Twitter @twitter	47.8 million
	Michael Moore @MMFlint	1.9 million
	Noam Chomsky @daily_chomsky	0.24 million
	Jeremy Corbyn @jeremycorbyn	0.31 million

Source: Data from www.socialbakers.com/statistics/twitter/profiles/ (accessed on 29 October 2015).

the myth of Twitter revolutions.[2] Can meaningful political debates be based on 140-character short messages? Short text invites simplistic arguments and is an expression of the commodification and speed-up of culture. Table 5.3 shows that nine out of the ten most followed Twitter user accounts are entertainment-oriented. Barack Obama is the only exception in the top ten. But Table 5.3 also shows that politics has a stratified attention economy on Twitter: whereas Barack Obama has a very large number of followers, the number is much lower for representatives of alternative politics, such as Michael Moore, Noam Chomsky and Jeremy Corbyn.

THE LIMITS OF PINTEREST

Pinterest is a photo-sharing social media platform, on which users create postings ("pins") as parts of pin-boards. Users can follow each other, like, share and comment on pins. Founded in 2010, Pinterest has become one of the most popular social media platforms. Pinterest is especially popular among those interested in design, fashion, photography, beauty and colours. Table 5.4 presents an overview of the ten most popular Pinterest profiles.

First, there are fashion and design companies or artists such as Joy Cho, L.L. Bean and Nordstrom on Pinterest, who advocate their own products. Second, there are commercial Pinterest curators who earn money by posting images of certain commodities on Pinterest and are paid for advertising products. Maryann Rizzo's Curated Style Shop explains how this business strategy works: "[W]e use contextual affiliate links in posts and/or banner ads across a variety of social media platforms. This means if you click on the link and purchase the item a small commission is earned on featured products."[3]

---

2 www.theatlantic.com/daily-dish/archive/2009/06/the-revolution-will-be-twittered/200478/ (accessed on 20 August 2011).

3 http://curatedstyleshop.com/Odisclaimer (accessed on 29 October 2015).

TABLE 5.4 Pinterest user profiles with the highest number of followers

Rank	User	Username	Type of profile	Number of followers
1	Joy Cho/Oh Joy!	ohjoy	Oh Joy: graphic design studio that sells branded products	13,064,307
2	Maryann Rizzo	maryannrizzo	Curated Style Shop: presents images and designer products and links where to buy them	9,297,932
3	Bonnie Tsang	bonnietsang	Pinterest curator of design products	7,178,150
4	L.L. Bean	llbean	L.L. Bean: clothing and recreation equipment retailer	5,180,732
5	Stephanie Brinkerhoff	stephanieannb	Hair stylist, make-up artist and beauty blogger who curates products on Pinterest	5,091,647
6	Nordstrom	nordstrom	Nordstrom: upscale fashion retailer	4,363,713
7	Aimee Hieber	contrary72	Non-commercial Pinterest curator of food and recipes	4,232,341
8	Igor Mamantov	igori	Non-commercial Pinterest user posting travel-related images	4,204,533
9	Mike Catalonian	leyre50	Non-commercial Pinterest user posting about art and photography	4,203,469
10	Maiysha Kai	maiyshakai	Musician who curates fashion on Pinterest	4,096,046

Source: Data http://pinauthority.com/pinterest_users/top100 (accessed on 29 October 2015).

Marketing services such as RewardStyle, Share-a-Sale, eBay Partner Network or Amazon Associates are so-called affiliate marketing services in which curators linking on their WWW profiles to company products earn commission for each product sold after someone has followed a product link on the curator's site and made a purchase.

> Affiliate programs, used by many online retailers, blogs and media sites for a decade or more, are gaining new ground for bloggers as they expand to social media platforms like Instagram, Pinterest and Twitter. Terms of the deals typically are based on how many readers a blog has, and how much interaction it gets. Commissions range from 3% to more than 20% of sales. For bloggers, also known as "influencers," whose readers are loyal and eager to shop, there is real money to be made.[4]

Third, there are Pinterest users who do not have commercial interests in their usage of the site, but are fond of certain aspects of life such as travelling, photography, art, colours, etc. and share images about these interests. Pinterest is a mixture of commercial and non-commercial visual culture.

---

4 How style bloggers earn sales commissions, one click at a time. *Wall Street Journal Online*, 11 February 2015.

Some popular Pinterest curators, such as Maryann Rizzo and Stephanie Brinkerhoff, Danaë Vokolos (Veanad) or Bekka Palmer, obtained millions of Pinterest followers because they were early-day users whom Pinterest suggested to new users as recommended curators in order to increase the activities on its site and the potential profits it makes by selling promoted pins and other featured pins.[5] Promoted pins are a form of native advertising (advertisements that look like ordinary, "native" content) in which special pins are featured when users enter search terms on Pinterest.

Many, but certainly not all of the top Pinterest users have chosen to make use of affiliate marketing to earn money. In addition, large companies are active on Pinterest and Pinterest operates its own form of targeted native advertising. To a certain degree Pinterest is also the home of non-commercial visual cultures. Affiliate marketing and native advertising on social media have resulted in a hybridization of commercial and non-commercial content. Sometimes it is difficult to tell whether a specific profile or posting is commercial in nature or not and if someone earns money by clicks or not. Advertisements thereby become more sophisticated, liquid and covert.

THE CORPORATE COLONIZATION OF SOCIAL MEDIA

Such examples make clear that corporations and their logic dominate social media and the Internet and that the Internet is predominantly capitalist in character. Social media is not exclusively an expression of commercial culture, but Pinterest is populated to a significant degree by companies, advertising, celebrities, commercial entertainment and consumer culture that all share the feature of wanting to sell commodities in order to accumulate profits. Social media do not automatically constitute a public sphere or participatory democratic space in a capitalist world. The dominant tendency is that corporations and capitalist logic colonize social media. Multimedia companies, celebrities and advertising dominate attention and visibility. Politics is a minority issue on social media. Georg Lukács argues that ideology "by-passes the essence of the evolution of society and fails to pinpoint it and express it adequately" (Lukács 1923/1972, 50). An ideology is a claim about a certain status of reality that does not correspond to actual reality. It deceives human subjects in order to forestall societal change. It is false consciousness (Lukács 1923/1972, 83). Public social spaces that celebrate consumption and entertainment and disregard politics aim at creating such a consciousness of happy consumption in a false world.

Habermas's (1989c, 175–195) main concern about advertising is that it has the potential to de-politicize the public. This would on the one hand be due to particularistic interests: "The public sphere assumes advertising functions. The more it can be deployed as a vehicle for political and economic propaganda, the more it becomes unpolitical as a whole and pseudo-privatized" (Habermas 1989c, 175). On the other hand the influence of economic logic on the media would result in tabloidization: "Reporting facts as human-interest stories, mixing information with entertainment, arranging material episodically, and breaking down complex relationships into smaller fragments – all of this comes together to form a syndrome that works to depoliticize public communication" (Habermas 1996, 377). The

---

5 https://medium.com/backchannel/how-people-youve-never-heard-of-got-to-be-the-most-powerful-users-on-pinterest-206770326006#.24lmlcbld (accessed on 29 October 2015).

more advertising and commodity logic shapes social media communication, the less there is space for non-commercially-oriented communication that focuses on fostering not the logic of brands, corporations and commodity consumption, but of the public sphere and the common good.

Social media are not inherently an expression of neoliberal culture. There are many different platforms, designed in different ways. Facebook and Twitter, two particularly important platforms, are built around individual profiles and are based on the accumulation of reputation via likes, favourites, re-tweets, the number of followers and friends. They foreground the logic of presenting the individual self, not the formation of collective identities. Such designs could certainly be changed from "me-media" to "we-media", from individualism to collectivism, from Facebook, MySpace and YouTube into OurBook, OurSpace and OurTube. Wikipedia, for example, is based on a much more collective logic. The rise of individualistically designed social media does not accidentally take place at a time when we experience the erosion of public services, public spaces and public media. At the same time movements that want to foreground the logic of the commons and the public have challenged these developments.

Although there is some importance of small public spheres of communication that foster social connections in specialist interest groups, there clearly is also a need for large public spheres that reach vast amounts of people in society. Social media are convergent media that can have a potential for creating and sustaining larger publics. If we all only lived in micro publics, then public communication would be entirely fragmented and it would become difficult to organize public life. So also in the age of social media, there is a need for large mediated public spheres. Certainly public service media could take the idea of user-generated content more seriously than they do at the moment in order to engage citizens more into content production. My point is that micro publics on the Internet alone are not enough and threaten to fragment the public sphere.

The Internet and social media are today to a significant degree stratified, non-participatory spaces. An alternative, non-corporate Internet is needed (see Fuchs 2011b, Chapters 7, 8 and 9). Large corporations colonize social media and dominate its attention economy. Even though Twitter and mobile phones supported the political rebellions, protests and revolutions in countries like Algeria, Bahrain, Egypt, Iran, Jordan, Libya, Morocco, Tunisia and Yemen in early 2011, and the publishing of videos about the effects of domination (as the video about the death of Neda Soltani in the Iranian protests in 2009 or the video about the death of Ian Tomlinson at the London anti-G20 protests in 2009) can support the communication of protest, one should not overestimate these potentials. There are no Twitter, Facebook or YouTube revolutions. Only people who live under certain societal conditions and organize collectively can make rebellions and revolutions. Technology is, in itself, not a revolution.

On corporate social media, the liberal freedom of association and assembly are to significant degrees suspended: big corporate and, to a lesser extent, political actors dominate and therefore centralize the formation of speech, association, assembly and opinion on social media. Liberal freedoms turn capitalist social media into their opposite. Given the importance of capitalism on social media, it seems both necessary and feasible to theorize "web 2.0" not as a participatory system, but in manners that employ more negative, critical terms such as class, exploitation and surplus value. This requires us to ground the analysis of social media in the works of the founding figure of critical political economy – Karl Marx.

5.2 THE CYCLE OF CAPITAL ACCUMULATION

Karl Marx's opus magnum *Capital: A Critique of Political Economy* was written in the nineteenth century. But Marx was a very visionary thinker who thought about the implications of the new media of his time (such as the telegraph) for the economy and society, was a practising critical journalist, analysed modern technology's dialectic, and anticipated the emergence of knowledge work and what some today call the information society. This is why reading and interpreting Marx's *Capital* and other works by him from a media and communication studies perspective in the information age can give us important critical insights about digital capitalism and informational capitalism. I have therefore written a chapter-by-chapter companion to Marx's *Capital, Volume 1* that provides a media and communication studies perspective: *Reading Marx in the Information Age: A Media and Communication Studies Perspective on "Capital Volume 1"* (Fuchs 2016c). In the three volumes of *Capital* (1867, 1885, 1894), Marx analyses the accumulation process of capital. This process, as described by Marx, is visualized in Figure 5.1.

In the accumulation of capital, capitalists buy labour power and means of production (raw materials, technologies, etc.) in order to organize the production of new commodities that are sold with the expectation to make money profit that is partly reinvested. Marx distinguishes two spheres of capital accumulation: the circulation sphere and the sphere of production. In the circulation sphere, capital transforms its value form. First, money M is transformed into commodities (from the standpoint of the capitalist as buyer): the capitalist purchases the

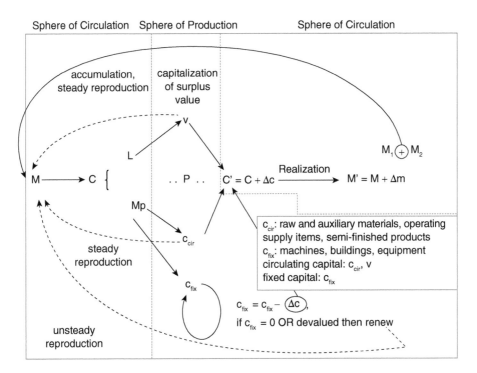

FIGURE 5.1   The accumulation/expanded reproduction of capital

commodities labour power L and means of production Mp. The process M-C is based on the two purchases M-L and M-Mp. This means that due to private property structures workers do not own the means of production, the products they produce or the profit they generate. Capitalists own these resources. In the sphere of production, a new good is produced: the value of labour power and the value of the means of production are added to the product. Value takes on the form of productive capital P. The value form of labour is variable capital v (which can be observed as wages), the value form of the means of production constant capital c (which can be observed as the total price of the means of production/producer goods).

In the sphere of production, capital stops its metamorphosis so that capital circulation comes to a halt. There is the production of new value V' of the commodity. V' contains the value of the necessary constant and variable capital and surplus value Δs of the surplus product. Unpaid labour generates surplus value and profit. Surplus value is the part of the working day that is unpaid. It is the part of the working day (measured in hours) that is used for producing profit. Profit does not belong to workers, but to capitalists. Capitalists do not pay for the production of surplus. Therefore the production of surplus value is a process of exploitation. The value V' of the new commodity after production is $V' = c + v + s$.

The commodity then leaves the sphere of production and again enters the circulation sphere, where capital conducts its next metamorphosis: It is transformed from the commodity form back into the money form by being sold on the market. Surplus value is realized in the form of money. The initial money capital M now takes on the form $M' = M + \Delta m$; it has been increased by an increment Δm. Accumulation of capital means that the produced surplus value/profit is (partly) reinvested/capitalized. The end point of one process M' becomes the starting point of a new accumulation process. One part of M', M_1, is reinvested. Accumulation means the aggregation of capital by investment and the exploitation of labour in the capital circuit M-C.. P.. C'-M', in which the end product M' becomes a new starting point M. The total process makes up the dynamic character of capital. Capital is money that is permanently increasing due to the exploitation of surplus value-generating labour.

Commodities are sold at prices that are higher than the investment costs so that money profit is generated. Marx argues that one decisive quality of capital accumulation is that profit is an emergent property of production that is produced by labour, but owned by the capitalists. Without labour, no profit could be made. Workers are forced to enter class relations and to produce profit in order to survive, which enables capital to appropriate surplus. The notion of exploited surplus value is the main concept of Marx's theory, by which he intends to show that capitalism is a class society. "The theory of surplus value is in consequence immediately the theory of exploitation" (Negri 1991, 74). One can add: The theory of surplus value is the theory of class and, as a consequence, the political demand for a classless society.

Capital is not money per se, but is money that is increased through accumulation – "money which begets money" (Marx 1867, 256). Marx argues that the value of labour power is the average amount of time that is needed for the production of goods that are necessary for survival (necessary labour time). Wages represent the value of necessary labour time at the level of prices. Surplus labour time is labour time that exceeds necessary labour time, remains unpaid, is appropriated for free by capitalists, and transformed into money profit. Surplus value "is in substance the materialization of unpaid labour-time. The secret of the self-valorization of capital resolves itself into the fact that it has at its disposal a definite quantity of the unpaid labour of other people" (Marx 1867, 672). The production of surplus value is "the *differentia specifica* of capitalist production" (Marx 1867, 769) and the "driving force and the final result of the capitalist process of production" (Marx 1867, 976).

5.3 CAPITAL ACCUMULATION AND SOCIAL MEDIA

PROSUMPTION

Alvin Toffler (1980) introduced the notion of the prosumer in the early 1980s. It means the "progressive blurring of the line that separates producer from consumer" (Toffler 1980, 267). Toffler describes the age of prosumption as the arrival of a new form of economic and political democracy, self-determined work, labour autonomy, local production and autonomous self-production. But he overlooks that prosumption is used for outsourcing work to users and consumers who work without payment. Thereby corporations reduce their investment costs and labour costs, jobs are destroyed, and consumers who work for free are extremely exploited. They produce surplus value that is appropriated and turned into profit by corporations without paying wages. Notwithstanding Toffler's uncritical optimism, his notion of the "prosumer" describes important changes of media structures and practices and can therefore also be adopted for critical studies.

Ritzer and Jurgenson (2010) argue that web 2.0 facilitates the emergence of "prosumer capitalism", that the capitalist economy "has always been dominated by presumption" (14), and that prosumption is an inherent feature of McDonaldization. The two authors overlook that prosumption is only one of capitalism's many tendencies, not its only quality and not the dominant quality. Capitalism is multidimensional and has multiple interlinked dimensions. It is at the same time finance capitalism, imperialistic capitalism, informational capitalism, hyperindustrial capitalism (oil, gas), crisis capitalism and so on. Not all of these dimensions are equally important (Fuchs 2011b, Chapter 5). Critical scholars have introduced concepts such as consumption work (Huws 2003) and Internet prosumer labour (Fuchs 2010c) for stressing how the boundaries between leisure and work, as well as production and consumption, have become more liquid in contemporary capitalism.

DALLAS SMYTHE, THE AUDIENCE COMMODITY AND INTERNET PROSUMER COMMODIFICATION

In 1977, Dallas Smythe published his seminal article "Communications: Blindspot of Western Marxism" (Smythe 1977), in which he argued that Western Marxism has not given enough attention to the complex role of communications in capitalism. The article's publication was followed by an important foundational debate of media sociology that came to be known as the *Blindspot Debate* (Livant 1979; Murdock 1978; Smythe answered with a rejoinder to Murdock: Smythe 1994, 292–299), and by another article by Smythe on the same topic (*On the Audience Commodity and its Work*: Smythe 1981/2006, 22–51). In the age of targeted online advertising and digital capitalism, Smythe's work has attracted new significance (Fuchs 2012a; McGuigan and Manzerolle 2014).

Dallas Smythe (1977, 1981/2006) suggests that in the case of media advertisement models, media companies sell the audience as a commodity to advertisers: The

> material reality under monopoly capitalism is that all non-sleeping time of most of the population is work time. […] Of the off-the-job work time, the largest single block is time of the audiences, which is sold to advertisers. […] In "their" time which is sold to advertisers workers (a) perform essential marketing functions for the producers of consumers' goods, and (b) work at the production and reproduction of labour power. (Smythe 1977, 3)

> Because audience power is produced, sold, purchased and consumed, it commands a price and is a commodity. [. . .] You audience members contribute your unpaid work time and in exchange you receive the program material and the explicit advertisements. (Smythe 1981/2006, 233, 238)

With the rise of user-generated content, free-access social networking platforms, and other free-access platforms that yield profit by online advertisement – a development subsumed under categories such as web 2.0, social software and social networking sites – the web seems to come close to accumulation strategies employed by capital on traditional mass media like TV or radio. Users who upload photos and images, write wall posting and comments, send mail to their contacts, accumulate friends or browse other profiles on Facebook, constitute a peculiar form of the audience commodity that is sold to advertisers. The difference between the audience commodity on traditional mass media and on the Internet is that in the latter case the users are also content producers, there is user-generated content, and the users engage in permanent creative activity, communication, community building and content production. The fact that the users are more active on the Internet than in the reception of TV or radio content is due to the decentralized structure of the Internet, which allows many-to-many communication. Due to the permanent activity of the recipients and their status as prosumers, we can say that in the case of corporate social media the audience commodity is a big data commodity created by Internet prosumers (Fuchs 2010c).

Dallas Smythe (1977) argued that on commercial broadcasting, audiences conduct labour that creates an audience commodity. On corporate social media, we can speak of a big data commodity produced by Internet prosumers' digital labour (Fuchs 2014a, Chapters 4 and 11). It is qualitatively different from the audience commodity in a number of respects:

- *Creativity, prosumption, social relations*: Audiences produce meanings of content, social media users also produce data, content and social relations.
- *User surveillance*: Measuring audiences has in broadcasting and print traditionally been based on studies with small samples of audience members. Measuring user behaviour on corporate social media is constant, total and algorithmic. Audience commodification on social media is based on the constant real-time surveillance of users.
- *Targeting*: Advertising on social media is targeted and personalized.
- *Predictive algorithms*: User measurement uses predictive algorithms (if you like A, you may also like B because 100,000 people who like A also like B).
- *Algorithmic auctions*: User prices are often set based on algorithmic auctions (pay per view, pay per click)

CONTROVERSIAL OPINIONS ABOUT ONLINE ADVERTISING

As part of a research project, I conducted focus groups with data experts.[6] One topic was what they think about online advertising and whether they think there should be opt-in to or opt-out from targeted online advertising. It was the most controversially discussed issue in our focus groups.

Focus group participant A, founder of an ICT consultancy who finds data protection issues to be of crucial importance, argued:

> Opt-in. [...] It has to be opt-in. Things ought to be set that they are by default secure. Otherwise you are making decisions for people. [...] The default start has to be default secure. I don't think there is any other way it can be done if you are responsibly looking after people. Obviously, if the industry does not like that, it worries about its income. [...] The default should be that one is opted out. That is my view.

D, who is the Chief Technology Officer (CTO) of an online advertising company, argued

> The challenging part is how to convey that [opt-in information] in a way that is easy for consumers, for an end-user who has not an idea of what technology means, does not want to go through a hundred options or 200 options because they want something much easier but at the same time gives an amount of flexibility for advertisers to work with that user.

D added that opt-in could have very negative impacts for companies:

> You need to think about what powers the Internet? [...] It's advertising. Advertising makes it possible for all of us to consume services like Google Search. It allows us to connect to other people on Facebook. Facebook exists not because it is a benevolent entity of the connected people, it is doing that for advertising. It is the same thing with Twitter and email. Why is it free for all of us? Why is information freely accessible as well?

B responded and pointed out that the capitalist and targeted-ad model of the Internet is not the only possibility:

> I agree that this is definitely how things work at the moment. But it would be a shame if every good that was produced in the economy would completely be holding to the current business model. We can imagine lots of different ways that all sorts of goods might be funded. And historically this is what has happened.

---

6 EU FP7 project PACT: Public Perception of Security and Privacy: Assessing Knowledge, Collecting Evidence, Translating Research into Action (2012–2015), grant agreement number 285635.

ADVERTISING AND SOCIETY

The discussion was a very good example of discourses about advertising's advantages and disadvantages for individuals and society (see Pardun 2014). A typical pro-advertising argument that was also found in the focus groups is that advertising allows free and cheap access to culture, technology and media and that without it there would be no Internet, culture and media. Critics hold that such an argument confuses the dominant reality of the Internet and culture with how it could be different; that is, the essence and potentials of the media world and its capitalist reality. Specifically focus group participants pointed out that there once was an Internet without advertising that worked and that there are non-advertising-based and non-commercial applications and platforms on the Internet. Some participants pointed out that opting into advertising might result in less convenience and a more difficult user experience. Further arguments in favour of targeted ads are that targeted ads are more relevant than non-targeted ones and that opt-in results in a waste of advertisers' money. The critics of online advertising point out that the issue at hand is a much larger one, having to do with capitalism and society and the question of whether we want to live in a society that is dominated by capitalism and advertising or of whether we shouldn't create alternatives to it and social spaces that are free from advertising and commodity logic.

Carol J. Pardun's (2014) book *Advertising and Society* presents controversies around advertising in such a form that a pro-advertising argument is opposed to a counter-argument. One chapter focuses on Facebook and social media. It shows that academic controversies about online targeted ads follow the same line of controversy as our focus groups. Joe Bob Hester argues in the pro-position that targeted online advertising "greatly reduces waste" (of money, time, attention) (in Pardun 2014, 165), is "more relevant" (167), enables interfaces that are "less cluttered by advertising" (167) and "services free of cost to users" (167). Tom Weir holds against Hester that targeted ads are a "violation of individual privacy" (170), that they show that "Orwell was right" (173) and that they display how freedom reduced to ownership and consumption turns into slavery (173). One can add to Weir's argument that theories of audience labour and audience commodification in the age of social media hold that the users of corporate social media constitute a class of unremunerated and exploited digital workers who produce value and a data commodity that is sold to advertisers. Both the academic debate and our empirical research confirm the controversial and antagonistic nature of social media advertising.

CAPITAL ACCUMULATION ON CORPORATE SOCIAL MEDIA

Figure 5.2 shows the process of capital accumulation on corporate social media platforms that are funded by targeted advertising. Social media corporations invest money (M) for buying capital: technologies (server space, computers, organizational infrastructure, etc.) and labour power (paid employees). These are the constant capital (c) and the variable capital v_1 outlays. The outcome of the production process P_1 is not a commodity that is directly sold, but rather social media services (the specific platforms) that are made available without payment to users. As a consequence of this circumstance, management literature has focused on identifying how to make profit from gratis Internet services.

The waged employees, who create social media online environments that are accessed by users, produce part of the surplus value. The users employ the platform for generating content

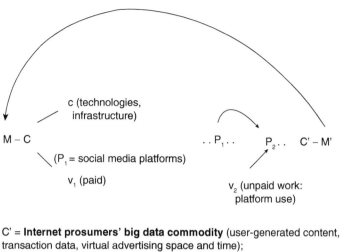

c (technologies, infrastructure)

M – C

$(P_1$ = social media platforms)

v_1 (paid)

$.. P_1 ..$ $P_2 ..$ C' – M'

v_2 (unpaid work: platform use)

C' = **Internet prosumers' big data commodity** (user-generated content, transaction data, virtual advertising space and time); most social media services are free to use, they are not commodities.
User data and the users are the social media commodity.

FIGURE 5.2   Capital accumulation on corporate social media platforms that are based on targeted advertising

that they upload (user-generated data). The constant and variable capital invested by social media companies (c, v_1) that is objectified in the online environments is the prerequisite for their activities in the production process P_2. Their products are user-generated data, personal data and transaction data about their browsing behaviour and communication behaviour on corporate social media. They invest a certain labour time v_2 in this process.

Corporate social media sell the users' data commodity to advertising clients at a price that is larger than the invested constant and variable capital. Partly the users and partly the corporations' employees create the surplus value contained in this commodity. The difference is that the users are unpaid and therefore infinitely exploited. Once the Internet prosumers' data commodity that contains the user-generated content, transaction data, and the right and possibility to access and target virtual advertising space and time is sold to advertising clients, the commodity is transformed into money capital and surplus value is transformed into money capital. A counter-argument to the insight that commercial social media companies exploit Internet prosumers is that the latter, in exchange for their work, receive access to a service. One can here, however, interpose that service access cannot be seen as a salary because users cannot "further convert this salary [. . .] [They] cannot buy food" (Bolin 2011, 37) with it.

THE PROFIT RATE AND SOCIAL MEDIA

For Marx (1867), the profit rate is the relation of profit to investment costs:

$p = s / (c + v)$ = surplus value / (constant capital (= fixed costs) + variable capital (= wages)).

135

If Internet users become productive web 2.0 prosumers, then in terms of Marxian class theory this means that they become productive labourers who produce surplus value and are exploited by capital because, for Marx, productive labour generates surplus value (Fuchs 2010c). Therefore the class of exploited digital workers includes not just web 2.0 companies' employees, who programme, update and maintain the software and hardware or perform marketing activities, but also the users and prosumers who engage in the production of user-generated content.

New media corporations do not (or hardly) pay the users for the production of content. One accumulation strategy is to give them free access to services and platforms and allow them to produce content, and accumulate a large number of prosumers whose user-generated content data and meta-data are sold as a commodity to third-party advertisers. No product is sold to the users, but the users' data is sold as a commodity to advertisers. The more users a platform has, the higher the advertising rates can be set. The productive labour time that capital exploits involves, on the one hand, the labour time of the paid employees and, on the other hand, all of the time that is spent online by the users. Digital media corporations pay salaries for the first type of knowledge labour. Users produce data that is used and sold by the platforms without payment. They work for free. There are neither variable nor constant investment costs. The formula for the profit rate needs to be transformed for this accumulation strategy:

$$p = s / (c + v_1 + v_2)$$

s: surplus value, c: constant capital, v_1: wages paid to fixed employees, v_2: wages paid to users

The typical situation is that $v_2 => 0$ and that v_2 substitutes v_1 ($v_1 => v_2 = 0$). If the production of content and the time spent online were carried out by paid employees, the variable costs (wages) would rise and profits would therefore decrease. This shows that prosumer activity in a capitalist society can be interpreted as the outsourcing of productive labour to users (in management literature the term "crowdsourcing" has been established; see Howe 2008) who work completely for free and help maximize the rate of exploitation:

$$e = s / v = surplus value / variable capital$$

THE RATE OF EXPLOITATION AND SOCIAL MEDIA

The rate of exploitation (also called the rate of surplus value) measures the relationship of workers' unpaid work time and paid work time. The higher the rate of exploitation, the more work time is unpaid. Users of commercial social media platforms have no wages ($v = 0$). Therefore the rate of surplus value converges towards infinity. Capital infinitely exploits Internet prosumer labour. This means that capitalist prosumption is an extreme form of exploitation in which the prosumers work completely for free. Marx (1867) distinguishes between necessary labour time and surplus labour time. The first is the time a person needs to work in order to create the money equivalent for a wage that is required for buying goods that are needed for survival. The second is all additional labour time. Users are not paid on corporate social media (or for consuming other types of corporate media), hence they cannot generate money for buying food or other goods needed for survival. Therefore, all online time on corporate social media like Google, Facebook, YouTube or Twitter is surplus labour time.

The outsourcing of work to consumers is a general tendency of contemporary capitalism. Facebook has asked users to translate its site into other languages without payment. Javier Olivan, international manager at Facebook, commented that it would be cool to use the wisdom of the crowds: "We thought it'd be cool."[7] Some users, such as Valentin Macias from California, however, argued that such crowdsourcing is in the case of Facebook a form of exploitation: "[Wikipedia is] an altruistic, charitable, information-sharing, donation-supported cause. [. . .] Facebook is not. Therefore, people should not be tricked into donating their time and energy to a multimillion-dollar company so that the company can make millions more—at least not without some type of compensation."[8]

Pepsi started a competition in which one could win US$10,000 for the best design of a Pepsi can. Ideabounty is a crowdsourcing platform that organizes crowdsourcing projects for corporations such as RedBull, BMW and Unilever. In such projects, most of the employed work is unpaid. Even if single individuals receive symbolic prize money, most of the work time employed by users and consumers is fully unpaid, which allows companies to outsource paid labour time to consumers or fans that work for free.

THE LAW OF VALUE ON SOCIAL MEDIA

Marx formulated the law of value as saying that "the greater the labour-time necessary to produce an article, [. . .] the greater its value" (Marx 1867, 131). It also applies in the case of commercial social media: the more time a user spends on commercial social media, the more data about her/his interests and activities are available and the more advertisements are presented to him/her. Users spending a lot of time online create more data and more value (work time) that is potentially transformed into profit.

Time dimensions play a crucial role in determining the price of an ad: the number of times people click on an ad, the number of times an ad or target URL has already been viewed, the number of times a keyword has been entered, the time that a specific user group spends on the platform, the number of times an ad is presented. Furthermore, the bidding maximums used as well as the number of ad clients competing for ad space influence the ad prices. In the pay-per-view method, Facebook and Google earn more with an ad that is targeted at a group that spends a lot of time on Facebook. The larger the target group, the higher Facebook's and Google's profits tend to be. In the pay-per-click method, Facebook and Google only earn money if users click on an ad. According to studies, the average click-through rate is 0.1 per cent.[9] This means that Facebook and Google tend to gain more profit if ads are presented to more users (in the pay-per-view method) and if more users spend time clicking on ads (in the pay-per-click-method).

---

7 www.msnbc.msn.com/id/24205912 (accessed on 30 October 2015).
8 www.msnbc.msn.com/id/24205912 (accessed on 30 October 2015).
9 Comscore. 2012. *The power of Like2: How social marketing works*. White Paper. www.comscore .com/ger/Press_Events/Presentations_Whitepapers/2012/The_Power_of_Like_2-How_Social_ Marketing_Works (accessed on 27 June 2012).

Generally, we can say that the higher the total attention time (clicks on ads, views of ads) given to ads, the higher Google's and Facebook's profits tend to be. The size of a target group and the average time this group spends on the platforms determines attention time. Online time on corporate social media is both labour time and attention time: the platforms monitor all activities that result in data commodities. On corporate social media, users produce commodities online during their online time. In the pay-per-view mode, specific online time of specifically targeted groups is also attention time that realizes profit for Facebook or Google. In the pay-per-click mode, attention time that realizes profit is only the portion of the online time that users devote to clicking on ads that are presented to them. In both cases, online time is crucial for (a) the production of data commodities, and (b) the realization of profit derived from the sales of the data commodities. Both surveillance of online time (in the sphere of production) and attention time (in sphere of circulation) given to advertisements play an important role in corporate social media's capital accumulation model.

Fixed constant capital (e.g. buildings, machines) is capital that the capitalist acquires and fixes in the production process for a longer time period (Marx 1885, Chapter 8). Circulating constant capital is in contrast a raw material that is immediately used up in production and must be renewed (Marx 1885, Chapter 8). The paid employees of a social media corporation that uses targeted advertising (v1), such as Facebook, produce the software platform that enters the production process as fixed capital that the users use in order to create data (profile data, communication data, content, social network data, browsing behaviour data). Whenever a user (= unpaid worker, v2) is online on Facebook, s/he transfer parts of the value of the platform and of the value of his/her existing personal data to a data commodity and s/he creates new value in the form of newly spent online time that creates additional data that enters the data commodity C' in the formed of stored data. The Facebook platform is a means of informational production – a fixed constant capital. It enables user labour that generates data. This data is stored and when a user accesses the platform, the stored data is used for generating the profile. So personal data is part of fixed constant capital. Big data remains fixed in the production process and enables user activity. The same data is also the starting point for the users' online activities on their profiles. They create new content based on existing content, contacts and communications. Therefore personal data is simultaneously fixed constant capital and circulating constant capital – a means of production that enables information, communication and networking and the resource based on and out of which user labour creates new data. On Facebook, circulating constant capital and fixed constant capital tend to converge. All uploaded content and generated data is stored on the platform's servers. This stored data (such as one's contacts, images, postings) forms an integral part of the platform that the users employ as instruments that enable online activities and help them create further data, content and communications. Users also build on previous contacts, postings, images, and communications that they further extend. Data and content are therefore simultaneously a constant good that is fixed and stored in the platform and a circulating good that is fluid, in flux and evolving through users' activities.

The users' labour (= online activity) creates the value (the total time spent online by the user) and the new content (the newly generated and stored data) of the data commodity. The whole commodity becomes part of Facebook's fixed capital that is reinvested in the production process: the existing data is used for organizing the user's Facebook profile and is re-used in the creation of an updated user profile. The user's profile is stored in a database and updated by the user whenever s/he logs into Facebook or whenever s/he visits a website that is connected to Facebook.

An advertising client selects a specific number of users when setting up targeted ads on Facebook. The client buys specific portions of the screen display of specific users that only exist while the user is on Facebook, which means that the user generates these spaces by his/her online behaviour and the data s/he generates and has previously generated. Users produce advertising spaces themselves. These spaces are either sold as commodity when the users click on them (pay per click) or when they are online (pay per view). They, however, are commodities in the moment that they are generated; that is, the moment a targeted ad is algorithmically generated and visualized on the screen. In the pay-per-click mode, the question is whether or not this commodity can be sold; that is, to which degree do users click on the presented ads? What is the value of a single ad space? It is the average number of minutes that a specific user group spends on Facebook divided by the average number of targeted ads that is presented to them during this time period. Facebook's ad clients fill the ads with their use-value promises that want to convince users to buy specific commodities. This means that the labour Facebook users perform enters the capital accumulation process of other companies in the realm of circulation, where commodities C' are transformed into money capital M' (C'-M'). Facebook users' labour is an online equivalent of transport work – their online activities help transporting use-value promises to themselves. Marx considered transport workers as productive circulation workers. Facebook users are productive online transport workers who organize the communication of advertising ideologies on the Internet.

THE SOCIAL MEDIA-DATA COMMODITY'S PRICE

How is the social media prosumer commodity's price determined and how is value transformed into money profit? Advertising clients are interested in the access to specific groups that can be targeted with individualized advertising that fit their interests. Access to this group and data about their interests (e.g. who is a member of a specific consumer group that shares certain interests) is sold to advertisers. On Google and Facebook, advertisers set a maximum budget for one campaign and a maximum they are willing to pay for one click on their advertisement or for 1,000 impressions (= presentations of an ad on a profile). The exact price for one click or for 1,000 impressions is determined in an automated bidding process, in which all advertisers interested in a specific group (all ads targeted at this specific group) compete. In both models, every user is offered as a commodity and commodified, but only certain user groups are sold as a commodity. In the pay-per-click model, value is transformed into money (profit is realized) when a user clicks on an ad. In the pay-per-view model, value is transformed into money (profit is realized) when an ad is presented on a user's profile. Value and price of the social media prosumer commodity do not coincide; the price is mathematically determined by an algorithm and based on bids. The number of hours spent online by a specific group of users determines the value of the social media prosumer commodity. The price of this commodity is algorithmically determined.

All hours spent online by users of Facebook, Google and comparable corporate social media constitute work time, in which data commodities are generated, and potential time for profit realization. The maximum time of a single user that is productive (i.e. results in data commodities) is 100 per cent of the time spent online. The maximum time that the same user contributes to profit realization by clicking on ads or viewing ads is the time that s/he spends on a specific platform. In practice, users only click on a small share of presented ads. So in the pay-per-click accumulation model, work time tends to be much larger than profit realization time. Online labour creates a lot of commodities that are offered for sale; only a certain share of it is sold and results in profits. This share is still large enough for companies like Google and Facebook to be able to generate significant profits. Online labour time is at the same time potential profit realization time. Capital tries to increase profit realization time in order to accumulate capital; that is, to make an ever-larger share of productive labour time also profit realization time.

On Google AdWords, advertisements compete against each other in an auction. Each bidder enters a maximum bid s/he is willing to pay per click as well as associated keywords. For each ad, an Ad Rank[10] is calculated based on the bid amount, an estimation of how often the ad will be clicked on (expected click-through rate), an assessment of the relevance of the landing page, the ad content's relevance to users' keywords and the quality of the ad format. This means that higher bids, high expected click-through rates and high ad relevance influence the ad positions. The ad with the highest Ad Rank gets the best position, the one with the second highest Ad Rank the second best, and so on. In determining the ad cost when a user clicks on an ad, the maximum bid of the next lower ranked ad plays a role. The price is set in such a way that it is a bit higher than this value. Google's chief advertiser Hal R. Varian describes the basic principle of Google's ad bid mechanism in the following way:

> In general, the search engine would like to sell the most prominent positions – those most likely to receive clicks – to those ads that have the highest expected revenue. To accomplish this, the ads are ranked by bid times expected click-through rates, and those ads with the highest expected revenue are shown in the most prominent positions. (Varian 2009, 430)

Let us assume a situation where certain brands are all having high-quality landing pages and highly-relevant ads. We can assume that among professional online advertisers this is the standard because advertisers are unlikely to spend money on irrelevant, badly written or badly designed ads or if they associate the advertisers with keywords that do not fit the advertised commodity. They also tend to have their own ad departments specializing in such issues. If advertisers in this situation now compete for clicks on certain very popular search keywords that reach lots of users, then given they have information on how popular keywords and ad-clicks associated with certain keywords are (which Google allows viewing with the help of a traffic estimator that advertisers can use in order to calculate expected impressions and click-through rates), we can assume that for popular keywords and keywords that reach many clicks, advertisers will be willing to set higher bids. High average bids also increase the profits Google makes per click. We can therefore assume that there is a tendency that the amount of time users spend searching for a particular keyword and the frequency of clicking on ads associated with this keyword (which is also a matter of time, namely time spent clicking on ads) influences the average profits that Google makes in the pay-per-click system that is Google's by-far dominant advertising sales method (pay-per-view is much less used).

---

10 For an explanation of how Ad Rank is calculated, see Insights on the AdWords Auction, www.youtube.com/watch?v=PjOHTFRaBWA (accessed on 30 October 2015).

One experimental study found in 2015 that keywords attracting on average very high costs-per-click relate to legal services, water damage, insurance, drugs and alcohol rehabilitation, online education and business services.[11] Another analysis found that in 2011 insurance-related keywords had the highest average CPC of US$ 54.91.[12] A third experimental study conducted in 2015 found that among the tested keywords, "car insurance quote" was the one that achieved the highest average CPC, namely US$70.03.[13]

If there is some truth in these findings, then they indicate that searches for commercial services that are in general popular on the Internet tend to result in high click-through rates. If someone searches for keywords about commercial or financial services (insurances, mortgages, buying something, etc.), then it is often likely that s/he does so with the plan to make a specific purchase soon. Companies such as legal firms, insurances and other financial companies may be willing to pay high average ad rates. Users searching for financial and professional services online are quite likely to buy such commodities and therefore to also follow links provided by ads. In the case of financial and professional services, users spend significant amounts of time searching and clicking on ads and there is significant demand by the industry to spend money for targeted ads, which results in relatively high average cost-per-click rates. One can say that the competition around certain keywords, which depends on their popularity and advertisers' expectations about popularity, and the average number of clicks per 1000 impressions (click-through rate) are important aspects of targeted online advertising. If

> an auction has fewer bidders than available slots, or just enough bidders to fill the available slots, we say it is "undersold". If it has more bidders than slots we say it is "oversold". [...] over sold pages are far more profitable than partially sold pages not just because there are more bidders, but also because the forces of competition are much stronger. (Varian 2006, 19–20)

In its targeted ad auctions, Facebook uses an algorithm comparable to the one by Google. One can either set the maximum bid oneself, or let Facebook decide based on a pacing algorithm that estimates how to set the maximum bid based on how user activities and ad competition are distributed over 24 hours. Facebook and Google's ad bid algorithms make use of the Vickrey–Clarke–Groves mechanism: the bidders do not know each other's bids. The auction mechanism charges a bidder A who makes the race not his maximum bid, but a value that is close to the bid value of the closest competitor B, which in turn depends on the maximum bid of the closest competitor of C, and so on.

> In the VCG mechanism: 1) each agent reports a value; 2) the search engine assigns agents to slots to maximize total value of the assignment; 3) each agent *a* then pays a charge equal to the total value accruing to the other agents if *a* is present minus the total value accruing to the other agents if *a* is absent. Thus each agent pays an amount equal to the cost that it imposes on the other agents. (Varian 2006, 17–18)

11 http://blog.hubspot.com/marketing/most-expensive-keywords-google (accessed on 27 September 2016).

12 www.statista.com/statistics/195680/share-of-keywords-prices-in-google-adwords-advertising (accessed on 27 September 2016).

13 www.truthin7minutes.com/most-expensive-keywords/ (accessed on 30 October 2015).

If there are, for example, two competitors and A's maximum bid is £100, B's £50, and A wins, then the cost will be somewhat more than £50. If B's maximum bid is, however, £90, then the cost will be larger than £90 and smaller than £100. If there are three bidders, then B's bid value depends on C's bid value, which again has an impact on A's bid value.

THE GENDERED COMMODITY AUDIENCE ON SOCIAL MEDIA

Eileen Meehan has introduced the concept of the gendered commodity audience. Advertisers are primarily interested in bona fide consumers who have "the disposable income, access, and desire to loyally purchase brand names and to habitually make impulse purchases [...] The larger the number of bona fide consumers viewing, the higher the price charged by networks" (Meehan 2002, 244).

> The overvaluing of a male audience reflects the sexism of patriarchy as surely as the overvaluing of an upscale audience reflects the classism of capitalism. [...] From this perspective, television is structured to discriminate against anyone outside the commodity audience of white, 18- to 34-year-old, heterosexual, English-speaking, upscale men. [...] television is an instrument of oppression. (Meehan 2002, 248)

Based on Meehan, Tamara Shepherd (2014) introduces the concept of the gendered commodity audience on social media. She argues that "like women who work often invisibly to maintain the cycle of reproduction and production, user labor on Facebook is elided in order to keep the site viable as a communication network predicated upon the site content that users contribute" (Shepherd 2014, 162). Advertising on social media would just like on television be gendered: the categorizations of targeted ad groups "based on gender (and also other stereotypical features of class, race, ethnicity, and age) function as a kind of discrimination by assigning differential value to these different target markets" (164).

Kylie Jarrett (2015, 2016) takes a Marxist-feminist approach for comparing housework and social media users' digital labour:

> Firstly, the work involved in both forms of labour is physical, but features significant cognitive, affective and communicative elements. [...] Moreover, consumer labour occupies a similar position in relation to the generation of surplus-value as domestic work. [...] Thus, there is more than the superficial resemblance between the types of activities involved in consumer labour and that associated with domestic work. They both operate in a regime of almost total exploitation, generating surplus by reducing the costs of production. Additionally, and this is important to emphasize, they are both involved in reproducing society. (Jarrett 2015, 209, 210–212)

SOCIAL MEDIA AND CRISIS

That surplus value generating labour is an emergent property of capitalist production means that production and accumulation will break down if this labour is withdrawn. It is an essential part of the capitalist production process. That prosumers conduct surplus-generating labour can also be seen by imagining what would happen if they stopped using Facebook: the number of users would drop, advertisers would stop investments because there would be no objects for their advertising messages and therefore no potential customers for their products, the profits of the new media corporations would drop, and they would go bankrupt. If such activities were carried out on a large scale, a new economy crisis would arise. This thought experiment shows that users are essential for generating profit in the new media economy. Furthermore, they produce and co-produce parts of the products, and therefore parts of the use value, value and surplus value that are objectified in these products.

A crisis of capitalism, however, not only is caused by workers' struggles, but can also have objective contradictions at its core. Venture capital firms are companies that organize a venture capital fund that they use for investments, often into start-up companies. They acquire ownership shares in companies and hope that future operations will yield large profits and dividends so that they accrue financial profits. Venture capital firms are financial investment firms. They have played an important role in the funding of Silicon Valley Internet corporations. So for example in the case of Facebook, large investors that funded the company's early development were the US venture capital firm Accel Partners, which owned around 15 per cent by investing US$12.7 million in 2005 and Mail.ru that invested US$200 million in 2009. In 2010, Accel Partners sold its Facebook ownership share for US$35 billion.[14] Mail.ru sold its Facebook shares in 2013 for US$525 million.[15] These examples show a typical strategy of financial capital: investing in start-up companies and selling ownership shares after these firms have increased their capital or market value in order to make a profit.

Companies sometimes use venture capital injections to increase their capital assets to a degree that allows them to make an initial public offering on a stock market and hence become publicly traded stock market companies. Stock market values depend on the complex and unpredictable laws of the financial markets, whereas actual profits depend on the amount of commodities sold, the rate of exploitation, the necessary investment costs and the productivity level. If a company has high stock values, then this does not imply that it makes lots of profits, but only that investors expect it to make high profits some time in the future and therefore make and keep up investments. If there is a longer or growing divergence between share values and profits, then investors may lose their confidence. If they start pulling out their invested capital and this behaviour spreads, then collapse of one company can be the result. The collapse of one key company can result in a panic and imitation behaviour that causes similar removals of investments. The outcome can be a crisis of an entire industry.

Financialization, that is the increasing dependence of companies, industries and capitalism on financial capital, is a result of capital's drive for achieving large profits and to escape crisis. Financial markets are, however, high risk markets, which is why financialization tends to increase capitalism's crisis-proneness. Marx (1894) speaks in this respect of fictitious capital, and David Harvey (2005b) talks of a temporal overaccumulation fix that results in the deference of "the re-entry of capital values into circulation into the future" (109) so that the difference between profits and asset price can result in financial bubbles. Just like there can be a difference between value and price of a commodity, there can be a difference between profit and financial market worth of a financial asset.

---

14 http://techcrunch.com/2010/11/19/accel-facebook-chunks-of-stock/.

15 Russia's Mail.Ru sells remaining Facebook stock. *Reuters* online, 5 September 2013. www.reuters.com/article/2013/09/05/us-mailru-results-idUSBRE98409720130905 (accessed on 27 September 2016).

The Internet economy's financialization resulted in the so-called dot-com crisis in 2000. There were large financial investments in Internet companies that became publicly listed on the stock markets but made constant losses. The result was a financial bubble that burst in 2000 and resulted in a crisis of the Internet economy. eToys.com is an online toy retail website founded in 1997. Based on large venture capital injections by investors such as Highland Entrepreneurs' Fund III Limited Partnership, DynaFund L.P., idealab! Capital Partners, Bessemer Venture Partners, Sequoia Capital Moore Global Investments Ltd, Remington Investment Strategies L.P. and Multi-Strategies Fund it made an Initial Public Offering (IPO) on the stock market in 1999. It made huge losses of up to US$200 million and had to file for chapter 11 bankruptcy in 2001. eToys is just one of many Internet corporations that exploded during the 2000 dot-com crisis. The new economy crisis 2000/2001 made financial capitalists reluctant to invest in new Internet companies. Web 2.0 and later social media were ideological strategies to create the impression that the WWW was re-invented and became entirely new so that new business opportunities had emerged. Social media was founded as an ideology aimed at convincing finance capitalists to invest in Internet companies and to attract advertising clients.

Google and Facebook are very profitable social media corporations. The two microblogs Twitter and Weibo in contrast struggle to make profits. Given that both Twitter and Weibo have been listed on the stock market without being profitable shows that the social media industry is also susceptible to financial bubbles. Targeted advertising is the dominant capital accumulation model in this industry. It is a high-risk model because the number of clicks per 1,000 advertisements tends to be low and is difficult to predict in respect of specific online advertising campaigns. And even if users click on an ad, this does not mean that they buy something on the page they land on. There is no guarantee that advertisers will in the future continue to trust that targeted advertising on social media is a good way to increase profits. In the event of them losing such confidence and the targeted advertising model entering crisis, this could have economic consequences for the social media industry.

5.4 FREE LABOUR AND SLAVE LABOUR

THE iSLAVE BEHIND THE IPHONE

Apple, according to the Forbes 2000 list of the largest transnational companies, was the world's 12th largest company in 2015.[16] Its profits were US$37.0 billion in 2012, US$39.5 billion in 2013 and US$44.5 billion in 2014.[17] In 2014, iPhones accounted for 56 per cent of Apple's net sales, iPads for 17 per cent, Macs for 13 per cent and iTunes, software and services for 10 per cent.[18] According to calculations, the Chinese labour involved in manufacturing an iPhone makes up only 1.8 per cent of the iPhone's price, Apple's profits 58.5 per cent (Chan et al. 2013, 107), and the profits of Apple's suppliers, such as the Taiwanese company Hon Hai Precision that is also known as Foxconn, 14.3 per cent. So the iPhone 6 Plus does not cost US$299 because of labour costs, but rather because Apple on average earns US$175 profits, Foxconn US$43 profits and the workers assembling the phone in a

---

16   www.forbes.com/global2000/list (accessed on 22 December 2014).
17   Apple SEC filings, form 10-K, 2014.
18   Apple SEC filings, form 10-K, 2014.

Foxconn factory in total US$5. The high costs are a consequence of a high profit rate and a high rate of exploitation that are achieved by organizing digital labour within an international division of digital labour.

According to the CNN Global 500 2012 list,[19] Foxconn is the fifth largest corporate employer in the world. In 2011 Foxconn had enlarged its Chinese workforce to a million, a majority being young migrant workers coming from rural areas (Students & Scholars Against Corporate Misbehaviour (SACOM) 2011). Foxconn assembles, for example, the iPad, iMac, iPhone, the Amazon Kindle and various consoles (by Sony, Nintendo, Microsoft).

SACOM[20] reported that Chinese Foxconn workers who produce iPhones, iPads, iPods, MacBooks and other ICTs are facing the withholding of wages, forced and unpaid overtime, exposure to chemicals, harsh management, low wages, bad work safety conditions, lack of basic facilities and so on. In 2010, 18 Foxconn employees attempted suicide, with 14 of them succeeding.[21] SACOM describes Foxconn workers as the "iSlave Behind the iPhone".[22] This example shows that the exploitation and surveillance of digital labour, that is labour that is needed for capital accumulation with the help of ICTs, is in no way limited to unpaid user labour, but includes various forms of labour – user labour, wage labour in Western companies for the creation of applications, and slave-like labour that creates hardware (and partly software) in developing countries under inhumane conditions (Chan 2013; Chan and Pun 2010; Chan et al. 2013; Fuchs 2014a; Hong 2011; Qiu 2009, 2012; Sandoval 2013, 2014; Zhao 2008).

Surveillance of Foxconn workers is direct, coercive, disciplinary and Taylorist. "Foxconn's stringent military-like culture is one of surveillance, obedience and not challenging authority. Workers are told obey or leave."[23]

> Supervisors yell at workers with foul language. Workers experience pressure and humiliation. Workers are warned that they may be replaced by robots if they are not efficient enough. Apart from scolding by frontline supervisors, other forms of punishment include being required to write confession letters and copying the CEO's quotations. A majority of workers have to stand for ten hours during work shifts. There is no recess as promised by Foxconn. Some workers suffer from leg cramps after work. Workers have extra workloads or have to skip the second meal break under the arrangement of "continuous shifts". [. . .] At the entrance of each building, there is a worker station to check the identities of the workers.[24]

---

19 http://money.cnn.com/magazines/fortune/global500/2012/full_list/ (accessed on 29 October 2013).

20 Students & Scholars Against Corporate Misbehaviour (SACOM), iSlave Behind the iPhone: Foxconn Workers in Central China. http://sacom.hk/wp-content/uploads/2011/09/20110924-islave-behind-the-iphone.pdf (accessed on 3 July 2013).

21 http://en.wikipedia.org/wiki/Foxconn_suicides (accessed on 16 April 2013).

22 Ibid.

23 CNN Online, Apple Manufacturing Plant Workers Complain of Long Hours, Militant Culture. http://edition.cnn.com/2012/02/06/world/asia/china-apple-foxconn-worker/index.html (accessed on 30 October 2015).

24 SACOM, iSlave Behind the iPhone.

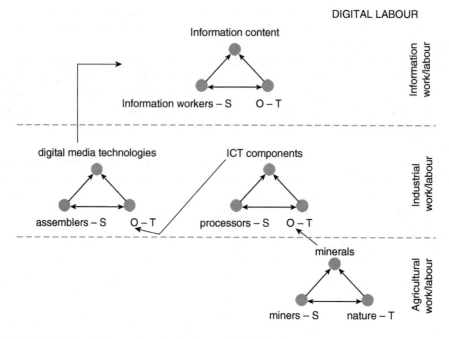

FIGURE 5.3   The international division of digital labour

Sources: Fuchs 2014a, 2015a.

In autumn 2014 SACOM published a new report on working conditions at Apple's supplier Pegatron in Jinagsu[25] where tens of millions of the iPhone 6 have been manufactured. Undercover scholars conducted the research.

> Workers told SACOM researchers that they sometimes have to work very long hours till early morning, often 12 to 15 hours a day, and sometimes even up to 17 to 18 hours a day. In other words, the total amount of overtime hours can be up to 170 to 200 hours a month, which, in turn, means that workers have to work more than 360 hours a month. (SACOM 2014, 2)

Also in 2014, Apple's profits were based on the exploitation of Chinese labour.

THE JOY OF THE PHONE AND COMPUTER IN THE WEST IS THE BLOOD AND SWEAT OF AFRICANS AND ASIANS

iPhones, iPads, iMacs, Nokia phones and so on are also "blood phones", "blood pads" and "blood Macs" in another sense: many smartphones, laptops, digital cameras, mp3 players and so on are made out of minerals (e.g. cassiterite, wolframite, coltan, gold, tungsten, tantalum,

---

25 See also the 2013 investigation by China Labor Watch: www.chinalaborwatch.org/report/68. (accessed on 27 September 2016). A comparable case is the iPhone 6 assemblage at Jabi in Wuxi: www.chinalaborwatch.org/report/103 (accessed on 27 September 2016).

tin) that are extracted from mines in the Democratic Republic of Congo and other countries under slave-like conditions (Fuchs 2014a, Chapter 6). Delly Mawazo Sesete describes the production conditions:

> These minerals are part of *your* daily life. They keep your computer running so you can surf the internet. [. . .] While minerals from the Congo have enriched your life, they have often brought violence, rape and instability to my home country. That's because those armed groups fighting for control of these mineral resources use murder, extortion and mass rape as a deliberate strategy to intimidate and control local populations, which helps them secure control of mines, trading routes and other strategic areas.[26]

THE INTERNET AS GLOBAL DIVISION OF LABOUR

The existence of the Internet in its current dominant capitalist form is based on various forms of labour: the relatively highly-paid wage work of software engineers, low-paid proletarianized labour in Internet companies, the unpaid labour of users, highly-exploited bloody Taylorist work, highly-toxic e-waste labour that disassembles ICTs, and slave work in developing countries producing hardware and extracting "conflict minerals" (Fuchs 2014a). There is a class conflict between capital and labour that is constituted through exploitation.

International communications in the form of the telegraph and international news agencies already played a role in the imperialism of the World War I era. They helped organize and co-ordinate trade, investment, accumulation, exploitation, and war at the international level. One hundred years later, qualitatively different means of information and communication, such as the computer, the laptop, tablets, the Internet, mobile phones and social media, have emerged. The production of information and information technology is embedded in an international division of information labour. There are new technologies, but capitalism, imperialism, class and exploitation continue to form the heart of society and international relations and shape the modes of information production, distribution and consumption that have become so important in the twenty-first century.

THE INTERNATIONAL DIVISION OF DIGITAL LABOUR

Critical scholars introduced the notion of the new international division of labour (NIDL) in the 1980s in order to stress that developing countries had become cheap sources of manufacturing labour and the rise of transnational corporations (TNCs) (Fröbel et al. 1981). The NIDL is at the heart of the information and digital economy that produces information and ICTs. Specific forms of physical work produce information technologies that are then used by workers in the media and cultural industries for creating informational content (music, movies, data, statistics, multimedia, images, videos, animations, texts, articles, etc.) in digital form. Informational content is produced, disseminated and consumed with the help of

---

26 *Guardian* online, Apple: Time to make a conflict-free iPhone. www.guardian.co.uk/commentis free/cifamerica/2011/dec/30/apple-time-make-conflict-free-iphone (accessed on 30 October 2015).

information technologies. Technology and content are dialectically interconnected so that the information economy is both physical and non-physical at the same time. The information economy is neither a superstructure nor immaterial, but rather a specific form of the organization of the productive forces that cuts across the base/superstructure divide and makes information and information technology immediate productive forces.

Figure 5.3 shows a model of the major production processes that are involved in the international division of digital labour. Each production step/labour process involves human subjects (S) using technologies/instruments of labour (T) on objects of labour (O) so that a new product emerges. The very foundation of digital labour is a labour cycle in which miners extract minerals. These minerals enter the next production process as objects so that processors based on them in physical labour processes create ICT components. These components enter the next labour cycle as objects: assemblage workers build digital media technologies and take ICT components as inputs. Processors and assemblers are industrial workers involved in digital production. The outcome of such labour are digital media technologies that enter various forms of information work as tools for the production, distribution, circulation, prosumption and consumption of diverse types of information.

"Digital labour" is not only a term that describes the production of digital content. It is a category that rather encompasses the whole mode of digital production that contains a network of agricultural, industrial and informational forms of work that enables the existence and usage of digital media. The subjects involved in the digital mode of production (S) – miners, processors, assemblers, information workers and related workers – stand in specific relations of production that are either class relations or non-class relations. So what is designated as S in Figure 5.3 is actually a relationship $S_1 - S_2$ between different subjects or subject groups. In contemporary capitalist society, most of these digital relations of production tend to be shaped by wage labour, slave labour, unpaid labour, precarious labour and freelance labour.

The international division of digital labour is a complex network that involves global interconnected processes of exploitation, such as the exploitation of Congolese slave-miners who extract minerals that are used as the physical foundation for ICT components that are manufactured by millions of highly-exploited Fordist wage-workers in factories such as Foxconn, low-paid software engineers in India, highly-paid and highly-stressed software engineers at Google and other Western software and Internet corporations, or precarious freelancers in the world's global cities who are using digital technologies to create and disseminate culture, poisoned eWaste workers who disassemble ICTs and thereby come in touch with toxic materials, and so on. (Fuchs 2014a, 2015a).

There is a difference between the exploitation of slaves and sweatshop workers and Facebook users: the first and the second face the threat of dying because of the physical and structural violence exerted against them, whereas violence in the case of the exploitation of Facebook-users is much more subtle, cultural and social in nature. It is a mistake to conclude from these differences in the form of violence that Facebook users are not exploited. Drawing this conclusion legitimates Google, Facebook and others' commodification of data. The conditions and consequences of exploitation vary from context to context, but workers in the international division of digital labour are connected to each other in a global production network that enables digital media companies' profits.

DIGITAL WORKERS IN THE INTERNATIONAL DIVISION OF DIGITAL LABOUR, UNITE!

Many forms of labour in the international division of labour are insecure and precarious. They feature low-paid or unpaid labour, long working hours, lack of social security and so on. Many digital workers share the feature that they are 'housewifized' workers (Fuchs 2014a, 2015a; Jarrett 2016) labouring in capitalism's inner colonies of ongoing primitive accumulation that yield high profits by high exploitation of labour. In analysing the international division of labour, one should focus on these commonalities in order to show that no matter how different the contexts of exploitation in the international division of digital labour, the exploitation of workers in this division has the same root cause: global capitalism. To point out the connectedness of these workers stresses the importance of international organization of the working class in struggles against exploitation. Why is it important to have such a unified concept of digital labour? Nick Dyer-Witheford (2014, 175) provides an answer: "To name the global worker is to make a map; and a map is also a weapon."

The rate of exploitation is varied depending on the type and location of activity. In the case of the salaried knowledge worker aristocracy, capital pays relatively high wages in order to try to gain their hegemonic consensus, whereas low-paid knowledge workers, users, hardware and software producers and mineral extractors in developing countries are facing precarious work conditions and varying degrees and forms of slavery and exploitation that, as a whole, help advance the profits of capital by minimizing the wage costs. Free-labouring Internet users and the workers in conflict mines have in common that they are unpaid. The difference is that the former gain pleasure through their exploitation, whereas the latter suffer pain and die through their exploitation which enables the pleasure of the former. The main benefit from this situation is monetary and goes to companies like Google, Apple and Facebook that are the contemporary exploiters, slaveholders and slave masters (Qiu 2016).

Different forms of control are needed for exploiting digital labour. Self-control and 'playbour' that feel like fun but create parts of the value constitute only one part of the labour process that has its foundation in a racist mode of production and exploitation of workers in developing countries. The exploitation of play workers in the West is based on the pain, sweat, blood and death of workers in developing countries. The corporate Internet needs for its existence both playbour and toil, fun and misery, biopolitical power and disciplinary power, self-control and surveillance. The example of the Foxconn factories and Congolese conflict minerals shows that the exploitation of Internet playbour needs as a precondition, and is coupled with, the bloody Taylorist exploitation of workers in the developing world.

5.5 CONCLUSION

The main results of this chapter can be summarized as follows:

- Contemporary social media are not participatory: large companies that centralize attention and visibility and marginalize politics, especially alternative politics, dominate them.
- Management gurus, marketing strategies and uncritical academics celebrate the democratic potentials of social media and neglect aspects of capitalism. Their assumptions are ideologies that reinforce capitalist domination.

- Corporate social media use capital accumulation models that are based on the exploitation of the unpaid labour of Internet users and on the commodification of user-generated data and data about user behaviour that is sold as commodity to advertisers. Targeted advertising and economic surveillance are important aspects of this accumulation model. The category of the audience commodity becomes, in the realm of social media, transmogrified into the category of the big data commodity that Internet prosumer's digital labour produces.

- The exploitation of the Internet prosumers' digital labour is an expression of a stage of capitalism, in which the boundaries between play and labour have become fuzzy and the exploitation of play labour has become a new principle. Exploitation tends to feel like fun and becomes part of free time.

- The existence of digital media is based on various forms of labour and different degrees of the exploited: the digital labour aristocracy of highly-paid workers in Internet companies, low-paid precarious knowledge workers, unpaid Internet users, highly-exploited workers in developing countries, slave workers extracting minerals that are used as raw materials, etc.

- Commercial social media are spheres of the exploitation of user play labour and at the same time objects of ideological mystifications that idealize social media in order to detract attention from their class character or advance the attraction of investors and the creation and expansion of spheres of capital accumulation. Commercial social media show that exploitation/capital accumulation and ideology are two important and entangled dimensions of the media in capitalism (Golding and Murdock 1978).

RECOMMENDED READINGS AND EXERCISES

The political economy of social media can best be approached by reading and discussing classical and newer texts that focus on aspects of labour and activity in the context of audiences and users. The recommended readings focus on the so-called Blindspot Debate, a classical foundational debate in Media and Communication Studies. Other readings introduce a debate on the digital labour theory of value between Adam Arvidsson and me, as well as four different positions on how to assess YouTube.

THE BLINDSPOT DEBATE

Smythe, Dallas W. 1977. Communications: Blindspot of Western Marxism. *Canadian Journal of Political and Social Theory* 1 (3): 1–27.

Smythe, Dallas W. 1981/2006. On the audience commodity and its work. In *Media and cultural studies*, ed. Meenakshi G. Durham and Douglas M. Kellner, 230–256. Malden, MA: Blackwell.

Murdock, Graham. 1978. Blindspots about Western Marxism: A reply to Dallas Smythe. In *The political economy of the media I*, ed. Peter Golding and Graham Murdock, 465–474. Cheltenham: Edward Elgar.

In 1977, Dallas Smythe published his seminal article "Communications: Blindspot of Western Marxism", in which he argued that Western Marxism has not given enough attention to the complex role of communications in capitalism. The article's publication was followed by an important foundational debate of media sociology that came to be known as the Blindspot Debate (Livant 1979; Murdock 1978; Smythe answered with a rejoinder to Murdock: Smythe 1994, 292–299), and by another article by Smythe on the same topic, *On the Audience Commodity and its Work* (Smythe 1981, 22–51).

Ask yourself:

- What are Dallas Smythe's main arguments?
- What are Graham Murdock's main points of criticism?
- There are different types of media commodities. Think about different for-profit media and the way they make money. What is their commodity? Try to construct a complete and systematic typology of media commodities.
- How does the commodity in the case of corporate social media differ from other media commodities?

THE SOCIAL MEDIA VALUE DEBATE

Fuchs, Christian. 2010. Labor in informational capitalism and on the Internet. *The Information Society* 26 (3): 179–196.

Arvidsson, Adam and Elanor Colleoni. 2012. Value in informational capitalism and on the Internet. *The Information Society* 28 (3): 135–150.

Fuchs, Christian. 2012. With or without Marx? With or without capitalism? A rejoinder to Adam Arvidsson and Eleanor Colleoni. *tripleC: Communication, Capitalism & Critique: Journal for a Global Sustainable Information Society* 10 (2): 633–645.

In 2010 I published an article about the relevance of Marx, his value and labour concepts for understanding social media. I presented excerpts from the article at the conference *The Internet as Playground and Factory* (New School, New York, 12–14 November 2009, www.digitallabor.org). Conference organizer Trebor Scholz conveyed a pre-conference discussion on the mailing list of the Institute for Distributed Creativity (IDC). Adam Arvidsson, in this discussion, first formulated criticism of my insistence on the importance of Marx for understanding value creation on social media. Three years later he published this criticism in an article co-authored with Eleanor Colleoni. Arvidsson and Colleoni argue that the law of value no longer exists and cannot be applied online. I responded to their claims in another article.

Ask yourself:

- What is the law of value?
- Summarize Fuchs's arguments on why the law of value is applicable to social media.
- Summarize Arvidsson and Colleoni's arguments on why the law of value is not applicable to social media. Discuss the differences between the two approaches.
- The law of value has to do with labour time. Discuss what roles time plays on social media and what the differences are if one spends little or a lot of time on social media. Is time a fundamental determinant of the profits that social media companies make or not? Why? Why not? What is the role of reputation and emotions for the generation of profit on social media?

(Continued)

(Continued)

My 2010 article in *The Information Society* resulted in an entire special issue of the journal *The Information Society*:

Proffitt, Jennifer M, Hamid R. Ekbia and Stephen D. McDowell, eds. Special forum on monetization of user-generated content – Marx revisited. In *The Information Society* 31 (1): 1–67.

- Read the articles in this special issue.
- Make a list of arguments and claims found in these diverse articles that argue for or against the assumption that capitalist social media companies such as Facebook exploit users' digital labour and commodify their data. Compare the different perspectives with each other and with the one I have advanced in Chapter 5. What commonalities and differences are there?

In 2014, Eran Fisher and I organized the workshop "Marx's Labour Theory of Value in the Digital Age" at the Open University of Israel. It focused on the topic of how to use Marx's labour theory of value for understanding digital labour. The contributions have been published in a collected volume:

Fisher, Eran and Christian Fuchs, eds. 2015. *Reconsidering value and labour in the digital age*. Basingstoke: Palgrave Macmillan.

- Read the chapters in this volume.
- Discuss: How do the authors in this book use concepts such as value, productive labour, rent and reproductive labour for analysis digital labour? What are the commonalities and differences of the approaches in the book?
- Which of these concept(s) do you find most feasible for analysis digital labour? Why?

Andrejevic, Mark. 2009. Exploiting YouTube: Contradictions of user-generated labor. In *The YouTube reader*, ed. Pelle Snickars and Patrick Vonderau, 406–423. Stockholm: National Library of Sweden.

Miller, Toby. 2009. Cybertarians of the world unite: You have nothing to lose but your tubes! In *The You Tube reader*, ed. Pelle Snickars and Patrick Vonderau, 424–440. Stockholm: National Library of Sweden.

Gauntlett, David. 2011. *Making is connecting: The social meaning of creativity, from DIY and knitting to YouTube and Web 2.0.* Cambridge: Polity Press. Chapter 8: Web 2.0 not all rosy?

Jenkins, Henry, Sam Ford and Joshua Green. 2013. *Spreadable media: Creating value and meaning in a networked culture*. New York: New York University Press. Chapter 1: Where web 2.0 went wrong + pp. 125–128 (Audiences as commodity and labour).

These four contributions to discussions about social media present different interventions in the digital labour debate and partly refer to each other. They are written by four important scholars who study contemporary media and whose approaches to certain degrees overlap and diverge: Mark Andrejevic, David Gauntlett, Henry Jenkins and Toby Miller.

Work in groups and present your results:

- Summarize the basic arguments of each contribution.
- Compare the four contributions to each other. What are the commonalities and differences?
- What are the crucial points of difference between the authors? How do you individually think about these differences? Try to justify your opinion with theoretical arguments, statistics, concrete examples and political reasoning.

6 GOOGLE: GOOD OR EVIL SEARCH ENGINE?

KEY QUESTIONS

- How does Google's political economy work?
- How has Google been criticized?
- What ideologies exist about Google? How does Google see itself and how does it want to be seen by others? What is the reality behind Google ideologies?

KEY CONCEPTS

Digital labour

Surveillance

Ideology

Googology (Google ideology)

New spirit of capitalism

Biopolitical exploitation

Internet solutionism

Internet fetishism

Technological online rationality

Rational discrimination

Cumulative disadvantage

Moral panics

Privacy policy

Targeted advertising

Sensitive personal data

Terms of use

Play labour (playbour)

Antagonism between the productive forces and the relations of production

Tax avoidance

OVERVIEW

In the early days of the World Wide Web, there were many search engines that users employed for navigating the web. Some of them featured text-based searches. Others were ordered directories. Examples were Altavista, Excite, Infoseek, Lycos, Magellan, Yahoo! At the end of the second millennium, Google's search engine emerged. It uses an algorithm called PageRank that orders the results of a search based on how many links lead to each result page. It uses automated software agents that crawl the WWW and count links to specific sites and analyse their results. Over the years, Google has become the world's dominant search engine. Google's search is based on a single box as user interface, which makes a search intuitive and easy for most users.

This chapter analyses Google's power, its advantages and disadvantages and the opportunities and risks it poses. A critical analysis of Google goes beyond moral condemnation or moral celebration, but rather tries to understand the conditions and contradictions that shape its existence and its users. This chapter therefore also wants to make a contribution to contextualizing normative questions about Google in the political economy of contemporary society. First, an introduction is given (in section 6.1). In section 6.2, I analyse Google's capital accumulation model. In section 6.3, I discuss the ideological implications of Google. Section 6.4 analyses the working conditions at Google. Section 6.5 discusses the good and bad sides of Google. Section 6.6 focuses on Google's relations to the state, especially concerning questions that concern its monopoly power in the search engine market and the circumstance that it has avoided paying taxes. I draw some conclusions in section 6.7.

6.1 INTRODUCTION

THE UBIQUITY OF GOOGLE

Tim O'Reilly (2005a) argues that Google is "the standard bearer" for web 2.0 and social media because it is not sold in different versions as are traditional software products, but is "delivered as a service" with "continuous improvement" and "context-sensitive" advertising. In 2012/2013, Google was the most accessed web platform: 45.8 per cent of worldwide Internet users accessed Google in a three-month period in 2012–2013 (data source: alexa. com, 2 March 2013). Also in 2015, Google was the world's most accessed web platform (data source: alexa.com, 1 November 2015). In autumn 2015, six of Google's services had more than one billion monthly active users (Google Search, YouTube, Google Maps, the mobile operating sytem Android, the web browser Chrome, Google Play).[1]

Google has become ubiquitous in everyday life – it is shaping how we search, organize and perceive information in contexts like the workplace, private life, culture, politics, the household, shopping and consumption, entertainment, sports and so on. The phrase "to google" has even found its way into the vocabulary of some languages. The *Oxford English Dictionary* defines "to google" as "search for information about (someone or something) on the Internet, typically using the search engine Google" and remarks that the word's origin is "the proprietary name of a popular Internet search engine".[2]

TABLE 6.1 Google's ranking in the list of the world's largest public companies

2004	2005	2006	2007	2008	2009	2010	2011	2012	2013	2014	2015	2016
904	439	289	213	155	120	120	120	103	68	52	39	27

Source: Data from Forbes Global 2000, various years; the ranking is based on a composite index of profits, sales, assets and market value). The year indicated refers to the year the respective Forbes ranking was published. Forbes uses financial data from the preceding calendar year for its ranking.

---

1 Here are all the Google services with more than 1 billion users. *Tech Insider*, 23 October 2015.
2 http://oxforddictionaries.com/view/entry/m_en_gb0342960#m_en_gb0342960 (accessed on 1 November 2015).

6.2 GOOGLE'S POLITICAL ECONOMY

GOOGLE'S ECONOMIC POWER

Google, which was founded in 1998 by Larry Page and Sergey Brin, was transformed into a public company on 19 August 2004 (Vise 2005, 4). Google acquired many other companies, including the video-sharing platform YouTube for US$1.65 billion in 2006, the online advertising service company DoubleClick for US$3.1 billion in 2008 (Stross 2008, 2), Motorola Mobility in 2012 for US$12 billion (that Google sold to Lenovo in 2014) and the artificial intelligence company DeepMind for around US$400 million.

In 2012, Google was, after IBM, the second largest computer service company in the world (Forbes Global 2000, 2012 list). In 2015, its profits, capital assets and market value were larger than those of IBM and it was the world's largest computer service corporation (Forbes 2000, 2015 list). In the list of the world's largest companies, Google has rapidly increased its ranking (Table 6.1). Its profits in 2014 were US$14.4 billion (Google SEC filings, Form 10-K, Annual Report 2014), the largest amount since the company's creation in 1998. Since 2004, Google's annual profits have rapidly increased (see Figure 6.1). Google's 2014 sales of US$66 billion (data source: Forbes 2000 [2015]) were larger than 124 countries' gross domestic product in the same year (data source: World Bank DataBank).

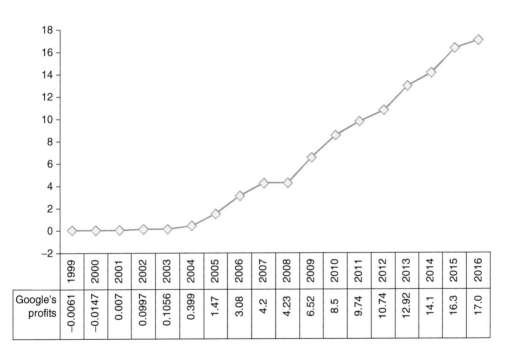

FIGURE 6.1 The development of Google's profits, in billion US$

Source: Data from SEC-filings, from 10-k, various years.

GOOGLE AND THE CAPITALIST CRISIS

In 2008, the year that a new world economic crisis hit capitalism, Google's market value dropped from US$147.66 billion (2007) to US$106.69 billion (data source: Forbes Global 2000, lists for the years 2007 and 2008). Google's profits remained constant in this period of world economic crisis (2007: $4.2 billion, 2008: $4.23 billion, Forbes Global 2000, lists for the years 2007 and 2008). In 2009, Google's market value increased to $169.38 billion (data source: Forbes Global 2000, year 2009). Google's profits reached a new all-time high of US$6.52 billion in 2009 and skyrocketed to $8.5 billion in 2010, $9.75 billion in 2011, $10.74 billion in 2012, $12.92 billion in 2013, $14.1 billion in 2014, $16.3 billion in 2015, and $17.0 billion in 2016 (data source: Google SEC filings, annual reports various years). So Google's profits were not harmed by the economic crisis that started in 2008. The company stabilized its profits in 2008 in comparison to 2007, achieved a 54.1 per cent growth of its profits in 2009, 30.4 per cent in 2010, 14.6 per cent in 2011, 10.3 per cent in 2012, 20.3 per cent in 2013, 11.5 per cent in 2014, 15.6 per cent in 2015, and 4.3% in 2016.

An economic crisis results in the shrinking of the profits of many companies, which can have negative influences on advertising markets because companies with declining profits have less money to spend for marketing purposes. As a result, many advertising-financed media companies' profits declined in the financial years 2008 and 2009 (Fuchs 2011b, Chapter 6). Google may have benefited from the crisis because at such times "advertisers are more concerned about the costs and direct results of their advertising campaigns" and Google offers good ways of "controlling and measuring [. . .] [a] campaign's effectiveness" (Girard 2009, 215). In non-marketing research language, this means that Google provides a form of advertising that is based on the close surveillance of users. Google advertising clients know a lot about who clicks when on their ads. Surveillance makes Google advertising predictable. Capitalist companies seek to control unpredictability of investments, especially in times of crisis, and therefore welcome Google advertising because it is based on a form of economic user surveillance that promises economic security in an insecure world of crisis.

GOOGLE, FACEBOOK, BAIDU: NO COMMUNICATIONS COMPANIES, BUT SOME OF THE WORLD'S LARGEST ADVERTISING AGENCIES

Table 6.2 shows the development of the global advertising revenues. Whereas the share of broadcast advertising (radio and television) has in the years from 2010 until 2014 slightly declined from 44.3 per cent to 42.0 per cent; the decline was more drastic in the print industry (newspapers and magazines), where the share went from 29.4 per cent to 21.2 per cent. At the same time, the share of Internet advertising increased from 17.8 per cent to 28.4 per cent. These statistical data give grounds to the assumption that advertisers find online advertising more secure than other forms of advertising because it can be targeted and personalized, and it is based on consumer- and user-surveillance. The new capitalist crisis may have accelerated this shift from traditional advertising to online advertising because corporations are then especially afraid of bankruptcy and making losses. In the UK in the year 2014, 37.1 per cent of the advertising revenue was spent in the online industry, 28.3 per cent in broadcasting, 18.7 per cent in the print industry, 9.5 per cent on direct mail advertising, 5.3 per cent on outdoor ads, and 1.0 per cent in the movie industry (Ofcom 2015b, 375). In 2015, the share of Internet advertising further increased to 41.1% and the shares of broadcasting advertising and print advertising dropped to 25.1% and 15.9% (Ofcom 2016, 211)

TABLE 6.2   The development of global advertising revenue, in £ billion and % of total ad revenue

	2010	2011	2012	2013	2014
Newspapers	48.04	47.00	44.94	43.28	41.96
Consumer magazines	20.65	20.49	19.76	18.94	18.14
Television	84.78	88.02	91.99	93.59	98.52
Radio	18.69	19.11	19.36	19.78	20.48
Cinema	1.35	1.41	1.49	1.55	1.6
Outdoor	18.5	19.35	19.98	20.89	22.04
Internet	41.58	50.57	58.68	68.88	80.27
Total	233.6	245.9	256.2	266.9	283
Newspapers	20.6%	19.1%	17.5%	16.2%	14.8%
Consumer magazines	8.8%	8.3%	7.7%	7.1%	6.4%
Television	36.3%	35.8%	35.9%	35.1%	34.8%
Radio	8.0%	7.8%	7.6%	7.4%	7.2%
Cinema	0.6%	0.6%	0.6%	0.6%	0.6%
Outdoor	7.9%	7.9%	7.8%	7.8%	7.8%
Internet	17.8%	20.6%	22.9%	25.8%	28.4%

Source: Data from Ofcom, 2015c, 26.

According to estimations, in 2015 Google controlled 54.5 per cent of the total online search ad revenues, Baidu 8.8 per cent, Microsoft 4.2 per cent, Yahoo! 2.3 per cent, Sohu 0.6 per cent and others 29.5 per cent.[3] In 2014, Google had a share of 31.10 per cent in the global digital ad revenue, Facebook 7.75 per cent, Baidu 4.68 per cent, Alibaba 4.66 per cent, Microsoft 2.72 per cent, Yahoo! 2.36 per cent, IAC 1.00 per cent, Twitter 0.84 per cent, Tencent 0.83 per cent, AOL 0.81 per cent, Amazon 0.70 per cent, Pandora 0.50 per cent, LinkedIn 0.49 per cent, SINA 0.38 per cent, Yelp 0.24 per cent and Millennial Media 0.08 per cent.[4] Such data indicate that Google, Facebook and Baidu are the key beneficiaries of Internet advertising's growth. One should not be mistaken: Google, Facebook and Baidu are not communications companies. They do not sell digital content or access to online platforms. They are some of the world's largest advertising companies. They sell user data as commodity to advertisers, who in return can present targeted ads to users. In 2014, 89 per cent of Google's revenues came from advertising (data source: SEC filings Google, Form 10-K 2014). In the case of Facebook this figure was 92 per cent in 2014 (data source: SEC filings Facebook, Form 10-K 2014), for Baidu it was in the same year 98.9 per cent online marketing services (data source: SEC filings Baidu, Form 20-F 2014).

ABCDEFGOOGLE: FROM GOOGLE INC. TO ALPHABET INC.

In 2015, Google reorganized its corporate structure and formed the parent company Alphabet Inc. It appointed Larry Page as CEO, Sergey Brin as President and Eric Schmidt as the

---

3 Google will take 55 per cent of search ad dollars globally in 2015. *eMarketer*, 31 March 2015.
4 China's leading ad sellers to take 10 per cent of the worldwide digital market this year. *eMarketer*, 16 December 2014.

Executive Chairman of the Board of Directors. Google Inc.'s shares were converted into Alphabet Inc. shares. Google that focuses on Alphabet's core search business is one of the new company's subsidiaries. Sundar Pichai was appointed Google's CEO in October 2015. Other subsidiaries are Calico (longevity, biotechnology), Google X (Artificial Intelligence), Fiber (broadband Internet and cable television), Google Capital (profit-oriented venture capital investments in tech companies), Google Ventures (venture capital) and Nest Labs (smart technologies).

Why did Google change its company structure? Part of the answer may be that a large corporation that controls a tremendous amount of capital and is active in many realms is difficult to manage as one central unit. Another aspect may be that parts of Google's activities form the core business that should be profitable, whereas other parts are more strategic and partly experimental activities that are not necessarily expected to be profitable, at least not in the short or medium term. Having several subsidiaries that make losses may prove to yield more tax advantages than having one large company that combines profits and losses. If profitable and unprofitable or not so profitable parts of a corporation can be kept separate, then it may be easier to attract investors by focusing their attention on the positive financial data. Google as the core business now reports its results separately from other non-search- and non-advertising-related investments, which is a better way to keep investors happy. Google came under pressure in the European Union, which started anti-trust action against Google in June 2015, arguing that its search engine favours its own online commerce activities. So restructuring may also have been an attempt on the part of Google to appease its critics in legal battles by showing that it is willing to change organizationally and becoming equipped to argue that the changed company structure means less capital concentration. This thought is also evident from the letter that Larry Page wrote to the public in order to explain Alphabet's founding:

> Our company is operating well today, but we think we can make it cleaner and more accountable. So we are creating a new company, called Alphabet. [...] Alphabet is mostly a collection of companies. The largest of which, of course, is Google. This newer Google is a bit slimmed down, with the companies that are pretty far afield of our main Internet products contained in Alphabet instead.[5]

Alphabet's non-Google part has created the company's separate corporate legs as venture capitalist and inventor company, which are both risky businesses. Separating the risks of the venture inventor and the inventive venture from the Google's thus far relative secure and continuous growth of Google's search and related operations is a way of risk management that aims at increasing long-term capital accumulation capacities. Time will tell whether from an economic perspective this strategy will be successful or develop its own contradictions and limits.

The formation of Alphabet is not the only example of a split of one large transnational corporation splitting into smaller units. In 2013, Rupert Murdoch's News Corp was split into 21st Century Fox that focuses on the profitable broadcast and film business on the one

---

5 https://abc.xyz (accessed on 2 November 2015).

hand and News Corporation that takes care of the less profitable, scandal- and crisis-ridden publishing business. The publishing industry, because of its commercialization, the digitization of print and reading, and the rise of online advertising, has been in crisis. The reputation of the publishing part of Murdoch's media empire was furthermore suffering under the *News of the World* phone-hacking scandal.

THE WEALTH AND POWER OF GOOGLE'S OWNERS

Ken Auletta (2010, 19) claims in his book *Googled* that Google is an egalitarian company and that Brin, Page and Schmidt have modest salaries. Can one speak of economic modesty if four persons control around 70 per cent of a corporation's voting power and more than 90 per cent of its key common stock (Table 6.3)? Page and Brin increased their personal wealth by a factor of eight in the years 2004–2015, Schmidt by a factor of seven (Figure 6.2). They are among the richest Americans. Google is not more or less "evil" than any other capitalist company (Table 6.3). It is an ordinary capitalist company that accumulates profit and, as a result, the personal wealth of a few also grows because of the exploitation of many.

HOW GOOGLE ACCUMULATES CAPITAL

These data show that Google is one of the world's most profitable media companies. But how exactly does it achieve this profit? How does it accumulate capital? Answering this question requires a political economy analysis of Google's capital accumulation cycle.

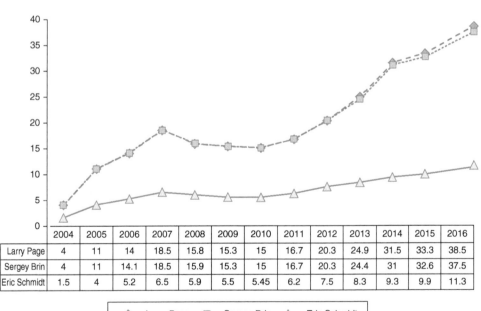

	2004	2005	2006	2007	2008	2009	2010	2011	2012	2013	2014	2015	2016
Larry Page	4	11	14	18.5	15.8	15.3	15	16.7	20.3	24.9	31.5	33.3	38.5
Sergey Brin	4	11	14.1	18.5	15.9	15.3	15	16.7	20.3	24.4	31	32.6	37.5
Eric Schmidt	1.5	4	5.2	6.5	5.9	5.5	5.45	6.2	7.5	8.3	9.3	9.9	11.3

--◆- Larry Page --■-- Sergey Brin --△- Eric Schmidt

FIGURE 6.2 Development of the wealth of Google's three richest directors, in billion US$

Source: Data from Forbes 400 List of the Richest Americans.

TABLE 6.3 Development of the ranking of Google's three richest directors in the list of the 300 richest Americans

	2004	2005	2006	2007	2008	2009	2010	2011	2012	2013	2014	2015	2016
Larry Page	43	16	13	5	14	11	11	15	13	13	13	10	9
Sergey Brin	43	16	12	5	13	11	11	15	13	14	14	11	10
Eric Schmidt	165	52	51	48	59	40	48	50	45	49	49	48	36

Source: Data from Forbes 400 List of the Richest Americans.

Some existing analyses of Google stand in the political economy tradition.[6] In section 5.3 of this book, I introduced, based on Dallas Smythe's (1981/2006) concept of the audience commodity, the notion of Internet prosumer commodification for analysing the political economy of social media. Google relates to Internet prosumer commodification in two ways. On the one hand, it indexes user-generated content that is uploaded to the web and thereby acts as a meta-exploiter of all user-generated content producers. Without user-generated content by unpaid users, Google could not perform keyword searches. Therefore Google exploits all users who create WWW content. On the other hand, users employ Google services and thereby conduct unpaid productive surplus-value generating labour.

Such labour includes, for example, searching for a keyword on Google's search portal, maintaining a social network on Google+, searching for a keyword on Google, sending an email via GMail, uploading or searching for a video on YouTube, searching for a book on Google Print, looking for a location on Google Maps or Google Earth, creating or editing a document on GoogleDocs, maintaining or reading a blog on Blogger/Blogspot, uploading images to Picassa, translating a sentence with Google Translate, playing a game developed by Google Game, searching for academic papers on Google Scholar, sharing data in Google's cloud via Google Drive, creating images on Google Draw, producing slides on Google Slides, conducting calculations on Google Sheets, organizing surveys on Google Forms, managing mailing lists via Google Groups, conducting video-conferences via Google Hangouts, and so on.

Google generates and stores data about the usage of these services in order to enable targeted advertising. It sells these data to advertising clients, who then provide advertisements that are targeted at the activities, searches, contents and interests of the users of Google services. Google engages in the economic surveillance of user data and user activities, thereby commodifying and infinitely exploiting users, and selling users and their data as Internet prosumer commodity to advertising clients in order to generate money profit. Google is the ultimate economic surveillance machine and the ultimate user-exploitation machine. It instrumentalizes all users and all of their data for creating profit.

Google does not pay for the circumstance that it uses web content as a resource, although results are provided to users when they search for keywords so that data about user interests are generated that are sold to advertising clients. It benefits monetarily from the expansion of the web and user-generated content. The more websites and content there are on the WWW,

---

6 See, for example, Bermejo 2009; Jakobsson and Stiernstedt 2010; Kang and McAllister 2011; Lee 2011; Mager 2012, 2014; Pasquinelli 2009; Petersen 2008; Vaidhyanathan 2011; Wasko and Erickson 2009.

the more content and pages Google can index in order to provide search results. The more and the better search results there are, the more likely users are to use Google and to be confronted with advertisements that match their searches, on which they might click.

The more users of Google's services there are, the more data about the services' users is stored and assessed. Google sells advertisements that match search keywords to ad clients that bid for advertising positions (Google AdWords). There are auctions for ad space connected to certain keywords and screen locations. Google sets the minimum bids. Ads that are clicked more frequently tend to be displayed at a better position on the Google result pages (Girard 2009, 31; see also the detailed description of Google's advertising auction algorithm in Chapter 5). Users who conduct searches containing specific keywords are targeted by specific advertisements. Google AdSense enables website operators to include Google adverts on their websites and to achieve revenue for each click on an advertisement. Google shares parts of the ad revenue with the website operators that participate in the AdSense programme. Advertisements can be presented in a targeted way to specific groups of users. For doing so, Google collects a lot of information about users. It engages in user surveillance. It is important to study what kind of data about users Google collects, monitors and commodifies.

GOOGLE AS A SURVEILLANCE MACHINE AND CONTROL APPARATUS

Surveillance of user data is an important part of Google's operations. It is, however, subsumed under Google's political economy; that is, Google engages in user surveillance for the end of capital accumulation. Google surveillance is therefore a form of economic surveillance. In 2013, Edward Snowden revealed the existence of a surveillance-industrial Internet complex, in which large communications companies such as Google and Facebook co-operate with secret services such as the National Security Agency (NSA). Snowden's revelations and their implications are analysed in detail in Chapter 7 of this book. They show that economic and political surveillance are strongly interlinked.

Google uses a powerful search algorithm. The details of the PageRank algorithm are secret. Basically small, automated programmes (web spiders) search the WWW, the algorithm analyses all found pages, counts the number of links to each page, identifies keywords for each page and ranks its importance. The results can be used for free via the easy user interface that Google provides. Google develops ever-newer services that are again offered for free. The PageRank algorithm is a form of surveillance that searches, assesses and indexes the WWW.

Google has become a culture of search, expressed by the fact that if people want to find out something, they say "I'll google it", "I'll have to investigate this on Google" or "I'll conduct some research about it [meaning that they'll google it]". The same culture of search and its political effects became evident when US President-elect Donald Trump argued in November 2015, after he had won the election: "You're always running, running, running, [. . .] There were so many times that I made a mental note to Google Obamacare but I just never got around to it". The problem of this culture of search is that it is based on a proprietary algorithm owned by Google whose source code is not publicly accessible and that has not been commonly developed. It is therefore open to manipulation and in general privileges those actors who have lots of online visibility over those who are culturally less powerful. The principle of privileging the culturally powerful means that if users do not find someone or something on Google's first or second result page, they sometimes tend to declare it is non-existent. Google has thereby become a powerful mechanism for constructing what users consider reality to be like. That something is not on Google's first result page does not, however, rule out that it is meaningful and important for a lot of people. Astrid Mager (2012, 2014) characterizes Google's search algorithm as algorithmic ideology that is built into the algorithm and is hegemonically reproduced by users' search practices.

The discussion shows not just that Google is economically powerful, but that its economic power and surveillance is interlinked with political surveillance and cultural control of reality definition. Google is a surveillance machine and an apparatus of control.

6.3 GOOGOLOGY: GOOGLE AND IDEOLOGY

THE IDEOLOGY OF GOOGLE'S PRIVACY POLICY

Google is a legally registered company with headquarters in Mountain View, California, United States. Its privacy policy is a typical expression of a self-regulatory privacy ideology, in which businesses can largely define themselves according to how they process personal user data. Privacy self-regulation by businesses is voluntary, therefore the number of organizations engaging in it tends to be very small (Bennett and Raab 2006, 171): "Self-regulation will always suffer from the perception that it is more symbolic than real because those who are responsible for implementation are those who have a vested interest in the processing of personal data." Google's terms of service and privacy policy are the legal foundations of economic user surveillance.

Google's privacy policy defines that the company is allowed to view commodity users' personal data in order to show them targeted advertisements:

> We use the information we collect from all of our services to provide, maintain, protect and improve them, to develop new ones, and to protect Google and our users. We also use this information to offer you tailored content – like giving you more relevant search results and ads. (Google Privacy Policy, version from 19 August 2015)

Google makes use of privacy policies and terms of service that enable the large-scale economic surveillance of users for the purpose of capital accumulation. Advertising clients of Google that use Google AdWords are able to target ads, for example by keyword searches, by country, by the exact location of users and by the distance from a certain location, by the language users speak, by the type of device used (desktop/laptop computer, mobile device (specifiable)), by the mobile phone operator used (specifiable), by gender or age group.

As of February 2016, Google offers two opt-out options for targeted ads: one can opt out from targeted ads on Google search ads and from the display of Google-based ads on other websites (http://www.google.com/settings/ads). The point, however, is that targeted ads are enabled and the user needs to take action in order to change that. Opting out will not result in freedom from online ads, but rather in the provision of non-targeted ads.

COMPLEX TERMS OF USE

Google's 2011 privacy terms (version from 20 October 2011) had 10,917 characters, whereas its 2012 privacy terms (version from 27 July 2012) had 14,218 characters, which is an increase of around 30 per cent. The version from 19 August 2015 consists of 17,380 characters, which is an increase of 22 per cent in comparison with the 2012 edition. The main privacy terms have grown in complexity.

SOCIAL MEDIA PLATFORMS' PRIVACY POLICY: THE COMMODIFICATION OF PERSONAL DATA

Google is not the only social media corporation that, based on a neoliberal pro-business policy regime, is able to define its own privacy policy in order to legally safeguard the commodification of personal data. Here are some examples. Legally, targeted advertising is enabled by privacy policies and terms of use that are published on the websites of the platforms and to which users agree when registering their profiles.

- From Facebook's Data Use Policy: "We use the information we have to improve our advertising and measurement systems so we can show you relevant ads on and off our Services and measure the effectiveness and reach of ads and services."[7]
- From the microblog Twitter's Terms of Service: "The Services may include advertisements, which may be targeted to the Content or information on the Services, queries made through the Services, or other information."[8]
- From the photo sharing platform Pinterest's Privacy Policy: "We also use the information we collect to offer you customized content, including: [...] Showing you ads you might be interested in. For example, if you purchased a camping tent on Pinterest, we may show you ads for other outdoorsy products."[9]
- From the blog platform Tumblr's Privacy Policy: "We may use this information about how you and others interact with the Services for a number of things generally related to enhancing, improving, protecting, and developing new Services, including but not limited to: providing users with personalized content; providing users with targeted advertising."[10]
- FromWeChat's[11] Terms of Service: "You also agree that, as explained in more detail in our *WeChat Privacy Policy*, we use targeted advertising to try to make advertising more relevant and valuable to you. [...] We may use your information for the purpose of sending you advertising or direct marketing (whether by messaging within our services, by email or by other means) that offer or advertise products and services of ours and/or selected third parties."[12]

---

7   www.facebook.com/full_data_use_policy, version from 30 January 2015 (accessed on 2 November 2015).
8   https://twitter.com/tos, version from 18 May 2015 (accessed on 2 November 2015).
9   https://about.pinterest.com/en/privacy-policy, version from 28 June 2015 (accessed on 3 November 2015).
10 www.tumblr.com/policy/en/privacy, version from 27 January 2014 (accessed on 9 February 2016).
11 Tencent Holdings Limited is a Chinese company operating online services such as the instant messenger QQ (launched in 1999) and the mobile phone-chat application WeChat (launched in 2011). WeChat is one of the first Chinese social and mobile media applications that is fully available in English and is therefore aimed at commodifying personal data on an international market of users.
12 www.wechat.com/en/service_terms.html, version from 4 September 2014 (accessed on 3 November 2015).

- From the photo-sharing site Flickr's Privacy Policy: "By bringing content and advertising to you that is relevant and tailored to your interests, Yahoo! provides a more compelling online experience."[13]
- From the video-messaging app Snapchat's Privacy Policy: "What do we do with the information we collect? [...] personalize the services by, among other things, suggesting friends or profile information or providing advertisements, content, or features that match user profiles, interests, or previous activities."[14]

This overview shows that many social media companies use relatively similar terms of use and privacy policies that allow them to use and commodify a multitude of personal user data for commercial purposes. These companies' privacy policies and terms of use not only share similar economic goals, but also use a comparable ideological language that presents targeted advertising as advantageous for users by speaking for example of "relevant ads" or "ads you might be interested in". Advertising and targeting are presented as desirable because they would allow users to get information about and to purchase relevant commodities. This ideology of "relevant ads" masks that advertising can have negative effects, such as the concealment of negative features and effects of products, the discrimination against competing products, the advancement of the concentration of the economy, the manipulation of human needs and desires, the statistical sorting of users into consumer groups so that the weak, the poor, people with low purchasing power and people of colour are discriminated against, the enforcement of, for example, racist or sexist stereotypes, the fostering of mass consumption of non-renewable resources that generate waste and aggravate the ecological crisis (for an overview see the contributions in Turow and McAllister 2009).

An interesting exception is the mobile chat application WhatsApp that says in its Terms of Service: "We are not fans of advertising. WhatsApp is currently ad-free and we hope to keep it that way forever. We have no intention to introduce advertisement into the product, but if we ever do, will update this section."[15] "These days companies know literally everything about you, your friends, your interests, and they use it all to sell ads. [...] Remember, when advertising is involved you the user are the product."[16] Given this criticism of advertising, it is interesting that WhatsApp was sold to Facebook for US$19 billion in February 2014.[17] In 2014, Facebook derived 92 per cent of its revenues from advertising.[18] WhatsApp will be compelled to find a commodification strategy that allows for making profits and the future will tell whether this will mean the introduction of advertising and a change of WhatsApp's values towards advertising or not. No matter which capital accumulation a corporation uses, capitalist commodity production always involves the exploitation of some type of labour. In August 2016, WhatsApp changed its terms of use

---

13 Yahoo! owns Flickr. https://policies.yahoo.com/us/en/yahoo/privacy/products/flickr/index.htm (accessed on 3 November 2015).
14 www.snapchat.com/privacy, version from 28 October 2015 (accessed on 3 November 2015).
15 www.whatsapp.com/legal/, version from 7 July 2012 (accessed on 3 November 2015).
16 http://blog.whatsapp.com/index.php/2012/06/why-we-dont-sell-ads/ (accessed on 9 April 2014).
17 www.theguardian.com/technology/2014/feb/19/facebook-buys-whatsapp-16bn-deal (accessed on 9 April 2014).
18 Facebook SEC filings, Form 10-K for financial year 2014.

and privacy policy, enabling advertising: "We joined the Facebook family of companies in 2014. As part of the Facebook family of companies, WhatsApp receives information from, and shares information with, this family of companies. We may use the information we receive from them, and they may use the information we share with them, to help operate, provide, improve, understand, customize, support, and market our Services and their offerings" (WhatsApp Privacy Policy, version from August 25, 2016). Also marketing messages can now be sent to WhatsApp-users' mobile phones: "We may provide you marketing for our Services and those of the Facebook family of companies, of which we are now a part" (WhatsApp Privacy Policy, version from August 25, 2016). The change of WhatsApp's privacy policy shows that in a capitalist world, an organisation that becomes part of a capitalist corporation faces pressure to introduce strategies of commodification and capital accumulation. In the case of WhatsApp, capitalist logic resulted in the app-makers' drop of the moral claim that it does not like and favour advertising.

6.4 WORK AT GOOGLE

WORK AT GOOGLE: FUN AND GOOD FOOD?

What is it like to work at Google? In the description of its company culture, Google promises that it is fun and play to work for them. Furthermore, the food will be great and free and interesting people will come and visit the company:

> The Googleplex has grown over the years. We're fond of doing things differently, so you'll find unique places scattered around the Googleplex. Creative environments like our flexible workspace—we call it the Garage—allow Googlers to get out from the behind their desks, experiment and find inspiration for their projects. Local childcare options help working moms and dads put family first, while our gFit physical fitness programs and onsite gyms allow Googlers to improve their work-life balance (as well as their actual balance) and make up for all the great food available in our gourmet cafes. As we've grown as a company, we've expanded our local offices, offering a variety of Bay Area jobs across many skills and product areas.[19]

THE REALITY OF WORK AT GOOGLE: WORKING LONG HOURS

Is the reality of working at Google as the company promises? I tested these claims empirically.

Glassdoor is "a free jobs and career community that offers the world an inside look at jobs and companies"[20] (www.glassdoor.com/about/index_input.htm). It has collected millions of reviews of how work, interviewing and salaries are conducted in specific companies. I analysed job reviews for Google that contained a job title related to the keyword "software". This resulted in a total of 307 postings that were written between 5 February 2008 and 15 December 2012. In addition, I analysed a thread on the social news site reddit (www.reddit.com/) that asked people to report anonymously on working conditions

---

19   www.google.co.uk/about/careers/locations/mountain-view/ (accessed on 4 November 2015).
20   www.glassdoor.com/about/index_input.htm (accessed on 15 March 2013).

at Google.[21] I searched for and analysed postings in which workers talked about working time issues. This resulted in a sample of 75 postings, 10 from the reddit thread and 65 from Glassdoor.

Glassdoor calculates salary averages for certain job positions. On 17 January 2013, the average salary for a Google software engineer in the USA was \$112,915 (N = 2,744) and for a senior software engineer \$144,692 (N = 187). In November 2015, the average salary for a Google software engineer in the USA was \$127,227 (N = 4879) and for a senior software engineer \$162,171 (N = 435).[22] Given that the mean salary of an application software developer was \$105,806 in California in 2012 and \$121,646 in 2015 (data source: State of California Employment Development Department[23]), Google seems to pay salaries that are above the average.

Quite a lot of postings say nothing about working time, but rather focus on aspects such as free food. They therefore had to be excluded from the working time analysis.

In the conducted analysis, 18 postings mentioned positive aspects of working time at Google: 14 (78 per cent) of them said that they value that there are flexible working times. A minority said that there is a good work–life balance (3 = 17 per cent) or that they work a regular eight hours a day (1 = 5 per cent). Fifty-eight postings mentioned negative aspects of working times at Google. The issue that all of these 58 postings exclusively focused on in relation to working time were long working hours and a resulting bad work–life balance.

The picture that emerges from this analysis is that people tend to work long hours at Google, feel that the nice working environment that features free food, sports facilities, restaurants, cafés, events, tech-talks and other perks encourages employees to stay and work longer, that working long hours is not something that is formally dictated by the management, but that it is rather built into the company culture. There is a lot of competitive peer pressure to work long hours. One tends not to have enough time to make use of the 20 per cent work for one's own projects or has to add these hours to more than 100 per cent of working time. Google indirectly admits when describing its company culture that working days can be atypical: "Despite our size and expansion, Google still maintains a start-up culture. Google is not a conventional corporation, and our workdays are not the typical 9 to 5."[24]

I updated the analysis in 2015 by again searching on Glassdoor for reviews of software engineers' work at Google. I looked at all comments posted between the start of 2013 and November 2015. The comments about working time were very similar to the ones made in the previous analysis that I conducted at the end of 2012. There were no positive comments about the working time and work–life balance. All comments made pointed out that the long working hours and the lack of work–life balance are a downside of work at Google. Here are some example comments:

---

21 www.reddit.com/r/AskReddit/comments/clz1m/google_employees_on_reddit_fire_up_your_throw away (accessed on 26 September 2016).

22 www.glassdoor.com (accessed on 4 November 2015).

23 www.edd.ca.gov/.

24 Google culture. www.google.com/intl/en/jobs/students/lifeatgoogle/culture/ (accessed on 15 March 2013).

- "Work/life balance. What balance? All those perks and benefits are an illusion. They keep you at work and they help you to be more productive. I've never met anybody at Google who actually takes time off on weekends or on vacations. You may not hear management say, 'You have to work on weekends/vacations' but, they set the culture by doing so – and it inevitably trickles down."
- "Cons: Working long hours and work/life balance can be sometimes tricky."
- "Pros: Great food, strong rewards and great co-workers. Cons: Sometimes working long hours can be a bit of a hassle."
- "Cons: It's hard to have a life separate from work – the entire ecosystem is designed to make it more comfortable and compelling than home! Now the 'small, less interesting project' purge seems to be over, maybe let people start to experiment with their ideas in 20% time, again?"
- "You will work long hours – usually till 7pm."
- "Finally don't expect to have much of a life outside of the company."
- "Cons: Always changing, fast paced, performance focused environment. Might prove testing for people who don't manage their work/life balance well."
- "Almost 0% work-life balance."
- "I would say the main downside is that people work such long hours. Perhaps this is because the environment is so competitive."
- "Too many working hours."
- "Don't expect much of a home life at times – when you're up against it, it's expected you'll stay there all hours."
- "For one, deadlines – they are very stressful to meet. Secondly, the amount of hours is huge."
- "Quite often [you] have to work overtime."
- "Long hours, tight deadline."

In the period between 2012 and 2015 things have not changed at Google: employees enjoy the idea of working in a high-reputation company, tend to find their work tasks interesting, like the perks such as free food, but tend to complain about the long working hours, a lot of overtime and the lack of work–life balance. Labour at Google means life at Google: Google as your labour, Google as your leisure, Google as your life.

WORKING LONG HOURS? NEVER MIND, JUST SLEEP UNDER YOUR DESK, AS FORMER GOOGLE VICE-PRESIDENT MARISSA MAYER DOES . . .

Where can long working hours lead to? To the fact that employees sleep under their desks in order to maximize performance. Former Google vice-president Marissa Mayer reports about her time at Google: "Part of Google was it was the right time and we had a great technology, but the other part was we worked really, really hard. [. . .] It was 130 hour weeks. People say, 'there's only 168 hours in a week, how can you do it?' Well, if you're strategic about when you shower and sleeping under your desk, it can be done."[25] The ultimate consequence of

---

25 http://it-jobs.fins.com/Articles/SBB0001424052702303404704577309493661513690/How-Google-s-Marissa-Mayer-Manages-Burnout (accessed on 16 March 2013).

such behaviour is that there is no life outside Google – life becomes Google and is, thereby, one-dimensional.

On the one hand, Google employees tend to have long working hours and make a lot of overtime, whereas on the other hand, office hours are completely flexible and management does not see it as a negative feature if somebody does not work from 9 to 5. What is very striking about Google is a management strategy that uses soft and social forms of coercion: there is no formal contractual requirement to work overtime, but the company culture is based on project-based work, social pressure between colleagues, competition, positive identification with the job, a fun and play culture, performance-based promotion, incentives to stay for long periods at the workplace (sports, restaurants, cafés, massages, social events, lectures, etc.) and a blurring of the boundaries between work and play. As a result, employees tend to work long hours, the work–life balance is damaged and Google tends to become synonymous with life itself: life time becomes work time and time spent creating value for Google. Google is a prototypical company for the realization of what Luc Boltanski and Éve Chiapello (2005) call the new spirit of capitalism[26] – the anti-authoritarian values of the political revolt of 1968 and the subsequently emerging New Left, such as autonomy, play, freedom, spontaneity, mobility, creativity, networking, visions, openness, plurality, informality, authenticity and emancipation, are subsumed under the logic of capital.

In the early times of capitalism that Marx describes in *Capital, Volume 1* (1867), the lengthening of the working day was achieved by control, surveillance, disciplinary measures and legitimation by state laws (see Fuchs 2016c, Chapter 10, for a detailed discussion of Marx's analysis of the working day in capitalism and struggles for the reduction of working hours). The price was an increase of class struggles that pressed for a reduction in working hours. Google's main way of increasing surplus value production is also absolute surplus value production, that is the lengthening of the working day, but it takes a different approach: the coercion is ideological and social, is built into the company's culture of fun, playbour (play labour), employee services and peer pressure. The result is that the total average working time and unpaid working hours per employee tend to increase. Marx described this case as a specific method of absolute and relative surplus value production, in which the productivity and intensity of labour remain constant, whereas the length of the working day is variable: if the working day is lengthened and the price of labour (wages) remain the same, "the surplus-value increases both absolutely and relatively. Although there is no absolute change in the value of labour-power, it suffers a relative fall. [. . .] Here, [. . .] the change of relative magnitude in the value of labour-power is the result of the change of absolute magnitude in surplus-value" (Marx 1867, 663). What Marx explains in this passage is that the wages tend to relatively decrease the more hours employees work unpaid overtime, because they then create additional surplus value and profit. This can be illustrated for the case of Google: 12 of the analysed postings indicated average working hours per week, which allows calculation of an average weekly working time of 62 hours.[27]

This evidence is certainly only anecdotal, but given the large number of comments that stated that working long hours is common at Google, this result seems to be indicative. The Fair US Labor Standards Act (Section 13 (a) 17) provides an exemption from overpay

---

26 For an application of this concept to the critique of Internet ideologies, see Fisher 2010a, 2010b.

27 For example, if an employee wrote that s/he works 55–70 hours per week, then this circumstance was coded as an average of 62.5 hours.

for computer systems analysts, software engineers or similar workers if they earn at least US$27.63 an hour.

This means that if it is assumed that software engineers at Google, on average, work 22 hours overtime per week, that their salary average of US$127,227 stands for a 155 per cent employment, which means that 55 per cent of the working time is unpaid extra work time. During these 22 hours a week, the employee creates surplus value and profit for Google. If we assume 47 weeks of work per year, then the unpaid overtime lengthens work on average by 1,034 hours a year.

6.5 GOOGLE: GOD AND SATAN IN ONE COMPANY

Many popular science accounts of Google are celebratory, whereas a lot of social science analyses point out the dangers of the company. One should go beyond one-sided assessments of Google and think dialectically: Google is at the same time the best and the worst that has ever happened on the Internet. Google is evil like the figure of Satan and good like the figure of God. It is the dialectical Good Evil. Google is part of the best Internet practices because its services can enhance and support the everyday life of humans. It can help them to find and organize information, to access public information, to communicate and co-operate with others. Google has the potential to greatly advance the cognition, communication and co-operation of humans in society. It is a manifestation of the productive and socializing forces of the Internet. The problem is not the technologies provided by Google, but the capitalist relations of production that organize these technologies and shape their design. The problem is that, in providing its services, Google necessarily has to exploit users and engage in the surveillance and commodification of user-oriented data.

MARX AND THE ANTAGONISM BETWEEN PRODUCTIVE FORCES AND RELATIONS OF PRODUCTION

Marx spoke of an antagonism of the productive forces and the relations of production: "the material productive forces of society come into conflict with the existing relations of production. [. . .] From forms of development of the productive forces these relations turn into their fetters. Then begins an era of social revolution" (Marx 1859, 263).

> In the development of productive forces there comes a stage when productive forces and means of intercourse are brought into being, which, under the existing relationships, only cause mischief, and are no longer productive but destructive forces (machinery and money); and connected with this a class is called forth, which has to bear all the burdens of society without enjoying its advantages, which, ousted from society, is forced into the most decided antagonism to all other classes; a class which forms the majority of all members of society. (Marx and Engels 1846, 60)

The class relations framing Google, in which all Google users and web users are exploited by Google and in which the privacy of all of these individuals is necessarily violated by Google's business activities, are destructive forces – they destroy consumer privacy and people's interest in being protected from exploitation.

GOOGLE IN AND BEYOND CAPITALISM

Google's cognitive, communicative and co-operative potentials point beyond capitalism. The social and co-operative dimension of corporate social media anticipates and points towards "elements of the new society with which old collapsing bourgeois society itself is pregnant" (Marx 1871, 277); new relations, which mature "within the framework of the old society" (Marx 1859, 263); "new forces and new passions" that "spring up in the bosom of society, forces and passions which feel themselves to be fettered by that society" (Marx and Engels 1848, 928); "antithetical forms", which are "concealed in society" and "mines to explode it" (Marx 1857/1858, 159).

Google is a sorcerer of capitalism. It calls up a spell that questions capitalism itself: "Modern bourgeois society with its relations of production, of exchange, and of property, a society that has conjured up such gigantic means of production and of exchange, is like the sorcerer who is no longer able to control the powers of the nether world whom he has called up by his spells" (Marx and Engels 1848, 214).

At the level of the technological productive forces, we see that Google advances socialization, the co-operative and common character of the online-productive forces: Google tools are available for free, Google Documents allows the collaborative creation of documents; G+, GMail and Blogger enable social networking and communication, YouTube supports sharing videos, Google Scholar and Google Books help to establish better access to worldwide academic knowledge, and so on. These are all applications that can give great benefits to humans. But at the level of the relations of production, Google is a profit-oriented, advertising-financed money-making machine that turns users and their data into a commodity. And large-scale surveillance and the immanent undermining of liberal democracy's intrinsic privacy value are the result. Liberal democratic values thereby constitute their own limit and immanent critique. So on the level of the productive forces, Google and other web 2.0 platforms anticipate a commons-based public Internet from which all benefit, whereas at the same time Google enables a form of freedom (free service access) that works by online surveillance and user commodification that threaten consumer privacy. Google is a prototypical example of the antagonisms between networked productive forces and capitalist relations of production in the capitalist information economy (Fuchs 2008a).

"The conditions of bourgeois society are too narrow to comprise the wealth created by them" (Marx and Engels 1848, 215). Google's class character limits its immanent potentials that can enhance human life. These potentials cannot be realized within capitalism. The critical discussion that maintains that Google advances the surveillance society points towards Google's immanent limit as a capitalist company.

Google is an antagonistic way of organizing human knowledge. Marx pointed out that knowledge and other productive forces constitute barriers to capital:

> The barrier to *capital* is that this entire development proceeds in a contra-
> dictory way, and that the working-out of the productive forces, of general
> wealth etc., knowledge etc., appears in such a way that [. . .] this antithetical
> form is itself fleeting, and produces the real conditions of its own suspension.
> (Marx 1857/1858, 541–542)

Google has created the real conditions of its own suspension. It is a mistake to argue that Google should be dissolved, or to say that alternatives to Google are needed or that its services are a danger to humanity. Rather, Google would lose its antagonistic character if it were expropriated and transformed into a public, non-profit, non-commercial organization that serves the common good. Such repurposed technologies would also have to be redesigned so that they overcome the logic of individualism, competition, ranking and power inherent in them today and fully reflect the logic of the common good. Google's search algorithm would have to be turned into an open source, the principle of privileging powerful actors would have to be re-thought, buying attention via targeted ads would have to be abolished, and new ways of visualizing results beyond a focus on the first ten results would have to be found. Google permanently expropriates and exploits Internet users by commodifying their content and user data.

The best solution is the expropriation of the Google expropriator – the transformation of Google into a public search engine. Google stands at the same time for universal and particular interests on the Internet. It represents the idea of the advancement of an Internet that benefits humanity and the reality of the absolute exploitation of humanity for business purposes. Google is the universal exploiter and has created technologies that can advance a universal humanity if, in an act of universal appropriation, humans act as a universal subject and free themselves and these technologies from exploitative class relations.

6.6 GOOGLE AND THE STATE: MONOPOLY POWER AND TAX AVOIDANCE

THE CONCENTRATION OF SEARCH

Table 6.4 shows estimates of search engines' shares in globally conducted web searches.

The Herfindahl-Hirschman Index (HHI) is a mathematical method for calculating how strongly concentrated a market is. It uses the following formula (Noam 2009, 47):

$$HHI_j = \sum_{i=1}^{f} S_{ij^2}$$

f = number of firms participating in an industry j,
Sij = each firm i's market share in the industry j.
HHI < 1,000: low market concentration
1,000 < HHI < 1,8000: moderately concentrated market
HHI > 18,000: highly concentrated market

For calculating the HHI, one squares the market share of each company and then sums up all the squared values. If one does so for the global search engine market based on the data in table 6.4, then one finds that the HHI is larger than 5072, which is an indication that this online industry has an extremely high concentration.

TABLE 6.4   Share of specific search engines in the web searches conducted globally in October 2015

Search engine	Share	Squared value
Google	69.24%	4,794.18
Bing	12.26%	150.31
Yahoo!	9.19%	84.46
Baidu	6.48%	41.99
AOL	1.11%	1.23
Ask	0.24%	0.06
Other	1.48%	
	HHI:	>5,072.22

Source: Data from www.netmarketshare.com/search-engine-market-share.aspx?qprid=4&qpcustomd=0 (accessed on 5 November 2015).

MONOPOLY POWER

The European Union defines a market as concentrated if one player has a significant market power of 40 per cent or more. Given that Google's share has in 2015 been almost 70 per cent, it is no surprise that anti-trust action has been taken against the company. In 2012, the US Federal Trade Commission started investigating whether it should open an anti-trust action against Google, but ended the investigation. In spring 2015, the European Union filed anti-trust charges against Google. It argued that Google manipulated search results in favour of its own shopping services.

News Corporation's Chief Executive Robert Thomson wrote in a letter to the EU about Google:

> The company has evolved from a wonderfully feisty, creative Silicon Valley start-up to a vast, powerful, often unaccountable bureaucracy. [...] This development reflects the exponential evolution from a company that is open to one that is selectively closed and willing to exploit its dominant market position to stifle competition.[28]

News Corp is the publishing arm of Rupert Murdoch's empire. It is like many publishing companies affected by the crisis of the news industry and the shift of advertising investments from print to online. This is also one of the reasons why News Corp in 2013 was split into two companies: News Corporation (publishing) and the more profitable 21st Century Fox that is active in the TV and film industry. News Corporation sells newspapers, magazines and access to online newspapers. It is part of the content industry that sells content as a commodity. Google in contrast is part of what could be termed the openness industry that provides open access to content, but uses targeted advertising or other mechanisms for accumulating capital. That News Corp supports anti-trust action against Google shows that there is competition and a contradiction between the

---

28   News Corp. and Google in a war of words. *New York Times Online,* 18 September 2014.

capitalist content industry and the openness industry. Both compete for profits in the capitalist media industry. Large companies in these industries that are prone to high concentration tend to see their competitors' profits as a threat to their own profitability. Such rivalry is, however, one about market dominance. One media capitalist company envies the power of another monopolist and wishes to be in the latter's position. Such logic does not question the capitalist logic of media markets. Both the content and the openness industry are based on the logic of commodification and capital accumulation that harms the public sphere as such.

Google has legally challenged the EU's anti-trust charges. It argued, for example, that it cannot take advantage of its users and abuses its market dominance because there is no trade relationship between Google and its users. "The [EU's] objections fails to take proper account of the fact that search is provided for free. [. . .] A finding of abuse of dominance requires a 'trading relationship' as confirmed by consistent case law. No trading relationship exists between Google and its users."[29] The problem of this argument is that users are entangled in Google's market relations in complex ways: Google targets its users based on their search and online behaviour. It trades behavioural data as commodity. Google thereby takes advantage of users and exploits them. If it is true that it manipulates result rankings in favour of its own shopping sites, then this means that besides exploiting users, Google also wants to preferentially direct them towards specific Google-owned sites in order to shop, which further increases its profits. This means a double strategy of trying to control user-attention in such a way that they click on targeted ads, and in the case of searching for specific products to purchase are directed towards Google's own online shops.

INQUIRIES INTO TAX AVOIDANCE

Google has its European headquarters in Ireland, from where it organizes its European revenues. From Ireland profits are transferred to the Netherlands and from there to the Bermuda islands, where Google does not need to pay any corporation tax. This tax-avoidance strategy has also become known as the "Double Irish".

Companies such as Google, Amazon and Starbucks had to appear before the UK Public Accounts Committee in late 2012 to discuss the question of whether they avoided paying taxes in the UK.[30] Amazon has 15,000 employees in the UK, but its headquarters are in Luxembourg, where it has just 500 employees.[31] In 2011, it generated revenues of £3.3 billion in the UK, but only paid £1.8 million corporation tax (0.05 per cent).[32] Facebook paid £238,000 corporation tax on a UK revenue of £175 million (0.1 per cent) in 2011.[33]

29 Google says EU antitrust charges don't take into account that search is free. *The Verge*, 4 November 2015.
30 Starbucks, Google and Amazon grilled over tax avoidance. *BBC Online*. 12 November 2012. www.bbc.co.uk/news/business-20288077 (accessed on 27 September 2016).
31 Ibid.
32 Amazon: £7bn sales, no UK corporation tax. *Guardian* online. 4 April 2012. www.guardian.co.uk/technology/2012/apr/04/amazon-british-operation-corporation-tax (accessed on 27 September 2016). Google, Amazon, Starbucks: The rise of "tax sharing". BBC Online. 4 December 2012 www.bbc.co.uk/news/magazine-20560359 (accessed on 27 September 2016).
33 Should we boycott the tax-avoiding companies? *Guardian* online. Shortcuts Blog. 17 October 2012. www.guardian.co.uk/business/shortcuts/2012/oct/17/boycotting-tax-avoiding-companies (accessed on 27 September 2016).

Google has its headquarters in Dublin, but employs around 700 people in the UK.[34] Google's Managing Director for the UK and Ireland, Matt Brittin, admitted that this choice of location is due to the circumstance that the corporation tax is just 12.5 per cent in Ireland,[35] whereas in the UK it was 26 per cent in 2011.[36] Google had a UK turnover of £395 million in 2011, but only paid taxes of £6 million (1.5 per cent).[37] While large media companies only pay a very low share of taxes, governments argue that state budgets are small, implement austerity measures and as a result cut social and welfare benefits that hit the poorest in society.

In 2013, Google UK made a turnover of 642.4 million. Its Annual Report 2013[38] says that it had administrative expenses of £569.9 million, a profit before taxes of £70.8 million, paid £21.6 million in corporation tax, and made a profit after taxes of £49.2 million. Google UK's taxes paid in 2013 amount to 30.5 per cent of its declared profits before taxes, but only to 3.4 per cent of its turnover. The company argues in its 2013 financial report that there were advertising and promotional expenses of £137.0 million, which is 21.3 per cent of the total revenue, and share-based compensation expenses of £67.5 million. Given a total of 1835 employees, this amounts to an average bonus of £37,000 per employee. In the 18 months ending on 30 June 2015, Google had a turnover of £1.2 billion. Its Annual Report 2015[39] argues that it had administrative expenses of £1 billion and therefore only a profit of £106 million. It paid taxes of £14.1 million for this period, which amounts to 1.2 per cent of its turnover. The administrative expenses include fees that allow Google to escape taxation in Britain.

Facebook UK Limited says in its Annual Report and Financial Statements 2014[40] that it made a turnover of £105.0 million in 2014, had costs of sales of £1.9 million, administrative expenses of £131.6 million, made a loss of £28.5 million and paid £4,327 in corporation tax. The report says that Facebook had 362 employees in 2014 and paid £35.4 million in shares to employees, which is on average around £98,000 per employee. These data indicate that the amounts of deductions due to bonuses and "administrative expenses" have remained high in companies such as Google and Facebook.

---

34   Google and auditor recalled by MPs to answer tax questions. *Guardian* online. 1 May 2013. www.guardian.co.uk/technology/2013/may/01/google-parliament-tax-questions (accessed on 27 September 2016).
35   Starbucks, Google and Amazon grilled over tax avoidance. *BBC Online*. 12 November 2012. www.bbc.co.uk/news/business-20288077 (accessed on 27 September 2016).
36   In the UK, the main rate of corporation tax that applies for profits exceeding £1,500,000, was reduced from 28 per cent in 2010 to 26 per cent in 2011, 24 per cent in 2012, 23 per cent in 2013, 21 per cent in 2014, 20 per cent in 2015.
37   www.bbc.co.uk/news/business-20288077 (accessed on 27 September 2016).
38   Google UK Limited: Annual Report and Financial Statements. 31 December 2013. Retrieved from: https://companycheck.co.uk (accessed on 27 September 2016).
39   Google UK Limited: Report and Financial Statements. Period ended 30 June 2015. Retrieved from: https://companieshouse.gov.uk.(accessed on 27 September 2016).
40   Facebook: Annual Report and Financial Statements for the Year Ended 31 December 2014. Retrieved from https://companycheck.co.uk (accessed on 27 September 2016).

GOOGLE: "BERMUDA IS A LOW-TAX ENVIRONMENT . . ."

The House of Commons Public Accounts Committee inquired into the matter of transnational corporations' tax avoidance and put forward a very clear view of its causes in a report published in 2013:

> Google generated US $18 billion revenue from the UK between 2006 and 2011. Information on the UK profits derived from this revenue is not available but the company paid the equivalent of just US $16 million of UK corporation taxes in the same period. Google defends its tax position by claiming that its sales of advertising space to UK clients take place in Ireland – an argument which we find deeply unconvincing on the basis of evidence that, despite sales being billed from Ireland, most sales revenue is generated by staff in the UK. It is quite clear to us that sales to UK clients are the primary purpose, responsibility and result of its UK operation, and that the processing of sales through Google Ireland has no purpose other than to avoid UK corporation tax. (House of Commons Committee of Public Accounts 2013a, 5)

In an interview with the Accounts Committee's inquiry, Google's then UK Managing Director Matt Brittin admitted that this structure serves to pay low taxes. He said in the inquiry session conducted on May 16, 2013: "We talked about Bermuda in the last hearing, and I confirmed that we do use Bermuda. Obviously, Bermuda is a low-tax environment."[41] Confronted with Google's low level of corporation tax paid in the UK, its Chairman Eric Schmidt said that "people we [Google] employ in Britain are certainly paying British taxes."[42] His logic here is that Google does not have to pay taxes because its employees do.

THE "GOOGLE TAX"

Whereas social media corporations advocate openness, sharing of user data and an end of privacy in order to maximize profits, they claim closure, secrecy and financial privacy when it comes to their own global finance, profit and tax issues.

In 2015, the so-called diverted profits tax, also called the "Google tax", came in effect under the Conservative British government. The law's goal is to challenge large transnational companies' avoidance to pay taxes in Britain. The government expects additional annual tax revenues of around £350 million. The diverted profits tax law's basic idea is to tax all profits that a company makes in the UK, but diverts to a foreign affiliate or mother company with 25 per cent. Given that the corporation tax rate was 20 per cent in 2015, the idea is that a diverted profits tax rate of 25 per cent will be an incentive for companies to tax their profits in the UK and not to transfer them out of the country.

The Public Accounts Committee also reports that tax avoidance has become an industry and that there are large accountancy firms – Deloitte, Ernst & Young, KPMG and Price

---

41 www.publications.parliament.uk/pa/cm201314/cmselect/cmpubacc/112/130516.htm (accessed on 13 December 2013).

42 www.bbc.co.uk/news/business-22245770 (accessed on 13 December 2013).

WatherhouseCoopers – that together have more resources and employees than HM Revenue & Customs (HMRC) that is in charge of collecting taxes in Britain and tackling tax avoidance (House of Commons Committee of Public Accounts 2013a, 2015). HMRC has faced continuous resource cut, but has answered to the Committee's questions about its resourcing that it is adequately resourced for tackling tax avoidance (House of Commons Committee of Public Accounts 2015, 5). The Committee expresses its view that HMRC's relationship with large companies is too cozy and that it does not undertake enough prosecutions of companies and wealthy individuals' tax evasion and avoidance (House of Commons Committee of Public Accounts 2015). The Committee's argument is that HMRC is not well resourced for tackling and prosecuting tax avoidance. As a result, if large companies simply ignore paying the diverted profits tax and continue with their avoidance practice, it may be difficult to prosecute them. Critics also express the doubt that the Google tax only tackles a minor share of the actually avoided tax payments based on a narrow definition of what the law defines as profits that are "artificially shifted" abroad.[43]

Google's Vice-President for Sales and Operations in Northern and Central Europe, Matt Brittin, argued in contrast to Margaret Hodge in the Public Account Committee's inquiry that the search engine's British employees do not execute transactions or trade. The sale would rather be concluded via an online auction algorithm. He also argued that the rights for Google's platform are owned by Google Ireland and that the UK employees therefore "can't sell what they don't own" and that the "trade is executed with Ireland where the intellectual property is owned". Brittin said that Google's 17,000 engineers in the USA "create the economic value for Google", that one needs to "pay tax where the economic value is created", and in contrast to last week's session that Google Bermuda "holds the rights to our intellectual property" and that it therefore is liable for paying taxes there.[44]

Google draws from these arguments the conclusion that it is not legally obliged to pay corporation tax in the UK. The Income and Corporation Taxes Act 1988 specifies that a company not resident in the UK must pay corporation tax if it "carries on a trade in the United Kingdom through a branch or agency", which means obtaining "income arising directly or indirectly through or from the branch or agency, and any income from property or rights used by, or held by or for, the branch or agency" (§11). Location is a central issue in this definition that brings up the legal question of what it means to operate an online business in the UK.

GOOGLE'S SWEETHEART TAX DEAL

In January 2016, HMRC and Google agreed that the company should pay back taxes of £130 million for the period from 2005 to 2015. It has been estimated that the total UK profits Google made in this decade amount to £7.2 billion.[45] Tax expert Prem Sikka made the following calculations:[46] Including previously paid taxes, Google paid a total of £200 million in UK taxes in ten years. This amounts to just 2.8 per cent of its profits, although the average corporation tax

---

43   George Osborne's Google tax doesn't add up to a radical reform. *Guardian* online, 3 December 2014.
44   Amazon, Google and Starbucks accused of diverting UK profits. *Guardian* online, 12 November 2012.
45   Google's £130m tax deal lambasted as "derisory" by expert. *The Guardian Online*, 23 January 2016.
46   http://visar.csustan.edu/aaba/Googletax23Jan2016.html (accessed on 9 February 2016).

rate was around 25 per cent. Sikka commented that Google only paid £200 million instead of £1.8 billion in corporation tax: "The settlement seems to be a sweetheart deal by HMRC to collect something rather than what may be owed."

The Conservative UK chancellor George Osborn spoke of a "major success".[47] Shadow chancellor John McDonnell in contrast commented:

> This deal looks like mate's rates for taxes. It's totally unacceptable that while most of us pay the taxes expected of us – recognising that part of living in a civilised society is ensuring that everyone who can makes a fair contribution to vital public services – a major multinational can, first, pay virtually no corporation taxes for a decade, and then pay what is a tiny amount relative to its deep pockets. [...] The so-called Google tax had its sights set on precisely those major tech firms making most assiduous use of accountancy devices. [...] The Google tax is a dead letter: and if Google can so easily duck this tax, with its own Tory tax deal, what exactly will stop any other tech firm doing the same?[48]

DIGITAL LABOUR AND CORPORATE TAXATION OF INTERNET GIANTS

For setting up a targeted ad on Google, a customer first selects whether the ad will be run on Google and/or partner sites and in which countries the ad will be presented. S/he also specifies the maximum bid in the advertising space auction and the maximum amount to be spent per day. In the next step one designs the ad and identifies associated search keywords. If a user conducts a search, Google AdWords' algorithm determines which ads are associated with the entered keyword(s) and conducts an automated algorithmic auction between these ads in order to determine their screen positions. The auction price is set as the amount the customer has to pay when a user clicks on its ad. This means that in the pay-per-click mode, a payment is executed if a user who has searched for a specific keyword clicks on an ad that is targeted at him/her and associated with her/his entered keyword. Let's assume there is an ad client who resides in the UK. And the ads are targeted at users in both the UK and Ireland.

A company not resident in the UK is liable to pay corporation tax in the UK if "it carries on a trade in the United Kingdom through a branch or agency". The decisive legal question is therefore what it means to carry on a trade in the UK. A trade is an exchange of two goods or services in a specific quantitative relationship. In monetary economies commodity sales are mediated with the help of money; that is, commodities are exchanged with money in specific quantitative relationships. Google's argument that the platform and algorithm are owned in Bermuda, and that the sale of its UK advertisements therefore takes place there, is mistaken because the search engine and the auction algorithm are not sold, that is they are not commodities. A specificity of a commodity is that you can only get access to it if you pay for it.

47 George Osborne insists Google's UK tax deal is "major success". *The Guardian Online*, 28 January 2016.
48 John McDonnell, These mate's rates from George Osborne let Google off the hook on tax. *Guardian* online, 3 February 2016.

The search engine can be used by anybody without payment. It is no commodity. Whenever I type keywords into Google, I see not only results, but also advertisements. I never click on these advertisements, so Google does not earn any money from me and Google's clients who present these ads to me do not pay any money to Google for the presentation of these ads. The presentation of advertisements itself is not a commodity.

If I click on an advertisement, I am transferred to one of Google's ad clients' specific websites and give my attention to it. The ad client hopes that I will buy a product there or conduct specific activities. This means that the actual commodity trade takes place the moment I click on the targeted ad. Neither the search engine nor the auction algorithm is sold or rented, but Google rather sells my attention to the client's website as well as data about my location and interests. My search activity generates the data and my click activity and online behaviour the attention that I give to the client's website. This means that without user activities there is no commodity that Google can sell. Users create large parts of Google's value and profits by their searching, clicking and online behaviour. The sale of the users' attention as commodity is executed by the users' clicks.

Given that a user is located in the UK, which is determined and defined in the online realm by the IP address of the computer one uses, the trade between Google and its advertising client on whose ad the user clicks is executed in the UK. Google in this case carries on a trade in Britain because it trades the transaction data (my location, keywords, etc.) and user attention that are generated by a user who is located in the UK. Users are located in specific countries at specific points of time. It is therefore feasible to use the location of the user who clicks on an advertisement as a factor determining in which country Google achieves its profits. Google users are unpaid Google workers who create large parts of Google's value and profits. More and more online businesses create value by relying on users' distributed value-creating activities.

The Internet is a globally distributed technological space of information, communication and collaboration that naturally extends beyond national boundaries. Online interactions and business operations therefore tend to stretch across time zones and countries. Internet service providers, companies storing applications, users who are active by using such applications and businesses investing online are often located in different countries. Taxation operates mainly on a national basis, which creates an ambiguity between the global network and nation states that is expressed in the question of where Google and other companies should pay taxes. Internet users are not consumers or audiences, they are active creators, productive consumers (prosumers) and consumption workers, who create content, social relations, transaction data and attention. The specific nature of the Internet requires us to take users' important role into account when determining in which country a trade takes place and where an online company such as Google should be taxed.

The conclusion from the point I have tried to make is that it is feasible to assume that Google should pay taxes in the UK for all the profits it generates with the help of clicks conducted on computers that are physically located in the UK. Determining where Google would have to pay taxes on specific shares of its annual profits could either be accomplished by an exact breakdown of ad clicks per country or by dividing the overall profits by the average annual share of Google's users in specific locations. Taking this criterion seriously could help put an end to online corporations' tax avoidance strategies.

6.7 CONCLUSION

We can summarize the main results of this chapter as follows:

- Google's accumulation model is based on the exploitation and commodification of users through the economic surveillance of users' interests and activities (demographic, technological, economic, political, cultural, ecological data), communications, networks and collaborations. User data is sold for the purpose of accumulating money capital by way of targeted advertising.
- Google's internal company ideology is based on the advancement of play labour. Google does not show sensitivity for privacy issues, which contradicts its philosophy of wanting to do no evil.
- Google says that work in its offices is fun and play. Empirical analysis indicates that work at Google is highly paid and based on working long hours, which can result in a lack of work–life balance and feelings of stress.
- Many analyses of Google are undialectical. They miss that Google's activities are embedded into the capitalist antagonism between networked productive forces and class relations. Google advances the socialization of the networked productive forces and at the same time uses these as destructive forces for exploiting users.
- Google, just like other transnational corporations, including Facebook, Amazon and Starbucks, has avoided paying taxes by making use of complex company and financial networks that divert profits to countries and islands with low and no tax regimes. Whereas the capitalist economy and the Internet via which Google, Amazon and Facebook conduct their businesses are global, taxation takes place within the nation state. Neoliberal governance has advanced the possibilities of companies to avoid taxes and to not prosecute them for it, which at the time of austerity measures that result in public expenditure cuts, is especially cynical.

One should think about Google in terms of commodity logic and ideology, but at the same time one should see how, from this very logic, potential alternatives emerge. Karl Marx stressed that the globalization of production and circulation necessitates institutions that allow individuals to inform themselves about complex conditions. He said that "institutions emerge whereby each individual can acquire information about the activity of all others and attempt to adjust his own accordingly" and that these "interconnections" are enabled by "mails, telegraphs etc." (Marx 1857/1858, 161). Is this passage not the perfect description of the concept of the search engine? We can therefore say that Larry Page and Sergey Brin did not invent Google, but that rather Karl Marx was the true inventor of the search engine and of Google. But if Marx's thinking is crucial for the concept of the search engine, shouldn't we then think about the concept of a public search engine?

What could a public search engine look like? Google services could be run by non-profit organizations, for example universities (Maurer et al. 2007, 74), and be supported by public funding. A service like Google Books could then serve humanity by making the knowledge of all books freely available to all humans without drawing private profit from it. A public search engine does not require advertising funding if it is a non-profit endeavour. In this way, the exploitation and surveillance of users and the privacy violation issues that are at the heart of Google could be avoided. Establishing a public Google could lead to the dissolution of the private business of Google. This may only be possible by establishing a commons-based Internet in a commons-based society as well as re-designing Google's software services in such a way that they fully reflect the logic of the commons. Doing so will require the first steps in the class struggle for a just humanity and a just Internet to be taken. These include, for example, the suggestion to require Google by law to make advertising an opt-in option and to surveil the surveillor by creating and supporting Google watchdog organizations that document the problems and antagonisms of Google. Google's 20 per cent policy is, on the one hand, pure capitalist ideology that wants to advance profit maximization. On the other hand, it makes sense that unions pressure Google to make the 20 per cent of work time really autonomous from Google's control. If this could be established in a large company like Google, then a general demand for a reduction of labour time without wage decreases would be easier to attain. Such a demand is a demand for the increase of the autonomy of labour from capital.

Another Google is possible, but this requires class struggle for and against Google in order to set free the humanistic (cognitive, communicative, co-operative) potentials of Google by overcoming its class relations.

RECOMMENDED READINGS AND EXERCISES

For understanding Google it makes sense to engage with classical (Stuart Hall, Herbert Marcuse) and newer (Evgeny Morozov) versions of ideology critique. More exercises follow on Google's terms of service, privacy policy and financial data.

Hall, Stuart, Chas Critcher, Tony Jefferson, John Clarke and Brian Roberts. 1978. *Policing the crisis: Mugging, the state and law and order*. London: Macmillan. Chapter 9: The law-and-order society: towards the "exceptional state" (273–323).

Marcuse, Herbert. 1941/1998. Some social implications of modern technology. In *Technology, war and fascism*, ed. Douglas Kellner, 39–65. London: Routledge.

Morozov, Evgeny. 2013. *To save everything, click here: Technology, solutionism and the urge to fix problems that don't exist*. London: Allen Lane. Chapter 1: Solutionism and its discontents. Chapter 2: The nonsense of "the Internet" – and how to stop it.

Stuart Hall is one of the most important representatives of Cultural Studies. Herbert Marcuse was, besides Horkheimer and Adorno, the major representative of Frankfurt School Critical Theory. Evgeny Morozov is a writer who is critical of Internet fetishism and techno-centrism.

Ask yourself:

* What do Stuart Hall et al. describe as characteristic elements of ideologies and moral panics during the crisis of the 1970s?
* Make a list of the characteristics of technological rationality that Herbert Marcuse identifies.

- Try to define what Evgeny Morozov understands by Internet solutionism and Internet centrism. Try to find some examples in the daily press. Try to also find examples that relate to Google.
- Discuss if, and how, the notions of technological solutionism and Internet centrism are connected to Stuart Hall et al.'s analysis of ideologies in times of crisis and Herbert Marcuse's notion of technological rationality.

Read Google's latest Terms of Service and ask yourself:

- What rights do Google have in relation to the content that you create on its services?
- If you feel treated in an illegal manner by Google, how can you hold it legally reliable? Which court is responsible?
- Try to find more information on how national regulations (e.g. the ones in your home country) work for a global system like the Internet?

Read Google's latest Privacy Policy and ask yourself the following questions:

- Make a systematic and ordered list of data that Google collects about users.
- Discuss which data Google uses for targeted advertising. Find out how exactly this form of advertising works. Which data does Google use about you for targeted advertising?
- Are there mechanisms for limiting targeted advertising on Google? Do you think they are sufficient? Why? Why not?
- How do you politically assess targeted advertising?
- Are there alternative organization models for social media that do not use targeted advertising? Which ones? How do you think social media should best be organized?

Read Google's latest Proxy Statement and its Annual Financial Report. You can find both on its website under SEC filings. Ask yourself:

- How do Google present itself in these documents?
- Try to make sense of and interpret the financial data presented in the reports. What do Google's ownership structure and financial operations look like?
- According to these reports, what role does advertising play in Google's operations?

Work in groups and then present the results to the class:

- Search for videos, documents, press releases, blog posts, etc. in which Google presents itself. What kind of image does Google construct of itself? What are the major themes in the discourse? What is the role of corporate responsibility in Google's public relations?
- Search for documents, interviews, news articles, reports by critical scholars, critical journalists, civil society representatives, privacy and data protection advocates, consumer protection advocates and organizations as well as watchdog organizations that criticize the topics that Google presented in a positive light in the material you found earlier. Summarize the basic points of criticism. Compare them to how Google presents itself. Discuss which assessments you find more convincing and provide reasons for your assessments.

(Continued)

(Continued)

Work in groups and present the results to the class:

- Select a specific Internet or social media company. Try to find out how the company presents the working conditions of its employees in public discourse. Register at glassdoor.com (you have to write a review of an employer to get full access to other reviews). Collect reviews about a specific job category at your selected company. Conduct a content analysis to assess what the working conditions are like at this company.

Read the following book as discussion input:

Murphy, Richard. 2015. *The joy of tax. How a fair system can create a better society*. London: Bantam Press.

Work in groups and discuss the results in class:

- Why is taxation an important principle of the welfare state?
- Why do certain companies avoid paying taxes?
- What measures can and should be taken against companies' tax avoidance and tax evasion?

7 FACEBOOK: SURVEILLANCE IN THE AGE OF EDWARD SNOWDEN

KEY QUESTIONS

- How does Facebook's political economy work?
- How has Facebook been criticized?
- What ideologies exist on and about Facebook? How does Facebook present itself to the world? What is the reality behind Facebook ideologies?
- What are the implications of Edward Snowden's revelation of the existence of a surveillance-industrial complex in the age of social media?
- Are there alternatives to Facebook?

KEY CONCEPTS

Digital labour

Privacy

Social media and privacy

Facebook ideologies

Privacy fetishism

Privacy policy

Opt-out

Targeted advertising

Instant personalization

Commodification

Private property

Alternative social media

Surveillance-industrial complex

OVERVIEW

Facebook is the most popular social networking site (SNS). SNSs are web-based platforms that integrate different media, information and communication technologies that allow at least the generation of profiles that display information describing the users, the display of connections (connection list), the establishment of connections between users displayed on their connection lists, and communication between users (Fuchs 2009b).

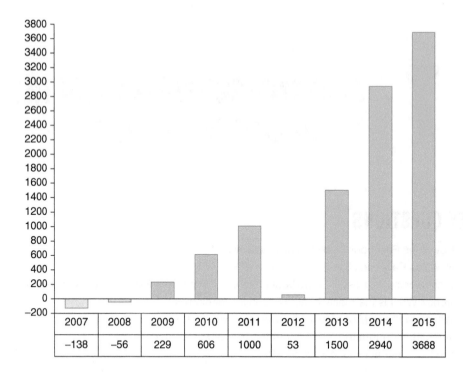

	2007	2008	2009	2010	2011	2012	2013	2014	2015
	−138	−56	229	606	1000	53	1500	2940	3688

FIGURE 7.1   The development of Facebook's profits, 2007–2015, in million US$

Source: Data from SEC filings, Form-S1 Registration Statement: Facebook, Inc., Form 10-K: Annual Reports

Mark Zuckerberg, Eduardo Saverin, Dustin Moskovitz and Chris Hughes, who were then Harvard students, founded Facebook in 2004. The movie *The Social Network* (Columbia Pictures, 2010) describes the history of Facebook as a bunch of talented Harvard students, who because of a good idea made it to be billionaires and realized the American Dream of becoming rich and famous. The movie frames the story in individualistic terms, neglecting to show that it, like most large Silicon Valley tech companies, received millions in venture capital, from Peter Thiel, Accel Partners, Jim Breyer and others, which allowed its expansion as a company. The movie advances the ideological view that in the American Dream a good idea such as Facebook can make anyone famous and popular. In reality, of course only a very small elite has the luck of becoming rich and famous precisely because others are not wealthy. In 2006, Facebook was turned from a college network into a general social network open to everyone. From then on the users of Facebook increased rapidly.

This chapter's task is to discuss the power of Facebook, the role of surveillance and implications for privacy. First, I discuss Facebook's economic development (section 7.1). Section 7.2 introduces the notion of privacy. Then, I criticize the dominant kind of analysis of Facebook privacy by characterizing it as a form of privacy fetishism (section 7.3). In section 7.4, I analyse Facebook's political economy. Section 7.5 discusses Edward Snowden's revelations. Finally, I draw some conclusions and outline strategies for alternative online privacy politics in section 7.6, and the alternative social networking site Diaspora* is introduced.

7.1 FACEBOOK'S FINANCIAL POWER

FACEBOOK'S PROFITS

Facebook became a public company on 1 February 2012. Facebook says that it generates "a substantial majority" of its "revenue from advertising": 98.3 per cent in 2009, 94.6 per cent in 2010, 85 per cent in 2011, 84 per cent in 2012, 89 per cent in 2013, 92 per cent in 2014 and 95 per cent in 2015.[1] It says: "We generate a substantial majority of our revenue from advertising. The loss of marketers, or reduction in spending by marketers with Facebook, could seriously harm our business."[2] Facebook's self-assessment of this risk shows that it is coupled to the broader political economy of capitalism: an advertising-based capital accumulation model depends on a constant influx of advertisement investments and the belief of companies that specific forms of advertisement on specific media can increase their profits. A general economic crisis that results in decreasing profits can result in a decrease of advertisement investments.

Figure 7.1 shows the development of Facebook's profits in the years 2007–2014. Since 2007, the company's annual profits have increased from US$–138 million in 2007 to US$3.69 billion in 2015. There was a slump in 2008 (–$56 million), which was due to the big economic crisis that took effect in 2008 all over the world. Since 2009, Facebook's profits have grown massively. At the same time, there was an increase of users: the number of monthly active users was 197 million in March 2009, 431 million in March 2010, 680 million in March 2011, 845 million in December 2011, 1.06 billion in December 2012, 1.23 billion in December 2013, 1.19 billion in December 2014 and 1.59 billion in December 2015.[3] On 17 May 2012, Facebook became a public company. Its shares were offered at an initial price of $38 per piece.

FACEBOOK'S ACQUISITION OF OTHER COMPANIES

Facebook's acquisition strategy is to buy other online technology providers that could either compete with Facebook directly or that allow the company to enhance its own platform and services in other technological realms. The most important acquisitions have been the mobile phone instant messaging app provider WhatsApp (2014, US$19 billion), the online video advertising company LiveRail (2014, US$500 million), Oculus Virtual Reality that produces head-mounted displays (2014, US$2 billion), the photo-sharing platform Instagram (2012, US$1 billion), the face recognition software company Face.com (2012, US$100 million), the advertising technology company Atlas (2013, US$100 million) and the mobile app developer Snaptu (2011, US$70 million).

WhatsApp and Instagram are examples of social media that competed with Facebook, which meant that Facebook became horizontally integrated in social media after acquiring the companies. The acquisitions of Atlas, Snaptu and Face.com are examples of vertical integration whereby Facebook extended its services into other realms, such as advertising, mobile phones and photo tagging. The acquisition Oculus is another example whereby

---

1 Facebook SEC filings, Form 10-K, financial years 2014+2015.
2 Ibid.
3 Ibid., 44.

Facebook extended its business into the virtual reality market. Taken together, these purchases constitute a case of conglomeration within the media technology sector.

The purchase of WhatsApp in 2014 gave Facebook a strong presence in the mobile online communication market. Instagram has become an increasingly popular social network that is focused on image sharing. Its acquisition allowed Facebook to strengthen its presence in the realm of content-sharing networks. Atlas strengthens Facebook's provision and use of targeted advertising. Snaptu developed the Facebook app for use on all mobile phones, which increased Facebook's presence on mobile phones. Face.com's photo tagging applications are direct enhancements for Facebook that take into account the fact that people use their mobile phones as digital cameras and want to share the images they take with others. Facebook's purchase of Oculus may have been driven by Google's development of Google Glass, which may have raised Facebook's fears about missing out on profits in the augmented reality market.

Whereas Instagram uses a targeted advertising-based capital accumulation model just like Facebook, WhatsApp and Oculus have different strategies: the first charges subscription/access fees, the second sells hardware. Although Facebook uses predominantly targeted advertising (i.e. the commodification of user data, as capital accumulation model), it has also created a presence in the commodification of hardware and of the access to online services. But Facebook also engages in horizontal integration: LiveRail specializes in providing video advertising, an area where YouTube is the market leader. Facebook hopes to better compete with Google's YouTube by specializing in video ads with LiveRail.

7.2 THE NOTION OF PRIVACY

DIFFERENT DEFINITIONS OF PRIVACY

Tavani (2008) distinguishes between the restricted access theory, the control theory, and the restricted access/limited control theory of privacy. The restricted access theory of informational privacy sees privacy as achieved if one is able to limit and restrict others from access to personal information. The classical form of this definition is Warren and Brandeis's notion of privacy: "Now the right to life has come to mean the right to enjoy life – the right to be let alone" (Warren and Brandeis 1890, 193). They discussed this right especially in relation to newspapers and spoke of the "evil of invasion of privacy by the newspapers". Although some scholars argue that Warren and Brandeis's (1890) paper is the source of the restricted access theory (e.g. Bloustein 1964/1984; Rule 2007, 22; Schoeman 1984b; Solove 2008, 15–16), already John Stuart Mill had formulated the same concept 42 years before Warren and Brandeis in his 1848 book *Principles of Political Economy* (Mill 1965, 938). This circumstance shows the inherent connection of the modern privacy concept and liberal ideology. The control theory of privacy sees privacy as control and self-determination over information about oneself (Tavani 2008).

Westin (1967, 7) provided the most influential control definition of privacy: "Privacy is the claim of individuals, groups or institutions to determine for themselves when, how, and to what extent information about them is communicated to others" (Westin 1967, 7). In a control theory of privacy, there is privacy even if one chooses to disclose all personal information about oneself. In an absolute restricted access theory of privacy, there is only privacy if one lives in solitary confinement without contact with others.

The restricted access/limited control theory (RALC) of privacy tries to combine both concepts. It distinguishes "between the concept of privacy, which it defines in terms of restricted access, and the management of privacy, which is achieved via a system of limited controls for individuals" (Tavani 2008, 144; see also Moor 2000).

All three kinds of definitions of informational privacy have in common that they deal with the moral questions of how information about people should be processed, who shall have access to this data, and how this access shall be regulated. All have in common the normative value that some form of data protection is needed.

CRITICISMS OF PRIVACY

Etzioni (1999) stresses that it is a typical American liberal belief that strengthening privacy can cause no harm. He stresses that privacy can undermine common goods (public safety, public health). Countries like Switzerland, Liechtenstein, Monaco and Austria have a tradition of relative anonymity of bank accounts and transactions. One sees money and private property as aspects of privacy about which the public should have no information. In Switzerland, the Federal Banking Act (§47) defines the bank secret. The Swiss Bankers' Association sees bank anonymity as a form of "financial privacy"[4] that needs to be protected and speaks of "privacy in relation to financial income and assets".[5] Most countries treat information about income and the profits of companies (except for public companies) as a secret, a form of financial privacy. The privacy-as-secrecy conception is typically part of the limited access concept of privacy (Solove 2008, 22).

Control theories and limited access/control theories of privacy, in contrast, do not stress absolute secrecy of personal information as desirable, but rather highlight the importance of self-determination in keeping or sharing personal information and the different contexts in which keeping information to oneself or sharing it is considered important. In this vein, Helen Nissenbaum argues that the "right to privacy is neither a right to secrecy nor a right to control but a right to appropriate flow of personal information" (Nissenbaum 2010, 127). In all of these versions of privacy theories, secrecy of information plays a certain role, although the exact role and desirability of secrecy is differently assessed.

The problem of secret bank accounts/transactions and the intransparency of richness and company profits is not only that financial privacy can support tax evasion, black money and money laundering, but also that it hides wealth gaps. Financial privacy reflects the classical liberal account of privacy. So, for example, John Stuart Mill formulated a right of the propertied class to economic privacy as "the owner's privacy against invasion" (Mill 1965, 232). Economic privacy (the right to keep information about income, profits or bank transactions secret) protects the rich, companies and the wealthy. The anonymity of wealth, high incomes and profits makes income and wealth gaps between the rich and the poor invisible and thereby ideologically helps legitimizing and upholding these gaps. It can therefore be considered an ideological mechanism that helps to reproduce and deepen inequality.

---

4 www.swissbanking.org/en/home/qa-090313.htm (accessed on 24 August 2011).

5 www.swissbanking.org/en/home/dossier-bankkundengeheimnis/dossier-bankkundengeheimnis-themen-geheimnis.htm (accessed on 24 August 2011).

THE CONTRADICTIONS OF PRIVACY IN CAPITALISM: FACEBOOK AND GOOGLE

Social media corporations' managers often express the view that privacy is outdated. Google's Executive Chairman Eric Schmidt said for example: "If you have something that you do not want anyone to know, maybe you should not be doing it in the first place."[6] Facebook's co-founder and CEO Mark Zuckerberg said: "The goal of the company is to help people to share more in order to make the world more open and to help promote understanding between people."[7] Schmidt and Zuckerberg argue for massive data sharing on social media. They do not, however, mention that this sharing is not primarily a sharing of data with friends and the public, but a sharing with Google and Facebook that are the largest data processors and data commodifiers in the world – which explains not just the recent rise of the term "big data", but also their interest in hiding their commercial interests ideologically behind the ideas of sharing and openness. Their claims are double-edged if one considers, for example, that Mark Zuckerberg in 2013 bought four estates that surround his house in Palo Alto's Crescent Park neighbourhood for US$30 million. He is concerned about his privacy. Zuckerberg's logic is as simplistic as it is mistaken: "Privacy is good only if you can pay for it, it is not good if it makes Facebook or Google obtain less profits."

Whereas social media corporations advocate openness, sharing of user data and an end of privacy in order to maximize profits, they claim closure, secrecy and financial privacy when it comes to their own global finance, profit and tax issues. Social media is facing an economic antagonism between users' interest in data protection and corporate tax accountability on the one side and corporations' interest in user data's transparency/commodification and corporate secrecy on the other side.

PRIVACY: A BOURGEOIS VALUE?

It would be a mistake to dismiss privacy rights as bourgeois values. Liberal privacy discourse is highly individualistic. It always focuses on the individual and his/her freedoms. It separates the public and private sphere. Privacy in capitalism can best be characterized as an antagonistic value that is, on the one side, upheld as a universal value for protecting private property, but is at the same time permanently undermined by corporate surveillance into the lives of people for profit purposes and by political surveillance for administrative purposes, defence and law enforcement. Capitalism protects privacy for the rich and companies, but at the same time legitimates privacy violations of consumers and citizens. It thereby undermines its own positing of privacy as a universal value.

PRIVACY AND SURVEILLANCE

In modern society, privacy is inherently linked to surveillance. Based on Foucault's (1977, 1994) notions of surveillance as disciplinary power, one can define surveillance as a specific kind of information gathering, storage, processing, assessment and use that involves potential or actual harm, coercion, violence, asymmetric power relations, control, manipulation,

---

6 www.youtube.com/watch?v=A6e7wfDHzew (accessed on 9 November 2015).
7 http://fuchs.uti.at/409/ (accessed on 9 November 2015).

domination or disciplinary power (Fuchs 2011a, 2011c). Surveillance is instrumental and a means for trying to derive and accumulate benefits for certain groups or individuals at the expense of other groups or individuals. Surveillance is based on the logic of competition. It tries to bring about or prevent certain behaviours of groups or individuals by gathering, storing, processing, diffusing, assessing and using data about humans so that potential or actual physical, ideological or structural violence can be directed against humans in order to influence their behaviour. This influence is brought about by coercive means and brings benefits to certain groups at the expense of others. In modern societies, privacy is an ideal rooted in the Enlightenment.

Capitalism is grounded in the idea that the private sphere should be separated from the public sphere and should not be accessible by the public, and that therefore autonomy and anonymity of the individual are needed in the private sphere. The rise of the idea of privacy in modern society is connected to the rise of the central ideal of the freedom of private owner-ship. Private ownership is the idea that humans have the right to as much wealth as they want, as long as it is inherited or acquired through individual achievements. There is an antagonism between private ownership and social equity in modern society. Many contemporary societies treat how much and what exactly a person owns as an aspect of privacy. Keeping ownership structures secret is a precautionary measure against the public questioning of or the political and individual attack against private ownership.

Capitalism requires anonymity and privacy in order to function. But full privacy is also not possible in modern society because strangers enter social relations that require trust or enable exchange. Building trust requires knowing certain data about other persons, especially in capitalist market relations. It is therefore checked with the help of surveillance procedures whether or not a stranger can be trusted. This means that companies try to find out as much as possible about job applicants, workers, consumers and competitors and that various forms of monitoring and espionage are common means for doing so. Corporations have the aim of accumulating ever more capital. That is why they have an interest in knowing as much as possible about their workers (in order to control them) and the interests, tastes and behaviours of their customers. This results in the surveillance of workers/employees and consumers.

The ideals of modernity (such as the freedom of ownership) also produce phenomena such as income and wealth inequality, poverty, unemployment, precarious living and work-ing conditions, crime and so on. The establishment of trust, socio-economic differences and corporate interests are three qualities of modernity that necessitate surveillance. Therefore, on the one hand modernity advances the ideal of a right to privacy, but on the other hand it must continuously advance surveillance that threatens to undermine privacy rights. An antagonism between privacy ideals and surveillance is therefore constitutive of capitalism.

AN ALTERNATIVE NOTION OF PRIVACY

When discussing privacy on Facebook, we should therefore go beyond a bourgeois notion of privacy. A socialist notion of privacy attempts to strengthen the protection of consumers and citizens from corporate surveillance. Economic privacy is posited as undesirable in those cases where it protects the rich and capital from public accountability, but as desirable where it tries to protect citizens from corporate surveillance. Public surveillance of the income of the rich, and of companies and public mechanisms that make their wealth transparent, is

> **Auschwitz Memorial / Muzeum Auschwitz**
> 1 November at 19:00 · ⊜
>
> On 1 November 1942 around 1:30 a.m. a transport of Jews from the
> Netherlands with 659 people arrived. After the selection all people were
> sent to the gas chambers. On the same day the 28th transport of Jews from
> Berlin arrived at the camp with 1,014 people, mostly women and old people.
> After the selection 37 women were registered in the cmap. 977 people were
> killed in the gas chambers.
>
> 👍 Like   💬 Comment   ↗ Share
>
> 248 people like this.   Top Comments ▾

FIGURE 7.2   An example of 'likes' on Facebook

desirable for making wealth and income gaps in capitalism visible, whereas privacy protection from corporate surveillance is also important. In a socialist privacy concept, the existing privacy values have to be reversed. Whereas today we mainly find surveillance of the poor and of citizens who are not owners of private property and surveillance for the protection of private property, a socialist privacy concept focuses on surveillance of capital and the rich in order to increase transparency and privacy protection of consumers and workers.

A socialist privacy concept conceives privacy as the collective right of dominated and exploited groups that need to be protected from corporate domination that aims at gathering information about workers and consumers for accumulating capital, disciplining workers and consumers, and for increasing the productivity of capitalist production and advertising. The liberal conception and reality of privacy as an individual right within capitalism protects the rich and the accumulation of ever more wealth from public knowledge. A socialist privacy concept as the collective right of workers and consumers can protect humans from the misuse of their data by companies. The question therefore is, privacy for whom? Privacy for dominant groups in regard to the ability to keep wealth and power secret from the public can be problematic, whereas privacy at the bottom of the power pyramid for consumers and normal citizens can be a form of protection from dominant interests. Privacy rights should therefore be differentiated according to the position people and groups occupy in the power structure.

7.3 FACEBOOK AND IDEOLOGY

LIKE AS FACEBOOK IDEOLOGY: "I LIKE AUSCHWITZ"

Facebook advances an ideology of liking in the form of its "Like button". For a long time, it was only possible to like pages and postings, but not to dislike them. Facebook wants to spread an affirmative atmosphere, in which people only agree and do not disagree or express discontent and disagreement. It was a common long-term criticism of Facebook that users complained about the one-dimensionality of the Like button. Zuckerberg said in 2010 that Facebook is "definitely thinking about" introducing a dislike button.[8] In

---

8 Should Facebook add a dislike button? CNN Online, 22 July 2010.

September 2015, Zuckerberg argued that Facebook is testing ways of allowing users to express empathy.[9] On 24 February 2016, Facebook introduced new reaction buttons that besides "Like" also include "Love", "Haha", "Wow", "Sad" and "Angry". It should be noted that there is a bias towards positive emotions in the design of these buttons: Four of the six buttons express positive emotions and only two negative ones ("Sad", "Angry"). Furthermore, they are organized in the form of one button called "Like": If one quickly clicks on this button, then the "Like" option is activated. Only if one puts the cursor on the "Like" button without clicking do all six buttons pop up and one can click on one of them. In this pop-up button dialogue, the "Like" symbol is closest to the cursor and the "Angry" symbol far away. This design makes "Likes" more likely than the expression of anger. Advertisers, brands and companies running campaigns on Facebook pages can therefore feel more assured that users are more likely to like than to dislike their products and postings.

Figure 7.2 shows an example of the problem of Facebook's like-ideology. Many people liked a posting on the Facebook page of the Auschwitz Memorial page that says that on 1 November 1942, 659 Durch Jews were killed in the gas chambers in Auschwitz.[10] One can assume that most of the users who pressed "like" are not neo-Nazis, but rather wanted to express their dismay about what had happened. Facebook's "happy-go-like" ideology does not allow for expressing negative emotions. It turns Auschwitz mourners into Auschwitz likers. Likes sell, whereas dislikes contain the risk that companies obtain negative assessments. So it is more profitable for Facebook, by design, to make people like companies and also to make them "like" Auschwitz. "The page of the Auschwitz Memorial Museum on Facebook is a good example to sketch out how our social discourses are now subject to Facebook's affirmation – if you want to be part of the new digital public, you need to be on Facebook" (Bunz 2013, 139).

Figure 7.3 shows an example of the re-designed reaction buttons from Coca-Cola's Facebook page. Coca-Cola is one of the world's largest corporations: In 2016 it was ranked number 83 in the Forbes list of the world's largest transnational companies. Its 2015 profits amounted to US\$ 7.3 billion.[11] Given such profits, Coca-Cola can also invest a lot into its branding, marketing and advertising strategy. It is also one of the most powerful and most visible companies on Facebook: In late 2016, Coca-Cola's Facebook page had around 100 million "Likes". In the example posting, there are 97 emotional reactions to a posting that advertises the launch of Coca-Cola Zero Sugar: 91 "Likes", 5 "Loves" and 1 "Haha". There is no negative reaction. The design and structure of brand pages on Facebook invites positive and discourages negative reactions.

THE LIBERAL FETISHISM OF PRIVACY

Liberal privacy theories typically talk about the positive qualities that privacy entails for humans or speak of it as an anthropological constant in all societies, without discussing the particular role of privacy in capitalist society. Solove (2008, 98) summarizes the positive

---

9 'Dislike' button coming to Facebook. BBC Online, 16 September 2015.
10 The "I like Auschwitz" Facebook example was introduced to academic discourse by Bunz (2013, 138).
11 Data source: Forbes 2000, 2016 list, http://www.forbes.com/global2000 (accessed on 26 September 2016).

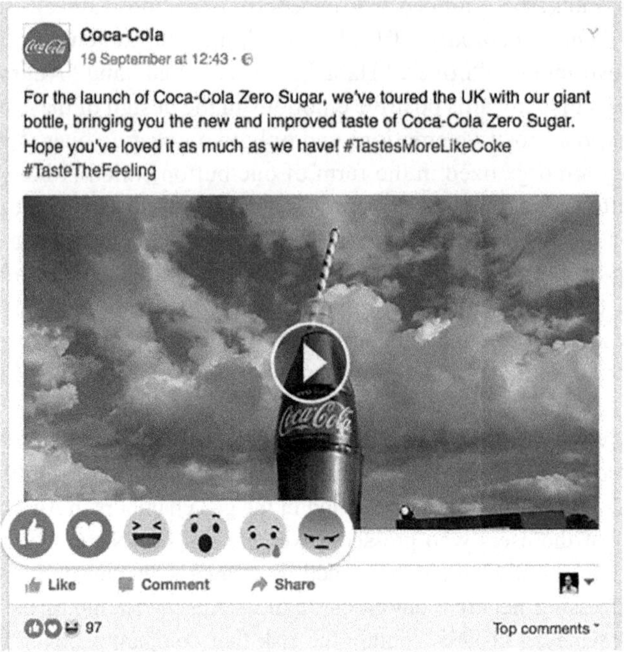

FIGURE 7.3   An example of response buttons on a Facebook page

values that have been associated with privacy in the existing literature: autonomy, counter-culture, creativity, democracy, eccentricity, dignity, freedom, freedom of thought, friendship, human relationships, imagination, independence, individuality, intimacy, psychological well-being, reputation, self-development. The following values can be added to this list (see the contributions in Schoeman 1984a): emotional release, individual integrity, love, personality, pluralism, self-determination, respect, tolerance, self-evaluation, trust.

Analyses that associate privacy with universal positive values tend not to engage with actual and possible negative effects of privacy or the relationship of modern privacy to private property, capital accumulation and social inequality. They give unhistorical accounts of privacy by arguing that privacy is a universal human principle that brings about positive qualities for individuals and society. They abstract from issues relating to the political economy of capitalism, such as exploitation and income/wealth inequality. But if there are negative aspects of modern privacy, such as the shielding of income gaps and of corporate crimes, then such accounts are problematic because they neglect negative aspects and present modern values as characteristic for all societies.

Karl Marx characterized the appearance of the "definite social relation between men themselves" as "the fantastic form of a relation between things" (Marx 1867, 167) as fetishistic thinking. Fetishism mistakes phenomena that are created by humans and have social and historical character as being natural and existing always and forever in all societies. Phenomena such as the commodity are declared to be "everlasting truths" (Marx 1867, 175, fn. 34). Theories of privacy that do not consider privacy as historical, that do not take into account the relation of privacy and capitalism or only stress its positive role, can, based on Marx, be characterized as privacy fetishism. In contrast to privacy fetishism, Barrington Moore (1984) argues – based on anthropological and historical analyses of privacy – that it is not an anthropological need "like the need for air, sleep, or nourishment" (Moore 1984, 71), but "a socially created need" that varies historically (Moore 1984, 73). The desire for privacy, according to Moore, develops only in societies that have a public sphere that is characterized by complex social relationships, which are seen as "disagreeable or threatening obligation" (72). Moore argues that this situation is the result of stratified societies in which there are winners and losers. The alternative would be the "direct participation in decisions affecting daily lives" (79).

PRIVACY FETISHISM IN RESEARCH ABOUT FACEBOOK

A specific form of privacy fetishism can also be found in research about Facebook and social networking sites in general. The typical standard study of privacy on Facebook and other social networking sites focuses on the analysis of information disclosures by users (in many cases younger users). Bourgeois scholars argue that users' privacy is under threat because they disclose too much information about themselves and thereby become targets of criminals and harassment. Such approaches see privacy as an individual phenomenon that can be protected if users behave in the correct way and do not disclose too much information. Such approaches ignore all issues relating to the political economy of Facebook, such as advertising, capital accumulation, the appropriation of user data for economic ends, and user exploitation. One can therefore characterize such analyses as Facebook privacy fetishism.

Marx has stressed that a critical theory of society does "not preach *morality* at all" (Marx and Engels 1846, 264) because human behaviour is an expression of the conditions individuals live in. Critical theorists "do not put to people the moral demand: love one another, do not be egoists, etc.; on the contrary, they are very well aware that egoism, just as much selflessness, *is* in definite circumstances a necessary form of the self-assertion of individuals" (264). The implication of uncritical analyses of social networking sites is moral condemnation and the simplistic conclusion that it is morally bad to make personal data public. Paraphrasing Marx, critical theorists, in contrast, do not put moral demands on users not to upload personal data to public Internet platforms, because they are very well aware that this behaviour is, under capitalist circumstances, a necessary form of the self-assertion of individuals. More than that, uploading and sharing information about oneself is also a form of communication, by which humans connect to others. The reason why many users do not find the idea of keeping their profiles invisible and closed infeasible is that they want to be seen and contacted by others.

One can also characterize Facebook privacy fetishism as victimization discourse. Such research concludes that social networking sites pose threats that make users potential victims of individual criminals, such as in the case of cyberstalking, sexual harassment, threats by mentally ill persons, data theft, data fraud and so on. Frequently, these studies also advance the opinion that the problem is a lack of individual responsibility and knowledge, and that as a consequence users put themselves at risk by putting too much private information online and not making use of privacy mechanisms, for example by making their profile visible for all other users. One problem of the victimization discourse is that it implies young people are irresponsible, passive and ill informed, that older people are more responsible, that the young should take the values of older people as morally superior and as guidelines, and especially that there are technological fixes to societal problems. It advances the view that increasing privacy levels will technologically solve societal problems and ignores that this might create new problems because decreased visibility may result in less fun for the users, fewer contacts and therefore less satisfaction, as well as in the deepening of information inequality. Another problem is that such approaches implicitly or explicitly conclude that communication technologies as such have negative effects. These are pessimistic assessments of technology that imply that it carries are inherent risks.

The causality underlying these arguments is one-dimensional: it assumes that technology causes only one negative effect on society. But both technology and society are complex, dynamic systems (Fuchs 2008a). Such systems are to a certain extent unpredictable and their complexity makes it unlikely that they will have only one effect (2008a). It is much more likely that there will be multiple, at least two, contradictory effects (2008a). The techno-pessimistic victimization discourse is also individualistic and ideological. It focuses on the analysis of individual usage behaviour without seeing or analysing how this use is conditioned by the societal context of information technologies, such as surveillance, the global war against terror, corporate interests, neoliberalism and capitalist development.

In contrast to Facebook privacy fetishism, Critical Internet Studies' task is to analyse Facebook privacy in the context of the political economy of capitalism.

7.4 PRIVACY AND THE POLITICAL ECONOMY OF FACEBOOK

PRIVACY AND PRIVATE PROPERTY

Karl Marx positions privacy in relation to private property. The liberal concept of the private individual and privacy would see man as "an isolated monad, withdrawn into himself. [. . .] The practical application of the right of liberty is the right of private property" (Marx 1843c, 235). Modern society's constitution would be the "constitution of private property" (Marx 1843a, 166).

For Hannah Arendt, modern privacy is an expression of a sphere of deprivation, where humans are deprived of social relations and "the possibility of achieving something more permanent than life itself" (Arendt 1958, 58). "The privation of privacy lies in the absence of others" (58). Arendt says that the relation between private and public is "manifest in its most elementary level in the question of private property" (61).

Habermas (1989c) stresses that the modern concept of privacy is connected to the capitalist separation of the private and public realms. Habermas sees privacy as an illusionary ideology – "pseudo-privacy" (157) – that in reality functions as a community of consumers (156) and enables leisure and consumption as a means for the reproduction of labour power so that it remains vital, productive and exploitable (159).

The theories of Marx, Arendt and Habermas have quite different political implications, but all three authors stress the importance of addressing the notions of privacy, the private sphere and the public by analysing their inherent connection to the political economy of capitalism. A critical analysis should not simply discuss privacy on Facebook as the revelation of personal data, but also inquire into the political economy and ownership structures of personal data on Facebook. Most contemporary analyses of privacy on web 2.0 and social networking sites neglect this dimension that Marx, Arendt and Habermas stressed. These three authors remind us that it is important to focus on the political economy of privacy when analysing Facebook.

Facebook is a capitalist company. Therefore its economic goal is to achieve financial profit. It does so with the help of targeted personalized advertising, which means that it tailors advertisements to the consumption interests of the users. Social networking sites are especially suited for targeted advertising because they store and communicate a vast amount of personal likes and dislikes of users that allow surveillance of these data for economic purposes and to identify and calculate which products the users are likely to buy. This explains why targeted advertising is the main source of income and the business model of most profit-oriented social networking sites.

Facebook uses mass surveillance because it stores, compares, assesses and sells the personal data and usage behaviour of several hundred million users. But this mass surveillance is personalized and individualized at the same time, because the detailed analysis of the interests and browsing behaviour of each user and the comparison to the online behaviour and interests of other users allow Facebook to sort the users into consumer interest groups and to provide each individual user with advertisements that, based on algorithmic selection and comparison mechanisms, are believed to reflect the users' consumption interests. Facebook surveillance is mass self-surveillance (Fuchs 2011a). Mass self-surveillance (Fuchs 2011a) is the shadow side of mass self-communication (Castells 2009) under capitalist conditions. The users' permanent input and activity is needed for this form of Internet surveillance to work. The specific characteristics of web 2.0, especially the upload of user-generated content and permanent communicative flows, enable this form of surveillance.

In order to understand the political economy of Facebook, one needs to analyse both its legal-political framework and its accumulation model.

FACEBOOK'S PRIVACY POLICY

The use of targeted advertising and economic surveillance is legally guaranteed by Facebook's privacy policy. In this section of the chapter, I will conduct a qualitative analysis of those parts of the Facebook data policy that are focused on advertising.[12]

Facebook can largely regulate itself in what it wants to do with user data because it is a company that is legally registered in Palo Alto, California, USA. Facebook's data policy is a typical expression of a self-regulatory privacy regime, in which businesses largely define themselves by how they process personal user data. The general perception in privacy and surveillance studies is that there is very little privacy protection in the United States and that the United States lags behind Europe in protecting privacy (Tavani 2010, 166; Wacks 2010, 124; Zureik and Harling Stalker 2010, 15). Also, US data protection laws only cover government databanks and, due to business considerations, leave commercial surveillance

---

12 Facebook Data Policy, version from 30 January 2015.

untouched in order to maximize profitability (Ess 2009, 56; Lyon 1994, 15; Rule 2007, 97; Zureik 2010, 351).

Facebook's terms of use and its data policy are characteristic of the liberal US data protection policies that are strongly based on business self-regulation. They also stand for the problems associated with a business-friendly self-regulatory privacy regime – if privacy regulation is voluntary, the number of organizations engaging in it tends to be very small (Bennett and Raab 2006, 171): "Self-regulation will always suffer from the perception that it is more symbolic than real because those who are responsible for implementation are those who have a vested interest in the processing of personal data." "In the United States, we call government interference domination, and we call marketplace governance freedom. We should recognize that the marketplace does not automatically ensure diversity, but that (as in the example of the United States) the marketplace can also act as a serious constraint to freedom" (Jhally 2006, 60).

Joseph Turow (2006, 83–84) argues that privacy policies of commercial Internet websites are often complex, written in turgid legalese, but formulated in a polite way. They would first assure the user that they care about his/her privacy and then spread over a long text advance elements that mean that personal data is given to (mostly unnamed) "affiliates". The purpose would be to cover up the capturing and selling of marketing data. Turow's analysis can be applied to Facebook. In another work, Turow (2011, 190) argues that targeted online advertisers create "reputation silos: flows of advertising, information, entertainment, and news designed to fit profiles about individuals and people who statistically seem similar". Consumer culture would have resulted in a shift from society-making media to segment-making media:

> Segment-making media are media that encourage small slices of society to talk to themselves, while society-making media are those that have the potential to get all those segments to talk to each other. [...] [Segment-making media allow advertisers] to search out and exploit differences between consumers. (Turow 2011, 193)

PRIVACY POLICY

Facebook wants to assure users that it deals responsibly with their data and that users are in full control of privacy controls. Therefore as an introduction to the privacy issue, it wrote: "We give you the power to share as part of our mission to make the world more open and connected."[13] Facebook uses targeted advertising in which it sells user data to advertisers: "We want our advertising to be as relevant and interesting as the other information you find on our Services. With this in mind, we use all of the information we have about you to show you relevant ads."

In its privacy policy Facebook avoids speaking of selling user-generated data, demographic data and user behaviour. It instead uses the phrase "sharing information" with third parties ("third parties we can share information with about you"), which is a euphemism for the commodification of user data. The words sharing/share appear 36 times in

---

13 www.facebook.com/privacy/explanation.php (accessed on 9 November 2015).

Facebook's data policy from January 2015, the terms sell/selling/sale/commodity not a single time.

UNAMBIGUOUS CONSENT?

There are no privacy settings on Facebook that allow users to disable advertisers' access to their data (there are only minor privacy settings relating to "social advertising" in Facebook friend communities). Facebook does not ask users whether they find targeted advertising necessary and agree to it.

Facebook in general uses targeted advertising. There is an opt-out in the advertising preferences option for Facebook's use of data from across the web (e.g. which websites a user visits and which apps s/he uses on her/his mobile phone). Even if one opts out from this option, Facebook continues to target ads based on the user's Facebook behaviour and profile data and continues to present the same amount of ads.

"If you turn off online interest-based adverts you'll still see the same number of adverts, but they may be less relevant to you."[14] Facebook assumes that its targeting algorithm can calculate and predict interests and tastes. Its strategy excludes that some users may not at all want to have their data monitored, analysed and commodified.

Users must agree to the privacy terms in order to be able to use Facebook and thereby they agree to the use of their self-descriptions, uploaded data and transaction data to be sold to advertising clients. Given the fact that Facebook is the second most used web platform in the world, it is unlikely that many users refuse to use Facebook because doing so will make them miss the social opportunities to stay in touch with their friends and colleagues, to make important new contacts, and may result in being treated as outsiders in their communities. Facebook coerces users into agreeing to the use of their personal data and collected user behaviour data for economic purposes.

If you do not agree to the privacy terms that make targeted advertising possible, you are unable to use the platform. Users are not really asked if their data can be sold to advertisers, therefore one cannot speak of user consent. Facebook utilizes the notion of "user consent" in its privacy policy in order to mask the commodification of user data as consensual. It bases its assumption on a control theory of privacy and assumes that users want to sacrifice consumer privacy in order to be able to use Facebook.

EXPLOITATION ON FACEBOOK

Based on Dallas Smythe's (1977, 1981/2006) notion of the audience commodity, the concept of the Internet prosumer commodity was introduced in section 5.3 of this book. Internet prosumer commodification in combination with economic surveillance that enables targeted advertising is at the heart of many commercial social media's capital accumulation strategy.

COMMODIFICATION AND DIGITAL LABOUR ON FACEBOOK

Surveillance on Facebook is surveillance of prosumers, who dynamically and permanently create and share user-generated content, browse profiles and data, interact with others,

---

14   Facebook adverts settings (accessed on 9 November 2015).

join, create and build communities, and co-create information. The corporate web platform operators and their third-party advertising clients continuously monitor and record personal data and online activities; they store, merge and analyse collected data. This allows them to create detailed user profiles and to know about the personal interests and online behaviours of the users. Facebook sells its prosumers' data as a commodity to advertising clients. Money is exchanged for the access to user data that allows economic surveillance of the users. The exchange value of the Facebook data commodity is the money value that the operators obtain from their clients. Its use value is the multitude of personal data and usage behaviour that is dominated by the commodity and exchange value form. Corporations' surveillance of the prosumers' permanently produced use values, that is personal data and interactions, allows targeted advertising that aims at luring the prosumers into consumption and at manipulating their desires and needs in the interest of corporations and the commodities they offer.

First, corporate platform operators commodify Facebook users' data. The latter are sold as commodities to advertising clients. Second, this process results in the users' intensified exposure to commodity logic. They are double objects of commodification: the products of their subjectivity are commodities and through this commodification their consciousness becomes, while online, permanently exposed to commodity logic in the form of advertisements. Most online time is advertising time. On Facebook, targeted advertising makes use of users' personal data, interests, interactions, information behaviour, and also interactions with other websites. So while you are using Facebook, it is not just you interacting with others and browsing profiles – all of these activities are framed by advertisements presented to you. These advertisements come about by permanent surveillance of your online activities. Such advertisements do not necessarily represent consumers' real needs and desires because the ads are based on calculated assumptions, whereas needs are much more complex and spontaneous. The ads mainly reflect marketing decisions and economic power relations: the ads do not simply provide suggestions to buy certain commodities, they provide suggestions by companies that have enough money for buying advertising for specific commodities, whereas other companies or non-profit organizations cannot purchase ads, which shows how selective and driven by financial power advertising actually is.

7.5 EDWARD SNOWDEN AND THE SURVEILLANCE-INDUSTRIAL COMPLEX

SURVEILLANCE

David Lyon (2015, 3) defines surveillance as "any systematic and routine attention to personal details, whether specific or aggregate, for defined purpose. That purpose, the intention of the surveillance practice, may be to protect, understand, care for, ensure entitlement, control, mange or influence individuals or groups". There are several problems which such a general definition of surveillance (Fuchs 2011c, 2013a). When a Nazi henchman monitors Jews in Auschwitz who are sent to the gas chamber on the next day, then given this definition, this is a form of surveillance. But also operating a babyphone that monitors a sleeping baby, an electrocardiogram or an earthquake detection system are seen as forms of surveillance. Such a broad concept of surveillance is not suited for a critical theory of society. For countering this tendency, we need a purely negative concept of surveillance, in which surveillance is a specific form of control that forms one dimension of domination, exploitation, class, capitalism, patriarchy, racism, and similar negative phenomena (Fuchs 2011c, 2013a). Just like Adorno (1973/2003) was calling for a negative dialectic, we need based on Foucault and Marx negative surveillance studies. A problem of the general understanding of surveillance is also that it makes surveillance categorically synonymous with information collection and processing so that no differentiation can be drawn between surveillance theory and information theory. Thomas Mathiesen (2013, 17–18, 23) therefore draws a distinction between information systems and surveillance systems. Surveillance stems etymologically from the French term "*surveiller*", which means to oversee and watch over. Watching *over* implies that there is a social hierarchy between persons, in which one person exerts power over the other.

Michel Foucault did not give a clear definition of surveillance, but he characterized it as a negative and repressive form of power. For Foucault, surveillance is a form of disciplinary power. Disciplines are "general formulas of domination" (Foucault 1977, 137). Disciplinary power includes penal mechanisms (177), it encloses humans into institutions such as schools, orphanages, training centres, the military, towns, factories, prisons, reformatories, houses of correction, psychiatry, hospitals, asylums and so on in order to control their behaviour, to partition and rank them (141–149; see also 1994, 57–58, 75–76) and to normalize, punish, hierarchize, homogenize, differentiate and exclude (Foucault 1977, 183–184). Foucault argues that in order to secure domination, disciplines make use of certain methods such as the hierarchical observation, the normalizing judgement and the examination (170–194). Surveillance is based on "a principle of compulsory visibility" that is exercised through the invisibility of disciplinary power (187), it "must see without being seen" (171), is "capable of making all visible, as long as it could itself remain invisible" (214), it is a "system of permanent registration" (196) in which "all events are recorded" (197), a "machine for dissociating the see/being seen dyad" (202).

Surveillance is the systematic collection and use of information in order to dominate individuals and groups. It can operate as a mere threat and be overt in order to discipline behaviour. Or it can be covert so that it is unknown that it takes place. In any case it is a form of domination, that is a social relation, in which one group or individual derives power (money, control, influence, reputation) at the expense of others. Marx had the insight that accumulation is a key principle of modern society. Generalizing Marx's analysis of capitalism, we can say that modern domination aims at the accumulation of money (economic power), decision-power (political power) and reputation/definition-power (cultural and ideological power). Combining Marx and Foucault, we can say that surveillance is a systematic collection and use of information for the accumulation of power (see also Fuchs 2013a).

CORPORATE AND STATE SURVEILLANCE

The dominant forms of surveillance in modern society are a) corporate surveillance of workers, consumers, applicants and competitors, and b) state surveillance of citizens as well as of perceived internal and external enemies of the state. Corporate and state surveillance are also interlinked: the state may collaborate with private security technology and service providers. It can obtain access to data gathered by corporations. Corporations' economic surveillance activities are to certain degrees enabled and constrained by state laws. The regulation of surveillance refers, for example, to questions like: Are employers allowed to use CCTV camera surveillance at workplaces for monitoring employees? Should the surveillance of consumer behaviour for advertising purposes be legal or illegal? What is the penalty for industrial espionage? Should it be legal that employers search for data about job applicants and base their employment decisions on these data?

Economic surveillance has a relation to the state's role in internal and external defence. Internal defence involves activities like policing, the prison system and intelligence activities directed towards a state's citizens. Policing relates to property questions by guaranteeing the protection of private property. Property crime is one specific type of crime. Surveillance of citizens is used for locating people who have committed property crimes and increasingly also for pre-emptive purposes, which raises questions about the legal principle of the presumption of innocence: all citizens are considered to be potential criminals until proven not guilty by pre-emptive surveillance methods. The prison system makes use of surveillance of criminals in order to hinder them escaping. Internal intelligence makes use of surveillance technologies for monitoring the activities of citizens and political groups that are under suspicion of actually or potentially questioning the foundations of the state system. The history of the working-class movement has also been accompanied by a history of surveillance of this movement. Examples are the surveillance and control of trade unionists, communists and social democrats in the McCarthy era, and the systematic surveillance of socialist and civil rights organizations in the US COINTELPRO (Counter Intelligence Programme). Surveillance of socialist movements and for the defence of property rights has a relatively direct link to the capital accumulation cycle, although it is part of the political system. It protects from disruption of the capital accumulation cycle by protests or the disappearance of resources.

External defence and intelligence is related to the opposition of the state to external threats by military means. Surveillance here is the surveillance of other nation states, institutions and political groups in other countries. It serves predominantly the defence of the existence of the nation state. Any war or external threat is always a threat to the whole societal system. It is also a threat to the capitalist economy. So surveillance for reasons of external defence in capitalist societies is also a defence of the capitalist economy, just as it is a defence of the state, the educational system, the health care system, the welfare system and so on. It indirectly serves capitalist purposes.

It is important to stress that the state is not always a "class state" that serves capitalist interests by conducting and enabling surveillance. Given the right kind of government, states can also pass legislation that protects consumers' and employees' privacy from surveillance that serves corporate interests. The state, for example, has the power to potentially ban or considerably limit all workplace surveillance and consumer surveillance, and to thereby strengthen privacy rights. This requires, however, consumer- and worker-oriented politics.

THE SURVEILLANCE STATE

The security industry has especially been growing since 9/11 (Lyon 2003, 2007), which resulted in an increased interest in the application of surveillance technologies that is guided by the technological-deterministic belief that crime and terrorism can best be stopped by creating a surveillance society. David Lyon (2007, 184) suggests that the welfare state is being superseded by "the safety state". There is an increased focus on law and order politics. 9/11 has resulted legally in the definition of "states of exception", "most notably for preemptive war, domestic surveillance, and the torture of terrorist suspects; and practically" in "the establishment of elaborate surveillance rituals for citizens (for example, airport screening) and the outsourcing of lucrative security contracts to private industries" (Monahan 2010, 6). "Capturing terrorists before they strike became an obsessive goal of many governments after 9/11" (Lyon 2003, 52). Since 9/11, also European security politics have "been mainly oriented towards the right for governments to strengthen coercive and surveillance security measures" (Bigo 2010, 265–266).

Stuart Hall et al. (1978) describe how a moral panic about street robbery ("mugging") developed in the UK in the 1970s. They argue that this panic must be seen in the context of the crisis of the mid-1970s. Hall et al. (1978) stress that the moral panics of the 1970s were used for creating and enforcing law and order politics that not only tackled criminals, but especially the working class, the black working class and social movements. The result was the rise of what Hall calls a "law & order society". In the political constellation characterizing the first decade of the twenty-first century, something comparable happened: 9/11 was indicative of a crisis of the hegemony of Western thought that was questioned by people and groups in Arab countries that put religious ideology against Western liberal and capitalist ideology.

The "war against terror", the security discourse and the intensification of surveillance resulted in a political crisis, in which war and terrorism tend to reinforce each other mutually, which results in a vicious cycle that intensifies hatred and conflict. Financialization and neoliberalism made capitalism more unjust (which constitutes a social crisis) and also crisis-prone, which resulted in a new world economic crisis that started in 2008. Western societies have faced a multidimensional crisis in the first two decades of the twenty-first century. One of the ideological responses was to erect a surveillance society that is based on law and order politics and omnipresent surveillance. This new surveillance not only tackles criminals and terrorists, but erects a visibility of everyone and everything that also allows (actually or potentially) the control of political protests (that are on the rise in situations of crisis), which not only undercuts the liberal values of freedom of speech and assembly and thereby shows how modern society contradicts and limits its own values on which it is built.

Thomas Mathiesen (2013, 61) argues that three "new enemy images replaced the enemy image of communism when this vanished or lost its impetus towards the end of the 1980s": "the struggle against terrorism, the struggle against organized crime, and the effective control of the EU's common external borders". The exaggerated public presentation of these enemy images would have resulted in a constant extension and intensification of surveillance. Key terrorist events would have resulted in law and order politics and more surveillance as responses, which, however, would only have prevented further terrorism in single cases. Mathiesen argues for strengthening human security in the form of democracy and social security as the best antidotes to violence. Writing several months before Edward Snowden made his revelations in June 2013, Mathiesen (2013, 155) argued that the "development of mass surveillance systems covering 'everyone' may be viewed as a final surveillance stage".

SNOWDEN'S REVELATIONS AND THE SURVEILLANCE SOCIETY

Surveillance is not just a necessary feature of capitalism, but also an inherent feature of modern society and modern politics: it involves activities of state institutions such as secret services and the police that monitor criminals, political activists, enemies of the state, as well as companies that track workers, customers and competitors. The purpose is not only to collect data, but to use this data to exert social control. The rise of consumer culture and computing have in the twentieth century brought about some qualitative changes of surveillance such that it has become more networked, ubiquitous, focused on everyday life and consumption, and organized in real time.

In June 2013, Edward Snowden revealed with the help of the *Guardian* the existence of large-scale Internet and communications surveillance systems such as Prism, XKeyscore and Tempora. According to the leaked documents, the National Security Agency (NSA), a US secret service, in the PRISM programme obtained direct access to user data from seven online/ICT companies: AOL, Apple, Facebook, Google, Microsoft, Paltalk, Skype and Yahoo![15] The Powerpoint slides that Edward Snowden leaked refer to data collection "directly from the servers of these U.S. Service Providers".[16] Snowden also revealed the existence of a surveillance system called XKeyScore that the NSA can use for reading emails, tracking web browsing and users' browsing histories, monitoring social media activity, online searches, online chat, phone calls and online contact networks, and following the screens of individual computers. According to the leaked documents, XKeyScore can search both meta-data and content data.[17] The documents that Snowden leaked also showed that the Government Communications Headquarters (GCHQ), a British intelligence agency, monitored and collected phone and Internet communications data from fibre optic cables and shared such data with the NSA.[18] According to the leak, the GCHQ, for example, stores phone calls, emails, Facebook postings and the history users' website access for up to 30 days and analyses these data.[19] Further documents indicated that, in co-ordination with the GCHQ, also intelligence services in Germany (Bundesnachrichtendienst, BND), France (Direction Générale de la Sécurité Extérieure, DGSE), Spain (Centro Nacional de Inteligencia, CNI) and Sweden (Försvarets radioanstalt, FRA) developed similar capacities.[20]

David Lyon (2015, 18–20) gives a comprehensive overview of the surveillance practices that Snowden uncovered by distinguishing three levels of surveillance: the surveillance of a) data from physical cables that transport communications data, b) user data stored by communications companies such as AOL, Apple, Facebook, Google, Microsoft, PalTalk, Skype or Yahoo!, c) data on individual computers with the help of spyware. Computer-mediated communication requires the transmission of data from one computer to at least one other via a network. So individual computers are involved that connect via networks. Software

---

15 NSA Prism program taps in to user data of Apple, Google and others. *Guardian* online. 7 June 2013. www.theguardian.com/world/2013/jun/06/us-tech-giants-nsa-data (accessed on 27 September 2016).
16 Ibid.
17 XKeyscore: NSA tool collects "nearly everything a user does on the internet'. *Guardian* online. 31 July 2013. www.theguardian.com/world/2013/jul/31/nsa-top-secret-program-online-data (accessed 26 September 2016).
18 GCHQ taps fibre-optic cables for secret access to world's communications. *Guardian* online. 21 June 2013. www.theguardian.com/uk/2013/jun/21/gchq-cables-secret-world-communications-nsa?guni=Article:in%20body%20link (accessed 26 September 2016).
19 Ibid.
20 GCHQ and European spy agencies worked together on mass surveillance. *Guardian* online. 1 November 2013. www.theguardian.com/uk-news/2013/nov/01/gchq-europe-spy-agencies-mass-surveillance-snowden (accessed 26 September 2016).

applications that run on the Internet and/or individual computers enable online communication. Part of the data also tends to be stored online on servers ("in the cloud"). The surveillance-industrial Internet complex that Snowden uncovered is capable of conducting surveillance at all levels of computer-mediated communication: individual computers, communications companies' servers and network cables. The conducted surveillance is, according to Lyon (2015, 80–89), automated, anticipatory (the use of predictive analytics for predicting who could be or become a terrorist, which puts innocent people at risk of being suspected of terrorism, undermines the liberal principle of the presumption of innocence and relies on algorithms that are error-prone) and adaptive (data and meta-data generated in certain contexts are put together, repurposed and decontexutalized).

Various scholars have worked on the critical analysis of Internet and social media surveillance (Andrejevic 2007, 2013; Fuchs and Trottier 2015; Fuchs et al. 2012; Mathiesen 2013; Trottier 2012, 2014; Trottier and Fuchs 2015). Given the intensification and extension of surveillance and law and order politics and surveillance ideology since 9/11 (Ball and Webster 2003; Chomsky 2011; Lyon 2003; Mathiesen 2013; Rockmore 2011), Snowden's revelations did not come as a surprise. The Internet surveillance that the NSA and other secret services conduct are forms of Deep Packet Inspection surveillance that have been analysed before Snowden (Fuchs 2013b). What came as a surprise for many, however, was the extent and dimensions Internet surveillance has taken on. We can therefore without a doubt assert that the twenty-first century information society is not just a capitalist society, but also a mass surveillance society.

THE SURVEILLANCE-INDUSTRIAL COMPLEX AND THE POWER ELITE

Edward Snowden's revelations about the existence of surveillance systems such as Prism, XKeyScore and Tempora have shed new light on the extension and intensity of state institutions' Internet and social media surveillance. The concept of the military-industrial complex stresses the existence of collaborations between private corporations and the state's institutions of internal and external defence in the security realm. C. Wright Mills argued in 1956 that there is a power elite that connects economic, political and military power:

> There is no longer, on the one hand, an economy, and, on the other hand, a political order containing a military establishment unimportant to politics and to money-making. There is a political economy linked, in a thousand ways, with military institutions and decisions. [...] there is an ever-increasing interlocking of economic, military, and political structures. (Mills 1956, 7–8)

Edward Snowden has confirmed that the military-industrial complex contains a surveillance-industrial complex (Hayes 2012), in which social media are entangled: Facebook and Google each have more than 1 billion users and have likely amassed the largest collection of personal data in the world. They and other private social media companies are first and foremost advertising companies that appropriate and commodify data on users' interests, communications, locations, online behaviour and social networks. They make profit out of data that users' online activities generate. They continuously monitor usage behaviour for this economic purpose. Vincent Mosco (2014) speaks of a military information complex (7) in which surveillance capitalism and the surveillance state interact (10): both capitalism and the state engage in mass surveillance of communications so that big data is "big surveillance" (146). David Lyon (2015, 13) argues that Snowden's revelations show that "surveillance is carried out by government and commercial agencies acting together. [...] Big government and big business dominate these processes".

Since 9/11 there has been a massive intensification and extension of surveillance that is based on the naïve technological-deterministic surveillance ideology that monitoring technologies, big data analysis and predictive algorithms can prevent terrorism. The reality of the murder of a soldier that took place in the South-East London district of Woolwich in May 2013 shows that terrorists can use low-tech tools such as machetes for targeted killings. High-tech surveillance will never be able to stop terrorism because most terrorists are smart enough not to announce their intentions on the Internet. It is precisely this surveillance ideology that has created intelligence agencies' interest in the big data held by social media corporations. Evidence has shown that social media surveillance not just targets terrorists, but has also been directed at protestors and civil society activists.[21] State institutions and private corporations have long collaborated in intelligence, but the access to social media has taken the surveillance-industrial complex to a new dimension: it is now possible to obtain detailed access to a multitude of citizens' activities in converging social roles conducted in converging social spaces.

Yet the profits made by social media corporations are not the only economic dimension of the contemporary surveillance-industrial complex: the NSA has subcontracted and outsourced surveillance tasks to approximately 2000 private security companies[22] that make profits by spying on citizens. Booz Allen Hamilton, the private security company that Edward Snowden worked for until recently, is just one of these firms that follow the strategy of accumulation-by-surveillance. According to financial data,[23] it had 22,500 employees in 2015 and its profits increased from US$25 million in 2010 to US$84 million in 2011, US$239 million in 2012, US$219 million in 2013, US$232 million in 2014 and US$233 million in 2015. Surveillance is big business, both for online companies and those conducting the online spying for intelligence agencies.

Users create data on the Internet that is private, semi-public and public. In the social media surveillance-industrial complex, companies commodify and privatize user data as private property, and secret services such as the NSA driven by a techno-determinist ideology obtain access to the same data for trying to catch terrorists that may never use these technologies for planning attacks. For organizing surveillance, the state makes use of private security companies that derive profits from organizing the monitoring process.

User data is in the surveillance-industrial complex first externalized and made public or semi-public on the Internet in order to enable users' communication processes, then privatized as private property by Internet platforms in order to accumulate capital, and finally particularized by secret services who bring massive amounts of data under their control that are made accessible and analysed worldwide with the help of profit-making security companies.

---

21 Spying on Occupy activists. *The Progressive Online*. June 2013. http://progressive.org/spying-on-ccupy-activists (accessed on 27 September 2016).

22 A hidden world, growing beyond control. *Washington Post Online*. http://projects.washingtonpost.com/top-secret-america/articles/a-hidden-world-growing-beyond-control (accessed on 27 September 2016).

23 Booz Allen Hamilton. SEC filings, form 10-K for various years.

With the rise of digital media and networked communication technologies, it has become easier for everyday people to conduct surveillance. Everyone can easily turn a mobile phone into a tool for audio-visual surveillance. It is, however, a mistake to assume that surveillance thereby has become "democratic" or "participatory". The Snowden case shows that big corporations and big state institutions dominate surveillance. They have more powerful surveillance technologies than others and legal rights that enable them access to data that others have no access to. So although information technologies have become more decentralized and networked, big government and big corporations understand how to use them for big surveillance and big data surveillance.

Thomas Mathiesen therefore argues that the polyoptical communication of social media and networked media, in which there are multiple sources of information, have not abolished panoptic surveillance: "But the panoptical form has not disappeared. Power is still around. The blossoming of the several/many ways profile, the Polyoptical profile, has not supplanted the one-way phase, but has merged with – and you might say improved on – the one-way phase" (Mathiesen 2013, 44). In the surveillance-industrial complex, the world's most powerful state institutions have collaborated with the world's most powerful communications companies to implement totalitarian surveillance systems. It is a system that centralizes control by monitoring decentralized technologies with multiple technologies and networking the obtained data. The result is centralized surveillance that as whole is a sum that is larger than its parts.

DEEP PACKET INSPECTION SURVEILLANCE TECHNOLOGIES

The Internet surveillance technologies, whose existence Snowden uncovered, are so-called deep packet inspection surveillance technologies. Data transmission on the Internet is based on the TCP/IP Protocol (Transmission Control Protocol/Internet Protocol). TCP/IP is an application of the so-called Open-Systems Interconnection (OSI) Model of network data transimission to the realm of the Internet. Whereas the OSI Model consists of seven dimensions of transmission, TCP/IP maps these seven dimensions to five (Comer 2004; Stallings 1995).

Each device (like a computer or a printer) in a network connected to the Internet has a specific IP address. In the Internet protocol version 4 (IPv4), each IP address is a unique 32-bit long identifier (such as 170.12.252.3). For enlarging the available IP address space, the identifier length has been increased to 128 bit in version 6 of the Internet protocol (Ipv6). In order for data to be transmitted over the Internet, a source and destination IP address are needed. If a user, for example, searches for data on Google, he enters a search keyword into the Google search box. This is at the application level.

At the TCP level, the Transmission Control Protocol (TCP) takes the data, adds a communication port number (an address, by which the application is addressed) and breaks the data into packets. TCP identifies ports, the sequence number of a packet and a checksum and provides a reliable transport service (Comer 2004, 386). At the IP level, the IP address of the destination is determined as well as the routing over the Internet are determined. The Internet Protocol (IP) "specifies addressing: IP divides each Internet address into a two-level hierarchy: the prefix of an address identifies the network to which the computer attaches, and the suffix identifies a specific computer on the network" (Comer 2004, 301). At the lower levels, the data is transmitted. The data is routed over the various routers of the Internet until it finally arrives in our example in Google's network, where it is treated in the opposite sequence (from the lowest level to the highest layer) so that data that correlates with the search query is generated and is then in the same way sent back to the user who requested the information.

A TCP/IP packet is a "small, self-contained parcel of data sent across a computer network. Each packet contains a header that identifies the sender and recipient, and a payload area that contains the data being sent" (Comer 2004, 666). The payload is "the data being carried in a packet" (667), the header contains data like the network address of source and destination. In the TCP/IP protocol that the Internet uses, the packet is called an IP datagram. It consists of "a header that identifies both the sender and receiver and a payload area that contains the data being carried" (658).

Deep packet inspection (DPI) surveillance technologies are communications surveillance tools that are able to monitor the traffic of network data that is sent over the Internet at all seven layers of the OSI Reference Model of Internet communication, which corresponds to the five layers of the TCP/IP Protocol. This means that DPI surveillance includes the surveillance of Internet content data. Important features of DPI are the recognition of objects on the network that may trigger notification and manipulation (Mueller et al. 2012).

THE SURVEILLANCE-INDUSTRIAL COMPLEX

The events of 9/11 have resulted in "the misguided and socially disruptive attempts to identify terrorists and then predict their attacks" (Gandy 2009, 5).

> In this generalized control society, governed by the managerial model, the ability to anticipate individual behaviour, identify the probability of a specific behaviour and construct categories based on statistical frequency is the common thread among the "styles" of marketing specialists, the 'scores' of financiers and the 'profiles' of the police. (Mattelart 2010, 184)

Policing looks for security by algorithms in a world of high insecurity. It advances a fethishism of technology – the belief that crime and terrorism can be controlled by technology. Technology promises an easy fix to complex societal problems. This explains the results that the security industry tends to justify the selling of surveillance technologies, such as DPI, with reference to the ideological assumption that more surveillance is needed for fighting crime and terror.

The post-9/11 situation has resulted not only in the intensification of surveillance (Lyon 2003), but at the same time in the growth of the security industry. DPI Internet surveillance as well as communication surveillance must be placed in the context of the post 9/11 moral panic about terrorism, the rise of a security-industrial complex, the new imperialistic vicious cycle of war and terrorism, and the neoliberal politics of privatization and commodification of everything.

The interconnection of state surveillance and corporate surveillance that is expressed in examples such as DPI surveillance must be seen in the context of the rise of neoliberal governmentality that has generalized the principles of markets, competition, the enterprise, commodification, individual responsibility and the ideology of the homo economicus to large realms of society. The capitalist economy has thereby become an important principle that governs the life and conduct of populations and interacts with other apparatuses of government such as the state. Surveillance in the climate of neoliberalism has taken on commercial forms and become a central principle of consumer culture. After 9/11, Western states tried to erect panoptic surveillance mechanisms in order to control and gain insights into the world population's communication based on the naïve belief that technological methods of surveillance can prevent the societal problem of terrorism. The context of these surveillance state endeavours is the situation of neoliberal governmentality, which requires that states gain access to privately gathered data in order to build a panopticon that makes citizens' communicative activities visible for the state. The visibility erected by companies is coupled to state activities. The results have been policies like the EU's Data Retention Directive that requires EU Internet service providers and telecommunications companies to store identification and connection data of all users of phones and the Internet so that the police can gain access to data about suspected terrorist or criminal activities. Surveillance after 9/11 has acquired its own specific form of political economy that connects economic surveillance and state surveillance.

"The surveillance *state* [...] now uses the dispersed systems and devices of surveillance *society*" (Lyon 2003, 37). Foucault uses the notion of governmentality for non-state forms of governing. In policing, governing the population has taken on a new governmentality regime that is based on the access of the state to surveillance data gathered by private actors and the state use of surveillance technologies produced by the capitalist security industry. The state–capital nexus is a central feature of the contemporary political economy of surveillance.

Ben Hayes (2009, 2010) speaks in this context of the emergence of the security-industrial complex. He argues that there is a "close bond between corporate and political elites in the homeland-security sector" and that on an ideological level one finds "the inherently neocon-servative appeal to the defence of the homeland" (Hayes 2010, 148).

> Neocon ideology is centred upon the "right to limitless profit-making", which is at the very heart of the EU's desire to create a lucrative Homeland Security industry. The EU's security policies are premised on the neocon philosophy of global policing and intervention in failed states to both pre-empt "threats" to security and further the spread of the free market and western-style democracy around the world. (Hayes 2009, 7)

The security-industrial complex on the one hand wants to make a business out of develop-ing military and surveillance technologies, and on the other hand advances the large-scale application of surveillance technologies and the belief in managing crime, terrorism and crises by technological means. DPI Internet surveillance is part of this political-economic complex that combines profit interests, a culture of fear and security concerns, and surveillance technologies.

7.6 CONCLUSION

We can summarize the main results of this chapter as follows:

* The modern concept of privacy is a highly individualistic ideology that legitimates pri-vate property relations and social inequality. It is a universal Enlightenment ideal that finds its own limit and its critique in capitalism's immanent tendencies for the surveil-lance of employees and consumers in the economy and the surveillance of citizens by the state that enable the accumulation of money capital and power.

- Facebook's privacy policy is the legal mechanism that enables prosumer exploitation. It is complex, an expression of the self-regulatory US privacy regime and sugar-coats the surveillance of users' personal data.
- Facebook's capital accumulation model commodifies the digital labour of users.
- Edward Snowden has revealed that Facebook and other communications corporations are entangled in a surveillance-industrial complex that is driven by the combination of the corporate commodification and state surveillance of big data.

ELLO: A SELF-PROCLAIMED "ALTERNATIVE" TO FACEBOOK

In 2014, the social network Ello presented itself as alternative to Facebook and to targeted advertising ("simple, beautiful & ad-free"), which attracted users and made it the 6,112th most accessed website in the world on 4 October 2014.[24] On 10 February 2016, it had lost some popularity and was ranked at position 19,608.[25] In February 2015, the news platform Vice asked: "Who the hell is still using Ello?"[26] Ello's capital accumulation model was to sell special features. Venture capital firm Fresh Tracks invested around US$435,000 into Ello in 2014. Ello in the same year also attracted venture capital of US$5.5 million from Bullet Time Ventures, the Foundry Group and FreshTracks Capital. It became a so-called B corporation (public benefit corporation). These are for-profit companies that "must create value for society, not just shareholders".[27] The B corporation concept is an ideology: every for-profit company is necessarily driven by the need to accumulate capital and to exploit labour. When it exploits labour it is definitely not doing good to society, but benefits a class of owner at the expense of workers. Ello has committed to not using advertising as Facebook does:

> Every post you share, every friend you make and every link you follow is tracked, recorded and converted into data. Advertisers buy your data so they can show you more ads. You are the product that's bought and sold. We believe there is a better way. We believe in audacity. We believe in beauty, simplicity and transparency. We believe that the people who make things and the people who use them should be in partnership. We believe a social network can be a tool for empowerment. Not a tool to deceive, coerce and manipulate—but a place to connect, create and celebrate life. You are not a product.[28]

Ello's current privacy policy rules out advertising: "Ello does not make money from selling advertising on the site, serving ads to you, or selling information about our users to third parties, including advertisers, data brokers, search engines, or anyone else."[29] Ello published a charter that says:

---

24 Data source: alexa.com.
25 Data source: alexa.com.
26 Who the hell is still using Ello? *Vice Online*, 11 February 2015.
27 www.bcorporation.net/what-are-b-corps/why-b-corps-matter (accessed on 10 November 2015).
28 https://ello.co/beta-public-profiles (accessed on 10 November 2015).
29 https://ello.co/wtf/policies/privacy-policy/ (accessed on 10 November 2015).

1) Ello shall never make money from selling ads; 2) Ello shall never make money from selling user data; and 3) In the event that Ello is ever sold, the new owners will have to comply by these terms. In other words, Ello exists for your benefit, and will never show ads or sell user data.[30]

Once venture capital enters a company, there is pressure to sooner or later accumulate capital. So Ello needs to sell something as commodity. It can, for example, sell premium services, premium memberships, or wait until it has a large user base and then charge for access. In any case, it does not transcend the logic of labour-exploitation. In any of these cases, it exploits the employees or freelancers who produce these services for a wage and create not just the platform as use-value, but also the company's (potential) profits. If such commodification strategies do not work, it may even be the case that Ello has to introduce advertising and to renounce its own manifesto promises. Even if Ello does not exploit users, it has to exploit some form of labour in order to make profits and to be profitable, which is also an imperative for a B company. Thus far the low level of success of Ello shows that it is difficult to compete with a monopoly capitalist such as Facebook. Given that there is little interest, no business model may work at all. Ello cannot be profoundly different from Facebook because it also follows a capitalist logic and can therefore only make profits by exploiting some form of labour. It can commit to not exploit users, but it cannot commit to not use exploitation as long as it is a for-profit company.

Ello is not fundamentally different from Facebook because both are capitalist social media. Being ad-free is not enough – the point is that you have to be non-capitalist in order to be an alternative to Facebook.

DIASPORA*: AN ALTERNATIVE TO FACEBOOK?

One strategy of socialist Internet politics is to establish and support non-commercial, non-profit Internet platforms. It is not impossible to create successful non-profit Internet platforms, as the example of Wikipedia – which is advertising-free, provides free access and is financed by donations – shows. The best-known alternative social networking site project is Diaspora*, which tries to develop an open source alternative to Facebook. Other examples are Budypress, Crabgrass, Cryptocat, Elgg, Friendica, kaioo, Lorea, N-1 and Occupii (see Allmer 2015; Cabello et al. 2013; Sevignani 2012, 2013, 2016). Diaspora* is a project created by four New York University students – Dan Grippi, Maxwell Salzberg, Raphael Sofaer and Ilya Zhitomirskiy. Diaspora* defines itself as a "privacy-aware, personally controlled, do-it-all, open source social network".[31] It is not funded by advertising, but by donations. The three design principles of Diaspora* are choice, self-ownership of data and simplicity.[32]

The Diaspora* team is critical of the control of personal data by corporations. It describes Facebook as "spying for free".[33] The basic idea of Diaspora* is to circumvent

---

30   https://ello.co/wtf/about/pbc/ (accessed on 10 November 2015).
31   www.joindiaspora.com (accessed on 11 November 2010).
32   www.joindiaspora.com (accessed on 21 March 2011).
33   Four nerds and a cry to arms against Facebook. *The New York Times* online, 10 March 2013 (accessed on 27 September 2016).

the corporate mediation of sharing and communication by using decentralized nodes that store data that is shared with friends.[34] Each user has his/her own data node that s/he fully controls. As Ilya Zhitomirskiy states: "On Diaspora, users are no longer dependent on corporate networks, who want to tell you that sharing and privacy are mutually exclusive."[35]

So Diaspora* aims to enable users to share data with others and at the same time to protect them from corporate domination and from having to sacrifice their data for corporate purposes in order to communicate and share. Diaspora* can therefore be considered as a socialist Internet project that practically tries to realize a socialist privacy concept. The Diaspora* team is inspired by the ideas of Eben Moglen, author of the *dotCommunist Manifesto* (2003). He says that an important political goal and possibility today is the "liberation of information from the control of ownership" with the help of networks that are "based on association among peers without hierarchical control, which replaces the coercive system" of capitalist ownership of knowledge and data (Moglen 2003). "In overthrowing the system of private property in ideas, we bring into existence a truly just society, in which the free development of each is the condition for the free development of all" (2003).

Diaspora* is explicitly a non-profit project. It is based on donations. On 10 February 2016 it was the world's 355,396th most frequently visited website, whereas Facebook was the second most accessed site.[36] This circumstance shows that there is an asymmetry between Facebook's monopoly power and alternative social networks. Facebook's users are socially "locked in" because they have invested a large labour of love, emotion and connection into their profiles. It they leave it, they may lose important contacts, content and advantages they have built up. They also only have limited time available to use multiple social networking sites. This puts alternative sites such as Diaspora* at a disadvantage. Diaspora* is also financially more volatile because it does not sell data, but rather depends on donations, which is a logic that transcends the commodity form, but is organized within a society ruled by instrumental reason.

Some Facebook users have diffuse feelings of discontent with Facebook's privacy practices that have manifested themselves into groups against the introduction of Facebook Beacon, news feed, mini-feed and so on, the emergence of the web 2.0 suicide machine (http://suicidemachine.org/), or the organization of a Quit Facebook Day (www.quitfacebookday.com/). These activities are mainly based on liberal and Luddite ideologies, but if they were connected to ongoing class struggles against neoliberalism (like the ones that have taken place throughout the world in the aftermath of the new global capitalist crisis) and the commodification of the commons, they could grow in importance.

On Facebook, the "audience" is an exploited worker-consumer. How can socialist privacy protection strategies be structured? The overall goal is to drive back the commodification of user data and the exploitation of prosumers by advancing the decommodification of the Internet and society.

---

34 http://vimeo.com/11242736 (accessed on 10 March 2013).
35 http://vimeo.com/11099292 (accessed on 10 November 2015).
36 Data source: alexa.com (accessed on 10 November 2015).

RECOMMENDED READINGS AND EXERCISES

For understanding Facebook, it makes sense to engage with its statement of rights and responsibilities, data use policy, financial statements as well as criticisms of the platform.

Read Facebook's latest Statement of Rights and Responsibilities and discuss the following questions in groups. Ask yourself:

- What rights does Facebook have in relation to the content that you create on its services?
- If you feel you have been treated in an illegal manner by Facebook, how can you hold it legally reliable? Which court is responsible?
- Try to find more information on how national regulations (e.g. the ones in your home country) work for a global system like the Internet?

Read Facebook's latest Data Use Policy and ask yourself the following questions:

- Make a systematic and ordered list of data that Facebook collects about users.
- Discuss which data Facebook uses for targeted advertising. Find out how this form of advertising works. Which data does Facebook use about you for targeted advertising?
- Are there mechanisms for limiting targeted advertising on Facebook? Do you think they are sufficient? Why? Why not?
- How do you politically assess targeted advertising?
- Are there alternative organization models for social media that do not use targeted advertising? Which ones? How do you think social media should best be organized?

Read Facebook's latest Proxy Statement and its Annual Financial Report. You will find both on its website under SEC filings. Ask yourself:

- How does Facebook present itself in these documents?
- Try to make sense of and interpret the financial data presented in the reports. What do Google's ownership structure and its financial operations look like?
- According to these reports, what role does advertising play in Facebook's operations?

Work in groups and present the results of the following exercises to the class.

Facebook has faced a lot of criticism. These exercises focus on engagement with this criticism.

- Search for videos, documents, press releases, blog posts, etc. in which Facebook presents itself. What kind of image does Facebook construct of itself? What are the major themes in its discourse?
- Search for documents, interviews, news articles, reports by critical scholars, critical journalists, civil society representatives, privacy and data protection advocates, consumer protection advocates and organizations as well as watchdog organizations that criticize the topics that

(Continued)

(Continued)

Facebook presented in a positive light in the material you found earlier. Summarize the basic points of criticism. Compare them to how Facebook presents itself. Discuss which assessments you find more convincing and provide reasons for your assessments.

- The initiative Europe vs. Facebook filed a complaint about Facebook to the Irish Data Protection Commissioner. First, read the basic complaint documents and the Irish Data Protection Commissioner's audit. Conduct a search about how Facebook, Europe vs. Facebook and other data protection commissioners (e.g. Thilo Weichert in Germany and others) have reacted to the audit report. Document the discussion and its basic arguments. Position yourself on the involved political issues. Present your results.

Fuchs, Christian. 2011. How to define surveillance? *MATRIZes* 5 (1): 109–133.

Gandy, Oscar H. 1996. Coming to terms with the panoptic sort. In *Computers, surveillance & privacy*, ed. David Lyon and Elia Zureik, 132–155. Minneapolis, MN: University of Minnesota Press.

Mathiesen, Thomas. 1997. The viewer society: Michel Foucault's "Panopticon" revisited. *Theoretical Criminology* 1 (2): 215–334.

Fuchs, Christian. 2013. Political economy and surveillance theory. *Critical Sociology* 39 (5): 671–687.

Allmer, Thomas. 2011. Critical surveillance studies in the information age. *tripleC: Communication, Capitalism & Critique: Open Access Journal for a Global Sustainable Information Society* 9 (2): 566–592.

These readings deal with the notion of surveillance in the context of computing. Read the texts and ask yourself:

- How should surveillance best be defined?
- What is the relevance of Michel Foucault's works for studying surveillance?
- What is the panoptic sort? What is the synopticon?
- Do the panoptic sort and the synopticon matter for understanding social media? Try to find examples that you can analyse with the help of these concepts.
- What are aspects of the political economy of surveillance on social media? Try to give some examples.

Arendt, Hannah. 1958. *The human condition* (2nd edition). Chicago, IL: University of Chicago Press. Chapter 8: The private realm: property. Chapter 9: The social and the private.

Habermas, Jürgen. 1989. *The structural transformation of the public sphere*. Cambridge, MA: MIT Press. Chapter 17: The polarization of the social sphere and the intimate sphere.

Fuchs, Christian. 2011. Towards an alternative concept of privacy. *Journal of Information, Communication and Ethics in Society* 9 (4): 220–237.

Allmer, Thomas. 2011. A critical contribution to theoretical foundations of privacy studies. *Journal of Information, Communication and Ethics in Society* 9 (2): 83–101.

Fuchs, Christian. 2012. The political economy of privacy on Facebook. *Television & New Media* 13 (2): 139–159.

Ask yourself:

* What are Arendt and Habermas's basic criticisms of privacy? In which respect do these criticisms matter for understanding Facebook and other social media critically?
* In light of the criticisms of privacy, do you think there is anything that is politically valuable about this concept? If so, why and what? If not, why not?
* Discuss what the advantages and disadvantages of the privacy concept are and how they relate to Facebook and other social media.

Fuchs, Christian, Kees Boersma, Anders Albrechtslund, Marisol Sandoval, eds. 2012. *Internet and surveillance: The challenges of web 2.0 and social media*. New York: Routledge. Chapter by Christian Fuchs: Critique of the political economy of web 2.0 surveillance. Chapter by Mark Andrejevic: Exploitation in the data mine. Chapter by Daniel Trottier and David Lyon: Key features of social media surveillance.

Ask yourself:

* Make a systematic and ordered typology of characteristics of social media surveillance. Give a name to each dimension and take care that the dimensions are not overlapping. Constructing such a typology presupposes that you understand and can define the terms "social media" and "surveillance".
* Have a look at your characteristics of social media surveillance. Give two examples that relate to specific platforms for each dimension.

Atton, Chris. 2002. *Alternative media*. London: SAGE. Chapter 1: Approaching alternative media: Theory and methodology. Chapter 2: The economics of production.

Sandoval, Marisol. 2009. A critical contribution to the foundations of alternative media studies. *Kurgu – Online International Journal of Communiation Studies* 1: 1–18.

Fuchs, Christian. 2010. Alternative media as critical media. *European Journal of Social Theory* 13 (2): 173–192.

Sandoval, Marisol and Christian Fuchs. 2010. Towards a critical theory of alternative media. *Telematics and Informatics* 27 (2): 141–150.

Sevignani, Sebastian. 2012. The problem of privacy in capitalism and the alternative social networking site Diaspora*. *tripleC: Communication, Capitalism & Critique: Open Access Journal for a Global Sustainable Information Society* 10 (2): 600–617.

Social networking sites like Diaspora* and N-1 are alternative social networking sites. Read first the given articles. Then make a list of ten alternative social networking sites. This presupposes that you have an understanding of what an alternative medium is. Ask yourself:

* What is an alternative medium? Discuss different meanings of the term and devise a working definition.

(Continued)

(Continued)

- In which respect can the social networking sites that you selected be considered as being alternatives to Facebook? What does the term "alternatives" mean here? In what respect are the platforms different from Facebook?
- Compare the terms of use and privacy policy of these platforms to the ones of Facebook. What are the differences and commonalities?

Rushkoff, Douglas. 2013. Why I'm quitting Facebook. *CNN*, February 25, 2013. http://edition.cnn.com/2013/02/25/opinion/rushkoff-why-im-quitting-facebook (accessed on 4 July 2013).

Scholz, Trebor. 2010. Facebook as playground and factory. In *Facebook and philosophy*, ed. Dylan E. Wittkower, 241–252. Chicago, IL: Open Court.

Kiss, Jemina. 2010. Facebook should be paying us. *Guardian*, 9 August. www.guardian.co.uk/media/2010/aug/09/facebook-users-union-demands-payment (accessed 26 September 2016).

Ask yourself:

- What are the basic points of criticism of Facebook formulated by Douglas Rushkoff, Trebor Scholz and Richard Buchanan?
- Which strategies of resistance are mentioned? What commonalities and differences are there? What other strategies are there? What do you think about such strategies?
- One strategy is to demand a wage from Facebook for platform usage. This demand is based on the assumption that Facebook usage is labour that creates value. Another strategy is to build, use and support alternative non-commercial platforms such as Diaspora*. What are the differences between these strategies? What do you think about them? What are their ultimate goals?

Edward Snowden's revelations about the existence of a surveillance-industrial Internet complex have given a new dimension to social media surveillance. Work in groups:

- Search for interviews with and talks by Edward Snowden and read, listen to and watch them. Ask yourself: Why did Snowden make these revelations? What does he see as the dangers of communications surveillance? What personal risks did he take? In which cases would you take personal risks for political reasons? Can you give examples?
- Do you think Edward Snowden is a hero who should be commended for letting the public know that our governments are running electronic surveillance programmes that threaten people's privacy, or a villain who threatens the West's national security by revealing secret services' covert surveillance actions? Give reasons for your answers.

Read the following chapter in Thomas Mathiesen's book *Towards a Surveillant Society*. Mathiesen is a Norwegian sociologist whose works have been very influential in the critical study of surveillance and in critical criminology. In this chapter, he describes the aftermath of Anders Breivik's fascist terrorist attacks in Norway on 22 July 2011. Breivik first detonated a bomb in a government building in Oslo that killed eight people, and then shot dead 69 young social democrats on Utøya Island. Discuss in groups.

Mathiesen, Thomas. 2013. *Towards a surveillant society: The rise of surveillance systems in Europe*. Hook: Waterside Press. Chapter 5: Epilogue: The bomb and the massacre (pp. 205–258).

- What are possible responses to terrorism and organized crime? What are the most common responses?
- What are differences between right-wing and left-wing responses? How does Mathiesen position himself in this respect?
- How did Norway respond to the July 2011 terrorist attacks? If you compare it to the USA's response to 9/11, what differences can be found? How do you assess the two different responses? Which one is more appropriate? Why?

8 TWITTER AND DEMOCRACY: A NEW PUBLIC SPHERE?

KEY QUESTIONS

- What is a public sphere?
- Does Twitter contribute towards the creation of a public sphere?
- How has Twitter been criticized?
- What are the political-economic limits of Twitter?
- Is Twitter emancipatory? What are the limits of political communication on Twitter?
- Can the 2011 rebellions (Arab spring, Occupy, etc.) be called Twitter revolutions and Twitter protests?

KEY CONCEPTS

Public sphere
Jürgen Habermas's concept of the public sphere
Political communication
Public sphere as immanent critique
Private sphere
Communicative capitalism

Slacktivism and clicktivism
Visibility on Twitter
Pseudo public sphere
Manufactured public sphere
Technological determinism
Social revolution
Social media revolutions

OVERVIEW

A blog is a website that features periodically published postings that are organized in reverse chronological order so that the newest postings are shown first. A microblog is a further development of the blog concept: one shares short messages with the public and each user has a contact list of persons who are following these messages. Microblogging is like sending SMS online to a large number of people. A microblog is "an Internet-based service in which: (1) users have a public profile where they broadcast short public messages/updates [...] (2) messages become publicly aggregated together across users; and (3) users can decide whose messages they wish to receive, but not necessarily who can receive their messages" (Murthy 2013, 10). The two most popular microblogs in the world are Twitter and Weibo. The Chinese company SINA owns Weibo, which was created in 2009. Twitter was created in 2006. It is owned by Twitter Inc., a company founded by Jack Dorsey that is based in San Francisco.

Lotan et al. (2011) analysed 168,663 tweets from the Tunisian revolution and 230,270 from the Egyptian one. They found that journalists and activists were the main sources of retweets and that bloggers and activists were the most active retweeters. However, it is hard to see why the presented evidence should support the authors' claim that "the revolutions were, indeed, tweeted" (1401). The analysis says nothing about what role these tweets had in mobilizing activists on the streets and how relevant Twitter was for street activists. In contrast to surveys and interviews with Egyptian activists, the analysis of tweets cannot provide conclusive evidence about the role of social media in a revolution. In March 2011, only 0.00158 per cent of the Egyptian population used Twitter (Murthy 2013, 107). It is therefore likely that "much of Twitter's prominence in relation to the 'Arab Spring' arose from individuals in the West tweeting and retweeting" (Murthy 2013, 112), which may have helped to "raise global awareness" (113), but cannot be considered to have caused a revolution.

Twitter revolution claims imply that Twitter constitutes a new public sphere of political communication that has emancipatory political potentials. This chapter questions these assumptions. It asks the question: Is Twitter a political public sphere? Lindgren and Lundström (2011, 1015) argue that Twitter and the Internet have "a particularly strong potential" to create a space for what Ulrich Beck terms subpolitics: politics that are not "governmental, parliamentary, and party politics", but take place in "all the other fields of society" (Beck 1997, 52). This chapter questions how large this potential is and what its limits are. Its analysis belongs to the field of political Twitter research, in which the topic of the public sphere has thus far been rather neglected.

Concepts of the public sphere are strongly connected to Jürgen Habermas's theory (see Calhoun 1992a; Roberts and Crossley 2004a). Dealing with the posed research question requires, therefore, a close engagement with Habermas's concept of the public sphere and a discussion of its relation to the Internet (section 8.1). Section 8.2 discusses how some scholars conceive the impact of social media on the public sphere. I will discuss the approaches of Clay Shirky, Zizi Papacharissi, Jodi Dean, Malcolm Gladwell and Evgeny Morozov and argue that the public sphere has two main aspects: political communication and political economy. Based on the theory framework, I present in section 8.3 an empirical analysis of the role of Twitter and social media in the public sphere's political communication. Section 8.4 discusses uncivil communication as Twitter's dark side. Section 8.5 shows how Twitter and social media's political economy impact the public sphere. Section 8.6 connects these results to Habermas's theory. Section 8.7 draws some conclusions.

8.1 HABERMAS'S CONCEPT OF THE PUBLIC SPHERE

WHAT IS THE PUBLIC SPHERE?

Habermas has defined the notion of the public: "We call events and occasions 'public' when they are open to all, in contrast to close or exclusive affairs" (Habermas 1989c, 1). Habermas

(1989c, 6) argues that the concept of the public is related to the notion of the common that is associated with ideas like *Gemeinschaft* (German), community, the common use of resources like a marketplace or a fountain and communal organization (in German: *Genossenschaftliche Organisation*).

Habermas characterizes some important dimensions of the public sphere (1989b, 136, 1989c, 27):

- Formation of public opinion.
- All citizens have access.
- Conference in unrestricted fashion (freedom of assembly, freedom of association, freedom of expression and publication of opinions) about matters of general interest.
- Debate over the general rules governing relations.

Habermas's original concept of the public sphere is grounded in Marxian political theory (see 1989c, 122–129). In his discussion of Marx's relevance for the concept of the public sphere, Habermas stresses:

- Private property and skills are required for participating in the public sphere, but wage-workers have been excluded from these resources.
- The bourgeois class serves and advances particular interests (its own profit interests), not the general interests of society.
- Marx imagined alternatives to the bourgeois state that serves class interests when he described the Paris Commune (March–May 1871) as a specific kind of public sphere.

THE WORKING-CLASS CRITIQUE OF THE PUBLIC SPHERE CONCEPT

There have been two common critiques of Habermas's theory of the public sphere: the working-class critique, the feminist as postmodernist critique, and the critique of cultural imperialism. The *working-class critique* stresses that Habermas focuses on the bourgeois movement and neglects other popular movements that existed in the seventeenth, eighteenth and nineteenth centuries, such as the working-class movement. Oskar Negt's and Alexander Kluge's (1972/1993) notion of a proletarian (counter) public sphere can be read as both a socialist critique and a radicalization of Habermas's approach (see Calhoun 1992b, 5; Jameson 1988).

Such criticism should, however, see that Habermas acknowledged in the preface of *Structural Transformation* the existence of a "plebeian public sphere", like in the Chartist movement or the anarchist working class (Habermas 1989c, xviii), and that he pointed out that the "economically dependent masses" would only be able to contribute "to the spontaneous formation [. . .] of opinion [. . .] to the extent to which they had attained the equivalent of the social independence of private property owners" (Habermas 1992, 434).

THE FEMINIST CRITIQUE OF THE PUBLIC SPHERE CONCEPT

The feminist critique points out that the public sphere has been a sphere of educated, rich men, juxtaposed to the private sphere that has been seen as the domain of women. Women, gays and lesbians, and ethnicities would have been excluded from the public sphere. It would therefore today be more promising that struggles against oppression take place in multiple subaltern counter publics than in one unified sphere. The criticism also stresses that an egalitarian society should be based on a plurality of public arenas in order to be democratic and multicultural (Eley 1992; Fraser 1992; Roberts and Crossley 2004b). Habermas agrees that his early account in *The Structural Transformation of the Public Sphere* (1989c), published in 1962, has not enough focused on proletarian, feminist and other public spheres (1992, 425–430).

The danger of pluralistic publics without unity is, however, that they will in social struggle focus on mere reformist identity politics without challenging the whole, which negatively affects the lives of all subordinated groups, and that in an egalitarian society common communication media are needed for guaranteeing cohesion and solidarity and a strong democracy. Postmodernists and post-Marxists are so occupied with stressing difference that they do not realize that difference can become repressive if it turns into a plurality without unity. One needs unity in diversity in order to struggle for participatory democracy and for maintaining this condition once it is reached. It is preferable and more effective to have a few widely accessible and widely consumed broad critical media than many small-scale special interest media that support the fragmentation of struggles. Nicholas Garnham argues in this context for the need of a single public sphere and says that the postmodernists risk "cultural relativism" if they do not see that democracy is in need of "some common normative dimensions" and "more generalized media" (Garnham 1992, 369).

THE CRITIQUE OF THE PUBLIC SPHERE CONCEPT AS CULTURAL IMPERIALISM

The *cultural imperialism critique* stresses that the public sphere is a Western enlightenment concept that Western societies use for trying to impose their political, economic and social systems on other countries. Jim McGuigan formulates in this context a criticism of Nicholas Garnham's interpretation of Habermas: "we have to entertain the possibility that the global public sphere is a Western fantasy and perhaps a last gasp of its otherwise shaky bid for or to sustain global hegemony" (McGuigan 1998, 96).

Concerning the question of whether there is a global public sphere, Colin Sparks (1998) stresses that broadcasting is mainly national. "Global" stations such as CNN and BBC World would reach limited audiences that are mainly located in the West. They would also predominantly have Western-made and Western-focused contents. He therefore suggests abandoning the term global public sphere and that the term "imperialist, private sphere" would be better (Sparks 1998, 122). The public sphere is not only about information and communication, but also about ownership. Therefore the existence of transnational forms of media and communication doesn't imply the existence of a global public sphere.

Public spaces and public spheres are not specific to the West. The public teahouse is an old cultural practice and space in many parts of the world, such as in China, Japan, Iran, Turkey and the UK. Di Wang (2008) compares the early twentieth-century Chinese teahouse to the British public houses. It is a common space where people from all walks of life go for different purposes. The Chinese word for teahouse is 茶館 (*cháguǎn*). Chengdu (成都) is the capital of the Southwestern Chinese province Sichuan (四川). It has about 7.7 million inhabitants in its urban core. "Teahouses in Chengdu, however, were renowned for their multiclass orientation. One of the 'virtues' of Chengdu teahouses was their relative equality" (Wang 2008, 421). Women were at first excluded, but by 1930 fully accepted. These teahouses were not just cultural spaces, but also political meeting points where political debates took place and political theatre pieces were performed, which attracted not only citizens, but also government spies. Wang (2008) discusses the role of the Chengdu teahouses during the 1911 Railroad Protection Movement. Public meeting places are spheres of civil engagement that can turn into political spaces of communication and protest. The example shows that public spheres are something quite universal that is not limited to the West.

The public sphere is both process and space: "In periods of mobilization, the structures that actually support the authority of a critically engaged public begin to vibrate. The balance of power between civil society and the political system then shifts" (Habermas 1996, 379). Juha Kovisto and Esa Valiverronen (1996) see the public sphere not as domain, but as process of counter-hegemonic struggles. A public sphere emerges where people struggle for a better society and their struggle is a process of constituting the public that creates spatial domains of resistance in the public. The public sphere is simultaneously process and space. Social organization turns into a public sphere when people act politically in common for a joint goal that fosters participatory democracy instead of economic and state power and when they use grassroots organizations and/or the occupation or creation of public space as political strategy. Neo-Nazis do not form a public sphere because their organization structures and goals are authoritarian and opposed to participatory democracy.

The various Occupy movements are movements where protests and spaces of occupation converge. They have created public spheres of political communication that they controlled in a self-managed manner: Tahrir Square in Cairo, Egypt; Syntagma Square in Athens, Greece; Puerta del Sol in Madrid, Spain; Plaça Catalunya in Barcelona, Spain; Zuccotti Park in New York City; St Paul's Cathedral's and Finsbury Square in London. This creation of public spheres did not just take place in the West, but also in many parts of the world in times of global capitalist and social crisis. In 2011, there were revolutions in Tunisia and Egypt and Yemen as well as major protests in countries such as Albania, Algeria, Armenia, Australia, Azerbaijan, Bahrain, Belarus, Belgium, Bolivia, Burkina Faso, Canada, Chile, China, Colombia, Cyprus, Czech Republic, Denmark, Djibouti, Finland, France, Georgia, Germany, Greece, Hong Kong, Hungary, India, Iran, Iraq, Ireland, Israel, Italy, Jordan, Kuwait, Lebanon, Libya, Macedonia, Malawi, Malaysia, Maldives, Mauritania, Mexico, Mongolia, Morocco, the Netherlands, New Zealand, Nigeria, Norway, Oman, Palestine, Portugal, Russia, Saudi Arabia, Slovenia, Somalia, South Africa, South Korea, Spain, Sri Lanka, Sudan, Switzerland, Syria, Turkey, the United Kingdom, the United States, Vietnam and Western Sahara. Common aspects of these protests were that many of them used the tactic of making space public and political and that they took place in a common crisis of society. Resistance is as old as class societies, so public spheres have been formed as resisting publics throughout the history of class societies.

THE PUBLIC SPHERE: POLITICAL COMMUNICATION AND POLITICAL ECONOMY

In discussions about the Internet and the public sphere, many authors have stressed the potential for or limit of the Internet to advance political communication (e.g. Benkler 2006;

Dahlberg 2001, 2004; Dahlgren 2005, 2009; Papacharissi 2002, 2009), whereas a smaller number have also stressed that aspects of the political economy of the media and the Internet relate directly to the concept of the public sphere (e.g. Garnham 1992; Sparks 2001).

It is important to see that Habermas stresses both aspects of (a) political communication and (b) political economy as being constitutive for the public sphere. So he points out (a) that the proper task of the public sphere is that "society [is] engaged in critical public debate" (1989c, 52). But he also points out (b) that the public sphere is a question of the command of resources (property, intellectual skills) by its members:

> But even under ideally favorable conditions of communication, one could have expected from economically dependent masses a contribution to the spontaneous formation of opinion and will only to the extent to which they had attained the equivalent of the social independence of private property owners. (Habermas 1992, 434)

Habermas stresses that Marx's work is especially relevant for the second dimension of the public sphere. Marx's

> critique demolished all fictions to which the idea of the public sphere of civil society appealed. In the first place, the social preconditions for the equality of opportunity were obviously lacking, namely: that any person with skill and "luck" could attain the status of property owner and thus the qualifications of a private person granted access to the public sphere, property and education. The public sphere with which Marx saw himself confronted contradicted its own principle of universal accessibility. (Habermas 1989c, 124)

HABERMAS: NO IDEALIZATION OF THE PUBLIC SPHERE, BUT RATHER PUBLIC SPHERE AS CONCEPT OF IMMANENT CRITIQUE

Habermas does not idealize the bourgeois public sphere, but rather applies an elegant dialectical logic to show that the bourgeois ideals and values find their own limits in the existence of stratification and class. Habermas showed, based on Marx (critique of the political economy: class character of the public sphere) and Horkheimer (ideology critique: manipulated public sphere), how the very principles of the public sphere are stylized principles that in reality within capitalist society are not realized due to the exclusory character of the public sphere and the manipulation of the public sphere by particularistic class interests.

Habermas's theory of the public sphere is an ideology-critical study in the tradition of Adorno's (1951/2003) method of immanent critique that confronts the ideals of the public sphere with its capitalist reality and thereby uncovers its ideological character. The implication is that a true public sphere can only exist in a participatory society.

Liberal ideology postulates individual freedoms (of speech, opinion, association, assembly) as universal rights, but the particularistic and stratified class character of capitalism undermines these universal rights and creates inequality and therefore unequal access to the public sphere. There are specifically two immanent limitations of the bourgeois public sphere that Habermas discusses:

- The limitation of freedom of speech and public opinion: individuals do not have the same formal education and material resources for participating in the public sphere (Habermas 1989c, 227).
- The limitation of freedom of association and assembly: big political and economic organizations "enjoy an oligopoly of the publicistically effective and politically relevant formation of assemblies and associations" (Habermas 1989c, 228).

The bourgeois public sphere creates its own limits and thereby its own immanent critique.

For discussing whether the Internet or certain Internet platforms constitute a public sphere, one should take both the level of political communication and the level of political economy into account. This allows asking specific questions that can help to determine whether we can speak of the existence of a public sphere:

1) Analysis of the political-economic dimension of mediated communication:

   1(a) Ownership:
   Is there a democratic ownership of the media organization and resources?
   1(b) Censorship:
   Is there political and/or economic censorship?
   1(c) Exclusion:
   Is there an overrepresentation of viewpoints of corporate elites or of uncritical and pro-capitalist viewpoints? To which degree are critical viewpoints present?
   1(d) Political content production:
   Who can produce content? How visible, relevant and influential is the produced content?

2) Analysis of political communication:

   2(a) Universal access:
   How relevant/frequently used are political communication sites or political communication forums/features/contents within more general platforms? Who has access and who uses the sites for political communication (income, education level, age, gender, ethnicity, origin, etc.)? How relevant is political communication in relation to other forms of communication (e.g. as pure entertainment)? Who has access and who uses the sites for political communication (income, education level, age, gender, ethnicity, origin, etc.)?
   2(b) Independence:
   How independent are the sites and discussions from economic and state interests?
   2(c) Quality of political discussion:
   How valid (right, true, truthful, understandable), inclusive, attentive, sincere, reflexive and inclusive is political online discussion?

COMMERCIAL MEDIA AND THE PUBLIC SPHERE

Habermas (1989c) describes and criticizes the commercialization of the press since the middle of the nineteenth century, that the idea of profit generation was introduced to the media and advertising became common. The public sphere of the media would thereby have become undemocratic and a privatized realm controlled by powerful actors instead of citizens:

> The communicative network of a public made up of rationally debating private citizens has collapsed, the public opinion once emergent from it has partly decomposed into the informal opinions of private citizens without a public and partly become concentrated into formal opinions of publicistically effective institutions. Caught in the vortex of publicity that is staged for show or manipulation the public of nonorganized private people is laid claim to not by public communication but by the communication of publicly manifested opinions. (Habermas 1989b, 248)

In a media world dominated by capitalism, the "world fashioned by the mass media is a public sphere in appearance only" (Habermas 1989c, 171). Habermas critically observes that in capitalist media, publicity is not generated from below, but from above (177).

James Curran (1991) argues that before the 1850s there was a rich history of radical newspapers in the UK and that it was easy and cheap to create such newspapers. Examples of the radical nineteenth-century UK press are: *Liberator, London Dispatch, Northern Star* (a Chartist newspaper that existed from 1837 until 1852 and had a circulation of around 50,000), *Political Register, Poor Man's Guardian, Reynolds News, Trades Newspaper, Twopenny Trash, Voice of the People, Voice of West Riding, Weekly Police Gazette* (Curran and Seaton 2010, Chapter 2). The radical press had an important role in radical politics and was associated with civil society groups such as the National Union of the Working Classes, the Chartist Movement and the Society for Promoting the Employment of Women. Later, advertising arose and it became ever more expensive to run a newspaper, so the press shifted towards the right and the labour press came to an end in the twentieth century. Curran argues that the nineteenth-century press had "a radical and innovatory analysis of society" and "challenged the legitimacy of the capitalist order" (Curran 1991, 40). Habermas would dismiss the role of the radical press, whereas the nineteenth-century London press consisted of "conflicting public spheres" (Curran 1991, 42). Curran's position can be characterized as being close to Negt and Kluge's (1972/1993) stress on a proletarian public sphere.

One should, however, see that Habermas's stress on the economic colonization of the lifeworld and the feudalization of the media system show his concerns about capitalist media and his preference for non-capitalist media. Habermas's notion of the feudalized public sphere reflects Marx's (1842, 175) concern that the *"primary freedom of the press lies in not being a trade"*. Slavko Splichal (2007) stresses in this context that Ferdinand Tönnies and Karl Bücher shared Marx's insight that media can only constitute a public sphere if they are non-commercial. The public sphere has never materialized "because of unequal access to communication channels, uneven distribution of communicative competence, and the reduction of public debates to a legitimisation of dominant opinions created by either the 'business type' or the 'government type' of power elites" (Splichal 2007, 242).

There are several problems of how capitalist media limit the public sphere:

- *Media concentration*: There is a tendency that market competition results in concentration. In the commercial media landscape, the mechanism of the advertising-circulation spiral enforces media concentration (Furhoff 1973).
- *Commercialized and tabloidized content*: Advertising-financed media tend to focus more on entertainment than news, documentaries and educational programmes because this content is better suited for attracting advertisers (Jhally 1987; Smythe 1954; Williams 1990).

- *Power inequalities*: There are power differentials in commercial media that disadvantage individuals and groups that do not have significant shares of money, political influence and reputation. Commercial media often disempower by invisibility and partial visibility.

    a) Private media ownership gives owners the possibility to influence media content.
    b) For-profit and advertising logic makes media organizations dependent on market and commodity logic and prone to exclude voices that question these logics.
    c) There is an educational and economic gap that can privilege educated and wealthy individuals in the consumption of demanding and costly culture.

Habermas's (1989c, 175–195) main concern about advertising is that it has the potential to de-politicize the public. This would on the one hand be due to particularistic interests: "The public sphere assumes advertising functions. The more it can be deployed as a vehicle for political and economic propaganda, the more it becomes unpolitical as a whole and pseudo-privatized" (175). On the other hand the influence of economic logic on the media would result in tabloidization: "Reporting facts as human-interest stories, mixing information with entertainment, arranging material episodically, and breaking down complex relationships into smaller fragments – all of this comes together to form a syndrome that works to depoliticize public communication" (Habermas 1996, 377).

CAPITALIST MEDIA, PUBLIC MEDIA, CIVIL SOCIETY MEDIA

Commercial and advertising-funded media are a dominant model of media organization, but not the only model. There are also public service and civil society media that face their own problems in a capitalist world, but also have potentials to transcend capitalist media control. Graham Murdock (2011) distinguishes between three political economies of the media in modern societies. Media can take on the form of commodities organized by capital, public goods organized by the state and gifts organized by civil society (see Table 8.1).

Information media are specifically cultural in that they enable the creation, co-creation, diffusion and interpretation of symbols, by which humans make meaning of the world. Raymond Williams has argued against cultural idealism and for cultural materialism: he opposes "the separation of 'culture' from material social life" (Williams 1977, 19). We "have to emphasise cultural practice as from the beginning social and material" (Williams 1989, 206). The production of culture is an economic activity of production that creates ideas and meanings as use-values. So culture is on the one hand always an economic process of production. On the other hand, culture is not the same as the economy, it is more than the sum of various acts of work, it has emergent qualities – it communicates meanings in society – that cannot be found in the economy alone. The economy is preserved in culture: culture is not independent from work, production and physicality, but requires and incorporates all of them. Based on Williams we can therefore say that information media have a) their specific culture that stores and communicates information in public and helps produce meaning and b) a specific mode of economic organization of culture, a political economy of culture, which enables the ownership, control, production, diffusion and consumption of information. The media have an economic and a political dimension, they are owned in specific ways and are channels for political information and debate. Table 8.1 distinguishes two levels of the organization of information media

TABLE 8.1 Two levels of the three political economies of the media

	Capitalist media	Public service media	Civil society media
Economy (ownership)	Corporations	State institutions	Citizen control
Culture (public circulation of ideas)	Content that addresses humans in various social roles and results in meaning-making	Content that addresses humans in various social roles and results in meaning-making	Content that addresses humans in various social roles and results in meaning-making

and introduces based on Graham Murdock's typology a distinction between capitalist media, public media and civil society media.

The media system has a public role for making information public. Public culture is however mediated by political economy and ownership structures (see Table 8.1):

- *Capitalist media* are companies that are privately owned by single individuals, families or shareholders. They are culturally located in the public sphere, but at the same time they are part of the capitalist economy and therefore produce not only public information, but capital and monetary profit by selling audiences/users and/or content.
- *Public media* are funded by or with the help of the state and/or are created and maintained by a specific statute. They are seen as a public service that plays the role of providing political, educational and entertainment information to citizens. They are as organizations located close to the state system or on the intersection of civil society and the state.
- *Civil society media* are full parts of the public sphere. They are economically related to the state if they receive subsidies and often stand in an antagonistic relation to the capitalist economy and governments because as alternative media they tend to reject for-profit and commercial logic and to express alternative points of view that challenge governments and corporations. Civil society media are media that are run, owned and controlled by citizens as common projects. They express alternative points of view on the level of culture and have alternative organization models at the level of political economy (Fuchs 2011; Sandoval and Fuchs 2010).

Media *make information public* on their *cultural* level, but only some of them are *publicly controlled on the economic level* by state-supported institutions or civil society, whereas *capitalist media* are profit-making corporations based on *private ownership*.

Table 8.2 introduces a model of public service media (PSM) that operates on three dimensions. There are economic, political and cultural dimensions of public service media: organization, participation and content. On each level there is the production, circulation and use of a specific good that is organized in line with the logic of public service. So, for example, public ownership of public service media is an economic aspect of the means of communicative production.

On the economic level, PSM are means of production, circulation and consumption. PSM's means of production are publicly owned. The circulation of information is based on a not-for-profit logic. Consumption is made available in principle to everyone by giving citizens easy access to PSM's technology and information. On the political level, PSM make

TABLE 8.2 A model of public service media

Sphere	Media	Production	Circulation	Use
Culture: social meaning	Content	Independence, unity in diversity, educational content	Cultural communication and debate	Cultural dialogue and understanding
Politics: collective decisions	Participation	Independence, unity in diversity (representation of minority interests and common affinity and reference points for society), political information	Political communication and debate	Political dialogue and understanding
Economy: property	Organization and technology	Public ownership	Non-profit, non-market	Universal access, universal availability of technology

available inclusive and diverse political information that can support political debate and the achievement of political understanding. On the cultural level, PSM provide educational content that has the potential to support cultural debate and the achievement of understanding in society.

8.2 TWITTER, SOCIAL MEDIA AND THE PUBLIC SPHERE

The rise of blogs (e.g. Wordpress, Blogspot, Tumblr), social networking sites (e.g. Facebook, LinkedIn, Diaspora*, VK), microblogs (e.g. Twitter, Weibo), wikis (e.g. Wikipedia) and content-sharing sites (e.g. YouTube, Flickr, Instagram) has resulted in public discussions on the implications of these media for the political realm. There are, on the one hand, more optimistic and, on the other hand, more sceptical views. This section introduces five approaches that have in common that they focus on discussing the role of social media in politics.

CLAY SHIRKY: SOCIAL MEDIA AS RADICALLY NEW ENHANCERS OF FREEDOM

Clay Shirky argued in 2008 that the political use of "social media" ultimately enhances freedom:

> Social tools create what economists would call a positive supply-side shock to the amount of freedom in the world. [. . .] To speak online is to publish, and to publish online is to connect with others. With the arrival of globally accessible publishing, freedom of speech is now freedom of the press, and freedom of the press is freedom of assembly. (Shirky 2008, 172)

Whereas one assumption in this discourse is that new media have predominantly positive effects, another one is that they bring about radical change: "Our social tools are dramatically improving our ability to share, co-operate, and act together. As everyone from working biologists to angry air passengers adopts those tools, it is leading to an epochal change" (Shirky 2008, 304).

ZIZI PAPACHARISSI: THE PRIVATE SPHERE

Papacharissi (2010, 21) has advanced an approach that is comparable to the one by Shirky, in which she argues that political activities that were in former times "activities pursued in the public realm" are today practised in the private realm "with greater autonomy, flexibility, and potential for expression". Social media like Twitter would make the private sphere "a sphere of connection and not isolation, as it serves primarily to connect the personal to the political, and the self to the polity and society" (164).

New forms of politics would include tweeting, "participating in a MoveOn.org online protest, expressing political opinion on blogs, viewing or posting content on YouTube, or posting a comment in an online discussion group" (131). Such online activities would constitute

> an expression of dissent with a public agenda. [. . .] these potentially powerful acts of dissent emanate from a private sphere of interaction, meaning that the citizen engages and is enabled politically through a private media environment located within the individual's personal and private space. (Papacharissi 2010, 131)

Papacharissi assumes that social media such as Twitter have resulted in a collapse of the boundaries between the private sphere and the political public sphere so that the private sphere becomes the realm of the political. But co-presence and physicality matter also in a networked world. A huge mass of people gathering in physical places is a visible threat to those in power and it can have material effects (like blocking streets, occupying squares and buildings, etc.).

It is no surprise that the main protests during the new global capitalist crisis have been associated with physical spaces: Tahrir Square in Cairo, Egypt; Syntagma Square in Athens, Greece; Puerta del Sol in Madrid, Spain; Plaça Catalunya in Barcelona, Spain; Zuccotti Park (Liberty Plaza Park) in New York, USA. Physical spaces allow an agglomeration of individuals that gives them a visibility that those in power likely perceive as a threat. They also provide opportunities for building and maintaining interpersonal relations that involve eye contact, communication of an emotional aura and bonding activities (such as singing songs, drinking a beer or coffee together) that are important for the cohesion of a political movement and can hardly be communicated over the Internet.

Papacharissi reduces collective action to individual action and the public sphere to the private sphere. This point does not imply social media never matter. I rather want to stress that social media cannot replace collective action that involves spatio-temporal presence. Social media can – given a good organization, high interest and a lot of resources – serve as protest co-ordination and organization tools. However, the reality of protests shows that they cannot replace collective protest action and experience.

Online activism can cause material and symbolic harm and be a threat to the powerful, as the hacking activities of the Anonymous group show (e.g. blocking of the sites of Amazon, MasterCard, PostFinance, PayPal and Visa as revenge for the companies' blocking of payments to WikiLeaks, blocking of government websites in Tunisia, Egypt, Libya and Syria in solidarity with the Arab Spring, the hacking of sites by Koch Industries that supported anti-union groups as part of the 2011 Wisconsin protests), but a lot of "online politics" is harmless (writing a blog, posting a tweet or YouTube video, signing an online petition, joining a Facebook group, etc.) and can simply be ignored by the powerful.

danah boyd (2010, 39) defines a networked public as "(1) the space constructed through networked technologies and (2) the imagined collective that emerges as a result of the intersection of people, technology, and practice". Expressions in networked publics would be persistent (recorded, archived), replicable, scalable and searchable. Audiences in these publics would often be invisible, social contexts collapsed and the boundary between public and private would often blur. For boyd, Facebook and Twitter are prototypes of networked publics. Whereas Papacharissi tends to idealize private individuals' political use of social media as new forms of the public sphere, boyd generalizes the notion of the public from a political context to the whole realm of social media so that the notion of the public (sphere) loses any critical dimension. The notion of the networked public is not only an apolitical concept; it is at the same time one that idealizes corporate social media: the notions of being public and being networked create a purely positive image of human activity without conceptualizing potential problems. As a consequence, the concept of social media as "networked publics" predominantly creates positive associations. It lacks a critical dimension that addresses power asymmetries, the exploitation of digital labour, asymmetric visibility, commercial culture and targeted advertising, corporate and state surveillance, and other problems that manifest themselves on dominant social media platforms.

JODI DEAN: SOCIAL MEDIA POLITICS AS IDEOLOGY

Jodi Dean (2005) argues, therefore, that the Internet has in the context of communicative capitalism become a technological fetish that advances post-politics. What Papacharissi (2010) calls the emergence of a political private sphere is, for Dean, the foreclosure of politics proper. "File sharing is political. A website is political. Blogging is political. But this very immediacy rests on something else, on a prior exclusion. And, what is excluded is the possibility of politicization proper" (Dean 2005, 65).

> Busy people can think they are active – the technology will act for them, alleviating their guilt while assuring them that nothing will change too much. [. . .] By sending an e-mail, signing a petition, responding to an article on a blog, people can feel political. And that feeling feeds communicative capitalism insofar as it leaves behind the time-consuming, incremental and risky efforts of politics. [. . .] It is a refusal to take a stand, to venture into the dangerous terrain of politicization. (Dean 2005, 70)

MALCOLM GLADWELL: SOCIAL MEDIA – NO NATURAL ENEMIES OF THE STATUS QUO

In response to the techno-euphoria about social media, Malcolm Gladwell (2010) argues that activists in revolutions and rebellions risk their lives and risk becoming victims of violence conducted by the police or the people their protest is directed at. Taking the courage to face these dangers would require strong social ties and friendships with others in the movement. Activism would involve high risks. "The kind of activism associated with social media isn't like this at all. The platforms of social media are built around weak ties" (Gladwell 2010, 45).

Facebook and Twitter activism would only succeed in situations that do not require people "to make a real sacrifice" (Gladwell 2010, 47), such as registering in a bone-marrow database or getting back a stolen phone. "The evangelists of social media", such as Clay Shirky, "seem to believe that a Facebook friend is the same as a real friend and that signing up for a donor registry in Silicon Valley today is activism in the same sense as sitting at a segregated lunch counter in Greensboro in 1960" (46). Social media would "make it easier for activists to express themselves, and harder for that expression to have any impact" (49). Social media "are not a natural enemy of the status quo" and "are well suited to making the existing social order more efficient" (49).

EVGENY MOROZOV: SOCIAL MEDIA AND SLACKTIVISM/CLICKTIVISM

Evgeny Morozov (2009) speaks in line with Gladwell's argument of slacktivism as:

> feel-good online activism that has zero political or social impact. It gives those who participate in "slacktivist" campaigns an illusion of having a mean-ingful impact on the world without demanding anything more than joining a Facebook group. [. . .] "Slacktivism" is the ideal type of activism for a lazy generation: why bother with sit-ins and the risk of arrest, police brutality, or torture if one can be as loud campaigning in the virtual space?

Morozov (2010) argues that the notion of "Twitter revolution" is based on a belief in cyber-utopianism – "a naive belief in the emancipatory nature of online communication that rests on a stubborn refusal to acknowledge its downside" (xiii) that, combined with Internet-centrism, forms a techno-deterministic ideology

SHIRKY'S RESPONSE TO GLADWELL AND MOROZOV

In an article that can be read as a kind of response to criticism, Clay Shirky (2011b, 29), men-tioning both Gladwell and Morozov, acknowledges that the use of social media "does not have a single preordained outcome". Social media would be "coordinating tools for nearly all of the world's political movements, just as most of the world's authoritarian governments (and, alarmingly, an increasing number of democratic ones) are trying to limit access to it" (30). Shirky admits that there are attempts to control, censor and monitor social media, but argues at the same time that these attempts are unlikely to be successful in the long run and that social media are "long-term tools that can strengthen civil society and the public sphere" (32).

Social media would facilitate shared awareness and result in "the dictator's dilemma"/"the conservative dilemma" (36):

> The dilemma is created by new media that increase public access to speech or assembly; with the spread of such media, whether photocopiers or Web brows-ers, a state accustomed to having a monopoly on public speech finds itself called to account for anomalies between its view of events and the public's. The two responses to the conservative dilemma are censorship and propaganda.

But neither of these is as effective a source of control as the enforced silence of the citizens. The state will censor critics or produce propaganda as it needs to, but both of those actions have higher costs than simply not having any critics to silence or reply to in the first place. But if a government were to shut down Internet access or ban cell phones, it would risk radicalizing otherwise pro-regime citizens or harming the economy. (Shirky 2011b, 36–37)

Shirky sees two sides of social media, but argues that the positive side over-determines the negative one and that in the last instance social media have positive effects on democracy. So although acknowledging contradictions in order to make his argument more complex, Shirky postulates the techno-deterministic equation: social media = more democracy = more freedom. Shirky (2011b, 38) argues that the slacktivism argument is irrelevant because "the fact that barely committed actors cannot click their way to a better world does not mean that committed actors cannot use social media effectively".

In a response to Shirky, Gladwell wrote that Shirky "has to convince readers that in the absence of social media, those uprisings would not have been possible" (Gladwell and Shirky 2011, 153). Shirky answered that "social media allow insurgents to adopt new strategies" that are crucial, "allow committed groups to play by new rules" and that "as with the printing press", social media "will result in a net improvement for democracy" (154). So, asked for clarification, Shirky confirmed the view that, although acknowledging complexity, the formula remains in the last instance "the Internet = increase of democracy".

Clay Shirky and Zizi Papacharissi, on the one hand, and Jodi Dean, Malcolm Gladwell and Evgeny Morozov, on the other, have opposing views on the question of whether Twitter and other social media, under the given societal context, advance or harm the political public. For readers of this book, it will be obvious that I am sceptical of the first position and have sympathies with the second one. But one can only give a definitive answer to this question by empirical inquiries that cover aspects of both political communication and political economy.

8.3 POLITICAL COMMUNICATION ON TWITTER

THE STRATIFICATION OF TWITTER AND MICROBLOG USAGE

The typical Twitter user was, in 2013, between 18 and 34 years old, held a university degree and had no children. The relative majority of users came from the USA (20.9 per cent).[1] In contrast, 92.4 per cent of Weibo's users are located in China.[2] In the United States, the typical Twitter user was, in 2013, part of a younger age group of up to 34 years (62 per cent), white (67 per cent) and earned more than US$100,000 per year (58 per cent).[3]

Stratification patterns that are created by age, ethnicity and class shape the use of Twitter and microblogs in general. The hypothesis of the end of information inequality (what is in a misleading way often called the "digital divide") due to the rapid adoption of the Internet (e.g. as claimed by Compaine 2001) is a myth. Stratification no longer so much concerns

---

1 www.alexa.com/siteinfo/twitter.com (accessed on 4 March 2013).
2 www.alexa.com/siteinfo/weibo.com (accessed on 4 March 2013).
3 www.quantcast.com/twitter.com (accessed on 4 March 2013).

physical access to the Internet, but rather the use of this technology and the skills required for this use. As long as there is a stratified society, information inequality will exist.

This pattern is not only specific to Twitter use in Western countries; as already mentioned, 93.4 per cent of all Weibo users live in China. The typical user is 25–34 years old, has attended university and has no children.[4] Just like in the West, the urban middle class also dominates microblogging in China, whereas workers, farmers, old people and others are rather excluded. Inequality in China and the West is a feature that shows that a similar neoliberal logic shapes both systems (Zhao 2008).

THE ASYMMETRICAL POWER OF VISIBILITY ON TWITTER

In 2009, only 7 per cent of the top Twitter trend topics were political topics and 38 per cent were entertainment-oriented topics. In 2010, only 3 per cent were about politics, 28 per cent about entertainment and 40 per cent about hashtags (#). An analysis of the most used hashtags in 2010 shows that politics was marginal and that music and dating were the most used hashtag topics.[55] Table 8.3 documents the top Twitter trends in 2009, 2010, 2011 and 2012. The statistics show that Twitter topics are dominated by entertainment. Table 8.4 shows the top hashtags during one month in 2015. Politics is not a particularly important topic in contrast to entertainment that is the dominant issue. Table 5.3 in Chapter 5 of this book shows a ranking of Twitter users ordered by number of followers. Celebrities from the entertainment business, particularly pop stars, dominate attention measured by the number of Twitter followers. Politics is much less represented and mainly in the form of influential political actors, such as Barack Obama, CNN and *The New York Times*, that dominate the political field in terms of influence, resources and reputation. Alternative political figures, such as political documentary producer Michael Moore, have far fewer followers, which is an expression of the asymmetrical political attention economy of capitalism that discriminates critical voices by lack of resources and attention: those who have a lot of reputation, fame, money or power tend to have many more followers than everyday people. Their tweets also tend to be much more often re-tweeted than common people's tweets.

Dhiraj Murthy (2013, 31) argues that "the influence of ordinary people on Twitter" may be minimal, but that "the medium can potentially be democratizing in that it can be thought of as a megaphone that makes public the voices/conversations of any individual or entity". The important question is, however, how society needs to be changed so that asymmetrical visibility disappears. Capitalist structures of accumulation operate not just in the economy, but also in culture, where they result in the accumulation of reputation, visibility and attention of a few. Murthy continues to argue that tweets circulate in the form of re-tweets and that as a result a single individual's voice "can potentially be amplified exponentially" if other users pick up their tweets and re-tweet them (21). This potential does not, however, mean that Twitter is a democratic medium because the power of amplification is also stratified: highly visible users determine what gets amplified and what does not. Twitter's reality is one of asymmetric visibility. Its democratic potentials are limited by the reality of stratified attention and the visibility characteristic for a capitalist culture.

---

4 www.alexa.com/siteinfo/weibo.com (accessed on 3 March 2013).
5 http://mashable.com/2010/12/22/top-twitter-trends-2010-charts (accessed on 12 November 2015).

TABLE 8.3 Top trends on Twitter

#	2012 top Twitter trends	Type	2011 top Twitter trends	Type	2010 top Twitter trends	Type	2010 top hashtags	Type	2009 top Twitter hashtags	Type
1	Olympics	EV	Justin Bieber	E	Gulf oil spill	C	#rememberwhen	E	#musicmonday	E
2	Election 2012	P	Soccer/ Sport	E	FIFA World Cup	E	#slapyourself	E	#iranelection	P
3	Justin Bieber	E	Lady Gaga	E	Inception	E	#confessiontime	E	#sxsw	E
4	Hurricane Sandy	C	NBA	E	Haiti earthquake	C	#thingsimiss	E	#swineflu	C
5	MTV Music Awards	E	Jonas Brothers		Vuvuzela	I	#ohjustlikeme	E	#nevertrust	E
6	Euro 2012	EV	Christmas	EV	Apple iPad	T	#wheniwaslittle	E	#mm	E
7	Super Bowl	EV	Super Junior	E	Google Android	T	#haveuever	E	#rememberwhen	E
8	Whitney Houston	E	Britney Spears	E	Justin Bieber	E	#icantlivewithoutit	E	#3drunkwords	E
9	Kony		Japan Earthquake	C	Harry Potter & the Deathly Hallows	E	#thankful	E	#unacceptable	E
10	One Direction	E	One Direction	E	Pulpo Paul	E	#2010disappointments	E	#iwish	E

Note: C = crisis, E = entertainment, I = instrument, T = technology, P = politics, EV = event

Sources: Data from 2012: http://blog.hootsuite.com/twitter-trends-2012/; data from 2011: http://mashable.com/2011/12/06/top-twitter-trends-2011/; data from 2010: http://mashable.com/2010/12/13/top-twitter-trends-2010/, http://yearinreview.twitter.com/trends/; data from 2009: http://3.bp.blogspot.com/_14cEenKeR04/SygI8Gp0F9I/AAAAAAAAADY/hELPQB1mQKo/s1600-h/2009trends_large.png.

THE DEGREE OF INTERACTIVITY OF POLITICAL COMMUNICATION ON TWITTER

For analysing the degree of information, communication and interactivity of political Twitter use, I have selected two cases: WikiLeaks and the Egyptian revolution. WikiLeaks was in the news media all over the world in December 2010 after it had released the diplomatic cables on 28 November, and a European-wide arrest warrant was issued against Julian Assange on 6 December. I collected 985,667 tweets that have the hashtag #wikileaks from the archive http://twapperkeeper.com (time period: 28 November 2010, 00:00:00–1 January 2011, 00:00:00).

The revolution in Egypt began on 25 January 2011, with mass protests in Cairo and other cities. On 11 February President Mubarak resigned. I collected 73,395 tweets with the

TABLE 8.4   Top trends on Twitter, 12 October–11 November 2015

#	Most popular hashtag	Description	Type
1	#EMABiggestFans1D	MTV Europe Music Awards	EV, E
2	#ALDubEBTamangPanahon	Benefit concert	EV, E
3	#EMABiggestFansJustinBieber	MTV Europe Music Awards	EV, E
4	#AMAs	American Music Awards	EV, E
5	#PushAwardsKathNiels	Push Awards	EV, E
6	#gameinsight	Online and mobile games	E, T
7	#android	Mobile operating system	T
8	#مغرد_بذكر_الله	Singing the remembrance of Allah (Arabic)	R
9	#トレクル	Torekuru (Japanese): role-playing game	E, T
10	#RT	Russia Today	P

Note: C = crisis, E = entertainment, I = instrument, T = technology, P = politics, EV = event, R = religion.

Source: Data from http://hashtagify.me/popular (accessed on 12 November 2015).

hashtag #25jan (time period: 25 January 2011, 00:00:00–12 February 2011, 00:00:00) from Twapper Keeper. Twitter users employed this hashtag for communication about the Egyptian revolution.

For addressing other users, it is common that one uses the "@" symbol followed by the username in tweets. There are two types of addressing: the re-posting of a Twitter message ("re-tweet") and the commenting on another posting. Twitter does not allow making downloadable archives of its posts. Twapper Keeper outputs a maximum of 25,000 results on screen. I manually generated these lists and copied them into Excel files that were then further analysed. I analysed the Twitter streams by identifying all tweets that address somebody ("@"). Then I decided for each of these tweets whether it was a re-tweet or not by looking for the identifier "RT @", which signifies a re-tweet in the output generated by Twapper Keeper. This procedure allowed me to identify which average share of postings is purely informational, a re-tweeting of another post or a comment on another tweet. The results are displayed in Table 8.5.

The results show that more than 50 per cent of the postings are re-tweets in both cases and there is a low level of commenting (23.1 per cent and 12.9 per cent respectively).

TABLE 8.5   Levels of information and communication for tweets relating to WikiLeaks and the Egyptian revolution

Hashtag	Number of tweets	Time period	Comment	Re-tweets	Information
#wikileaks	985,667	11-28-2010, 00:00:00 – 01-01-2011 00:00:00	23.1%	51.3%	25.6%
#25jan	73,395	time period: 01-25-2011, 00:00:00 – 02-12-2011, 00:00:00	12.9%	54.4%	32.7%

As re-tweeting is also a form of information, the total level of information provision was 76.9 per cent in the WikiLeaks case and 87.1 per cent in the Egyptian case.

Communication can be one-way or two-way (McQuail 2010, 552). In the first case, one person talks to the other, who does not talk back or does not have the means to do so. In two-way communication (interaction; McQuail 2010, 560), there is mutual meaningful symbolic interaction. In order to get a first idea of the quality of communication of postings, I analysed all postings in the #wikileaks stream that were posted in the time period 28 November 2010, 00:00:00–01:00:00 that mentioned other users. There were a total of 110 postings, of which there were 44 re-tweets (40 per cent), one mutual interaction consisting of two postings (1.8 per cent) and 64 informational postings (58.2 per cent). This sample is an indication that mutual symbolic interaction is rare in political Twitter communication and that Twitter communication mostly consists of one-way comments. Single messages like the following ones were typical interactions:

> @userA @userB A large number of your countrymen would disagree with you. Most humans disagree with you. http://bit.ly/i7pJy0 #wikileaks Sun Nov 28 00:27:26

> @userC @userD <————————#Racist #idiot #wikileaks Sun Nov 28 00:00:43

> @userE @userF <————————SPAM Don't retweet #wikileaks #SPAM Sun Nov 28 00:58:52

Re-tweets typically contained links or information that users assessed as important. For example:

> @userG RT @userH: #Wikileaks next release contains 251,287 diplomatic cables: report [ibtimes] http://j.m . . . Sun Nov 28 00:45:17

> @userI RT @userF: UK Sunday papers have got it all wrong about #wikileaks #embassy cables. Not worth reading. Wait for the #guardian! Sun Nov 28 00:56:00

The only mutual interaction in the analysed stream section of #wikileaks was a short dialogue:

> @userJ @userK #Assange is a traitor to whom? He is not a citizen of the US. He is a whistle blower #wikileaks Sun Nov 28 00:07:10

> @userK @userJ You misunderstood my tweet. . . . #Assange #wikileaks Sun Nov 28 00:19:28

In 2015 I collected a Twitter dataset about Jeremy Corbyn with the help of the software platform Discovertext. The data gathering took place during the final three weeks of his campaign for becoming the leader of the British Labour Party. I used keywords that Corbyn's opponents typically used in their smear campaigns against him (see Table 8.6). The dataset consisted of a total of 32,298 tweets. An analysis showed that 33.9 per cent of the tweets were

TABLE 8.6 Levels of information and communication for tweets relating to Jeremy Corbyn

Search	Number of tweets	Time period	Comment	Re-tweets	Information
Corbyn AND anti-Semite OR anti-Semitic OR chaos OR clown OR commy OR communism OR communist OR loony OR Marx OR Marxist OR pinko OR red OR reds OR socialism OR socialist OR Stalin OR Stalinist OR terrorist OR violent OR violence	32,298	From: 08-22-2015, 23:25 BST Until: 09-13-2015, 12:35 BST	10.0%	43.9%	33.9%

purely informational, 43.9 per cent were re-tweets and 10.0 per cent comments. It confirmed the tendency that Twitter is not a communication system, but an information medium used for spreading content and links.

THE 2011 PROTESTS AND REVOLUTIONS: TWITTER AND FACEBOOK REVOLUTIONS?

The question of whether the 2011 revolutions and protests were Twitter or Facebook revolutions also has to do with Internet access rates. Since 2008 the Internet access rate in the countries where such protests took place varies between 3.1 per cent (Mauritania) and 97.8 per cent (Iceland), and the Facebook usage rate varies between 2.6 per cent of the population (Yemen) and 69.1 per cent (Iceland) (see Table 8.7). Given such different conditions of Internet usage, the question arises as to whether one can really so easily generalize, as some observers do, that the Internet and social media created and amplified revolutions and rebellions. Data on media use in the Egyptian revolution show that the revolutionaries considered phone communication and face-to-face talk were much more important for spreading information than "social media" (Wilson and Dunn 2011). In December 2011, 26.4 per cent of the Egyptian population had access to the Internet and in June 2012, 13.6 per cent of the Egyptian population were Facebook users (data source: internetworldstats.com, accessed on 28 October 2012). The Facebook page "We are all Khaled Said" that has been moderated by Whael Ghonim (see Ghonim 2012), is said to have played a role in spreading the protests after Khaled Said was beaten to death by Egyptian police forces on 6 June 2010. It had 2.5 million likes (Arabic version; English version: 278,000) on 8 December 2012. However, it is unclear how many of the likes come from Egyptian users who participated in the Tahrir Square occupation and protests.

eMarketing Egypt conducted a survey about the Internet and the revolution in Egypt.[6] Of the respondents, 71 per cent said that Facebook was the prime medium "used to tie up with events and news". The problem is, however, that the survey only focused on Egyptian Internet users, who make up a minority of the population (26.4 per cent, see Table 8.7), and not on the Egyptian population as a whole. The results are therefore necessarily techno-centric.

---

6 For more details, see www.emarketing-egypt.com/1st-study-about-the-Internet-and-the-Egyptian-Revolution:-Survey-Results/2/0/18 (accessed on 13 November 2015).

TABLE 8.7   Internet penetration rate and Facebook usage rate (relative to the entire population) in selected countries that witnessed revolutions or rebellions in 2011

Country	Internet access rate (%)	Facebook usage rate (% of population)
Algeria	13.4	9.5
Bahrain	77.0	30.0
Egypt	26.4	13.6
Greece	46.9	33.1
Iceland	97.8	69.1
Jordan	38.1	38.1
Kuwait	74.2	31.2
Lebanon	52.0	38.0
Libya	5.9	10.0
Mauritania	3.1	2.7
Morocco	49.0	14.2
Oman	68.8	16.9
Portugal	50.7	38.8
Saudi Arabia	49.0	20.9
Spain	65.6	33.5
Sudan	9.3	n/a
Syria	22.5	n/a
Tunisia	36.3	28.9
United Arab Emirates	70.9	38.6
United Kingdom	84.1	48.6
United States	78.1	46.4
Western Sahara	n/a	n/a
Yemen	14.9	2.6

Source: Data from www.internetworldstats.com (accessed on 30 October 2012); n/a = not available.

THE ROLE OF SOCIAL MEDIA IN THE EGYPTIAN REVOLUTION

The Tahrir Data Project conducted a survey with Tahrir Square activists (N = 1056). Wilson and Dunn (2011) present some results from the survey that focused on activists' media use. Interestingly, Castells (2012) ignores Wilson and Dunn's results in his techno-deterministic analysis of social media in the Arab spring, although they were published in the *International Journal of Communication* that he co-founded. The survey shows that face-to-face interaction (93 per cent) was the most important form of activists' protest communication, followed by television (92 per cent), phones (82 per cent), print media (57 per cent), SMS (46 per cent), Facebook (42 per cent), email (27 per cent), radio (22 per cent), Twitter (13 per cent) and blogs (12 per cent). Interpersonal communication, traditional media and telecommunications were more important information sources and communication tools in the revolution than social media and the Internet. Another part of the survey showed that Egyptian revolutionaries perceived phone communication followed by face-to-face talk as most important for their own protest, most informative and most motivating for participating in the protests. Facebook, eMail and Twitter were considered to be less important, less informative, less used and less motivating. The study illustrates that "digital media was not as central to protester communication and organization on the ground as the heralds of Twitter revolutions would have us hyperbolize" (Wilson and Dunn 2011, 1252). James Curran (2012, 53) argues that the Arab Spring has "deep-seated economic, political and religious causes". Digital media "contributed to the build-up of dissent, facilitated the actual organisation of protests, and disseminated news of the protests across the region and to the wider world. If the rise of digital communications technology did not cause the uprisings, it strengthened them" (Curran 2012, 54).

THE ROLE OF SOCIAL MEDIA IN THE OCCUPY MOVEMENT

I conducted a survey among Occupy activists in order to study the role of social media and other media in their protest information, communication and mobilization practices. The results were published in detail in the book *OccupyMedia! The Occupy Movement and Social Media in Crisis Capitalism* (Fuchs 2014b). Here I will only mention one aspect of the entire dataset: one important dimension of social movements' knowledge structures is how activists communicate with each other. In order to find out, the OccupyMedia! Survey contained the question: "If you think back to a month, in which you were involved in Occupy protests, then how often did you use any of the following media for communicating or discussing the protests with other activists?" The results are shown in Table 8.8.

The data provides indications that the personal conversation is the most frequent form of communication in the Occupy movement, followed by communication on Facebook, email, mailing lists and Twitter. SMS and mobile phones were less frequently used for movement communication than face-to-face communication, email and social media (Facebook, Twitter). Using Spearman's rho, I conducted a correlation analysis of the Occupy protest communication variables. The results are presented in Table 8.9.

TABLE 8.8   Frequency of usage per month of specific social media for communicating or discussing the protests with other activists

	Infrequently (0–3) (%)	Medium (4–8) (%)	Frequently (> 9) (%)
Personal conversation	24.90	14.50	60.60
SMS	57.90	14.80	27.40
Phone calls	54.90	21.40	23.70
Personal emails	41.40	21.90	36.60
Email mailing lists	49.70	17.90	32.50
Occupy movement chat	70.00	14.90	15.20
Twitter	56.30	11.20	32.50
Facebook group	37.20	17.30	45.40
YouTube comments	79.90	11.20	8.90
Riseup communication tools	83.40	7.90	8.80
InterOccupy teleconferences	90.40	5.80	3.80
OccupyTalk voice chat	95.50	1.30	3.30

Source: Fuchs (2014b).

TABLE 8.9 Correlations between frequency of specific forms of protest communication for discussion, activism intensity as well as political positioning (Spearman's rho)

	Personal conversation	SMS	Phone calls	Personal emails	email mailing lists	Occupy movement chat	Twitter	Facebook	YouTube	Riseup	InterOccupy teleconferences	OccupyTalk
Intensity of activism, significance	0.532**, 0.000	0.442**, 0.000	0.495**, 0.000	0.515**, 0.000	0.417**, 0.000	0.312**, 0.000	0.304**, 0.000	0.375**, 0.000	0.161**, 0.005	0.314**, 0.000	0.346**, 0.000	0.177**, 0.002
Political positioning, significance	−0.013, 0.824	0.039, 0.503	−0.050, 0.379	−0.065, 0.254	−0.019, 0.737	0.061, 0.285	−0.012, 0.828	0.077, 0.169	0.036, 0.537	−0.037, 0.735	0.019, 0.735	0.102, 0.075
Personal conversation, significance	—	0.392**, 0.000	0.520**, 0.000	0.540**, 0.000	0.367**, 0.000	0.272**, 0.000	0.209**, 0.000	0.243**, 0.000	0.194**, 0.009	0.149**, 0.009	0.157*, 0.006	0.013, 0.820
Facebook, significance	0.243**, 0.000	0.348**, 0.000	0.251**, 0.000	0.338**, 0.000	0.289**, 0.000	0.333**, 0.000	0.313**, 0.000	—	0.397***, 0.000	0.116*, 0.043	0.261**, 0.000	0.182**, 0.001
email mailing lists, significance	0.367**, 0.000	0.448**, 0.000	0.502**, 0.000	0.740**, 0.000	—	0.211**, 0.000	0.228**, 0.000	0.289**, 0.000	0.179**, 0.002	0.301**, 0.000	0.256**, 0.000	0.176**, 0.002
Twitter, significance	0.209**, 0.000	0.398**, 0.000	0.176**, 0.002	0.203**, 0.000	0.228**, 0.000	0.233**, 0.000	—	0.313**, 0.000	0.338**, 0.000	0.207**, 0.000	0.246**, 0.000	0.180**, 0.002

Source: Fuchs (2014b).

Correlation analysis shows that the intensity of activism is positively correlated with the frequency of all forms of protest communication at a significant level. The political positioning of the respondents in contrast does not correlate with their protest communication frequency. People who are more active in protests tend to engage more in communication with other activists in personal conversations, on the phone, in email mailing lists, chats, on Twitter, Facebook, YouTube and other communication media. Correlation analysis also shows that different forms of protest communication do not substitute, but complement each other: the frequency of personal communications is significantly positively correlated with the frequency of most other forms of protest communication; the frequencies of the use of Facebook, Twitter, email mailing lists and other online media for protest communication are significantly positively correlated with each other. Note that the respondents were activists, so these results say nothing about the role of social media in inhibiting or supporting the mobilization of protestors. They rather show that Occupy activists tend to make use of multiple forms of online and offline media for communicating about the protests with other activists and that these forms of protest communication tend to complement each other.

These empirical results deconstruct the myth that the Arab Spring was a Twitter revolution, a Facebook revolution, a social media revolution or revolution 2.0. Social media and the Internet played a role as one among several media (especially interpersonal communication), but empirical evidence does not sustain the assumption that social media were necessary conditions of the revolution. The Arab revolutions and other protests (such as the ones by Occupy) were not tweeted, blogged or liked. Social media played a role in protest communication, but it was one role among different media types.

8.4 UNCIVIL COMMUNICATION ON TWITTER

ONLINE HATRED AND ONLINE VIOLENCE ON SOCIAL MEDIA

In August 2014, the Islamic State (IS) spread a video on the Internet that showed how one of its members beheaded the American journalist James Foley, who was kidnapped in Syria in 2012. IS has continuously published and diffused images and videos of such killings online and has for this purpose not just used YouTube and Twitter, but also newer platforms such as justpaste.it, an image- and text-sharing platform that is among the world's 8,500 most accessed WWW sites. Panos Kompatsiaris and Yiannis Mylonas (2015) show that the Golden Dawn uses social media for Goebbels-style Nazi propaganda. Right-wing movements are no less active and no less capable of using social media than left-wing ones. There have been repeated reports about misogyny against women and hatred and threats against minorities on Twitter.

One reaction to online hatred have repeated calls for total surveillance and rapid censorship. Such discussions miss the point, however. Attempts to censor the Internet misunderstand its nature: if somebody recalls contaminated chickens or bottles of poisoned beer from supermarkets, then nobody can eat and drink these goods any longer and the harm can be contained. Information on the Internet behaves completely differently: it can be copied and spread easily, quickly and cheaply all over the world because it is a peculiar good; information is not used up in consumption and it is difficult to exclude people from its consumption and from copying it. Given the characteristics of information, it is impossible to censor online information, which makes such political ideas infeasible and a tilt at windmills. The censors of this world fundamentally misunderstand the nature of the Internet and are trapped in the right-wing ideological illusion that surveillance and censorship technologies can solve the world's social and political problems.

In 2003, Barbara Streisand tried to legally suppress images of her Malibu house that had been posted online. The effect was that thousands of people re-posted the pictures and hundred of thousands viewed them. This so-called "Streisand effect" shows that censorship attempts in the world of media spectacle create more attention for the censored information. The more platforms and politicians try to censor IS, the more the horrifying images and videos will spread.

What is an appropriate political reaction to online threats, fascism and violence? There is a continuum between the two extremes of the politics of laissez-faire and control politics. The one extreme of laissez-faire does not take seriously that there are a number of anonymous posts that make users feel terrified. Such actual experiences of threat need to be taken seriously. The other extreme of control politics believes that tough laws, surveillance, imprisonment and the death penalty are adequate responses. It overlooks that crime has concrete social causes and that superficial measures do not eliminate social problem's root causes. Even after the introduction of the toughest sentences, comparable threats are likely to occur at a different time in a different context. So what can best be done?

Right-wing media, politicians and observers often use online fascism, bullying, child pornography, paedophiles' online grooming of children, online misogyny and terrorism as occasions for creating moral panics that call for wide-ranging surveillance of the Internet and tough prison sentences. But imagine a world of total surveillance. The police and secret services analyse everything one does and communicates online and on the phone. Predictive algorithms analyse all obtained text and voice data in order to foresee whether someone could become a criminal, terrorist, online bully and so on. If there are indications, then the user is automatically imprisoned for several years. Why? An algorithm identified him or her as risk. The algorithm is considered as the ultimate judge, so also no trial and no evidence is needed. A step further is the connection of thoughts to the Internet so that we can automatically search online by just thinking and so on. Google and Facebook would certainly love to know our inner thoughts in order to deliver advertisements directly to our brains. But also the police and secret services would be interested in these data. Their predictive algorithms could analyse what citizens think, and if there are indications that they could become criminals, they could immediately be put behind bars or be executed by a firing squad or by electrocution. Such a world is a totalitarian world without any justice, a world of fascist policing.

Imagine an antagonistic world without policing: A civil society activist receives 500 fascist online death threats per day. He alarms the police, who just tell him: "Policing the Internet is fascist. People like you want to advance politics of control and surveillance. That's right-wing bullshit. You are a right-wing extremist!" The activist becomes ever more frightened and feels abandoned by the state. The threats do not stop and almost drive him mad. Finally, he jumps from the fifth floor of his flat because the fear resulted in a persecution complex so that he interpreted every sound in his environment as a possible attack.

LEFT REALISM IN TACKLING THE INTERNET'S PROBLEMS

Both scenarios of total control and of total lack of policing are of course extreme, but show what happens if we take a conservative and a liberal position on policing crime to the end. We need a left realist approach to tackling online crime, as is often suggested in critical criminology. If people are threatened online, then the police should step in. Social media should offer user-friendly ways for users to report threats. The police should employ enough personnel for handling and checking such reports, blocking abusive, terrorist, racist, misogynistic, fascist, etc. users immediately, and offering to help the victims report the incidents to the police. The police should then look into the matter, and demand – based on a warrant signed by a judge – access to the abusive users' personal data on the social media platform and the respective Internet service provider. They should be able to respond quickly and in a competent manner, which requires specially trained, highly-skilled personnel working in well-resourced departments. These policewomen and policemen should very well understand the social, legal, ethical, economic, cultural and technical dimensions of the Internet and constantly update their knowledge. Based on police investigations, public prosecutors should then take legal action. If there is a grounded suspicion that a specific user is involved in terrorism or organized crime, then a judge can issue a warrant that enables the police to conduct targeted surveillance of the individual's communications. All of this is legally and technically possible today without having to undertake mass surveillance of all users, all their communications connection data and all their communications content data.

It is, however, naïve to assume that policing, blocking users and messages, and targeted surveillance in specific cases always works. If users are tech-savvy, then they can use technologies for masking their IP addresses and communicating anonymously. Nor will policing alone ever solve the underlying causes of crime, fascist ideology, racism, sexism and terrorism. Overcoming problems in society requires changes that address the causes of societal problems. For addressing measures that aim at overcoming problems one should neither be naïve nor disillusioned.

Potential reforms can include: criminal justice reforms, enhancement of full and quality employment, higher minimum wages, educational opportunities, social services and programmes, using new technologies for public relations, support for civil society mechanisms that watch and report the abuse of power by powerful institutions, a culture of support for risk groups (DeKeseredy 2011, Chapter 4), affordable quality day care, housing subsidies, improved public transport (DeKeseredy et al. 2006), equal opportunity policies, positive recognition and fostering of interaction between different cultures and identities (Young 2002), development policies that enhance living and working conditions in developing countries, and so on.

8.5 TWITTER'S POLITICAL ECONOMY

TWITTER'S TERMS OF SERVICE AND TARGETED ADVERTISING

Twitter started as a profit-oriented corporation without a business model. At first it did not use advertising. In September 2009 it revised its terms of use, so that advertising and targeted advertising became possible. But advertising was not used. In April 2010, Twitter announced that advertising would be introduced in the near future.[7] Twitter's terms of use significantly grew in length and complexity, and set out the company's ownership rights with respect to user-generated content. In 2011, Twitter's business model that is based on targeted advertising came into full effect.

CAPITAL ACCUMULATION ON TWITTER

Twitter's capital accumulation model uses three mechanisms: *promoted tweets*, *promoted trends*, *promoted accounts*. Promoted tweets are advertising tweets that appear at the top of search result lists for searches conducted by specifically targeted user groups. "Use Promoted Trends to drive conversations and interest around your brand or product by capturing a user's attention on Twitter."[8] "The Promoted Account is featured in search results and within the Who To Follow section. Who To Follow is Twitter's account recommendation engine and identifies similar accounts and followers to help users discover new businesses, content, and people on Twitter."[9]

---

7 See http://news.bbc.co.uk/2/hi/8617031.stm (accessed on 13 November 2015).
8 http://business.twitter.com/advertise/promoted-trends (accessed on 4 March 2013).
9 http://business.twitter.com/advertise/promoted-accounts (accessed on 4 March 2013).

When one searches on Twitter for content or a hashtag, current tweets, people results/accounts and worldwide Twitter trends are displayed. Twitter's advertising strategy manipulates the selection of Twitter search results, displayed accounts and trends. Those tweets, accounts and trends that attain most attention are not displayed, but preference is given to tweets, accounts and trends defined by Twitter's advertising clients. Twitter advances a class-structured attention economy that privileges economically powerful actors over everyday users. If you are a large company with a huge advertising budget, then it is easy for you to buy attention on Twitter. If you are an everyday user without an advertising budget and without much time, you will, in contrast, have a much harder time promoting your tweets and your accounts as trends on Twitter.

Users who tweet constitute an audience commodity (Smythe 1977, 1981/2006) that is sold to advertisers (see Chapter 5 in this book). The difference between the audience commodity on traditional mass media and that on Twitter is that in the latter case the users are also content producers; there is user-generated content and the users engage in permanent creative activity, communication, community building and content production (Fuchs 2010c). The fact that the users are more active on Twitter than in the reception of TV or radio content is due to the decentralized structure of the Internet, which allows many-to-many communication. Because of the permanent activity of the recipients and their status as prosumers, we can say that in the case of the Internet the audience commodity is a prosumer data commodity. The category of the prosumer data commodity does not signify a democratization of the media towards a participatory or democratic system, but the total commodification of human creativity. Twitter users work for free, without payment; they generate surplus value by creating tweets and log data that are sold as commodity to advertisers that then target their ads to specific user groups. In order that capital accumulation can work on Twitter, the economic surveillance of user data is needed (Fuchs 2011a). Twitter surveillance is subsumed under the capitalist political economy.

TWITTER ON THE STOCK MARKET

Twitter was just like many other Silicon Valley tech companies first supported by venture capital firms such as Institutional Venture Partners, Benchmark Capital, Union Square Ventures, Spark Capital or Insight Venture Partners. On 7 November 2013, Twitter made its Initial Public Offering (IPO) on the New York Stock Exchange. It became a publicly traded corporation listed on the stock market. The initial share price was US$45.10. Twitter's share price increased by 73 per cent on its first trading day and its entire stock market value thereby was 24 times its projected 2014 earnings. In February 2016, Twitter's share price had fallen to around US$14.5.

Twitter has, however, made large losses that amounted to US$577.8 million in the financial year 2014[10] and US$521.0 million in 2015.[11] Twitter in 2014 and 2015 derived 90 per cent of its revenue from advertising.[12] Like Facebook and Google it is an advertising agency, not a communications company. Targeted advertising is uncertain and high risk. The speed

---

10   Twitter SEC filings, form 10-K, financial year 2014.
11   Twitter SEC filings, form 8-K, 10 February 2016.
12   Twitter SEC filings, form 8-K, 10 February 2016.

of information flow is extremely high on Twitter, which makes it even more difficult to sell targeted ads. That Twitter has not been profitable, but is listed on the stock market, makes it a high-risk financial venture.

8.6 @JÜRGENHABERMAS #TWITTER #PUBLICSPHERE

THE PUBLIC SPHERE AND POLITICAL COMMUNICATION ON TWITTER

Habermas argues that political communication and political economy are two important aspects of the public sphere. According to Habermas (1989b, 1989c), the public sphere is a sphere of political debate. It is therefore important to test how communicative political Twitter use is. What is the role of political communication on Twitter? Twitter is dominated by the young, educated middle class and excludes other groups, such as workers, farmers and elderly people. Those with higher incomes and better education, who are more politically interested and informed, dominate political communication. The result is "a rather homogenous climate of opinion" (Habermas 1989c, 213).

Politics is a minority topic on Twitter. Twitter is a platform dominated by entertainment. It is predominantly an information medium, not a communication tool. It is predominantly about entertainment, not about politics. Celebrities from the entertainment industry have the most-followed profiles on Twitter. Concerning political profiles, mainly established high-profile political actors with a lot of resources have a large number of followers, whereas critical political actors have much less visibility and fewer followers. An analysis of a large number of tweets from three political events (discussions about WikiLeaks in 2010, the Egyptian revolution in 2011, the Jeremy Corbyn campaign in 2015) has shown that political tweets tend to be primarily information-based postings, especially re-tweets, and not conversations. The interactive postings are mainly one-way comments and not two-way interactions.

There is a limitation of freedom of speech and public opinion on Twitter: individuals do not have the same formal education or material resources for participating in the public sphere (Habermas 1989c, 227). The proper task of a public sphere, a "society engaged in critical public debate" (Habermas 1989c, 52) about politics, is not achieved on Twitter in the current societal context. One important question arises in this context: Can meaningful political debates be based on 140-character short messages? Short text may invite simplistic arguments and be an expression of the commodification and speeded-up nature of culture.

TWITTER: FROM 140 TO 10,000 CHARACTERS?

In early 2016, there were reports that Twitter may expand its character limit from 140 to 10,000 (Fuchs 2016b). At the time you are reading this chapter, this may or may not have become reality. Twitter seems to assume that changing its technological design will fix its own economic crisis. But there is no technological fix to capitalist crisis. Capitalism is itself the crisis. It may indeed be a fallacy to assume that increasing the *potential* length of tweets will increase their *actual average length* and the *actual average attention span* for single tweets. Twitter users have over the past ten years become used to Twitter's logic and may simply continue to use it the way they have done in a long time. Twitter's reasoning seems to be that tweets of up to 10,000 characters will fix users' attention for a longer time on single postings so that personalized adverts can be better presented and targeted and that as a result it will become profitable. This strategy may not work out. Twitter is in a dilemma: neither its current nor an alternative design promise large profits.

The logic of social media capitalism is flawed. Twitter's change is not radical enough because it does not think of changing social media's political economy. A more radical and the only feasible step would be to turn Twitter into a non-commercial, non-profit platform that stops using advertising, does not aim at accumulating capital, and substitutes the focus on the logic of accumulation with the logic of trying to foster sustained political communication. Non-commercial logic works for Wikipedia. Why shouldn't it also work for Twitter? What we need are radical social and political innovations in the realm of social media communication that de-commodify and de-commercialize online communication. This would require both fundamental design and political-economic changes of Twitter and other social media. It also requires thinking of alternative funding models beyond profit-making.

The important task is not to make profits on the Internet, but to foster political debate and understanding in a world of global violence. The logic of profit and capital displaces the logic of conversation. We should think of going from social media capitalism towards public sphere social media and commons-based social media. Only then could social media become truly social.

THE PUBLIC SPHERE AND THE VISIBILITY OF THE POWERFUL ON TWITTER

In 2013 Twitter had around 180 million unpaid users and a rather small number of waged employees that together create surplus value. At the end of 2015, Twitter had around 320 million unique monthly users.[13] Twitter's political economy is stratified in two ways:

a) Twitter users and waged employees are exploited, which generates a dispossessed and non-owning class that is opposed to the Twitter-owning class. Given these circumstances, it is no surprise that Twitter's 2010 revenue of US$45 million[14] grew to $139.5 million in 2011,[15] $269.4 million in 2012, $594.5 million in 2013, $1.23 billion in 2014 and $2.2 billion in 2015.[16]

b) Twitter is a profit-oriented commercial company that stratifies visibility of tweets, profiles and trends in favour of advertising clients and at the expense of everyday users in order to accumulate capital.

The analysis of Twitter's political economy shows that Twitter's stratified economy is detrimental to the character of a public sphere. On Twitter, the powerful (especially entertainers and celebrities) "enjoy an oligopoly of the publicistically effective and politically relevant

---

13 Twitter SEC filings, form 8-K, financial year 2015.

14 http://online.wsj.com/article/SB10001424052748703716904576134543029279426.html?KEY WORDS=twitter (accessed on 13 November 2015).

15 www.emarketer.com/newsroom/index.php/strong-2011-twitter-ad-revenues-grow-86-259-mil lion-2012/ (accessed on 13 November 2015).

16 www.emarketer.com/newsroom/index.php/strong-2011-twitter-ad-revenues-grow-86-259-million-2012/, accessed on 13 November 2015. + Twitter SEC filings, form 10-K for financial year 2014, form 8-K for 2015.

formation of assemblies and associations" (Habermas 1989c, 228). There is a limitation of freedom of association and assembly.

THE PSEUDO AND MANUFACTURED PUBLIC SPHERE

These results allow no other conclusion than the one that Twitter is not a public sphere. Twitter shows the continued importance of Habermas's argument that the bourgeois public sphere has created, as Marx has already observed, its own limits and thereby its own immanent critique. "The public sphere with which Marx saw himself confronted contradicted its own principle of universal accessibility" (Habermas 1989c, 124). Habermasian public sphere analysis with the help of the epistemological method of immanent critique compares an actual public sphere (political economy and political communication) to the ideal and values of the public sphere that bourgeois society promises (freedom of speech, freedom of public opinion, freedom of association, freedom of assembly). The immanent analysis conducted in this chapter found that Twitter's reality contradicts the promises of bourgeois society. Twitter is a "pseudo-public sphere" (162) and a "manufactured public sphere" (217).

8.7 CONCLUSION

One of the reasons why critical theory is important for analysing media, technology and information is that it allows us to question and provide alternatives to technological determinism and to explain the causal relationship of media and technology on the one hand, and society on the other, in a complex way that avoids one-dimensionality and one-sidedness. Technological determinism is a kind of explanation of the causal relationship of media/technology and society that assumes that a certain medium or technology has exactly one specific effect on society and social systems (see Figure 8.1). In the event of this effect being assessed positively, we can speak of techno-optimism. In the event of the

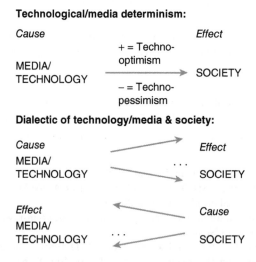

FIGURE 8.1 Two logics of the relationship between media technology and society

effect being assessed negatively, we can speak of techno-pessimism. Techno-optimism and techno-pessimism are the normative dimensions of technological determinism.

The problem of techno-optimistic and techno-pessimistic arguments is that they are only interested in single aspects of technology and create the impression that there are only one-sided effects (see Figure 8.1). They lack a sense of contradictions and the dialectics of technology and society and can therefore be described as technological deterministic forms of argumentation. Technological determinism is a fetishism of technology (Robins and Webster 1999), "the idea that technology develops as the sole result of an internal dynamic, and then, unmediated by any other influence molds society to fit its pattern" (Winner 1980/1999, 29).

Technological determinism overestimates the role of technology in society; it ignores the fact that technology is embedded into society and that it is the people living under and rebelling against power relations, not the technology, who conduct unrest and revolutions. The rise of new technologies often creates an "eruption of feeling that briefly overwhelms reason" (Mosco 2004, 22). Technological determinism ignores the political economy of events. Social media determinism is an expression of the digital sublime, the development that "cyberspace has become the latest icon of the technological and electronic sublime, praised for its epochal and transcendent characteristics and demonized for the depth of the evil it can conjure" (Mosco 2004, 24).

An alternative that avoids technological and social determinisms is to conceptualize the relationship of technology and society as dialectical (see Figure 8.1): society conditions the invention, design and engineering of technology and technology shapes society in complex ways. Technology is conditioned, not determined by society, and vice versa. This means that societal conditions, interests and conflicts influence which technologies will emerge, but technology's effects are not predetermined because modern technologies are complex wholes of interacting parts that are to certain extents unpredictable. Technology shapes society in complex ways, which means that frequently there are multiple effects that can stand in contradiction with each other. Because society and technology are complex systems, which means that they have many elements and many interactions between these elements, it is unlikely that the interaction of the two complex systems of technology and society will have one-dimensional effects. Technology is a medium (enabling and constraining) and outcome of society.

A DIALECTICAL CONCEPT OF TECHNOLOGY AND SOCIETY

A critical theory of media and technology is based on dialectical reasoning (see Figure 8.1). This allows us to see the causal relationship of media/technology and society as multidimensional and complex: a specific media/technology has multiple, at least two, potential effects on society and social systems that can co-exist or stand in contradiction to each other. Which potentials are realized is based on how society, interests, power structures and struggles shape the design and usage of technology in multiple ways that are also potentially contradictory.

Social media in a contradictory society (made up of class conflicts and other conflicts between dominant and dominated groups) are likely to have a contradictory character: they do not necessarily and automatically support/amplify or dampen/limit social change, but rather pose contradictory potentials that stand in contradiction with influences by the state, ideology and capitalism.

SUMMARY

We can summarize the main results of this chapter as follows:

- Habermas's concept of the public sphere stresses that a public sphere is (a) a space of political communication and (b) that access to resources that allow citizens to participate in the public sphere is crucial.
- Habermas's notion of the public sphere is a critical concept that helps to analyse whether modern society lives up to its own expectations. It allows testing whether the freedom of speech and public opinion are realized or rather limited by the distribution of educational and material resources. Furthermore, it enables the same test for the values of freedom of association and assembly by analysing whether there are powerful actors that dominate visibility and influence.
- Twitter is not a public sphere. It should neither be the subject of hope for the renewal of democracy and publication nor the cause of concerns about violence, terrorism, crime, misogyny, online harassment and bullying and riots. What should first and foremost concern us is inequality in society and how to alleviate inequality. Habermas's notion of the public sphere has not primarily been about the media, but about the creation of a concept that allows the criticism of structures that lack public concerns about common goods and limit the availability of the commons for all people.
- Social media are embedded into contradictions and the power structures of contemporary society. They have contradictory characteristics in contradictory societies: they do not necessarily and automatically support/amplify or dampen/limit social change, but rather pose contradictory potentials that stand in contradiction with influences by the state, ideology, capitalism and other media.
- Social media are in antagonistic societies antagonistic communication systems. In antagonistic societies, there are opposing interests expressed in power relations. These interests shape the use of technologies, including social media. Given that there are various opposing interests in an antagonistic society, different interests in how to use technologies exist. These uses also have unpredictable dimensions and consequences. As a result, technologies tend to have complex, contradictory impacts on society. They have both progressive political potentials as well as a dark side. The latter features phenomena such as online fascism, right-wing extremism online, bullying, online misogyny, etc. It is important not to overestimate these phenomena and to avoid moral panics about them. A left realist approach to tackling the Internet's dark side is the most feasible approach that can be taken.

Contemporary societies are today experiencing highly-damaged common goods and services as the result of decades of neoliberalism. The result has been a global crisis of capitalism that allows us to also think about the possibility of strengthening the commons. Strengthening the commons requires common struggle, which also involves, among other things, common communication. The struggle for a commons-based society that overcomes neoliberalism should also be the struggle for communication commons. The stratified structures of Twitter are an expression of the limits of the public sphere. Another society is possible. Is another Twitter possible?

RECOMMENDED READINGS AND EXERCISES

For critically understanding Twitter, it is useful to engage with works by Jürgen Habermas and debates about Twitter's role in politics.

Habermas, Jürgen. 1989. *The structural transformation of the public sphere*. Cambridge, MA: MIT Press.

Jeffrey, Stuart. 2010. A rare interview with Jürgen Habermas. *Financial Times Online*, 30 April 2010.

There are many myths about Habermas's famous book *The Structural Transformation of the Public Sphere*. I therefore recommend that you read the entire book in order to understand its content and the notion of the public sphere. Ask yourself:

* What is the public sphere according to Habermas? How has it developed historically?
* What are characteristics and limits of the bourgeois public sphere?
* How is the notion of the public sphere connected to Karl Marx's thinking?
* What does Habermas mean by refeudalization of the public sphere?
* Think of social media in contemporary politics and society: Which aspects of political communication, limits of the public sphere and refeudalization are there? Try to find examples.
* How do you interpret the fact that a fake Habermas posted about the public sphere on Twitter under Habermas's name and caused some irritation? What are the implications for the public sphere?

Morozov, Evgeny. 2009. The brave new world of slacktivism. http://www.npr.org/templates/story/story.php?storyId=104302141 (accessed on 24 November 2016).

Gladwell, Malcolm. 2010. Small change: Why the revolution will not be tweeted. *The New Yorker*, October: 42–49.

Morozov, Evgeny. 2010. *The net delusion: How not to liberate the world*. London: Allen Lane. Chapter 7: Why Kierkegaard hates slacktivism.

Shirky, Clay. 2011. The political power of social media. *Foreign Affairs* 90 (1): 28–41.

Gladwell, Malcolm and Clay Shirky. 2011. From innovation to revolution: Do social media make protests possible? *Foreign Affairs* 90 (2): 153–154.

These readings focus on a debate between Clay Shirky, Malcolm Gladwell and Evgeny Morozov concerning the question of whether digital media help to liberate the world and strengthen democracy or not.

* Summarize and compare the basic arguments of Shirky, Gladwell and Morozov about social media's role in politics.
* Try to find logical, theoretical and empirical evidence to describe what the relationship between social media, politics and protests looks like.

Identify Twitter hashtags for a current political event and a current entertainment event. Observe, collect and store all postings for these two hashtags for one day (using e.g. an online

(Continued)

(Continued)

data collection service such as Discovertext). Conduct a content and discourse analysis that focuses on the topics of discussion and their frequency, the interactivity of the tweets (the degree of re-tweeting/information/communication), the overall number of tweets, the number of participants, the number of postings per participant and the share of tweets for each participant in the total number of tweets, the use of emoticons, abbreviations and affects. If there are disagreements, how are they expressed? Are these disagreements further discussed? Observe also how the number of followers of the most active participants changes during the day. How many new followers does s/he gain?

- Interpret the results of your small study in the light of Habermas's public sphere theory.

Examples for the dark side of communication on Twitter and social media include online fascism, misogyny and terrorist communication. Work in groups. Each group searches for a severe example of a disturbing use of social media. Each group analyses its example case and discusses the following questions:

- What would right-wing politicians, who favour law-and-order and control-politics, suggest in order to hinder something like this occurring again in the future?
- Why are such right-wing arguments wrong?
- What does a left realist strategy in contrast look like?

9 WEIBO: POWER, IDEOLOGY AND SOCIAL STRUGGLES IN CHINESE CAPITALISM

KEY QUESTIONS

- What are the Chinese economy's key features?
- How does neoliberalism matter in China?
- What is the role of the working class in China?
- How does the Chinese working class relate to digital media?
- What are the features of the political economy of Chinese social media platforms such as Weibo?
- How does the financialization of the Internet work in China?
- What is the role of the political control of the Internet in China and the West?

KEY CONCEPTS

Neoliberalism
Neoliberalism with Chinese characteristics
Labour
Labour share
International division of digital labour
Financialization

Financialization of social media
Ideology
Engaging/connecting/sharing-ideology
Network society
Working class
Working-class network society

OVERVIEW

If you look at lists of the world's most widely used Internet platforms, you will realize that quite a few Chinese ones are among them. An analysis of social media in China is therefore an important task. Weibo is one of the most popular social media platforms in China. It is a kind of Chinese Twitter. This chapter asks: What are the features of the political economy of Chinese social media platforms such as Weibo in the context of the development of the Chinese economy and Chinese society?

The Chinese economy has often been celebrated for its large growth. Along with it, also its Internet economy has been presented as being the largest online market of users in the world. Weibo is not just a symbol of Chinese media, but also of the promises of Chinese capitalism. Chinese capitalism, however, is special because the state plays an important role in it. We therefore need to understand the relationship of the economy, the state and the Internet in China.

Chinese companies operate some of the world's most accessed web platforms such as Baidu, QQ, Taobao, Sina, Weibo, TMall, Hao123. Baidu is a search engine, the Chinese equivalent of Google. It also operates Hao123 that provides online listings. Tencent Holdings owns and operates QQ, a web portal and instant messenger. The Alibaba Group provides both Taobao and TMall, two online shopping platforms. They are like Chinese versions of Amazon and eBay. Sina Corp operates the web portal Sina and the microblog platform Weibo. Baidu, Sina, Tencent and Alibaba are among China's most powerful media companies. There are also Chinese equivalents of video-sharing platforms such as YouTube and Vimeo: Tudou, Youku; and of social networking sites such as Facebook and LinkedIn: Douban, Kaixin001, QZone and RenRen.

CHINA AND THE WEST

The development of the Chinese Internet economy is linked to China's general economic development. The gross domestic product (GDP) measures an economy's total size. China's GDP had the following values:

* 2013: US$16.5 trillion;
* 2014: US$18.0 trillion;
* 2015: US$19.4 trillion;
* 2016: US$20.9 trillion;
* 2017: US$22.5 trillion;
* 2018: US$24.3 trillion;
* 2019: US$26.3 trillion[1]

The USA's GDP had in contrast the following values:

* 2013: US$16.7 trillion;
* 2014: US$17.4 trillion;
* 2015: US$18.0 trillion;
* 2016: US$18.6 trillion;
* 2017: US$19.3 trillion;
* 2018: US$20.1 trillion;
* 2019: US$21.0 trillion.

The Western press has been fascinated by China's economic growth. Western magazines' front-cover headlines about China have included:

* "Made in China: New, improved and stronger than ever" (*The Economist*, 14 March 2015),
* "Buying up the world: The coming wave of Chinese takeovers" (*The Economist*, 13 November 2010),

---

1 Data source: IMF World Economic Outlook Database, April 2016; GDP in US$ with purchasing-power parity (PPP).

- "China: Dawn of a new dynasty" (*Time*, 22 January 2007),
- "How China runs the world economy" (*The Economist*, 30 July 2005),
- "China's new revolution: Remaking our world, one deal at a time" (*Time*, 27 June 2005).

CHINA AND THE USA

Table 9.1 shows the specific shares of China's and the USA's economy in the worldwide GDP.

Such data should of course be considered with caution because it is partly based on predictions. It is difficult to predict economic development because economies are complex, dynamic systems. But the data certainly indicate that the total size of the Chinese economy has for the first time exceeded the one of the USA in 2014. This fact is impressive, but should also be interpreted with caution because China's population was in 2016 4.4 times larger than that of the United States: China had around 1.4 billion inhabitants, the United States around 320 million.[2] Taking population size into account, the GDP per capita in 2016 was around US$15,095 in China and US$57,220 in the USA. If one takes population into account, then the projection for China's GDP per capita in 2020 is US$20,190 and that for the USA US$67,238.[3] China's immense economic size is certainly not just an issue of growth, but also one of population. GDP data is also misleading because the GDP is the sum of capital investments, salaries and profits. This variable can therefore say nothing about inequality in a country. For measuring inequality one needs to take the distribution of wealth between labour and capital into account.

This chapter first discusses tendencies in the development of Chinese capitalism (section 1). It then analyses Weibo's political economy (section 2) and ideology (section 3). Section 4 focuses on social struggles in China and their relations to the Internet. This chapter's focus on Weibo does not indicate that Weibo is necessarily China's most important Internet platform. Weibo is, however, certainly besides QQ a key Chinese social media platform. The limited space in this book does not allow for covering more than one Chinese platform. But certainly more critical analyses of non-Western Internet economies and platforms are needed.

TABLE 9.1   China and the USA's shares of the worldwide GDP

	China (%)	USA (%)
2013	16.0	16.1
2014	16.6	15.9
2015	17.2	15.9
2016	17.7	15.8
2017	18.1	15.6
2018	18.5	15.5
2019	18.9	15.2
2020	19.3	14.9

Data source: IMF World Economic Outlook, October 2015; GDP measured in international US$ with purchasing-power-parity.

---

2   Data source: UN Statistics, http://data.un.org (accessed on 16 November 2015).
3   Data source: IMF World Economic Outlook Database, April 2016; Gross domestic product based on purchasing-power-parity (PPP) per capita GDP

9.1 CHINA'S CAPITALISM

In the West, the information about the Chinese economy is often very sensationalist and superficial. In everyday news, one can hardly read in-depth analyses of the world's largest country's economic structures. In China itself, Marxist theory is today predominantly an orthodoxy and not a critical tool of thought. For understanding the role of social media in China, we need to take a closer look at the structure of China's economy. China has a peculiar form of capitalism. We can identify several key features.[4]

EXPORT-ORIENTATION

China's economy is strongly export-oriented. There is comparatively little export of services. Manufactured and agricultural products dominate China's exports. China's most important export products are computers, mobile phones, integrated circuits and clothes.

FOREIGN DIRECT INVESTMENT

Foreign direct investment (FDI) into the Chinese economy has been undergoing a large growth since 1978, when Deng Xiaoping opened up China to foreign capital.

NEOLIBERALISM WITH CHINESE CHARACTERISTICS

Neoliberalism is an ideology and a form of politics that wants to treat everything as a commodity that is sold for money on markets. China's political economy has been shaped by a neoliberalism with Chinese characteristics that combines privatization, deregulation, commodification and financialization with an authoritarian state.

LOW-WAGE ECONOMY

Chinese exports and foreign direct investment into the country are based on a low-wage manu-facturing economy. Rural migrants form an important workforce in China's low-wage economy.

INDUSTRIALIZATION AND INFORMATIZATION

At the macroeconomic level, employment in manufacturing has remained relatively constant. Service employment has been increasing. The agricultural sector's share in occupations has been declining.

UNEVEN URBAN/RURAL DEVELOPMENT

China's rural areas are the focus of agricultural production. The urban metropolises are centres of industrial production, services, the information industry and finance.

---

4 For example analyses, consult: Amin 2013a, 2013b; Arrighi 2007; Chase-Dunn 2010; Foster and McChesney 2012; Hart-Landsberg 2010; Harvey 2007, 2012; Huang 2008; Hung 2009, 2012; Li 2008a, 2008b; Lin 2013; Nolan 2012; Nolan and Zhang 2010; Panitch 2010; Qi 2014.

URBANIZATION

There has been a strong urbanization of China that is linked to economic centralization, uneven geographical economic development and the large flows of migration from rural areas to metropolises.

URBAN INFRASTRUCTURE AND OVERPRODUCTION

China has made massive investment in creating an urban infrastructure for transport, housing, offices, highways, subways, shopping malls, high-speed rail links, dams, airports, science parks, amusement parks, sports facilities and so on. This development has resulted in a boom of and overproduction in the cement, aluminium, real estate, steel and car industries. Overproduction means that goods and services are produced that are not consumed. Invested capital can therefore not be turned into profits.

INEQUALITY

Rising income inequality has resulted in underconsumption accompanying overproduction. Underconsumption means that there is an abundance of goods, but many people do not have incomes high enough to purchase them.

FINANCIALIZATION

Financialization means that certain parts of the economy are turned into assets that are traded on financial markets. China's economic development has also created a speculative real estate market that has seen a large increase of housing prizes and has created an asset bubble.

ECOLOGICAL PROBLEMS

China's economic development has resulted in ecological problems such as air and water pollution, desertification and reduced biodiversity.

WORKING-CLASS STRUGGLES

Social inequality and high exploitation rates have resulted in a large amount of strikes and protests by the Chinese working class.

Capitalism and socialism are two models that in China have been articulated in a complex manner. In Marxist political economy, there are two distinct positions on the question of whether China is today a capitalist or a socialist country.

POSITION 1: CHINA HAS A SOCIALIST MARKET ECONOMY

Some Marxist authors argue that the Chinese economy is not a form of capitalism, but continues to be socialist in character. Samir Amin and Giovanni Arrighi are two of the most important thinkers representing this position.

Samir Amin is a well-known theorist and analyst of global society and development issues, who has published dozens of books about global capitalism. Giovanni Arrighi is one of the most important world systems theorists. He wrote a well-known book about China titled *Adam Smith in Beijing*.

SAMIR AMIN ON CHINA

Samir Amin says that China is not a capitalist country: "The capitalist road is based on the transformation of land into a commodity" (Amin 2013a, 16). Chinese peasants would not defend "the principle of private property" (Amin 2013a, 29). China's economy would involve an important role of petty production and small agricultural family production. The Chinese welfare state and the modernization of the Chinese economy would have resulted in China's rise. "I argue that if China is indeed an emerging power, this is precisely because it has not chosen the capitalist path of development pure and simple" (Amin 2013a, 25). Although there would be inequality in the country, China would have vastly reduced poverty. Amin argues that China's rise is part of capitalism's "long period of decline" (Amin 2013b, 107), a "wave of independent initiatives of the countries of the South", in which "the 'emerging' countries and others, like their peoples, are fighting the ways in which the collective imperialism of the Triad [North America, Europe, Japan] tries to perpetuate its domination" (117).

GIOVANNI ARRIGHI: ADAM SMITH WAS A BRITISH ECONOMIST, BUT TODAY HE IS ALSO CHINESE

Giovanni Arrighi (2007, 4) said that China's increasing power could result in "an eventual equalization of power between the conquering West and the conquered non-West". The USA would continue to be the globally hegemonic military power. But China would have strongly challenged the USA's economic power. China's share of global value would have increased and the USA's economy would be strongly based on Chinese exports and credits. Arrighi (2007) shares Amin's assessment that

> socialism in China has thus far neither won nor lost [...] as long as the principle of equal access to land continues to be recognized and implemented, it is not too late for social action in contemporary China to steer evolution in a non-capitalist direction [...] even if socialism has already lost out in China, capitalism, by this definition, has not yet won. (Arrighi 2007, 16, 24)

Arrighi (2007) characterizes contemporary China as a socialist market economy, a model that Adam Smith would have envisioned and that has advanced and maintained health care, education and welfare (16). He therefore titled one of his books *Adam Smith in Beijing* (Arrighi 2007).

> Contrary to widespread belief, the main attraction of the PRC for foreign capital has not been its huge and low-priced reserves of labor as such – there are plenty of such reserves around the world but nowhere have they attracted capital to the extent that they have in China. The main attraction, we shall argue, has been the high quality of those reserves – in terms of health, education, and capacity for self-management in combination with the rapid expansion of the supply and demand conditions for the productive mobilization of these reserves within China itself. (Arrighi 2007, 351)

DAVID HARVEY VS. GIOVANNI ARRIGHI: HOW TWO MARXISTS DISAGREE ON CHINA

Arrighi (2007) says that introducing competion in China did not mean the privatization of state-owned enterprises (SOEs), but exposing them to competition with new private firms, community-owned enterprises and international capital (356). David Harvey is a critical geographer, who is by many considered to be the most influential Marxist theorist today. Harvey (2007) argues that the Chinese economy is a specific authoritarian form of neoliberalism. He defines neoliberalism as accumulation by dispossession: citizens are dispossessed of income, wealth and access to public services.

Arrighi (2007, 361–367) disagrees with Harvey's assessment of China. He argues that China is facing accumulation without dispossession: the creation of communally-owned Township and Village Enterprises (TVEs) would have enabled a "relatively egalitarian distribution of land among households" (364). It would have absorbed the rural surplus labour force and advanced industrial production in rural areas. "China's economic success was built on the extraordinary social achievements of the Mao era" (370). This Maoist tradition that included the "economic and educational uplifting of peasantry" (374) would have also resulted in vast increases of per capita income, life expectancy and literacy. At the same time China would, however, face rising inequality between social groups and rural and urban areas (375), environmental degradation and the diversion of rural land into industrial, real estate or infrastructural zones, which would have advanced an "enormous upsurge of social unrest" (378).

Christopher Chase-Dunn (2010, 47–48) criticizes that even farmers not dispossessed of their land have become integrated into the capitalist world market and via outsourcing have become de facto wageworkers for large companies. Leo Panitch (2010, 84) points out in this context that "unequal class-relations" have also developed within township village enterprises and that "TVEs have now been marginalised as the foundation of China's economic development". Richard Walker (2010) says that Arrighi does not take into account that many township village enterprises and state-owned enterprises have collapsed since the late 1990s, which would have increased the urban proletariat. Arrighi would also neglect the privatization of land in Chinese cities and the growth of the speculative real estate market.

POSITION 2: CHINA'S ECONOMY IS A PECULIAR FORM OF CAPITALISM

A second group of Marxist authors stresses the rise of capitalism and neoliberal politics in China. They foreground discontinuities and how the logic of capitalism started penetrating China when Deng Xiaoping came to power in 1978. Lin Chun (2013, 47) argues for example: "Abandoning socialism in the name of reform, however, is precisely what has been happening and is openly advocated by an intellectual elite speaking for the wealthy and powerful." At the same time these reforms would have been accompanied by the rise of new anti-capitalist struggles so that Chinese socialism "makes more sense as protest than as official language" (47). "The persistence of sweatshops, the collusion of money and power, the dictatorship of capital, and the reign of developmentalism all violate socialist promises" (87).

Slavoj Žižek is a Slovenian philosopher whom many consider to be one of the most influential thinkers today. He has written on virtually almost all imaginable topics. He therefore also has something to say on China and it is interesting to listen to him: "China as the emerging superpower of the twenty-first century thus seems to embody a new kind of capitalism: disregard for ecological consequences, disdain for workers' rights, everything subordinated to the ruthless drive to develop and become the new world force" (Žižek 2008, 191).

Ho-fung Hung identifies "triple transformations of global capitalism in the late twentieth century" (Hung 2009, 13) that has shaped China: "(1) the advent of a new international division of labor, (2) the twin decline of U.S. hegemony and the Cold War order, and (3) the general decline of antisystemic movements in the form of working-class-based, state-power-oriented mass politics" (Hung 2009, 2).

DAVID HARVEY: NEOLIBERALISM WITH CHINESE CHARACTERISTICS

David Harvey (2007) argues China has implemented a neoliberalism with Chinese characteristics. This model relies on heavy foreign direct investments combined with a low-wage economy and special economic zones focused on foreign direct investments, the fostering of urban and rural private companies as well as rural township village enterprises, state-owned corporation-managers' ownership of surplus products and extra-profits, the transformation of state enterprises into shareholding companies for fostering entrepreneurialism, competition and free markets, an export-oriented growth strategy focusing on the export of light industrial products (textiles, toys, plastics) and electronic consumer goods combined with low wages.

Hundreds of millions of rural migrants have fled poverty and the dispossession of land that is turned into private property. They have become highly-exploited workers in China's urban centres. Especially the rural land around larger cities has been dispossessed for being turned into export-processing zones or urban modernization projects (Harvey 2007, 146). "This labour force is vulnerable to super-exploitation and puts downward pressure on the wages of urban residents" (Harvey 2007, 127). China's urbanization would have made the country dependent on the import of cement, coal, steel, oil and various metals. It would also have resulted in a growth of urban/rural income and wealth inequality.

> Almost every city in the world has witnessed a building boom for the rich – often of a distressingly similar character – in the midst of a flood of impoverished migrants converging on cities as a rural peasantry is dispossessed through the industrialization and commercialization of agriculture. (Harvey 2012, 12)

The Chinese state and Chinese municipalities have to a large degree debt-financed the growth by making large investments in urbanization projects involving a focus on real estate and construction, highways, subways, high-speed rail links, dams, shopping malls, airports, science parks, amusement parks, gated communities, golf courses and so on. These investments would have resulted in overbuilding, a speculative real estate market that drove up urban housing prices and the creation of an asset bubble. "The danger lurks of a severe crisis of over-accumulation of fixed capital (particularly in the built environment)" (Harvey 2007, 141). The "overaccumulation of capital has been or is about to be transformed into an overaccumulation of investments in the built environment" (Harvey 2012, 58). Many assets in the built environment would be overvalued (Harvey 2012, 65). So Harvey says that in China the composition of total capital changes in such a way that ever more infrastructure investments are made, especially in buildings, infrastructure and land. At the same time agri-cultural and manufacturing jobs tend to disappear via dispossessions and privatizations. The result has been "unoccupied capital on the one hand and an unemployed working population on the other" (Marx 1894, 359) in China.

The new world economic crisis had an impact on China because its exports to a large degree go to the USA. As a result, Chinese exports declined in 2009 by 20 per cent (Harvey 2012, 61), to which the Chinese government reacted with further investments in urban and infrastructure projects in order to absorb the unemployed surplus labour set free in the export industry (62). "Many investments, such as the huge shopping mall close to Dongguan, stand almost empty, as do quite a few of the high-rises that litter the urban landscape almost every-where. And then there are the empty new cities waiting for populations and industries to arrive" (62). The expansion would have meant the rise of more and more irregular urban employment in China and the privatization of Chinese state companies.

CAPITALISM AND/OR SOCIALISM?

The discussion shows that Marxist political economists do not agree about the character of China's economy. The question of whether China is capitalist and/or socialist is, however, not just a theoretical question. One should also try to sustain it by data. This is a difficult task because of the limited availability of reliable data. One should therefore always compare several data sources.

The National Bureau of Statistics of China (2015) reports on the structure of the Chinese industry:

> The profits made by the industrial enterprises above the designated size in 2014 were 6,471.5 billion yuan, an increase of 3.3 percent over the previous year. Of this total, the profits of the state-owned and state-holding enterprises were 1,400.7 billion yuan, down by 5.7 percent; that of the collective enterprises were 53.8 bil-lion yuan, up by 0.4 percent; that of the share-holding enterprises 4,296.3 billion yuan, up by 1.6 percent; that of the enterprises by foreign investors and investors from Hong Kong, Macao and Taiwan 1,597.2 billion yuan, up by 9.5 percent; and that of private enterprises were 2,232.3 billion yuan, a rise of 4.9 percent.

According to this data, the capitalist character of Chinese industry dominates in the form of share-holding enterprises, foreign-owned enterprises and private Chinese companies. State-owned enterprises continue to play a significant but not dominant role. Collective enterprises play a minor role. There were no foreign investors and almost 100 per cent collective and stated-owned enterprises in 1978 (Qiu 2009, 89: Table 4.2). Huang (2008, 79) shows that the share of large privately-owned township village enterprises (TVEs) in total TVE employ-ment increased from 6.8 per cent in 1985 to 26.3 per cent in 2002. That of collectively-owned township village enterprises decreased from 59.5 per cent in 1985 to 28.6 per cent in 2002. The number of township village enterprises run by small households increased from 33.7 per cent in 1985 to 45.0 per cent. A decreasing share of collective ownership and increasing shares of private-capitalist and small private enterprises shape the structure of rural companies.

Huang (2008, 13–19) uses two different data sets (Organization for Economic Co-operation and Development (OECD), Guangdong Statistical Manual) for assessing the Chinese economy. Value-added is a measure of new economic activities during a certain time period in an economy. Huang concludes that based on the first data set the share of capitalist value-added in China increased from 28.9 per cent in 1998 to 44.7 per cent in 2001 and 71.2 per cent in 2005. In the second data set, it increased from 31.8 per cent in 1998 to 38.8 per cent in 2001 and 50.8 per cent in 2005. In both cases, indigenous and foreign-owned companies were included. Both analyses conclude that China's economy has an increasing share of capitalist ownership and is predominantly capitalist. State-owned and collective enterprises that have a mixed ownership status so that only a part of it is shareholder-owned were in both analyses counted as being capitalist if the capital share in ownership was larger than 50 per cent. One can therefore say that the estimates are conservative and that the actual share of capitalist ownership in the total Chinese economy exceeds these estimations. If a company is, for example, 49 per cent owned by capitalist shareholders and 51 per cent by workers it is to a significant degree shaped by capitalist ownership.

If the data are correct, then both Arrighi and Amin overstate the socialist character of the Chinese economy. Capitalist, state and collective (worker-controlled) forms of ownership and combinations thereof each control specific shares of the Chinese economy. There are indications that non-capitalist ownership is not dominant and has decreased. If this is the case, then China is today at least predominantly a capitalist society.

A CRISIS OF THE CHINESE ECONOMY?

A stock market index measures the total financial value of the companies listed on a particular financial market. In summer 2015, China saw a drop of its stock market values:

- The Shanghai Stock Exchange Composite Index dropped from 5,166 points on 12 June to 3,887 on 3 July and 2,927 on 26 August.
- The Shenzen Stock Exchange Composite Index decreased from 2,464 points on 30 June to 1955 on 9 July and 1,696 on 26 August.
- The Hong Kong-based Hang Seng Index fell from 27,993 points on 26 May to 23,517 on 8 July and 20,584 on 7 September.
- Business observers in the West interpreted these developments as the end of the Chinese boom: The *Financial Times* wrote that the "Chinese model is nearing its end" (*FT Online*, 21 August 2015).
- *The Economist* spoke of the "Great Fall of China" (*The Economist*, 29 August 2015).

24 August was termed "Black Monday" because Chinese stock exchanges dropped particularly heavily on this day. Commodity prices for oil, gold, food, iron, metal and coal fell on the world market. Currencies of emerging economies lost in exchange value. The Chinese economy's growth rate slowed down. Also Western stock markets were negatively affected by the Chinese financial turmoil. The Chinese government stopped new companies from making initial public offerings. It prohibited the short-term sale of stock, backed large funds to buy shares, closed down the trading of a significant amount of corporations on Chinese stock markets, and banned owners of large amounts of shares from selling these for a six-month period.

MICHAEL ROBERTS: SOCIALISM WITH CHINESE CHARACTERISTICS AND ECONOMIC CRISIS

The Marxist political economist Michael Roberts (2015a, 2015b) argues that the stock market turmoil had to do with the financialization of the Chinese property market, a stock market bubble, high inequality and the super-rich's tax evasion. Roberts is critical of neo-liberal economists' argument that the Chinese economy is crisis-prone because of state control. He argues to the contrary that this control has enabled China's growth. Socialism with Chinese characteristics with a strong role of state-owned corporations in the economy and a high level of state intervention into and state direction of the economy would protect China from sliding into a severe crisis. "The great Chinese economic 'miracle' is not exhausted quite yet" (Roberts 2015b). "China is still growing faster than any other major capitalist country and nearly all the so-called emerging economies" (Roberts 2015a).

MINQI LI: NEOLIBERALISM WITH CHINESE CHARACTERISTICS AS CRISIS FACTOR

Minqi Li (2016) argues that global capitalism since the 1970s has been volatile to crisis. An attempt to increase profits would in this context have been to outsource labour to China in order to "lower the global labor cost" and revive "the global rate of profit" (78). Li follows Immanuel Wallerstein, a prominent sociologist and historian, who founded world systems theory. Wallerstein argues for a profit squeeze theory of capitalist crisis. This theory says that capitalist crisis can result from a rise in wages, infrastructural and environmental costs, and increased capital taxation. With capitalist development in China, this profit squeeze tendency would have started to operate (Li 2006, 80). Chinese neoliberalism would, however, via lay-offs, privatization and wage repression, have managed to increase its profits.

The transfer of agricultural population to industrial labour, on which the Chinese low-wage economy and its export orientation are built, would sooner or later reach limits. The bad treatment of these workers would call forth struggles for higher wages, which would together with ecological constraints put pressure on China's economic growth. Furthermore China would be compelled to make heavy investments into infrastructure and equipment because its economy is export-oriented. Working-class struggles and environmental devastation would have resulted in increasing wage and taxation costs and a decrease of the profit rate in China since 2005.

Li (2016, 98) predicts that China will see a major economic and financial crisis by the 2020s or earlier. Given that the world economy, including China, depends strongly on fossil fuels, especially oil, natural gas and coal, but non-renewable resources are in limited supply, Li assumes that there will be negative effects on the world economy and also the Chinese economy in the near future. These limits would exhaust the possibility of China continuing to act as a fix to the crises of global capitalism.

> Within the current capitalist world system, Chinese capitalism specializes in manufacturing exports based on the exploitation of a large cheap labor force and the massive consumption of natural resources. As labor and resources costs rise, Chinese capitalism begins to be squeezed between rising costs and the relatively low value-added commodities it sells in the global capitalist market. This is a fundamental contradiction that Chinese capitalism cannot overcome. (Li 2016, 180)

CHINA, CAPITALISM, CRISIS

Both Michael Roberts and Minqi Li are Marxist political economists. Yet their positions on the Chinese economy's crisis-proneness are quite opposed: Roberts argues that China is relatively crisis-proof and will continue to grow because it has maintained the model of socialism with Chinese characteristics. Li in contrast holds that the Chinese economy is highly antagonistic because it has adopted neoliberalism with Chinese characteristics and therefore will inevitable enter a major crisis. It is interesting to see that the basic disagreement about capitalism and/or socialism that we identified earlier in Marxist theory can also be found in the discussion of China and the economic crisis. The disagreement furthermore extends to the question of whether the BRICS countries (Brazil, Russia, India, China and South Africa) challenge and/or reproduce capitalism and imperialism. Immanuel Wallerstein (2015, 271–272) summarizes this debate: The BRICS countries

> have also become a very controversial subject. There are those who think of BRICS as the avant-garde of anti-imperialist struggle. There are those who, quite to the contrary, think of the BRICS as sub-imperialist agents of the true North (North America, Western Europe and Japan). And there are those who argue that they are both.

The preceding analysis in this chapter indicated that China is predominantly capitalist. Its capitalism is indeed neoliberalism with Chinese characteristics. If this is the case, then Chinese capitalism is necessarily an antagonistic system. Capitalism is inherently crisis-prone and given capitalist antagonisms, China's is unlikely to grow forever. That there are Chinese characteristics of capitalism means that China's political economy can be characterised as neoliberal state capitalism. There is state control of public opinion. The Chinese government tends to intervene into the economy. The way it actively intervened in financial markets in the 2015 Chinese stock market turmoil clearly demonstrates this political approach. The Chinese government may therefore to a certain extent be able to manage crises by deferring them into the future and shifting capitalism's contradictions around. Given capitalist domination and the integration of China into the capitalist world system, the Chinese government cannot, however, overcome crisis-proneness.

The media are institutions that organize the communication of information in society. In China, just like in the West, the media landscape has undergone transitions with the emergence of the computer, the Internet and mobile media. These changes of the media landscape interact with the Chinese economy and society.

CHINESE MEDIA

Yuezhi Zhao is the leading political economist of Chinese media. She argues that China is not simply opposed to Western cultural imperialism, but has a complex relationship with the West (Zhao 2011): it is neither completely different from Western capitalism, nor the same. She shows that since the reform period started in 1978 under Deng Xiaoping, China promoted ICTs and the commercialization of the media. The Chinese form of neoliberalism would combine commodification with state control and incorporate Western marketing and public relations. At the same time there would be a political and ideological legacy of Mao and socialism that could not be done away with and that would shape Chinese identity. There would also be a cultural form of nationalism and the media would celebrate the new urban middle class. Zhao speaks of the "challenge of China": China is "a poor country that has managed to rise up in the global capitalist order while dramatically increasing domestic class inequalities, and a nation with staggering ethnic, gender, urban-rural, and regional divides" (Zhao 2011, 563).

Joseph Nye (2004) has defined the power that is not exerted with the help of physical force, guns and bombs, but with the help of culture, the media and ideology as "soft power". Soft power is an odd concept that trivializes the presence of ideology and propaganda in international communication. Zhao analyses the Chinese "soft power strategy", in which Chinese media such as CCTV International, China Radio International, *China Daily* or the *Global Times* play an important role: "No longer content with merely critiquing American cultural imperialism, the Chinese state under the Hu Jintao leadership has embraced Joseph Nye's concept of 'soft power' and launched a multifaceted effort to project China abroad through its media and cultural institutions" (Zhao 2011, 574).

There is large number of migrant workers that form a new urban proletariat and a supply of cheap labour for China's export of consumer goods and consumer electronics to the West. At the same time, in social struggles these workers make use of blogs, Weibo, online video, social networks and so on (Qiu 2009, 2012).

CHINA IN THE INTERNATIONAL DIVISION OF DIGITAL LABOUR

Working conditions in China have attracted significant attention: there are, for example, the stories of textile workers, who face very harsh conditions. Comparable conditions are also present in the computer manufacturing industry. The suicides of Foxconn workers, who could not endure the difficult labour they performed, made this point very evident. Both China's textile and computer assemblage industries are huge.

China is the largest exporter of computer parts and accessories and computers and office machines: in 2014, Mainland China accounted for 23.6 per cent of the world's exports of this product type and Hong Kong for 20.0 per cent, which combined is 43.6 per cent of the worldwide exports in this economic segment.[5] The second largest exporter was the United States with a share of 12.4 per cent.[6] In 2014, China also accounted for 46.5 per cent of the exports of automatic data processing machines.[7] The United States was the second largest exporter with a share of 7.6 per cent. In the same year, China was also the world's largest exporter of mobile phones: it accounted for an export share of 60.5 per cent.[8] It was also the largest exporter of clothes: in 2014 China made 43.0 per cent of the world's exports of knit or crochet apparel items and 38.5 per cent of the world's exports in non-knit and non-crochet apparel articles.[9]

China's export-oriented manufacturing of computers, mobile phones and textiles indicates that both the information technology industry and the textile industry play an important

---

5 Data source: Trade Map – International Trade Statistics.
6 Ibid.
7 Ibid.
8 Ibid.
9 Ibid.

role in its economy. The textile industry is a classical industry, the information technology industry in contrast a rather new one. Both tend to be based on low-paid, low-skill labour. These manufacturing sectors are labour-intensive. That a good is labour-intensive means that it takes comparatively many working hours to produce it.

Given China's low-wage economy, in which young rural migrants play a very important role, the two sectors of textiles and information technology have therefore become of key importance for Western capitalist corporations' investments. By outsourcing labour to China, they aim at reducing their production costs in order to maximize their profits.

THE INTERNATIONAL DIVISION OF DIGITAL LABOUR

The digital media industry is a global industry that is based on an international division of digital labour (IDDL; see the discussion in Chapter 5 of this book). China's role in the international division of digital labour is that predominantly it is a source of cheap labour that manufactures computers, mobile phones and computing equipment. Our everyday use of computers and phones is based on highly-exploited Chinese labour. Many of these workers are young rural migrants who face harsh working conditions. The conditions in Foxconn factories described in Chapter 5 are prototypical for China's integration into the international division of digital labour and its global circuits. A 2015 report by China Labor Watch (2015, 2) that analyses the working conditions in Apple's Chinese supply companies concludes:

> Apple constantly claims that it is monitoring suppliers' compliance with Apple labor standards. Research of Pegatron workers' pay stubs reveals average of 60+ working hours per week, 52% of workers completed more than 90 hours of overtime per month, even working as many as 132 hours of overtime. Workers desire overtime because their base wages are too low; base wages cannot meet the local living standard. [...] Apple has sufficient profits to improve workers' treatment. Apple executives make public commitments to workers, yet poor labor conditions remain unresolved. Earning three-fifths of the profit in the industry, and with $178 bn in cash reserves, if Apple doesn't reform labor conditions, who will?

The same report found that Apple's total labour costs accounted in 2014 for only 3.4 per cent of its total revenue, whereas profits were at a high level of 24.1 per cent (China Labor Watch 2015, 3). This circumstance is an indication that Apple achieves massive profits and a very large profit rate by a high rate of exploitation in China.

PARALLELS TO NINETEENTH-CENTURY BRITAIN

The situation in the Chinese information technology and textile industries is not so dissimilar from the conditions of the working class in nineteenth-century Britain that Marx and Engels analysed. Engels in 1846 published his analysis of *The Condition of the Working Class in England*. Read this quote and see how much it resonates with the descriptions of labour conditions in Chinese factories producing Apple iPhones:

Of all the workers in competition with machinery, the most ill-used are the hand-loom cotton weavers. They receive the most trifling wages, and, with full work, are not in a position to earn more than ten shillings a week. One class of woven goods after another is annexed by the power-loom, and hand-weaving is the last refuge of workers thrown out of employment in other branches, so that the trade is always overcrowded. Hence it comes that, in average seasons, the hand-weaver counts himself fortunate if he can earn six or seven shillings a week, while to reach this sum he must sit at his loom fourteen to eighteen hours a day. Most woven goods require moreover a damp weaving-room, to keep the weft from snapping, and in part for this reason, in part because of their poverty, which prevents them from paying for better dwellings, the work-rooms of these weavers are usually without wooden or paved floors. I have been in many dwellings of such weavers, in remote, vile courts and alleys, usually in cellars. Often half-a-dozen of these hand-loom weavers, several of them married, live together in a cottage with one or two work-rooms, and one large sleeping-room. Their food consists almost exclusively of potatoes, with perhaps oatmeal porridge, rarely milk, and scarcely ever meat. Great numbers of them are Irish or of Irish descent. (Engels 1846, 433–434)

Young rural migrants in China's urban agglomerations are the contemporary Chinese equivalent to nineteenth-century Irish migrant workers in Britain. They work in sweatshops for producing commodities that are sold by Western corporations. They live in cellars or poor dwellings, work long hours, and have low wages. Hard labour makes them ill and kills them.

iSLAVERY IN DIGITAL CAPITALISM

Modes of production do not develop in a dualist manner so that one (such as capitalism) simply eliminates older ones (such as feudalism and patriarchy). They rather develop in a dialectical manner. This means that newer stages in economic history "sublate" older ones, that is, incorporate them, change them and at the same time go beyond them by new emergent qualities (see Fuchs 2014a, Chapter 6, 2015a, Chapter 6).

JACK QIU: A KEY CRITICAL THINKER OF THE INTERNET IN CHINA

Jack Qiu (2016, 53) in his book *Goodbye iSlave: A Manifesto for Digital Abolition* applies this understanding to slavery, arguing that "rather than pre-modern or anti-modern, slavery […] is part and parcel of capitalist modernity", which means that it continues to exist in specific forms in digital capitalism.

"The so-called 'rise of China' would have been impossible without European technologies and Japanese investment, Middle-Eastern oil and African minerals, Australian coal and Russian timber, and above all, American consumption" (Qiu 2016, 15). Jack Qiu (2016) focuses in his analysis especially on two nodes in the international division of digital labour: the manufacturing iSlaves and manufactured iSlaves: "Gadgets made by Foxconn's manufacturing iSlaves are […] sold to manufactured iSlaves who play and labor in cyberspace, another set of New World plantations" (Qiu 2016, 179).

Conceptually, the manufacturing mode of iSlavery consists of all the labor force required in the productive processes of digital media industries. It can be waged or unwaged, formal or informal, handling mostly tasks of material manipulation. There are many modes of manufacturing iSlave be they Congolese mine workers or Indonesian child labor. (Qiu 2016, 54)

Manufactured iSlaves represent a deceptive, prevalent, and indispensable mode of iSlavery that operates in the realm of cultural consumption. It refers more specifically to those who are constantly attached to their gadgets, playing games, updating 'status', 'liking' other people's updates (Qiu 2016, 91).

THE SOCIAL CONSEQUENCES OF APPLE: SUICIDE JUMPERS AND ORGAN SALES

As the epitome of manufacturing iSlaves, Qiu tells the story of Tian Yu, a young Foxconn worker who survived jumping from a Foxconn building after she could no longer stand the harsh working conditions: the enslavement of workers by transnational corporations such as Apple and Foxconn that exploit them, military drill, forced internships, keeping workers from being able to quit the job by bureaucratic procedures, the humiliation of workers, dangerous working and living conditions, and so on.

Jack Qiu also tells the story of the Chinese teenager Yangi Ni in Huangshan, who sold one of his kidneys in order to buy an iPhone and an iPad. Such tragic events are for Qiu an expression of manufactured iSlaves – the enslavement of consumers and users by consumer culture, the effect of a consumer culture, in which prosumption (productive consumption) means that corporations exploit audiences, users and consumers' activities and turn them into audience workers, user labour and consumer labour. Qiu stresses that Yangi Ni is a prosumer in the most cynical way: "While consuming the gadgetry, he also consumed his kidney and health to produce a most tragic, and much circulated, marketing ploy for Apple, in China and worldwide" (Qiu 2016, 105).

CAPITAL/LABOUR INEQUALITY IN CHINA AND INDIA

This dialectic of wealth and poverty has today become quite evident in China. Capitalist development with Chinese authoritarian characteristics has resulted in an increase of the GDP per capita from US$190 in 1978 to US$7,380 in 2014. Life expectancy has increased from 65 to 75 years. The mortality rate of under-5s has decreased from 7 per cent to 1.3 per cent. Capitalist development, however, was accompanied by a decrease of the income share held by the poorest 20 per cent from 8 per cent in 1987 to 4.7 per cent in 2010[10] and an increase of Gini income inequality from around 0.3 to more to around 0.5 today (Sicular 2013). The top 10 per cent have incomes 12 times as large as those of the bottom 10 per cent, which means a doubling of inequality since the early 1990s. "China is now among the least equal 25 percent of countries worldwide. Very few Asian countries belong to this group" (Sicular 2013, 1). China's export-oriented economy has become a source of cheap manufacturing labour in the international division of labour that spurs the profits of Western corporations, while its economy has built up massive unused overcapacities of infrastructure and a financialized property market prone to crisis.

---

10 Source of all data: Worldbank Data.

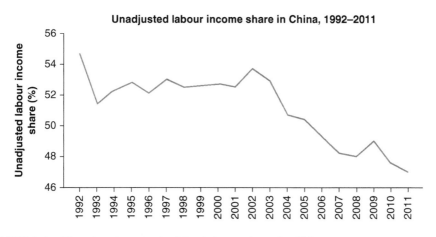

Unadjusted labour income share in China, 1992–2011

FIGURE 9.1   The development of the labour share in China

Source: ILO 2015, 27.

The labour share is the share of the wage sum in the total economy. The higher the wage share, the better the working class is doing in an economy. The data in Figure 9.1 show that in China the labour share decreased from around 65 per cent in the early 1990s to slightly above 45 per cent in 2011 (International Labour Organization (ILO) 2015, 27). This means that the Chinese working class is doing in relative terms much worse today than in the early 1990s.

Just like China, India is also a very large country whose economy has attracted interest in the West as investment opportunity. Indian software exports form one realm of particular interest for Western capital because Indian employees tend to be highly qualified and low paid. The data for India in Figure 9.2 shows that the labour share decreased from around 20 per cent in the early 1990s to around 10 per cent in the late 2000s. The profit share (the share of profits in the GDP) increased from around 30 per cent to 55 per cent (ILO 2010, 91). This means that in India, capital's economic power has massively increased and the working class's power has been weakened.

SOCIAL INEQUALITY IN CHINA AND INDIA

The Gini coefficient is a measure of social inequality in a country. The Gini coefficient takes on a value between 0 and 1. A level of 0 means strong equality, a level of 1 strong inequality.

> China's Gini coefficient (a measure of inequality ranging from zero, which represents perfect equality, to one, perfect inequality) rose from about 0.3 in the early 1980s to more than 0.45 in the early 2000s. After 2000, the Gini rose further to a high of 0.49 in 2008. Since then it has declined slightly, but remains well above 0.45. With a Gini approaching 0.5, China's level of income inequality is in the same ballpark as that of relatively high-inequality Latin American countries such as Mexico (0.51), Nicaragua (0.52), and Peru (0.48), although still lower than Brazil and Honduras (0.56–0.57). China is now among the least equal 25 percent of countries worldwide. Very few Asian countries belong to this group. (Sicular 2013, 1)

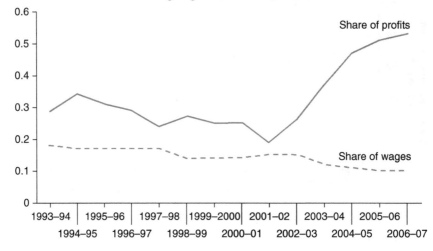

FIGURE 9.2   The development of the labour and profit shares in India

Source: ILO 2010, 91.

China's rising inequality has to do with the fast growth of the wealth of the rich, urban/rural differences, and the dominant class's income from private property. Income inequality measured by the Gini index increased in India from a level of 32 per cent in the early 1990s to 38 per cent in 2011.[11] The top 10 per cent have incomes 12 times as large as the ones of the bottom 10 per cent, which is a doubling since the early 1990s.[12] The cases of India and China show that rising overall economic growth does not automatically mean an increase of wage and income equality. In both countries the opposite has been the case.

China and India have been among the countries with the highest economic growth rates in the world measured in terms of the increase of GDP. The GDP is, however, a deceptive macroeconomic variable because it mixes together profits and wages. A class analysis requires the disentangling of these components and a look at the global relationship between capital and labour. The data presented in this chapter show that in recent decades capital has expanded its power at the expense of labour through neoliberal class struggle. This development has in the BRICS countries especially taken place in China and India so that economic growth and productivity have in relative terms predominantly benefitted the capitalist class. One should in this context bear in mind that the decisive criterion for analysing the deepening or reduction of capitalist class domination are the relative shares in the total economy.

---

11   http://timesofindia.indiatimes.com/india/Indias-income-inequality-has-doubled-in-20-years/articleshow/11012855.cms (accessed on 27 September 2016).

12   Ibid.

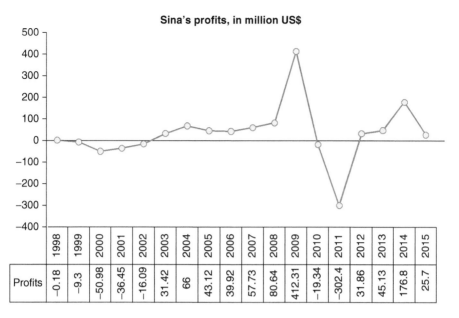

FIGURE 9.3   The development of Sina's profits

Source: SEC filings, forms 10-K, 20-F.

9.2 WEIBO'S POLITICAL ECONOMY

SINA'S PROFITS

Sina is a Chinese web portal founded in 1998. Sina Corp owns and operates it. Sina became a public company listed on the NASDAQ in 2000.[13] Its share-offering price was US$17.[14] It launched the microblog Weibo in 2009. Weibo Corp that operates Weibo is a subsidiary of Sina. Figure 9.3 shows that Sina has been struggling and making losses during the new economy crisis in 2000. It then consolidated and increased its profits up to US$412 million in 2009. During the global economic crisis it made again losses in 2010 and 2011. In 2012, 2013 and 2014 it again achieved profits.

Weibo can be seen as the Chinese microblogging equivalent of Twitter. Some comparative data:

- On 31 December 2013, Weibo had 129.1 million monthly active users (Weibo SEC filings, form F-1, registration statement) and Twitter 240.9 million (Twitter SEC filings, form 10-K: annual report for 2013).
- In December 2014, Weibo had 175.7 million monthly active users (Weibo SEC filings, form 20-F for financial year 2014).
- In the same month, Twitter had on average 288 million users (Twitter SEC filings, form 10-K for financial year 2015).

13   www.nasdaq.com/symbol/sina, accessed on 6 April 2014 (accessed on 27 September 2016).
14   http://chinastockresearch.com/company-profiles/company-summaries/item/196-sina-corporation-sina/196-sina-corporation-sina.html (accessed on 6 April 2014).

TWITTER AND WEIBO'S LOSSES

Twitter has been struggling financially: it became a stock-traded public company in November 2013, although its annual net losses were US$645.32 million in 2013 (Twitter SEC filings, form 10-K 2013). Table 9.2 shows the development of Weibo and Twitter's annual profits/ losses. Weibo – a subsidiary of Sina – made losses of US$116.74 million in 2011, US$102.47 million in 2012, US$38.12 million in 2013 and US$62.7 million in 2014 (Weibo SEC filings, form F-1 registration statement). Twitter's losses amounted in 2015 to US$521 million (Twitter SEC filings, form 10-K 2015).

WEIBO AND TWITTER ON THE STOCK MARKET

Just like Twitter in 2013, Weibo became a stock-marketed listed corporation in April 2014 when it made its Initial Public Offering (IPO) on the NASDAQ stock exchange. The NASDAQ is one of the United States' major stock exchanges, where shares in corporations are traded. Initial Public Offering is a term used in the finance industry for indicating that a company becomes a stock-trading corporation, listed on a stock exchange. Like Twitter, Weibo became a strock-trading corporation, although it had made significant losses in the previous years and continued to make a total loss of US$62.6 million in financial year 2014. Table 9.3 shows the development of the share value of both Weibo and Twitter since their IPO.

Weibo and Twitter's share values have been fluctuating. In December 2014, eight months after its IPO, Weibo's share value dropped below its initial value of US$17. The same happened to Twitter's share value in August 2015, when it dropped below the initial value of US$26. Both shares have been fluctuating.

Twitter and Weibo are not communications companies, but predominantly large advertising agencies. Targeted advertising is their main revenue source. A total of 85 per cent of Twitter's revenues came from advertising in 2012, 89 per cent in 2013, 89.5 per cent in 2014 and 90.0 per cent in 2015 (Twitter SEC filings, form 10-K: annual report for 2013; form 8-K from 10 February 2016). In 2015, 78.8 per cent of Weibo's revenues were derived from advertising and marketing, 12.2 per cent from games and 5.9 per cent from VIP membership services (Weibo SEC filings, form F-1, registration statement). In 2014, Weibo generated 79 per cent of its revenue from advertising and marketing (ibid.). The rest of the revenue was made from online games and data licensing (ibid.). Given that Weibo increased its profits during the first and second quarter of 2016, its share-values started to rise (see Table 9.3) Given the uncertainties of the targeted advertising business model, it is however uncertain if Weibo will be able to make large profits over time. If not, then the expectations expressed in the rising share value may be disappointed.

TABLE 9.2 Weibo and Twitter's profits/losses

Year	Weibo	Twitter
2012	US$–102.5 million	US$–79.5 million
2013	US$–38.1 million	US$–645.3 million
2014	US$–62.6 million	US$–577.8 million
2015	US$37.5 million	US$–521.0 million

Sources: Data from Weibo's and Twitter's SEC filings.

TABLE 9.3   The development of Weibo and Twitter's share values

Date	Weibo	Twitter
7 November 2013		US$26 (IPO)
2 December 2013		US$44.95
3 February 2014		US$54.35
7 April 2014		US$40.05
17 April 2014	US$17 (IPO)	
19 May 2014	US$19.55	US$30.50
14 July 2014	US$19.25	US$37.05
29 September 2014	US$19.21	US$53.94
1 December 2014	US$17.26	US$38.49
26 January 2015	US$13.05	US$37.53
6 April 2015	US$13.20	US$51.94
26 May 2015	US$15.67	US$36.67
13 July 2015	US$15.09	US$35.67
17 August 2015	US$13.09	US$25.87
21 September 2015	US$11.81	US$25.29
12 October 2015	US$13.52	US$31.15
16 November 2015	US$16.98	US$25.41
9 February 2016	US$12.73	US$14.40
16 June 2016	US$27.01	US$15.87
23 September 2016	US$49.15	US$21.79
23 November 2016	US$49.95	US$18.22

Source: Data from Yahoo! Finance.

THE HIGH-RISK FINANCIALIZATION OF SOCIAL MEDIA

Financialization means that a company or resource becomes financial capital that is traded on financial markets such as a stock exchange. Weibo and Twitter are high-risk financial companies because they have been listed on the stock market without making profits. The share value is the amount of money one piece of stock in a corporation costs on a financial market. Weibo and Twitter's share values are positive, but they tend not to make profits. There is a divergence between profits and share values. Both companies hope that their large number of users attracts advertisers and financial investors. They assume that they will make large profits in the future and that this hope will keep investors confident.

The risks these companies face is two-fold: on the one hand they face a highly competitive online advertising market, in which Google and Facebook dominate in the West and Baidu is a big player in China. Microblog communication has an immensely high speed and short attention span. It is difficult to place targeted ads on them and to make users click on them. It is not easy to make profits with targeted advertising because the average click-through rate is around 0.1 per cent (Comscore 2012): users tend to only click on every 1000th online ad presented to them. And even then it is not sure if such clicks on targeted ads tend to result in purchases or not.

"FINANCIAL BUBBLES"

It takes a critical political economy perspective to understand that Twitter and Weibo are evidence that the social media economy is highly financialized and investments in it are insecure.

Twitter and Weibo's political economy is an indication that the social media economy is highly financialized. Investments in it are insecure. We speak of a "financial bubble" when there is a large gap between the profits of corporations in a specific economic sector and their financial values. If this gap grows, then it is like a bubble that gets larger and larger and at a certain point of time can no longer stand the pressure and explodes. Financial crises can start if finance bubbles burst because there is a large divergence between actual profits and stock market valuation. Normally such bursts take place when lots of investors lose confidence and pull out their invested capital. The dot-com crisis in 2000 was an earlier expression of the high financialization of the Internet economy, in which actual profits could not keep up with the promises of high stock market values. A new round of financialization in the Internet industry has enabled the rise of social media, while the ongoing world economic crisis showed us how crisis-prone financial markets are. Targeted advertising, is a high-risk business. Users only click on a small share of advertisements. It is uncertain whether and how often they purchase something on the landing pages to which they are transferred.

The future of the social media economy in China and the West is uncertain. It is clear that social media is both in China and the West a highly financialized capitalist industry that depends on the influx of investments on finance markets and the confidence of advertisers that advertising works. There are many uncertainties associated with advertising capital accumulation models, especially concerning users' privacy concerns, the use of ad-block technologies and other limits to advertising, and the question of whether targeted ads are effective or not. The possibility of a dwindling confidence of investors after some trigger event and a resulting social media crisis cannot be ruled out. The financialization and corporatizing of the Internet has been accompanied by huge risks that both China and the West are facing.

WEIBO AND TWITTER'S ACKNOWLEDGEMENT OF BEING HIGH-RISK

Both Weibo and Twitter have acknowledged in their financial reports that they operate high-risk businesses:

> *Weibo*: We generate a substantial majority of our revenues from advertising and marketing. A decline in our advertising and marketing revenues could harm our business. We cannot guarantee that the monetization strategies we have adopted can generate sustainable revenues and profit. As is common in the industry, our advertising and marketing customers do not have long-term commitments with us. In addition, our major brand customers typically purchase our advertising and marketing services through advertising agencies. (Weibo SEC-filings, form 20-F for financial year 2014)

> *Twitter*: The substantial majority of our revenue is currently generated from third parties advertising on Twitter. We generated 89% and 90% of our revenue from advertising in the fiscal years ended 31 December 2013 and 2014, respectively. We generate substantially

TABLE 9.4 Weibo and Twitter's boards of director

Weibo's board of directors	Involvement in other companies	Twitter's board of directors	Involvement in other companies
Charles Chao, Chairman		Omid Kordestani, Chairman	
Hong Du, Director		Jack Dorsey, CEO, Co-Founder	Square Inc. Walt Disney Company
Pehong Chen, Independent Director	BroadVision Inc.	Peter Chernin	Chernin Entertainment LLC, Chernin Group LLC CA Media
Frank Kui Tang, Independent Director	FountainVest Partners	Peter Currie	Currie Capital Schlumberger Ltd
Daniel Zhang, Director	Alibaba Group,	Peter Fenton	Benchmark Capital Yelp Inc.
		David Rosenblatt	1stdibs.com Inc. IAC/InterActive Corp
		Evan Williams	Medium Obvious Corp
		Marjorie Scardino	MacArthur Foundation

Sources: Data from Weibo and Twitter Investor Relations: http://ir.weibo.com, https://investor.twitterinc.com (accessed on 10 February 2016).

all of our advertising revenue through the sale of our three Promoted Products: Promoted Tweets, Promoted Accounts and Promoted Trends. As is common in our industry, our advertisers do not have long-term advertising commitments with us. In addition, many of our advertisers purchase our advertising services through one of several large advertising agency holding companies. Advertising agencies and potential new advertisers may view our Promoted Products as experimental and unproven, and we may need to devote additional time and resources to educate them about our products and services. (Twitter SEC-filings, form 10-K for financial year 2014)

WEIBO AND TWITTER'S BOARDS OF DIRECTORS

Table 9.4 shows that both Weibo and Twitter have directors who are members of either financial investment firms or other media companies in the sectors of mobile payments, entertainment, online shopping or online storytelling. This board structure shows the interlocking of financial capital, Internet capital and media capital.

9.3 WEIBO AND SOCIAL MEDIA IDEOLOGIES

PRIVACY POLICIES

Weibo and Twitter's terms of service and privacy policies enable the exploitation of users' digital labour and the commodification of personal data this labour generates.

Reading the following extracts from the Twitter and Weibo privacy statements clearly shows how commodification is implicitly embedded in their corporate language. While they don't transparently say they will sell and commodify users' data, like other social media platforms, they hide this by using the positive euphemisms of 'sharing' data and relevant advertisements

> User agrees that Sina reserves the right to insert or add various kinds of commercial advertising or other types of commercial information (including but not limited to put advertisement on any webpage of Weimeng website), and, user agrees to accept product promotion or other relevant business information sent by Weimeng through email or other measures. (Weibo User Agreement, accessed on November 18, 2015)

> Our Services are primarily designed to help you share information with the world. Most of the information you provide us through the Twitter Services is information you are asking us to make public. Your public information includes the messages you Tweet; the metadata provided with Tweets, such as when you Tweeted and the client application you used to Tweet; the language, country, and time zone associated with your account; and the lists you create, people you follow, Tweets you mark as likes or Retweet, and many other bits of information that result from your use of the Twitter Services. We may use this information to make inferences, like what topics you may be interested in, and to customize the content we show you, including ads. [...] We do this to help improve our Services, to provide more relevant advertising, and to be able to share aggregate click statistics such as how many times a particular link was clicked on. (Twitter Privacy Policy, accessed on 18 November 2015)

Neither of the legal agreements speak of selling and commodifying users' personal data, but rather use the positive euphemisms of sharing data and relevant advertisements: "relevant business information", we "help you share information with the world", we "provide more relevant advertising", and so on.

WEIBO AND TWITTER'S IDEOLOGICAL SELF-UNDERSTANDINGS

How does Weibo define itself? Its Chairman Charles Chao[15] argues that social media makes information and communication easier and allows everyone to participate:

> But with microblog, with Weibo, people start to not only create content themselves, but also to distribute content themselves. [...] In the future, you don't need a TV station to do the live broadcasting. Everybody with a mobile phone can do live broadcasting. [...] We want to make it easy for people to access information, to share information.

An associated claim is that social media make communication more open and transparent: Charles Chao says Weibo is a space where users "talk, where they think, where they exchange intents of their ideas, their opinion", that it is "a very free platform for people to express

---

15 www.youtube.com/watch?v=tlliivJKHk8 (accessed on 25 November 2015).

themselves and exchange ideas" and that it helps China to "progress into a more open, more transparent society".[16] Chao argues that Weibo enables transparency and enables a system of

> check and balance in society, which makes China's society much better. [...] Everybody will have the ability to report news and report what is happening. So it is made impossible almost to withhold information. [...] It makes information wider available. [...] This makes society much more open. [...] It makes everything much more transparent.[17]

Twitter uses an ideology that is quite similar to the one of Weibo. For Twitter, the freedom of social media is "to connect with people, express yourself and discover what's happening"[18] and "give everyone the power to create and share ideas and information instantly, without barriers".[19] "Connect with your friends—and other fascinating people. Get in-the-moment updates on the things that interest you. And watch events unfold, in real time, from every angle."[20]

THE ENGAGING/CONNECTING/SHARING IDEOLOGY

So a common ideology that Chinese and Western corporate web platforms and their CEOs associate with social media is that it enables everyone to get and share information, to communicate, engage, produce and distribute content, connect with others. A further claim is that producing, connecting, sharing, communicating, engaging via social media enhances humans' quality of life and society's quality and transparency. In the analysed statements, there is an underlying assumption that social media makes society necessarily more open, transparent, connected. Aspects of closure and power are not considered and if they are considered. Social media is only framed as empowering users.

The engaging/connecting/sharing ideology is not just typical for Chinese corporate social media. It is a universal capitalist social media ideology that is used by social media companies, management gurus and uncritical scholars and observers. They do so in order to justify the capitalist character of corporate social media as acceptable and good. They argue that social media capitalism is fun for the users and allows them to do something with these platforms. It would be a form of cultural imperialism to describe this ideology as specific to China. It is in fact an ideology that comes along with the commodity form of social media.

The engaging/connecting/sharing ideology is immanent to structures of representation of capitalist social media both in China and the West. The problem is that capitalism is a class-divided society and that therefore inevitably not everyone benefits from it. Social media ideologies do not talk about outcasts, the poor, the unemployed and the exploited. It ignores issues such as the exploitation of free labour, negative consequences of capitalism, advertising and consumer culture, the fact that users create value on social media platforms but do not own

---

16 Talk Asia. 2011. Interview with Charles Chao. CNN Online transcript, CNN Talk Asia, 3 August 2011, http://transcripts.cnn.com/TRANSCRIPTS/1108/03/ta.01.html.
17 www.youtube.com/watch?v=tlliivJKHk8 (accessed on 25 November 2015).
18 https://about.twitter.com/company (accessed on 10 April 2014).
19 https://about.twitter.com/company (accessed on 17 November 2015).
20 https://about.twitter.com (accessed on 17 November 2015).

these platforms, the asymmetrical power of visibility on social media that gives celebrities, companies and governments much more visibility and attention than ordinary users.

SOCIAL MEDIA IS BULLSHIT!

B.J. Mendelson (2012), in his book *Social Media is Bullshit*, critically reflects on his ten years of experience as an Internet consultant that marketers want people to believe that social media can help organizations and individuals to increase their reputation. But "almost nothing" works, "unless you have a multimillion-dollar budget and a healthy media presence" (Mendelson 2012, 11). Generating social media visibility requires "a big budget, lots of time, a team of people who know what they're doing, media exposure" (13), because the WWW "is essentially run by major corporations" (23). "The truth is that it's almost impossible for you to reach an audience of any significance [...] unless you a strong network, millions to spend on advertising and publicity, or if the media likes you" (44). Mendelson argues that myths about the Internet that he based on Harry G. Frankfurt (2005) calls "bullshit" spread through an "asshole-based economy" (Mendelson 2012, 54) that is furthered by cyber hipster, tech media and marketers, analysts, corporations, mainstream media and users (74).

The engaging/connecting/sharing ideology is grounded in an individualistic and consumerist notion of freedom that sees freedom as social media's enablement of single users to communicate, create, consume and share more. Corporate social media have hijacked the concept of free access and turned it into an ideology that tries to conceal the existence of a mode of capital accumulation that is based on the commodification of personal data and targeted advertising. Corporate social media present themselves as free, open and social, but are in reality unfree, closed and particularistic machines for the commodification of personal data that produce and sell targeted ads.

THE INTERNET SHOPPING MALL AS THE ANTITHESIS OF FREEDOM

The problem is that Internet companies, consultants, managers and those who believe in their ideology do not see that freedom is, as Karl Marx stressed, a "realm of freedom" (Marx 1894, 958) that is not based on the logic of profitability and accumulation, but on the principle "From each according to his ability, to each according to his needs!" (Marx 2000, 615). This principle implies that the "first freedom" of the media "consists in not being a trade" (Marx 1974, 41). The consequences of the reduction of the WWW's freedom to freedom of property, the market and trade have been that the WWW is today first and foremost a shopping mall and a huge advertising space, in which the world's largest advertising agencies disguise themselves as "social media" and "mobile media" in order to garner and commodify personal data as "big data".

The WWW is the world's biggest narcissistic self-presentation machine and individualizing spectacle, in which users are not connected to WeTube, OurBook, OurSpace, but to YouTube, Facebook, MySpace, Weibo and Renren in order to advertise their own selves to others. So Chinese social media platforms' individualism is not so different from social media individualism in the West. The task is to gain competitive advantages and accumulate reputation in order to be better "employable" and more successful. Individualism is designed into corporate "social" media platforms and has become a strategy of survival for many workers who tend to see themselves not as an exploited class, but reflect their existence as individual freelancers by conceiving themselves not as precarious workers, but as "knowledge professionals", "middle class", "makers" and "creatives".

THE INTERNET'S POLITICAL CONTROL

Another limit that the engaging/connecting/sharing ideology hides is the political control of the Internet. We have seen in Chapter 7 how Edward Snowden's revelations have revealed the existence of a Western surveillance-industrial complex that secret services such as the NSA use for mass surveillance of communications, the Internet and social media. Given these revelations, the argument that the Internet is politically free in the West and politically controlled in China has become ridiculous. Both in China and the West the Internet and social media are highly controlled by economic and political power. The Chinese Internet is controlled by both the state and capital. Weibo does not deny that there is state control of users' communication. Weibo outlines in its 2014 financial report how Chinese state control works. The following passage shows that the Chinese state can both monitor and censor Weibo content:

> The Ministry of Public Security has the authority to order any local internet service provider to block any internet website at its sole discretion. From time to time, the Ministry of Public Security has stopped the dissemination over the internet of information which it believes to be socially destabilizing. (Weibo SEC filings, form 20-F for financial year 2014).

9.4 CHINESE SOCIAL STRUGGLES IN THE AGE OF WEIBO

WORKING-CLASS NETWORK SOCIETY

China is not a monolithic society, but one with a very active and vivid working class that struggles against exploitation. Jack Qiu (2009, x) argues that China has "the largest exploited working class of the global information age". The Chinese working class uses digital media in its struggles (Qiu 2009). Qiu characterizes China as undergoing a change that has resulted in the emergence of a working-class network society that is especially characterized by what he terms the "information have-less: low-end ICT users, service providers, and laborers who are manufacturing these electronics" (3–4). This class would consist of migrant workers (who have migrated from rural to urban areas), unemployed and underemployed workers, micro entrepreneurs, youth, students and retirees struggling to make a living, who to a certain degree are "grey-collar" workers with highly repetitive jobs in industries such as software engineering, design, marketing, advertising, telecommunications or customer services (93, 104–105, 113).

WORKER-GENERATED CONTENT

Slaves tend to seek ways to resist and struggle for abolition. Jack Qiu (2016, Chapter 5), in his analysis of iSlavery in the context of working-class struggles and in contradistinction to the term user-generated content (UGC), introduces the term worker-generated content (WGC). This category means "alternative expressions, social networking, and cultural formation beyond the scope of UGC (user-generated content), the latter of which is governed by corporate goals and/or the logic of state surveillance" (Qiu 2016, 132). Workers at specific spatial points of the international division of digital labour for particular time periods appropriate digital, social and mobile media for organizing in a way that strengthens questioning corporate and state power.

There are seven types of worker-generated content that Qiu (2016, Chapter 5) distinguishes. It can be collective or individual, activist or non-activist, empowering or non-empowering. The only logical possibility excluded from the eight possible combinations of these three variables is user-generated content: user-generated content would be individual, not activism-oriented and not empowering. The ideal type of worker-generated content is collective activism using digital, social and mobile media for political goals and empowering workers. QQ, WeChat and Weibo would be examples of popular media in "the toolkit of working-class struggle against iSlavery" (Qiu 2016, 153).

TOWARDS DIGITAL WORKER CO-OPERATIVES

Workers in social struggles should make use of all communications tools that are available and that can advance their struggles. Using communications technologies that are under corporate and/or state control, however, brings along the risks of censorship, control, surveillance, exploitation and repression (see Fuchs 2014b for a detailed discussion). Foxconn workers going on strike and co-ordinating their protests via Weibo work as part of their protest for yet another capitalist company in the international division of digital labour. And they risk being monitored by state institutions. The example shows that worker-generated content in and outside of protests is not enough. The political goal and strategy should involve creating a worker-owned, worker-controlled and worker-operated media landscape and society (see Sandoval 2016).

Worker co-operatives are needed everywhere in the international division of digital labour's mines, factories, offices, homes, social systems and digital spaces in order to politically challenge this division. A commons-based, worker-controlled society that rids itself of class divisions is the goal. Setting up worker co-operatives should be part of the struggle for achieving such a society.

WORKING-CLASS PUBLIC SPHERES

Working-class struggles create, as Jack Qiu (2016) argues based on Negt and Kluge (1972/1993), working-class public spheres, "digitally networked action – actions of collective will, connective power, discursively and on the ground" (Qiu 2016, 187). Public spheres are not, however, just public political spaces of collective struggle, they are also the germs of publicly-controlled commons-based social systems, social systems controlled by the people for the people. Working-class public spheres are not just communicative and political, but productive in and through communication; they are "counter-products of a proletarian public sphere" (Negt and Kluge 1972/1993, 79–80).

Working-class public spheres produce proletarian counter-products: "idea against idea, product against product, production sector against production sector" (Negt and Kluge 1972/1993, 80). Worker-generated ideas against capitalist ideas! Common products against capitalist products! Common technologies against capitalist technologies! A commons-based peer production sector against the capitalist production sector! A working-class public sphere of the digital age that challenges capitalist media and capitalist society! This is the essence of class struggle from below in the digital age.

THE KEY POLITICAL ECONOMIST OF CHINESE COMMUNICATION YUEZHI ZHAO ASKS: AFTER BICYCLES, WHAT? AFTER MOBILE PHONES, WHAT?

The Canadian political economist of communication Dallas Smythe visited China in the early 1970s. On this occasion he wrote the article "After bicycles, what?" (Smythe 1994, 230–244), in which he deals with communications in China. In this paper, he speaks of the need for a "two-way system in which each receiver would have the capability to provide either a voice or voice-and-picture response. [...] a two-way TV system would be like an electronic tatzupao system" (Smythe 1994, 231–232). These thoughts parallel Hans Magnus Enzensberger's (1970/1997) concept of emancipatory media use, Walter Benjamin's (1934, 1936/1939) idea of the reader/writer and Bertolt Brecht's (1932/2000) notion of an alternative radio in his radio theory.

Yuezhi Zhao (2011) points out the relevance of Smythe's article and his ideas of an alternative non-capitalist communication system for China. Given a world dominated by the logic of neoliberal capitalism (both in the West and China), she stresses – inspired by Smythe – the importance of establishing communications and societies that are based on non-capitalist logic. Zhao (2007, 92) argues that Smythe raised the question "After bicycles, what?" "in the context of China's search for a socialist alternative to capitalist modernity, with the hope that China would avoid the capitalist path of development". She says that although Smythe misjudged the political situation in China in the 1970s on a number of points, his intervention would continue to "offer a useful point of departure in analyzing not only the deployment and development of ICTs in China during the reform era, but also the broad path of China's post-Mao development strategy and its sustainability" (Zhao 2007, 96). The question one would have to ask today about Chinese media in Dallas Smythe's manner would be: After mobile phones, what? (Zhao 2007).

Smythe answered the question "After bicycles, what?" by saying that China should create a media structure that favours "public goods and services [...] against goods and services for individual, private use" (Smythe 1994, 243). Zhao, based on Smythe, writes that ICTs not only serve capitalist purposes, but are "by their very nature" social. They allow "alternative uses", including collective political action (Zhao 2007, 96). The reality of ICTs in China shows the antagonistic character of these technologies as means of both domination and protest.

9.5 CONCLUSION

We can summarize the main results of this chapter as follows:

- China's export-oriented economy focuses especially on manufacturing computing hardware, mobile phones and clothes. It is integrated into the international division of (digital) labour and is a source of cheap labour that helps maximize global corporations' profits. China is also shaped by a neoliberalism with authoritarian characteristics.

- Rising inequality in China and wage repression have been accompanied by working-class struggles.
- Although China has seen large economic growth, its economy is contradictory and crisis-prone. Financialization, overproduction, underconsumption and overaccumulation have fostered such crisis tendencies.
- Weibo and Twitter's political economies are financialized and characterized by a divergence of share values and profits/losses. Both companies are indications of a social media financial bubble.
- China is a working-class network society: it has a very large working class that uses the Internet and mobile phones for different purposes. The question is whether the logic of the commons that the working class in essence stands for will in the future become the dominant model of communications in global society or not.
- There is a quite strong form of political control of Internet communication in China, which should be seen critically. One should, however, at the same time avoid idealizing the Internet in the West. Edward Snowden's revelations have shown that there is also Internet control in Western countries.

RECOMMENDED READINGS AND EXERCISES

In this chapter you have read a lot about the Chinese economy and the Internet in China. There are a number of very good texts that can help you to further deepen your knowledge. I therefore recommend you read these texts and engage in the following exercises.

Read the following text:

Harvey, David. 2005. *A brief history of neoliberalism*. Oxford: Oxford University Press. Chapter 5: Neoliberalism "with Chinese characteristics".

Work in groups:

- Search for articles, chapters and books that have been published in the past two years and provide a Marxist analysis of China's political economy. Compare the analysis to Harvey's analysis and ask yourself: How has China's economy changed since Harvey wrote his analysis? What are commonalities and differences between the Marxist works you found and Harvey's analysis?

In this chapter I presented a political-economic analysis of Weibo that focused on commodification, ideology and politics.

Work in groups:

- Each group chooses one popular Chinese social media platform and conducts a critical political economy analysis. Present the results and compare them.

Read the following two texts:

Smythe, Dallas W. 1994. *Counterclockwise*. Boulder, CO: Westview Press. Chapter: After bicycles, what?

Zhao, Yuezhi. 2007. After mobile phones, what? Re-embedding the social in China's "digital revolution". *International Journal of Communication* 1: 92–120.

Ask yourself and discuss:

- How did Smythe characterize the role of the media in China in the early 1970s?
- How have Chinese media and society changed?
- What could an alternative Internet look like and how can it best be achieved?

Read the following two texts:

Qiu, Jack, Linchuan Qiu, Melissa Gregg and Kate Crawford. 2014. Circuits of labour: A labour theory of the iPhone era. *TripleC: Communication, Capitalism & Critique* 12 (2): 486–563.

Fuchs, Christian. 2013. Theorising and analysing digital labour: From global value chains to modes of production. *The Political Economy of Communication* 1 (2): 3–27. http://polecom.org/index.php/polecom/article/view/19

Ask yourself and discuss:

- What is the role of China in the international division of digital labour and the global circuits of labour?
- What role do Foxconn and Apple have in the global circuit and division of labour?
- What role do social media have in the global circuit and division of labour? How is their labour connected to the Foxconn workers' labour?
- How can digital workers of the world politically unite in order to struggle for a fair, participatory and just Internet and society?

10 AIRBNB AND UBER: THE POLITICAL ECONOMY OF ONLINE SHARING PLATFORMS

KEY QUESTIONS

- What is the political economy of sharing platforms such as the commercial flat-sharing platform Airbnb and the taxi-location-sharing app Uber?
- What is the role of online sharing in contemporary capitalism?
- What is the role of the ideology of sharing in contemporary capitalism?
- What are the potentials of non-capitalist sharing to challenge capitalism?
- How have labour conditions been transformed due to the rise of the sharing economy?
- What problems face those who work in the sharing economy?
- On what kind of ideologies is the capitalist sharing economy based?

KEY CONCEPTS

Sharing economy
Capitalist sharing economy
Pay per service model of online sharing
Rent on rent model of online sharing
Freemium model of online sharing
Wage share
Capital share

Digital imperialism
Non-profit online sharing platforms
Commodity fetishism
Commodity fetishism in the capitalist sharing economy
Reverse commodity fetishism
Commons-based sharing and gift economy

OVERVIEW

Commuting from place A to place B is part of our everyday life. In a city, it is part of work and leisure. In our leisure time, it involves travelling to places where we do not regularly live. Transport and tourism have become two important industries in modern society. Taxis and hotels are two key aspects of these industries. Digital media have transformed the worlds of both transportation and accommodation. Uber and Airbnb are two manifestations of these changes.

Uber is a San Francisco-based tech company that was founded in 2009. It developed a taxi app that shares the location of drivers and customers in order to organize rides. Airbnb is a company that is also based in San Francisco. It was founded in 2008. It hosts an online platform that shares information about the availability of short-term rentals of rooms and apartments in specific cities. Travellers share their travel dates and search for available accommodation.

Have you used either Airbnb or Uber? What was your experience? What did you like about it? Can you think of aspects of these companies that may be problematic? This chapter will try to show that there is a negative reality hidden behind the positively seeming consumer experience of these platforms.

Both platforms are about sharing location-based information. But this sharing is not just a sharing of information, but a capitalist business: the capitalist sharing economy.

Sharing is a positively connoted term. We share our feelings of happiness and grief with friends and loved ones. We share a bottle of wine as a gift. Love is about altruistic sharing of space and time along with very strong positive feelings. Sharing is a positive emotional activity. What makes the capitalist sharing economy so problematic is that it turns a term that has to do with love, family, care and friendship into an ideology and capital accumulation model. Shares are, however, also ownership shares in a company. We share because we care. Some share because they care only about their own welfare. In the capitalist sharing economy, the economic and the emotional understanding of sharing converge into a capital accumulation model and ideology. This chapter will show that the kind of sharing created on Airbnb, Upwork and Uber is very different from sharing as we know it from elsewhere.

A survey (N = 2,238) showed that in 2016, 21 per cent of the British population looked for labour as crowdworkers online on platforms such as Upwork, Uber, Handy, Freelancr, Clickworker or PeoplePerHour (Huws and Joyce 2016). 11 per cent succeeded in finding such work. A significant proportion of the population is involved in conducting self-employed freelance labour in the sharing economy.

This chapter analyses Airbnb and Uber in order to explain how the capitalist sharing economy works. I will first discuss Uber's model of the sharing economy (section 1). Section 2 focuses on an analysis of Airbnb and its context. Section 3 broadens out the topic and shows why the sharing economy is a capitalist ideology. Section 4 asks whether there can be a non-capitalist sharing economy.

10.1 UBER: THE PAY PER SERVICE SHARING MODEL

In 2009, Travis Kalanick, Garrett Camp and Paulina Kopinska founded Uber. It is active in hundreds of cities, including metropolises from San Francisco, London and Los Angeles all the way to Moscow, Beijing and Singapore. At least until the end of 2015, the company never made any profits. During the first three-quarters of 2015, it had revenues of US$1.2 billion and made losses of US$1.7 billion.[1]

---

1   Facing a price war, Uber bets on volume. Bloomberg Business Online, 21 January 2016. http://www.bloomberg.com/news/articles/2016-01-21/facing-a-price-war-uber-bets-on-volume (accessed on 26 September 2016).

Uber argues that its business model and mobile app bring advantages to both drivers and passengers. The company says about Uber drivers:[2] "Work for yourself: Drive when you want, make the money you need. Set your own schedule. Make money on your own terms. Let the app lead the way. Watch the money add up fast." And it promises to customers: "Always the ride you want. The best way to get wherever you're going. Tap a button, get a ride. No cash, no tip, no hassle. You rate, we listen. There's a ride for every price. And any occasion."

Uber's promises are highly individualistic. The company promises convenience to customers. And it promises to taxi workers that they can become self-determined wealthy entrepreneurs. On the one hand there is no guarantee or proof that this is true. On the other hand there is no reflection on whether Uber may have negative impacts on society at large. The company says that it helps "to curb drunk driving", and that encouraging taxi sharing fosters "sustainable cities" and "helps revitalize local economies. In London, nearly a third of driver-partners live in areas where unemployment rates are highest." Drunk driving can only be curbed if those who are drunk can be convinced to use taxis. Whether they do so is a social issue, not a technical one that is decided by the availability of an app. Whether local economies can be revitalized depends on whether working people such as Uber drivers can earn a decent living or not and whether companies pay taxes or not. The environmental impacts of transportation depend on how many cars are on the street for which total amount of time. It is in general an odd idea that driving cars has a positive environmental impact. The only real measure for reducing the carbon dioxide emissions of transportation is to advance public transportation and to make it gratis or very cheap so that fewer and fewer people rely on cars.

ONLINE SHARING CAPITAL ACCUMULATION MODEL #1: PAY PER SERVICE

Uber is an example of a specific model of the capitalist sharing economy. *The first capitalist sharing economy model is based on pay per service*. It is the pay per service model.

Companies that use the same sharing economy model as Uber include, for example, BlaBlaCar, TaskRabbit, Upwork, PeoplePerHour and Amazon MTurk. These companies describe their platforms on their websites the following way:

- "**Uber** is evolving the way the world moves. By seamlessly connecting riders to drivers through our apps, we make cities more accessible, opening up more possibilities for riders and more business for drivers."
- **Upwork**: "The best companies win with the best talent. But great people can be hard to find. We've created an online workplace for the world – connecting clients with top freelance professionals from San Francisco to Sao Paulo. Our mission: To create economic and social value on a global scale by providing a trusted online workplace to connect, collaborate, and succeed."
- "**BlaBlaCar** is a trusted community marketplace that connects drivers with empty seats to passengers looking for a ride."

---

2 All of the following quotes were taken from Uber's website: www.uber.com (accessed on 11 February 2016).

- "**TaskRabbit** is the smart way to get things done by connecting you with others in your neighbourhood." "TaskRabbit allows you to live smarter by connecting you with safe and reliable help in your neighbourhood. Outsource your household errands and skilled tasks to trusted people in your community. It's an old-school concept – neighbours helping neighbours – reimagined for today."
- "**PeoplePerHour** is a community of talent available to work for you remotely, online, at the click of a button."

Let us have a look at how the pay per service model works.

HOW DOES THE PAY PER SERVICE SHARING MODEL WORK?

Uber charges 20–25 per cent commission on taxi drives mediated by its app. A driver performs work that s/he sells to passengers in order to make a profit. His/her main forms of investment good are the car and petrol. On work expertise sharing sites, not one company monopolizes the skills of one person. The skills are rather offered to multiple customers. The commodity that is sold is a service, often the creation, collection or manipulation of information.

- BlaBlaCar charges reservation fees for passengers (10 per cent of the total fee for a ride plus VAT).
- TaskRabbit charges a 20 per cent service fee on each work task.
- Upwork receives 10 per cent of the total payment per task.
- On PeoplePerHour, sellers of tasks pay a service fee of 3.5 per cent plus 15 per cent VAT on all work above the first £175 and £7 for short work tasks. Promotion of tasks costs £5.
- On MTurk, Amazon collects 10 per cent of a work task's price on top as commission.

The task performers on platforms such as Upwork, PeoplePerHour and MTurk tend to be freelancers, that is worker-capitalists who are not employed by others, but are workers and capitalists in one person. Marx (1867, 423) points out that if a capitalist participates "directly in the process of production, […] he is only a hybrid, a man between capitalist and worker, a 'small master'". A freelancer owns all capital (that is typically low or non-existent) and exploits himself/herself. S/he is a hybrid worker-capitalist. A significant amount of capital is required for a freelancer to become able to employ and exploit others (Marx 1867, 423). Marx says that there is a certain sum of capital that poses a point at which "merely quantitative differences pass over by a dialectical inversion into qualitative distinctions" (423) so that the capitalist can become a pure capitalist, not a worker-capitalist, and devotes himself/herself to management and control purposes. "The capitalist, who is capital personified, now takes care that the worker does his work regularly and with the proper degree of intensity" (424). Many freelancers never acquire enough capital to become capitalists that separate the tasks of capital and labour. So, for example, a freelance driver, who is formally self-employed but struggles to makes ends meet and does not employ others, is certainly not a capitalist.

RENT AND THE PAY PER SERVICE MODEL

A rent is a fee that one pays for the temporary use of a resource. The most common form of rent is the rent paid for living in an apartment or house. BlaBlaCar, TaskRabbit, Upwork,

PeoplePerHour, MTurk and Uber charge a rent for each service that is communicatively mediated by their platforms. They thereby reduce the profit that those who perform the services make. Given that many of these worker-capitalists are freelancers, it becomes difficult to distinguish between wage and profit, which tend to fall into one. Sharing platforms accumulate rent by reducing the income of many freelancers.

Given that a larger number of freelancers are present, the rent is a kind of profit taken away from freelancers, who often struggle to survive and have difficulties earning a living. Broadcast Now conducted the UK Freelancer Survey in the media and cultural industries in 2012 (N = 656).[3] A total of 21 per cent of the respondents worked more than 60 hours a week, nearly 50 per cent more than 50 hours and 56 per cent 10 hours or more a day; 47 per cent earned less than £25,000. Freelancers exploit themselves. If they use commercial sharing platforms for offering services, then the rent they pay is turned into a profit for the platform owners. One can say that the platforms exploit the freelancers because one can imagine the paid commission as a surplus-value that is created by the freelancers and expropriated by the platforms. The rest of their income is then their wage. The crucial quality that these cases have in common and that allows us to speak of the existence of surplus-value is the circumstance that freelancers perform labour that creates new use-values.

THE CONTRADICTIONS OF UBER CAPITALISM: STRUGGLES IN THE SHARING ECONOMY

The world of for-profit online sharing platforms is far from frictionless. Its contradictions are displayed by the circumstance that new struggles have emerged around platforms such as Airbnb and Uber. There is a struggle over economic value between capitalist sharing businesses, traditional businesses in industries such as tourism and transport, freelancers, and employees. The capitalist sharing industry's profits tend to reduce other industries' profits as well as the wages and income of freelancers and employees, which results in struggles over the distribution of value.

In June 2014, taxi drivers in London, Berlin, Paris and Madrid went on strike to protest against Uber.[4] In the summer of 2015, taxi drivers all over France and in Rio de Janeiro also went on strike against Uber. They blocked roads, airports and train stations. In September 2015, taxi drivers in Brussels went on strike against Uber and blocked roads. In January 2016, there was again a nationwide anti-Uber strike of taxi drivers all over France.

One of their fears associated with Uber is that its lower customer prices dumps taxi drivers' wages and creates a low-wage economy. Steve McNamara from the Licensed Taxi Drivers Association (LTDA) says that Uber is illegal and out for making big profits, which would be backed by the City of London:

---

3 www.broadcastnow.co.uk/freelancer/freelancer-survey-2012-i-cant-do-this-much-longer/5043075. article (accessed on 12 December 2013).
4 Taxi drivers in European capitals strike over Uber – as it happened. *Guardian* online, 11 June 2014. www.theguardian.com/politics/2014/jun/11/taxi-drivers-strike-uber-london-live-updates (accessed on 27 September 2016).
   Taxi drivers to bring London to standstill over Uber app. *Guardian* online, 11 June 2014. www. theguardian.com/uk-news/2014/jun/11/taxi-drivers-london-standstill-uber-app (accessed on 27 September 2016).

They operate totally in contradiction to the legislation that relates to taxis and private hire in London. It has been allowed to get away with it by Transport for London purely because Uber is backed by Google, Amazon, Goldman Sachs; seventeen billion dollars worth of finance. Transport for London are frightened of them. They have allowed them to do exactly what they want.[5]

The RMT union that represents taxi drivers in the UK argues that Uber is dumping taxi drivers' wages:

The latest undermining of the Private Hire Laws by apps such as Uber is just another attempt to casualise and weaken the professional and safe licensed taxi trade and the long-established regulations around the right to ply for hire, coming after the exposure of the illegal ranks around London and the drive to destroy the airport services.[6]

Benita Matofska from the platform The People Who Share disagrees with assessments that point out the risks of the capitalist sharing economy:

The founders of Airbnb, Uber and the other 7,400 sharing economy initiatives around the world aren't building businesses based on law-breaking and tax evasion, they're responding to a changing landscape where people no longer need to rely on big business for products and services.[7] (Matofska 2014)

Evgeny Morozov is a journalistic writer and critic of technological determinism. In the following quote, he draws a picture that is less optimistic than the one given by Matofska and other sharing ideologues.

Given vast youth unemployment, stagnating incomes, and skyrocketing property prices, today's sharing economy functions as something of a magic wand. Those who already own something can survive by monetising their discomfort: for example, they can earn cash by occasionally renting out their apartments and staying with relatives instead. Those who own nothing, on the other hand, also get to occasionally enjoy a glimpse of the good life – built entirely on goods they do not own. [...] There's no denying that the sharing economy can – and probably does – make the consequences of the current financial crisis more bearable. However, in tackling the consequences, it does nothing to address the causes. It's true that, thanks to advances in the information technology, some of us can finally get by with less – chiefly, by relying on more effective distribution of

---

5 http://taxileaks.blogspot.co.uk/2014/06/watch-steve-mcnamara-and-geoffrey.html (accessed on 9 November 2014).

6 www.rmt.org.uk/news/rmt-backs-london-taxi-protest-on-wednesday/ (accessed on 9 November 2014).

7 Matofska's definition of the sharing economy is that it is "a socio-economic ecosystem built around the sharing of human and physical resources. It includes the shared creation, production, distribution, trade and consumption of goods and services by different people and organisations". www.thepeoplewhoshare.com/blog/what-is-the-sharing-economy/ (accessed on 16 November 2015).

existing resources. But there's nothing to celebrate here: it's like handing everybody earplugs to deal with intolerable street noise instead of doing something about the noise itself. (Morozov 2014)

THE EARNINGS OF UBER DRIVERS

In 2015, Uber released data[8] that claims that in the USA Uber drivers on average make US$19.04 per hour in comparison to the national hourly taxi driver wage of US$12.90. Uber's calculation does not, however, deduct its drivers' costs for gasoline, car maintenance and insurance, and so on. Therefore such data is rather manipulative.

In 2015, data about average net earnings (i.e. after deduction of the Uber commission) were collected from Uber drivers in 15 US cities.[9] The average hourly net earnings were US$11.15. From this value, one must also deduct the average hourly costs for insurance, gasoline and car maintenance. In the year 2015, the average hourly wage of taxi drivers and chauffeurs was US$12.35 in the USA (data source: Occupational Employment Statistics (OES)). So there are indications that Uber drivers' net earnings before deduction of fixed costs are lower than the average taxi driver wage. In 2015, the GMB Union, which, among other workers, also represents professional drivers in the UK, calculated that the average net income (after taxes and deducing all fixed costs) of an Uber driver was £5.68, £1 below the 2015 British minimum wage of £6.70. Uber seems to dump taxi drivers' wages.[10]

In 2015, Uber paid only £22,134 corporation tax on a UK profit of £866,000 by transferring profits to the Netherlands, where the tax rate is lower.[11] So it paid an effective tax rate of 2.6 per cent even though the British corporation tax rate was 20 per cent in the UK. Given low average wages and tax avoidance, one cannot say that Uber strengthens, but rather that it weakens local economies.

ONLINE SHARING CAPITAL ACCUMULATION MODEL #2: FREEMIUM

A second form of online sharing is the freemium model. Freemium means that a certain basic or initial use of a service is gratis, but that for continued or full use, a service fee is charged.

An example is NeighborGoods. It is a platform for the sharing of goods with friends and neighbours. NeighborGoods describes itself the following way: "NeighborGoods is a safe community where you can save money and resources by sharing stuff with your friends. Need a ladder? Borrow it from your neighbor. Have a bike collecting dust in your closet? Lend it out and make a new friend"; "Not only does NeighborGoods provide a way to save money and resources – it also connects neighbors in meaningful ways making for happier, healthier neighborhoods".

---

8   Uber reveals how much its drivers really earn … Sort of. *Time* online, 22 January 2015. http://time.com/money/3678389/uber-drivers-wages (accessed on 26 September 2016)

9   http://uberdriverdiaries.com/how-much-do-uber-drivers-really-make/ (accessed on 11 February 2016).

10 www.gmb.org.uk/newsroom/new-uber-drivers-pay-down-by-one-pound (accessed on 17 February 2016).

11 Uber pays £22,000 tax on £866,000 UK profit. *Guardian* online, 20 October 2015 (accessed on 27 September 2016).

NeighborGoods has a free basic use and charges a one-time fee (US$9.99) for an upgrade account that allows users to access more shared goods. Neighbours typically do not charge each other for sharing goods, but rather the platform supports a community spirit of peer-to-peer sharing without exchange-value. NeighborGoods, however, is a for-profit platform that wants to make profit by making users pay a premium fee. The profits earned by it are a kind of rent for platform use that stems either from wages or capitalists' profits and therefore workers' surplus-value in the case of the registering user being a capitalist. And the profits are a reduction of wages in the case of the user being an employee. In the case where the user is a freelancer, the reduction is a profit-wage. This distinction is based on the difference between capitalists, employees and freelancers, whose source of revenue is respectively profit, wages and a profit-wage.

WHY DO USERS FIND SHARING SERVICES SUCH AS UBER ATTRACTIVE?

Answering this question requires us to have a look at economic development. The wage share is the share of total wages in an economy's total value. The profit share is the share of total profits in an economy's total value. And the capital share is the share of total capital in an economy's total value. Comparing the development of these indicators allows us to analyse the economic power relationship between capital and labour in an economy.

The new great recession that started in 2009 has resulted in a rise of global unemployment from 6.1 per cent in 2008 to 8.5 per cent in 2010 (ILO 2012, 2) and a contraction of real wage growth (ibid.). In the period from 1990 to 2009, the share of labour compensation in the GDP (the so-called labour share) declined in 26 of the 30 OECD countries (ILO 2012, 42). The median labour share in these countries decreased from 66.1 per cent to 61.7 per cent during this time period (ibid.). There were also declines of the labour share in Asia, North Africa and Latin America (ibid.). In a combination of 16 developed countries, the decline of the average labour share was from around 75 per cent in the mid-1970s to about 65 per cent before the crisis started (ibid.). In a combination of 16 developing and emerging economies the decrease was from 62 per cent in the early 1990s to 58 per cent before the crisis (ibid.). Also, in China the wage share decreased from around 65 per cent in the early 1990s to slightly above 45 per cent in 2008 (ILO 2012, 45). Wages have risen much slower than productivity, which has resulted in a growth of the capital share at the expense of the labour share (ILO 2012, 44–48). The data show that in recent decades capital has expanded its power at the expense of labour through neoliberal class struggle.

THE DEVELOPMENT OF THE WAGE SHARE AND THE CAPITAL SHARE IN THE USA AND THE EU

From the early 1960s until the mid-1970s, the wage share increased in both the USA and the EU (see Figure 10.1), which signified an increasing power of the working class and relatively successful class struggles during this period that compelled capital to increase wages. In the mid-1970s a period of wage repression started in both the EU and the USA, which resulted in significant drops of the wage share. At the same time, the share of capital in the total economy increased (see Figure 10.2). Class struggle determines how large the working class's exploitation and its poverty (understood as non-ownership) is and the share of the economy it can control. The period that started in the mid-1970s has seen a defeat of the working class and as

FIGURE 10.1   The wage share in the USA and the EU, 1960–2015

Source: AMECO

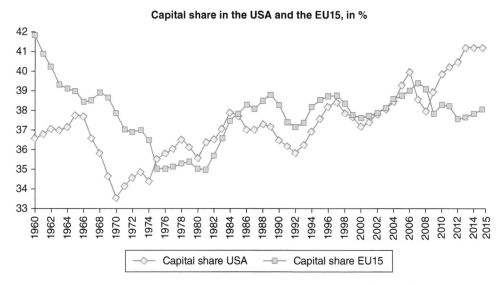

FIGURE 10.2   The capital share in the USA and the EU, 1960–2015

Source: AMECO

a result an increasing level of its expropriation. The working class has the power to resist, but does not automatically organize collectively and does not automatically win battles.

Given that many employees in many parts of the world are worse off than they were some decades before and that much labour today is precarious, the promise of entrepreneurial self-employment that Uber and other companies make sounds to a significant number of people like a way out of precarity. And given relatively low wages, also taxi passengers may find Uber attractive in order to save money. There are, however, as we have seen, indications that Uber is not at all a way out of precarity, and that charging rents drives average earnings down and weakens local economies.

The Uber users find location-based services attractive because they can be used any time from any place on a mobile. Furthermore, they tend to be cheaper than regular services. But these qualities come at the social price of a low-wage economy. At the same time, some drivers may certainly think Uber is a good opportunity, but the overall picture of working conditions at Uber and similar sharing economy services is not at all rosy, but the reality of precarious labour in the neoliberal age.

10.2 AIRBNB: THE CAPITALIST SHARING ECONOMY'S RENT-ON-RENT MODEL

In the previous section we discussed two specific capitalist sharing economy models: pay per service and freemium. *A third organization form of the capitalist sharing economy is the rent-on-rent model.* Airbnb is an example of this model.

HOW DOES AIRBNB UNDERSTAND ITSELF?

Brian Chesky, Joe Gebbia and Nathan Blecharczyk founded Airbnb in 2008. In 2016, Airbnb was active in more than 34,000 cities in 190 countries. It describes itself on its website in the following way:

> Whether a flat for a night, a castle for a week, or a villa for a month, Airbnb connects people to unique travel experiences, at any price point, in more than 34,000 cities and 190 countries. And with world-class customer service and a growing community of users, Airbnb is the easiest way for people to monetise their extra space and showcase it to an audience of millions.[12]

Airbnb says it helps people to "belong anywhere". "Airbnb hosts create a sense of belonging around the world." "Airbnb is a trusted community marketplace for people to list, discover, and book unique accommodations around the world – online or from a mobile phone."

Airbnb is not the only such model. There are others too that are worth discussing.

RENTING ROOMS, DOGS AND BIKES

Examples for sharing platforms that are comparable to Airbnb include DogVacay, BorrowMyDoggy and Spinlister. These companies describe themselves in the following way:

- "BorrowMyDoggy is a trusted community where local dog lovers help take care of dogs for walkies, playdays, weekends, and happy holidays."

---

12 www.airbnb.co.uk (accessed on 11 February 2016).

- "DogVacay is an online community that has tens of thousands of hosts vetted and insured dog sitters across the country ready to care for your dog like a member of their family. It's a safe, convenient and affordable way to make sure your best friend is in good care." "DogVacay is an online community where dog lovers can connect with one another to find and provide superior, safe, convenient, and affordable ways to care for their best friend."
- Spinlister: "Rent a bike from someone like you. Save money, meet awesome people, and consume less."

HOW DO SUCH PLATFORMS MAKE MONEY?

Airbnb charges 3 per cent of the host's total revenue and a 6–15 per cent booking fee for guests. DogVacay makes dog owners pay and keeps a certain percentage (15 per cent) of the price. BorrowMyDoggy charges annual platform access fees for both dog owners and borrowers. The bike-sharing platform Spinlister keeps 17.5 per cent of the bike rental price.

Dogs, bikes, flats and rooms are not reproduced by constant labour inputs. They are more conservative forms of private property. Their owners rent them out to leasers and charge a certain rent for this use. This rent stems from profits in the event of the leaser being a capitalist, from wages if s/he is an employee, or a non-differentiable profit-wage if s/he is a freelancer. In the case of a capitalist being the renter, the source of rent is the surplus-value created by the capitalist's employees. If the renter is a worker, then the rent is charged on wages. If several people rent a good together, then combinations of different rent sources are also possible. The sharing platforms charge a specific annual fee or percentage share on the rental price. The platform is rented out for the service of mediating the renting of physical goods for a specific time period. The platform owners charge a rent on rent.

WHAT IS COMMODITY FETISHISM?

Commodity fetishism is a term that Marx introduces in *Capital, Volume 1* in order to critically analyse the ideological illusions that the commodity form produces. Given that in the sharing economy we also have to do with commodities, the question arises as to what role commodity fetishism has in it.

The world of capitalism is rational in the sense that it involves companies' inherent compulsion to exploit labour and increase productivity in order to accumulate ever more capital. Labour power and technology are means to the end of accumulation. Human activity thereby becomes instrumentalized. The creation of various use-values satisfies human needs in society and enables humans to relate to each other. One specific use-value of media systems is that they enable the sharing of information and communication in society. They have an inherently social character. People socialize at the workplace and connect through the joint production and consumption of use-values.

This social quality of capitalism at the level of use-value is for Marx (1867), however, subsumed under the logic of value, commodities and capital accumulation that renders social relations to the status of mere instruments for partial purposes that constitute and reproduce the structures of class society. The commodity is a "strange" thing (Marx 1867, 163).

Commodity producers do not relate to each other directly, but relate only in exchange in the form x commodity A = a money M, y commodity B = b money M. Therefore "the relationship between the producers [...] take on the form of a social relation between the products of labour" (164). The "definite social relation between men themselves" assumes "the fantastic form of a relation between things" (165).

Marx stresses explicitly the important role that money plays in commodity fetishism:

> It is however precisely this finished form of the world of commodities – they money form – which conceals the social character of private labour and the social relations between the individual workers, by making those relations appear as relations between material objects, instead of revealing them plainly. (169).

Given that money and exchange-value mediate social relations in capitalism, direct social relations between producers and between producers and consumers do often not take place, which creates a void of meaning: social meaning of commodities is not created by communicative relations between producers and consumers. Ideology can therefore fill this symbolic void left by commodity fetishism with imaginary meanings devoid of reality. Public relations, marketing, advertising, branding, corporate and strategic communication, and corporate social responsibility are practices that create commodity's ideologies and use-value promises (Fuchs 2015a).

AIRBNB AND COMMODITY FETISHISM

The Airbnb model of capitalist online sharing promises to users that they can engage with others and be social. This sociality, due to commodity fetishism, cannot normally be experienced in the purchase and consumption of commodities. Airbnb promises a de-alienated world without questioning the existence of capitalism as such. The reason why a significant share of consumers may find such ideological meanings appealing is not just that Airbnb promise to overcome commodity fetishism, but that they also promise to overcome the loss of community that many have experienced in neoliberalism's highly individualized culture. Airbnb promises to enable community, connection between humans, belonging, family, friendship, neighbourhood and environmental sustainability. It also presents itself as reinventing and evolving the world. Airbnb promises a radical makeover of the world and to reverse commodity fetishism so that the social that is hidden behind the commodity becomes the primary feature of consumer culture.

The problem is, however, that these promises mask the fact that Airbnb and similar projects are for-profit capitalist businesses aiming at making monetary profits. They organize a form of gifting or trading between users that tends to involve a direct, non-anonymous communicative and social encounter. To access the possibility of social sharing, one or both sides of the established social relations have to pay a fee to the platform. Sharing thereby becomes itself a commodity. The language that capitalist sharing platforms use is often ideological because it hides profit interests and commodity logic behind social promises. Sharing thereby becomes an ideology, from which somebody in the end benefits monetarily and accumulates capital.

CAPITALIST SHARING: TURNING THE NON-INSTRUMENTAL INTO THE INSTRUMENTAL

Online platforms are useful tools for bringing together people who want to share a good or provide gifts to others. The essential logic of sharing and gifting is that it is non-instrumental and altruistic. By turning sharing and gifting into an instrument for capitalist purposes, Airbnb inverts the non-instrumentality of gifting and sharing and renders them instrumental. The profit logic is an alien and unnecessary third in the social encounter of sharing and gifting. The social relations enabled by sharing platforms are not automatically forms of gifting, but are within a capitalist world often based on exchange-value.

Renting a bike, dog or flat, finding cheap expertise or a cheap taxi ride means an exchange between a person's money on one side and another person's good or service on the other side. These are not true forms of gifting and sharing. There is, however, a potential that online sharing platforms transcend and negate the logic of exchange and enable non-instrumental sociality. Many people may indeed be willing to share a good, give people a lift in their car or host them for a couple of nights on their couch because they enjoy the social encounter, community and communication with others.

An argument against the organization of non-instrumental sociality with strangers is that money is a means for organizing trust between strangers. How can you trust that someone you have not met before is a responsible driver, host or pet sitter? The problem of money and exchange-value is that they render goods and services inaccessible to those who cannot afford paying the set prices and is therefore embedded into structures of unequal access. Gifts and public services in contrast enable a logic of sharing that can create a world of equal rights, equal possibilities and equal access. A comment system, using online social networks, that allows users to share their experiences with specific sharers can foster trust and community. Such an online system is a sufficient communicative means of trust that can substitute monetary exchanges.

WHY DO USERS FIND INTEREST IN AIRBNB AND SIMILAR SERVICES?

We live in a world of high risk, high precarity, crises, austerity and debt. We need to understand the transformations of capitalism in order to answer the posed question.

FINANCIALIZATION

Financialization means that specific resources are turned into goods that are traded on financial markets. Financialization has been rising in capitalist economies, especially since the 1970s (Harvey 2007).

After the new economy crisis in 2000, the US wanted to boost the economy by low interest rates and cutting the federal funds rate successively from 6 per cent down to 1 per cent so that as a result capital would flow into the housing market (Bischoff 2008; Foster and Magdoff 2009, 93–94, 96; Lapavitsas 2013, 271). There was a combined double process of fictionalization. The mortgages given to short-term lenders did not produce immediate profits for banks, but based on certain interest rates (that were variable, typically low in the beginning and increasing after some years) promised future profits over a continuous time. This was the first process of fictionalization. Part of this fictionalization was also the re-mortgaging of existing mortgages; that is, the practice of taking a new mortgage for paying off an existing one.

The creation of new high-risk securities that were sold on financial markets to investors who expected to achieve high rates of return was the second process of fictionalization. Asset-backed securities combined both forms of fictitious capital. They were double fictitious capital based on mortgages and high-risk securities. As Marx knew, such an "artificial system" (Marx 1894, 649) must sooner or later result in a "violent outbreak" (572). The outbreak was built into the financial system, but was finally triggered once a critical mass of low-income mortgage borrowers were unable to pay their rates, which caused the breakdown of the artificial system. This situation was also caused by a stagnation of real wages that drove up profit rates and made it necessary that low-wage workers took out loans in order to buy homes and other commodities that they needed for their survival. The drive to accumulate drove down wages and created high-risk securities coupled with high-risk mortgages. This deadly combination triggered the crisis. Class relations are one central aspect of this crisis. Marx argued in this context that the "ultimate reason for all real crises always remains the poverty and restricted consumption of the masses, in the face of the drive of capitalist production to develop the productive forces as if only the absolute consumption capacity of society set a limit to them" (615).

FINANCIAL AND ECONOMIC CRISIS

In the US subprime housing market, many subprime mortgages were combined into new commercial papers, so-called asset-backed securities (ABS), which were traded on the stock market. ABS are high-risk papers. Many banks from all over the world have over the past years and decades bought high-risk papers, which explains the domino effect by which the crisis spread from the US housing market to all parts of the world so that many economies and all economic realms became affected. The asset-backed securities in the sub-prime housing market turned parts of the wages of mortgage holders into an asset that was traded. The arising financial profits were a financial expropriation of workers' wages, a form of secondary exploitation that reduced the wages that workers needed in order to finance their everyday lives.

The crisis took on a transnational scope and also turned into a crisis of the Eurozone. Lapavitsas (2013, Chapter 9) argues that the Eurozone consists of a core (especially Germany and France) whose banks have provided low-interest liquidity to banks in the periphery (especially Greece, Spain, Portugal and Ireland) so that the result was a rise of external debt-funded domestic lending and domestic household debts.

BAILOUT AND AUSTERITY

The main reaction of Western states to the crisis was a bailout of banks and financial capital by providing securities in the form of taxpayers' money. At the political level, the consequence was an intensification of neoliberal cuts and privatizations as well as the discourse of having to reduce state expenditures. Neoliberal politicians first dispossessed the majority of citizens from access to public services that were increasingly privatized and commodified. In a second step after the crisis, parts of their taxes and future taxes were dispossessed for saving banks and capitalism and an intensified hyper-neoliberalism continued to commodify, expropriate and privatize common and public goods and services. "Across the periphery, but also increasingly in the core, public spending has been cut, taxes have been increased, wages have been reduced, markets have been further deregulated, and public enterprises have been lined up for privatization" (Lapavitsas 2013, 304).

Lapavitsas (2013) argues that since the 1970s many capitalist countries and regions such as the USA, the EU and Japan have experienced a large growth of the derivatives markets and an accruing debt of private households to finance housing, consumption, health, education and transport. An important aspect of financialization has been the "financialization of the personal revenue of workers and households across social classes. This phenomenon refers both to increasing debt (for mortgages, general consumption, education, health) and to expanded holdings of financial assets (for pensions, insurance, money market funds)" (Lapavitsas 2013, 38–39). The causes include "rising income inequality", "the retreat of public provision across a range of services, including housing, pensions, education, health, transport, and so on" (Lapavitsas 2013, 39).

Lapavitsas (2013, Chapter 7) shows for the USA, the UK, Japan and Germany that a combination of low GDP growth, weak productivity growth, decreasing wage shares, higher unemployment and rising income inequality has spurred the financialization of the economy, which included the financialization of the personal incomes and wealth of households in order to finance everyday life.

> The bulk of household indebtedness in the period of financialization in mature countries has been for mortgage purposes. [...] The evidence shows that financialization of households has meant, above all, heavy reliance on private providers of finance – banks, or institutions associated with banks – to obtain housing. (Lapavitsas 2013, 238, 240)

INCREASING PERSONAL DEBT

The data in Table 10.1 show the share of the total loan sum (consumer credit, lending for house purchase, other loans) in the annual GDP. It indicates a pronounced increase of private household debt in the period 1995–2013 in almost all analysed countries, with individual exceptions, such as Germany and Japan. The data show that wage repression and rising inequality have forced more and more people to take out loans in order to finance housing and consumption, which has increased debt and spurred financialization.

AIRBNB AND CHANGES OF CAPITALISM

The interest of citizens in Airbnb and comparable sharing platforms can be explained by the changes of the capitalist economy. A relative lack of time, income, resources and adequate housing makes consumers look for ways to reduce their debt, expenditures on transport, travelling, commuting, holidays, household goods, services and so on. The online sharing economy promises saving such expenditures and enabling additional incomes for those who own specific goods (such as houses, flats, cars, etc.) that can be shared. The extension of the online sharing economy stands in the context of the neoliberalization, financialization and crisis of capitalism, as well as decreasing labour shares. Those who are facing rising personal debt, increasing costs for rents, interest on loans and mortgages,

TABLE 10.1 The share of loans in the annual GDP in selected countries (%)

	1995	1997	2000	2002	2004	2006	2008	2010	2012	2013
Australia	49.5	48.9	49.2	59.0	96.9	109.0	103.9	160.7	171.6	148.2
Austria	53.3	43.7	38.3	44.1	58.8	59.7	62.7	62.1	58.6	
Belgium	45.0	37.9	32.2	34.1	48.2	51.0	58.3	58.5	60.4	
Canada	50.6	50.2	48.7	48.3	68.6	75.3	81.1	111.2	116.6	
Czech Republic	4.2	2.8	2.8	4.9	8.7	12.6	18.7	21.4	21.8	
Denmark	119.8	104.9	92.8	112.2	161.9	172.4	195.3	189.7	187.8	192.5
Estonia	0.8	2.8	3.6	7.0	15.7	28.2	38.3	36.6	30.1	
Finland	45.4	31.7	28.5	35.1	53.9	60.2	65.5	72.2	75.7	
France	44.3	35.8	29.7	33.6	49.7	52.4	59.6	61.5	62.4	
Germany	82.4	70.4	63.8	68.9	83.9	71.8	67.2	62.9	59.0	
Greece	4.9	5.8	8.2	14.7	28.5	39.0	50.4	58.3	57.7	57.3
Hungary	2.6	1.8	2.2	5.7	13.7	17.2	24.8	23.6	18.1	
Iceland					148.0	169.7	97.4	114.2	102.7	
Ireland				58.0	100.0	123.4	148.9	131.7	115.4	
Italy	16.9	16.1	17.2	22.8	35.5	39.2	42.9	45.5	44.3	
Japan	112.5	86.6	93.1	80.7	83.9	67.6	80.3	85.4	76.6	
Korea	0.0	0.0	0.0	42.1	47.4	57.7	45.6	55.8	64.0	
Luxembourg			25.7	31.9	47.3	54.3	61.9	66.3	67.2	
Netherlands	70.2	65.1	67.2	84.8	126.1	126.5	130.6	135.0	132.9	
Norway	80.6	66.9	54.3	82.1	101.7	97.9	90.4	126.9	134.3	128.8
Poland			3.1	6.1	8.1	11.4	18.6	21.0	20.3	
Portugal	22.4	29.7	38.4	49.3	73.5	72.7	79.7	76.2	72.5	70.9
Slovak Republic	1.5	1.4	1.4	2.3	5.0	9.0	16.0	17.2	19.1	
Slovenia					13.3	17.0	22.4	25.8	24.0	
Spain	30.3	27.2	31.2	39.8	66.2	76.1	83.6	82.2	74.5	72.1
Sweden	61.4	55.0	48.0	57.8	83.0	88.2	81.6	109.0	114.1	115.7
Switzerland			123.1	143.1	181.3	158.9	160.0	189.9	192.2	
Turkey	0.4	0.7	1.7	0.7	3.0	5.6	7.3	9.8	11.3	11.2
UK	64.0	66.3	64.7	79.2	109.7	116.2	93.3	104.8	104.5	104.8
USA	63.0	64.0	68.6	76.7	86.4	93.9	93.5	88.4	81.1	79.1

Source: Data from OECD Stats; loans in US$ (current prices, current exchange rates) [dataset: households' financial and non-financial assets and liabilities], gross domestic product in US$ (current prices).

everyday goods and services, and relatively decreasing personal income and wealth are looking for ways to increase their income and to decrease their expenditures. The online sharing economy promises both, but also results in new costs that the access to the sharing services on these platforms costs and that funds the profits of capitalist online sharing businesses.

AIRBNB'S CONTRADICTIONS

Airbnb had to pay fines in Barcelona and has faced legal disputes in several cities because most hosts do not charge hotel taxes that are due in many cities. In some cities hosts must stay in the same flat or house when renting it out, but in practice stay abroad while renting out their property.

> Most cities and states both tax and regulate hotels, and the tourists who stay in hotels are usually an important source of tax revenue (since governments have long recognized that a modest hotel tax is not likely to discourage most visitors nor provoke the ire of constituents). But many of Airbnb's customers are not paying the taxes required under the law. [...] Insofar as Airbnb is allowing people to evade taxes and regulations, the company is not a net plus to the economy and society – it is simply facilitating a bunch of rip-offs. Others in the economy will lose by bearing an additional tax burden or being forced to live next to an apartment unit with a never-ending parade of noisy visitors, just to cite two examples. (Baker 2014)

An empirical study of data from Airbnb and the hotel industry in Texas concludes that Airbnb's "entry into the Texas market has had a quantifiable negative impact on local hotel revenues" (Zervas et al. 2014, 22) and that "lower-end hotels as those that are most vulnerable to increased competition from rentals enabled by firms like Airbnb" (23).

AIRBNB AND THE HOUSING CRISIS

Think of a city like London that has a highly speculative and financialized property market. In 2016, the average home cost £500,000 in London. Many average income earners cannot afford the necessary down payments to get mortgages and get onto the property ladder. They are forced to rent property.

A family of two people with one child needs at least a two-bedroom flat. In February 2016, the average monthly rent for such a property measures across all London postcode districts was £2,300 per month.[13] The average London wage in late 2015 was £711 before taxes per week and £542.85 after taxes (data source: Office for National Statistics (ONS)). An average London couple with two full-time workers therefore earns around £4,700 per month. This sounds like a good income, but is offset by the fact that this couple has to pay on average 50 per cent for rent, on average around £800 for childcare, up to £500 per month for public transport and so on. So at the end of the month, they will not have saved any money.

The average Londoner will therefore never be able to buy a house or flat, except if s/he has rich relatives or wins a fortune. At the same time there is the phenomenon of buy-to-let: rich property owners buy ever more flats and houses in order to rent them out and make ever more money. At the same time more and more affordable council homes have been privatized and the number of new homes built is only a fraction of those required.[14]

---

13 Calculation based on data obtained from www.londonpropertywatch.co.uk/average_rental_prices.html (accessed on 11 February 2016).
14 The housing crisis in charts. *Guardian* online, 12 January 2015. https://www.theguardian.com/money/2015/jan/12/the-housing-crisis-in-charts (accessed on 26 September 2016).

AIRBNB IN LONDON

Imagine what happens in a financialized property market like the one in London when Airbnb enters: it is not predominantly everyday citizens who rent out property on Airbnb. Because of the unaffordable housing prices, everyday people in cities like London tend to rent and not to own property. It is rather the class of rich property owners and landlords – the buy-to-let class (the class owning and renting out flats and houses) that uses Airbnb as a medium of rent accumulation. The members of this class devote a certain share of their property to Airbnb rentals and take care to make more money with these short-term rentals than by renting out long-term to regular tenants.

There are indications that this is indeed happening:

> Data [...] suggests that professionals and buy-to-let investors with empty properties have carved out a huge presence on the site. The analysis of more than 13,000 Airbnb listings in London – by far the site's biggest UK market – shows more than 6,600 are leasing out an entire home or flat, rather than a spare room. More than 1,500 people listing properties on the site have multiple listings, with 180 listing five or more properties or rooms across London. Some of the site's super users have dozens of properties across the city at once: one, who went by the name Petra, had 127 active listings on Thursday.[15]

The effect is that rich property owners become richer and the housing shortage and housing crisis are intensified. Aribnb is likely to make housing crises worse. The only solution of such crises is to build more affordable community-owned houses and flats, to strictly regulate the maximum rent that can be charged per square metre, and to pass a bill that legislates that in crisis-prone housing areas such as London a person owning a private property must also live in it and cannot own more than one property.

Airbnb says that it wants "London to be an incredible place to live and to visit" and that it allows Londoners to "make some extra cash and pursue new ventures, and will allow guests to benefit from unique accommodation in all corners of this amazing city".[16] The reality is that Airbnb helps the rich to get richer and advances the housing crisis.

10.3 THE SHARING ECONOMY: A CAPITALIST IDEOLOGY

ONLINE SHARING: A SOCIAL MEDIA IDEOLOGY

The blogger and journalist Jeff Jarvis (2011) argues in the book *Public Parts: How Sharing in the Digital Age Improves the Way We Work and Live* that "Facebook is at the core of its own new industry, built on sharing" (2) and that "Facebook, Twitter, Flickr, YouTube, Foursquare" and other social media platforms form "the sharing industry" (9) that is based on the principle "the more we share, the more we benefit from what others share" (3). Facebook

---

15 A deep data dive into how Airbnb is changing London lodging. skift.com, 21 June 2014.
16 http://publicpolicy.airbnb.com/london-reveals-new-policy-home-sharing (accessed on 27 September 2016).

says it provides "the power to share and to make the world more open and connected".[17] Twitter argues that it helps to "give everyone the power to create and share ideas and information instantly".[18] Instagram says it is a "fast, beautiful and fun way to share your life with friends and family".[19] Tumblr claims it enables you to "share the things you love".[20] The idea of sharing is indeed a core ideology of social media platforms that masks that companies such as Google and Facebook are from a political economy perspective first and foremost among the world's largest advertising agencies.

For Clay Shirky (2008, 21), social media (such as social networks, blogs, wikis) are tools that result in an "increase in our ability to share, to co-operate with one another, and to take collective action". Shirky is aware that the sharing of common property such as natural resources has a long history (Shirky 2011a, 112–133). But he focuses on how social media enable new forms of sharing knowledge. He speaks in this context of the "economics of sharing" (Shirky 2011a, 140): "Our new tools provide an opportunity to create new cultures of sharing" (Shirky 2011a, 143). Shirky does not much focus on the sharing of physical goods, in which the co-ordination is mediated by digital technologies.

MESH BUSINESSES

Sharing on capitalist social media serves the specific purpose of serving ads to users and commodifying data. Social media platforms that allow the sharing of ideas and multimedia content are certainly a very important part of the sharing economy. This specific form of economy, however, goes beyond the online world and social media. It also includes the sharing of ownership, means of production, workplaces, means of distribution and consumption. The Internet entrepreneur Lisa Gansky, therefore, in her book *The Mesh: Why the Future of Business is Sharing*, speaks of the emergence of mesh businesses that she defines as being represented by "four characteristics: sharing, advanced use of Web and mobile information networks, a focus on [sharing] physical goods and materials, and engagement with customers through social networks" (Gansky 2012, 15–16). One should add that one can also share informational goods, services and physical products.

COLLABORATIVE CONSUMPTION

Rachel Botsman and Roo Rogers (2011) speak in their book *What's Mine is Yours* about the emergence of collaborative consumption, which they define as "peer-to-peer exchanges between producer and consumer, seller and buyer, lender and borrower, and neighbour and neighbour" (Botsman and Rogers 2011, xiii). It includes "traditional sharing, bartering, lending, trading, renting, gifting and swapping, redefined through technology and peer communities" (xv). "Simply put, people are sharing again with their community – be it an office, a neighbourhood, an apartment building, a school or a Facebook network" (xv).

There are several problems with the analyses presented by authors such as Jarvis, Shirky, Ganski and Botsman/Rogers.

---

17 www.facebook.com/FacebookUK/info (accessed on 16 November 2015).
18 https://about.twitter.com/company (accessed on 16 November 2015).
19 http://instagram.com (accessed on 16 November 2015).
20 www.tumblr.com/ (accessed on 16 November 2015).

PROBLEM 1 OF THE SHARING ECONOMY LITERATURE: THE LACK OF CLASS ANALYSIS

A first tendency in the sharing economy literature is that the notion of the sharing economy is used in an undifferentiated manner. Sharing is presented as a moral value in itself independent of class and capital.

So, for instance, Botsman and Rogers (2011, xvii–xviii) mention on one page Zopa, Freecycle, U-Exchange, thredUP, Landshare, Couchsurfing, Zipcar, WhipCar, Airbnb, CrashPadder and Zilok as examples of online collaborative sharing. This lists masks that although most of these examples are for-profit companies, there are exceptions. Freecycle is a non-profit network where people can give away things without payment. Landshare.net is a non-profit online platform run by British broadcaster Channel 4 that brings together people who have or seek access to land in order to grow vegetables or fruits and keep farm animals. Couchsurfing.org was founded in 2003 as a non-profit hospitality network that enabled users to share and search for a couch in a living room, flat or house that is available for a limited time during a visit without payment. In 2011, it was turned into a for-profit corporation and raised venture capital. Users criticized this commodification of community and travel commons by, for example, saying in an Avazz petition that "we, the community of CouchSurfing, are the ones who built everything from scratch in voluntary work [. . .] we won't just watch how this all is destroyed by the profit-seeking share holders".[21] The other projects are for-profit. Also Beth Buczynski (2012) mixes together for-profit and non-profit sites in a list of 59 online sharing platforms. Her main stress is that these are sites for forms of "collaborative consumption" that are "changing the way we work, play and interact with each other" (Buczynski 2012, 96).

THE SHARING ECONOMY'S IDEOLOGUES

Lisa Gansky (2012, 122) argues that "WhipCar and CouchSurfing allow an individual to get more use for only marginally greater cost from his car and, well, couch" so that one can "achieve better personal yield management" (Gansky 2012, 122). Gansky identifies the commonality of a car- and couch-sharing platform by the circumstance that individuals can better manage their individual finances, but ignores that at the point of time that her book was first published (2010), CouchSurfing was a non-profit organization, whereas WhipCar was from its founding in 2009 until its closure in 2013 a venture-capital funded for-profit car-sharing company. In addition, the idea of CouchSurfing is not to rent out a couch for money. Its idea is rather to offer a free couch to someone without payment. Gansky mixes up for-profit and non-profit initiatives and characterizes both as "mesh networks".

Gansky (2012, 16) says that a mesh is a network in which all nodes are connected. She compares mesh businesses to "minds" and "DNA, nerve cells" (17). She thereby equates aspects characteristic of all humans with organizations in capitalism. She fetishizes, that is naturalizes, capitalism by creating the impression that something particular to a specific society is a universal feature of humanity. She speaks of threefold benefits – "greener commerce and greater profits" and "social benefits" so that an "ethic of doing well while

---

21 https://secure.avaaz.org/en/petition/For_a_strong_Community_behind_CouchSurfing (accessed on 10 February 2016).

doing good" is practised (29). Capitalism is based on the exploitation of labour that produces commodities. Workers do not own the products they produce. These products contain what Marx terms surplus-value: unpaid labour time. Capitalists' individual monetary benefit is based on the expropriation of others. Larger profits therefore do not bring about social benefits for the working class. Corporate social responsibility is an immanently ideological project (Sandoval 2014).

SHARING ECONOMY-HYPE

Some observers, such as the journalist Tina Rosenberg, assume that the sharing economy is the next big thing in business. She only identifies advantages without thinking of contradictions and potential negative impacts:

> What's new is that the sharing economy is deepening and spreading. Thousands of new businesses now sell access rather than ownership. For the young, hip and urban, collaborative consumption is a way to live light, waste less, to protect the environment, to create and associate with a community of like-minded people. But it's not just a phenomenon of the hip. For everyone, it's a way to de-clutter and save money. (Rosenberg 2013)

Lisa Gansky (2012, 3) is enthusiastic about the sharing economy's for-profit business opportunities: She says that "there is gold in giving people convenient access to shared goods". She also writes that sharing businesses have "extraordinary competitive advantages" (Gansky 2012, 5). She is honest in admitting that the only interest of mesh entrepreneurs is profit-making: "The central strategy is, in effect, to 'sell' the same product multiple times. Multiple sales multiply profits, and customer contacts" (5). "The successful Mesh companies will be the ones that delight customers, grow trust in the brand and business itself, and make a profit" (72).

The focus for Rosenberg, Gansky and others is that sharing is the newest big thing, whereas a discussion of how sharing may best be organized and whether all manners of doing so are equally desirable is absent. For-profit companies such as Airbnb are meshed together with non-profits such as Wikipedia when Rosenberg discusses examples:

> The list is long and eclectic: Airbnb and Home Exchange, Wikipedia and open-source software, peer-to-peer banks such as Lending Club, time banks. There are countless local tool exchanges, clothing swaps and neighbor-to-neighbor taxi services. You can share your Wi-Fi. You can share a dog. You can even share a baby. (Rosenberg 2013)

Thomas Friedman (2013) argues that Airbnb "set off [...] the 'sharing economy'", an economy that for him is all about people "building their own branded reputations". For Friedman, there are only positive aspects of the sharing economy and he thinks of it in terms of capitalist business opportunities. A London-based initiative called The People Who Share defines as its goal "to enable sharing, to make it easy for people who need, to connect with people who have, and build a global community of sharers".[22]

---

22 www.thepeoplewhoshare.com/ (accessed on 11 November 2014).

SHARING FETISHISM

Fetishism is according to Marx (1867) the naturalization of social phenomena. They are presented as inherently necessary and natural. Fetishism ignores the power relations underlying phenomena. Sharing fetishism sees sharing as a goal in itself that is independent of the political-economic structures that contextualize it. It tends to ignore the fundamental difference between a for-profit and a non-profit economy: the first is necessarily based on class and therefore on exploitation; that is, the enrichment of an owning class by a non-owning class. We have seen earlier in this chapter that sharing businesses that foster sharing among humans and earn profits by it, exploit employees (access fees) or users (advertising funding), or charge a rent on the exploitation of one user by another (freelancer platforms), or a rent on rent (rental platforms such as Airbnb), or a rent on the commercial provision of services (service apps and platforms such as Uber), in which labour is exploited. The effect is that contradictions and class conflicts are not transcended, but persist and are repositioned. As a result, for example, the tourist industry opposes Airbnb and the taxi industry feels challenged by Uber because new forms of competition between capitalists have emerged that the Internet and mobile apps mediate. The principle that someone wants to make a monetary profit persists and the net effect is that some groups are better off and some groups worse off. Such inequality is a necessary consequence in any economic system based on exchange, class and profitability.

PROBLEM 2 OF THE SHARING ECONOMY LITERATURE: THE REDUCTION OF SHARING TO A MORAL PHENOMENON

A second tendency in the sharing economy literature is to interpret sharing as a purely moral phenomenon that people engage in because they cherish the moral values of togetherness, community and loving their neighbours.

Botsman and Rogers (2011, 45) describe the sharing economy as "reclaiming old virtues" (45), "belief in 'the commons'" (88) and "changing the consumer mind-set" (213). Brands "can make us want more of the sustainable values and benefits attached to Collaborative Consumption. These values include relationships, respect, support, skills, happiness, new habits, space and even time" (199–200). The result would be that economic value would turn into moral value. Botsman and Rogers speak of a re-definition of value so that capitalist companies create communities. "[W]e will trust them more" (220). A "multidimensional notion of value" (221) emerges. The net effect would be the "democratization and flowering of new companies" (221).

Moralizations of the sharing economy ignore the materiality of all morality: the desire of humans to share in contemporary capitalism does not come from autonomous moral conviction or conversion to a faith, cult or religion of sharing, but is rather grounded in contemporary capitalism's political economy, that is, in phenomena such as crisis, class relations, inequality, lack of ownership, consumer debt, wage repression, exploitation, precarity, unemployment, high social insecurity among the young, the financialization of land and housing, and so on.

PROBLEM 3 OF THE SHARING ECONOMY LITERATURE: TECHNOLOGICAL DETERMINISM

A third tendency is that sharing economy literature reduces the emergence of the sharing economy to being a consequence of the Internet or to seeing technology as the driving factor.

So, for example, Botsman and Rogers (2011, 51) write that ICTs, social networks and mobile devices are "driving us towards a 'we' mind-set". The "values that tie them [participants in collaborative consumption] together – openness, community, accessibility, sustainability, and, most importantly, collaboration – come straight of the digital culture" (180). "To explain this hyper-evolution, of which Collaborative Consumption is a part, we can look at the range of communication platforms that are changing our world" (212). "The new share businesses are bolstered and built on social media" (Gansky 2012, 3). Gansky (2012, 4) says that "mobile networks" bring sharing as a "*disruption* to physical goods and venues". "Mesh businesses are thriving on the growth of social media, the Internet, wirless networks, and mobile phones" (15). The "rapid growth of mobile and social networks energizes the Mesh model" (28). She also says that online meshes represent "a new stage in the information revolution" (41). Gansky views the social through technology and therefore says that mesh networks mean "the birth of a new social operating system" (168).

Digital, online, social and mobile technologies certainly constitute a factor that reflects and influences the logic of sharing. But it is a one-dimensional and techno-deterministic logic to causally reduce the sharing economy to technological changes. Sharing has many dimensions, economic, political, cultural, ecological and technological ones. It is not only a phenomenon of the digital age.

SHARING IN TRADITIONAL SOCIETIES

Marshall Sahlins observes in an analysis of anthropological studies from various traditional societies: "That food is the item so often shared is significant. Examples that indicate sharing in favor of need between socially distant parties – those who would ordinarily enter balanced exchange – especially underscore" the phenomenon of generosity (Sahlins 1972, 264). Food is so basic that it is a particular symbol of hospitality, sociality, caring and welcoming. "Direct and equivalent returns for food are unseemly in most social settings: they impugn the motives both of the giver and of the recipient" (Sahlins 1972, 215). Given that food sharing is an ancient human practice that does not require modern communication technologies, but is rather one of the most basic technologies of communication itself, one cannot claim that it is communication technology or other technology that creates sharing. Sharing rather seems to be an essential feature of humans and society.

MICHAEL TOMASELLO: SHARING AS BASIC HUMAN CAPACITY, HUMANS AS SHARING, CARING, CO-OPERATIVE BEINGS

The development psychologist and evolutionary anthropologist Michael Tomasello (2008) has, according to Jürgen Habermas (2009), written a "groundbreaking book": *Origins of Human Communication* shows that the combination of mutual requesting, reciprocal informing and the cultural sharing of attitudes distinguishes humans from animals. These features enable human co-operative communication. Shared intentionality and the sharing of food would have played an important role in the evolution of the human (Tomasello 2008, 239–240).

Tomasello argues that the three anthropological communicative motives of requesting, informing and sharing would also emerge early in an infant's development:

> In the months before their first birthdays, and before they begin acquiring language in earnest, most infants in Western culture begin pointing [...] they point to request things (imperatives) and to share experiences and emotions with others (declaratives). [...] Our contention is thus that recent research on infant pointing establishes three general classes of social intention or motive, just as in the case of adults: (1) sharing (they want to share emotions and attitudes with others); (2) informing (they want to help others by informing them of useful or interesting things); and (3) requesting (they want others to help them in attaining their goals). (Tomasello 2008, 111, 112, 123)

Infants imitate adults' gestures and thereby start communicating with their attachment figures. Tomasello provides evidence that humans are anthropologically sharing, caring and co-operating beings. Given that capitalism is based on individual private property and competition, it is a society that contradicts humans' anthropological essence.

The question that remains to be answered is whether there is potential for an alternative sharing economy.

10.4 AN ALTERNATIVE SHARING ECONOMY BEYOND CAPITALISM?

CHARLES LEADBEATER: WE-THINK SYSTEMS

For Charles Leadbeater (2009), free software, open access, social networks, blogs, wikis and user-generated content sites are relatively new forms of sharing (Leadbeater 2009, Chapter 2, 65–68, 157–159). He is aware that there is a long history of sharing, including the sharing of physical resources and common goods (such as land as natural commons or languages as cultural commons) and their enclosure (48–60).

> The spread of the web invites us to look at the future from a different vantage point, to see that what we share is as important as what we keep for ourselves; [...] The biggest change the web will bring about is in allowing us to share with one another in new ways and particularly to share ideas. (6)

Leadbeater uses the term We-Think for systems that support that humans "think, play, work and create" together (19). We-Think systems are based on five principles, five Cs: the existence of a core community that contributes, is connected, collaborates, and co-creates (68–87).

The crucial political-economic question is how these systems relate to ownership and capitalism. Leadbeater (2009, Chapter 4) draws a clear distinction between capitalist and non-capitalist forms of We-Think (as well as hybrid forms). He speaks of "corporate models of We-Think" (97) on the one hand, and "digital communes" (126), "shared ownership" that "flies in the face of the conventional wisdom that private ownership – usually by companies with shareholders – is the best way" (119), a digital gift economy of "*sharing* that is deeply at odds with the idea that private property animates our economies" (225), as well as "collaborative and open forms of ownership" (124) on the other hand. This distinction is elaborated in the form of a typology that distinguishes between private and public ownership combined with open and closed systems of production (127). Leadbeater also thinks about how public services can be organized in a new way (Public Service 2.0; 141–153), by which he does not mean the erosion of public funding and privatization, but rather the opening of publicly funded services to citizen participation to a specific degree.

But Leadbeater has a clear political preference for hybrid models: "The most exciting business models of the future will be hybrids that blend elements of the company and the community, of commerce and collaboration" (91). "The most exciting organisational models of the future will mix collaboration and commerce, community and corporation" (227). "Successful organisations will have a foot in both camps. The most successful will find ways to make money from enabling the circulation of ideas" (228). What one considers as "exciting" clearly depends on political judgements.

CAPITALISM = IMPERIALISM

Charles Leadbeater overlooks capitalism's imperialist character that stems from the fact that capital has to be accumulated in order not to cease to exist. It therefore expands into non-commodified realms and tries to transform them into realms of capital accumulation and commodity production. In this context, Rosa Luxemburg developed based on Marx (1867, Chapter 28) the idea of ongoing primitive accumulation: "capital feeds on the ruins of such organisations, and, although this non-capitalist milieu is indispensable for accumulation, the latter proceeds, at the cost of this medium nevertheless, by eating it up" (Luxemburg 1913/2003, 363). As a result, "capital must go all out to obtain ascendancy over […] territories and social organizations" (Luxemburg 1913/2003, 346). Capitalism means permanent competition, which makes it hard for non-capitalist, commons-based projects that do not commodify something, to survive.

Leadbeater makes a helpful distinction between private and public online sharing, but disregards capitalism's imperialistic character, which makes his vision a somewhat naïve version of digital social democracy, although it is not completely ideological and not impossible to relate in some way to his ideas. It is unlikely that there is a peaceful co-existence between capitalist and non-capitalist forms of organization and online sharing. The first try to destroy the second, which means a form of class struggle, to which they latter can best respond by trying to destroy the former and to establish democratic-communist forms of organization and self-organization for the twenty-first century.

THREE POLITICAL ECONOMIES OF INFORMATION

Leadbeater's distinction between public and private forms of organizing communications is helpful, but can be further differentiated. Graham Murdock (2011) distinguishes between three political economies of the media in modern societies. Media can take on the form of commodities organized by capital, public goods organized by the state or with the help of state power and gifts organized by civil society. Michael Hardt and Antonio Negri draw a similar distinction: "The multitude of producing subjectivities must today be autonomous from either private/capitalist and public/state authority in order to produce and develop the common" (Hardt and Negri 2009, 302).

TABLE 10.2   A typology of the political economies of information and examples

Ownership organization of production and distribution	PR: Private	PU: Public	CO: Commons
O: Open (OP: Open Production, OD: Open Distribution)	Facebook, Twitter, YouTube, commercial open access publishing using article processing charges, Ubuntu (Linux), Fedora (Linux), Red Hat Enterprise (Linux), openSUSE (Linux), Creative Commons Commercial	Public Service 2.0, open government licence	Wikipedia, Debian (Linux), Creative Commons Non-Commercial Derivatives, non-commercial open access publishing
C: Closed (CP: Closed Production, CD: Closed Distribution)	Microsoft, Apple	BBC	Creative Commons Non-Commercial Attribution No Derivatives

Table 10.2 provides an overview of different models for the organization of information production and circulation. Ownership can be private, public or common. The production process can be rather open (everyone can contribute, the source can be changed and re-developed) or closed (only selected people can contribute, the source cannot be altered). The same can be said of the distribution process that can either be more open (everyone can re-distribute content) or closed (there is a monopoly or oligopoly of distribution). An important aspect of distribution is furthermore the question of whether the original source has to be attributed or not.

Open content is not necessarily a common good and fully open. It is a model that is well suited for commons-based open production, as examples such as non-commercial Creative Commons licences, Debian Linux and Wikipedia show. These are projects that are relatively open: everyone can contribute in the case of Debian and Wikipedia. Creative Commons Derivative licences allow the remixing, transformation and re-distribution of commons. If you for example write a book or article and do not want others to be able to change them, then one can still make distribution a commons, but restrict production to the No Derivatives option, which makes production more closed. The Creative Commons Non-Commercial Attribution No Derivatives licence makes production closed, ownership common and distribution open (everyone can distribute the good for non-commercial purposes). Creative Commons also has one version that allows commercialization of the content and therefore introduces aspects of private profit. Production is open (everyone can contribute), but the overall organization is oriented towards making monetary profits from selling something. Also open access publishing has taken on different forms. The main distinction is between those that use article-processing charges in order to make profits and non-commercial projects. Both of them have open distribution, but vary according to the question of whether the organization's ownership is for-profit, which implies private ownership, or non-profit, which means that it is commons-based. An example of dubious for-profit open-access is the publishing of more than 100 open access journals by the company Bentham Open. *tripleC: Communication, Capitalism & Critique* is in contrast an example of a non-profit, non-commercial open access journal. Corporate social media such as YouTube and Facebook are relatively open in term of access and production as they encourage user-generated content, but are closed and proprietary in terms of their own organizations' ownership.

There are also for-profit and non-profit versions of Linux. Whereas Debian is a non-profit project, for-profit companies organize Ubuntu (Canonical Ltd), Fedora (Red Hat Inc.), Red Hat Enterprise (Red Hat Inc.) or openSUSE (SUSE). Both models are based on open co-production and (relatively) open distribution, but the for-profit Linux companies try to accumulate capital by selling, for example, support services, hardware, merchandise or bundles of free/open source software. Public media such as the BBC have had traditionally closed production, open access to the spectrum and a licence fee. Openness is restricted to access, but has tended to be restricted in terms of the re-use and re-development of content. In the age of more open and commons-based media, models such as open government licences or Public Service 2.0 have emerged that allow more re-use, re-distribution and re-development by citizens.

DIGITAL IMPERIALISM

The typology is not static. In reality, there are hybrid forms and conversions from one model in another. The PR/O and PR/C models tend to be privileged in terms of power because they can command financial investments and capital, which allows them to purchase labour power, resources, voice, attention and visibility. Digital imperialism means attempts and strategies to transform non-PR models into PR/O or PR/C models. The fact that there are for-profit communications companies in realms such as social media, open access and open source shows digital imperialism's tendency to try to subsume the logics of the public, the commons and openness under the imperative of capital accumulation. Digital imperialism is a form of class struggle, to which public service and commons-based projects can best respond not by collaborating with for-profit companies, but by reversing class struggle for trying to extinguish the logic of capitalism and to expand the logics of the non-profit public and non-profit commons. In this respect, networks, collaborations and hybrid public/common projects can also act as a form of empowerment. It is, for example, feasible to make use of the logic of the state in order to introduce a media fee that is funded by a progressive tax on profits in order to create a participatory budget for non-commercial communications projects run by civil society (Fuchs 2015a, Chapter 8). Neoliberal politics has promoted public–private partnerships in order to commodify public and common goods and services. Class struggle against neoliberalism and capitalism should make use of public–commons partnerships, hybrids and convergence in order to challenge the logic of capital.

PLATFORM CO-OPERATIVES

Trebor Scholz (2016) suggests that online platform co-operatives could be a foundation of a solidarity economy. He says that "platform cooperativism is about structural change, a change of ownership" (14; see also Scholz 2017, Chapter 7), about solidarity and benefits for all. He defines ten principles of platform co-operatives: They are collectively owned, for example by users, workers, prosumers, municipalities, the state or hybrid forms. They provide secure and decent pay and an appreciative working atmosphere. They are transparent and participatory and provide legal protection of workers, portable worker benefits and protection against arbitrary behaviour. They avoid workplace surveillance and define a right to log off.

Scholz makes an important point. If we imagine Facebook owned by its users, Upwork owned by the freelancers working in it and Amazon owned by its warehouse workers, then there are clear benefits. The Facebook users would have the potential to abolish targeted ads and turn the company into a non-profit organization. Upwork freelancers would not have to pay commission and could keep what the platform now charges to freelancers as a rent. The Amazon workers could socialize the company's profits in order to increase their wages.

THE FAILURES OF PLATFORM CO-OPERATIVISM

There are also, however, problems with concepts such as platform co-operativism. A co-operative is not a solutionist app that can abolish capitalism's problem when combined with Internet technologies. There are already well-established definitions of what a co-operative is, so providing new definitions is confusing. The Worker Co-Operative Code defines a co-op as being voluntary, open, autonomous, transparent, having democratic member control, member economic participation, fostering education and training, co-operation among co-operatives and concern for community.[23]

Co-operative ownership and democratic control of property and finances are inherent features of such definitions. But this is enough. A co-op can democratically decide that the profit is owned and paid out to some single individuals: "Members decide how to use surpluses (profits)" (Worker Co-Operative Code). Such co-operatives use democracy, but do not question inequality in society and in their own organization.

MARISOL SANDOVAL: TOWARDS RADICAL CO-OPS

Marisol Sandoval (2016, 59–60), who studies the political economy of cultural co-operatives, argues in this context: "Turning workers into capitalists might improve the conditions of individual workers but does not solve other structural problems of capitalism that lead to huge social inequalities, economic and environmental crises."

A more radical principle would be to understand co-ops as inherently non-profit projects that either do not make any monetary profit or always socialize it. The problem in mainstream definition co-ops can be for-profit ventures. It is therefore no wonder that even neoliberals like David Cameron love co-ops. He said: "The Co-op is also a wonderful business model that's given amazing service to communities, staff and customers alike. [...] It's a very powerful business model and one I admire."[24] It is a real danger that co-ops replace the welfare state by voluntary activity.

It is also not enough that drivers own Uber and Airbnb is owned by its users or municipalities. Even if this is the case, the problems of congested streets, environmental pollution, smog, unaffordable housing, financialized housing markets and so on may persist. Democratic collective control as a principle of democratic socialism is ineffective if limited to Internet platforms. It also needs to be extended all over society, including to the transportation and housing sector. The problem of civil society co-ops is that they often stay marginal and cannot challenge the power of large corporations.

---

23   The Worker Co-operative Code. Downloaded from www.uk.coop, 20 February 2016.
24   Prime Minister backs Co-Op. *Manchester Evening News*, 3 April 2014.

CLASS STRUGGLE NETWORKS OF RADICAL COMMUNAL CO-OPS, RADICAL PUBLIC SERVICES AND RADICAL MUNICIPAL SERVICES AS FOUNDATIONS OF DEMOCRATIC SOCIALISM

Co-ops therefore should also see the power relations they are part of and politically challenge them in social struggles. In the final instance, a better society is a question of political struggles. There should be hybrid forms of public- (state-ownership, municipality-ownership) and community-controlled organizations. We need a co-operation and hybridization of radical co-ops and radical public service not just on the Internet, but throughout society.

We need the common control and ownership of society so that it benefits all. The Uber and Airbnb problems can only be resolved by free public transport for everyone and affordable municipally-controlled housing. Radical co-ops, radical municipalism and radical public service could, as organizations engaged in political-economic struggles, become foundations of a democratic-socialist society. Co-ops are not enough. We do not need the co-op app society. We need political class struggle networks of democratic-socialist co-ops, municipalities and public services.

Radical co-op researcher Marisol Sandoval argues in this context:

> [A]s the neoliberal take on co-ops as a form of self-help and entrepreneurial initiative illustrates, co-ops are not immune from being incorporated and made productive for capitalism. [...] A radical concept of worker co-operatives keeps alive the possibility of real alternatives. [...] Improving these conditions requires political reforms, which need to be demanded by broad movement for social change that can include social movements and other forms of political activism, radical political parties and a reinvigorated union movement. (Sandoval 2016, 68, 61, 68)

NON-PROFIT ONLINE SHARING PLATFORMS: EXAMPLES

The concepts of open production, open distribution, public ownership and common ownership can also be applied to online sharing platforms that enable the sharing of non-informational goods and services. Freecycle[25] is a global network and online sharing platform that enables people to give away goods for free to others. It uses the Internet for organizing a 'freeconomy'. The platform and initiative is a non-profit civil society project with common ownership of the platform, closed production of goods that are shared (people don't produce things together, but rather pre-existing things are shared), and open distribution in the sense that those who look for and give away goods do not engage in monetary or other exchanges, but in gifting.

THE FREECYCLE NETWORK

> The worldwide Freecycle Network is made up of many individual groups across the globe. It's a grassroots movement of people who are giving (and getting) stuff for free in their own towns. Freecycle groups match people who have things they want to get rid of with people who can use them. Our goal is to keep usable

---

25 http://uk.freecycle.org.

items out of landfills. By using what we already have on this earth, we reduce consumerism, manufacture fewer goods, and lessen the impact on the earth. Another benefit of using Freecycle is that it encourages us to get rid of junk that we no longer need and promote community involvement in the process.[26]

STREETBANK

A similar commons-based online sharing project with open distribution and gifting is Streetbank.

> Streetbank is a site that helps you share and borrow things from your neighbours. Streetbank is meant for everyone. It is not for private benefit – for individuals to make a profit or professionals to sell their services. It is for the common good. Of course, you may already share things with your neighbours, in which case, don't let us stop you![27]

> The aim is to get people involved in their community, to foster altruism, a generosity of spirit and volunteerism. It is to help local needs to be met by local solutions, reducing poverty by building community. It makes sense environmentally. It helps people to reuse things, and for things that are under-used to be used more, and that all helps to reduce consumption. It also makes sense economically. If there are 100 houses on your road and each of them uses a ladder maybe once a year to clean the guttering, they probably don't all need their own ladder. One ladder shared between everyone should be enough.[28]

Streetbank is at the moment a non-profit project. There are, however, indications that it could be commodified in the future: "How do you make money then? We don't, we probably won't ever, but if it were to get really successful we'll turn it into a social enterprise."[29]

FAB LABS

In these examples sharing is open, but the creation of products closed. One can also imagine projects where people come together and share knowledge and skills and together make and create things. This is the idea underlying so-called fab labs.

> Fab labs are a global network of local labs, enabling invention by providing access to tools for digital fabrication. [...] Fab labs share an evolving inventory of core capabilities to make (almost) anything, allowing people and projects to be shared. [...] Fab labs are available as a community resource, offering open access for individuals as well as scheduled access for programs. [...] Designs and processes developed in fab labs can be protected and sold however an inventor chooses, but should remain available for individuals to use and learn from.[30]

---

26 http://uk.freecycle.org/ (accessed on 17 November 2015).
27 www.streetbank.com (accessed on 17 November 2015).
28 www.streetbank.com/faq?locale=en-GB (accessed on 17 November 2015).
29 Ibid.
30 www.fablabsuk.co.uk/ (accessed on 17 November 2015).

The creation process in fab labs is open and involves the principle that knowledge should be shared. The distribution can be, but is not necessarily, open. Innovations can be commodified and sold. Fab labs provide open production, but only partly open distribution and common ownership. One can also imagine publicly funded projects that provide non-profit opportunities for open creation and distribution as well as public funding for non-profit civil society sharing and making projects.

TOWARDS A COMMONS-BASED SHARING AND GIFT ECONOMY

The sharing economy has today a predominantly capitalist and imperialist character. Online and offline projects have emerged that foster for-profit and non-profit sharing of digital and non-digital goods and services in order to make monetary profits. At the same time, there are potentials and foundations of commons-based and public service projects that foster digital and non-digital gifting, co-production, open production, open distribution and a 'freeconomy'. Such projects are foundations of a commons-based sharing and gift economy that can challenge the capitalist sharing industry. If such projects remain apolitical, they risk being destroyed by sharing imperialism. They are germs of a commons-based society, but may only be able to survive if they expand and engage in a political-economic struggle against the capitalist economy.

Capitalism is based on an antagonism between productive forces and class relations:

> At a certain stage of development, it [the capitalist mode of production] brings into the world the material means of its own destruction. From that moment, new forces and new passions spring up in the bosom of society, forces and passions which feel themselves to be fettered by that society. (Marx 1867, 928)

The sharing economy is an expression of how capitalist development socializes the forces of production that within class relations foster new forms of exploitation of the commons and the public, but have the potential to become the foundation of a democratic commons-based economy and society.

10.5 CONCLUSION

We can summarize the main results of this chapter as follows:

* Social media are often explained in the context of the sharing economy and a culture of sharing information.
* Capitalist sharing ideology ("the sharing economy") tends to lack class analysis, reduce sharing to a moral phenomenon, ignore the political economy of sharing, conflate for-profit and non-profit models, be techno-determinist in character.
* Important capital accumulation models in the online sharing economy include the pay per service model, the rent on rent model and the 'freemium' model.
* The extension of the online sharing economy stands in the context of the neoliberalization, financialization and crisis of capitalism, as well as decreasing labour shares.
* A world of high risk, high precarity, crises, austerity and debt is the context of the capitalist sharing economy.

- The sharing economy is not inherently negative. The history of humans is also a history of sharing beyond the commodity form. The problem today is that alternative, non-exchange-based, altruistic sharing is not the economy's mainstream.
- Airbnb and other social experience-oriented sharing platforms promise a radical make-over of the world and to reverse commodity fetishism so that the social that is hidden behind the commodity becomes the primary feature of consumer culture. The reality is that these promises are empty and capitalist sharing is in many respects not social at all, but rather highly instrumental.

RECOMMENDED READINGS AND EXERCISES

This chapter has introduced various capitalist models of online sharing. You have read in it about how the sharing economy is in contemporary capitalism both a capital accumulation model and an ideology. You have also seen that there are some alternatives that have, however, thus far not challenged the capitalist sharing economy. The following readings and exercises are intended to help you deepen your knowledge and critique of the sharing economy.

Work in groups: each group selects one online sharing platform not discussed in this chapter that is popular in the city you live in.

- Try to find out as much as possible about the economic model the platform uses. Search for information on the platform's website, read its terms of use and privacy policy, look for inter-views with people working for the platform, and consider conducting such interviews yourself. Ask yourself: What kind of economic model does this platform use? How does it work?
- Discuss the platform's self-understanding: To what degree is it ideological and a form of sharing ideology?

Read the following two examples of an ideological account of the sharing economy:

Gansky, Lisa. 2012. *The mesh: Why the future of business is sharing*. London: Penguin. Chapter 1: Getting to know the mesh.

Botsman, Rachel and Roo Rogers. 2011. *What's mine is yours: How collaborative consumption is changing the way we live*. London: Collins. Introduction: What's mine is yours.

Business consultants such as Gansky, Botsman and Rogers often advance an ideological concept of the sharing economy. Conduct a search for other works that discuss the sharing economy in business and management literature and the business press. Ask yourself:

- What are the main claims that these works make about the sharing economy?
- Are these claims ideological in character? Why? How do they express the sharing ideology?
- How can the capitalist sharing ideology best be deconstructed and criticized?

Read the following two texts:

Rosenberg, Tina. 2013. It's not just nice to share, it's the future. *New York Times* online. 5 June.

Morozov, Evgeny. 2014. Don't believe the hype, the 'sharing economy' masks a failing economy. *Guardian* online. 28 September.

Work in groups. Ask yourself and discuss:

- What are the main points that Rosenberg and Morozov make about sharing economy platforms such as Airbnb and Uber?
- What are the main differences between the two positions?
- How do you assess each of the two positions?

The following text by political economist of communication Graham Murdock gives an introduction to two alternatives to the commodity logic: common goods and public services.

Murdock, Graham. 2011. Political economies as moral economies: Commodities, gifts, and public goods. In *The handbook of the political economy of communications*, ed. Janet Wasko, Graham Murdock and Helena Sousa, 13–40. Chicester: Wiley-Blackwell.

First read Graham Murdock's text. Afterwards, work in groups. There are also alternative, non-capitalist online sharing platforms. Each group searches for one alternative, non-capitalist online sharing platform that has not been discussed in this chapter. Ask yourself and discuss:

- What economic model does the platform use?
- How does this model differ from comparable capitalist platforms?
- What is the platform's self-understanding?
- In what respects is this self-understanding different from the capitalist sharing ideology?

11 WIKIPEDIA: A NEW DEMOCRATIC FORM OF COLLABORATIVE WORK AND PRODUCTION?[1]

KEY QUESTIONS

* How does Wikipedia work and how does it differ from corporate social media such as Facebook?
* Positivistic or utopian? Exploitative or emancipatory? What are the political implications of Wikipedia's organization model?
* What is a commons-based Internet and why should we think about this model?
* What are criticisms of Wikipedia?

KEY CONCEPTS

Collaborative work

Communal production

Commons

Participatory democracy

Well-rounded individuality

Communication commons

OVERVIEW

This chapter's task is to analyse the political economy of Wikipedia and its implications for economic democracy. In 2015, Wikipedia was the seventh most visited web platform in the world.[2] It was founded in 2001. It deviates strongly from other dominant web platforms, such as Google, Facebook, YouTube, Yahoo, Baidu, Twitter, QQ, MSN, Weibo and LinkedIn, because it is operated by a non-profit organization (the Wikimedia Foundation) and is advertising-free.

1 Acknowledgement: This chapter is based on and further extends my contributions to the following article: Firer-Blaess, Sylvain and Christian Fuchs. 2014. Wikipedia. An info-communist manifesto. *Television & New Media* 15 (2): 87–103.

2 Data source: alexa.com (accessed on 20 November 2015).

Wikipedia describes itself in the following way:

> Wikipedia [. . .] is a multilingual, web-based, free-content encyclopedia project based on an openly editable model. [...] Wikipedia is written collaboratively by largely anonymous Internet volunteers who write without pay. Anyone with Internet access can write and make changes to Wikipedia articles, except in certain cases where editing is restricted to prevent disruption or vandalism. [...] Since its creation in 2001, Wikipedia has grown rapidly into one of the largest reference websites, attracting 374 million unique visitors monthly as of September 2015. There are more than 70,000 active contributors working on more than 35,000,000 articles in more than 290 languages. As of today, there are 5,013,392 articles in English. [...] Wikipedia is a live collaboration differing from paper-based reference sources in important ways. Unlike printed encyclopedias, Wikipedia is continually created and updated, with articles on historic events appearing within minutes, rather than months or years. Older articles tend to grow more comprehensive and balanced; newer articles may contain misinformation, unencyclopedic content. Any article may contain undeteced vandalism. Awareness of this helps the reader to obtain valid information and avoiding recently added misinformation.[3]

Wikipedia is based on general principles, the *Five Pillars of Wikipedia*:[4]

- "Wikipedia is an onencyclopedia. [...]
- Wikipedia is written from a neutral point of view. [...]
- Wikipedia is free content that anyone can use, edit, and distribute. [...]
- Editors should interact with each other with respect and civility [...]
- Wikipedia has no firm rules: Wikipedia has policies and guidelines, but they are not carved in stone; their content and interpretation can evolve over time."

This chapter advances the argument that Wikipedia's mode of production bears a strong resemblance to what Marx and Engels described as communism. First, I discuss the renewal of the idea of communism undertaken by thinkers such as Slavoj Žižek and Alain Badiou and give an overview of Marx's principles of communism (section 11.1). Then I discuss the relationship between communism and communication (section 11.2) and present an analysis of Wikipedia's political economy (section 11.3). Section 11.4 discusses some of the criticisms of Wikipedia.

The literature published on Wikipedia (for an overview, see: http://en.wikipedia.org/wiki/Wikipedia:Wikipedia_in_academic_studies) lacks attention to societal implications, economic property, economic production and participatory democracy. It is very positivist and hardly has a critical focus. One of the exceptions is Erik Olin Wright's (2010) book *Envisioning Real Utopias*, in which he briefly discusses Wikipedia based on a critical framework and points out its implications for "real utopias". He discusses four emancipatory aspects of Wikipedia:

---

3 http://en.wikipedia.org/wiki/Wikipedia:About (accessed on 20 November 2015).
4 http://en.wikipedia.org/wiki/Wikipedia:Five_pillars (accessed on 20 November 2015).

1   non-market relations (voluntary, unpaid contributions, free access);
2   egalitarian participation;
3   direct deliberative interactions;
4   democratic governance and adjunction. (Wright 2010, 194–203)

The problem is that Wright ignores aspects of ownership of Wikipedia's content (its Creative Commons licence) and the contradictory nature of free labour as a source of both unlimited exploitation for corporate ends and communist potentials. While he asserts the emancipatory characteristics of Wikipedia's mode of governance, he does not seem to see the potential of Wikipedia in terms of political economy and its mode of production. Wikipedia is important in the sense that it is a new way of producing, owning, consuming and distributing goods and a new way of collaborative decision-making.

11.1 THE COMMUNIST IDEA

THE RETURN OF MARX

One interesting thing about Marx is that he keeps coming back at moments when people least expect it, in the form of various Marxisms that keep haunting capitalism like ghosts, as Jacques Derrida (1994) has stressed. It is paradoxical that more than 25 years after the end of the Soviet Union, capitalism seems to have falsified itself because its neoliberal mode of development has intensified global problems, and caused severe poverty and a rise of unequal income distribution. As a result we have also seen a return of the economic in the form of a worldwide economic crisis and with it a re-actualization of the Marxian critique of capitalism. Although a persistent refrain is "Marx is dead, long live capitalism", Marx has come back again today.

The Marxian focus on machinery, means of communication and the general intellect anticipated the importance of technology, knowledge and the media in contemporary capitalism (see e.g. Dyer-Witheford 1999; Fuchs 2011b, 2008a, 2016c). The new global economic crisis that started in 2008 has shown that Marxist crisis theory is still important today (Foster and Magdoff 2009). Capitalism seems to be inherently crisis-ridden.

The renewed discussion about the relevance of Marx's critique of the political economy (see Eagleton 2011; Žižek 2008) as an analytical tool for understanding the crisis of capitalism has been accompanied by a discussion about the need for establishing a democratic form of communism as an alternative to capitalism (Badiou 2008; Dean 2012; Hardt and Negri 2009; Harvey 2010a, 2010b, 2012; Žižek and Douzinas 2010; for a detailed discussion see Fuchs 2011b, Chapter 9).

THREE DIMENSIONS OF COMMUNISM

The negation of class is the classless society – communism. Marx and Engels did not mean by the term communism a totalitarian society that monitors all human beings, operates forced labour camps, represses human individuality, installs conditions of general shortage, limits the freedom of movement and so on. Rather, they saw communism as a society that strengthens common co-operative production and common ownership of the means of production, and enriches the individual sphere of activities and thereby individuality. We will discuss each of these three aspects that constitute communism (Fuchs 2011b, Chapter 9). In production, human subjects engage in co-operative social relations (subjective dimension) and by making use of the means of production (technologies, resources) create a new good or service (objective dimension). The overall process has effects on individuals and on society. The production process has a subjective, an objective and an effects dimension. All three dimensions are transformed by the transition from a capitalist to a communist society.

THE SUBJECTIVE DIMENSION

1. The subjective dimension of production: communism as the co-operative form of production.

For Marx and Engels, communism is a community of co-operating producers that operate in a highly productive economy, use the means of production together to produce use values that satisfy the needs of all, and take decisions in the production process together.

Marx speaks of communism as "general co-operation of all members of society" (Marxs and Engels Collected Works (MECW) 4, 177[5]), "communal production" (Marx 1857/1858, 172) and the "positing of the activity of individuals as immediately general or social activity" (Marx 1857/1858, 832).

THE OBJECTIVE DIMENSION

2. The objective dimension of production: communism as the common ownership of the means of production.

Communism does not mean, for Marx and Engels, that there are no longer any private goods for consumption. Its main difference from capitalist society is rather that there is no longer only a small group of owners, but all producers own and control the means of production (the technologies of production, the firms, the decision power in firms, etc.). Communism is a democratic form of organizing industry and the economy. It extends economic property from a small group to all producers. Communist firms are self-managed and do not have a power division between owners and workers – all workers are at the same time owners.

Marx and Engels extended the notion of the commons to all means of production. Marx spoke of "an association of free men, working with the means of production held in common, and expending their many different forms of labour-power in full self-awareness as one single social labour force" (Marx 1867, 171). In this association, machines are the "property of the associated workers" (Marx 1857/1858, 833) so that "a new foundation" of production emerges. This new system implements "the common use of all instruments of production and the distribution of all products according to common agreement, or the so-called community of property" (MECW 6, 348).

Marx and Engels described communism using terms such as "social property" (Marx 1867, 930), "conditions of production" as "general, communal, social conditions" (Marx 1894, 373), "common appropriation and control of the means of production" (Marx 1857/1858, 159),

---

5 Translated from German to English by CF.

"common ownership of the means of production" (Marx and Engels 1968, 305), "industry controlled by society as a whole" (Marx/Engels Werker (MEW) 4, 376[6]), "a system in which all these branches of production are operated by society as a whole" (MEW 4, 370[7]), or by speaking of individuals who "appropriate the existing totality of productive forces" (MECW 5, 87).

For Marx, individuals in capitalism are not yet fully developed social beings because they do not co-operatively own the means of production and operate the production process. He therefore speaks of the emergence of "social individuals" in communism (Marx 1857/1858, 832). Communism is "the complete return of man to himself as a social (i.e. human) being" (Marx 1844, 102). For Marx, communism is a not a dictatorship, but a form of humanism; it is the "advent of practical humanism" (164).

Marx argued that it is not the capitalists who produce money capital and commodities: the activities of many producers and "the united action of all members of society" that contribute diverse activities enable production. Therefore, it is not only a small class of capitalists who should profit from production, but all should benefit.

Communism does not put an end to private consumption, but an end to the exploitation of the labour of individuals: "Communism deprives no man of the power to appropriate the products of society; all that it does is to deprive him of the power to subjugate the labour of others by means of such appropriation" (Marx and Engels 1968, 48).

A communist economy is not based on money and the exchange of goods: "money would immediately be done away with" (Marx 1885, 390); "producers do not exchange their products" (Marx and Engels 1968, 305). Rather the economy is so productive that consumers receive all goods for free. In communism, the "productive forces have also increased with the all-round development of the individual, and all the springs of common wealth flow more abundantly", which allows the economy to be based on the principle: "from each according to his abilities, to each according to his needs" (Marx and Engels 1968, 306).

COMMUNISM = PARTICIPATORY DEMOCRACY

Marx's notion of a communist economy is what Crawford Macpherson (1973) and Carole Pateman (1970) describe as participatory democracy in the economic realm. Participatory democracy involves the intensification of democracy and its extensions into realms beyond politics. It also involves the insight that the capitalist economy is an undemocratic dictatorship of capital that should be democratized. Democracy is, in capitalism, limited to the realm of voting and parliament. Participatory democracy theory asks the questions why democratic ideals are given up once one enters the realm of the workplace and how one can speak of a democratic society if the economy is excluded from the realm of democracy. It wants to go beyond a narrow understanding of the concept of democracy and broadens its meaning and practice. Macpherson and Pateman argue that participatory democracy requires that the means and the output of labour are no longer private property, but become common property. Pateman (1970) terms the grassroots organization of firms and the economy in a participatory democracy "self-management".

---

6 Translated from German to English by CF.
7 Translated from German to English by CF.

THE SUBJECT-OBJECT DIMENSION

3. The effect dimension of production: communism as the emergence of well-rounded individuals.

When a subject interacts with an object, some change is the result. A new quality on some organizational level of the overall system or an entirely new system emerges. Hegel (1991) terms this outcome the subject-object. The subject-object is the unity of the subjective and the objective (Hegel 1991, §212). In the economy, the human subject with the help of the means of production as object creates an economic subject-object, a new use-value that satisfies human needs (Fuchs 2016c, Chapter 1). In capitalism, use-values have exchange-value and are sold in order for capitalists to accumulate monetary profit. In a democratic communist economy, collaborative work based on an associated means of production is connected to a high level of productivity. The result is the emergence of a new form of work organization.

For Marx and Engels, communism also means a condition where productivity has developed to such a high degree that, in combination with common ownership of the means of production and the abolition of the division of labour, the time for self-directed activities can be enlarged so that humans can engage in many-sided activities and can thereby realize and develop creative potentials that benefit society as a whole. A new form of work organization emerges. For Marx, a true form of individuality develops through the co-operative character of production.

With the technological increase of the productivity of labour in communism, "the part of the social working day necessarily taken up with material production is shorter and, as a consequence, the time at society's disposal for the free intellectual and social activity of the individual is greater" (Marx 1867, 667). There is a "general reduction of the necessary labour of society to a minimum, which then corresponds to the artistic, scientific etc. development of the individuals in the time set free" (Marx 1857/1858, 706). Based on the development of the productive forces, "the realm of freedom really begins only where labour determined by necessity and external expediency ends" (Marx 1894, 958–959). Freedom here is the freedom to determine one's own activities.

Reducing necessary labour time by high technological productivity is, for Marx, a precondition of communism. "Real economy" consists "of the saving of labour time" (Marx 1857/1858, 711). "The multiplicity of its [society's] development, its enjoyment and its activity depends on economization of time. Economy of time, to this all economy, ultimately reduces itself" (Marx 1857/1858, 173).

Wealth would then result from the free activities of humans: "When the limited bourgeois form is stripped away, what is wealth other than the universality of individual needs, capacities, pleasures, productive forces etc., created through universal exchange" (Marx 1857/1858, 488). "Labour in the direct form has [then] ceased to be the great wellspring of wealth" (Marx 1857/1858, 705). "The measure of wealth is then not any longer, in any way, labour time, but rather disposable time" (Marx 1857/58, 708). "Disposable time will grow for all" (Marx 1857/1858, 708). "For real wealth is the developed productive power of all individuals" (Marx 1857/1858, 708).

Marx sees high technological productivity and the increase of disposable time as the foundation for rich human individuality. He spoke of the emergence of the well-rounded individual. The "highest development of the forces of production" is "the richest development of the individuals" (Marx 1857/1858, 541). "The saving of labour time [is] equal to an increase of free time, i.e. time for the full development of the individual" (Marx 1857/1858, 711).

> The appropriation of these forces is itself nothing more than the development of the individual capacities corresponding to the material instruments of production. The appropriation of a totality of instruments of production is, for this very reason, the development of a totality of capacities in the individuals themselves. (MECW 5, 87)

The best-known passage that describes the emergence of "complete individuals" (MEW 3, 68), "well-rounded human beings" (MECW 5, 88), and of "a society in which the full and free development of every individual forms the ruling principle" (Marx 1867, 639) can be found in the *German Ideology*:

> In communist society, where nobody has one exclusive sphere of activity but each can become accomplished in any branch he wishes, society regulates the general production and thus makes it possible for me to do one thing today and another tomorrow, to hunt in the morning, fish in the afternoon, rear cattle in the evening, criticise after dinner, just as I have a mind, without ever becoming hunter, fisherman, herdsman or critic. (MECW 5, 47)

Guattari and Negri (1990) stress that real communism is based on a dialectic of community and rich individuality.

For discussing the notion of communism, I have deliberately used many quotations by Marx and Engels in order to show that they see communism not as a repressive and totalitarian society, but as a form of humanism that is based on co-operation, participatory economic democracy and well-rounded human individuality. Communism is not the Soviet Union, Stalin, Mao and the Gulag, but participatory democracy. Stalin, Mao and the Soviet Union called themselves communist, but had nothing in common with participatory democracy and therefore were alien to the Marxian idea of communism. Communism was, for Marx, the "battle of democracy" (MECW 6, 504). By democracy, Marx means a specific kind of democracy – participatory democracy.

11.2 COMMUNICATION AND COMMUNISM

THE COMMUNICATION COMMONS

Raymond Williams (1983, 70–72) points out that the term "commons" stems from the Latin word *communis*, which means that something is shared by many or all. The notion has to do with the generality of humankind and that something is shared. Williams (73) argues that there are affinities and overlaps between the words "communism" and "commons". The notion of the commons is also connected to the word "communication" because to communicate means to make something "common to many" (72).

Communication is an essential feature of human society. There can be no society without communication; humans create and maintain social relationships by communication and thereby continuously reproduce their social existence. Media, such as the Internet, are a means of communication. They are tools that enable the production of communication and human sociality. Means of communication, such as the Internet, are therefore essential necessary features of human society, just like nature, education, love, care, knowledge, technology, affects, entertainment, language, transportation, housing, food, cities, cultural goods and traditions, and so on. Communicative social relations and the means of communication are part of the commons of society – all humans continuously create, reproduce and use them in order to exist. Denying humans the means to communicate is like denying them fresh air to breathe. It undermines the conditions of their survival. Therefore the commons of society should be available free (without payment or other access requirements) to all and no class should own them privately.

The freedom of the commons includes the creation of a commons-based Internet: the communist Internet. The communist Internet is an association of free prosumers (productive consumers) that is critical, self-managed, surveillance-free, beneficial for all, freely accessible for all, fostering wealth for all, co-operative, classless and universal. On the communist Internet there is no profit and no advertising and there are no corporations. In a communist Internet age programmers, administrators and users control Internet platforms by participatory self-management. Network access is provided free to all. There are no corporate Internet service providers. Internet literacy programmes are widely available in schools and adult education in order to enable humans to develop capacities that allow them to use the Internet in meaningful ways that benefit themselves and society as a whole. All humans have free access to web platforms, computer software and hardware. Computing is non-profit, non-commercial, non-commodified and advertising-free. There is no corporate mediation of Internet communication; humans engage more directly with each other over the Internet without the mediation by corporations that own platforms and exploit communicative labour.

THE COMMONS-BASED INTERNET

On the commons-based Internet:

1. humans co-create and share knowledge;
2. humans are equal participants in the decision-making processes that concern the platforms and technologies they use;
3. the free access to and sharing of knowledge, the remixing of knowledge, and the co-creation of new knowledge help to create well-rounded individuals.

A commons-based Internet is only possible in a commons-based society. If, for example, you make all copyrighted knowledge available for free on the Internet within a capitalist society, this will result in either precarious working conditions for cultural producers or an accumulation strategy based on targeted advertising and massive surveillance. A true communist Internet therefore requires together with a redesign of the Internet (e.g. the abolishment of targeted ads and other similar commercial design principles) the end of wage labour, the common ownership of all means of production, the free availability of all goods instead of exchange and money, the end of the division of labour, the abolition of classes and so on.

11.3 WIKIPEDIA'S POLITICAL ECONOMY

David Harvey argues that "communists are all those who work incessantly to produce a different future to that which capitalism portends. [. . .] If, as the alternative globalization movement of the late 1990s declared, 'another world is possible', then why not also say 'another communism is possible'" (Harvey 2010b, 259). My claim is that, based on Harvey, we can say that one of these communist practices is the production and usage of Wikipedia, which means that Wikipedians are prototypical contemporary communists. Communism is not a distant society. It exists to a certain degree in each society. Communism is a dream that the world has always possessed. In this context, Marx says that "the world already possesses the dream of a thing, of which it has only to possess the consciousness to possess it truly" (Marx/Engels-Gesamtausgabe (MEGA), Section 3, Vol. 1, 56[8]). There are communist elements in contemporary society of which Wikipedia is one such form. These communist cell-forms need to be developed, extended and intensified in order to create a communist Internet and a communist society. Wikipedia should be seen as a communist project that anticipates a communist mode of production. The mode of production at work in Wikipedia goes beyond the production of the collaborative encyclopedia and is also present in the production of, for instance, free software. This mode of production, which bears so many resemblances to the model of communism, works based on the production of information. This is why it can be called *info-communism*.

According to Marx (1859, 263; Marx and Engels 1846, Chapter I.A), a mode of production is a combination of (see Fuchs 2016c, Chapter 10, for a discussion of how Marx defines the mode of production):

* The productive forces: (a) labour power, the capacity to systematically transform nature and create use-values in work processes; (b) the means of production, materials, land, or objectified crystallization of previous labour power, namely tools, infrastructures and other technologies.
* The relations of production: ways in which humans relate to one another to determine how work is organized, how property is distributed, who controls the productive forces, etc.

THE SUBJECTIVE DIMENSION OF WIKIPEDIA PRODUCTION: CO-OPERATIVE LABOUR

Info-communism relies heavily on intellectual work. In Wikipedia, thousands of intellectual user-workers constitute the labour force. Wikipedians are today mainly Western youth and "elite workers": the highly educated students, white-collar workers and programmers who have sufficient income, skills and time to work on Wikipedia in their leisure time (Glott et al. 2010; Jullien 2011). Wikipedia in 2011 conducted an Editor Survey: it showed that 20 per cent of the editors came from the USA, 12 per cent from Germany, 7 per cent from Russia, 6 per cent from the UK, 4 per cent from Italy, 3 per cent each from India, France, Poland, Spain and Canada. Of the editors 91 per cent were male and 62 per cent held an academic degree; 76 per cent contributed to editing the English Wikipedia version, 20 per cent

---

8 Translated from German to English by CF.

to the German version, 13 per cent to the French one, 12 per cent to the Spanish one, 11 per cent to the Russian one, 6 per cent to the Italian one, 5 per cent to the Polish one, 4 per cent each to the Portuguese and Simple English editions, 3 per cent to the Ukrainian version, and 3 per cent to the Chinese version; 55 per cent of the editors were 29 years old or younger.[9] These distributions reflect the general stratification patterns of capitalism and show that a truly info-communist mode of production requires a communist society in which free time, skills and material wealth become universal.

The work on Wikipedia is co-operative. No one can reclaim the authorship of an article, as it is often the result of dozens of people writing and debating together about what should be written. Most of the articles have between seven and 21 co-authors (Auray et al. 2007, 194). Wikipedians use a decision-making process that is based on debate and consensus. This method is supported and enabled by the wiki web software, which generates webpages that can be edited by anyone and that supports discussion between the users. Each article has a talk page that is used for discussions of how to change articles. A temporary consensus is achieved if an article or passage in it stays unchanged for some time. If there is disagreement over a passage, then users have to discuss and try to find a solution and a joint formulation. Each Wikipedia article has an edit page and a discussion page. Also its history is documented.

THE OBJECTIVE DIMENSIONS OF WIKIPEDIA PRODUCTION: THE COMMON OWNERSHIP OF THE MEANS OF PRODUCTION

Wikipedia uses the free software MediaWiki for its website. The Wikimedia Foundation, which is a public, non-profit charity under US regulations, operates Wikipedia. Its self-defined purpose is to "empower and engage people around the world to collect and develop educational content under a free license or in the public domain, and to disseminate it effectively and globally".[10] In the period from 1 July 2013 until 30 June 2014, Wikipedia received donations of US$49.6 million.[11] Around 2.5 million supporters contributed donations.[12] Wikipedia's expenses are mainly funded by individual donations made by users. There is no advertising on Wikipedia and Wikipedia does not have a business model. Wikipedia's terms of use[13] and privacy policy[14] therefore do not mention advertising – there is no need for commercial income.

In info-communism, the means of production belong to the workers. Programmes and servers can be considered as common property managed by the Wikimedia Foundation. MediaWiki is based on a copyleft licence that makes it a free software commons:

- The code is free to use and to analyse.
- The users can copy and share the software with others.
- The code can be modified, and modified copies can be distributed.

---

9 Data source: https://upload.wikimedia.org/wikipedia/commons/7/76/Editor_Survey_Report_-_April_2011.pdf (accessed on 21 November 2015).
10 Bylaws of the Wikimedia Foundation, Article II. http://goo.gl/2Wdy2 (accessed on 21 November 2015).
11 https://annual.wikimedia.org/2014/ (accessed on 21 November 2015).
12 Ibid.
13 http://wikimediafoundation.org/wiki/Terms_of_use (accessed on 27 September 2016).
14 http://wikimediafoundation.org/wiki/Privacy_policy (accessed on 27 September 2016).

- It is illegal to use and/or modify part of a code under copyleft without the resulting work being implemented under the copyleft licence, which prevents a future proprietary enclosure of the commons.

Wikimedia's servers are becoming de facto public goods for the community of workers running the project because the users control the production of and access to Wikipedia content. Wikipedia does not serve capital accumulation purposes. The Wikipedia community elects the top managers of the Wikimedia Foundation and thereby has some control over the Foundation.

RELATIONS OF PRODUCTION: PARTICIPATORY DEMOCRACY IN THE ECONOMIC REALM

In the info-communist mode of production, workers manage production themselves. They make all decisions together and control the production process, which is an expression of economic participatory democracy. In order to avoid over-complexity, they can also democratically decide to delegate certain activities to specific persons or groups. In Wikipedia, Wikipedians decide about the rules structuring co-operation in common. The same debate/consensus decision-making process is applied as in the editing process to bring about Wikipedia's rules.[15] A policy proposal usually emerges from a discussion at the village pump – the general Wikipedia forum.[16] Policy proposals are then discussed. Other than in liberal representative democracy, it is not the vote but consensus that constitutes the mode of decision-making. Wikipedia's decision modus therefore parallels grassroots democracy.

WIKIPEDIA'S USE-VALUE: FREE CONTENT

The use of the means of production by workforces within definite relations of production results in the creation of use-values that serve human needs. In capitalism, these use-values are exchange values and commodities. In communism, they are commonly owned and all people can access them without payment.

The motto of Wikipedia is: "Imagine a world in which every single person on the planet is given free access to the sum of all human knowledge."[17] This shows that Wikipedia's intrinsic reason for production is different from that of capitalism. Capitalism is based on profit interests, whereas Wikipedia is based on voluntary work and users' desire and pleasure to work on the provision of encyclopedic knowledge as a common good that is available without payment to all. Wikipedia's products are collaboratively authored articles, which are available to the world without payment. Their character is dynamic and open. They are not a one-time product, but a product in flux that invites users to participate in developing the content, and therefore can potentially change according to the number of participants who become involved in its development.

---

15 http://en.wikipedia.org/wiki/Wikipedia:CONPOL#CONPOL gives an overview of Wikipedia's policies.

16 http://en.Wikipedia.org/wiki/Wikipedia:Village_pump (accessed on 21 November 2015).

17 Wikimedia Foundation, Annual report 2009–2010. http://upload.wikimedia.org/wikipedia/commons/9/9f/AR_web_all-spreads_24mar11_72_FINAL.pdf (accessed on 21 November 2015).

According to Wikipedia's terms of use, articles are licensed under the Creative Commons Attribution-ShareAlike License and the GNU Free Documentation License. These licences grant the users the same rights we described earlier for free software that uses a copyleft licence: the right to freely use the Wikipedia content, to share it with others, and to modify it as long as the resulting work is under the same licence. As a result of a decision by Wikipedia founder Jimmy Wales (Enyedy and Tkacz 2011, 114), only the GNU Free Documentation License (GFDL) is applied to Wikipedia content. In June 2009, Wikipedia adopted, in addition, the Creative Commons Attribution-ShareAlike (CC-BY-SA) License,[18] that allows the commercial use of content as long as others are allowed to use and distribute the content under the same conditions. A vote taken in April 2009 resulted in the decision to introduce this licence. Voting, not consensus, was used in this case as the decision mechanism to broaden participation. Of a total of 15,071 voters, 87.9 per cent were in favour of the adoption of the new licence.

It is therefore allowed that somebody can print and sell a book that contains Wikipedia articles as long as others are granted the right to copy, share and remix/edit the content. So a commercial publishing house could publish a book or paper encyclopedia that is sold for making a profit and that contains Wikipedia articles. Wherever such a commodification of Wikipedia knowledge happens, the work of Wikipedians is infinitely exploited (see Chapter 5 of this book and Fuchs 2010c) because the users create surplus value that is fully unpaid, which results in the circumstance that the rate of surplus value $rs = s/v$ (surplus value/variable capital, profit/wages) converges towards infinity. This means that commodified Wikipedia work is extremely exploited and unremunerated. This circumstance shows that Wikipedia is to a certain degree entangled in the capitalist relations of production. In order to go beyond them, Wikipedians would, among other things, have to change Wikipedia's licence from a Creative Commons Attribution-ShareAlike Unported License to a Creative Commons Attribution-NonCommercial Unported License, which would prohibit the commercial exploitation of Wikipedia. Selling Wikipedia articles in book form has limited feasibility because they change dynamically, whereas a book has a more static character.

WIKIPEDIA PRODUCTION'S EFFECT DIMENSION: THE PLEASURE OF CO-OPERATIVE INTELLECTUAL WORK

Why do Wikipedians work voluntarily and without payment for the project? Studies have shown that their main incentive is that they derive pleasure from intellectual and co-operative work and believe in the importance of making encyclopedic knowledge available to the world as common good (Bauwens 2003; Foglia 2008; Hars and Ou 2002). In the 2011 Wikipedia Editor Survey, 71 per cent of the participating Wikipedia editors said that they contribute to Wikipedia because they liked the idea of volunteering to share knowledge, and 69 per cent said an important motivation for them was that they thought information should be freely available.[19]

---

18 http://meta.wikimedia.org/wiki/Licensing_update/Result (accessed on 22 November 2015).

19 https://upload.wikimedia.org/wikipedia/commons/7/76/Editor_Survey_Report_-_April_2011. pdf (accessed on 22 November 2015).

The work process is self-determined. Wikipedians work on whatever article they choose according to their time, resources and own preferences. Wikipedia work, in contrast to capitalist wage labour, is not coercive; it is not conducted for survival by earning a wage that allows the buying of food and other nutrition. The Wikipedia workforce is non-commodified, it has no exchange value, it is not exchanged against money, but has a voluntary character. The time Wikipedians work on Wikipedia is self-determined work time, an expression and anticipation of the communist mode of production, in which all work is self-determined and an expression of well-rounded individuality.

At the same time, Wikipedia work is stratified today. Those who have the time and skills required for Wikipedia production are part of a well-educated elite. Not all have the intellectual skills and the wealth of time needed to actively contribute to Wikipedia because global capitalism is a class society that creates classes of wealthy and poor people: the wealthy are rich in material resources, skills, time, relations, networks and so on, and the poor are deprived of these. These class structures are fluid, overlapping and many-folded (the material rich are not automatically the culturally rich or most educated, although they can use money to try to convert money capital into cultural capital, etc.). Wikipedia is embedded into global capitalism. A global elite that can afford its own elite status operates and contributes to the platform. A truly democratic and communist Wikipedia can only be achieved if we overcome class society and establish a classless society in which all humans have wealth in terms of resources, time, skills, networks, relations, capacities and so on – a society of well-rounded individuals.

11.4 CRITICISMS OF WIKIPEDIA

WIKIPEDIA: A TWENTY-FIRST-CENTURY ONLINE BUREAUCRACY?

Mathieu O'Neil (2009, 2011) criticizes that Wikipedia is built on a hierarchy, in which administrators have a more important role and more power than everyday users and contributors. Wikipedia would have a bureaucracy that consists of hundreds of pages of policies, such as policies on neutral point of view, no original research, verifiability of information, article titles, biographical information, citing sources, the three revert rule and so on. Administrators' "primary concern is now for the health of the project itself; they have become custodians. This division between content-oriented and process-oriented users can cause tensions" (O'Neil 2009, 156) when administrators, for example, constantly point editors towards lots of different Wikipedia rules and thereby hinder the updating of content. "Wikipedia's editorial process, understood as the herding or disciplining of autonomous content providers, cannot but generate bad blood, in the shape of participants who feel they have been ill treated, or even humiliated, by editors and admins" (163). One could also formulate this criticism by saying that on Wikipedia there is a hierarchic division of labour between productive producers of content and unproductive administrators who exert control over editors.

> Wikipedia similarly claims that it is "not a bureaucracy" [...] Nonetheless Wikipedia, like most large peer produced projects, comprises typically bureaucratic features such as the maintenance of archives of decisions, the existence of

rules, and the separation of roles and persons: any Wikipedia editor can become an "administrator" and hence exercise authority over other participants; these officers can be replaced by some-one else. [...] Participants have occasionally alleged that exclusionary power in Wikipedia has been concentrated in the hands of a core group of administrators. Whilst no evidence exists of systematic abuse, it seems logical that people benefiting from such advantages as incumbency, intimate knowledge of site procedures, networks of supporters, and in some cases administrative tools, would be statistically more likely to see their point of view prevail during disputes, irrespective of the correctness of their position. (O'Neil 2011)

Vasilis Kostakis (2010) argues in this context:

Decisions are being made in secret and power is being accumulated. Authority, corruption, hidden hierarchies and secrecy subvert the foundations of peer governance, that is openness, heterachy, transparency, equipotentiality and holoptism – the very essence of *Wikipedia*. [...] *Wikipedia* is constantly at risk of transforming itself into an inflexible, despotic hierarchy, while new disputes are emerging about the mode of content creation and governance.

José van Dijck (2013, 139) stresses the role of bots in the policing of Wikipedia content and that they impose

a uniform regime of delegated tasks aimed at perfect execution. Such regimented protocols, critics contend, preclude dissent and nonconsensual behavior. [...] Wikipedia's users worry about their site becoming a semiautomated, impermeable operational system that prohibits discord and favors consensus at the expense of a variety of opinions.

She argues that Wikipedia has "a rank-and-file techno-bureaucratic system grounded in Wikipedia's normative patrol of content" (137).

Nicholas Carr has an overall negative assessment of Wikipedia as a bureaucratic and autocratic system:

Where once we had a commune, we now have a gated community, "policed" by "good editors". So let's pause and shed a tear for the old Wikipedia, the true Wikipedia. Rest in peace, dear child. You are now beyond the reach of vandals. [...] Wikipedia is beginning to look something like a post-revolutionary Bolshevik Soviet, with an inscrutable central power structure wielding control over a legion of workers. [...] Maybe it should call itself 'the encyclopedia that anyone can edit on the condition that said person meets the requirements laid out in Wikipedia Code 234.56, subsections A34-A58, A65, B7 (codicil 5674), and follows the procedures specified in Wikipedia Statutes 31 - 1007 as well as Secret Wikipedia Scroll SC72 (Wikipedia Decoder Ring required). (Carr 2011, 193, 196, 200)

WIKIPEDIA EDIT WARS AND VANDALISM

New users' experience on Wikipedia can certainly be frustrating, especially if admins repeatedly delete added content by referring them to various policies. Such activities create the impression that admins destroy more than help create content and that they have a more destructive than constructive role. In an antagonistic society that is based on class and other social conflicts, there are conflicts of interest. It is therefore very likely that conflicts of interest reflect themselves also in a popular encyclopedia project like Wikipedia. On Wikipedia, typical manifestations of social interest conflicts are vandalism and edit wars. One example is the disagreement about the name of the Polish city Gdańsk (Polish)/Danzig (German) that resulted in long-lasting edit war. The city has both a German- and a Polish-speaking population, and throughout history for some periods belonged to Germany and for others to Poland. The users, for example, disagreed in the following way:

> User A: "The city is called Gdańsk (in English) and that is how it should be referred to regardless of the time period, especially since the page deals mostly with the current city (not its 14th Century Prussian ancestor)." User B: "Polish nationalistic propaganda again. This user should be banned." User A: "Me? Aren't you the one who posted pro-Nazi remarks all over various pages and was banned? I'm simply trying to resolve an issue (which wasn't even an issue until ppl like you started a revert war)."[20]

A Wikipedia discussion and vote was held in 2005 that decided that for the period from 1793 to 1945 the city should in Wikipedia articles be referred to as Danzig (votes for Danzig: 56, votes for Gdańsk: 8) and for the period after 1945 as Gdańsk (votes for Danzig: 3, votes for Gdańsk: 67).[21] Also, vandalism of articles is present on Wikipedia:

> A person from Łódź was attacking Polish Wikipedia throughout 2006 and early 2007, inserting profanity and pictures of penises and anuses into pages (especially ones related with Catholicism or Polish politicians), without any reaction from his internet provider, Neostrada. The vandal's activity finished when he was deprived of his internet connection, but not before the entire city of Łódź had to be blocked from editing Wikipedia for three days. [...] In May 2012, media critic Anita Sarkeesian created a Kickstarter project, intending to raise money to make a series of videos exploring sexism in digital gaming culture. The idea evoked a hostile response, which included repeated vandalism of Sarkeesian's Wikipedia article with pornographic imagery, defamatory statements, and threats of sexual violence. More than 12 anonymous editors contributed to the ongoing vandalism campaign before editing privileges were revoked for the page. [...] In July 2015, presidential candidate Donald Trump's entire Wikipedia page was deleted and replaced with the solitary sentence "Let's be fair, nobody cares about him".[22]

---

20 https://en.wikipedia.org/wiki/Talk:Gda%C5%84sk/Naming_convention (accessed on 22 November 2015).

21 https://en.wikipedia.org/wiki/Talk:Gdansk/Vote#Results_on_VOTE:_Period_from_1793_to_1945 (accessed on 22 November 2015).

22 https://en.wikipedia.org/wiki/Vandalism_on_Wikipedia (accessed on 22 November 2015).

IDEALIST CRITIQUES OF WIKIPEDIA LACK POLITICAL ECONOMY

Criticisms of Wikipedia as bureaucracy are often not just quite cynical, but also fairly idealist and fail to consider the broader political-economic context of a heteronomous society in which the online encyclopedia has to operate. Given social conflicts in society that are reproduced on Wikipedia, some form of arbitration mechanism is needed. That administrators have more power than others is necessary for a mechanism that can manage edit wars, vandalism and so on. Without such a hierarchy, Wikipedia could in an antagonistic society become unmanageable and the site of constant vandalism and edit wars. In a society that requires only little policing, the situation would be different. Admins can protect pages so that only certain users or user groups can edit them, block disruptive users, delete articles and so on. Admins are not appointed arbitrarily, but are democratically elected: anyone can apply to become an admin. After application, a discussion takes place for seven days, during which users can ask questions and the candidates can answer. The users can express their approval or objection. Finally an uninvolved user decides whether consensus has been reached or not. As "a general descriptive rule of thumb most requests above ~80% approval pass and most below ~70% fail".[23]

If an admin deletes lots of content by Wikipedia newcomers, then the latter will easily be frustrated. When this happens, then the admin violates one of Wikipedia's policies, the "Please do not bite the newcomers" rule that says:

> We have a set of rules, standards, and traditions, but they must not be applied in such a way as to thwart the efforts of newcomers who take that invitation at face value. [...] If a newcomer seems to have made a small mistake (*e.g.*, forgetting to put book titles in italics), try to correct it yourself: do not slam the newcomer. A gentle note at their user page explaining the Wikipedia standard and how to achieve it in the future may prove helpful, as they may be unfamiliar with the norm or merely how to achieve it. Remember, this is a place where anyone may edit and therefore it is each person's responsibility to edit and complement, rather than to criticize or supervise others. If you use bad manners or curse at newcomers, they may decide not to contribute to the encyclopedia again. If you feel that you must say something to a newcomer about a mistake, please do so in a constructive and respectful manner.[24]

Electing admins democratically and defining rules of conduct for them are very feasible policies. In practice, it can, however, happen that such rules are not strictly followed. More experienced users can also file a "Request for Admin Recall". Such a Recall will trigger a vote whether the admin should be "desysopped". So overall Wikipedia's hierarchy is created and managed in a very democratic manner. O'Neil has made suggestions of how to improve Wikipedia's governance: "Possible solutions include reassessing the role of anonymity on the project as well as the drafting of a Constitution which would more clearly lay out the roles and responsibilities of authority-holders (both these suggestions contradict core elements of the Wikipedia ethos)" (O'Neil 2011).

---

23 https://en.wikipedia.org/wiki/Wikipedia:Administrators (accessed on 22 November 2015).

24 https://en.wikipedia.org/wiki/Wikipedia:Please_do_not_bite_the_newcomers (accessed on 22 November 2015).

WIKIPEDIA: A FORM OF DIGITAL CULTURAL IMPERIALISM?

Mark Graham (2011) argues that uneven geographies, directions and politics shape Wikipedia.

> The country with the most articles is the United States [...] Almost all of Africa
> is poorly represented in Wikipedia. Remarkably, there are more Wikipedia arti-
> cles written about Antarctica than all but one of the 53 countries in Africa. [...]
> The large spike at the left hand side of the graph is the English version with
> about three million articles. There are then about twenty language editions that
> contain a few hundred thousand articles. The rest of the graph is characterized
> by the amount of content dropping off sharply until the far right-hand side
> (representing the many Wikipedia language versions that only host a handful
> of articles). [...] The geography of authorship is also reportedly highly uneven,
> thus allowing for voices and opinions from certain parts of the world to be
> disproportionately visible. [...]
>
> It is conceivable that not only are many being left out of the palimpsests of
> place but that, in the words of Gayatri Spivak, the subaltern may not even have
> a voice in the representations that do exist. All knowledge is constituted in
> relation to omissions, absences, and asymmetries, and within Wikipedia there
> are inevitably places lacking representation and people lacking voice. Most
> worrisome, Western dominance of representation and voice is likely produced
> and reproduced in myriad sociospatial practices around the world. As such, we
> need to continue to expose unevenness in both voice and representation.
>
> There is enormous potential for Wikipedia to open participation in knowledge
> construction and loosen the West's entrenched grip on globally accessible rep-
> resentations. The platform, available in 271 languages, in theory allows mar-
> ginalized groups to be heard around the world. However, it is important not to
> overstate how Wikipedia has democratized digital representation and always
> to be aware of its uneven geographies, directions, and politics when integrating
> it into palimpsests of place. (Graham 2011, 273, 275, 277, 280)

It is certainly true, as the statistics mentioned earlier show, that Wikipedia editors come predominantly from Western countries, which means an uneven representation of voice. The vast
majority of Wikipedia articles are written in English. One cannot, however, blame Wikipedia
for global inequalities. China is the country with the world's largest number of inhabitants.
The Chinese government, however, has repeatedly blocked Wikipedia's English-language
version, permanently blocks access to articles about what it considers to be sensitive political topics and permanently blocks access to the Chinese version.[25] On 22 November 2015,
the English version of Wikipedia en.wikipedia.org could be accessed in China, whereas the
Chinese version zh.wikipedia.org was blocked.[26] It is therefore no wonder that the number of
Chinese Wikipedia articles is relatively low in comparison to English ones.

---

25 https://en.wikipedia.org/wiki/Censorship_of_Wikipedia (accessed on 22 November 2015).
26 According to a search on www.blockedinchina.net.

Wikipedia encourages many languages and does not have an English-language bias built into its design and interfaces. Wikipedia's unevenness also has to do with global resource inequalities. It would be cynical and techno-determinist to blame Wikipedia for the world's inequalities. The wiki is a flexible technology that can easily be adapted to different contexts. More could be done to integrate Wikipedia into education in, for example, developing countries so that more local knowledge could be created in schools, universities and other educational institutions in these countries.

SLAVOJ ŽIŽEK: ENGLISH IS NOT A COLONIAL LANGUAGE, WIKIPEDIA IS NOT AN IMPERIALIST PROJECT

That Wikipedia's main language is English is not necessarily a bad thing because it is a rather strange form of pseudo-pluralist reverse to argue that English is a cultural imperialistic language. One of the reasons why English is popular throughout the world is that in comparison to many other languages it is relatively easy to learn and has an easy grammar. Slavoj Žižek pinpoints this circumstance in a critique of postcolonial critiques of the English language:

> According to some Indian cultural theorists, the fact that they are compelled to use the English language is a form of cultural colonialism that suppresses their true identity [...] but this imposition of a foreign language itself created the very X which is "oppressed" by it; that is, what is oppressed is not the actual pre-colonial India, but the authentic dream of a new universalistic and democratic India. It is crucial to note that this role of the English language was clearly perceived by many intellectuals among the Dalits (the "untouchables"): a large number of Dalits welcomed the English language and indeed even the colonial encounter. [...] The point all these examples illustrate is not that there was nothing prior to the loss. Of course there was [...] This holds in general for all processes of lost and regained national identity. In the process of its revival, a nation-in-becoming experiences its present constellation in terms of a loss of precious origins, which it then strives to regain. In reality, however, there were no origins that were subsequently lost, for the origins are constituted through the very experience of their loss and the striving to return to them. [...] According to the standard liberal myth, the universality of human rights establishes the conditions for peaceful coexistence between the multiplicity of particular cultures. The reproach from the standpoint of the colonized is that such liberal universality is false, that in practice it merely facilitates the violent intrusion of a foreign culture that dissolves indigenous roots. Even if she admits there may be some truth in this, a liberal would continue to strive for a "universality without wounds," for a universal frame that would not impinge violently on particular cultures. From a properly dialectical perspective, we should strive for (or endorse the necessity of) the exact reverse of this approach: the wound as such is liberating – or rather, contains a liberatory potential. So while we should definitely problematize the positive content of the imposed universality (i.e., the particular content it secretly privileges), we should also fully endorse the liberating aspect of the wound

(to our particular identity) as such. [...] in the course of the dialectical process, a shift of perspective occurs which makes the wound itself appear as its
opposite – the wound itself is its own healing when seen from another standpoint. (Žižek 2014, 132–133, 136, 138, 141)

Just as English is often not experienced as a colonial language by the subaltern, but as something empowering that they adopt, transform and impurify, neither is the English Wikipedia
a colonial or cultural imperialist, but a universalist project. It has the potential to reflect not
just standard English, but also Hindish, Chinglish, Spanglish, Arablish, Heblish, Runglish,
Porglish and so on and the rich wealth of the world's linguistic heritage that is communicated in such linguistic dialectics. If all language versions of Wikipedia were of the same
size, then the project would be a quite fragmented public sphere of knowledge with many
microspheres. Just like a universal language adopted by all in specific local and regional
versions is an immense tool for international understanding and anti-nationalism, one universal Wikipedia that allows linguistic and cultural unity in diversity can foster international
collaboration and understanding. Wikipedia is not an imperialist, colonial or Western-centric
project, but a project that is designed to enable transnational cultural unity in diversity and to
bring together many people from all over the world in a common cultural project.

11.5 CONCLUSION

The main results of this chapter are as follows:

- Communism is not about the establishment of a repressive state-centred society, but the
  struggle for establishing a participatory democracy. There is a need for a renewed debate
  about democratic communism and a renewal of the critique of the political economy.
- Wikipedia has communist potentials that are antagonistically entangled into capitalist
  class relations.
- Wikipedia is based on co-operative work, grassroots decision-making and content
  that is made available without payment. Furthermore, a non-profit organization that
  is non-commercial (no use of advertisement) operates Wikipedia. Wikipedia work is
  voluntary, self-determined and non-commodified.
- These communist potentials are, however, antagonistic because of the use of the Creative
  Commons Attribution-ShareAlike licence that allows the selling of Wikipedia content as
  commodity. In those cases where an article is sold, all underlying voluntary work is
  unpaid labour and the involved Wikipedians are infinitely exploited.
- Wikipedia has faced multiple criticisms, such as that it has a bureaucratic and hierarchic
  structure, has an English-language bias and is Western-centric. Such issues are not, however, built into Wikipedia's design, which is why one cannot say that it is an authoritarian
  or imperialist project. Wikipedia is a progressive project that has to act in an imperfect
  and problem-ridden capitalist world.

A new mode of production develops within an old one. "The economic structure of capitalist
society has grown out of the economic structure of feudal society" (Marx 1867, 875). But

there is no guarantee that the roots of a new society can be realized because realization is a task of political practice. The social and co-operative dimension of Wikipedia points towards "elements of the new society with which old collapsing bourgeois society itself is pregnant" (Marx 1871, 277); new relations, which mature "within the framework of the old society" (Marx 1859, 263); "new forces and new passions" that "spring up in the bosom of society, forces and passions which feel themselves to be fettered by that society" (Marx and Engels 1848, 928); "antithetical forms", which are "concealed in society" and "mines to explode it" (Marx 1857/1858, 159). In order to compete with and supersede capitalism, the info-communist mode of production needs to grow in terms of the number of members engaging in it, the number of projects being part of it, and the resources controlled. Such a growth is only possible if info-communist seeds grow, expand in size, can command ever more resources and overcome their own antagonistic character.

There are therefore two possible futures for info-communism. In the first scenario, communist class struggle nourishes info-communism against capitalist hegemony so that info-communism drives back the capitalist mode of production. In the second scenario, some of the characteristics of info-communism, such as the principle of free access and free content provision and online mass collaboration, are absorbed by capitalism, which thereby destroys the communist character of info-communism.

Capitalism is a violent and imperialist system that has always colonized non-capitalist spaces and has always used the violence of the law and warfare to destroy alternatives. Informational communism is a potential and Wikipedia is the brightest communist star on the Internet's class struggle firmament. It is possible that capitalism subsumes the transcendent elements of info-communism just like it has done before with many anti-capitalist worldviews and practices (Boltanski and Chiapello 2005, Chapter 3). The primary political task for concerned citizens should therefore be to resist the commodification of everything and to strive for democratizing the economy, society and the Internet.

RECOMMENDED READINGS AND EXERCISES

For understanding Wikipedia, it is useful to engage with the idea of the commons and different assessments of the platform and to gather experiences of it that are systematically analysed.

Hardt, Michael. 2010. The common in communism. In *The idea of communism*, ed. Slavoj Žižek and Costas Douzinas, 131–144. London: Verso.

Žižek, Slavoj. 2010. How to begin from the beginning. In *The idea of communism*, ed. Slavoj Žižek and Costas Douzinas, 209–226. London: Verso.

Williams, Raymond. 1983. *Keywords*. New York: Oxford University Press. Entries: Common, Communication, Communism (pp. 70–75).

Fuchs, Christian. 2011. *Foundations of critical media and information studies*. New York: Routledge. Chapter 9: Conclusion (pp. 323–349).

These readings introduce the ideas of the commons and the communication commons. They are good foundations for thinking about the relevance of the commons in respect to the Internet. Ask yourself:

- What are the commons? What kinds of commons are there? Try to construct an ordered and systematic typology. Identify a theoretical category that you can use for distinguishing the categories in your typology. Take care that the types do not overlap and that the typology is complete (i.e. involves all forms of commons that exist).
- What are communication commons?
- In what respects is Wikipedia a communications commons?

Wright, Erik Olin. 2010. *Envisioning real utopias*. London: Verso. Chapter 1: Why real utopias? Chapter 8: Real utopias II: Social empowerment and the economy. Conclusion: Making utopias real.

Carr, Nicholas. 2011. Questioning Wikipedia. In *Critical point of view: A Wikipedia reader*, ed. Geert Lovink and Nathaniel Tkacz, 191–202. Amsterdam: Institute of Network Cultures.

O'Neil, Mathieu. 2010. Wikipedia and authority. In *Critical point of view: A Wikipedia reader*, ed. Geert Lovink and Nathaniel Tkacz, 309–324. Amsterdam: Institute of Network Cultures.

O'Neil, Mathieu. 2011. The sociology of critique in Wikipedia. *Critical Studies in Peer Production* RS 1.2: 1–11.

van Dijck, José. 2013. *The culture of connectivity: A critical history of social media*. Oxford: Oxford University Press. Chapter 7: Wikipedia and the neutrality principle.

The authors of these readings have different opinions of Wikipedia. Work in groups on the questions below and present your results to the class.

- Discuss how Wikipedia differs from Google Docs, Facebook, Twitter and YouTube.
- Make a list of commonalities and differences in the assessments of Wikipedia that these three authors give. Which criteria for assessing Wikipedia does each text employ?
- There are points of disagreement on the overall assessment of Wikipedia in the works of the four authors. Formulate your own opinion individually and a group opinion on these questions. Do you think that Wikipedia is the germ form of an alternative Internet? If so, in which respect? If not, why not?

Conduct a group project: select a topic that is currently hotly debated in society and whose Wikipedia entry at the moment is frequently updated. As a group, set yourselves the goal of contributing to the improvement of this article. Together as a group, conduct academic research on this topic. Try to make new additions to the article. Enter the world of Wikipedia and discuss with others on the article's talk page how to improve certain paragraphs. Continue this work for one week. In the next week, write down your experiences: What was positive? What was not so positive? What did it feel like to be actively contributing Wikipedians? How do you assess Wikipedia as a project? What did you learn as a group by working together on a knowledge project? Make a group presentation and discuss your results with the results of other groups.

III

FUTURES

12 CONCLUSION: SOCIAL MEDIA AND ITS ALTERNATIVES – TOWARDS A TRULY SOCIAL MEDIA

KEY QUESTIONS

- What common social media ideologies exist?
- How does the exploitation of digital labour undermine the social aspect of social media?
- What alternatives are there to corporate social media? What could truly public, social and common media look like?

KEY CONCEPTS

Corporate social media

Neoliberalism

Crisis

Alternative social media

Commons

Social media commons

Commons-based social media

12.1 SOCIAL MEDIA REALITY: IDEOLOGIES AND EXPLOITATION

IDEOLOGY

Social media have been the subject of lots of ideological myth-making, speculation, hopes and fears. It has been seen as bringing new forms of democracy, re-invigorating the public sphere, creating wealth, employment, job growth, political change, revolutions and so on. At the same time some have said it is the cause of crime, terror, misogyny, hatred and so on. Capitalism, crisis, class and unequal power relations are the main contexts of social media and society today. The mass media tend to present a simplistic picture about the role of the

Internet in society. It has become so obvious today that we do not simply live in a society, but that we live in capitalist societies and that capitalism needs to be considered as the context of the Internet.

Technological determinism overestimates the role of technology in society. It ignores the fact that technology is embedded in society, and that it is not technology, but humans living under and rebelling against power relations who create revolutions and unrest. The rise of new technologies often creates an "eruption of feeling that briefly overwhelms reason" (Mosco 2004, 22). Technological determinism ignores the political economy of events. Social media determinism is an expression of the digital sublime, the development that "cyberspace has become the latest icon of the technological and electronic sublime, praised for its epochal and transcendent characteristics and demonized for the depth of the evil it can conjure" (Mosco 2004, 24).

Critical theory and critical political economy of the media analyse how exploitation, domination, commodification and ideology interact in shaping media communication in society, what potentials for alternatives there are, and how struggles can use and advance these potentials.

Talking about social media requires that we engage with the concept of the "social" and social theory. It requires us to specify which notions of the social we are using. Applying a multidimensional understanding shows that we are experiencing at the same time continuity and discontinuity of the sociality of the media. The media's development is dialectical.

EXPLOITATION

I have stressed throughout this book the double logic of commodification and ideology that shapes corporate social media. Capital accumulation on corporate social media is based on user data commodification, the unpaid labour of Internet users, targeted advertising and economic surveillance. Google is the dominant player in this business. It is not a communications company, but the world's largest advertising agency. It has developed a sophisticated targeted advertising system that collects a multitude of data about user interests and activities (demographic, technological, economic, political, cultural, ecological information), communications, networks and collaborations. Facebook is the dominant social networking site. It has developed a commodification system that is especially based on commodifying networks, contacts, user profiles and user-generated content that are created by unpaid user labour. Twitter is a microblog platform that has become the object of political mythologizing. Edward Snowden has revealed how the class structures sustained by communications companies are embedded into a surveillance-industrial complex that stands in the context of the naïve right-wing belief that more surveillance and law-and-order politics can prevent and control terrorism and organized crime. In the surveillance-industrial complex, big brother, big capital and big data converge. The surveillance state fuses with surveillance capitalism.

The analysis has shown that politics is a minority issue on Twitter, that the urban middle class dominates the platform and that Twitter is not a political public sphere. Non-profit non-commercial Internet projects like Wikipedia advance the logic of common production, common control and common ownership. Alternative online media (such as WikiLeaks, Indymedia, AlterNet, Democracy Now!, OpenDemocracy, etc.) try to make alternative, critical information available and to foster critical debates (see Fuchs 2010a; Sandoval and Fuchs 2010).

SOCIAL MEDIA: ANTICIPATIVE AND LIMITED SOCIALITY

Management gurus, marketing strategists and uncritical academics have used the notions of "web 2.0", "social media" and "social software" as ideology that overemphasizes novelty and democratic potentials. One of the goals of this ideology has been to create new business models and attract financial capital investments. In contemporary capitalism, the boundaries between play and labour have become fuzzy. Google's management philosophy is characterized by stressing play labour (playbour), which is the expression of a new spirit/ideology of capitalism. Many analyses of Google are one-dimensional and therefore ideological in the sense that they only see positive or negative aspects. Google is a dialectical system reflecting the contradictions of contemporary capitalism. It advances the socialization of the networked productive forces and has thereby created new potentials for cognition, communication and co-operation, but within capitalist class relations limits and exploits these potentials for commodity purposes. The mainstream of social networking sites research is based on an individualistic and bourgeois privacy ideology that sees information sharing as necessarily bad and ignores the problems created by targeted advertising and user exploitation. Corporate social media use privacy policies and terms of use that legally legitimate Internet prosumer commodification. They are expressions of a privacy regime that is based on the ideology of corporate self-regulation of privacy. In these terms and policies, social media corporations tend to assure the users that they deal with user data responsibly, but at the same time define and enable consumer privacy violations so that these terms and policies become ideological documents. There are many claims about political social media use: that Twitter and other platforms revitalize the political public, cause political revolutions, are the source of violence and so on. Neither techno-optimism nor techno-pessimism is the appropriate method for analysing social media. Rather, one needs to decentre the analysis from technology and focus on the interaction of the power structures of the political economy of capitalism with social media.

Social media in their current forms advance the socialization of human activities. But these activities are on corporate social media trapped in private relations of ownership so that social media advance social production and private ownership of data in the form of commodification of data, human creativity and social relations. Corporate social media are incompletely social: they are controlled and owned in a particularistic manner by an elite, although their social form of production points towards an existence beyond capitalism. Social media anticipate a full sociality of human existence, but in their corporate form this potential is limited by capitalist structures of ownership and capital accumulation. Social media today have an anticipative and simultaneously limited sociality: they anticipate a full socialization of human existence that is limited by the capitalist reality of social media. Alternatives are needed.

JARON LANIER: TOTAL COMMODIFICATION OF THE INTERNET

Jaron Lanier (2013) shares digital labour theory's insight that corporate social media's "value comes from the millions of users who contribute to their network without being paid for it" (Lanier 2013, xii). His answer to this problem is, however, not the suggestion to abolish digital capitalism. He rather wants to deepen it. He argues that working for free has destroyed the "middle class" and that one should pay "people for information gleaned from them if that information turns out to be valuable" (4–5).

We want free online experiences so badly that we are happy to not be paid for information that comes from us now or ever. […] Siren Servers gather data from the network, often without having to pay for it. The data is analyzed using the most powerful available computers, run by the very best available technical people. The results of the analysis are kept secret, but are used to manipulate the rest of the world to advantage. […] The latest waves of high-tech innovation have not created jobs like the old ones did. Iconic new ventures like Facebook employ vastly fewer people than big older companies like, say, General Motors. […] The middle classes that have already lost their levees and economic dignity to Siren Servers are sometimes called the "creative classes." They include recording musicians, journalists, and photographers. There were also a significantly larger number of people who supported these types of creators, like studio musicians and editors, who enjoyed "good jobs" (meaning with security and benefits). […] anyone interested in liberal democracy must realize that without a dominant middle class, democracy becomes vulnerable. […] Valuing all the information on networks […] will create an economy that can continue to grow as more and more activity becomes software-mediated. […] A monetized version of a many-to-many network could create an organic path to middle-class wealth that would be better than the ad hoc mountain of levees that sustained middle classes in pre-digital capitalism. […] So, for instance, if Google placed the ads that referenced your marriage, and earned a certain amount based on auction and click-through results, your instant remuneration would be proportional to Google's. […] I am not condemning big business data, but celebrating it. […] In the world foreseen in this book, a Siren Server of any type would have to pay for the information gathered about you proportionally to the value of that information, as determined by expectations for future transactions. "Spying" on you would still occur, especially when you are the customer for a service related to you. However, in the event a company offers you something worth paying for over the network, that success would have to be based primarily on some creation of value beyond spying, based on the unique competence of the seller. (Lanier 2013, 12, 50, 51, 84, 200, 228, 234, 271, 282, 306)

In a capitalist world, wages and profits are both inherent parts of capital. If one believes in capitalism as the best way of wealth creation, one therefore has to increase profits for increasing wages. Lanier does not question, but fully believes in capitalism. He suggests deepening and totalizing capitalism and surveillance on the Internet in order to commodify the whole online world. All digital labour should then be remunerated. The problem is that a totally commodified world is also a class-based world of exploiters and the exploited. Lanier cannot any other political economy than capitalism. Non-profit public service and civil society media do not exist in his political universe. The middle class that Lanier would like to see re-emerge presupposes a distinction between the poor, the rich and the middle. Today, the poor as well as the rich often define themselves as middle class. The poor because they are ashamed to say they are poor, the rich in order to play down their wealth. Digital capitalism is based on a class conflict between digital capital and digital labour. The solution is not to introduce an additional class, but to question class on the Internet and in society.

12.2 SOCIAL MEDIA ALTERNATIVES

THE INTERNET AND THE LOGIC OF THE COMMONS

Exploitation and ideology can and should be questioned and challenged. Capitalism is not the end of history. The capitalist Internet is not the end of history. An alternative society is possible. An alternative Internet is possible. Changes to the design of both the Internet and society's fundamental structures are needed. But alternatives require struggles. We have seen that alternative platforms like Diaspora*, Wikipedia and WikiLeaks have a contradictory character. They are shaped by the logics of commodification and bourgeois ideology, but at the same time have potentials that point beyond capitalism and the capitalist Internet. They anticipate a commons-based Internet that is not based on capital accumulation, advertising, profit, ideology or a stratified attention economy, but rather enables knowledge, communication and collaboration for their own sake as social activities between humans. A commons-based Internet is possible – an Internet on which people share, communicate, decide, discuss, play, create, criticize, network, collaborate, find, maintain and build friendships, fall in love, entertain themselves and each other, educate themselves as a common activity without corporate mediation.

The logic of the commons is the logic of a common humanity that has realized that all humans should be equal participants and beneficiaries in society (see Dyer-Witheford 1999, 2007, 2009; Fuchs 2011b; Hardt and Negri 2009; Žižek 2010). Technology and the media are not the main aspect, but a part of society. Therefore all humans should be able to truly participate and benefit from media and technology, which is not the case today. Capitalism is a class society. The capitalist Internet is a class-structured Internet: corporations and other central actors dominate attention and symbolic, social and material benefits. A just society is a classless society. A just Internet is a classless Internet.

CAPITALISM, NEOLIBERALISM, CRISIS

All forms of capitalism are contradictory and create crises. The world economic crisis that started in 2008 was the result of decades of neoliberal capitalism. Neoliberalism is based on "the subordination of the totality of socio-economic fields to the accumulation process so that economic functions come to occupy the dominant place within the state" (Jessop 2008, 132). Neoliberal ideology's focus is almost exclusively on capital accumulation:

> Neoliberalism is in the first instance a theory of political economic practices that proposes that human well-being can be best advanced by liberating individual entrepreneurial freedoms and skills within an institutional framework characterized by strong private rights, free markets and free trade. [...] It holds that the social good will be maximized by maximizing the reach and frequency of market transactions, and it seeks to bring all human action into the domain of the market. This requires technologies of information creation and capacities to accumulate, store, transfer, analyze, and use massive databases to guide decisions in the global marketplace. (Harvey 2007, 2–3)

Negative social consequences are subordinated to economic logic: "The fundamental mission of the neoliberal state is to create 'a good business climate' and therefore to optimize conditions for capital accumulation no matter what the consequences are for employment or social well-being" (Harvey 2005a, 19). Capitalism is immanently crisis-ridden. The history of capitalism is also a history of economic and political crises. Neoliberalism has intensified inequality. We have also discussed in this book that non-Western countries do not automatically bring about an alternative framework to global capitalism and neo-liberalism. China has seen massive economic growth, but has at the same time to a significant degree adopted neoliberal policies and seen a strong increase of inequalities. In India, right-wing Hindu nationalism mixed with neoliberal politics has become the ruling party's dominant ideology.

STRUGGLES

The main political reaction to the crisis has been the rise of hyper-neoliberalism. Hyper-neoliberalism is an intensification of neoliberalism that uses employees' tax money for consolidating the financial system and, as a result, extends and intensifies budget cuts to social security, education, health care and the pension system, and has resulted in a shift towards the right and extreme right in elections in many countries. Large protests in countries such as Greece, Portugal and Spain, student protests in many countries, rebellions and revolutions in Arab and North African countries (e.g. Tunisia and Egypt), the emergence of various Occupy movements and riots have constituted another important, although weaker, consequence of the crisis. However different these consequences may be, they express discontent with capitalism and remind us that we need a classless society in order to overcome inequality. There seem to be only two options today: (a) continuance and intensification of the 200-year-old barbarity of capitalism or (b) socialism.

Struggles for a commons-based Internet need to be connected to struggles for socialism. In Chapter 8, I introduced the concept of socialist privacy protection. One can achieve privacy protection of consumers, prosumers and workers only in an economy that is not ruled by profit interests, but controlled and managed by prosumers, consumers and producers. If there were no profit motive on Internet platforms, then there would be no need to commodify the data and usage behaviour of Internet users. Achieving such a situation is, however, not primarily a technological task, but one that requires changes in society. Socialist privacy policies are part of a struggle for a just society. Oscar Gandy (2011, 183) argues that just as societies have, in respect to pollution, realized that "markets will not work on their own to insure the maintenance of healthy and sustainable environments" and "agree that the regulation of pollution and other threats to the environment should be treated as explicit and important public policy goals", they should realize the need for consumer protection in cyberspace as part of a policy that protects the information environment.

Seven strategies for achieving this goal are: (1) the use of data protection legislation; (2) the advancement of opt-in online advertising; (3) civil society surveillance of Internet companies; (4) digital labour unionism; (5) the establishment and support of alternative platforms; (6) corporate taxation and a participatory media fee; (7) the establishment of an alternative societal context of Internet use.

DATA PROTECTION LAWS

One strategy is to use existing data protection laws to force Internet corporations not to put profit interests above user interests, and to strive for strict data protection laws that protect consumer interests.

Struggles against the corporate and commercial character of the Internet can also make use of existing data protection laws. On 18 August 2011, members of the initiative "Europe vs. Facebook", which was founded by Austrian law students, filed a complaint against Facebook to the Irish Data Protection Commissioner. Facebook Europe is legally registered in Ireland. The initiative's members asked the Commissioner to check whether Facebook violates European data protection laws in these 16 privacy areas. The complaint was, however, relatively unsuccessful because the Irish data protection authorities accepted Facebook's commodification of personal data as legitimate economic strategy.

OPT-IN ADVERTISING POLICIES

Oscar Gandy (1993) argues that an alternative to opt-out solutions to targeted advertising are opt-in solutions that are based on the informed consent of consumers. Opt-in to advertising and automatically activated Do-Not-Track cookies in all web browsers as standard setting are progressive design principles that can help changing the problematic reality of the internet. Consumer organizations and data protectionists typically favour opt-in privacy policies, whereas companies and marketing associations tend to prefer opt-out and self-regulation advertising policies in order to maximize profit (Bellman et al. 2004; Federal Trade Commission 2000; Gandy 1993; Quinn 2006; Ryker et al. 2002; Starke-Meyerring and Gurak 2007). Socialist privacy legislation could require all commercial Internet platforms to use advertising only as an opt-in option, which would strengthen the users' possibility for self-determination.

Within capitalism, forcing corporations by state laws to implement opt-in mechanisms is certainly desirable, but at the same time it is likely that corporations will not consent to such policies because opt-in is likely to reduce the actual amount of surveilled and commodified user data significantly, which results in a drop in advertising profits. Organizing targeted advertising as an opt-in instead of an opt-out or no option does not establish economic user privacy, but is a step towards strengthening the economic privacy of users.

CORPORATE WATCH PLATFORMS AS A FORM OF STRUGGLE AGAINST CORPORATISM

In order to circumvent the large-scale surveillance of consumers, producers and consumer-producers, movements and protests against economic surveillance are necessary. Kojin Karatani (2005) argues that consumption is the only space in capitalism where workers become subjects that can exert pressure by consumption boycotts on capital. I do not think that this is correct because strikes also show the subject position of workers that enables them to boycott production, to cause financial harm to capital, and to exert pressure in order to voice political demands. However, Karatani in my opinion correctly argues that the role of the consumer has been underestimated in Marxist theory and practice. The fact that in the contemporary media landscape media consumers become media producers who work and create surplus value shows the importance of the role of consumers in contemporary capitalism and of "the transcritical moment where workers and consumers intersect" (Karatani 2005, 21). For political strategies this brings up the actuality of an associationist movement that is "a transnational association of consumers/workers" (295) and engages in "the class struggle against capitalism" of "workers qua consumers or consumers qua workers" (294).

Critical citizens, critical citizens' initiatives, consumer groups, social movement groups, critical scholars, unions, data protection specialists/groups, consumer protection specialists/groups, critical politicians and critical political parties should observe closely the surveillance and exploitation operations of Internet corporations and document these mechanisms, as well as the instances where corporations and politicians take measures that threaten privacy or increase the surveillance of citizens. Such documentation is most effective if it is easily accessible to the public. The Internet provides the means for documenting such behaviour. It can help to watch the watchers and exploiters and to raise public awareness. In recent years, corporate watch organizations that run online watch platforms have emerged. Examples for corporate watch organizations are:

- CorpWatch Reporting (www.corpwatch.org)
- Transnationale Ethical Rating (www.transnationale.org)
- The Corporate Watch Project (www.corporatewatch.org)
- Multinational Monitor (www.multinationalmonitor.org)
- Responsible Shopper (www.greenamerica.org/programs/responsibleshopper)
- Endgame Database of Corporate Fines (www.endgame.org/corpfines.html)
- Corporate Crime Reporter (www.corporatecrimereporter.com)
- Corporate Europe Observatory (www.corporateeurope.org)
- Corporate Critic Database (www.corporatecritic.org)
- Students and Scholars against Corporate Misbehaviour (http://sacom.hk)
- China Labor Watch (www.chinalaborwatch.org)
- Center for Media and Democracy's PR Watch (www.prwatch.org)

For example, Transnationale Ethical Rating aims at informing consumers and research about corporations. Its ratings include quantitative and qualitative data about violations of labour rights, violations of human rights, lay-off of employees, profits, sales, earnings of CEOs, boards, president and managers, financial offshoring operations, financial delinquency, environmental pollution, corporate corruption and dubious communication practices. Dubious communication practices include an "arguable partnership, deceptive advertising, disinformation, commercial invasion, spying, mishandling of private data, biopiracy and appropriation of public knowledge".[1] Corporate watchdog organizations' task is to document corporate irresponsibility. Corporate watch platforms can not only monitor ICT corporations and the corporate media (as well as corporations in general), but can also situate corporate behaviour in the larger political-economic context of corporate social irresponsibility (the counterpart of the corporate social responsibility (CSR) ideology).

Figure 12.1 shows as an example an article about Google from the corporate watchdog platform Corpwatch.org. The article argues:

> Children have become lucrative targets for data mining companies [...] Just weeks after Google settled a lawsuit for selling student data for advertising, the publication revealed an entire industry devoted to marketing data gathered from Internet applications offered to students and their teachers.

---

1 www.transnationale.org/aide.php (accessed on 22 November 2015).

On the one hand, it is important that watchdog organizations document and gather data about the corporate irresponsibility of Internet corporations. On the other hand, it looks like these data are not very complete and not many Internet corporations are thus far included. So one could, for example, also document Google's targeted advertising practices and many other irresponsible practices (see Chapter 7). These practices are highly opaque to users and they leave it unclear for the single user what data exactly about her/him is stored and commodified. In any case, more efforts are required in order to advance the documentation of corporate social irresponsibility of Internet corporations and to contextualize privacy violations within the process of watching the watchers.

Corporate watch platforms are attempts by those resisting asymmetric economic power relations to struggle against the powerful class of corporations by documenting data that should make economic power transparent. Online corporate watchdog organizations document and gather data about the corporate irresponsibility of corporations. Making data about corporate irresponsibility available to the public does not abolish exploitation and oppression. It can, however, be a useful tool in the struggle against exploitation and oppression. Action is always related to events. If there is no knowledge about oppressive practices because they are hidden from the public, then reactions to it are unlikely. Watching the powerful does not necessarily result in struggles, but it can make struggles more likely. This also requires that watchdog organizations do not present examples of corporate irresponsibility as exceptions from the rule and bad practices, but rather as necessary irresponsibilities and necessary bad practices that are caused by the systemic logic of corporate irresponsibility that is inherent in capitalism. Marisol

FIGURE 12.1   An example page about Google from www.corpwatch.org

Sandoval (2015) argues in this context that the ideology of CSR is not just masking corporate social irresponsibility, but shows a need for the responsibility to socialize corporations (RSC):

> In order to discover its "rational kernel" within the "mystical shell," CSR must be turned from its head to its feet; turned from its head to its feet, corporate social responsibility (CSR) turns into the responsibility to socialize corporations (RSC). [...] Whereas CSR entails idealistic hopes about reconciling corporate and social goals within capitalism, RSC highlights that material transformations are necessary to achieve a truly socially responsible and socially just economy. [...] RSC is a reminder of the possibility of socially responsible economic alternatives beyond capitalism, which realize collective decision power and satisfy social needs rather than individualized profit goals. (Sandoval 2015, 619, 620, 621)

Also WikiLeaks is an online watchdog platform that tries to make power transparent by leaking secret documents about political and economic power. Watchdog organizations (just like alternative media in general; see Fuchs 2010a; Sandoval and Fuchs 2010) try to exert counter-power. But they are facing resource asymmetries that result in antagonism between resource precariousness and political autonomy. They are facing three serious limits in capitalism:

a) They are frequently based on precarious, self-exploitative labour.
b) They often lack resources.
c) Resource provision by politics or the economy may threaten their political autonomy and make them vulnerable to corporate or political filtering of their contents.

Curbing these limits requires affirmative action politics that tries to overcome the economic censorship (lack of attention, lack of money, lack of resources) of alternative media by providing guaranteed funding to these media. Thereby the problem of potential pressures by the state on alternative media is posed, and this can only be overcome by installing socialist governments that acknowledge the importance of civil society for democracy and social transformation.

Worker-owned and -controlled factories, so-called co-operatives, are alternatives that start in the here-and-now as germ forms of a socialist economy. Marx stressed their importance, but also saw their problems within capitalism:

> We speak of the cooperative movement, especially the cooperative factories raised by the unassisted efforts of a few bold "hands". The value of these great social experiments cannot be over-rated. By deed, instead of by argument, they have shown that production on a large scale, and in accord with the behests of modern science, may be carried on without the existence of a class of masters employing a class of hands; that to bear fruit, the means of labour need not be monopolised as a means of dominion over, and of extortion against, the labouring man himself; and that, like slave labour, like serf labour, hired labour is but a transitory and inferior form, destined to disappear before associated labour plying its toil with a willing hand, a ready mind, and a joyous heart. In England, the seeds of the cooperative system were sown by Robert Owen; the same working men's experiments, tried on the Continent, were, in fact, the practical upshot of the theories, not invented, but loudly proclaimed, in 1848. (MECW 21, 330–331)

The cooperative factories of the labourers themselves represent within the old form the first sprouts of the new, although they naturally reproduce, and must reproduce, everywhere in their actual organisation all the shortcomings of the prevailing system. But the antithesis between capital and labour is overcome within them, if at first only by way of making the associated labourers into their own capitalist, i.e., by enabling them to use the means of production for the employment of their own labour. They show how a new mode of production naturally grows out of an old one, when the development of the material forces of production and of the corresponding forms of social production have reached a particular stage. Without the factory system arising out of the capitalist mode of production there could have been no cooperative factories. (MECW 37, 438)

On social media, both software engineers creating the platforms and users who create content and social relations are workers. They both create use-values. If social media are operated as advertising-funded corporations, then capital exploits both paid workers and user-workers. Turning a social media platform into a co-operative then requires democratic control and decision-making that brings together all workers, including the user-workers.

DIGITAL LABOUR UNIONS

A trade union is a collective worker organization for the struggle to improve working conditions.

Marx stressed the importance of the unions:

> The *trade unions* aim at nothing less than to prevent the *reduction of wages* below the level that is traditionally maintained in the various branches of industry. That is to say, they wish to prevent the *price* of labour-power from falling below its *value*. (Marx 1867, 1069)

In a trade union, "workers *combine* in order to achieve *equality* of a sort with the capitalist in their *contract concerning the sale of their labour*" (1070). Trade unions are "insurance societies formed by the workers themselves" (1070).

Not just those who earn a wage are workers. Late twentieth- and twenty-first-century capitalism has been shaped by many different forms of atypical labour, including precarious freelancers in the media/cultural/digital industries and other sectors. They do not earn a lot of money, have high individual risks and tend to work atypical and at times very long hours in order to survive. There are also, however, unremunerated workers, such as homeworkers, audience workers and digital workers, who also need unions in order to represent their interests as workers exploited by capital. Traditional labour unions tend to focus on wage-labour; they have yet to discover the importance of organizing digital and other "free" workers. A step in the right direction is the idea of an Immaterial Labour Union:

> The Immaterial Labor Union was born out of a desire to escape from the atomization of the individual into the collective, to think about alternatives to the neoliberal grey area of the multitude and its permanent state of insulation, to

negotiate terms of service and push for the protection of personal data on a trans-national scope. Framed within the context of social media monopolies such as Facebook, Twitter or Google+, the Union aims, on a short-term basis, to reddress privacy abuses and unfair working conditions perpetrated through the process-ing of our online data, and on a long-term basis to conceive and shape alterna-tive social networking solutions. [...] Increasingly, information is becoming the means of production of the digital age. The blurring of lines between work and leisure time means the commodification of the latter, and the monetization of our relationships and online activities becomes the rule. [...] Based on this assump-tions, equating social media activity with labour and stating this correspondence clearly becomes key to framing the necessity of a Union which can effectively state its demands in the context of digital economy.[2]

A digital labour union can organize temporary user-strikes, wage-demands in the form of a universal basic income as remuneration for the world's unpaid labour, argue for creating funds that support alternative, non-commercial platforms and so on.

ALTERNATIVE INTERNET PLATFORMS

Another attempt to resist corporate domination of the Internet is in the form of non-commercial, non-profit Internet platforms. It is not impossible to create successful non-profit Internet plat-forms, as the example of Wikipedia – which is advertising-free, provides free access and is financed by donations – shows. The most well-known alternative social networking site-project is Diaspora*, which tries to develop an open-source alternative to Facebook. The four New York University students Dan Grippi, Maxwell Salzberg, Raphael Sofaer and Ilya Zhitomirskiy created Diaspora* in 2010. The social networking site kaioo is not only non-commercial; the users can also discuss and edit its terms of use and privacy terms in a wiki.

These projects are facing the same dilemma as all alternative media in capitalism: the contradiction between alternative demands and the reality of resource precariousness and pre-carious labour. The demand to produce non-commercial and non-profit media is crucial for advancing a democratic media landscape, but the problem is at the same time that money is needed for organizing media within capitalism. Also, organizing media against capitalism needs to start within capitalism. Alternative media projects frequently operate with the help of precarious voluntary labour and face a lack of funds. They are confronted with a permanent threat of commercialization. State funding, donation models and subscription models can help, but have their own limitations. Donations and subscriptions are unstable and state funding can create political pressure that functions indirectly as censorship by way of economic means.

Robert Gehl (2014) suggests to reverse-engineer social media and to create socialized media, systems that involve "true two-way communication, decentralization, free and open-source software, and encryption", user participation in engineering and design (142). Such platforms would run on free hardware (143). The basic design principles that Gehl intro-duces for socialized media are users' equal capacity to transmit and receive information; a decentralized technological architecture; radical democratic pedagogy at the interface;

---

2 http://immateriallaborunion.net/ (accessed on 27 October 2015).

collaboration of users with and without technical skills; copyleft; platform independence; free hardware; anonymity; pseudonimity; identity shifts; play; an anti-archival system.

It is certainly very important to think about what alternative systems and an alternative future could look like. An alternative socialized media system is still a collective organization even though it uses decentralized data storage. Copyleft licences do not always rule out charging money for access. Therefore if, for example, a platform installation fee is introduced, monetary benefits could be derived and then the question of the ownership of the means of production is crucial. Robert Gehl's vision of socialized media is an "idealized design" (143) that is based on the "gap between the ideal design and the material implementation" (143). Alternatives cannot wait until the day after everything has changed. Utopian socialism dreams of another world, but the point is to change the world so that humans really possess and materialize this dream. We have to start and operate in the here-and-now, which means that alternatives face hard capitalist realities, such as the question of how they obtain money in order to organize their basic resources. Social movements that build and operate alternative social media are important, but civil society alone is not enough. Civil society and social movements need to co-operate with left-wing political parties in order to create legal frameworks that can help channel resources towards alternative media.

THE ADVERTISING TAX AND THE PARTICIPATORY MEDIA FEE

Astra Taylor (2014) in her book *The People's Platform: Taking Back Power and Culture in the Digital Age* makes suggestions for the strengthening of public culture. These include, for example, shortening the duration of copyright (170), fees for the limitation of the reuse of culture (171), the introduction of an initial copyright on culture that expires after a limited time so that cultural goods are turned into public goods (171), communal broadband initiatives (226), publicly funded digital archives (220), advertising-free search engines (222), alternatives to iTunes and Netflix that are operated as co-operatives (222), the introduction of press subsidies in the USA (226–227), the public funding of community centres as well as local book shops and movie theatres (175, 217, 228), the collection of taxes that global tech firms such as Google, Apple and Amazon that avoid paying (229), and the introduction of an advertising tax (229).

Corporate taxation has declined under neoliberal conditions. Neoliberal governments have argued that the left wants to create a big state that engages in tax-and-spend politics and has implemented politics that privilege corporations and the rich and cut public services and expenditures, meaning that everyday people are worse off. Global corporations have used tax loopholes and tax offshoring in order to avoid paying taxes. Taxing corporations constitute an important foundation for creating a post-neoliberal framework of society that fosters social justice. Robert McChesney (2013, 223, 232) argues in this context:

> efforts to reform or replace capitalism, but leave the Internet giants riding high will not reform or replace really existing capitalism. [...] Their massive profits are the result of monopoly privileges, network effects, commercialism, exploited labour, and a number of government policies and subsidies. [...] battles over the Internet are of central importance for all those seeking to build a better society.

States usually make companies pay capital taxes and social security contributions for employees. The theory of audience and digital labour assumes that the economic value of advertising-financed media is not simply created by these organizations' wage-labour, but also by their audiences, respectively users who create attention and data that are sold as commodity to advertising clients. Advertising corporations, including Google and Facebook, outsource value creation to consumption workers, whereby they increase their profitability and keep the number of their employees low. An advertising tax can be seen as a kind of tax on the exploitation of audience and digital labour. It is comparable to social security payments that companies pay to the state for their regular employees. It is important to think about advertising as a global phenomenon that is part of the production process and stands in the context of the critique of the totality of capitalism and the political demand for increasing the taxation of capital. An advertising tax exists, for example, in Austria, Italy, Greece, Belgium, Estonia, Croatia, Sweden, Portugal and Romania. Internet advertising tends to be excluded from this tax, although it has a rising share in total advertising. The consequence is that existing advertising taxes are rather ineffective.

Table 12.1 shows that a tax on advertising expenditures can fund a media cheque that amounts to €50–100 per household. Participatory budgeting could be used for providing such a cheque to households with the obligation that they have to donate the amount to non-commercial media organizations. The participatory media fee is one of the possible reforms that could strengthen public and alternative media. It can be designed in different ways, so the data I have provided should just be seen as an example calculation. Different models are imaginable.

Taxing large media corporations, channelling this income into non-commercial media and combining it with elements of participatory budgeting could allow every citizen to receive and donate a certain amount per year to a non-commercial media project. Elements of state action and civil society action could be combined: the power of the state would guarantee taxation of large companies; the distribution of this income to media projects would, however, be decentralized and put in the hands of citizens. Google, Facebook and other large online media companies hardly pay taxes in many countries. The insight that users are digital workers and create economic value on corporate social media that are financed by advertising allows changing global tax regulations: corporate social media platforms should have to tax in a specific country that share of their revenues that corresponds to the share of users or ad-clicks/views in that country. Avoiding corporations' tax evasion is a first step for strengthening the public sphere. The licence fee could be developed into a media fee paid by citizens and companies. It could be made more socially just than the licence fee by implementing it

TABLE 12.1   Example calculations for an advertising tax

	Advertising revenue 2014 (Austria: 2013)	Number of households	Advertising tax of 10%	Media cheque per household
Germany	€19.0 billion	39.9 million	€1.9 billion	€48
Austria	€3.2 billion	3.7 million	€317 billion	€86
UK	€19.7 billion	26.4 million	€1.97 billion	€75
USA	€125.93 billion	115.6 million	€12.6 billion	€109

Sources: Data from WARC, Statistisches Bundesamt, Statistik Austria, ONS, US Census Bureau.

not as a flat fee but a progressive one that varies based on salary and revenue levels. It is a matter of fairness that those who earn more should contribute more to the organization of the common interest and public good.

The media fee could partly be used for directly funding public service media's online presence and partly be used in the form of participatory budgeting to provide an annual voucher to every citizen that s/he must donate to a non-profit, non-commercial media organization. So participatory budgeting should not be used for deciding whether the BBC receives the full costs it needs for its operations. Additional income from the media fee could, however, be distributed to alternative media projects with the help of participatory budgeting. Non-profit versions of Twitter, YouTube and Facebook run by institutions such as the BBC and civil society based on such a model could serve the purpose of the public sphere and strengthen the democratic character of communications. Public service media such as the BBC would be strong in operating an alternative YouTube that requires large storage capacity, whereas non-profit civil society organizations are well suited to operate platforms that contain lots of personal data, such as an alternative Facebook and an alternative Twitter.

12.3 TOWARDS A TRULY SOCIAL MEDIA AND A NEW SOCIETY

The contradictions of the corporate Internet can only be resolved in a framework of society that overcomes inequalities. An alternative Internet requires, together with alternative design principles, an alternative societal setting: a solidary, co-operative information society – a participatory democracy. Calls for the strengthening of privacy in the light of corporate Internet domination are short-sighted and superficial because privacy is intended to protect humans from harm, not to overcome those conditions and structures that cause harms. Slavoj Žižek (2001, 256) suggests in this context not to "retreat into islands of privacy, but an ever stronger socialization of cyberspace" (256). Privacy is a contradictory value: it is proclaimed in liberal ideology, but at the same time constantly undermined by corporate and state surveillance. Privacy as a liberal value protects the rich and powerful from public accountability, which can help to increase and legitimatize inequality. The socialist philosopher Torbjörn Tännsjö (2010) stresses that liberal privacy concepts imply "that one can not only own oneself and personal things, but also the means of production" and that the consequence is "a very closed society, clogged because of the idea of business secret, bank privacy, etc." (186[3]).

The questions in discussions about privacy should therefore be: Who should be protected through privacy rights in order to be safe from harm? Whose privacy rights should be limited in order not to damage the public good? Privacy contradictions can never be resolved in capitalism (see Sevignani 2016). Tännsjö (2010) calls for the establishment of an "open society" that is based on equality and democracy instead of the strengthening of privacy rights. Tännsjö's use of the term "open society" is unfortunate because Karl Popper (1962a, 1962b) employed the same notion for defending the liberal ideology that Tännsjö criticizes. What Tännsjö actually means by an open society is a participatory democracy.

---

3 Translation from Swedish by the author.

Facebook and Google are only the two best-known examples of a more general contemporary economy that appropriates, expropriates and exploits the common goods (communication, education, knowledge, care, welfare, nature, culture, technology, public transport, housing, etc.) that humans create and need in order to survive. In the area of the Internet, a socialist strategy can try to resist the commodification of the Internet and the exploitation of users by trying to claim the common and participatory character of the Internet with the help of pro-tests, legal measures, alternative projects based on the ideas of free access/content/software and creative commons, wage campaigns, unionization of social media prosumers, boycotts, hacktivism, the creation of public service- and commons-based social media, and so on.

The exploitation of digital labour on the Internet is, however, a topic that is connected to the broader political economy of capitalism, which means that those who are critical of what social media companies like Facebook do with their data ought to be also critical of what contemporary capitalism is doing to humans throughout the world in different forms. If we manage to establish a participatory democracy, then a truly open society (Tännsjö 2010) might become possible that requires no surveillance, no protection from surveillance and no exploitation. A commons-based Internet requires commons-based design principles and a commons-oriented society (Fuchs 2011b, Chapters 8 and 9). It can give a new meaning to the sociality of society and the media. Humans are essentially social and societal beings. They need to collaborate in order to exist. A collaborative society requires participatory democracy and collective ownership and control of the means of production. Collaboration and co-op-eration are the fundamental meanings of the terms "social" and "society". Discussions about social media remind us of the need to think and act in respect of the question about what sociality, what society and what kind of media we want to have.

Truly public, social and common media require as one of their preconditions not only alternative design principles, but also a society that realizes the meaning of the terms "public", "social" and "common" – the public sphere and participatory democracy. Another Internet is possible. Social media are possible.

REFERENCES

Acquisti, Alessandro and Ralph Gross. 2006. Imagined communities: Awareness, information sharing, and privacy on the Facebook. In *Proceedings of the 6th Workshop on Privacy Enhancing Technologies*, ed. Phillipe Golle and George Danezis, 36–58. Cambridge: Robinson College.

Adorno, Theodor W. 1951/2003. Cultural criticism and society. In *Can one live after Auschwitz? A philosophical reader*, ed. Rolf Tiedemann, 146–162. Stanford, CA: Stanford University Press.

Adorno, Theodor W. 1973/2003. *Negative dialectics*. London: Routledge.

Adorno, Theodor W. 2000. *The Adorno reader*. Malden, MA: Blackwell.

Adorno, Theodor W. 2002. *Introduction to sociology*. Cambridge: Polity Press.

Agger, Ben. 2006. *Critical social theories: An introduction* (2nd edition). Boulder, CO: Paradigm.

Albarran, Alan B., ed. 2013. *The social media industries*. New York: Routledge.

Allen, Matthew. 2012. What was web 2.0? Versions and the politics of Internet history. *New Media & Society* 15 (2): 260–275.

Allmer, Thomas. 2015. *Critical theory and social media: Between emancipation and commodification*. London: New York.

Amin, Samir. 2013a. China 2013. *Monthly Review* 64 (10): 14–33.

Amin, Samir. 2013b. *The implosion of contemporary capitalism*. New York: Monthly Review Press.

Andrejevic, Mark. 2007. *iSpy: Surveillance and power in the interactive era*. Lawrence, KS: University Press of Kansas.

Andrejevic, Mark. 2013. *Infoglut: How too much information is changing the way we think and know*. New York: Routledge.

Andrejevic, Mark. 2014a. The big data divide. *International Journal of Communication* 8: 1673–1689.

Aouragh, Miriyam. 2012. Social media, mediation and the Arab revolutions. *tripleC: Communication, Capitalism & Critique: Journal for a Global Sustainable Information Society* 10 (2): 518–536.

Arendt, Hannah. 1958. *The human condition* (2nd edition). Chicago, IL: University of Chicago Press.

Arrighi, Giovanni. 2007. *Adam Smith in Beijing: Lineages of the twenty-first century*. London: Verso.

Arvidsson, Adam and Elanor Colleoni. 2012. Value in informational capitalism and on the Internet. *The Information Society* 28 (3): 135–150.

Auletta, Ken. 2010. *Googled: The end of the world as we know it*. London: Virgin.

Auray Nicolas, Celine Poudat and Pascal Pons. 2007. Democratizing scientific vulgarisation: The balance between co-operation and conflict in French Wikipedia. *Observatorio Journal* 3: 185–199.

Badiou, Alain. 2008. The communist hypothesis. *New Left Review* 49 (1): 29–42.

Badiou, Alain. 2012. *The rebirth of history: Times of riots and uprisings*. London: Verso.

Baker, Dean. 2014. Don't buy the 'sharing economy' hype: Airbnb and Uber are facilitating rip-offs. *Guardian* online. 27 May. https://www.theguardian.com/commentisfree/2014/may/27/airbnb-uber-taxes-regulation (accessed on 26 September 2016).

Ball, Kirstie and Frank Webster. 2003. The intensification of surveillance. In *The intensification of surveillance: Crime, terrorism, and warfare in the information era*, ed. Kirstie Ball and Frank Webster, 1–15. London: Pluto Press.

Barnes, Susan. 2006. A privacy paradox: Social networking in the United States. *First Monday* 11 (9). http://firstmonday.org/article/view/1394/1312 (accessed on 26 September 2016).

Bauwens, Michael. 2003. Peer-to-peer and human evolution. http://economia.unipv.it/novita/seminario/P2PandHumanEvolV2.pdf.

Baym, Nancy and danah boyd. 2012. Socially mediated publicness: An introduction. *Journal of Broadcasting & Electronic Media* 56 (3): 320–329.

Beck, Ulrich. 1997. Subpolitics: Ecology and the disintegration of institutional power. *Organization & Environment* 10 (1): 52–65.

Bellman, Steven, Eric J. Johnson, Stephen J. Kobrin and Gerald L. Lohse. 2004. International differences in information privacy concerns: A global survey of consumers. *The Information Society* 20 (5): 313–324.

Benjamin, Walter. 1934. Der Autor als Produzent. In *Medienästhetische Schriften*, 231–247. Frankfurt am Main: Suhrkamp.

Benjamin, Walter. 1936/1939. The work of art in the age of mechanical reproduction. In *Media and cultural studies KeyWorks*, ed. by Meenakshi Gigi Durham and Douglas M. Kellner, 18–40. Malden, MA: Blackwell.

Benkler, Yochai. 2006. *The wealth of networks*. New Haven, CT: Yale University Press.

Benkler, Yochai. 2013. WikiLeaks and the networked fourth estate. In *Beyond WikiLeaks: Implications for the future of communications, journalism and society*, ed. Benedetta Brevini, Arne Hintz and Patrick McCurdy, 11–34. Basingstoke: Palgrave Macmillan.

Bennett, Colin and Charles Raab. 2006. *The governance of privacy*. Cambridge, MA: MIT Press.

Bennett, W. Lance and Alexandra Segerberg. 2012. The logic of connective action. *Information, Communication & Society* 15 (5): 739–768.

Bennett, W. Lance and Alexandra Segerberg. 2013. *The logic of connective action: Digital media and the personalization of contentious politics*. Cambridge: Cambridge University Press.

Bermejo, Fernando. 2009. Audience manufacture in historical perspective: From broadcasting to Google. *New Media & Society* 11 (1/2): 133–154.

Bigo, Didier. 2010. Delivering liberty and security? The reframing of freedom when associated with security. In *Europe's 21st century challenge: Delivering liberty*, ed. Didier Bigo, Sergio Carrera, Elspeth Guild and R.B.J. Walker, 263–287. Farnham: Ashgate.

Bischoff, Joachim. 2008. *Globale Finanzkrise*. Hamburg: VSA.

Black, Edwin. 2001. *IBM and the Holocaust: The strategic alliance between Nazi Germany and America's most powerful corporation*. New York: Crown.

Bloustein, Edward J. 1964/1984. Privacy as an aspect of human dignity. In *Philosophical dimensions of privacy*, ed. Ferdinand David Schoeman, 156–202. Cambridge, MA: Cambridge University Press.

Boltanski, Luc and Éve Chiapello. 2005. *The new spirit of capitalism*. London: Verso.

Botsman, Rachel and Roo Rogers. 2011. *What's mine is yours: How collaborative consumption is changing the way we live*. London: Collins.

Bourdieu, Pierre. 1986. *Distinction: A social critique of the judgement of taste*. London: Routledge.

Bourdieu, Pierre. 1986/1997. The forms of capital. In *Education: Culture, economy, society*, ed. A.H. Halsey, Hugh Lauder, Phillip Brown and Amy Stuart Wells, 46–58. Oxford: Oxford University Press.

boyd, danah. 2009. "Social media is here to stay . . . Now what?" *Microsoft Research Tech Fest*, Redmond, Washington, DC, 26 February. www.danah.org/papers/talks/MSRTechFest2009.html (accessed on 26 September 2016).

boyd, danah. 2010. Social network sites as networked publics: Affordances, dynamics, and implications. In *A networked self: Identity, community, and culture on social network sites*, ed. Zizi Papacharissi, 39–58. New York: Routledge.

Brecht, Bertolt. 1932/2000. The radio as an apparatus of communications. In *Brecht on Film & Radio*, ed. Marc Silberman, 41–46. London: Methuen.

British Psychological Society (BPS). 2009. *Code of ethics and conduct*. Leicester: BPS.

British Sociological Association (BSA). 2002. *Statement of ethical practice*. https://www.britsoc.co.uk/equality-diversity/statement-of-ethical-practice (accessed on 26 September 2016).

Bruns, Axel. 2008. *Blogs, Wikipedia, Second Life, and beyond: From production to produsage*. New York: Peter Lang.

Buczynski, Beth. 2012. The Gen Y guide to collaborative consumption. In *Share or die: Voices of the get lost generation in the age of crisis*, ed. Malcolm Harris and Neal Gorenflo, 95–103. Gabriola Island: New Society Publishers.

Bunz, Mercedes. 2013. As you like it: Critique in the era of affirmative discourse. In *"Unlike us" reader: Social media monopolies and their alternatives*, ed. Geert Lovink and Miriam Rasch, 137–145. Amsterdam: Institute of Network Cultures.

Burston, Jonathan, Nick Dyer-Witheford and Alison Hearn, eds. 2010. Digital labour. Special issue. *Ephemera* 10 (3/4): 214–539.

Cabello, Florencio, Marta G. Franco and Alexandra Haché. 2013. Towards a free federated social web: Lorea takes the networks! In *"Unlike us" reader: Social media monopolies and their alternatives*, ed. Geert Lovink and Miriam Rasch, 338–346. Amsterdam: Institute of Network Cultures.

Caiani, Manuela and Patricia Kröll. 2015. The transnationalization of the extreme right and the use of the Internet. *International Journal of Comparative and Applied Criminal Justice* 39 (4): 331–351.

Calabrese, Andrew and Colin Sparks, eds. 2004. *Toward a political economy of culture*. Lanham, MD: Rowman & Littlefield.

Calhoun, Craig, ed. 1992a. *Habermas and the public sphere*. Cambridge, MA: MIT Press.

Calhoun, Craig. 1992b. Introduction: Habermas and the public sphere. In *Habermas and the public sphere*, ed. Craig Calhoun, 1–48. Cambridge, MA: MIT Press.

Calhoun, Craig. 1995. *Critical social theory*. Cambridge, MA: Blackwell.

Calhoun, Craig, Joseph Gertes, James Moody, Steven Pfaff and Indermohan Virk. 2007. General introduction. In *Classical sociological theory*, ed. Craig Calhoun, Joseph Gertes, James Moody, Steven Pfaff and Indermohan Virk, 1–16. Malden, MA: Blackwell.

Cammaerts, Bart. 2008. Critiques on the participatory potentials of web 2.0. *Communication, Culture & Critique* 1 (4): 358–377.

Carpentier, Nico. 2011. *Media and participation: A site of ideological-democratic struggle*. Bristol: Intellect.

Carpentier, Nico and Benjamin de Cleen. 2008. Introduction: Blurring participations and convergences. In *Participation and media production*, ed. Nico Carpentier and Benjamin de Cleen, 1–12. Newcastle: Cambridge Scholars.

Carr, Nicholas. 2011. Questioning Wikipedia. In *Critical point of view: A Wikipedia reader*, ed. Geert Lovink and Nathaniel Tkacz, 309–324. Amsterdam: Institute of Network Cultures.

Castells, Manuel. 2000. *End of millennium*. The information age: Economy, society and culture, Volume III (2nd edition). Malden, MA: Blackwell.

Castells, Manuel. 2004. *The power of identity*. The information age: Economy, society and culture, Volume II (2nd edition). Malden, MA: Blackwell.

Castells, Manuel. 2009. *Communication power*. Oxford: Oxford University Press.

Castells, Manuel. 2010. *The rise of the network society*. The information age: Economy, society and culture, Volume I (2nd edition with a new preface). Malden, MA: Wiley-Blackwell.

Castells, Manuel. 2012. *Networks of outrage and hope: Social movements in the Internet age*. Cambridge: Polity Press.

Castells, Manuel. 2015. *Networks of outrage and hope: Social movements in the Internet age* (2nd edition). Cambridge: Polity Press.

Castoriadis, Cornelius. 1991. *Philosophy, politics, autonomy*. Oxford: Oxford University Press.

Castoriadis, Cornelius. 1998. *The imaginary institution of society*. Cambridge, MA: MIT Press.

Chan, Jenny. 2013. A suicide survivor: The life of a Chinese worker. *New Technology, Work and Employment* 28 (2): 84–99.

Chan, Jenny and Ngai Pun. 2010. Suicide as protest for the new generation of Chinese migrant workers: Foxconn, global capital, and the state. *The Asia-Pacific Journal* 37 (2): 1–50.

Chan, Jenny, Ngai Pun and Mark Selden. 2013. The politics of global production: Apple, Foxconn and China's new working class. *New Technology, Work and Employment* 28 (2): 100–115.

Chandler, David. 2015. A world without causation: Big data and the coming age of posthumanism. *Millennium: Journal of International Studies* 43 (3): 833–851.

Chase-Dunn, Christopher. 2010. Adam Smith in Beijing: A world-systems perspective. *Historical Materialism* 18 (1): 39–51.

China Labor Watch. 2015. Analyzing labor conditions of Pegatron and Foxconn: Apple's low-cost reality. www.chinalaborwatch.org/upfile/2015_02_11/Analyzing%20Labor%20Conditions%20of%20Pegatron%20and%20Foxconn_vF.pdf (accessed on 26 September 2016).

Chomsky, Noam. 2011. *9-11: Was there an alternative?* New York: Seven Stories Press.

Coleman, Gabriella. *Hacker, hoaxer, whistleblower, spy: The many faces of Anonymous.* 2014. London: Verso.

Comer, Douglas E. 2004. *Computer networks and Internets.* Upper Saddle River, NJ: Pearson.

Compaine, Benjamin. 2001. Declare the war won. In *The digital divide: Facing a crisis or creating a myth?*, ed. Benjamin Compaine, 315–336. Cambridge, MA: MIT Press.

Comscore. 2012. *The power of Like2: How social marketing works.* White Paper. www.comscore.com/ger/Insights/Presentations_and_Whitepapers/2012/The_Power_of_Like_2_How_Social_Marketing_Works (accessed on 25 November 2015).

Couldry, Nick. 2002. *The place of media power.* London: Routledge.

Curran, James. 1991. Rethinking the media as a public sphere. In *Communication and citizenship: Journalism and the public sphere*, ed. Peter Dahlgren and Colin Sparks, 27–57. London: Routledge.

Curran, James. 2002. *Media and power.* London: Routledge.

Curran, James. 2012. Rethinking internet history. In *Misunderstanding the Internet*, ed. James Curran, Natalie Fenton and Des Freedman, 34–65. London: Routledge.

Curran, James, Natalie Fenton and Des Freedman. 2012. *Misunderstanding the Internet.* London: Routledge.

Curran, James and Jean Seaton. 2010. *Power without responsibility: Press, broadcasting and the Internet in Britain* (7th edition). London: Routledge.

Dahlberg, Lincoln. 2001. The Habermasian public sphere encounters cyber-reality. *Javnost* 8 (3): 83–96.

Dahlberg, Lincoln. 2004. Net-public sphere research: Beyond the "first phase". *Javnost* 11 (1): 27–44.

Dahlgren, Peter. 2005. The Internet, public spheres, and political communication. *Political Communication* 22 (2): 147–162.

Dahlgren, Peter. 2009. *Media and political engagement.* Cambridge: Cambridge University Press.

Dean, Jodi. 2005. Communicative capitalism: Circulation and the foreclosure of politics. *Cultural Politics* 1 (1): 51–74.

Dean, Jodi. 2010. *Blog politics.* Cambridge: Polity Press.

Dean, Jodi. 2012. *The communist horizon.* London: Verso.

DeKeseredy, Walter S. 2011. *Contemporary critical criminology.* London: Routledge.

DeKeseredy, Walter S., Shahid Alvi and Martin D. Schwartz. 2006. Left realism revisited. In *Advancing critical criminology*, ed. Walter S. DeKeseredy and Barbara Perry, 19–41. Lanham, MD: Lexington.

della Porta, Donatella and Alice Mattoni. 2015. Social networking sites in pro-democracy and anti-austerity protests. Some thoughts from a social movement perspective. In *Social media, politics and the state: Protests, revolutions, riots, crime and politics in the age of Facebook, Twitter and YouTube*, ed. Daniel Trottier and Christian Fuchs, 39–63. New York: Routledge.

Derrida, Jacques. 1994. *Specters of Marx.* New York: Routledge.

Deuze, Mark. 2007. *Media work*. Cambridge: Polity Press.

Deuze, Mark. 2008. Corporate appropriation of participatory culture. In *Participation and media production*, ed. Nico Carpentier and Benjamin de Cleen, 27–40. Newcastle: Cambridge Scholars.

Durkheim, Émile. 1982. *Rules of sociological method*. New York: Free Press.

Dwyer, Catherine. 2007. Digital relationships in the "MySpace" generation: Results from a qualitative study. In *Proceedings of the 40th Hawaii International Conference on System Sciences*. Los Alamitos, CA: IEEE Press.

Dwyer, Catherine, Starr Roxanne Hiltz and Katia Passerini. 2007. Trust and privacy concern within social networking sites: A comparison of Facebook and MySpace. In *Proceedings of the 13th Americas Conference on Information Systems*. Redhook, NY: Curran.

Dyer-Witheford, Nick. 1999. *Cyber-Marx: Cycles and circuits of struggle in high-technology capitalism*. Urbana, IL: Universiy of Illinois Press.

Dyer-Witheford, Nick. 2007. Commonism. *Turbulence* 1. http://turbulence.org.uk/turbulence-1/commonism/ (accessed on 3 July 2013).

Dyer-Witheford, Nick. 2009. *The circulation of the common*. www.globalproject.info/it/in_movimento/nick-dyer-witheford-the-circulation-of-the-common/4797 (accessed on 22 November 2015).

Dyer-Witheford Nick. 2014. The global worker and the digital front. In *Critique, social media and the information society*, ed. Christian Fuchs and Marisol Sandoval, 165–178. New York: Routledge.

Dyer-Witheford, Nick. 2015. *Cyber-proletariat: Global labour in the digital vortex*. London: Pluto Press.

Eagleton, Terry. 2011. *Why Marx was right*. London and New Haven, CT: Yale University Press.

Eley, Geoff. 1992. Nations, public and political cultures: Placing Habermas in the nineteenth century. In *Habermas and the public sphere*, ed. Craig Calhoun, 289–339. Cambridge, MA: MIT Press.

Elliott, Anthony. 2009. *Contemporary social theory*. London: Routledge.

Engels, Friedrich. 1843/1844. Outlines of a critique of political economy. In *Economic and philosophic manuscripts of 1844 and the Communist Manifesto*, 171–202. Amherst, MA: Prometheus.

Engels, Friedrich. 1846. The condition of the working class in England. In *MECW, Volume 4*, 295–596. New York: International Publishers.

Engels, Friedrich. 1886. *Dialectics of nature*. New York: International Publishers.

Enyedy, Edgar and Nataniel Tkacz. 2011. "Good luck with your wikiPAIDia": Reflections on the 2002 Fork of the Spanish Wikipedia. An interview with Edgar Enyedy. In *Critical point of view: A Wikipedia reader*, ed. Geert Lovink and Nathaniel Tkacz, 110–118. Amsterdam: Institute of Network Cultures.

Enzensberger, Hans Magnus. 1970/1997. Baukasten zu einer Theorie der Medien. In *Baukasten zu einer Theorie der Medien: Kritische Diskurse zur Pressefreiheit*, 97–132. München: Fischer.

Ess, Charles. 2009. *Digital media ethics*. Cambridge: Polity Press.

Etzioni, Amitai. 1999. *The limits of privacy*. New York: Basic Books.

Federal Trade Commission. 2000. *Privacy online: Fair information practices in the electronic marketplace*. www.ftc.gov/reports/privacy2000/privacy2000.pdf (accessed on 3 July 2013).

Feenberg, Andrew. 2002. *Transforming technology: A critical theory revisited*. Oxford: Oxford University Press.

Fenton, Natalie. The internet and social networking. In *Misunderstanding the Internet*, ed. James Curran, Natalie Fenton and Des Freedman, 123–148. London: Routledge.

Findahl, Olle. 2012. *Swedes and the Internet*. Stockholm: SE.

Fisher, Eran. 2010a. Contemporary technology discourse and the legitimation of capitalism. *European Journal of Social Theory* 13 (2): 229–252.

Fisher, Eran. 2010b. *Media and new capitalism in the digital age: The spirit of networks*. Basingstoke: Palgrave Macmillan.

Fogel, Joshua and Elham Nehmad. 2009. Internet social network communities: Risk taking, trust, and privacy concerns. *Computers in Human Behavior* 25 (1): 153–160.

Foglia, Marc. 2008. *Wikipedia, média de la connaissance démocratique?* Limoges: FYP.

Foster, John Bellamy and Fred Magdoff. 2009. *The great financial crisis: Causes and consequences*. New York: Monthly Review Press.

Foster, John Bellamy and Robert W. McChesney. 2012. The global stagnation and China. *Monthly Review* 63 (9): 1–28.

Foucault, Michel. 1977. *Discipline and punish*. New York: Vintage.

Foucault, Michel. 1980. *Power/knowledge: Selected interviews and other writings, 1972–77*. Brighton: Harvester.

Frankfurt, Harry G. 2005. *On bullshit*. Princeton, NJ: Princeton University Press.

Fraser, Nancy. 1992. Rethinking the public sphere. In *Habermas and the public sphere*, ed. Craig Calhoun, 109–142. Cambridge, MA: MIT Press.

Freedman, Des. 2012. Web 2.0 and the death of the blockbuster economy. In *Misunderstanding the Internet*, ed. James Curran, Natalie Fenton and Des Freedman, 69–94. London: Routledge.

Freedman, Des. 2014. *The contradictions of media power*. London: Bloomsbury Academic.

Friedman, Thomas. 2013. Welcome to the "sharing economy". *The New York Times* online. 20 July. http://www.nytimes.com/2013/07/21/opinion/sunday/friedman-welcome-to-the-sharing-economy.html?_r=0 (accessed on 26 September 2016).

Fröbel, Folker, Jürgen Heinrichs and Otto Kreye. 1981. *The new international division of labour*. Cambridge: Cambridge University Press.

Fuchs, Christian. 2003a. Some implications of Pierre Bourdieu's works for a theory of social self-organization. *European Journal of Social Theory* 6 (4): 387–408.

Fuchs, Christian. 2003b. Structuration theory and self-organization. *Systemic Practice and Action Research* 16 (2): 133–167.

Fuchs, Christian. 2008a. *Internet and society: Social theory in the information age*. New York: Routledge.

Fuchs, Christian. 2008b. Review essay of "Wikinomics: How mass collaboration changes everything", by Don Tapscott and Anthony D. Williams. *International Journal of Communication* 2, Review Section: 1–11.

Fuchs, Christian. 2009a. Information and communication technologies and society: A contribution to the critique of the political economy of the Internet. *European Journal of Communication* 24 (1): 69–87.

Fuchs, Christian. 2009b. *Social networking sites and the surveillance society: A critical case study of the usage of studiVZ, Facebook, and MySpace by students in Salzburg in the context of electronic surveillance*. Salzburg/Vienna: Research Group UTI.

Fuchs, Christian. 2010a. Alternative media as critical media. *European Journal of Social Theory* 13 (2): 173–192.

Fuchs, Christian. 2010b. Grounding critical communication studies: An inquiry into the communication theory of Karl Marx. *Journal of Communication Inquiry* 34 (1): 15–41.

Fuchs, Christian. 2010c. Labor in informational capitalism and on the Internet. *The Information Society* 26 (3): 179–196.

Fuchs, Christian. 2010d. Social networking sites and complex technology assessment. *International Journal of E-Politics* 1 (3): 19–38.

Fuchs, Christian. 2010e. studiVZ: Social networking sites in the surveillance society. *Ethics and Information Technology* 12 (2): 171–185.

Fuchs, Christian. 2011a. Critique of the political economy of web 2.0 surveillance. In *Internet and surveillance: The challenges of web 2.0 and social media*, ed. Christian Fuchs, Kees Boersma, Anders Albrechtslund and Marisol Sandoval, 31–70. New York: Routledge.

Fuchs, Christian. 2011b. *Foundations of critical media and information studies*. New York: Routledge.

Fuchs, Christian. 2011c. How can surveillance be defined? *MATRIZes* 5 (1): 109–133.

Fuchs, Christian. 2012a. Dallas Smythe today – the audience commodity, the digital labour debate, Marxist Political Economy and Critical Theory: Prolegomena to a digital labour theory of value. *tripleC: Communication, Capitalism & Critique: Journal for a Global Sustainable Information Society* 10 (2): 692–740.

Fuchs, Christian. 2012b. Some reflections on Manuel Castells' book "Networks of outrage and hope: Social movements in the Internet age". *tripleC: Communication, Capitalism & Critique: Journal for a Global Sustainable Information Society* 10 (2): 775–797.

Fuchs, Christian. 2012c. With or without Marx? With or without capitalism? A rejoinder to Adam Arvidsson and Eleanor Colleoni. *tripleC: Communication, Capitalism & Critique: Journal for a Global Sustainable Information Society* 10 (2): 633–645.

Fuchs, Christian. 2013a. Political economy and surveillance theory. *Critical Sociology* 39 (5): 671–687.

Fuchs, Christian. 2013b. Societal and ideological impacts of Deep Packet Inspection (DPI) Internet surveillance. *Information, Communication and Society* 16 (8): 1328–1359.

Fuchs, Christian. 2014a. *Digital labour and Karl Marx*. New York: Routledge.

Fuchs, Christian. 2014b. *OccupyMedia! The Occupy movement and social media in crisis capitalism*. Winchester: Zero Books.

Fuchs, Christian. 2015a. *Culture and economy in the age of social media*. New York: Routledge.

Fuchs, Christian. 2015b. Reflections on Todd Wolfson's book "Digital Rebellion: The Birth of the Cyber Left". *tripleC: Communication, Capitalism & Critique* 13 (1): 163–168.

Fuchs, Christian. 2016a. *Critical theory of communication: New readings of Lukács, Adorno, Marcuse, Honneth and Habermas in the age of the Internet*. London: University of Westminster Press.

Fuchs, Christian. 2016b. Expanding tweets from 140 characters to 10,000? Not nearly radical enough. *The Conversation*, 7 January. https://theconversation.com/expanding-tweets-from-140-characters-to-10-000-not-nearly-radical-enough-52851 (accessed on 26 September 2016).

Fuchs, Christian. 2016c. *Reading Marx in the information age: A media and communication studies perspective on* Capital Volume 1. New York: Routledge.

Fuchs, Christian. 2016d. Red scare 2.0: User-generated ideology in the age of Jeremy Corbyn and social media. *Journal of Language and Politics* 15 (4): 369–398.

Fuchs, Christian, Kees Boersma, Anders Albrechtslund and Marisol Sandoval, eds. 2012. *Internet and surveillance: The challenges of web 2.0 and social media*. London: Routledge.

Fuchs, Christian and Wolfgang Hofkirchner. 2005. Self-organization, knowledge, and responsibility. *Kybernetes* 34 (1–2): 241–260.

Fuchs, Christian, Wolfgang Hofkirchner, Matthias Schafranek, Celina Raffl, Marisol Sandoval and Robert Bichler. 2010. Theoretical foundations of the web: Cognition, communication, and co-operation. Towards an understanding of web 1.0, 2.0, 3.0. *Future Internet* 2 (1): 41–59.

Fuchs, Christian and Vincent Mosco, eds. 2012. Marx is back – The importance of Marxist theory and research for Critical Communication Studies today. *tripleC: Communication, Capitalism & Critique* 10 (2): 127–632.

Fuchs, Christian and Vincent Mosco, eds. 2016a. *Marx in the age of digital capitalism*. Studies in critical social sciences, Volume 80. Leiden: Brill.

Fuchs, Christian and Vincent Mosco, eds. 2016b. *Marx and the political economy of the media*. Studies in critical social sciences, Volume 79. Leiden: Brill.

Fuchs, Christian and Daniel Trottier. 2015. Towards a theoretical model of social media surveillance in contemporary society. *Communications: European Journal of Communication Research* 40 (1): 113–135.

Furhoff, Lars. 1973. Some reflections on newspaper concentration. *Scandinavian Economic History Review* 21 (1): 1–27.

Galtung, Johan. 1990. Cultural violence. *Journal of Peace Research* 27 (3): 291–305.

Gandy, Oscar H. 1993. *The panoptic sort: A political economy of personal information*. Boulder, CO: Westview Press.

Gandy, Oscar H. 2009. *Coming to terms with chance: Engaging rational discrimination and cumulative disadvantage*. Farnham: Ashgate.

Gandy, Oscar H. 2011. Consumer protection in cyberspace. *tripleC: Communication, Capitalism & Critique: Journal for a Global Sustainable Information Society* 9 (2): 175–189.

Gansky, Lisa. 2012. *The mesh: Why the future of business is sharing*. London: Penguin.

Garnham, Nicholas. 1990. *Capitalism and communication*. London: SAGE.

Garnham, Nicholas. 1992. The media and the public sphere. In *Habermas and the public sphere*, ed. Craig Calhoun, 359–376. Cambridge, MA: MIT Press.

Garnham, Nicholas. 2000. *Emancipation, the media, and modernity: Arguments about the media and social theory*. Oxford: Oxford University Press.

Garnham, Nicholas. 2011. The political economy of communication revisited. In *The handbook of political economy of communication*, ed. Janet Wasko, Graham Murdock and Helena Sousa, 41–61. Malden, MA: Wiley-Blackwell.

Gauntlett, David. 2011. *Making is connecting: The social meaning of creativity, from DIY and knitting to YouTube and Web 2.0*. Cambridge: Polity Press.

Gehl, Robert. 2014. *Reverse engineering social media: Software, culture and political economy in new media capitalism*. Philadelphia, PA: Temple University Press.

Gerbaudo, Paolo. 2012. *Tweets and the streets: Social media and contemporary activism*. London: Pluto Press.

Ghonim, Wael. 2012. *Revolution 2.0: The power of the people is greater than the people in power. A memoir*. New York: Houghton Mifflin Harcourt.

Giddens, Anthony. 1981. *A contemporary critique of Historical Materialism. Vol. 1: Power, property and the state*. Basingstoke: Macmillan.

Giddens, Anthony. 1984. *The constitution of society: Outline of the theory of structuration*. Cambridge: Polity Press.

Giddens, Anthony. 1985. *A contemporary critique of Historical Materialism. Vol. 2: The nation-state and violence*. Cambridge: Polity Press.

Girard, Bernard. 2009. *The Google way: How one company is revolutionizing management as we know it*. San Francisco, CA: No Starch Press.

Gladwell, Malcolm. 2010. Small change: Why the revolution will not be tweeted. *The New Yorker* October: 42–49.

Gladwell, Malcolm and Clay Shirky. 2011. From innovation to revolution: Do social media make protests possible? *Foreign Affairs* 90 (2): 153–154.

Glott, Ruediger, Philipp Schmidt and Rishab Ghosh. 2010. *Wikipedia survey – Overview of results*. www.ris.org/uploadi/editor/1305050082Wikipedia_Overview_15March2010-FINAL.pdf (accessed on 22 November 2015).

Golding, Peter and Graham Murdock. 1997a. Introduction: Communication and capitalism. In *The political economy of the media I*, ed. Peter Golding and Graham Murdock, xiii–xviii. Cheltenham: Edward Elgar.

Golding, Peter and Graham Murdock, eds. 1997b. *The political economy of the media*. Cheltenham: Edward Elgar.

Goodwin, Jeff. 2001. *No other way out: States and revolutionary movements, 1945–1991*. Cambridge: Cambridge University Press.

Graham, Mark. 2011. Wiki space: Palimpsets and the politics of exclusion. In *Critical point of view: A Wikipedia reader*, ed. Geert Lovink and Nathaniel Tkacz, 269–282. Amsterdam: Institute of Network Cultures.

Green, Joshua and Henry Jenkins. 2009. The moral economy of web 2.0. Audience research and convergence culture. In *Media industries: History, theory, and method*, ed. Jennifer Holt and Alisa Perren, 213–225. Malden, MA: Wiley-Blackwell.

Gross, Ralph and Alessandro Acquisti. 2005. Information revelation and privacy in online social networks. In *Proceedings of the 2005 ACM workshop on privacy in the electronic society*, 71–80. New York: ACM Press.

Guattari, Félix and Antonio Negri. 1990. *Communists like us*. New York: Semiotext(e).

Habermas, Jürgen. 1971. *Knowledge and human interest*. Boston, MA: Beacon Press.

Habermas, Jürgen. 1984. *Theory of communicative action* (Vol. 1). Boston, MA: Beacon Press.

Habermas, Jürgen. 1987. *Theory of communicative action* (Vol. 2). Boston, MA: Beacon Press.

Habermas, Jürgen. 1989a. The horrors of autonomy: Carl Schmitt in English. In *The new conservatism: Cultural criticism and the historians' debate*, 128–139. Cambridge, MA: MIT Press.

Habermas, Jürgen. 1989b. The public sphere: An encyclopedia article. In *Critical theory and society: A reader*, ed. Stephen E. Bronner and Douglas Kellner, 136–142. New York: Routledge.

Habermas, Jürgen. 1989c. *The structural transformation of the public sphere*. Cambridge, MA: MIT Press.

Habermas, Jürgen. 1992. Further reflections on the public sphere and concluding remarks. In *Habermas and the public sphere*, ed. Craig Calhoun, 421–479. Cambridge, MA: MIT Press.

Habermas, Jürgen. 1996. *Between facts and norms*. Cambridge, MA: MIT Press.

Habermas, Jürgen. 2006. Political communication in media society: Does democracy still enjoy an epistemic dimension? The impact of normative theory on empirical research. *Communication Theory* 16 (4): 411–426.

Habermas, Jürgen. 2009. Es beginnt mit dem Zeigefinger. *Die Zeit* online 51, 22 December. www.zeit.de/2009/51/Habermas-Tomasello (accessed on 26 September 2016).

Hall, Stuart. 1981/1988. Notes on deconstructing "the popular". In *Cultural theory & popular culture: A reader*, ed. John Storey, 442–453 (2nd edition). Athens, GA: University of Georgia Press.

Hall, Stuart, Chas Critcher, Tony Jefferson, John Clarke and Brian Roberts. 1978. *Policing the crisis: Mugging, the state and law and order*. London: Macmillan.

Hardt, Michael and Antonio Negri. 2009. *Commonwealth*. Cambridge, MA: Belknap Press.

Hardy, Jonathan. 2010. The contribution of critical political economy. In *Media and society*, ed. James Curran, 186–209. London: Bloomsbury.

Hardy, Jonathan. 2014. *Critical political economy of the media: An introduction*. London: Routledge.

Hars, Alexander and Shaosong Ou. 2002. Working for free? Motivations for participating in open-source projects. *International Journal of Electronic Commerce* 6 (3): 25–39.

Hart-Landsberg, Martin. 2010. The U.S. economy and China: Capitalism, class, and crisis. *Monthly Review* 61 (9): 14–31.

Harvey, David. 2005a. *Spaces of neoliberalization: Towards a theory of uneven geographical development*. Heidelberg: Franz Steiner Verlag.

Harvey, David. 2005b. *The new imperialism*. Oxford: Oxford University Press.

Harvey, David. 2007. *A brief history of neoliberalism*. Oxford: Oxford University Press.

Harvey, David. 2010a. *A companion to Marx's* Capital. London: Verso.

Harvey, David. 2010b. *The enigma of capital*. London: Profile Books.

Harvey, David. 2012. *Rebel cities: From the right to the city to the urban revolution*. London: Verso.

Hayek, Friedrich August. 1948. *Individualism and economic order*. Chicago, IL: University of Chicago Press.

Hayek, Friedrich August. 1988. *The fatal conceit: The errors of socialism*. London: Routledge.

Hayes, Ben. 2009. *NeoConOpticon: The EU security-industrial complex*. Amsterdam: Transnational Institute/Statewatch.

Hayes, Ben. 2010. "Full spectrum dominance" as European Union security policy. On the trail of the "NeoConOpticon". In *Surveillance and democracy*, ed. Kevin D. Haggerty and Minas Samatas, 148–169. Abingdon: Routledge.

Hayes, Ben. 2012. The surveillance-industrial complex. In *Routledge handbook of surveillance studies*, ed. Kirstie Ball, Kevin D. Haggerty and David Lyon, 167–175. Abingdon: Routledge.

Hegel, Georg Willhelm Friedrich. 1991. *The encyclopaedia logic*. Indianapolis, IN: Hackett.

Held, David. 1980. *Introduction to critical theory*. Berkeley, CA: University of California Press.

Held, David. 2006. *Models of democracy* (3rd edition). Cambridge: Polity Press.

Hinton, Sam and Larissa Hjorth. 2013. *Understanding social media*. Los Angeles, CA: SAGE.

Hodge, Matthew J. 2006. The Fourth Amendment and privacy issues on the "new" Internet: Facebook.com and MySpace.com. *Southern Illinois University Law Journal* 31: 95–122.

Hofkirchner, Wolfgang. 2002. *Projekt Eine Welt: Kognition – Kommunikation – Kooperation: Versuch über die Selbstorganisation der Informationsgesellschaft*. Münster: LIT.

Hofkirchner, Wolfgang. 2013. *Emergent information: A unified theory of information framework*. Singapore: World Scientific.

Holzer, Horst. 1973. *Kommunikationssoziologie*. Reinbek: Rowohlt.

Holzer, Horst. 1994. *Medienkommunikation*. Opladen: Westdeutscher Verlag.

Hong, Yu. 2011. *Labor, class formation, and China's informationalized policy of economic development.* Lanham, MD: Lexington Books.

Horkheimer, Max. 1947. *Eclipse of reason.* New York: Continuum.

Horkheimer, Max. 2002. *Critical theory.* New York: Continuum.

Horkheimer, Max and Theodor W. Adorno. 2002. *Dialectic of enlightenment.* Stanford, CA: Stanford University Press.

House of Commons Committee of Public Accounts. 2013a. *Tax avoidance: Google.* London: The Stationery Office Limited.

House of Commons Committee of Public Accounts. 2013b. *Tax avoidance: The role of large accountancy firms.* London: The Stationery Office Limited.

House of Commons Committee of Public Accounts. 2015. *Improving.* London: The Stationery Office Limited

Howe, Jeff. 2008. *Crowdsourcing: Why the power of the crowd is driving the future of business.* New York: Three Rivers Press.

Huang, Yasheng. 2008. *Capitalism with Chinese characteristics: Entrepreneurship and the state.* Cambridge: Cambridge University Press.

Hung, Ho-fung, ed. 2009. *China and the transformation of global capitalism.* Baltimore, MD: Johns Hopkins University Press.

Hung, Ho-fung. 2012. Sinomania: Global crisis, China's crisis. *Socialist Register* 48: 217–234.

Hunsinger, Jeremy and Theresa Senft, eds. 2014. *The social media handbook.* New York: Routledge.

Huws, Ursula. 2003. *The making of a cybertariat: Virtual work in a real world.* New York: Monthly Review Press.

Huws, Ursula. 2014. *Labor in the global digital economy: The cybertariat comes of age.* New York: Monthly Review Press.

Huws, Ursula and Simon Joyce. 2016. Size of the UK's "gig economy" revealed for the first time. www.feps-europe.eu/assets/a82bcd12-fb97-43a6-9346-24242695a183/crowd-working-surveypdf. pdf (accessed on 17 February 2016).

International Labour Organization (ILO). 2010. *World of work report 2010.* Geneva: ILO.

International Labour Organization (ILO). 2012. *Global wage report 2012/2013.* Geneva: ILO.

International Labour Organization (ILO). 2015. *Global wage report 2014/2015.* Geneva: ILO.

Jakobsson, Peter and Fredrik Stiernstedt. 2010. Pirates of Silicon Valley: State of exception and dispossession in web 2.0. *First Monday* 15 (7). http://firstmonday.org/ojs/index.php/fm/article/view/2799 (accessed on 26 September 2016).

Jameson, Frederic. 1988. On Negt and Kluge. *October* 46: 151–177.

Jarrett, Kylie. 2015. Devaluing binaries: Marxist feminism and the value of consumer labour. In *Reconsidering value and labour in the digital age*, ed. Eran Fisher and Christian Fuchs, 207–223. Basingstoke: Palgrave Macmillan.

Jarrett, Kylie. 2016. *Feminism, labour and digital media. The digital housewife.* New York: Routledge.

Jarvis, Jeff. 2011. *Public parts: How sharing in the digital age improves the way we work and live.* New York: Simon & Schuster.

Jenkins, Henry. 1992. *Textual poachers: Television fans and participatory culture.* New York: Routledge.

Jenkins, Henry. 2006. *Fans, bloggers, and gamers.* New York: New York University Press.

Jenkins, Henry. 2008. *Convergence culture.* New York: New York University Press.

Jenkins, Henry. 2009. What happened before YouTube? In *YouTube*, ed. Jean Burgess and Joshua Green, 109–125. Cambridge: Polity Press.

Jenkins, Henry. 2014a. Participatory culture: From co-creating brand meaning to changing the world. *GfK Marketing Review* 6 (2): 34–39.

Jenkins, Henry. 2014b. Rethinking 'Rethinking convergence/culture'. *Cultural Studies* 28 (2): 267–297.

Jenkins, Henry and Nico Carpentier. 2013. Theorizing participatory intensities: A conversation about participation and politics. *Convergence* 19 (3): 265–286.

Jenkins, Henry, Sam Ford and Joshua Green. 2013. *Spreadable media: Creating value and meaning in a networked culture.* New York: New York University Press.

Jenkins, Henry, Xiaochang Li, Ana Domb Krauskopf and Joshua Green. 2009. *If it doesn't spread, it's dead: Eight parts.* www.henryjenkins.org/2009/02/if_it_doesnt_spread_its_dead_p.html (accessed on 1 August 2011).

Jenkins, Henry, Ravi Purushotma, Margaret Weigel, Katie Clinton and Alice J. Robison. 2009. Confronting the challenges of participatory culture. Chicago, IL: MacArthur Foundation.

Jessop, Bob. 2008. *State power: A strategic-relational approach.* Cambridge: Polity Press.

Jhally, Sut. 1987. *The codes of advertising.* New York: Routledge.

Jhally, Sut. 2006. *The spectacle of accumulation.* New York: Peter Lang.

Jin, Dal Yong and Andrew Feenberg. 2015. Commodity and community in social networking: Marx and the monetization of user-generated content. *The Information Society* 31 (1): 52–60.

John, Nicholas A. 2013. Sharing and web 2.0: The emergence of a keyword. *New Media & Society* 15 (2): 167–182.

Jullien, Nicolas. 2011. *Mais qui sont les Wikipédiens? Résultats d'études.* http://blog.wikimedia.fr/qui-sont-les-wikipediens-2961 (accessed on 3 July 2013).

Juris, Jeffrey S. 2012. Reflections on #occupy everywhere: Social media, public space, and emerging logics of aggregation. *American Ethnologist* 39 (2): 259–279.

Kang, Hyunjin and Matthew P. McAllister. 2011. Selling you and your clicks: Examining the audience commodification of Google. *tripleC: Communication, Capitalism & Critique: Journal for a Global Sustainable Information Society* 9 (2): 141–153.

Kant, Immanuel. 2002. *Groundwork for the metaphysics of morals.* New Haven, CT: Yale University Press.

Karatani, Kojin. 2005. *Transcritique.* Cambridge, MA: MIT Press.

Kellner, Douglas. 1989. *Critical theory, Marxism and modernity.* Baltimore, MD: Johns Hopkins University Press.

Kellner Douglas. 1995. *Media culture: Cultural studies, identity and politics between the modern and the postmodern.* London: Routledge.

Kellner, Douglas. 2009. Toward a critical media/cultural studies. In *Media/cultural studies: Critical approaches*, ed. Rhonda Hammer and Douglas Kellner, 5–24. New York: Peter Lang.

KhosraviNik, Majid. 2013. Critical discourse analysis, power, and new media discourse. *In Why discourse matters: Negotiating identity in the mediatized world*, ed. Yusuf Kalyango Jr. and Monika Weronika Kopytowska, 287–305. New York: Peter Lang.

Knoche, Manfred. 2005. Kommunikationswissenschaftliche Medienökonomie als Kritik der Politischen Ökonomie der Medien. In *Internationale partizipatorische Kommunikationspolitik*, ed. Petra Ahrweiler and Barbara Thomaß, 101–109. Münster: LIT.

Knoche, Manfred. 2016. The media industry's structural transformation in capitalism and the role of the state: Media economics in the age of digital communications. *tripleC: Communication, Capitalism & Critique* 14 (1): 18–47.

Kompatsiaris, Panos and Yiannis Mylonas. 2015. The rise of Nazism and the web: Social media as platforms of racist discourses in the context of the Greek economic crisis. In *Social media, politics and the state: Protests, revolutions, riots, crime and policing in the age of Facebook, Twitter and YouTube*, ed. Daniel Trottier and Christian Fuchs, 109–130. New York: Routledge.

Kostakis, Vasilis. 2010. Identifying and understanding the problems of Wikipedia's peer governance: The case of inclusionists versus deletionists. *First Monday* 15 (3).

Kovisto, Juha and Esa Valiverronen. 1996. The resurgence of the critical theories of public sphere. *Journal of Communication Inquiry* 20 (2): 18–36.

Kreilinger, Verena. 2014. *Research design & data analysis, presentation, and interpretation: Part two.* The Internet & Surveillance-Research Paper Series, Research Paper #14. Vienna: UTI Research Group.

Laclau, Ernesto and Chantalle Mouffe. 1985. *Hegemony and socialist strategy.* London: Verso.

Lanier, Jaron. 2013. *Who owns the future?* London: Allen Lane.

Lapavitsas, Costas. 2013. *Profiting without producing: How finance exploits us all.* London: Verso.

Lazarsfeld, Paul F. 1941/2004. Administrative and critical communications research. In *Mass communication and American social thought: Key texts, 1919–1968*, ed. John Durham Peters, 166–173. Lanham, MD: Rowman & Littlefield.

Leadbeater, Charles. 2009. *We-think: Mass innovation, not mass production* (2nd edition). London: Profile Books.

Lee, Micky. 2011. Google ads and the blindspot debate. *Media, Culture & Society* 33 (3): 433–447.

Lévy, Pierre. 1997. *Collective intelligence*. New York: Plenum.

Lewis, Kevin, Jason Kaufman and Nicholas Christakis. 2008. The taste for privacy: An analysis of college student privacy settings in an online social network. *Journal of Computer-Mediated Communication* 14 (1): 79–100.

Li, Minqi. 2008a. An age of transition: The United States, China, peak oil, and the demise of neoliberalism. *Monthly Review* 59 (11): 20–34.

Li, Minqi. 2008b. *The rise of China and the demise of the capitalist world economy*. London: Pluto Press.

Li, Minqi. 2016. *China and the 21st century crisis*. London: Pluto Press.

Lin, Chun. 2013. *China and global capitalism: Reflections on Marxism, history, and contemporary politics*. Basingstoke: Palgrave Macmillan.

Lindgren, Simon and Ragnar Lundström. 2011. Pirate culture and hacktivist mobilization: The cultural and social protocols of #WikiLeaks on Twitter. *New Media & Society* 13 (6): 999–1018.

Livant, Bill. 1979. The audience commodity: On the "blindspot" debate. *Canadian Journal of Political and Social Theory* 3 (1): 91–106.

Livingstone, Sonia. 2008. Taking risky opportunities in youthful content creation: Teenagers' use of social networking sites for intimacy, privacy and self-expression. *New Media & Society* 10 (3): 393–411.

Lotan, Gilad, Erhardt Graeff, Mike Ananny, Devin Gaffney, Ian Pearce and danah boyd. 2011. The Arab Spring! The revolutions were tweeted: Information flows during the 2011 Tunisian and Egyptian revolutions. *International Journal of Communication* 5: 1375–1405.

Lovink, Geert. 2008. *Zero comments: Blogging and critical internet culture*. New York: Routledge.

Lovink, Geert. 2011. *Networks without a cause: A critique of social media*. Cambridge: Polity Press.

Luhmann, Niklas. 1998. *Die Gesellschaft der Gesellschaft*. Frankfurt/Main: Suhrkamp.

Luhmann, Niklas. 2000. *Die Politik der Gesellschaft*. Frankfurt/Main: Suhrkamp.

Lukács, Georg. 1923/1972. *History and class consciousness*. Cambridge, MA: MIT Press.

Lund, Arwid. 2014. Playing, gaming, working and labouring: Framing the concepts and relations. *tripleC: Communication, Capitalism & Critique* 12 (2): 735–801.

Lupton, Deborah. 2015. *Digital sociology*. London: Routledge.

Luxemburg, Rosa. 1913/2003. *The accumulation of capital*. New York: Routledge.

Luxemburg, Rosa. 1916. The Junius pamphlet. In *Rosa Luxemburg speaks*, 371–477. New York: Pathfinder.

Lynd, Staughton. 1965. The new radicals and "participatory democracy". *Dissent* 12 (3): 324–333.

Lyon, David. 1994. *The electronic eye: The rise of surveillance society*. Cambridge: Polity.

Lyon, David. 2003. *Surveillance after September 11*. Cambridge: Polity.

Lyon, David. 2015. *Surveillance after Snowden*. Cambridge: Polity.

Macpherson, Crawford Brough. 1973. *Democratic theory*. Oxford: Oxford University Press.

Mager, Astrid. 2012. Algorithmic ideology: How capitalist society shapes search engines. *Information, Communication & Society* 15 (5): 769–787.

Mager, Astrid. 2014. Defining algorithmic ideology: Using ideology critique to scrutinize corporate search engines. *tripleC: Communication, Capitalism & Critique* 12 (1): 28–39.

Mandiberg, Michael. 2012. Introduction. In *The social media reader*, ed. Michael Mandiberg, 1–10. New York: New York University Press.

Manovich, Lev. 2009. Cultural analytics: Visualising cultural patterns in the era of "more media". http://manovich.net/content/04-projects/063-cultural-analytics-visualizing-cultural-patterns/60_article_2009.pdf (accessed on 26 September 2016).

Manyika, James et al. 2011. *Big data: The next frontier for innovation, competition, and productivity*. Washington, DC: McKinsey Global Institute.

Marcuse, Herbert. 1941. *Reason and revolution: Hegel and the rise of social theory* (2nd edition). London: Routledge.

Marcuse, Herbert. 1964. *One-dimensional man*. Boston, MA: Beacon Press.

Marcuse, Herbert. 1988. *Negations: Essays in critical theory*. London: Free Association Books.

Marwick, Alice. 2013. *Status update: Celebrity, publicity, and branding in the social media age*. New Haven, CT: Yale University Press.

Marx, Karl. 1842. Debates on the freedom of the press. In *Marx/Engels Collected Works (MECW), Volume 1*, 132–202. New York: International Publishers.

Marx, Karl. 1843a. Critique of Hegel's doctrine of the state. In *Early writings*, 57–198. London: Penguin.

Marx, Karl. 1843b. *Letter to Arnold Ruge*. https://www.marxists.org/archive/marx/works/download/Marx_Engels_Correspondence.pdf (accessed on 26 September 2016).

Marx, Karl. 1843c. On the Jewish question. In *Writings of the young Marx on philosophy and society*, 216–248. Indianapolis, IN: Hackett.

Marx, Karl. 1844. *Economic and philosophic manuscripts of 1844*. Mineola, NY: Dover.

Marx, Karl. 1857/1858. *Grundrisse: Foundations of the critique of political economy*. Harmondsworth: Penguin.

Marx, Karl. 1859. A contribution to the critique of the political economy. In *Marx/Engels Collected Works (MECW), Volume 29*, 257–417. New York: International Publishers.

Marx, Karl. 1867. *Capital. Volume I*. London: Penguin.

Marx, Karl. 1871. The civil war in France. In *Selected works in one volume*, 237–295. London: Lawrence & Wishart.

Marx, Karl. 1875. Critique of the Gotha programme. In *Selected works in one volume*, 297–317. London: Lawrence & Wishart.

Marx, Karl. 1885. *Capital. Volume II*. London: Penguin.

Marx, Karl. 1894. *Capital. Volume III*. London: Penguin.

Marx, Karl. 1974. *On freedom of the press & censorship*, ed. Saul K. Padover. New York: McGraw-Hill.

Marx, Karl. 1997. *Writings of the young Marx on philosophy and society*. Indianapolis, IN: Hackett.

Marx, Karl. 2000. *Selected writings*, ed. David McLellan (2nd edition). Oxford: Oxford University Press.

Marx, Karl and Friedrich Engels. 1846. *The German ideology*. Amherst, NY: Prometheus Books.

Marx, Karl and Friedrich Engels. 1848. The Communist Manifesto. In *Economic and philosophic manuscripts of 1844*, 203–243. Amherst, NY: Prometheus Books.

Marx, Karl and Friedrich Engels. 1968. *Selected works in one volume*. London: Lawrence & Wishart.

Mathiesen, Thomas. 2013. *Towards a surveillant society: The rise of surveillance systems in Europe*. Hook: Waterside Press.

Matofska, Benita. 2014. Critics of the sharing economy are missing the point altogether. *Guardian* online. 5 June. https://www.theguardian.com/media-network/media-network-blog/2014/jun/05/sharing-economy-critics-airbnb-uber (accessed on 26 September 2016).

Mattelart, Armand. 2010. *The globalization of surveillance*. Cambridge: Polity.

Maurer, Hermann, Tilo Balke, Frank Kappe, Narayanan Kulathuramaiyer, Stefan Weber and Bilal Zaka. 2007. *Report on dangers and opportunities posed by large search engines, particularly Google*. www.iicm. tugraz.at/iicm_papers/dangers_google.pdf (accessed on 22 November 2015).

Maxwell, Richard and Toby Miller. 2012. *Greening the media*. Oxford: Oxford University Press.

Mayer-Schönberger, Viktor and Kenneth Cukier. 2013. *Big data: A revolution that will transform how we live, work and think*. London: John Murray.

McChesney, Robert. 2008. *The political economy of media*. New York: Monthly Review Press.

McGuigan, Jim. 1998. What price the public sphere? In *Electronic empires: Global media and local resistances*, ed. Daya Kishan Thussu, 108–124. London: Hodder Arnold.

McGuigan, Lee and Vincent Manzerolle, eds. 2014. *The audience commodity in a digital age: Revisiting a critical theory of commercial media*. New York: Peter Lang.

McLuhan, Marshall. 2001. *Understanding media*. New York: Routledge.

McQuail, Denis. 2000. *McQuail's mass communication theory* (4th edition). London: SAGE.

McQuail, Denis. 2010. *McQuail's mass communication theory* (6th edition). London: SAGE.

MECW. 1975 et seq. *Marx/Engels Collected Works*. New York: International Publishers.

Meehan, Eileen. 2002. Gendering the commodity audience. Critical media research, feminism, and political economy. In *Media and Cultural Studies: KeyWorks*, ed. Meenakshi Gigi Durham and Douglas Kellner, 242–249 (2nd edition). Malden, MA: Wiley-Blackwell.

MEGA. 1975 et seq. *Marx/Engels Gesamtausgabe*. Berlin: Dietz.

Meikle, Graham. 2016. *Social media: Communication, sharing and visibility*. New York: Routledge.

Meikle, Graham and Sherman Young. 2012. *Media convergence: Networked digital media in everyday life*. Basingstoke: Palgrave Macmillan.

Mendelson, B. J. 2012. *Social media is bullshit*. New York: St. Martin's Press.

MEW. 1962 et seq. *Marx/Engels Werke*. Berlin: Dietz.

Mies, Maria. 1986. *Patriarchy & accumulation on a world scale: Women in the international division of labour*. London: Zed Books.

Mies, Maria, Veronika Bennholdt-Thomsen and Claudia von Werlhof. 1988. *Women: The last colony*. London: Zed Books.

Mill, John Stuart. 1965. *Principles of political economy* (2 volumes). London: University of Toronto Press.

Mill, John Stuart. 2002. *On liberty*. Mineola, NY: Dover.

Miller, Toby. 2008. "Step away from the croissant". Media Studies 3.0. In *The media and social theory*, ed. David Hesmondhalgh and Jason Toynbee, 213–230. London: Routledge.

Moglen, Eben. 2003. *The dotCommunist manifesto*. http://emoglen.law.columbia.edu/my_pubs/dcm.html#tex2html2 (accessed on 22 November 2015).

Monahan, Torin. 2010. *Surveillance in the time of insecurity*. New Brunswick, NJ: Rutgers University Press.

Moor, James H. 2000. Toward a theory of privacy in the information age. In *Cyberethics*, ed. Robert M. Baird, Reagan Ramsower and Stuart E. Rosenbaum, 200–212. Amherst, NY: Prometheus Books.

Moore, Barrington. 1984. *Privacy: Studies in social and cultural history*. Armonk, NY: M.E. Sharpe.

Morozov, Evgeny. 2009. The brave new world of slacktivism. www.npr.org/templates/story/story.php?storyId=104302141 (accessed on 13 November 2015).

Morozov, Evgeny. 2010. *The net delusion: How not to liberate the world*. London: Allen Lane.

Morozov, Evgeny. 2013. *To save everything, click here: Technology, solutionism and the urge to fix problems that don't exist*. London: Allen Lane.

Morozov, Evgeny. 2014. Don't believe the hype, the "sharing economy" masks a failing economy. *Guardian* online. 28 September. https://www.theguardian.com/commentisfree/2014/sep/28/sharing-economy-internet-hype-benefits-overstated-evgeny-morozov (accessed on 27 September 2016).

Mosco, Vincent. 2004. *The digital sublime*. Cambridge, MA: MIT Press.

Mosco, Vincent. 2009. *The political economy of communication* (2nd edition). London: SAGE.

Mosco, Vincent. 2014. *To the cloud: Big data in a turbulent world*. Boulder, CO: Paradigm.

Mosco, Vincent. 2016. Marx in the cloud. In *Marx in the age of digital capitalism*, ed. Christian Fuchs and Vincent Mosco, 516–535. Leiden: Brill.

Mosco, Vincent and Janet Wasko, eds. 1988. *The political economy of information*. Madison, WI: University of Wisconsin Press.

Mueller, Milton L., Andreas Kuehn and Stephanie Michelle Santoso. 2012. Policing the network: Using DPI for copyright enforcement. *Surveillance & Society* 9 (4): 348–364.

Murdock, Graham. 1978. Blindspots about Western Marxism: A reply to Dallas Smythe. In *The political economy of the media I*, ed. Peter Golding and Graham Murdock, 465–474. Cheltenham: Edward Elgar.

Murdock, Graham. 2011. Political economies as moral economies: Commodities, gifts, and public goods. In *The handbook of the political economy of communications*, ed. Janet Wasko, Graham Murdock and Helena Sousa, 13–40. Chicester: Wiley-Blackwell.

Murdock, Graham and Peter Golding. 1974. For a political economy of mass communications. In *The political economy of the media I*, ed. Peter Golding and Graham Murdock, 3–32. Cheltenham: Edward Elgar.

Murdock, Graham and Peter Golding. 2005. Culture, communications and political economy. In *Mass media and society* (4th edition), ed. James Curran and Michael Gurevitch, 60–83. London: Hodder.

Murthy, Dhiraj. 2013. *Twitter: Social communication in the Twitter age*. Cambridge: Polity Press.

National Bureau of Statistics of China. 2015. *Statistical communiqué of the People's Republic of China on the 2014 national economic and social development*. http://www.stats.gov.cn/english/PressRelease/201502/t20150228_687439.html (accessed on 25 November 2015).

Negri, Antonio. 1991. *Marx beyond Marx: Lessons on the Grundrisse*. London: Pluto Press.

Negt, Oskar and Alexander Kluge. 1972/1993. *Public sphere and experience: Toward an analysis of the bourgeois and proletarian public sphere*. Minneapolis, MN: University of Minnesota Press.

Nissenbaum, Helen. 2010. *Privacy in context*. Stanford, CA: Stanford University Press.

Noam, Eli. 2009. *Media ownership and concentration in America*. Oxford: Oxford University Press.

Nolan, Peter. 2012. *Is China buying the world?* Cambridge: Polity Press.

Nolan, Peter and Jin Zhang. 2010. Global competition after the financial crisis. *New Left Review* 64: 97–108.

Nye, Joseph. 2004. *Soft power: The means to success in world politics*. New York: Public Affairs.

O'Neil, Mathieu. 2009. *Cyberchiefs: Autonomy and authority in online tribes*. London: Pluto Press.

O'Neil, Mathieu. 2011. The sociology of critique in Wikipedia. *Critical Studies in Peer Production* RS 1.2: 1–11.

O'Reilly, Tim. 2005a. *What is web 2.0?* www.oreillynet.com/pub/a/oreilly/tim/news/2005/09/30/what-is-web-20.html?page=1 (accessed on 22 November 2015).

O'Reilly, Tim. 2005b. *Web 2.0: Compact definition*. http://radar.oreilly.com/2005/10/web-20-compact-definition.html (accessed on 22 November 2015).

O'Reilly, Tim and John Battelle. 2009. *Web squared: Web 2.0 five years on*. Special report. http://assets.en.oreilly.com/1/event/28/web2009_websquared-whitepaper.pdf (accessed on 22 November 2015).

Ofcom. 2014. *International communications market report 2014*. http://stakeholders.ofcom.org.uk/binaries/research/cmr/cmr14/icmr/ICMR_2014.pdf (accessed on 31 October 2015).

Ofcom. 2015a. *Adults' media use and attitudes*. http://stakeholders.ofcom.org.uk/binaries/research/media-literacy/media-lit-10years/2015_Adults_media_use_and_attitudes_report.pdf (accessed on 31 October 2015).

Ofcom. 2015b. *The communications market report 2015* [UK]. http://stakeholders.ofcom.org.uk/binaries/research/cmr/cmr15/CMR_UK_2015.pdf (accessed on 31 October 2015).

Ofcom. 2015c. The international communications market report 2015. http://stakeholders.ofcom.org.uk/binaries/research/cmr/cmr15/icmr15/icmr_2015.pdf (accessed on 27 September 2016).

Ofcom. 2016. The communications market report 2016 [UK]. http://stakeholders.ofcom.org.uk/binaries/research/cmr/cmr16/uk/CMR_UK_2016.pdf (accessed on 27 September 2016).

Orwell, George. 1945. *Animal farm*. Harlow: Heinemann.

PageFair and Adobe. 2015. *The cost of ad blocking. PageFair and Adobe 2015 ad blocking report*. http://downloads.pagefair.com/reports/2015_report-the_cost_of_ad_blocking.pdf (accessed on 31 October 2015).

Panitch, Leo. 2010. Giovanni Arrighi in Beijing: An alternative to capitalism? *Historical Materialism* 18 (1): 74–87.

Papacharissi, Zizi. 2002. The virtual sphere: The Internet as a public sphere. *New Media & Society* 4 (1): 9–27.

Papacharissi, Zizi. 2009. The virtual sphere 2.0: The Internet, the public shpere, and beyond. In *Routledge handbook of Internet politics*, ed. Andrew Chadwick and Philip N. Howard, 230–245. New York: Routledge.

Papacharissi, Zizi A. 2010. *A private sphere: Democracy in a digital age*. Cambridge: Polity.

Pardun, Carol J., ed. 2014. *Advertising and society*. Chicester: Wiley Blackwell.

Pasquinelli, Matteo. 2009. Google's PageRank algorithm: A diagram of cognitive capitalism and the rentier of the common intellect. In *Deep search: The politics of search beyond Google*, ed. Konrad Becker and Felix Stalder, 152–162. Innsbruck: StudienVerlag.

Pateman, Carole. 1970. Participation and democratic theory. Cambridge: Cambridge University Press.

Petersen, Søren Mørk. 2008. Loser generated content: From participation to exploitation. *First Monday* 13 (3). http://firstmonday.org/article/view/2141/1948 (accessed on 27 September 2016).

PewResearchCenter. 2015. Social media usage: 2005–2015. www.pewinternet.org/2015/10/08/social-networking-usage-2005-2015, accessed on 22 November 2015.

Popper, Karl. 1962a. *The open society and its enemies. Volume 2: Hegel and Marx*. Princeton, NJ: Princeton University Press.

Popper, Karl R. 1962b. Zur Logik der Sozialwissenschaften. *Kölner Zeitschrift für Soziologie und Sozialpsychologie* 14 (2): 233–248.

Qi, Hao. 2014. The labor share question in China. *Monthly Review* 65 (8): 23–35.

Qiu, Jack L. 2009. *Working-class network society: Communication technology and the information have-less in China*. Cambridge, MA: MIT Press.

Qiu, Jack L. 2012. Network Labor: Beyond the shadow of Foxconn. In *Studying mobile media: Cultural technologies, mobile communication, and the iPhone*, ed. Larissa Hjorth, Jean Burgess and Ingrid Richardson, 173–189. New York: Routledge.

Qiu, Jack L. 2015. Reflections on big data: "Just because it is accessible does not make it ethical". *Media, Culture & Society* 37 (7): 1089–1094.

Qiu, Jack L. 2016. *Goodbye iSlave: A manifesto for digital abolition*. Urbana, IL: University of Illinois Press.

Quinn, Michael. 2006. *Ethics for the information age*. Boston, MA: Pearson.

Ritzer, George and Nathan Jurgenson. 2010. Production, consumption, prosumption. *Journal of Consumer Culture* 10 (1): 13–36.

Roberts, John Michael and Nick Crossley, eds. 2004a. *After Habermas: New perspectives on the public sphere*. Malden, MA: Blackwell.

Roberts, John Michael and Nick Crossley. 2004b. Introduction. In *After Habermas: New perspectives on the public sphere*, ed. Nick Crossley and John Michael Roberts, 1–27. Malden, MA: Blackwell.

Roberts, Michael. 2015a. Is it all over? Michael Roberts looks at the implications of China's stock market collapse. *Weekly Worker*, 6 August. http://weeklyworker.co.uk/worker/1070/is-it-all-over (accessed on 27 September 2016).

Roberts, Michael. 2015b. Is there a economic bubble in China about to burst? *The Socialist Network*, 15 June, http://socialistnetwork.org/is-there-a-economic-bubble-in-china-about-to-burst (accessed on 27 September 2016).

Robins, Kevin and Frank Webster. 1999. *Times of the technoculture*. New York: Routledge.

Rockmore, Tom. 2011. *Before and after 9/11: A philosophical examination of globzliation, terror, and history*. New York: Continuum.

Rogers, Richard. 2013. *Digital methods*. Cambridge, MA: MIT Press.

Rosenberg, Tina. 2013. It's not just nice to share, it's the future. *The New York Times* online, 5 June. http://opinionator.blogs.nytimes.com/2013/06/05/its-not-just-nice-to-share-its-the-future (accessed on 27 September 2016).

Rushkoff, Douglas. 2010. *Program or be programmed: Ten commands for a digital age*. New York: OR Books. Kindle version.

Rushkoff, Douglas. 2013. Unlike – Why I'm leaving Facebook. www.rushkoff.com/blog/2013/2/25/cnn-unlike-why-im-leaving-facebook.html (accessed on 27 September 2016).

Ryker, Randy, Elizabeth Lafleur, Chris Cox and Bruce Mcmanis. 2002. Online privacy policies: An assessment of the fortune E-50. *Journal of Computer Information Systems* 42 (4): 15–20.

Sahlins, Marshall. 1972. *Stone age economics*. Chicago, IL: Aldine Atherton.

Salem, Sara. 2015. Creating spaces for dissent: The role of social media in the 2011 Egyptian revolution. In *Social media, politics and the state: Protests, revolutions, riots, crime and politics in the age of Facebook, Twitter and YouTube,* ed. Daniel Trottier and Christian Fuchs, 171–188. New York: Routledge.

Sandoval, Marisol. 2013. Foxconned labour as the dark side of the information age. Working conditions at Apple's contract manufacturers in China. *tripleC: Communication, Capitalism & Critique* 11 (2): 318–347.

Sandoval, Marisol. 2014. *From corporate to social media? Critical perspectives on corporate social responsibility in media and communication industries*. London: Routledge.

Sandoval, Marisol. 2015. From CSR to RSC: A contribution to the critique of the political economy of corporate social responsibility. *Review of Radical Political Economics* 47 (4): 608–624.

Sandoval, Marisol 2016. Fighting precarity with co-operation? Worker co-operatives in the cultural sector. *New Formations* 88: 51–68.

Sandoval, Marisol and Christian Fuchs. 2010. Towards a critical theory of alternative media. *Telematics and Informatics* 27 (2): 141–150.

Schmitt, Carl. 1996. *The concept of the political*. Chicago, IL: Chicago University Press.

Schoeman, Ferdinand David, ed. 1984a. *Philosophical dimensions of privacy*. Cambridge, MA: Cambridge University Press.

Schoeman, Ferdinand David. 1984b. Privacy: Philosophical dimensions of the literature. In *Philosophical dimensions of privacy*, ed. Ferdinand David Schoeman, 1–33. Cambridge, MA: Cambridge University Press.

Scholz, Trebor. 2008. Market ideology and the myths of web 2.0. *First Monday* 13 (3). http://firstmonday.org/article/view/2138/1945 (accessed on 27 September 2016).

Scholz, Trebor, ed. 2013. *Digital labor: The Internet as playground and factory*. New York: Routledge.

Scholz, Trebor. 2016. *Platform cooperativism: Challenging the corporate sharing economy*. New York: Rosa Luxemburg Stiftung New York Office.

Scholz, Trebor. 2017. *Uberworked and underpaid: How workers are disrupting the digital economy*. Cambridge: Polity.

Sevignani, Sebastian. 2012. The problem of privacy in capitalism and the alternative social networking site Diaspora*. *tripleC: Communication, Capitalism & Critique* 10 (2): 600–617.

Sevignani, Sebastian. 2013. Facebook vs. Diaspora: A critical study. In *"Unlike us" reader: Social media monopolies and their alternatives*, ed. Geert Lovink and Miriam Rasch, 323–337. Amsterdam: Institute of Network Cultures.

Sevignani, Sebastian. 2016. *Privacy and capitalism in the age of social media*. New York: Routledge.

Shepherd, Tamara. 2014. Gendering the commodity audience in social media. In *The Routledge companion to media and gender*, ed. Cynthia Carter, Linda Steiner and Lisa McLaughlin, 157–167. London: Routledge.

Shirky, Clay. 2008. *Here comes everybody*. London: Penguin.

Shirky, Clay. 2011a. *Cognitive surplus: How technology makes consumers into collaborators*. London: Penguin.

Shirky, Clay. 2011b. The political power of social media. *Foreign Affairs* 90 (1): 28–41.

Sicular, Terry. 2013. The challenge of high inequality in China. *Inequality in Focus* 2 (2): 1–5.

Smythe, Dallas W. 1954. Reality as presented by television. In *Counterclockwise: Perspectives on communication*, 61–74. Boulder, CO: Westview Press.

Smythe, Dallas W. 1977. Communications: Blindspot of Western Marxism. *Canadian Journal of Political and Social Theory* 1 (3): 1–27.

Smythe, Dallas W. 1981. *Dependency road*. Norwood, NJ: Ablex.

Smythe, Dallas W. 1981/2006. On the audience commodity and its work. In *Media and cultural studies*, ed. Meenakshi G. Durham and Douglas M. Kellner, 230–256. Malden, MA: Blackwell.

Smythe, Dallas W. 1994. *Counterclockwise*. Boulder, CO: Westview Press.

Solove, Daniel J. 2008. *Understanding privacy*. Cambridge, MA: Harvard University Press.

Sparks, Colin. 1998. Is there a global public sphere? In *Electronic empires: Global media and local resistances*, ed. Daya Kishan Thussu, 91–107. London: Hodder Arnold.

Sparks, Colin. 2001. The Internet and the global public sphere. In *Mediated politics: Communication in the future of society*, ed. W. Lance Bennett and Robert M. Entman, 75–95. New York: Cambridge University Press.

Splichal, Slavko. 2007. Does history matter? Grasping the idea of public service at its roots. In *From public service broadcasting to public service media: RIPE@2007*, ed. Gregory Ferrell Lowe and Jo Bardoel, 237–256. Gothenburg: Nordicom.

Stallings, William. 1995. *Operating systems* (2nd edition). Englewood Cliffs, NJ: Prentice-Hall.

Stallings, William. 2006. *Data and computer communications*. Englewood Cliffs, NJ: Prentice-Hall.

Standage, Tom. 2013. *Writing on the wall: Social media – The first 2,000 years*. London: Bloomsbury.

Stanyer, James. 2009. Web 2.0 and the transformation of news and journalism. In *Routledge handbook of Internet politics*, ed. Andrew Chadwick and Philip N. Howard, 201–213. New York: Routledge.

Starke-Meyerring, Doreen and Laura Gurak. 2007. Internet. In *Encyclopedia of privacy*, ed. William G. Staples, 297–310. Westport, CT: Greenwood Press.

Students & Scholars against Corporate Misbehaviour (SACOM). 2014. *The lives of iSlaves: Report on working conditions at Apple's supplier Pegatron*. http://sacom.hk/wp-content/uploads/2014/09/SACOM-The-Lives-of-iSlaves-Pegatron-20140918.pdf (accessed on 22 November 2015).

Stutzman, Frederic. 2006. An evaluation of identity-sharing behavior in social network communities. *iDMAa Journal* 3 (1).

Sullivan, Andrew. 2009. The revolution will be twittered. *The Atlantic*. www.theatlantic.com/daily-dish/archive/2009/06/the-revolution-will-be-twittered/200478 (accessed on 22 November 2015).

Tännsjö, Torbjörn. 2010. *Privatliv*. Lidingö: Fri Tanke.

Tapscott, Don and Anthony D. Williams. 2007. *Wikinomics: How mass collaboration changes everything*. New York: Penguin.

Tavani, Herman T. 2008. Informational privacy: Concepts, theories, and controversies. In *The handbook of information and computer ethics*, ed. Kenneth Einar Himma and Herman T. Tavani, 131–164. Hoboken, NJ: Wiley.

Tavani, Herman T. 2010. *Ethics and technolog: Controversies, questions and strategies for ethical computing*. Hoboken, NJ: Wiley.

Taylor, Astra. 2014. *The people's platform: Taking back power and culture in the digital age*. London: Fourth Estate.

Terranova, Tiziana. 2004. *Network culture*. London: Pluto.

Terranova, Tiziana and Joan Donovan. 2013. Occupy social networks: The paradoxes of corporate social media for networked social movements. In *"Unlike us" reader: Social media monopolies and their alternatives*, ed. Geert Lovink and Miriam Rasch, 296–311. Amsterdam: Institute of Network Cultures.

Terras, Melissa, Julianne Nyhan and Edward Vanhoutte, eds. 2013. *Defining digital humanities: A reader*. Farnham: Ashgate.

Thompson, John B. 1995. *The media and modernity: A social theory of the media*. Cambridge: Polity Press.

Toffler, Alvin. 1980. *The third wave*. New York: Bantam.

Tomasello, Michael. 2008. *Origins of human communication*. Cambridge, MA: The MIT Press.

Tönnies, Ferdinand. 1988. *Community & society*. New Brunswick, NJ: Transaction Books.

Trottier, Daniel. 2012. *Social media as surveillance: Rethinking visibility in a converging world*. Farnham: Ashgate.

Trottier, Daniel. 2014. *Identity problems in the Facebook era*. New York: Routledge.

Trottier, Daniel and Christian Fuchs. 2015. Theorising social media, politics and the state: An introduction. In *Social media, politics and the state: Protests, revolutions, riots, crime and policing in the age of Facebook, Twitter and YouTube*, ed. Daniel Trottier and Christian Fuchs, 3–38. New York: Routledge.

Tufekci, Zeynep. 2008. Can you see me now? Audience and disclosure regulation in online social network sites. *Bulletin of Science, Technology and Society* 28 (1): 20–36.

Turow, Joseph. 2006. *Niche envy: Marketing discrimination in the digital age*. Cambridge, MA: MIT Press.

Turow, Joseph. 2011. *The daily you: How the new advertising industry is defining your identity and your worth*. New Haven, CT: Yale University Press.

Turow, Joseph and Matthew McAllister, eds. 2009. *The advertising and consumer culture reader*. New York: Routledge.

Vaidhyanathan, Siva. 2011. *The Googlization of everything (and why we should worry)*. Berkeley, CA: University of California Press.

van Dijck, José. 2009. Users like you? Theorizing agency in user-generated content. *Media, Culture & Society* 31 (1): 41–58.

van Dijck, José. 2013. *The culture of connectivity: A critical history of social media*. Oxford: Oxford University Press.

van Dijck, José and David Nieborg. 2009. Wikinomics and its discontents: a critical analysis of web 2.0 business manifestos. *New Media & Society* 11 (5): 855–874.

van Dijk, Teun A. 1993. Principles of critical discourse analysis. *Discourse & Society* 4 (2): 249–283.

Varian, Hal R. 2006. The economics of internet search. *Rivista di politica economica 96* (11/12): 8–23.

Varian, Hal R. 2009. Online ad auctions. *American Economic Review* 99 (2): 430–434.

Vise, David A. 2005. *The Google story*. London: Macmillan.

Wacks, Raymond. 2010. *Privacy: A very short introduction*. Oxford: Oxford University Press.

Wallerstein, Immanuel. 2015. Whose interests are served by the BRICS? In *BRICS: An anti-capitalist critique*, ed. Patrick Bond and Ana Garcia, 269–273. London: Pluto Press.

Wang, Di. 2008. The idle and the busy: Teahouses and public life in early twentieth-century Chengdu. *Journal of Urban History* 26 (4): 411–437.

Warren, Samuel and Louis Brandeis. 1890. The right to privacy. *Harvard Law Review* 4 (5): 193–220.

Wasko, Janet. 2004. The political economy of communications. In *The SAGE handbook of media studies*, ed. John Downing, Denis McQuail, Philip Schlesinger and Ellen Wartella, 309–329. Thousand Oaks, CA: SAGE.

Wasko, Janet and Mary Erickson. 2009. The political economy of YouTube. In *The YouTube reader*, ed. Pelle Snickars and Patrick Vonderau, 372–386. Stockholm: National Library of Sweden.

Wasko, Janet, Graham Murdock and Helena Sousa, eds. 2011. *The handbook of political economy of communication*. Malden, MA: Wiley-Blackwell.

Weber, Max. 1978. *Economy and society*. Berkeley, CA: University of California Press.

Westin, Alan. 1967. *Privacy and freedom*. New York: Altheneum.

Wiggershaus, Rolf. 1995. *The Frankfurt school: Its history, theories and political significance*. Cambridge, MA: MIT Press.

Williams, Raymond. 1977. *Marxism and literature*. Oxford: Oxford University Press.

Williams, Raymond. 1983. *Keywords*. New York: Oxford University Press.

Williams, Raymond. 1989. *What I came to say*. London: Hutchinson Radius.

Williams, Raymond. 1990. *Television* (2nd edition). London: Routledge.

Wilson, Christopher and Alexandra Dunn. 2011. Digital media in the Egyptian revolution: Descriptive analysis from the Tahrir data sets. *International Journal of Communication* 5: 1248–1272.

Winner, Langdon. 1980/1999. Do artifacts have politics? In *The social shaping of technology*, ed. Donald MacKenzie and Judy Wajcman, 28–40. Maidenhead: Open University Press.

Winseck, Dwayne. 2011. The political economies of media and the transformation of the global media industries: An introductory essay. In *The political economies of media*, ed. Dwayne Winseck and Dal Yong Jin, 3–48. London: Bloomsbury Academic.

Winseck, Dwayne and Robert M. Pike. 2007. *Communication and empire*. Durham, NC: Duke University Press.

Wolfson, Todd. 2014. *Digital rebellion: The birth of the cyber left*. Urbana, IL: University of Illinois Press.

Wright, Erik Olin. 2010. *Envisioning real utopias*. London: Verso.

Young, Jock. 2002. Critical criminology in the twenty-first century. Critique, irony and the always unfinished. In *Critical criminology*, ed. Kerry Carrington and Russell Hogg, 251–271. Cullompton: Willian.

Zervas, Georgios, Davide Prosperio and John W. Byers. 2014. *The rise of the sharing economy: Estimating the impact of Airbnb on the hotel industry*. http://people.bu.edu/zg/publications/airbnb.pdf (accessed on 22 November 2015).

Zhao, Yuezhi. 2007. After mobile phones, what? Re-embedding the social in China's "digital revolution". *International Journal of Communication* 1: 92–120.

Zhao, Yuezhi. 2008. *Communication in China*. Lanham, MD: Rowman & Littlefield.

Zhao, Yuezhi. 2011. The challenge of China: Contribution to a transcultural political economy of communication in the twenty-first century. In *The handbook of the political economy of communications*, ed. Janet Wasko, Graham Murdock and Helena Sousa, 558–582. Chicester: Wiley-Blackwell.

Zimmer, Michael. 2010a. "But the data is already public": On the ethics of research in Facebook. *Ethics and Information Technology* 12 (4): 313–325.

Zimmer, Michael. 2010b. Is it ethical to harvest public Twitter accounts without consent? www.michaelzimmer.org/2010/02/12/is-it-ethical-to-harvest-public-twitter-accounts-without-consent/ (accessed on 22 November 2015).

Zimmer, Michael and Nicholas John Proferes. 2014. A topology of Twitter research: Disciplines, methods, and ethics. *Aslib Journal of Information Management* 66 (3): 250–261.

Žižek, Slavoj. 2001. *Did somebody say totalitarianism?* London: Verso.

Žižek Slavoj. 2008. *In defense of lost causes*. London: Verso.

Žižek, Slavoj. 2010. How to begin from the beginning. In *The idea of communism*, ed. Slavoj Žižek and Costas Douzinas, 209–226. London: Verso.

Žižek, Slavoj. 2012. *The year of dreaming dangerously*. London: Verso.

Žižek, Slavoj. 2014. *Absolute recoil: Towards a new foundation of dialectical materialism*. London: Verso.

Žižek, Slavoj and Costas Douzinas, eds. 2010. *The idea of communism*. London: Verso.

Zureik, Elia. 2010. Cross-cultural study of surveillance and privacy: Theoretical and empirical observations. In *Surveillance, privacy and the globalization of personal information*, ed. Elia Zureik, Lynda Harling Stalker, Emily Smith, David Lyon and Yolane E. Chan, 348–359. Montreal: McGill-Queen's University Press.

Zureik, Elia and L. Lynda Harling Stalker. 2010. The cross-cultural study of privacy. In *Surveillance, privacy and the globalization of personal information*, ed. Elia Zureik, Lynda Harling Stalker, Emily Smith, David Lyon and Yolane E. Chan, 8–30. Montreal: McGill-Queen's University Press.

INDEX